A Guide to Grants for Individuals in Need

A Guide to Grants for Individuals in Need

Edited by
David Casson
Paul Brown

Additional research by
John Smyth

A Directory of Social Change publication

A GUIDE TO GRANTS FOR INDIVIDUALS IN NEED

1994 Edition

Edited by David Casson & Paul Brown

Copyright © 1994 the Directory of Social Change

No part of this book may be stored in a retrieval system or reproduced in any form whatsoever without prior permission in writing from the publisher.

The Directory of Social Change is a registered charity no. 800517.

A Guide to Grants for Individuals in Need was first published in 1987. The second edition was published in 1990. The third edition was published in 1992. This fourth edition was published in 1994.

Published by the Directory of Social Change, Radius Works, Back Lane, London NW3 1HL (071-284 4364), from whom copies may be obtained.

British Library Cataloguing-in-Publication Data

A catalogue record for this book is available from the British Library.

ISBN 1 873860 45 5

Contents

Introduction	6
How to use this book	8
How to make an application	12
Model application form	14
Occupational charities	16
Service and ex-service charities	60
Army regimental associations	69
Sickness and disability charities	74
Advice organisations	87
Local charities	92
National and general charities	283
Charities for the relief of the poor	301
Index	304

Introduction

This book describes the work of over 2,000 charities. Together they give about £130 million a year in grants to individuals in need. For many, giving grants to individuals is not their only activity. Some give cash grants more widely (eg. education grants or to community and other groups), or have large financial commitments (often in providing housing). Whatever the overall work of the charity, we have concentrated on their grants to individuals in need.

What the book covers

We aim to include all publicly registered charities (plus those in Scotland and Northern Ireland) with a grant-making potential of at least £500 a year in grants to individuals in need. Most can give considerably more. This book excludes education grants as these are covered in the companion guide *The Educational Grants Directory*.

We have divided the entries into the following five categories (see also *How to use this book* on page 8 and the short introduction at the beginning of each section):

1. Occupational charities: This section contains over 270 charities whose combined annual grant total is over £42 million. Many are for professional people and/or their dependants, from actors and barristers to patent agents and teachers. Others cover whole industries.

2. Service and ex-service charities: 50 charities with a combined grant total of about £27 million. Together they represent an exceptionally well-organised voluntary welfare system. People who are eligible (and this includes most of the male population over the age of 60 as they will have done national service), and their dependants, can turn to trained local voluntary workers for advice and practical help. These workers in turn are backed up by professional staff and substantial resources.

We also list the army regimental associations in case members, former members or their dependants want to apply directly to the relevant regiment.

3. Sickness and disability charities: These 70 charities together give about £29 million in grants to people with specific illnesses or disabilities. Most give grants throughout Britain; some have a network of local branches which can also help. Further details are available from the central correspondents.

4. Local charities: There are about 1,600 local charities in the Guide giving about £20 million between them. Many are quite small (under £10,000 income a year). However, many of the main centres of population have at least one large trust able to give over £50,000 a year. Many of these trusts are restricted in who they can help only by geographical area (eg. parish, town or county), but some have other limiting conditions such as age or occupation.

5. National and general charities: The final section contains over 100 charities which operate nationally (or at least in more than one region) and which are not tied to a particular trade, occupation or disability. Often they can only benefit a certain age or religious group or offer a specific type of help, but they are among the best known and tend to be heavily over-subscribed. Together their grants total about £15 million.

How much money is available?

Although the combined grant total for the trusts in this Guide is £130 million, probably at least half is already committed in recurrent grants and pensions. A further, smaller proportion is tied to, for example, comforts for the elderly middle class rather than being more widely available to people in critical financial need. We estimate, therefore, it is unlikely that there is more than about £50 million a year available for new grants.

This compares with £38 billion of non-contributory statutory benefits in 1993/94 (DSS figures). It does not even cover the difference between the old single payments system and the Social Fund. It is clear, therefore, that charity cannot compensate for reductions in government expenditure.

Recommendation to charities

Much has been written in previous editions of this Guide and the companion *The Educational Grants Directory* about the eccentricities and shortcomings particularly of local charities in Britain. The following comments summarise the current position:

- Few local charities are actively seeking to expand their resources to meet new or more widespread needs.

- All trusts should check their investment policies to ensure they are making the most of the resources in their care. If you do not know an investment fund manager, you could write to the Charities Official Investment Fund (COIF), St Alphage House, 2 Fore Street, London EC2Y 5AQ (071-588 1815).

- Many local charities are still not sufficiently well-known in their area of benefit. We recommend that each charity (depending on its eligibility restrictions) writes to all welfare agencies, churches, community centres, schools and other public meeting points, and doctors' surgeries and health centres.

- Charities should develop a working relationship with welfare agencies, if only because:

    (a) The state is by far the largest provider of help to individuals in need. A call to a knowledgeable welfare rights officer ensures that every possible area of statutory support has been exhausted before the charity makes a payment.

    (b) When welfare agencies refer appropriate cases to the charity for prompt and sympathetic consideration, the charity knows that all possible sources of statutory provision have been examined and therefore the charity can save itself administrative time.

- Charities should establish the parameters of Social Fund provision in the area and let the Social Fund Officers know of their own resources and policies.

- Some charities persist in their policy of dividing their income by the number of pensioners in their area of benefit and giving them all a Christmas gift, usually of less than £10 each. This practice is in our view illegal. We believe that the role of a relief-in-need charity is to meet the most urgent needs prescribed by its trust deed. For example, instead of giving 1,600 people a £5 grant (as one trust in the Guide does), we believe that it would be better to ensure that 50 people in real need are warm and well fed.

- Charities should aim to ensure that needs can be met as rapidly as possible. For example empowering the clerk or a small group of trustees to make payments up to a certain limit.

- Charities should consult with other charities in the area so that while avoiding unnecessary duplication they can work together to meet as full a range of needs as possible.

- All charities should read carefully the Charity Commission leaflet CC4 entitled *Charities for the Relief of the Poor* reprinted in this Guide on page 301. We believe it reinforces many of the points made above.

The above comments are in no way meant to detract from the great benefits already resulting from the hard work of so many active and committed trustees, clerks and others involved in relief-in-need charities.

Organisations not included

Though there are exceptions, the following types of fund do not have entries in the Guide:

- Organisations which give grants to **members only** and not to their dependants;
- **Individual employer or company** welfare funds;
- **Friendly Societies;**
- **Local branches** of national charities, though they may raise money locally for cases of need;
- **Collecting charities** whose grant giving abilities vary from year to year and who are more likely to give support to organisations rather than individuals;
- **Local Lions/Rotaries and Masonic/other orders;**
- Organisations providing **services only.**

Getting help

Applying for grants can be a daunting experience. Especially if you are unfamiliar with the process, it is probably worth starting with the help of a sympathetic advisor. Most citizen's advice bureaux have money advice workers or volunteers trained in basic money advice work. If you find that you are in financial need try going to the nearest citizen's advice bureau and talk to them about your financial difficulties. They may be able to help write an application to an appropriate charity, know of a welfare benefit you could claim or be able to re-negotiate some of your debt repayments on your behalf. They will certainly be able to help you minimise your expenditure and budget effectively.

Acknowledgements

We are extremely grateful to the many people who have helped compile this Guide. To name them all would be impossible. 95% of the trusts either replied to our letters or spoke to us on the telephone, the vast majority of whom were very helpful. There were a few trusts who expressed their unequivocal wish not to be included in the Guide. Our policy remains unchanged; we include all publicly registered charities of relevance. Although drafts of all the entries were sent to the charities concerned, and any corrections noted and incorporated, the text and any mistakes within in, remains ours rather than theirs.

We are also once again indebted to the staff of the Liverpool office of the Charity Commission particularly Lol Grant and Tom Hitchings. We are similarly grateful to Margaret Harrison and Ashley Wood of the FWA for their continued help with parts of the editorial text.

Request for further information

The research for this book was done as carefully as we were able, but there will be relevant charities that we have missed and some of the information is incomplete or will become out-of-date. If any reader comes across omissions or mistakes in this Guide, please let us know so that future editions can rectify them. A telephone call to the Research Department of the Directory of Social Change Northern Office (051-708 0117) is all that is needed.

Conclusion

The money available from this book is small compared to government expenditure on social welfare. However, many of the needs that charities can cater for and which the state does not recognise require fairly small-scale help. If the average grant was £100, the charities in this book could be helping over 1 million people a year, and they would be those for whom other help was either inadequate or unavailable.

How to use this book

The following section contains:
- An article on how to identify all the relevant sources of help listed in the Guide.
- A table on page 10 summarising points made in the above article.
- An article on how individuals (or welfare agencies applying on behalf of individuals) should make a good, clear and relevant application.
- A model application form which can be used either as a check-list for people preparing a written application or, if preferred, it can be photocopied if the trust being applied to has no application form of its own.

Identifying Relevant Trusts

When individuals (or welfare agencies on behalf of individuals) are applying to charities for help, they should bear in mind three things:

1. To get help from charity you do not need to be on state benefits.
2. Hesitating for a few months because you do not like to ask or in the unlikely hope that the situation will improve only makes the problem worse for you and worse for the charity that would have preferred to help from the start.
3. There is no simple list of charities that will "pay off the debt" or "repair the roof". Different charities have different restrictions, but a flexible approach enables people in need to make relevant applications to trusts whose areas of activity are very diverse.

The limits of each charity's help

Every charity is bound by its trust deed (also called its constitution or governing instrument). This sets out, amongst other things, the charity's area of benefit and, in general terms, who it can help. The trustees of a charity are powerless to help anyone who falls outside the terms of the trust deed; applications from such people are a waste of time both for the applicant and the charity.

Furthermore, trustees can, within the often general terms of their trust deed, draw up their own criteria as to who and how they will help. Sometimes this means that they will only help people over a certain age, or people who have lived in the beneficial area or worked in a profession or served in a regiment for a certain number of years. However, the most common limits of help are the amount, type and category of grant given.

Amount and type of grant

One-off grants

Some trusts will give a one-off cash payment only. This means that they will award a single lump sum (say £50) which is paid by cheque/postal order either direct to the applicant, to the welfare agency applying on the person's behalf, or another suitable third party. No more help will be considered until the applicant has submitted a new application, and trusts are usually unwilling to give more than one one-off grant per person per year.

Recurrent grants

Other trusts will only pay recurrent grants, usually weekly allowances, often of up to the current "disregard" level, at present £10 a week in most cases. (The "disregard" level is the maximum income a person on Income Support can receive in addition to their state benefit before it affects their Income Support calculations). These payments can be made quarterly (so each year the applicant receives four grants of £130), or in smaller, more regular amounts.

Weekly payments can be much higher than £10, particularly if the applicant requires expensive treatment/medicine on a regular basis, or has some other high ongoing cost.

Some trusts will give either one-off or recurrent payments according to what is more appropriate for the applicant.

Grants in kind

Occasionally grants are given in the form of vouchers or are paid directly to a shop or store in the form of credit to enable the applicant to obtain food, clothing or other pre-arranged items. Some charities still deliver coal!

More commonly, especially with disability aids or other technical equipment, the charity will either give the equipment itself to the applicant (rather than the money to buy it) or loan it free of charge or at a low rental as long as the applicant needs it. More common items, such as telephones and televisions, can also be given as equipment rather than as a cash grant to enable the applicant to buy one, often because the charity can get better trade terms than the individual.

Category of grant

Some trust deeds state specifically what grants are to be given for (eg. holidays), but many define the type of person the trust should help (eg. a shipwrecked mariner, diabetic,

How to use this book

elderly widower) and it is up to the trustees what form this help will take. Typically this means that a trust will help with, for example, clothing, essential household items and holidays but not with rent/rate arrears and fuel/credit debts. Such policies are determined by a variety of factors, one of the most important being the trustees' perception of current state provision.

It should be stressed that many, particularly local, charities do not have such clear policies, but where clear policy statements are made in the Guide the applicant will be wasting time by applying for a grant outside of the areas listed; the trust simply will not help.

Grants from more than one source

Charities in the Guide have been divided into five sections. Applicants will usually find that they can approach more than one trust in each section, although it is very important to tailor the application to the type of trust being approached (see the following article on "How to make an application"). Applicants should also read the introduction to each of the five sections.

Occupational charities

These trusts benefit not simply the people who worked in the particular trade but also, in many cases, their widows/widowers and dependant children. Membership or previous membership of the particular association or institute can be required, but many are open to non-members. Length of service can also be taken into account.

Service and ex-service charities

There is an exceptionally thorough charitable provision for people who have served in the forces, whether as a regular or during national service. Again these are very important sources of help for widows/widowers and dependant children of service or ex-service personnel.

Sickness and disability charities

These trusts can help people (and occasionally families/carers of people) who are in financial need as a result of a particular illness or disability. Many of them also give advisory and other support.

Local charities

Local charities help people living within their defined area, although help may depend on how long you have lived there, your age, or perhaps your connection with some local activity or church.

National and general charities

Some national charities have very wide objects which enable them to benefit "people in need", "children" or "the elderly", or help foreign communities in Britain, people belonging to a religious denomination or a masonic/other order, refugees and other people in need. However these charities are still generally the best known and so receive the most applications.

An example

Therefore if, for example, a child of parents on low income needs an adaptor for his/her wheelchair, the parents (or welfare agency acting on their behalf) should establish:

- If there is a suitable local charity operating in the region, county, town or parish where the family is currently living, or (less commonly) a charity benefiting people born in the town of the child's/parents' birth (see the relevant local charities section of the Guide).

- If there is a charity covering the child's particular illness/disability, or if the child is (or the parents as carers are) eligible for help from one of the charities covering disability more generally (see the Sickness and disability charities section of the Guide).

- If either or both of the child's parents has worked or is working in a trade or occupation with a charity connected to it (see the Occupational charities section of the Guide).

- If either or both of the child's parents has served in the forces, including national service (see the Services and ex-services charities section of the Guide).

- If any of the national and general charities can help. For example, does either parent practice a religion or belong to a masonic lodge, or is either parent a refugee? Also, at the beginning of the National and general charities section of the Guide, there is an index of the charities classified (as far as possible) according to type of beneficiary. Are there any trusts under the children or general headings of that index that can help? (See the National and general charities section of the Guide.)

- If there any other possible sources of help (eg rotary, lions, churches etc.) - see page 10.

If the adaptor is expensive then the family will probably have to obtain varying levels of help from several charities to make up the total amount required. A flexible approach using different letters tailored to suit the different types of trusts being approached would therefore be essential.

The following table gives a summary of the above points and procedure for quick reference.

How to identify sources of help - quick reference chart

1. Occupation	Has the **person** or their **husband** or wife or their **parent** on whom they are dependent had a **trade** or long-term occupation (including some past connection with a trade or occupation)?	See **Occupational index** to identify the appropriate occupation in the alphabetical list of **Occupational charities**	*Page 16*
2. Service and ex-service	Have they at any time been a serving member of the **armed forces** (including national service)? For other kinds of help and advice:	See **Service and ex-service charities** and **Army regimental associations** Contact **SSAFA** (Soldiers', Sailors' & Airmen's Families Association)	*Page 60* *Page 69*
3. Sickness and disability	Has the person a specific **illness** or **disability**? There may be a specialist charity which makes grants: There may be a specialist charity which can help in other ways or which can give advice:	See index in the **Sickness and disability charities** section See **Advice organisations**	*Page 74* *Page 87*
4. Geographical area	What parish, town, county or area does the person **live in**? For advice and information on other sources of help locally:	See **map** to identify the appropriate geographical areas and the list of **local charities** arranged geographically Contact the local **citizen's advice bureau**	*Page 92*
5. Other sources of help	There are many other sources of help. Some national charities help with a wide range of needs; others specialise in certain groups of people (eg. the elderly, children)	See **National and general charities**	*Page 283*

Other sources of help

The charities listed in this book are not the only non-statutory sources of financial help to individuals in need, although they are the most organised in their giving. If applicants cannot obtain the necessary money from the trusts in the Guide they could also try the following:

Vicars, priests and ministers of religion
There may be informal arrangements within a church, mosque etc. to help people in need. Church of England vicars are often trustees of local charities which are too small to be included in the Guide or which we have missed.

Hospitals
Most hospitals have patient welfare funds, but they are little known about even within the hospitals and so are little used. It may take some time to locate an appropriate contact within the hospital. Start with the trust fund administrator or the treasurer's department of the health authority.

Past employers
Many employers are unhappy to see former members of staff, or their dependants, living in need or distress. Few have formal arrangements but a letter or telephone call to the personnel manager should establish if help is possible.

Local organisations
Rotary Clubs, Lions Clubs and Round Tables etc. are active in welfare provision. Usually they support groups rather than individuals and policies vary in different towns, but some welfare agencies (eg. citizen's advice bureaux) have a working relationship with these organisations and keep up-to-date lists of contacts. All enquiries should be made on behalf of the individual by a recognised agency.

Orders
Masonic and Buffalo lodges, Foresters Associations and other organisations exist for mutual benefit of their usually male members. Spouses and children of members (or deceased members) may also benefit, but people unconnected with these orders are unlikely to. Applications should be made to the lodge where the parent/spouse is or was a member.

Charity shops
Some charity shops will provide clothing if the applicant has a letter of referral from a recognised welfare agency.

How to make an application

By Margaret Harrison & Ashley Wood, The FWA

Once the appropriate charities have been identified, the next stage is the application itself. People often find making applications difficult and those who might benefit sometimes fail to do so because of the quality of the application submitted.

The following article gives guidelines both to individuals applying directly and to welfare agencies applying on behalf of individuals on how to make a good, clear and relevant application.

The Application Form

The first stage in submitting an application is the question of application forms. Applications on agency letter headings or personal letters direct from the applicant, no matter how well presented, are fairly pointless if the charity being approached has a specific application form which must be completed. This obvious point is often overlooked. It is frustrating when the application is returned with a blank form requesting substantially the same information as has already been submitted. The resulting delay can mean missing a committee meeting where the application would have been considered and a considerable wait until the next one.

Usually the Guide indicates where a particular application form is needed, but if there is any doubt the applicant should make a preliminary telephone call to the trust.

Who submits the application?

Again, it is important that the application is sent by an appropriate person. The Guide usually indicates whether an individual in need can apply on his/her own behalf, or whether a third party (professional or otherwise) must apply for them.

With the current trend towards "empowerment" of service users, advisory bodies sometimes simply advise families of funds they can approach themselves. However, some charities require applications to be made by, for example, a professional person. Therefore, the individual in need may need to press the agency to make an application on his/her behalf.

The Questions

When application forms are used, the questions asked sometimes cause problems, often because they do not appear relevant. Applicants sometimes fail to realise that all charities are governed by the criteria laid down in their trust deed and usually specific questions are designed to ensure these criteria are met.

For example questions concerning date and place of birth are often answered very vaguely. 'Date of birth' is sometimes answered with 'late 50s' or even worse, 'elderly'. Such a reply reflects the appearance of the person in question and not their age! If the charity can only consider applications for those below pensionable age, and the request was on behalf of a woman, then the above answers would be too imprecise. Equally 'Place of birth' is sometimes answered with 'Great Britain' which is not precise enough for funds whose area of benefit is regional or local. It is always better to state the place of birth as well as the town and county, even if they are different from the current home address.

Where application forms are not requested, it is essential to prepare clear concise applications which provide:

1. A description of the person or family and the need which exists

Although applications should be concise, they must provide sufficient detail, such as:

(a) The applicant's name, address, place and date of birth;

(b) The applicant's family circumstances (ie. married/co-habiting, separated/divorced/single parent, widow/widower, the number and ages of dependent children);

(c) The applicant's financial position (ie. a breakdown of weekly income and expenditure and, where appropriate DSS/housing benefits awarded/refused, savings, credit debts, rent/gas/electricity arrears etc.);

(d) Other relevant information such as how the need arose (eg. illness, loss of job, marital separation etc.) and why other sources (especially DSS/housing departments) have not helped. If applying to a disability charity, applicants should include details on the nature and effects of the disability (although see Medical information below); if applying to a local charity, how long they have lived in the locality.

How to make an application

The application which says "this is a poor family who need their gas reconnecting" is unlikely to receive proper consideration. It is also worth mentioning that applications are dealt with in the strictest confidence, so applicants should aim to provide as much information as is relevant. The form printed after this article may serve as a useful check list to ensure that all the relevant information is included for the particular application.

2. *How much money is requested and what it will be used for*

This second point appears to cause the most difficulty. Applications are often received without any indication of the amount required or without sufficient explanation as to the desired use of the money.

For example, an applicant may have multiple debts totalling over £1,000. A grant of £100 would clear one of the debts and free much-needed weekly income. So the applicant approaches a suitable charity for a grant of £100. If the application explains the situation clearly, trustees can see that a £100 grant in this instance would be an effective use of their charity's resources. However if it is not made clear, trustees can only guess at the possible benefits of the grant. Because they are not willing to take undue risks with charitable money, trustees may either turn down an incomplete application or refer it for more information with the inevitable delays involved.

Charity and the state

Charities are not supposed to give grants for items which are covered by statutory sources. However, recent changes in government legislation (eg. the introduction of the Social Fund) have made it increasingly difficult to say where statutory provision ends and charitable provision should begin.

Similarly, the introduction of assessments and means testing under Disabled Facilities Grants procedures is creating shortfalls between the amount that statutory sources will pay and the full costs of equipment and adaptations to houses. Sometimes assessments of what families can pay appear unrealistic. Changes arising from community care legislation are increasingly creating new areas of need.

If individuals are applying to charity because statutory provision is clearly no longer adequate they should make it clear in the application that they have exhausted all possible statutory sources of funding but they are still left with a shortfall. A supporting reference from a knowledgeable agency may be helpful.

Realism

It helps to be realistic. Sometimes families have contributed to their own situation. The applicant who admits this and seems not to expect miracles but rather seeks to plan afresh – even if with fingers crossed – will often be considered more sympathetically than the applicant who philosophises about the deprivation of the family or the imperfections of the then current political regime.

Likewise, the application which tries to make the trustees feel guilty and responsible for the impending doom which is predicted for the most vulnerable members of the family is unlikely to impress experienced trustees, however sympathetic. In general, be clear and factual, not moralising and emotional.

Applications to more than one charity

Where large amounts are being sought to send applications one at a time, awaiting the outcome of each before applying to another can take months. However, if a number of applications are being sent out together, a paragraph explaining that other charities are being approached should be included together with a commitment to return any surplus money raised.

The same application should not be sent off indiscriminately. For example, if someone is applying to a trade charity on behalf of a child whose deceased father had lengthy service in that particular trade, then a detailed description of the deceased father's service would be highly relevant. If an application for the same child was being made to a local charity, it would not.

Sometimes people who are trustees of more than one charity receive three or four identical letters, none tailored to the particular trust and none indicating that other trusts have been approached. The omission of such details and the neglect of explanations raises questions in the minds of trustees which in the end can result in delays or even refusal.

Timing

When applying to charities, remember the time factor, particularly in cases of urgent need. Committees often sit monthly, or even quarterly. Without knowledge but with 'luck', an application may be received the day before the meeting. If Murphy's Law operates it will always arrive the day after. For the lack of a little homework, applications may not be considered in time.

From experience, few organisations object to a telephone call being made to clarify criteria, dates of meetings or requests for application forms. So often it seems that the whole process is left to chance which leads to disillusionment, frustration and wasted time for all concerned.

Savings

When awarding a grant, most trustees take the applicant's savings into account. Some applicants may think this unnecessarily intrusive, but openness and honesty make for a better presented application and save time. However sometimes savings may not need to affect trustees' calculations.

For example, if a woman has a motor accident in which she was not at fault but which leaves her permanently disabled, she will receive compensation (often a once-off lump sum) through the guilty party's insurance company based on medical prognoses at the time. If her condition deteriorates faster and further than anticipated, requiring her to obtain an expensive item of equipment, it could well be argued that this should not be paid for out of the compensation awarded. The compensation was paid to cover factors such

How to make an application

as loss of earnings potential, a reduced quality of life, reduced ability to fulfil easily basic household tasks and a general loss of future security, not to pay for unexpected and expensive pieces of equipment. In such circumstances, the applicant should include a paragraph in the application to explain why his/her savings are not relevant to grant calculations.

Be clear

Two final points should be borne in mind. Firstly, social workers in particular often resort to the use of jargon when plain English would be more effective. There seems to be two extremes; one to present a report on the bases that the trustees are not very intelligent lay people who need to be educated, or alternatively that they are all psychotherapists who need to be impressed. Usually this only causes confusion.

Medical information

Secondly, medical information should not be presented without an accurate medical diagnosis to support it. Applicants' or social workers' presumptions on medical matters are not relevant. Often what is necessary is to explain why a financial need arises from a particular condition. This may be because of the rarity of the condition or the fluctuating nature of it. The medical information should be presented by a professional in that field. The task of the applicant or the welfare officer is to explain the financial implications of the condition.

Using the model application form for financial assistance

Over the page is a general purpose application form. It has been compiled with the help of the FWA. It can be photocopied and used whenever convenient and should enable applicants (and welfare agencies applying on behalf of individuals) to state clearly the basic information required by most trusts. Alternatively, applicants can use it as a check-list of points to include in a letter. Applicants using this form should note the following things in particular:

1. It is always worth sending a short letter setting out the request in brief, even when using this application form.

2. Because this form is designed to be useful to a wide range of people in need, not all the information asked for in the form will be relevant to every application. For example, not all applicants are in receipt of state benefits, nor do all applicants have credit debts. In such cases, applicants should write 'N/A' (not applicable) in the box or on the line in question.

3. Filling out the weekly income and expenditure parts of the form can be worrying or even distressing. Expenditure when itemised in this way is usually far higher than people expect. It is probably worth filling out this form with the help of a trained welfare rights worker.

4. You should always keep a copy of the filled out form in case the trust has a specific query.

5. This form should not be used where the trust has its own form which must be completed.

A model application form for financial assistance

PURPOSE FOR WHICH GRANT IS SOUGHT	AMOUNT SOUGHT FROM THIS APPLICATION £
APPLICANT (Name)	Occupation/School
Address	
Tel. no	
Date of birth / Age	Place of birth
Nationality	Religion (if any)

☐ Single ☐ Married ☐ Divorced ☐ Partnered ☐ Separated ☐ Widow/er

FAMILY DETAILS: Name	Age	Occupation/School
Husband/Wife	....	....
Partner	....	....
Children	....	....
Others (specify)	....	....

INCOME (weekly)	£	p	EXPENDITURE (weekly)	£	p
Father/husband's wage	....		Rent/mortgage	....	
Mother's/wife's wage	....		Council tax	....	
Partner's wage	....		Water rate	....	
Income Support	....		Electricity	....	
Sickness/invalidity benefit	....		Gas	....	
Child benefit	....		Coal/paraffin	....	
Family Credit	....		Insurance	....	
Attendance allowance	....		Fares/travel	....	
Disability living allowances	....		Household expenses (food, laundry etc.)	....	
Housing benefit	....		Clothing	....	
Maintenance payments	....		Maintenance	....	
Retirement pension	....		Childminding fees	....	
Occupational pension	....		HP commitments	....	
Other income (specify)	....		Telephone	....	
			TV rental	....	
			TV licence	....	
			Other expenditure (specify)	....	

TOTAL WEEKLY INCOME £ ☐   TOTAL WEEKLY EXPENDITURE £ ☐

Model application form

SAVINGS £ ....

DEBTS/ARREARS Rent, fuels, loans, HP etc.		Has applicant received help from any other source? YES/NO
Specify in detail	Amount owed	(If YES, please include details below)
		Sources of grant obtained Amount

.... £ .... £ ....

.... £ .... £ ....

.... £ ....   Other sources approached

.... £ ....

.... £ ....

TOTAL £ ....   TOTAL STILL REQUIRED £ ....

Has applicant ever received previous financial help from this trust?   YES/NO   If so, when?

REASON FOR THE APPLICATION

Continue on a separate sheet if necessary

FOR APPLICATIONS BEING SUBMITTED THROUGH A WELFARE AGENCY

Name of agency ....

Case worker ....

Address ....

....

Telephone ....

How long has the applicant been known to your department/organisation? ....

FOR ALL APPLICATIONS

Signature: Date:

15

Occupational charities

This section contains:
- An index of each charity connected with a particular trade or profession (including both independent charities and benevolent funds associated with trade unions or professional bodies). The categories of trades/professions are listed alphabetically.
- After the index, the entries themselves are arranged alphabetically.

Therefore, for example, people in need (or the spouse/dependants of such people) who are or have been hairdressers should first look in the index under the heading "Hairdressing". They will see three charities listed. They should then turn to and read carefully the respective entries to see if they are eligible and whether the charity gives the kind of help they need. Finally, they should check with their or their spouse's trade union to see if there is any welfare provision arising out of contributions made to the union or if there is any non-contributory welfare provision. Trades unions, even if they do not have their own separate benevolent funds, sometimes have resources available for members, former members or their dependents who are in need.

Local occupational charities, for example the Grimsby Fishermen's Dependants' Fund, are not listed in this section. They can be found in the relevant local section of the Guide.

Index of funds for particular trades or occupations

Accountancy
Certified Accountants' Benevolent Association
Chartered Accountants' Benevolent Association
Chartered Institute of Management Accountants' Benevolent Fund
Institute of Company Accountants Benevolent Fund
Institute of Financial Accountants Benevolent Fund

Actors (see Arts and Entertainment)

Advertising
National Advertising Benevolent Society

Agriculture & Forestry
Royal Agricultural Benevolent Institution
Rural, Agricultural & Allied Workers' Benevolent Fund
Timber Trades Benevolent Society

Air Travel
British Airline Pilots' Association Benevolent Fund
Guild of Air Pilots' & Navigators' Benevolent Fund

Ambulance Services
Ambulance Services Benevolent Fund

Antique Dealers
British Antique Dealers' Association Benevolent Fund

Architects
Architects Benevolent Society

Arts & Entertainment
Actors' Benevolent Fund
Actors' Charitable Trust
Artists' General Benevolent Institution
Authors' Contingency Fund
Concert Artistes' Association
Dance Teachers' Benevolent Fund
Eaton Fund for Artists, Nurses & Gentlewomen
English National Opera Benevolent Fund
Entertainment Artistes' Benevolent Fund
Equity Trust Fund
Grand Order of Water Rats Charities Fund (variety artists)
Francis Head Bequest (authors)
Incorporated Association of Organists Benevolent Fund
Incorporated Society of Musicians Benevolent Fund
International Dance Teachers' Association Benevolent Fund
King George's Pension Fund for Actors & Actresses
Magic Circle Benevolent Fund
Musicians Benevolent Fund
Musicians' Social & Benevolent Council
Evelyn Norris Trust
Pension Fund of the Incorporated Society of Authors, Playrights & Composers
Performing Rights Society Members' Fund (composers, authors, publishers of music)
Royal Ballet Benevolent Fund
Royal Literary Fund
Royal Opera House Benevolent Fund
Royal Society of Musicians
Royal Theatrical Fund
Theatrical Ladies Guild of Charity
Michael Tippert Musical Foundation

Atomic Energy
UK Atomic Energy Authority Benevolent Fund

Auctioneers
Incorporated Society of Valuers & Auctioneers Benevolent Fund

Bakers (see Food, Drink & Provision)

Banking
Bankers Benevolent Fund
Banking Insurance & Finance Union Benevolent Fund
Alfred Foster Settlement

Barristers (see Legal Profession)

Occupational charities

Book Retail
Book Trade Benevolent Society

Bookbinding
Bookbinders' Charitable Society

Bookmakers
Bookmakers Employees Benevolent Fund

Boxing
Jack Solomons Charity Fund

Brewing (see Food, Drink & Provision Trades)

British Rail (see Railways)

British Telecom (see Telecommunications)

Brush Trade
John Chamberlain Permanent Benevolent Fund for Aged & Infirm Members of Brush Trade

Building/Construction (see also Engineering)
Builders' Benevolent Institution
Lighthouse Club Benevolent Fund
Royal Metal Trades Benevolent Society

Butchers (see Food, Drink & Provision Trades)

Caravan Industry
National Caravan Council Ltd

Catering (see Hotel & Catering)

Ceramic Industry
Ceramic Industry Welfare Society

Chartered Secretaries & Administrators
Institute of Chartered Secretaries & Administrators Benevolent Fund

Chartered Surveyors
Royal Institution of Chartered Surveyors Benevolent Fund

Chemical Engineers
Chemical Engineers' Benevolent Fund

Chemistry (see Science)

Chiropody (see Medicine & Health)

Cinema (see Media)

Civil & Public Services
Benevolent Fund of HM Inspectors of Schools in England & Wales
Century Benevolent Fund
Civil & Public Services Association Benevolent Fund
Civil Service Benevolent Fund
Institution of Professionals, Managers & Specialists Benevolent Fund
Overseas Service Pensioners' Benevolent Society
Staines Trust
Unison Welfare Fund

Clayworkers
Institute of Clayworkers Benevolent Fund

Clergy/Christian workers
Aged & Infirm Ministers' Fund (Presbyterian, United Reformed, Baptist)
Mrs Frances Ashton's Charity (Anglican)
Auxiliary fund of Ministers' Retirement Fund of Methodist Church
Mrs Becker's Charity for Clergy (Anglican)
Church of England Pensions Board
Corporation of Sons of Clergy (Anglican)
Foundation of Edward Storey
Friends of Clergy Corporation (Anglican)
Arthur Hurst Will Trust
Methodist Local Preachers' Mutual Aid Association
Mylne Trust
Pyncombe Charity (Anglican)
Rev Dr George Richards Charity (Anglican)
Henry Smith's Charity Alfriston Estate (Anglican)
Silverwood Trust (Missionaries)
Society for Relief of Necessitous Protestant Ministers
Society for Relief of Poor Clergymen
Tancred's Charities (Anglican clergy in Armed Forces)
Thornton Fund (Unitarian church)
Widow's Fund of Three Denominations (Presbyterian, Independent, Baptist)

Clothing/Footwear
Boot Trade Benevolent Society
Master Tailors' Benevolent Association
Merchant Taylors' Company
Tailors' Benevolent Institute

Coal Industry
Coal Industry Benevolent Trust
Coal Trade Benevolent Association

Commercial Travellers
Commercial Travellers' Benevolent Institution
Manufacturing Confectioners' Commercial Travellers' Association Benevolent Fund

Confectionery (see Food, Drink & Provision Trades)

Cooperative Officials
National Association of Cooperative Officials' Benevolent Fund

Corn Exchange
Corn Exchange Benevolent Society

Cotton Industry (see Textiles)

Cricketers
Cricketers Association Charity
Hornsby Professional Cricketers Fund

Customs & Excise
Customs & Excise Family Fund

Dairy Trade (see Food, Drink & Provision Trades)

Dance (see Arts & Entertainment)

Domestic Servants
Domestic Servants Benevolent Institution

Dentists (see Medicine & Health)

Dock workers
Tim O'Leary Special Fund

Doctors (see Medicine & Health)

Drapers (see Textiles)

Drink (see Food, Drink & Provision Trades)

Driving Instructors
Driving Instructors Accident & Disability Fund

Electrical & Electronic Industries
Amalgamated Engineering & Electrical Union – Electrical, Electronic, Telecommunications & Plumbing Section
Electrical & Electronic Industries Benevolent Association
Institution of Electrical Engineers Incorporated Benevolent Fund

Engineering (see also Electrical & Electronic Industries)
Benevolent Fund of Institution of Mechanical Engineers
Chartered Institution of Building Services Engineers Benevolent Fund
Engineering Employers' Federation Benevolent Fund

● Occupational charities

Engineers' & Managers' Association (EMA) Benevolent Fund
Institution of Civil Engineers Benevolent Fund

Institute of Marine Engineers Guild of Benevolence
Institution of Plant Engineers Benevolent Fund
Institution of Structural Engineers Benevolent Fund

Entertainers (see Arts & Entertainment)

Farriers
Worshipful Company of Farriers Charitable Trust

Fire Services
Fire Services National Benevolent Fund

Fishermen
Royal National Mission to Deep Sea Fishermen
Shipwrecked Mariners' Society

Fishmongers (see Food, Drink & Provision Trades)

Flooring Industry
Sydney Simmons Pension Fund

Food, Drink & Provision Trades
Bakers' Benevolent Society
Butchers' & Drovers' Charitable Institution
Confectioners' Benevolent Fund
Fishmongers' & Poulterers' Institution
Sir Percival Griffiths' Tea Planters Trust
Incorporated Brewers' Benevolent Society
National Association of Master Bakers
National Dairymen's Benevolent Institution
National Federation of Fish Friers Benevolent Fund
National Grocers' Benevolent Fund
Oilseed, Oil & Feedingstuffs Trades Benevolent Association
Provision Trade Benevolent Institution
Society of Licensed Victuallers
Wine & Spirits Trade Benevolent Society
Wine Trade Foundation

Football
Football Association Benevolent Fund
Institute of Football Management & Administration Charity Trust
Professional Footballers Association Accident Fund
Professional Footballers Association Benevolent Fund
Referees Association Members Benevolent Fund

Forestry (see Agriculture)

Furnishing
Furnishing Trades Benevolent Institution

Gardening
Gardeners' Royal Benevolent Society
Horticultural Trades Association Benevolent Fund

General
Morden College
Professional Classes Aid Council
Royal United Kingdom Beneficent Association (RUKBA)

Glass Trade
Pottery & Glass Trade Benevolent Institution

Gold & Silver Smithing (see Metal Trade & Metallurgy)

Golf
PGA European Tour Benevolent Fund

Governesses (see Teaching)

Grocers (see Food, Drink & Provision Trades)

Hairdressing
Barbers' Amalgamated Charity
British Hairdressers' Benevolent & Provident Institution
Hairdressers' Children's Welfare Fund

Health Services
Institute of Health Services Management Benevolent Fund
National Health Service Pensioners Trust

Horse Racing
Bentinck Benevolent Fund (for flat race trainers & jockeys)
Beresford Trust (for horse racing employees)
Injured Jockeys Fund
Rendlesham Benevolent Fund (national hunt trainers & jockeys)
Stable Lads Welfare Trust

Horticulture (see Gardening)

Hotel & Catering
Hotel & Catering Benevolent Association

Insurance
Insurance Benevolent Fund
Insurance Orphans' Fund
Lloyd's Benevolent Fund
Worshipful Company of Insurers Charitable Trust Fund

Jewellery & Giftware
British Jewellery, Giftware & Leathergoods Benevolent Society
Goldsmiths' Silversmiths' & Jewellers' Benevolent Society

Journalism (see Media)

Launderers
Worshipful Company of Launderers Benevolent Trust

Leather
British Jewellery, Giftware & Leathergoods Benevolent Society
Leather & Hides Trades' Benevolent Institution

Legal Profession
Barristers' Benevolent Association
Institute of Legal Executives Benevolent Funds
Solicitors' Benevolent Association
United Law Clerks Society

Librarians
Library Association Benevolent Fund

Linen Trades (see Textiles)

Local Government
Unison Welfare Fund

Lock-keepers
Myrtle Cohen Trust Fund

London Transport (see Transport General)

Loss Adjusters
Chartered Institute of Loss Adjusters Benevolent Fund

Magicians (see Arts & Entertainment)

Market Research
Market Research Benevolent Association

Match Manufacture
Joint Industrial Council & the Match Manufacturing Industry Charitable Fund

Media
Chartered Institute of Journalists Orphan Fund
Cinema & Television Benevolent Fund
Grace Wyndham Goldie (BBC) Trust Fund
National Union of Journalists Provident Fund
Newspaper Press Fund

Occupational charities

Medicine & Health
Association of Optical Practitioners Charitable Fund
Barbers' Amalgamated Charity *(surgeons, physicians, dentists)*
British College of Optometrists Benevolent Fund
British Dental Association Benevolent Fund
Cameron Fund *(general medical practitioners)*
Edith Cavell & Nation's Fund for Nurses
Chartered Society of Physiotherapy Benevolent Fund
Eaton Fund for Artists, Nurses & Gentlewomen
Hastings Benevolent Fund
Junius S Morgan Benevolent Fund *(nurses)*
1930 Fund for District Nurses
Nurses Fund for Nurses
Pharmaceutical Society's Benevolent Fund
Queen's Nursing Institute
Royal College of Midwives Benevolent Fund
Royal Medical Benevolent Fund
Royal Medical Foundation of Epsom College
Society of Chiropodists Benevolent Fund
Society of Radiographers Benevolent Fund
Society for Relief of Widows & Orphans of Medical Men
Trained Nurses Annuity Fund

Metal Trades & Metallurgy
Institution of Mining & Metallurgy Benevolent Fund
British Jewellery, Giftware & Leathergoods Benevolent Society
Goldsmiths' Silversmiths' & Jewellers' Benevolent Society
Royal Metal Trades Benevolent Society

Millers
National British & Irish Millers' Benevolent Society

Motor Industry
Ben - Motor & Allied Trades Benevolent Fund
H T Pickles Benevolent Fund
Society of Motor Manufacturers & Traders Charitable Trust Fund

Motor Sport
British Motoring Sport Relief Fund
Grand Prix Mechanics Charitable Trust

Musicians *(see Arts & Entertainment)*

Naval Architects
Royal Institution of Naval Architects Benevolent Fund

Newsagents
National Federation of Retail Newsagents Convalescence Fund
Newsvendors' Benevolent Institution

Nuclear Industry *(see Atomic Energy)*

Nurses *(see Medicine & Health)*

Optical Practitioners *(see Medicine & Health)*

Patent Agents
Chartered Institute of Patent Agents' Incorporated Benevolent Association

Pawnbrokers
Pawnbrokers' Charitable Institution

Petroleum
Institute of Petroleum 1986 Benevolent Fund

Pharmaceutical Industry *(see Medicine & Health)*

Physics *(see Science)*

Physiotherapy *(see Medicine & Health)*

Pilots *(see Air Travel)*

Plaisterer
Worshipful Company of Plaisterers Charitable Trust

Plumbing
Amalgamated Engineering & Electrical Union – Electrical, Electronic, Telecommunications & Plumbing Section

Police
Gurney Fund for Police Orphans
Metropolitan Police Civil Staff Welfare Fund
Metropolitan Police Combined Benevolent Fund
Northern Police Orphans' Trust
Police Dependants' Trust

Post Office
Rowland Hill Benevolent Fund
National Federation of Sub-Postmasters Benevolent Fund
Second Post Office Relief Fund

Pottery
Pottery & Glass Trade Benevolent Institution

Poulterers *(see Food, Drink & Provision Trades)*

Printers
Printers' Charitable Corporation

Probation Workers
Edridge Fund

Provision Trades *(see Food, Drink & Provision Trades)*

Public Relations
Institute of Public Relations Benevolent Fund

Quarrying
Institute of Quarrying Benevolent Fund

Railways
Associated Society of Locomotive Engineers & Firemen (ASLEF) Orphans' Fund
British Rail Staff Assistance Fund
Railway Benevolent Institution
RMT (National Union of Rail, Maritime & Transport Workers) Orphan Fund

Retail
Royal Metal Trades Benevolent Society

Road Haulage
Road Haulage Association Benevolent Fund

Seafaring & Shipping
Baltic Exchange Charitable Society
Honourable Company of Master Mariners
Bonno Krull Fund
London Shipowners' & Shipbrokers' Benevolent Society
Marine Society
NUMAST Welfare Fund
Royal Alfred Seafarers' Society
Royal Liverpool Seamen's Orphan Institution
Royal Seamen's Pension Fund
Sailors' Families Society
Seamen's Hospital Society
Shipwrecked Mariners' Society
Trinity House Charities

Science
Institute of Physics Benevolent Trust
John Murdoch Trust
Royal Society of Chemistry Benevolent Fund
Scientific Relief Fund

Sewing Machines
Sewing Machine Trade Benevolent Fund

Occupational charities

Shipping (see Seafaring & Shipping)

Social Work
Social Workers' Benevolent Trust

Solicitors (see Legal Profession)

Sport General (see also individual sports)
Rugby Football Union Charitable Fund

Stationery & Office Equipment
British Office Systems & Stationery Federation Benevolent Fund

Stock Exchange
Stock Exchange Benevolent Fund
Stock Exchange Clerks Fund

Surgeons (see Medicine & Health)

Tallow Chandlers
Worshipful Company of Tallow Chandlers

Tax Inspectors
Association of Her Majesty's Inspectors of Taxes Benevolent Fund

Tea Planting (see Food, Drink & Provision Trades)

Teaching
Association of Teachers & Lecturers Benevolent Fund
Association of University Teachers Benevolent Fund
Church Schoolmasters & Schoolmistresses' Benevolent Institution
Incorporated Association of Preparatory Schools Benevolent Fund
Liverpool Governesses Benevolent Institution
National Association of Schoolmasters Union of Women Teachers Benevolent Fund
Schoolmistresses & Governesses Benevolent Institution
Society of Schoolmasters
Teachers' Benevolent Fund

Telecommunications
British Telecom Benevolent Fund
Amalgamated Engineering & Electrical Union – Electrical, Electronic, Telecommunications & Plumbing Section

Television (see Media)

Textiles
City of London Linen Trades Association
Cotton Industry Benevolent Fund
Drapers' Consolidated Charity
Textile Benevolent Fund

Timber Trades (see Agriculture & Forestry)

Tobacco
Tobacco Trade Benevolent Association

Transport (General)
RMT (National Union of Rail, Maritime & Transport Workers) Orphan Fund
Transport Benevolent Fund
(see also Air Travel, Railways, Seafaring & Shipping)

Travel Industry
ABTA Benevolent Fund
Guild of Guide Lecturers Benevolent Fund

Valuers
Incorporated Society of Valuers & Auctioneers Benevolent Fund

Veterinary Surgeons
Veterinary Benevolent Fund

Watch & Clock Makers
National Benevolent Society of Watch & Clock Makers

The ABTA Benevolent Fund

Eligibility: People who are or have been employed by ABTA members for at least three years and their dependants.

Types of grants: One-off and recurrent grants according to need. Grants have been given to help with schooling; a holiday for a disabled child, and to buy a wheelchair following a serious accident. Help is also given with bills, central heating and redecoration costs.

The fund does not generally help with costs arising from the failure of a business.

Annual grant total: In 1993, the fund gave grants ranging from £100 to £2,000 and totalling about £10,000 to £15,000.

Applications: On a form available from the correspondent. Suitable applicants are then visited by a trustee.

Correspondent: S F Robin, 5 Kensington High Street, London W8 5NP (071-937 1775).

The Actors' Benevolent Fund

Eligibility: Members or former members of the theatrical profession including actors, actresses, managers, stage managers, business managers, and their spouses and/or dependants.

Types of grants: One-off and recurrent grants, allowances and interest-free loans.

Annual grant total: About £235,000 (117 weekly allowances and 828 other grants).

Applications: On a form available from the correspondent.

Correspondent: Mrs Rosemary Stevens, General Secretary, 6 Adam Street, London WC2N 6AA (071-836 6378).

The Actors' Charitable Trust

Eligibility: Children of people in the theatrical profession who are in financial hardship or extreme circumstances, and elderly members of those professions in need of residential or nursing care.

Types of grants: One-off and recurrent grants according to need.

Annual grant total: About £61,000 in 1993.

Applications: In writing or by telephone, requesting an application form.

Correspondent: Althea Stewart, 19-20 Euston Centre, London NW1 3JH (071-608 6212).

Other information: The trust co-operates with other theatrical charities to help actors and actresses and their dependants both when disaster strikes and in old age.

Occupational charities

The trust also manages Denville Hall, its residential and nursing home for members of the theatrical profession who are in need of care in their old age.

The Aged & Infirm Ministers' Fund

Eligibility: Elderly and infirm Presbyterian, United Reformed and Baptist ministers in England and Wales.

Types of grants: One-off or recurrent grants according to need.

Annual grant total: £5,500 in 1993/94.

Applications: In writing to the correspondent.

Correspondent: Rev J McClelland, 14 Gordon Square, London WC1H 0AG (071-387 3727).

The Amalgamated Engineering & Electrical Union - Electrical, Electronic, Telecommunication & Plumbing Section

Eligibility: Union members, former members, and their dependants who are in financial distress caused by unemployment, ill-health or age.

Types of grants: Usually one-off grants.

Annual grant total: In 1992, the funds had assets of £574,000 and an income of £282,000. Expenditure totalled £241,000, but not all of this was given in grants to individuals for relief-in-need.

Applications: By letter to the local branch.

Correspondent: A Cunningham, Accountant, Hayes Court, West Common Road, Bromley, Kent BR2 7AU (081-462 7755).

Other information: The union's central office in Bromley does not have a benevolent fund, but is responsible for allocating resources to the 840 local branches, each of which has its own fund. Each branch assesses local needs autonomously. This trust was previously known as the Electrical, Electronic, Telecommunications & Plumbing Union (EETPU) Benevolent Funds.

The Ambulance Services Benevolent Fund

Eligibility: Present and former ambulancemen/women, who have been employed by the NHS ambulance services of England, Wales, Scotland, Ireland (North or South) and the Channel Islands, and their dependants.

Types of grants: One-off and recurrent grants according to need, for the relief of poverty, sickness or distress. Loans are no longer given following considerable problems with repayment in the past.

Annual grant total: In 1992/93, the trust had assets of £101,000 and an income of £29,000. Total expenditure was £6,400, of which £5,700 was given to 23 individuals in grants of at least £100. Christmas hampers may also be given.

Applications: Applications are considered throughout the year and should be made in writing to the correspondent by a recognised referral agency (social worker, citizen's advice bureau, doctor or ambulance officer/manager). The application should include verification from an ambulance officer/manager that the claim is genuine, dates and length of service, specific details of need, support received from other trusts, and any other relevant financial or other information which would support the claim.

Correspondent: S D Fermor, Secretary, Cherith, 31 East Beeches Road, Crowborough, East Sussex TN6 2AU (0892-655961).

The Architects Benevolent Society

Eligibility: People engaged or formerly engaged in the architectural profession, and their dependants.

Types of grants: One-off and recurrent grants (paid monthly) and loans.

Annual grant total: In 1991/92, 400 grants totalled £730,000.

Applications: On a form available from the correspondent. Applications can be submitted directly by the individual or through a welfare agency. They are considered throughout the year.

Correspondent: R P Roth, Charity Secretary, 66 Portland Place, London W1N 4AD (071-580 2823).

Other information: The society also runs homes for elderly beneficiaries.

The Artists' General Benevolent Institution

Eligibility: Professional painters, sculptors, engravers, illustrators, architects and other creative artists and their dependants.

Types of grants: All types of grants considered; renewable annually. The trusts cannot help artists with career difficulties or students with fees.

Annual grant total: About £392,000 in several hundred grants in 1993.

Applications: By letter in the first instance. Subsequent application must include career details of qualifying person and present financial position, and be supported by two referees.

Correspondent: Mrs C Rees, Secretary, Burlington House, Piccadilly, London W1V 0DJ (071-734 1193).

Mrs Frances Ashton's Charity

Eligibility: Church of England clergymen or their widows.

Types of grants: Grants vary between £250 and £600 and are paid once a year in September.

Annual grant total: £55,000 in about 120 grants in 1993.

Applications: In writing to the correspondent, by 1st June each year.

Correspondent: B J N Coombes, Receiver, 1 Dean Trench Street, London SW1P 3HB (071-799 3696).

The Associated Society of Locomotive Engineers & Firemen (ASLEF) Orphans' Fund

Eligibility: Any child or adopted child under 16 of an ASLEF member.

Types of grants: Regular grants of £2 a week. No other form of help is considered.

Annual grant total: There are about 30 beneficiaries who also receive a gift at the end of the year from funds donated by members which totalled £9,600 in 1993.

Applications: Through the local branches, where the secretary will automatically notify the Orphans' Fund committee of the death of a member.

Correspondent: The General Secretary, ASLEF, 9 Arkwright Road, Hamstead, London NW3 6AB (071-431 0275).

The Association of Her Majesty's Inspectors of Taxes Benevolent Fund

Eligibility: Tax inspectors and other senior officers in the Inland Revenue and their dependants.

Types of grants: One-off or recurrent grants according to need.

Annual grant total: In 1992/93, the trust had assets of £133,000, an income of about £9,000 and gave 27 grants totalling £4,400.

Applications: Can be submitted by the individual, in writing to the correspondent at any time.

● **Occupational charities**

Correspondent: R E Creed, Hon. Secretary, Room S23, West Wing, Somerset House, London WC2R 1LB (071-438 6105).

The Association of Optical Practitioners Charitable Fund

Eligibility: Present or past members of the association and their dependants.

Types of grants: One-off or recurrent grants according to need.

Annual grant total: In 1993, the trust had an income of about £4,500 and gave grants totalling about £3,000.

Applications: In writing to the correspondent.

Correspondent: The Secretary, Association of Optometrists, Bridge House, 233-234 Blackfriars Road, London SE1 8NW (071-261 9661).

The Association of Teachers & Lecturers Benevolent Fund

Eligibility: Members and former members of the association, and their dependants.

Types of grants: One-off and recurrent grants according to need.

Annual grant total: About 270 grants a year totalling £35,000 to £40,000.

Applications: Write to the correspondent for an application form. Proof of membership is necessary.

Correspondent: The Secretary, 7 Northumberland Street, London WC2N 5DA (071-930 6441).

The Association of University Teachers Benevolent Fund

Eligibility: Present or past members or employees of the Association of University Teachers and their dependants.

Types of grants: One-off grants most likely to be given for items such as essential household equipment or repairs, and to widows or former members left without occupational pension provision because of defects in the university pension scheme generally applicable before 1975. Grants are also made in connection with disablement, for example home or car adaptations. No loans are given.

Annual grant total: No information available.

Applications: In writing to the correspondent, describing the help needed, details of financial circumstances and evidence of eligibility.

Correspondent: Dr G R Talbot, Secretary, United House, 9 Pembridge Road, London W11 3JY (071-221 4370).

The Authors' Contingency Fund

Eligibility: Professional authors and their dependants in an emergency.

Types of grants: One-off grants according to need.

Annual grant total: £3,000 to £4,000 in about 10 grants.

Applications: On a form available from the correspondent.

Correspondent: The Secretary, 84 Drayton Gardens, London SW10 9SB (071-373 6642).

The Auxiliary Fund of the Ministers' Retirement Fund of the Methodist Church

Eligibility: Retired ministers of the Methodist church and their dependants.

Types of grants: All kinds of need (including emergencies) are considered.

Annual grant total: £350,000 in about 800 grants.

Applications: In writing to the correspondent.

Correspondent: Roy Foulds, Secretary, 1 Central Buildings, Westminster, London SW1H 9NH (071-222 8010).

The Bakers' Benevolent Society

Eligibility: People who have worked in the baking industry and its allied trades, and their dependants.

Types of grants: One-off and recurrent grants according to need.

Annual grant total: About £24,000.

Applications: On a form available from the correspondent.

Correspondent: Mrs M A Tisi, Clerk, The Mill House, 23 Bakers Lane, Epping, Essex CM16 5DQ (0992-575951).

Other information: The society also manages almshouses and sheltered housing for its beneficiaries.

The Baltic Exchange Charitable Society

Eligibility: Members of the society and their dependants.

Types of grants: One-off and regular grants paid quarterly, according to need. Additional grants are made to meet unexpected expenses, such as hospitalisation or a nursing home stay for three or four weeks.

Annual grant total: In 1993, regular grants totalled £162,000 to 43 people. 17 one-off grants totalled £28,000.

Applications: On a form available from the correspondent. When a member dies or experiences particularly hard times the society will approach the family to see if any support is needed.

Correspondent: Doug Painter, Secretary, 14-20 St Mary Axe, London EC3A 8BH (071-623 5501).

The Bankers Benevolent Fund

Eligibility: People in need who are working or have worked in a bank in the UK for at least five years, and their families and dependants. Applicants must not have capital in excess of £8,000 if living in their own home, or £3,000 if in a residential care or nursing home.

Types of grants: (a) Regular grants up to £520 a year, plus other non-recurring grants within the DSS rules, to those on Income Support and living in their own homes.

(b) Regular grants up to £35 a week to help with the cost of residential care or nursing home fees.

(c) One-off grants normally to meet items of a capital nature such as special equipment for disabled people.

(A significant proportion of the help provided by the fund is directed towards the education and maintenance of the children of deceased or incapacitated bank employees. See entry in *The Educational Grants Directory*).

Annual grant total: In 1992/93, the trust had assets of £22.6 million and an income of £1.2 million. Total expenditure was £1.2 million including £99,000 in relief-in-need grants to individuals. There were about 105 recipients of weekly grants.

Applications: On a form available from the correspondent. Applications can be submitted directly by the individual or a relative, or through a social worker or other welfare agency.

Correspondent: Peter G Oliver, Secretary, St Mary-le-Bow House, 54 Bow Lane, London EC4M 9DJ (071-236 6428).

The Banking Insurance & Finance Union Benevolent Fund

Eligibility: 1. Members, employees and former employees of the union and their dependants who are in need and generally living in the UK.

Occupational charities

2. Employees and pensioners of financial institutions who are in need.

Types of grants: Help towards outstanding bills for essential services such as gas and electricity, buying equipment for disabled people, council tax arrears, clothes for children, mortgage and payments. Recent grants have included £500 to a victim of domestic violence to set up a new home and £100 towards a special chair for someone with a back injury. The trust prefers not to pay for private fees such as physiotherapy, osteopathy etc. but with the decline in the availability of NHS treatments, this may occasionally be supported.

Annual grant total: In 1992, the trust had assets of £171,000 and an income of £24,500. Grants ranging from £100 to £500 were given to 54 individuals in need and totalled £24,000.

Applications: Applications can be submitted by the individual or through a recognised referral agency (social worker, citizen's advice bureau or doctor etc.) union organiser or seconded representative. They are considered throughout the year.

Correspondent: Mrs J Bogner, Hon. Secretary, c/o Banking & Finance Union, Sheffield House, 1b Amity Grove, Raynes Park, London SW20 0LG (081-946 9151).

The Barbers' Amalgamated Charity

Eligibility: Poor members of the medical, dental or nursing professions, the barbers or hairdressing trades, and their widows and children.

Types of grants: Pensions of up to £10 a week.

Annual grant total: About £15,000.

Applications: In writing to the correspondent at any time.

Correspondent: The Clerk, The Worshipful Company of Barbers, Barber-Surgeons' Hall, Monkwell Square, Wood Street, London EC2Y 5BL (071-606 0741).

The Barristers' Benevolent Association

Eligibility: Past or present practising members of the bar in England and Wales, and their dependants. No grants to those who when qualified went straight into commerce.

Types of grants: One-off grants, maintenance allowances and loans. The correspondent states that some form of grant is given in most cases.

Annual grant total: In 1992, the trust had assets of £2.7 million and an income of £343,000. Total expenditure was £283,000, of which £167,000 was for general grants and £24,000 was given to specific beneficiaries. This left a surplus of income over expenditure of £60,000. Loans totalling £222,000 were also given.

Applications: On a form available from the correspondent. Applications can be submitted by the individual or through a social worker or other welfare agency. They are considered at monthly meetings of the management committee.

Correspondent: Mrs R A Ashley, 2nd Floor, 14 Gray's Inn Square, Gray's Inn, London WC1R 5JP (071-242 4761).

Mrs Becker's Charity for Clergy

Eligibility: Retired clergy of the United Church of England and Ireland who have retired through sickness or age and who are in need, hardship or distress.

Types of grants: Annual grants up to £520.

Annual grant total: No information available.

Applications: On a form available from the correspondent, submitted directly by the individual. Applications are considered at any time.

Correspondent: A P Newman, Secretary, 71 Eastfield Avenue, Weston, Bath BA1 4HH (0225-424229).

Ben - Motor & Allied Trades Benevolent Fund

Eligibility: People from the UK or Republic of Ireland employed or formerly employed in the motor, agricultural engineering and cycle trades and allied industries, and their dependants.

Types of grants: One-off and weekly grants according to need, including care costs, heating, clothing, holidays and convalescence.

No grants will be given towards medical costs.

Annual grant total: The trust gave over 2,000 grants totalling £400,000 and between £50 to £500.

Applications: On a form available from the correspondent. Applications are considered monthly and can be submitted directly by the individual or through a welfare agency or another third party.

Correspondent: Mrs S M Cooper, Director Welfare Services, Lynwood, Sunninghill, Ascot, Berkshire SL5 0AJ (0344-20191).

Other information: The fund also manages an extensive range of residential accommodation for the elderly or disabled, including sheltered accommodation.

The Benevolent Fund of HM Inspectors of Schools in England & Wales

Eligibility: Present and retired HM Inspectors and their dependants who are in need.

Types of grants: One-off or recurrent grants according to need.

Annual grant total: In 1992, the trust had an income of £20,000. Grants to individuals totalled £4,750.

Applications: In writing to the correspondent, directly by the individual.

Correspondent: D J Lewis, Trustee, The Willows, Low Street, Bardwell, Bury-St-Edmunds, Suffolk IP31 1AS (0359-50845).

The Benevolent Fund of the Institution of Mechanical Engineers

Eligibility: Members/former members of the institution and their dependants.

Types of grants: Recurrent grants ranging from £520 to £2,000 a year to those on or near the Income Support level. A £10 weekly disregard grant is given to those on Income Support. Other grants according to need for essential house maintenance, to buy special equipment, such as wheelchairs for disabled people and towards respite care. Top up grants for residential/nursing home fees may also be awarded.

Grants are not given towards private education (unless their are exceptional circumstances), private medicine, or business loans or debts.

Annual grant total: In 1993, the trust had assets of £7.4 million and an income of £439,000. £435,000 was given to 215 beneficiaries.

Applications: On a form available from the correspondent, giving details of income, expenditure, capital, assets, property and debts. Initial enquiries are encouraged directly by the individual or through a third party such as spouse or dependant. Details of connection with the institute are required. Referrals by citizens advice bureau, social workers etc. are encouraged. Applications are considered in March, May, August and October. Emergency cases can be dealt with sooner.

Occupational charities

Correspondent: Wing Cmdr J A Mutsaars, Manager, Northgate Avenue, Bury St Edmunds, Suffolk IP32 6BN (0284-764875).

The Bentinck Benevolent Fund

Eligibility: Flat race trainers and jockeys, their widows and dependants who due to old age or illness are in need.

Types of grants: Allowances and grants paid twice-yearly; one-off grants for urgent needs and, occasionally, funeral expenses. One-off grants range from £200 to £460; bi-annual allowances are currently £130; bi-annual grants £100.

Annual grant total: £32,000 in 1993, including £17,500 in allowances and £14,500 in donations; 76 grants in total.

Applications: On a form available from the correspondent. Applications can be submitted directly by the individual or through a social worker, citizen's advice bureau or other welfare agency. They are considered throughout the year.

Correspondent: Mrs P Lewis, c/o The Jockey Club Charitable Trust, 121 High Street, Newmarket, Suffolk CB8 9AJ (0638-560763).

The Beresford Trust

Eligibility: Thoroughbred racing stable, racecourse and stud employees, and their dependants, who due to old age or illness are in need.

Types of grants: Quarterly allowances and grants, one-off grants for special needs and, occasionally, funeral expenses. Grants range from £200 to about £460. Quarterly allowances are currently £65 and quarterly grants £100.

Annual grant total: £61,000 in 1993, including £33,000 in £65 allowances, £26,000 in £100 allowances and £1,800 in one-off grants; 149 grants in total.

Applications: On a form available from the correspondent. Applications can be submitted directly by the individual or through a social worker, citizen's advice bureau or other welfare agency. They are considered throughout the year.

Correspondent: Mrs P Lewis, The Jockey Club Charitable Trust, 121 High Street, Newmarket, Suffolk CB8 9AJ (0638-560763).

The Book Trade Benevolent Society

Eligibility: People who have worked in the book trade in Great Britain for at least one year, and their dependants. Priority will be given to those who are chronically sick or 50 years of age or over.

Types of grants: One-off and recurrent grants according to need, generally to supplement weekly/monthly income for housekeeping and help with fuel bills in long spells of cold weather. Other support is given in a variety of ways (eg. assistance with telephone and television rental, medical aid, aids for disabled people and house repairs/redecoration). There is also a holiday fund to help a number of people who have not had a break for many years with the cost of a holiday or to visit family or friends. Christmas gift cheques are also given.

Grants are not given for nursing home fees.

Annual grant total: In 1992, the trust had assets of £1.1 million and an income of £153,000. Total expenditure was £162,000 including £13,000 in relief-in-need grants to individuals.

Applications: On a form available from the correspondent. Applications can be submitted by the individual or through a recognised referral agency (social worker, citizen's advice bureau, doctor etc.) and are considered quarterly.

Correspondent: Mrs A Brown, Dillon Lodge, The Retreat, Kings Langley, Hertfordshire WD4 8LT (0923-263128).

The Bookbinders' Charitable Society

Eligibility: Retired people in need who have worked in the bookbinding, printing and allied trades, and their dependants.

Types of grants: About 40 pensions of £31 paid four times a year totalling £4,800, in 1992. Three one-off grants were also given totalling over £500. One-off grants may be given to help buy essential or emergency items.

Annual grant total: Over £5,000 in grants and pensions.

Applications: In writing to the correspondent. People who meet the criteria will then be sent an application form.

Correspondent: The Secretary, 3 Bookbinders Cottages, Bawtry Road, Whetstone, London N20 0SS (081-368 4770).

Other information: The trust also has accommodation (26 homes/flats) in Whetstone for eligible people in need. Residents pay a small contribution towards maintaining the property.

The Bookmakers Employees Benevolent Fund

Eligibility: Employees or former employees of bookmakers and their dependants. Priority is given to elderly or infirm racecourse workmen in the south east of England. Applicants from other regions are usually transferred to other trusts such as the Archie Scott Benevolent Fund in the Midlands section of the book.

Types of grants: One-off and recurrent grants ranging from £50 to £100. 38 grants were given in 1992/93.

Annual grant total: In 1992/93, the fund had assets of £19,800, income of £8,900 and expenditure totalled £6,600. Relief-in-need grants totalled £3,900.

Applications: On a form available from the correspondent. Applications are considered throughout the year.

Correspondent: D S Saphir, Secretary, 117 Auckland Road, Upper Norwood, London SE19 2DT (081-653 8230).

The Boot Trade Benevolent Society

Eligibility: People who are working or have worked in the boot trade and their dependants.

Types of grants: One-off grants and allowances according to need.

Annual grant total: £80,000 in 1992/93.

Applications: In writing to the correspondent.

Correspondent: Ms V H S Jacob, Secretary, Eldan Chambers, 30 Fleet Street, London EC4Y 1AA (071-353 2970).

The British Airline Pilots' Association Benevolent Fund (BALPA)

Eligibility: Serving and retired pilots and navigators who are or have been members of BALPA, and their dependants.

Types of grants: One-off and recurrent grants and interest-free loans. The fund prefers to give grants for specific needs such as electricity bills, school books for children etc..

Annual grant total: About £15,000.

Applications: In writing to the correspondent requesting an application form. Applications are considered quarterly.

Correspondent: Peter Smith, Hon. Secretary, 81 New Road, Harlington, Hayes, Middlesex UB3 5BG (081-759 9331).

Occupational charities

The British Antique Dealers' Association Benevolent Fund

Eligibility: People closely related to, or having worked for, members or former members of the association.

Types of grants: One-off and recurrent grants according to need.

Annual grant total: About £5,000 in seven grants in 1990.

Applications: On a form available from the correspondent. Applications are considered in May and November, or as necessary.

Correspondent: The Secretary General, 20 Rutland Gate, London SW7 1BD (071-589 4128).

The British College of Optometrists Benevolent Fund

Eligibility: Members and former members (of any class) of the British College of Optometrists; former members of the British Optical Association; other members and former members of the optical/optometric profession, and their dependants.

Types of grants: Grants according to need. Some grants are paid monthly; some bills are also paid such as television and telephone. Help is occasionally given towards residence/nursing fees top-ups and Christmas grants.

No grants to students.

Annual grant total: In 1993, the trust had assets of £400,000 and an income of £20,000. Grants ranging from £20 to £100 were given to 30 individuals and totalled £15,000.

Applications: Application forms are available from the correspondent and a financial form must be completed. Applications are considered all year round and applicants are usually visited by a member of the profession.

Correspondent: Mrs D Leasow, Admin. Secretary, 10 Knaresborough Place, Earls Court, London W5 2JD (071-370 4765).

The British Dental Association Benevolent Fund

Eligibility: Dentists who are or have been on the UK dental register, and their dependants.

Types of grants: One-off and recurrent grants and loans according to need. The trust does not generally help people with a considerable amount of capital (it generally uses the DSS regulations as a guide, but this is flexible, especially in nursing home cases).

Help is not usually given with private medical fees or private school fees.

Annual grant total: In 1992, the trust had assets of over £900,000 generating an income of £159,000. Total expenditure was £140,000, of which £128,000 was given in 70 grants to individuals in need.

Applications: On a form available from the correspondent. Applications are considered as they are received.

Correspondent: Miss Priscilla Watt, 64 Wimpole Street, London W1M 8AL (071-935 0875).

The British Hairdressers' Benevolent & Provident Institution

Eligibility: Hairdressers or barbers over 18 years of age who are in need, and their dependants. Also eligible are people who have worked in associated industries, such as hairdressing retail and manufacture, and their dependants.

Types of grants: One-off and recurrent grants and loans according to need. Grants range from £260 to £520 and there are two main categories:

(a) People in nursing homes, needing help with a shortfall in fees;

(b) People in their own homes on very low incomes to help with television licence/rental etc..

One-off grants can also be given towards holidays, wheelchairs and computers.

The trust does not help with funeral expenses or towards tertiary education.

Annual grant total: In 1992, the trust had assets of over £400,000 which generated an income of about £58,000. Total expenditure was £65,000. Grants were given to 110 individuals and totalled £51,000.

Applications: On a form available from the correspondent. Applications are considered in any month except August. Include full details of hairdressing employment details. A supporting letter from a doctor/social worker etc. would be useful but not essential.

Correspondent: Alan Rapkin, Secretary, Phoenix House, 211-213b High Road, Benfleet, Essex SS7 5HZ (0268-759990).

The British Jewellery, Giftware & Leathergoods Benevolent Society

Eligibility: Elderly and infirm people who have worked in the manufacture or distribution of jewellery and giftware, manufacture of leathergoods and luggage, or processing of metal. Grants are also available to their dependants.

Types of grants: Regular allowances within the DSS "disregard" limit (at present £10 a week). One-off grants are also given towards the provision of essential needs such as a second hand fridge/freezer/washing mashine or towards bed linen or clothes etc..

Annual grant total: In 1992, grants totalled £33,400, distributed mainly in quarterly grants of £130.

Applications: In writing to the correspondent, requesting an application form.

Correspondent: Lynn B Snead, Federation House, 10 Vyse Street, Birmingham B18 6LT (021-236 2657).

The British Motoring Sport Relief Fund

Eligibility: People injured or disabled through participating or assisting in motor car sports, and their dependants.

Types of grants: One-off and recurrent grants according to need, offering short term help. Grants are generally towards medical expenses, towards rehabilitation, car/transport costs or occasionally to help with bills.

Annual grant total: In 1992/93, the fund had assets of about £62,000 and an income around £5,000. One relief-in-need grant of about £2,000 was given to an individual. The previous year three grants were given totalling around £6,000.

Applications: Applications should be made in writing giving details of the event at which the injury or disability occurred. A supporting letter from the organisers of the event would be useful.

Correspondent: Mr Grant, Financial Director, c/o BRDC, Silverstone Circuit, Silverstone, Nr Towcester, Northants NN12 8TN (0327-857271).

The British Office Systems & Stationery Federation Benevolent Fund

Eligibility: People working or who have worked in the stationery and office machines trade and are in need.

Types of grants: Quarterly pensions and one-off grants to help with items such as telephones, television licences and rentals, residential fees and occasionally holidays.

Annual grant total: In 1992, the trust had an income of £21,000; it gave £25,000 in grants.

● **Occupational charities**

Applications: In writing to the correspondent. A team of visitors assess the need and offer support to beneficiaries.

Correspondent: J S Roscoe, Secretary, 6 Wimpole Street, London W1M 8AS (071-637 7692).

The British Rail Staff Assistance Fund

Eligibility: Present and former staff of British Railways who were contributors to the above fund or the former Railway Staff Assistance Funds, and their dependants whose net income is under £3,346 a year.

Types of grants: One-off and recurrent grants according to need.

Annual grant total: £24,000 in 622 grants in 1992, including £23,000 to widows.

Applications: In writing to the correspondent.

Correspondent: The Secretary, Stooperdale Offices, Brinkburn Road, Darlington, Co Durham DL3 6EH (0325-343397).

The British Telecom Benevolent Fund

Eligibility: Serving and retired employees of British Telecom, and their dependants.

Types of grants: Regular grants up to £750 are given, usually quarterly or six-monthly to people on low incomes for all kinds of need. Loans and grants are also given towards a shortfall in residential or nursing home fees. Recent grants have included help with disability aids, holidays, arrears, clothing, redecoration and domestic equipment.

The trust does not give grants for private education or private medicine costs.

Annual grant total: In 1992, the trust had assets of £589,000 and an income of £403,000. Grants of up to £750 were given to 620 people and totalled £208,000.

Applications: Applications can be made to the correspondent via the local British Telecom welfare officer, through a welfare agency or directly by the individual. Applicants will be visited by a welfare officer. There is an application form and applications are considered every month.

Correspondent: Brian Upcroft, Room G023, 2-12 Gresham Street, London EC2V 7AG (071-356 7584).

Other information: This fund was originally set up in 1853 as the "Post Office Clerks Charitable Fund". The fund was formed when the Post Office and Telecommunications businesses separated in 1981.

The Builders' Benevolent Institution

Eligibility: Those who are or who have been master builders (employers in the building industry), and their dependants. Applicants with fewer than 10 years experience are not eligible.

Types of grants: Monthly payments of £5 to £12.50 a week; holiday grants of £100 a year; winter comforts grant of £120 a year; Christmas gifts of £35; telephone rental grants of £70 a year.

Annual grant total: Variable; in 1990, the trust had assets of £224,000 and an income of £42,000. Expenditure totalled £49,000.

Applications: On a form available from the correspondent, submitted directly by the individual, through a social worker, citizen's advice bureau or other welfare agency or third party. Applications are considered throughout the year.

Correspondent: The Secretary, c/o 82 New Cavendish Street, London W1M 8AD (071-636 3891).

The Butchers' & Drovers' Charitable Institution

Eligibility: People who have worked in the meat trade, normally for at least 15 years, and their dependants.

Types of grants: Pensions and one-off grants.

Annual grant total: The institution had an income of £173,000 in 1991, it is not known how much was given in grants to individuals.

Applications: In writing to the correspondent.

Correspondent: J Alistair Fordyce, Secretary, St Bartholomews Chambers, 61 West Smithfield, London EC1A 9EA (071-606 5711).

The Cameron Fund Limited

Eligibility: General medical practitioners and their dependants.

Types of grants: Help with general expenses, holidays, house repairs or to supplement nursing home fees.

Annual grant total: In 1992, the trust had assets of £2.33 million and an income of £280,000. Expenditure totalled £291,000 including £207,000 in relief-in-need grants to individuals.

Applications: On a form available from the correspondent. Applications can be submitted directly by the individual, through a social worker, citizen's advice bureau or welfare agency, or through a solicitor or person holding power of attorney. Applications are considered in February, May, August and November.

Correspondent: Mrs J Martin, Secretary, Tavistock House North, Tavistock Square, London WC1H 9JP (071-388 0796).

The Edith Cavell & Nation's Fund for Nurses

Eligibility: Registered nurses who are retired or unable to continue their chosen career owing to severe disability, with a minimum of 10 years experience.

Types of grants: Regular grants plus single grants in emergencies, generally £100 to £250. Grants are to assist with household expenses and essential equipment, television, telephone rental/installation, respite breaks and help towards provision of specialist aids and equipment.

No help with debt repayment, loans, rent or mortgage arrears.

Annual grant total: In 1993, the trust had assets of £2.2 million producing an income of £130,000. All of this was given in grants to about 1,000 individuals.

Applications: Applications can be submitted by the individual or through a recognised referral agency (social worker, citizen's advice bureau or other charitable organisation etc.). Applications are considered in February, April, June, August, October and December.

Correspondent: Mrs Maureen Proctor, Welfare Adviser, 3 Albemarle Way, Clerkenwell, London EC1V 4JB (071-490 1808).

Other information: Although most of the income is distributed to qualified nurses, the fund can make grants to untrained auxiliaries. See also the entry for the Queen's Nursing Institute.

The Century Benevolent Fund

Eligibility: Employees and ex-employees of the Government Communications Bureau.

Types of grants: One-off or recurrent grants according to need.

Annual grant total: In 1992/93, the trust's income was £46,000; grants totalled £53,000.

Applications: In writing to the correspondent.

Correspondent: The Secretary, 100 Westminster Bridge Road, London SE1 7XF (071-928 5600).

Occupational charities

The Ceramic Industry Welfare Society

Eligibility: People who are or have been employed in the ceramics industry. Membership of the Ceramic and Allied Trades Union is a condition as is payment when in work of 50p a week premium. No grants are payable beyond 12 months of the date of retirement.

Types of grants: Recurrent grants ranging from £28 to £45 per six week period depending on the circumstances of the applicant as identified by the visit of the society's representative. About 200 grants were given in 1992, that is about 24 people per six week period.

Annual grant total: In 1992, the trust had assets of £71,000 and an income of £14,000. Relief-in-need grants totalled £7,500.

Applications: In the first instance applications should be made through the Ceramic & Allied Trades Union, Hillcrest House, Garth Street, Hanley, Stoke-on-Trent ST1 2AB.

Correspondent: A McRae, Federation House, Station Road, Stoke-on-Trent ST4 2SA (0782-744631).

The Certified Accountants' Benevolent Association

Eligibility: Members of the association and their dependants.

Types of grants: One-off grants for all kinds of need (amount dependent on need), allowances, sometimes over £1,000 a year, and interest-free or low-interest loans on property.

Annual grant total: £63,000 not including loans. 45 to 55 grants are made each year.

Applications: On a form available from the correspondent.

Correspondent: R V Toncic, Hon. Secretary, 29 Lincoln's Inn Fields, London WC2A 3EE (071-242 6855).

The John Chamberlain Permanent Benevolent Fund for Aged & Infirm Members of the Brush Trade

Eligibility: Aged and infirm members of the brush trade.

Types of grants: Pensions and one-off grants.

Annual grant total: £3,000 in 1993, including 20 pensions of about £100 with an additional £50 Christmas gift.

Applications: The governing committee is trying to wind the fund down as far as possible; no new applications have been accepted since 1984.

Correspondent: A N Nisbet, Brooke House, 4 The Lakes, Bedford Road, Northampton NN4 7YD (0604-22023).

The Chartered Accountants' Benevolent Association

Eligibility: Members and former members of the Institute of Chartered Accountants in England and Wales and their dependants. Also former articled clerks disabled as a result of the 1939-45 war and their dependants.

Types of grants: One-off and recurrent grants depending on need.

Annual grant total: In 1992, a total of £789,000 was given to 580 people. A small proportion was given for educational purposes.

Applications: In writing to the correspondent.

Correspondent: P L P Humpage, Secretary, 301 Salisbury House, London Wall, London EC2M 5QQ (071-588 2662).

The Chartered Institute of Journalists Orphan Fund

Eligibility: Children in need provided one parent is a member of the institute.

Types of grants: One-off grants (including birthday/Christmas payments) and quarterly payments according to need.

Annual grant total: About £12,500 in about eight grants.

Applications: In writing to the correspondent.

Correspondent: The General Secretary, 2 Dock Offices, Surrey Quays Road, London SE16 2XN (071-252 1187).

The Chartered Institute of Loss Adjusters Benevolent Fund

Eligibility: Members of the institute and their dependants.

Types of grants: One-off and recurrent grants according to need.

Annual grant total: About £1,000.

Applications: In writing to the correspondent.

Correspondent: The Honorary Secretary, Manfield House, 376 Strand, London WC2R 0LR (071-836 6482).

The Chartered Institute of Management Accountants' Benevolent Fund

Eligibility: Present and past fellows and associates of the institute, their widows/widowers and dependants anywhere in the world.

Types of grants: Grants are generally one-off towards television licence/rental, telephone rental, motor insurance, tax, some repairs, household insurance and necessary household items eg. fridge, cooker etc..

No grants will be given towards private medical care or education, or to enhance property.

Annual grant total: In 1992, the trust had assets of £927,000 and an income of £108,000. Grants to 35 individuals ranged from £10 a week to £5,000 a year and totalled £35,000.

Applications: Can be submitted by the individual on a form available from the correspondent. Applications are considered each month and applicants are then visited.

Correspondent: Miss P Rushton, 63 Portland Place, London W1N 4AB (071-637 2311).

Other information: The fund was formerly known as the Institute of Cost & Management Accountants Benevolent Fund and the Institute of Cost & Works Accountants Benevolent Fund.

The Chartered Institute of Patent Agents' Incorporated Benevolent Association

Eligibility: British members and former members of the institute, and their dependants.

Types of grants: One-off and recurrent grants or loans according to need.

Annual grant total: In 1993, the trust had an income of £31,000 and gave grants totalling £18,000.

Applications: By letter, marked "Private and Confidential".

Correspondent: H G Hallybone, c/o Messrs Carpmaels & Ransford, 43 Bloomsbury Square, London WC1A 2RA (071-242 8692).

The Chartered Institution of Building Services Engineers Benevolent Fund

Eligibility: Members of the institution and their dependants (on death of member).

● **Occupational charities**

Types of grants: Grants for any kind of need. This includes house repairs, holidays and Christmas gifts. About 40 grants of £100 are made each quarter.

Annual grant total: In 1993, grants totalled about £20,000.

Applications: In writing to the correspondent including financial status. Applications are considered in February, May, August and November.

Correspondent: The Honorary Secretary, Delta House, 222 Balham High Road, London SW12 9BS (081-675 5211).

The Chartered Society of Physiotherapy Members' Benevolent Fund

Eligibility: Members of the society.

Types of grants: One-off grants for emergency needs. Recurrent grants, usually of £20 a month to help with living expenses, but in exceptional cases up to £101 a month to help with nursing home fees. The fund helps with telephone rental, household repairs, heating bills and road tax (where car use is essential). The fund also supplements low income.

Annual grant total: About £31,000 in 30 to 40 grants.

Applications: On a form available from the correspondent. Applications should be submitted directly by the individual and are considered in January, April, July and October.

Correspondent: Mrs J Turner, 14 Bedford Row, London WC1R 4ED (071-242 1941).

The Chemical Engineer's Benevolent Fund

Eligibility: Chemical engineers and their dependants. This includes all chemical engineers worldwide, not simply members or former members of the Institution of Chemical Engineers.

Types of grants: One-off grants and loans only. In 1990, awards were up to £1,500 and included a grant for a cataract operation and for computer equipment for a mentally disabled child.

No grants for students.

Annual grant total: In 1990, the trust had an income of nearly £6,000. Total expenditure was £4,000.

Applications: In writing by the individual or a family member for consideration in April and November.

Correspondent: Mrs S Kilner, Davis Building, 165-171 Railway Terrace, Rugby, Warwickshire CV21 3HQ (0788-578214).

The Church of England Pensions Board

Eligibility: Retired clergy and licensed layworkers of the Church of England, their widows/widowers and dependants.

Types of grants: Allowances to supplement incomes when they fall below pre-set limits and assistance with fees in residential or nursing homes. There are over 1,400 recipients of allowances and supplementary pensions.

Annual grant total: About £2.1 million.

Applications: On a form available from the correspondent.

Correspondent: R G Radford, Secretary, 7 Little College Street, London SW1P 3SF (071-222 2091).

Other information: The trust's main concern is the welfare of retired clergy and their spouses who need sheltered accommodation. It runs eight residential and nursing homes for these beneficiaries.

The Church Schoolmasters & Schoolmistresses' Benevolent Institution (CSSBI)

Eligibility: Past and present members of the teaching profession and/or their widows/orphans, who are members of the Church of England.

Types of grants: Grants according to need, although grants rarely exceed £100 and are not normally given for convalescence, travel, home adaptations or education.

Annual grant total: Over £1,000 in 1990/91. About 12 grants were given (out of about 35 to 40 applications).

Applications: On a form available from the correspondent. Cases are considered monthly except April and August. Recommendations to support applications are often received from social services, but most applications come direct from the individual.

Correspondent: Lt Col Norman E Smart, Administrator, Glen Arun, 9 Athelstan Way, Horsham, West Sussex RH13 6HA.

Other information: The institution owns a residential home in Horsham for 15 residents together with a nursing wing for a further 10 residents. All places in the home are subsidised.

This entry has not been confirmed by the trust, but is accurate according to the latest information on file at the Charity Commission.

The Cinema & Television Benevolent Fund

Eligibility: Anyone who has worked in any capacity in the British film, cinema or independent television industries, and their dependants.

Types of grants: One-off grants or weekly allowances (at present £10 a week maximum), and help with television licences and television and telephone rental charges. Cold weather grants are also given. Support both for members living in their own homes (single or married) or nursing homes. At Glebelands (the fund's residential home in Wokingham, Berkshire) the fund offers permanent residence plus convalescent facilities for eligible people (serving or retired) who have had recent surgery or illness.

Annual grant total: About £950,000 is given to about 1,200 regular beneficiaries plus about 100 one-off grants.

Applications: On a form available from the correspondent.

Correspondent: The Executive Director, 22 Golden Square, London W1R 4AD (071-437 6567).

The City of London Linen Trades Association

Eligibility: Members and former members of the association and their dependants.

Types of grants: One-off grants only (subject to review). The trust will contribute towards the cost of a holiday at one of the Textile Benevolent Association holiday homes.

Annual grant total: £3,500 in 1988.

Applications: Please note the correspondent states that "all people who are eligible are known to the trustees".

Correspondent: J R Bryceson, 3 Marston Drive, Bishop's Stortford, Hertfordshire CM23 5EJ (0279-652480).

The Civil & Public Services Association Benevolent Fund

Eligibility: Members of the association.

Types of grants: One-off grants to a maximum of £250, for the relief of hardship caused by sudden and unexpected problems such as accident or illness.

Annual grant total: £10,000 to £12,000 in about 100 grants.

Applications: Through local area offices of the association. All applications must be recommended by the branch secretary.

Correspondent: The General Treasurer, 160 Falcon Road, London SW11 2LN (071-924 2727).

The Civil Service Benevolent Fund

Eligibility: Serving and retired staff of the civil service and associated organisations, and their dependants.

Types of grants: Many types of need can be considered. Applications are considered individually and help is tailored to the applicant's needs.

Help to buy houses, legal costs, car repairs or replacement except in cases of serious disability is normally excluded.

Annual grant total: In 1993, the fund gave £2 million in direct financial assistance to individuals.

Applications: In writing to the correspondent. Applications can be submitted directly by the individual or through a social worker, citizen's advice bureau, other welfare agency or other third party such as a relative or friend. They are considered as they arrive.

Correspondent: The Cases Team, Fund House, Anne Boleyn's Walk, Cheam, Sutton, Surrey SM3 8DY (081-642 8511).

Other information: The fund runs 10 homes for elderly/infirm staff and their dependants throughout the UK. Convalescent and respite care can be provided in these homes.

The Coal Industry Benevolent Trust

Eligibility: Widows and dependants of deceased coal miners whose death was caused by or connected with their employment (see paragraph [a] below). For other mineworkers and their dependants see paragraph (b).

Types of grants: (a) There are extensive regulations governing maximum payments available in cases of death connected to employment in the coalmining industry. Amounts are relatively modest and do not continue indefinitely. For example, the widow of a former coalminer who died of an industry-related disease may receive an immediate grant of up to £600 and grants of not more than £400 in each of the next six years. Payments for dependent children, which are not time-limited, are up to a maximum of £200 a year (or £300 if disabled), according to the circumstances. A detailed account of the regulations is available from the trust.

(b) Additionally, applications are received which do not fall within the regulations governing the work of the Finance and Grants Committee but which are dealt with under the wider powers expressed in the trust deed. Such applications must be in respect of mineworkers who have ceased to be gainfully employed in the coal industry by reason of sickness or injury and who have not taken up further employment outside the coal industry, widows/dependants of deceased mineworkers, or mining families facing problems with disabled children.

Annual grant total: About £1.8 million in about 6,000 grants.

Applications: In writing to the correspondent for consideration by the Finance and Grants Committee.

Correspondent: The Secretary, 27 Huddersfield Road, Barnsley, South Yorkshire S70 2LX (0226-298871).

The Coal Trade Benevolent Association

Eligibility: Elderly and distressed non-manual workers of the solid fuel and allied trades, and their widows and orphans. (For National Coal employees see entry for the Coal Industry Benevolent Trust.)

Types of grants: Both recurrent (typically £260 a year) and one-off grants (generally £500 maximum) for most kinds of need. Assistance is given to people in nursing homes, for travel to hospital for treatment and towards special dietary needs, but not towards the costs of medicine.

Annual grant total: In 1993, £135,000 was given to about 400 beneficiaries.

Applications: On a form available from the correspondent.

Correspondent: The Secretary, Unit 6, Bridge Wharf, 156-156a Caledonian Road, London N1 9RD (071-278 3239).

The Myrtle Cohen Trust Fund

Eligibility: Lock-keepers, relief lock-keepers and boatmen either in active service on the non-tidal River Thames or who have retired from such service, and their widows or widowers who are in need. Children of lock-keepers are not eligible, nor are administrative staff of the National Rivers Authority who manage the Thames.

Types of grants: One-off grants according to need.

Annual grant total: In 1992, the trust had an income of £520. Two grants totalled £700.

Applications: In writing to the correspondent.

Correspondent: B Cohen, Trustee, 716 Endsleigh Court, Upper Woburn Place, London WC1H 0HW (071-387 6805).

The Commercial Travellers' Benevolent Institution

Eligibility: Commercial travellers, representatives and agents, and their dependants. It is not necessary to have been a member of any commercial travellers association, but grants are not given to door to door salespeople.

Types of grants: Grants usually of about £10 a week paid quarterly in advance. One-off grants are seldom given.

Annual grant total: About £300,000 to over 300 regular beneficiaries.

Applications: On a form available from the correspondent. Applications are considered quarterly and can be submitted directly by the individual, through a welfare agency or another third party (eg. citizen's advice bureau, nursing home etc.).

Correspondent: Maurice Bown, Secretary, Gable End, Mill Hill Road, Arnesby, Leicestershire LE8 3WG (0533-478647).

The Concert Artistes' Association

Eligibility: Artistes who have fallen on hard times.

Types of grants: One-off or recurrent grants according to need.

Annual grant total: No information available.

Applications: In writing to the correspondent.

Correspondent: The Secretary, 20 Bedford Street, Strand, London WC2 (071-836 3172).

The Confectioners' Benevolent Fund

Eligibility: Anyone who has been engaged in the manufacture, wholesale or retail of chocolates and sweets, or their dependants.

Types of grants: One-off and recurrent grants according to need. Grants can be given for television licences, telephone installation/rental, disability equipment, clothing, convalescence/holidays, house insurance and repairs.

Annual grant total: In 1992/93, the fund had assets of £760,000 and an income of £560,000. Total expenditure was £360,000 including £233,000 in relief-in-need grants to about 670 beneficiaries.

Occupational charities

Applications: On a form available from the correspondent submitted directly by the individual or through a third party. Applications are considered in February, May, August and November.

Correspondent: Mrs Christine Duncan, Director of Welfare, 11 Green Street, London W1Y 3RF (071-629 7107).

Other information: The fund also has a team of paid field welfare officers and volunteer visitors. The number of visitors has increased to over 150 throughout the UK, visiting elderly and vulnerable people on a regular basis.

The Corn Exchange Benevolent Society

Eligibility: Members of the society and their dependants. Limited funds are available for people working or who worked in the corn, grain, seed, animal feed stuffs, pulses, malt, flour or granary-keeping trades, and their dependants.

Types of grants: One-off and recurrent grants according to need. Additional grants are also made to meet unexpected items of expense, such as hospitalisation or going into a nursing home etc. for three or four weeks.

Annual grant total: In 1993, 18 people received £36,000 in regular grants and five people received special one-off grants totalling £10,000.

Applications: On a form available from the correspondent.

Correspondent: Doug Painter, Secretary, 14-20 St Mary Axe, London EC3A 8BH (071-623 5501).

The Corporation of the Sons of the Clergy

Eligibility: Anglican clergymen, their widows and dependants, and separated or divorced wives of such clergymen.

Types of grants: One-off grants to meet financial need as well as recurrent support where necessary. "The corporation is able to help in a variety of ways by making a discretionary grant to meet evinced need. Loans cannot be made for any purpose and grants are not made for the purchase or running costs of cars or property nor for holidays."

Annual grant total: £1.5 million in between 2,000 and 2,500 grants.

Applications: Write to or telephone the correspondent at any time.

Correspondent: R C F Leach, Registrar, 1 Dean Trench Street, Westminster, London SW1P 3HB (071-799 3696 or 071-222 5887).

The Cotton Industry Benevolent Fund

Eligibility: Current or former employees in the cotton and allied fibres textile manufacturing industry who are disabled (a) by service in the armed forces, merchant navy or civil defence or (b) through accident or disease occurring in the course of their employment in the industry. Qualifying dependants of the above may, in restricted circumstances, be eligible.

Types of grants: Grants according to need. Periods of convalescence are provided for eligible individuals (that is people who are medically certified ill or suffering from the effects of an accident, and who are sponsored by the relevant trade union/employer authorised signatory).

Annual grant total: £98,000 in 230 grants (out of 252 applications) in 1992.

Applications: Application forms for convalescence are obtainable from authorised signatories; applications for other grants should be made in writing to the correspondent via a social worker or other welfare agency.

Correspondent: J Platt, Hon. Secretary, 7 Link Lane, Garden Suburb, Oldham, Greater Manchester OL8 3AD (061-626 8282).

Other information: The trust also gives very substantial grants to educational bodies which encourage recruitment in to or efficiency in the industry, and to other organisations furthering the interests of the industry.

The Cricketers Association Charity

Eligibility: Members and former members of the association and any person who has played cricket on at least one occasion for any county which at the relevant time was recognised by the Test and County Cricket Board, and their dependants.

Types of grants: One-off or recurrent grants according to need.

Annual grant total: In 1991/92, the charity had an income of £20,000. Grants totalled £15,000.

Applications: In writing to the correspondent.

Correspondent: H Goldblatt, Goldblatt & Co, 60 Doughty Street, London WC1N 2LS (071-405 9855).

The Customs & Excise Family Fund

Eligibility: Members and former members of the Customs and Excise Department and their dependants who are in need.

Types of grants: One-off or recurrent grants according to need.

Annual grant total: In 1991/92, grants totalling £102,500 were made.

Applications: In writing to the correspondent.

Correspondent: The Hon. Secretary, 3rd Floor, Jubilee House, Farthingale Walk, Stratford, London E15 1AS.

Other information: This entry has not been confirmed by the trust. The contact address is the most up to date available at the Charity Commission.

The Dance Teachers' Benevolent Fund

Eligibility: Teachers and retired teachers of dance over the age of 28, who must have a minimum of eight years teaching experience with any recognised examining body. The fund does not give grants to students; it is not an educational charity.

Types of grants: The trust gives grants up to the DSS disregard level, helps with nursing home fees and gives other one-off grants.

Annual grant total: In 1992/93, the fund had assets of £165,000, income of £29,000 and gave about £7,500 in 16 grants.

Applications: On a form available from the correspondent. Details of training and teaching experience is required, together with evidence of pupil/students' examination results. Applications should be submitted directly by the individual, through a social worker, citizen's advice bureau or other welfare agency or third party. They are considered throughout the year, although the board meets quarterly in January, April, July and October.

Correspondent: Mrs Annette Awcock, c/o The Dancing Times, 45 Clerkenwell Green, London EC1R 0BE (0379-384091).

The Domestic Servants Benevolent Institution

Eligibility: People who have been in domestic service and who were members of the institution.

Types of grants: Pensions of £125 a quarter plus additional Christmas grants of £25.

Occupational charities

Annual grant total: £1,575 to three beneficiaries in 1993.

Applications: On a form available from the correspondent.

Correspondent: Alan Gibson, Secretary, The Royal Bank of Scotland, 7 Burlington Gardens, London W1A 3DD (071-615 4852).

The Drapers' Consolidated Charity

Eligibility: In order of priority:

1. Freemen of the Drapers' Company and their dependants.

2. People who are or have been engaged in the manufacture or sale of woollen cloth and their widows and dependants.

3. People who are or have been engaged in any trade or calling in Greater London and their widows and dependants.

4. Those generally in need or distress but note: "The Charity's funds are almost fully committed in responding to applications under the first three headings above; regrettably, therefore, it is unlikely that applicants under the fourth priority would receive help."

Types of grants: Both one-off and recurrent grants, with a preference for the former. Grants are usually up to £250.

Annual grant total: About £200,000 in just over 1,000 grants in 1991.

Applications: In writing to the correspondent via a social worker, medical staff or citizen's advice bureau.

Correspondent: The Clerk to the Drapers' Company, Drapers Hall, London EC2N 2DQ (071-588 5001).

The Driving Instructors Accident & Disability Fund

Eligibility: Driving instructors or former driving instructors (members of the Driving Instructors Association) who have been injured or disabled and their dependants. The association has about 10,000 members.

Types of grants: One-off grants of £150 to £250.

Annual grant total: £1,500 to £2,000.

Applications: In writing to the correspondent.

Correspondent: Yusuf Dosani, 2 Alford Close, Burpham, Guildford, Surrey GU4 7YL (0483-574542).

The Eaton Fund for Artists, Nurses & Gentlewomen

Eligibility: Artists, nurses and gentlewomen in need of financial help for one specific item or purpose.

Types of grants: Single grants given in cases of extreme hardship; no recurrent grants, nor for any matters whatsoever connected with education, training, courses etc..

Annual grant total: £8,000 in 1992/93.

Applications: On a form available from the correspondent on written request. Applications are considered quarterly, usually in January, April, July and October.

Correspondent: A A H Selwood, Clerk, 1 Pemberton Row, Fetter Lane, London EC4A 3EX.

The Edridge Fund

Eligibility: (a) Probation officers of all grades and all other people who are eligible to be members of the National Association of Probation Officers.

(b) Retired people of (a).

(c) Widows and dependants of (a) and (b).

Types of grants: Financial and welfare support is given. Generally one-off grants, typically £50 to £200, maximum £400, for hardship caused by accident, bills etc..

Annual grant total: About £40,000 in about 150 grants.

Applications: On a form available from the correspondent, submitted either directly by the individual, through local representatives of the fund, or through the area Chief Probation Officer.

Correspondent: Richard Martin, Secretary, The Limes, Lynn Road, Gayton, King's Lynn, Norfolk PE32 1QJ.

Other information: There are Edridge Fund representatives throughout the UK.

The Electrical & Electronic Industries Benevolent Association

Eligibility: Employees and former employees of the electrical and electronic industries and their dependants/close relatives, anywhere in the UK or Republic of Ireland. There are no age limits.

Types of grants: "To provide practical help and support in any form most appropriate to each individual applicant including one-off grants, on-going budget balancing grants, house repairs, aids for disabled people, holidays, motorised wheelchairs on permanent loan, television sets on loan, etc.."

No private health treatment.

Annual grant total: In 1992, the trust had assets of £3.6 million and an income of £1.6 million. About 15,000 grants were given to individuals in need totalling £517,000.

Applications: Direct or through referrals from any agency throughout the year. Applicants are then interviewed by regional welfare officers or welfare visitors.

Correspondent: J W Garner, Chief Executive, 8 Station Parade, Balham High Road, London SW12 9BH (081-673 0131).

Other information: In addition to supporting elderly beneficiaries in private residential and nursing homes, the association also operates a residential home in Derbyshire and warden controlled self-contained flats.

The Engineering Employers' Federation Benevolent Fund (including the Dyer Memorial Funds)

Eligibility: "The purpose of the fund is to enable federated employers to obtain financial assistance for their employees or their dependants. In order to be eligible the relevant employee should be or have been employed in a position of trust and this is normally taken to mean under-foreman or equivalent status."

Types of grants: Grants fall into the following categories:

(a) Income grants, where the applicant's income, after certain deductions, has fallen below the equivalent of a state pension (this can be increased when the applicant is elderly, infirm or has dependants). These grants range from £20 to £520.

(b) Property grants, generally to repair the applicant's home to enable them to continue living there.

(c) Convalescent grants, for the costs of a short stay in a convalescent home. The application must be accompanied by a doctor's certificate.

(d) Bereavement grants, payable in respect of the death of a spouse only, to assist with funeral costs.

(e) Mobility grants to help applicants in need of a wheelchair or to adapt other forms of transport.

All beneficiaries receive a £20 Christmas gift and a £20 "event" gift to celebrate an event of national importance. The annual

31

● **Occupational charities**

number of grants varies but is usually over 200.

The fund does not give loans.

Annual grant total: In 1991/92, the trust had assets of £1.3 million, income of £135,000 and gave 248 grants totalling almost £96,900.

Applications: All applications must be submitted through the applicant's former employer and federated association on a form available from the correspondent. Applications should be submitted by May in time for the annual trustees' meeting in June. Grants are paid in August/September. Urgent cases will be dealt with during the year. Applications for property or mobility grants must be accompanied by written estimates or receipts.

Correspondent: Paul Reynolds, Fund Manager, Broadway House, Tothill Street, London SW1H 9NQ (071-222 7777).

The Engineers' & Managers' Association (EMA) Benevolent Fund (& Associated Funds)

Eligibility: Members and retired members and their dependants.

Types of grants: One-off and maintenance grants.

Annual grant total: Probably about £2,000, although this has not been confirmed by the fund.

Applications: To the Benefits & Services Committee on the claim form available from the correspondent. Applications should be submitted directly by the individual and are considered at any time.

Correspondent: The General Secretary, Flaxman House, Gogmore Lane, Chertsey, Surrey KT16 9JS (0932-564131).

The English National Opera Benevolent Fund

Eligibility: People retired from or connected with the English National Opera and/or Saddlers Wells Companies.

Types of grants: Recurrent grants of up to £240 a month and discretionary one-off grants according to need.

Annual grant total: £73,000 to 45 individuals in 1992/93.

Applications: In writing to the correspondent.

Correspondent: The Secretary, London Coliseum, St Martin's Lane, London WC2N 4ES (071-836 0111).

The Entertainment Artistes' Benevolent Fund

Eligibility: Entertainment artistes (that is professional performers in variety, pantomime, revue, circus, concert party, cabaret, clubs, television, radio, making of records and light entertainment in general), and their dependants.

Types of grants: Regular allowances, one-off grants and loans to meet social needs (such as nursing home fees, gas, electricity and fuel bills, television licences and rentals, and telephone bills). Also help with funeral costs where necessary.

Annual grant total: About £105,000 in about 320 grants.

Applications: In writing to the correspondent. Applications can be made directly or through a social worker/welfare agency.

Correspondent: Peter Elliott, Executive Administrator, Brinsworth House, 72 Staines Road, Twickenham TW2 5AL (081-898 8164/5).

Other information: The fund has its own home for elderly entertainment artistes in need of care.

The Equity Trust Fund

Eligibility: Professional performers (members of Equity) and their dependants.

Types of grants: One-off grants only, to help with bills, accidents etc.. Grants range from £300 to £2,000.

Annual grant total: In 1992/93, 12 welfare grants totalled £24,000.

Applications: In writing to the correspondent, directly by the individual to be considered quarterly. Applications should include a full cv as an adult professional performer.

Correspondent: Carla Hanreck, Administrative Secretary, 114 Africa House, 64 Kingsway, London WC2B 6AH (071-404 6041).

Other information: The trust also gives grants for re-training (see *The Educational Grants Directory*).

The Fire Services National Benevolent Fund

Eligibility: People who are, or have been over a specified minimum period, active fire fighters (including volunteers and those in the wartime National Fire Service) and ancillary workers. Widows, orphans and disabled children of serving fire fighters are also eligible.

Types of grants: Grants according to need. Local county committees can pay immediate hardship grants of up to £300; regional committees can make grants of up to £900, and grants of up to £3,000 can be made at national level. Death grants of up to £600 are available for widows. Some allowances are paid to those disabled and in need. Limited assistance may be given to people in residential care homes or nursing homes if they are already in receipt of Income Support.

Annual grant total: About £1,255,000 in about 1,500 grants.

Applications: Applications should be made to the Fund Secretary at the local fire brigade headquarters on a form available from them.

Correspondent: R A Spackman, General Manager, Marine Court, Fitzalan Road, Littlehampton, West Sussex BN17 5NF (0903-717185).

Other information: This fund was founded in 1943 to help all types of fire fighters and their widows and orphans. It also provides short term convalescence but does not have sheltered housing, residential homes or nursing homes.

The Fishmongers' & Poulterers' Institution

Eligibility: People who are or who have been in the fish or poultry trades, and their dependants.

Types of grants: Generally weekly pensions; also one-off gifts.

Annual grant total: About £15,000.

Applications: On a form available from the correspondent. Applications can be submitted directly by the individual or by a third party such as a social worker or citizen's advice bureau. They are usually considered in January, May and September, but can be considered at the chairman's discretion at any time.

Correspondent: Mrs C M Fry, 88 Berkeley Road, Bishopston, Bristol BS7 8HG (0272-241063).

The Football Association Benevolent Fund

Eligibility: People who are in need and have or had connections with the game of Association Football (ie. player, referee or administrator), and their dependants.

Types of grants: One-off grants ranging from £250 to £2,000. 180 grants were given in 1992.

Occupational charities

Annual grant total: In 1992, the fund had assets of £775,000 and an income of £228,000. Grants totalled £45,200 leaving £180,000 unallocated in the year.

Applications: On a form available from the correspondent. Applications can be submitted directly by the individual or by the appropriate county football association who would normally visit the applicant. Applications are considered monthly.

Correspondent: Mike Appleby, 16 Lancaster Gate, London W2 3LW (071-262 4542).

The Alfred Foster Settlement

Eligibility: Employees and former employees of banks and their dependants who are in need.

Types of grants: Mainly one-off grants for specific purposes.

Annual grant total: In 1993, grants totalled £27,000. Not all were given to individuals in need.

Applications: Must be made by the employee's bank to their local regional office and NOT directly to the correspondent.

Correspondent: The Trust Officer, Barclays Bank Trust Co Ltd, Trust Management Office, Octagon House, PO Box 27, Gadbrooke Park, Northwich CW9 7RE (0606-40123).

The Foundation of Edward Storey

Eligibility: Unsupported women in need who are at least 40 years of age and who qualify for assistance under either or both of the undermentioned categories:

(a) Clergymen's Widows Branch: in the following order of priority:

1. Widows of clergymen of the Church of England;
2. Dependants of clergymen of the Church of England;
3. Women deacons and deaconesses of the Church of England;
4. Missionaries of the Church of England;
5. Other women closely involved with the work of the Church of England (including divorced, separated and deserted wives of clergymen of the Church of England).

(b) Parish Almspeople's Branch: eligible people living within the city of Cambridge boundary.

Types of grants: Grants and pensions (which are annually reviewed).

Annual grant total: £149,000 in 1992/93. Grants under category (a) totalled about £70,000 and under (b) about £25,000; pensions under (a) totalled about £30,000 (about 90 pensions) and under (b) £24,150 (about 60 pensions).

Applications: By application form and sponsorship by, for example, Diocesan Widows' Officers, Diocesan Visitors, clergy, social workers etc.. Applications are considered bi-monthly by trustees.

Correspondent: The Clerk to the Trustees, Storey's House, Mount Pleasant, Cambridge CB3 0BZ (0223-64405).

Other information: This entry is repeated in the Cambridge section of the book.

The Friends of the Clergy Corporation

Eligibility: Anglican clergy, their widows, children or other dependants, including separated or divorced wives (subject to certain conditions) and their children.

Types of grants: One-off cash grants (see below). Where there is severe financial distress costs of essential services or items, such as dental treatment, spectacles and hospital travel may be met in full. In 1992/93, 920 grants were made.

Annual grant total: Grants in 1992/93 were as follows:

Bereavement expenses	£26,634
Removal expenses	£45,185
Holidays	£270,756
Various (including medical, hospital etc.)	£95,479
Pensions and Christmas grants	£9,937
Debts	£34,633
Retirement	£7,700]
Repairs	£10,268
Total of all grants (including school clothing)	£576,042

Applications: On a form available from the correspondent to be submitted directly by the individual or by a social worker, dependant etc. if the individual is unable to do so. Applications are considered each month.

Correspondent: J M Greany, 27 Medway Street, London SW1P 2BD (071-222 2288).

Other information: The corporation also runs five self-catering holiday flats and a few retirement flats and bungalows for its beneficiaries.

The Furnishing Trades Benevolent Association

Eligibility: People who are or have been employed in any capacity in the furnishing and allied trades, and their families (and in some cases other relatives and dependants).

Types of grants: One-off and recurrent grants for example towards travel costs for hospital visits, wheelchairs, lifts, mortgage arrears, washing machine, telephone installation and heating. Sometimes beds have been donated by members of the association.

Annual grant total: In 1993, grants totalled £97,000. Weekly payments of £4 or £5 were given to 359 people and 64 received one-off grants generally of about £200. About £5,000 was also given for educational purposes.

Applications: In writing to the correspondent. Meetings are quarterly but a quick response is possible to emergency applications.

Correspondent: The Chief Executive, 50 Bedford Street, London WC2E 9HA (071-836 6082).

The Gardeners' Royal Benevolent Society

Eligibility: People who have made their living through gardening and horticulture and their surviving spouses. Applicants should be of retirement age, unless retired early through disability.

Types of grants: Beneficiary payments: Regular allowances of £364 a year paid quarterly.

Holidays: Disabled people receive grants to attend special holidays; able-bodied people attend the society's own holidays, which are run every year in the UK.

One-off grants towards personal or household items such as clothing, kitchen equipment, funeral expenses, removal expenses, telephone and television. The society also provides bed linen and towels.

No grants for items not allowable under DSS regulations, with special reference to people receiving Income Support.

Annual grant total: £225,000 in 1991, of which £177,000 was for beneficiary payments. There are about 440 regular beneficiaries.

Applications: On a form available from the correspondent. Applications are considered bi-monthly.

Correspondent: Kathleen Baker, Caseworker, Bridge House, 139 Kingston Road, Leatherhead, Surrey KT22 7NT (0372-373962).

Other information: The society also has its own nursing/residential home and various other types of accommodation.

Occupational charities

The Grace Wyndham Goldie (BBC) Trust Fund

Eligibility: Those who have worked in broadcasting or any associated activity, and their dependants.

Types of grants: One-off grants only; usual maximum £500.

Annual grant total: In 1988, the most recent year for which information is available, about £9,000 was given, mostly in educational grants. £5,000 remained unallocated for the year.

Applications: On a form available from the correspondent. Applications are considered from June to September.

Correspondent: Miss Alison Crowley, Pensions Services, Ty Oldfield, Cardiff CF5 2YQ (0222-572603).

The Goldsmiths' Silversmiths' & Jewellers' Benevolent Society

Eligibility: Members of trades connected with gold and silver smithing (including for example retail jewellers and jewellery designers) and their dependants; Liverymen Freemen of the Goldsmiths' Company and their dependants; Londoners in need, and some blind and partially-sighted people connected with the trade.

Types of grants: Regular payments of £470 a year are given to 110 people. Over 100 one-off grants usually of £35 to £500 were given for cookers, washing machines, bedding, redecoration etc.. Special grants can be given eg. £700 to a disabled person for a special electric bed. The trust is now supporting nursing home fees, up to £200 a month is paid direct to the home. The trust can only afford to support 20 people with nursing home fees, but it receives 50 new requests each year. The list is currently full.

Payments are not usually made for holidays and are not given for funeral costs or to pay off debts.

Annual grant total: In 1993, the trust gave £72,500 in regular payments, about £15,000 in one-off grants and £25,000 in nursing home fees.

Applications: On a form available from the correspondent. For individuals not connected with the trade or the Goldsmiths' Company, applications should be made through the appropriate social services department of the London area.

Correspondent: Malcolm Pullen, Goldsmiths' Hall, Foster Lane, London EC2V 6BN (071-606 3673).

The Grand Order of Water Rats Charities Fund

Eligibility: (i) People in need who are or have been connected with light entertainment and their dependants.

(ii) The fund also buys medical equipment for individuals and hospitals.

Types of grants: Grants according to need. No grants for the relief of public taxes or for educational purposes.

Annual grant total: In 1993, the trust gave grants totalling £150,000, of which, £80,000 was given to organisations such as homes and hospitals.

Applications: In writing to the correspondent. Applications can be submitted by the individual or through a social worker, citizen's advice bureau or other welfare agency or relevant third party. They are considered monthly.

Correspondent: John Adrian, Secretary, 328 Gray's Inn Road, London WC1X 8BZ (071-278 3248).

The Grand Prix Mechanics Charitable Trust

Eligibility: Past and present Grand Prix mechanics and their dependants who are in need.

Types of grants: One-off and recurrent grants according to need. In addition, the trust pays the premiums for medical and personal accident cover for Grand Prix mechanics.

Annual grant total: About £20,000 in 1992.

Applications: In writing to the correspondent.

Correspondent: The Secretary, Rawlinson & Hunter, 1 Hanover Square, London W1A 4SR (071-493 4040).

Sir Percival Griffiths' Tea Planters Trust

Eligibility: People who live in the UK who are or have been involved in tea planting in North-East India, and their dependants.

Types of grants: Monthly allowances and ad hoc payments two, three or four times a year. In 1992, grants ranged from £315 to £1,357.

Annual grant total: In 1992, the trust had assets of £50,000 and an income of £12,000. 15 grants totalled £15,000.

Applications: On a form available from the correspondent, to be submitted directly by the individual or through a social worker or other welfare agency or third party. Applications are considered in April and November.

Correspondent: K Mayes, Lawrie Plantation Services Ltd, Wrotham Place, Wrotham, Sevenoaks, Kent TN15 7AE (0732-884488).

The Guild of Air Pilots' & Navigators' Benevolent Fund

Eligibility: Those who have been engaged professionally as air pilots or air navigators in commercial aviation and who are British subjects by birth or naturalisation, and their dependants. The fund's main aim is to help disabled/incapacitated air pilots and navigators and families of those who have died or are disabled. Help is also given to past and present air pilots and air navigators in need.

Types of grants: Help can be given towards debts and fuel bills (usually on a one-off basis only); Christmas gifts are given to all beneficiaries and their dependants. Larger loans may be available (secured against the applicant's property). The guild has honorary medical advisers and can advise on entitlements for recently bereaved widows.

Annual grant total: £10,000 in about 40 grants in 1993.

Applications: On a form available from the correspondent. Applications are considered in January, April, July and October. The fund has helpers and visitors who can help applicants fill in the form (details required include the individual's financial situation and flying career). The board considering applications attaches great importance to the comments and recommendations of helpers.

Correspondent: Gp Capt John Tritton, 291 Gray's Inn Road, London WC1X 8QF (071-837 3323).

Other information: The fund works closely with the other aviation trusts for individuals (both military and civilian). If an applicant has approached another such trust, they should say so in their application to this fund.

The Guild of Guide Lecturers Benevolent Fund

Eligibility: Tourist Board registered (blue badge) guides, qualified for at least one year who are in need, and dependants of guides qualified for at least three years.

Types of grants: One-off grants. Grants are not given for "gambling debts, riotous living, or private hospital care".

Occupational charities

Annual grant total: In 1992, the trust had an income of £4,500. It is not known how much was given in grants to individuals in need.

Applications: In writing to the correspondent, including the tourist board with which the applicant was registered, whether any statutory bodies have been approached and the specific need. Applications can be made directly by the individual or by a third party to one of the trustees or the committee. They are considered at any time, after which the applicant is visited by a committee member.

Correspondent: Mrs Helen Clapp, Chairman, 25 Eglington Road, London E4 7AN (081-529 1140).

The Gurney Fund for Police Orphans

Eligibility: Children up to 18 of deceased or incapacitated police officers from subscribing forces in southern and south Midland areas of England and south and mid-Wales, excluding the Metropolitan Police.

Types of grants: Grants for all kinds of need including education (but not school fees). Grants range from £5.50 to £30 a week.

Annual grant total: About £250,000 to about 400 beneficiaries, most of which will be for educational purposes and not relief in need.

Applications: By letter to the correspondent. A force welfare officer/local representative will then assess the application for a later decision by the trustees. Applications are considered in February, May, August and November.

Correspondent: The Director, 9 Bath Road, Worthing, West Sussex BN11 3NU (0903-237256).

Hairdressers' Children's Welfare Fund

Eligibility: Children of hairdressers (up to 16 years old).

Types of grants: On-going grants for pocket money, winter clothing, Christmas presents etc.. In 1993, there were 40 to 50 regular beneficiaries, generally receiving £10 to £30 a month depending on the child's age. One-off grants are given towards the cost of computers/specialist equipment for disabled children.

No grants for education purposes.

Annual grant total: Probably about £10,000.

Applications: On a form available from the correspondent. The committee meets quarterly so ample time must be allowed for an application to be considered.

Correspondent: Alan Rapkin, Secretary, Phoenix House, 211-213b High Road, Benfleet, Essex SS7 5HZ (0268-759990).

The Hastings Benevolent Fund

Eligibility: Members of the medical profession and their dependants who have fallen on hard times.

Types of grants: Temporary help only through a one-off payment or a loan.

Annual grant total: The trust's income is about £40,000 a year.

Applications: On a form available from the correspondent.

Correspondent: The Case Secretary, BMA Charities, BMA House, Tavistock Square, London WC1H 9JP (071-383 6334).

The Francis Head Bequest

Eligibility: Professional authors over the age of 35 who live in the UK.

Types of grants: Emergency grants only.

Annual grant total: £10,000 in 5 to 10 grants.

Applications: On a form available from the correspondent.

Correspondent: The Secretary, 84 Drayton Gardens, London SW10 9SB (071-373 6642).

The Rowland Hill Benevolent Fund

Eligibility: Past and present Post Office employees and their dependants.

Types of grants: Weekly grants/loans to supplement living expenses. Normally up to £5 a week, except for people in residential/nursing homes where the maximum is £10 a week.

Also one-off grants/loans for specific purposes eg. £150 for the installation of a telephone for a sick person living alone.

Loans (but not grants) are either repayable from salary in the case of serving officers or from the estate in the case of pensioners or widows who own their own home. The latter loans attract interest (10% simple). The fund also sponsors nominees for places in certain rest and nursing homes and in certain sheltered accommodation schemes.

Annual grant total: In 1993, the trust gave grants and loans to 1,887 people totalling £312,000.

Applications: In writing to the correspondent. Applications can be received from the applicant or any third party and are considered twice every calendar month. Applicants are visited by Post Office welfare officers.

Correspondent: C C Trott, Secretary, Palmerston House, 80-86 Old Street, London EC1V 9PP (071-320 7525).

The Honourable Company of Master Mariners

Eligibility: Merchant Navy Officers and their dependants in need.

Types of grants: One-off and quarterly grants according to need.

Annual grant total: About 35 grants are given.

Applications: On a form available from the correspondent. Applications can be submitted directly by the individual, through a social worker, citizen's advice bureau, or other welfare agency, or by a friend or relative. They are considered throughout the year.

Correspondent: The Clerk, HQS Wellington, Temple Stairs, Victoria Embankment, London WC2R 2PN (071-836 8179).

The Hornsby Professional Cricketers Fund Charity

Eligibility: Former professional cricketers and their dependants who are in need.

Types of grants: Monthly, holiday, Christmas, winter, medical and educational grants are given.

Annual grant total: In 1989/90, the trust had an income of £12,000; grants totalled £6,800. No more recent information is available.

Applications: In writing to the correspondent.

Correspondent: A K James, Clerk, Dunroamin, 65 Keyhaven Road, Milford-on-Sea, Lymington, Hampshire SO41 0QX (0590-644720).

The Horticultural Trades Association Benevolent Fund

Eligibility: Nurserymen and seedsmen and their dependants who are in need.

Types of grants: Usually one-off grants.

Annual grant total: About £4,000.

Applications: In writing to the correspondent.

Occupational charities

Correspondent: A E Strickland, 19 High Street, Theale, Reading, Berkshire RG7 5AH (0734-303132).

The Hotel & Catering Benevolent Association

Eligibility: Those who are or have been engaged in the hotel and catering industry and their dependent relatives.

Types of grants: Weekly allowances and one-off grants for specific purposes.

Annual grant total: About £200,000 in about 450 grants.

Applications: In writing to the correspondent.

Correspondent: Robin Maddy, Director, 52 Ridgeway, Wimbledon, London SW19 4QR (081-946 7561).

Other information: The association has sheltered housing schemes throughout the country (one has an Extra Care Unit) and a residential club in London for young people entering the catering industry.

The Arthur Hurst Will Trust

Eligibility: Distressed gentlewomen, needy clergy who have been forced to give up their work because of ill health, and the widows of poor clergy for the education of their children.

Types of grants: One-off and recurrent grants according to need.

Annual grant total: £19,000.

Applications: By letter, either direct from the applicant or through a third party, giving full details of qualification and an outline of circumstances.

Correspondent: The Trust Officer (Ref P647/A9), The Trust Division, Public Trust Office, Kingsway, London WC2B 6JX (071-269 7433).

The Incorporated Association of Organists Benevolent Fund

Eligibility: Members and former members of any association or society affiliated to the Incorporated Association of Organists, and their dependants.

Types of grants: One-off and recurrent grants according to need. Welfare grants are mainly given to elderly organists who have fallen on hard times.

Annual grant total: In 1993, the trust gave 18 grants totalling £9,000.

Applications: On a form available from the correspondent. Applications can be submitted by the individual or the secretary of the local organists' association. They are considered throughout the year.

Correspondent: Anthony J Cooke, Hon. Secretary, 8 Wrenbury Avenue, Cookridge, Leeds LS16 7EQ (0532-671903).

The Incorporated Association of Preparatory Schools Benevolent Fund

Eligibility: Past and present members of the association and their dependants.

Types of grants: One-off and recurrent grants according to need.

Annual grant total: £14,500 in 1993.

Applications: In writing to the correspondent.

Correspondent: The Executive Trustee, 11 Waterloo Place, Leamington Spa, Warwickshire CV32 5LA (0926-887833).

The Incorporated Brewers' Benevolent Society

Eligibility: People employed or formerly employed in the brewing profession and their dependants.

Types of grants: Regular and one-off grants according to need.

Annual grant total: No information available.

Applications: On a form available from the correspondent.

Correspondent: The Secretary, 8 Ely Place, London EC1N 6SD (071-405 4565).

The Incorporated Society of Musicians Benevolent Fund

Eligibility: Members and former members of the society and their dependants.

Types of grants: One-off and recurrent grants according to need.

Annual grant total: In 1991/92, grants totalled £26,000. There were 32 beneficiaries.

Applications: On a form available from the correspondent.

Correspondent: Ms C Aldred, ISM Charities Officer, 10 Stratford Place, London W1N 9AE (071-629 4413).

The Incorporated Society of Valuers & Auctioneers Benevolent Fund

Eligibility: Members and former members of the society and their dependants.

Types of grants: One-off and recurrent grants and loans. Recurrent grants to members experiencing financial difficulties as a result of redundancy or unemployment and to retired members or the widows/widowers of former members whose income is insufficient for day-to-day living (grants are calculated so as not to affect any DSS benefit). One-off grants for one-off hardship (eg. funeral expenses, to buy equipment to help with a disability or to settle a particular debt). Loans are usually only made to members who have been seriously injured in the knowledge that the loan can be repaid when the claim for damages has been settled.

Annual grant total: In 1991/92, the trust had assets of £228,000 generating an income of £33,000. Relief-in-need grants to individuals totalled £16,000.

Applications: On a form available from the correspondent. Applicants may be visited by a representative of the local branch of the society.

Correspondent: The Chief Executive, ISVA, 3 Cadogan Gate, London SW1X 0AS (071-235 2282).

The Injured Jockeys Fund

Eligibility: Jockeys who have been forced to give up their career through injury, and their families. Applicants must hold (or have held) a licence to ride under the Rules of Racing.

Types of grants: Weekly or periodical grants to injured jockeys whose current income only gives them/their families a bare subsistence level of living (in 1992/93 the usual minimum weekly payment was £10); loans or mortgage to help buy a house or set up a small business; annual holidays for those who would otherwise never get a chance to leave home; help with the cost of education where children have special needs (eg. dyslexia); suitable transport for old or infirm jockeys (where necessary cars are adapted to the needs of the disabled).

The fund has a bulk account with a leading television rental company through which colour sets are hired for beneficiaries who, for some reason, are largely or totally confined to their home. These cost over £6,500 a year.

Whether or not an injury seems likely to force a jockey into retirement, the fund is always ready to pay for the best possible advice, treatment and rehabilitation. Injured jockeys are encouraged and assisted to seek retraining and the fund pays for accommodation of currently licensed jockeys who attend the well-known rehabilitation centre at Lilleshall.

Annual grant total: In 1992/93, the trust had assets of £6.5 million and an income of £232,000. Total expenditure was £527,000, of which £319,000 was given as grants to individuals in need.

Applications: On an application form to be sent, any month, direct to regional almoners, who are as follows:

The South: Mrs Susan Mills, Lower House, Little Barrington, Burford, Oxfordshire (0451-4312).

The North: Mrs Hilary Kerr, Garth House, 75 Levenside, Stokesley, Middlesbrough, Cleveland TS9 5BH (0642-710452).

Newmarket area: Mrs Serena Oxley, Flint Cottage, Gazeley, Nr Newmarket, Suffolk (0638-750975).

Correspondent: Jeremy Richardson, Secretary, PO Box 9, Newmarket, Suffolk CB8 8JG (0638-662246).

The Institute of Chartered Secretaries & Administrators Benevolent Fund

Eligibility: Members and former members of the institute or their widows, widowers, children or other dependants.

Types of grants: One-off and recurrent grants according to need, plus interest-free loans. No grants for higher education.

Annual grant total: £105,000 in 125 grants in 1993.

Applications: In writing to the correspondent. Local advisors visit beneficiaries where necessary.

Correspondent: A G Smith, Charities Officer, 16 Park Crescent, London W1N 4AH (071-580 4741 ext. 188).

The Institute of Clayworkers Benevolent Fund

Eligibility: People in need who had to retire early from the clay-working industry through accident or ill-health. Dependants of deceased clayworkers may also be eligible. The fund covers brick-making, roof tiles, clay drainage pipes and refractory industries, but not pottery workers.

Types of grants: One-off grants.

Annual grant total: In 1993, the trust had assets of £56,000 and an income of £4,500. Expenditure totalled £4,700 including £3,900 in relief-in-need grants to individuals. 15 grants of about £250 were made.

Applications: In writing to the correspondent, including age, length of service, date of termination of employment (if applicable), brief description (two or three sentences) of circumstances leading to application, and brief testimonial (a sentence or two) from a supervisor/manager if appropriate.

Correspondent: A McRae, Secretary, Federation House, Station Road, Stoke-on-Trent ST4 2SA (0782-744631).

The Institute of Company Accountants Benevolent Fund

Eligibility: Fellows and Associates of the institute and their close dependants.

Types of grants: One-off grants according to need.

Annual grant total: In 1991, the fund's income was £10,000; it gave grants of £3,000 leaving a surplus of £7,000.

Applications: In writing to the correspondent.

Correspondent: B T Banks, 40 Tyndalls Park Road, Clifton, Bristol BS8 1PL (0272-738261).

The Institute of Financial Accountants Benevolent Fund

Eligibility: Members or former members of the institute and their dependants.

Types of grants: One-off grants according to need. There is currently a preference for those who face hardship due to unemployment, serious illness or bereavement. Grants are usually of £300 to £500 but can be for up to £2,000 in exceptional circumstances towards items such as an electric wheelchair.

Annual grant total: In 1993, about 20 grants were given totalling £5,000 to £10,000.

Applications: On a form available from the correspondent and applications must include full income and expenditure details.

Correspondent: The Honorary Secretary, Burford House, 44 London Road, Sevenoaks, Kent TN13 1AS (0732-458080).

The Institute of Football Management & Administration Charity Trust

Eligibility: Members or former members of the institute (formerly the Football League Executive Staffs Association) who have worked for a Football League or Premier League club and who are in need, and their dependants.

Types of grants: One-off grants in particular cases of need, and Christmas hampers.

Annual grant total: In 1991/92, the trust had an income of £6,500. Expenditure totalled £5,000 including £4,500 in relief-in-need grants to individuals.

Applications: On a form available from the correspondent. Applications can be submitted directly by the individual or through family, friend or colleague.

Correspondent: O Dixon, Secretary, PO Box 52, Leamington Spa, Warwickshire CV32 4UF (0926-882313).

The Institute of Health Services Management Benevolent Fund

Eligibility: Members and former members of the institute and their dependants.

Types of grants: Emergency one-off grants (usually around £200); monthly grants (variable according to circumstances, presently £40 to £100 a month); special Christmas and summer holiday grants usually paid to people receiving regular grants (variable but with emphasis on dependent children); top-up nursing/residential home fees and similar.

Generally no grants given to students but some educational grants may be given to members of the institute, not their children.

Annual grant total: In 1993, the trust had assets of about £80,000 and an income of around £6,000, nearly all distributed in relief-in-need grants.

Applications: Should be submitted through a regional representative on the National Council of the Institute. Applications are considered on receipt.

Correspondent: Mr Stansby, Secretary, Warwickshire Health Authority, Westgate House, Market Street, Warwick CV34 4DE (0926-493491).

The Institute of Legal Executive Benevolent Funds

Eligibility: Members and former members of the institute in England and Wales, present and former solicitors' managing clerks, and the dependants of any of the above.

Types of grants: There are three funds administered by trustees on behalf of the Institute of Legal Executives: the Benevolent Fund, the Benevolent Fund Account and the SMCA (Charitable) Fund. They have similar objects and policies. Grants are usually one-off for specific purposes eg. telephone/fuel bills, payment towards nursing/residential care, medical equipment etc..

Occupational charities

Annual grant total: In 1992, the trusts had a combined income of £12,000, it is not known how much was given in grants to individuals.

Applications: In writing to the correspondent requesting an application form.

Correspondent: Mr Evans, Secretary, Kempston Manor, Kempston, Bedford MK42 7AB (0234-841000).

The Institute of Marine Engineers Guild of Benevolence

Eligibility: Members of the institute and the guild and their wives, widows and dependants. Engineers who possess a marine engineering qualification, their wives, widows and dependants, may also be eligible.

Types of grants: Both one-off and recurrent grants, typically £5 a week.

Annual grant total: Over £40,000 in about 100 grants.

Applications: In writing to the correspondent requesting an application form.

Correspondent: The Secretary, 76 Mark Lane, London EC3R 7JN (071-481 8493).

Other information: This fund was launched by the The Daily Chronicle when the Titanic sank in 1912, a disaster which no marine engineer survived.

The guild has a residential home at Littlehampton, West Sussex. Holiday accommodation is also available.

The Institute of Petroleum 1986 Benevolent Fund

Eligibility: Members and former members of the institute, and their dependants.

Types of grants: One-off grants according to need.

Annual grant total: In 1992, the fund had an income of £8,000; grants totalled £2,300.

Applications: In writing to the correspondent requesting an application form.

Correspondent: R Taylor, Secretary, 61 New Cavendish Street, London W1M 8AR (071-636 1004).

The Institute of Physics Benevolent Fund

Eligibility: Physicists and members of their family, in need. There is a preference for members of the society.

Types of grants: One-off and recurrent grants according to need.

Annual grant total: In 1992, grants totalled £35,000 to 200 beneficiaries.

Applications: In writing to the correspondent.

Correspondent: Mrs Dowling, Finance Manager, 47 Belgrave Square, London SW1X 8QX (071-235 6111).

The Institute of Public Relations Benevolent Fund

Eligibility: Members of the institute and dependants of members or deceased members.

Types of grants: One-off and recurrent grants according to need.

Annual grant total: About £6,000.

Applications: In writing to the correspondent.

Correspondent: J Lavelle, Director, The Old Trading House, 15 Northburgh Street, London EC1V 0PR (071-253 5151).

The Institute of Quarrying Benevolent Fund

Eligibility: Members or former members of the institute, and their dependants.

Types of grants: In 1992/93, grants ranged from £500 to £3,500. Awards can be granted for many years with one pensioner having received an annual grant since 1965.

Annual grant total: About £30,000 in about 17 grants.

Applications: On a form available from the correspondent.

Correspondent: The Honorary Secretary, 7 Regent Street, Nottingham NG1 5BY (0602-411315).

The Institution of Civil Engineers Benevolent Fund

Eligibility: Past and present members of the institution and their dependants. Also dependants of former members of the Institution of Municipal Engineers.

Types of grants: Regular or one-off grants to bring income up to a suitable level after receipt of state benefits, to top up nursing/care home fees, to buy equipment for disabled people or to help with temporary financial difficulties. Loans are also made, generally against security. In 1992, 200 cases (349 people) were assisted, 42 of which were new recipients. 160 cases received direct cash grants, 36 were accommodated in homes, 14 received both grant aid and accommodation and 18 received loans.

There were 20 cases (27 adults and 15 children) in 11 overseas countries; 13 were helped jointly with other organisations. Between 1989 and 1992, the number of cases assisted has increased by one-third, the number of individuals by nearly two-thirds, the amount paid out in grants has almost doubled (from £166,000 to £355,000) and the average grant has risen from £1,272 to £1,773.

No grants towards funeral expenses or higher education. Education grants are only given in very exceptional circumstances and then only to those under 16.

Annual grant total: In 1992, the trust had assets of £6.5 million and an income of £519,000. Expenditure totalled £575,000 including £355,000 in grants to individuals.

Applications: On a form available from the correspondent, sponsored by two members of the institution, or by solicitors, accountants and such like. Applications can be submitted directly by the individual or through a social worker, citizen's advice bureau or other welfare agency, or through a close relative, solicitor or similar third party. They are considered throughout the year.

Correspondent: Miss L E McCarthy, Suite 4, 27 Boltro Road, Haywards Heath RH16 1BP (0444-417979).

Other information: Rent free housing in West Sussex is offered to those in housing and financial difficulty. The fund also has nomination rights to the Hanover Housing Association and Crossways Trust.

The Institution of Electrical Engineers Incorporated Benevolent Fund

Eligibility: Members or former members, for not less than five consecutive years, of the institution, and/or their dependants.

Types of grants: One-off grants, loans and regular allowances according to need. The trust also owns a residential home in New Malden, Surrey for the benefit of its members.

Annual grant total: £220,000 in 250 grants.

Applications: In writing to the correspondent.

Correspondent: A D Baker, Clerk, Savoy Place, London WC2R 0BL (071-344 5497).

Occupational charities

The Institution of Mining & Metallurgy Benevolent Fund

Eligibility: Members of the institution and former members (who have paid their subscription to the institution for at least five years) and their dependants.

Types of grants: Recurrent, as well as one-off grants, according to need.

Annual grant total: Nine grants totalling £21,000 in 1991.

Applications: On a form available from the correspondent. Applicants can telephone or write for a form.

Correspondent: The Honorary Secretary, 44 Portland Place, London W1N 4BR (071-580 3802).

The Institution of Plant Engineers Benevolent Fund

Eligibility: Members/former members of the institution, and their dependants living in the UK.

Types of grants: One-off and recurrent grants according to need. Most grants are given to those who are financially stressed through serious illness. Grants can range from £50 to £500, but in practice they tend to be for £50.

Annual grant total: In 1992, the fund had assets of £100,000 and an income of £16,000. Total expenditure was £7,500 including £5,500 in about 100 relief-in-need grants to individuals.

Applications: Through local members acting as "Honorary Branch Almoners". Applications must be made on a form and are considered in March, July and November.

Correspondent: F D Chapman, Hon. Secretary, 77 Great Peter Street, London SW1P 2EZ (071-233 2855).

The Institution of Professionals, Managers & Specialists Benevolent Fund

Eligibility: Members and retired members of the institution (and the former Institution of Civil Servants), and their spouses, families, widows or widowers.

Types of grants: Generally one-off grants. Recurrent grants do not exceed £1,000. The trust does not make loans. The trustees aim to relieve immediate problems and point applicants to other channels and agencies for long-term solutions. Grants are usually sent to the applicant, but for speed and/or reliability, some awards are sent direct to the utility/body owed money. Occasionally this is processed through an agency or second party (eg. welfare officer, debt counsellor, branch officer or relative).

Annual grant total: In 1991, the trust made 52 grants totalling £31,000.

Applications: On a form available from the correspondent. Applications can be submitted directly by the individual, through employer's welfare officers or branch representative. Applications are considered throughout a year. Payments are usually made to successful applicants within a week of receiving the application (if a trustee is available urgent cases may only take one or two days).

Correspondent: The Chairman, 75-79 York Road, London SE1 7AQ (071-928 9951).

The Institution of Structural Engineers Benevolent Fund

Eligibility: Members of the institution and their dependants.

Types of grants: One-off and recurrent grants and loans according to need. Grants range from £500 to £6,000.

Annual grant total: About £53,000 in about 38 grants.

Applications: Application forms are available from the correspondent and can be submitted by the individual for consideration in March and November.

Correspondent: H S Kitching, 11 Upper Belgrave Street, London SW1X 8BH (071-235 4535).

The Insurance Benevolent Fund

Eligibility: Insurance employees, pensioners and their dependants suffering financial hardship as a result of misfortune. Applicants must usually have spent five years in the insurance industry with service taking place not more than 10 years before misfortune, retirement or event prompting application.

Types of grants: Regular allowances and one-off grants to meet emergency needs for people who do not own their homes. For people who own their homes, loans are available to help with day-to-day expenses and larger items of specific (usually capital) expenditure. Loans for day-to-day expenses are interest-free but loans for capital expenditure are normally on interest-bearing terms, although the interest is below the commercial rate.

There are currently over 650 recipients, 500 of whom receive continuing help.

Annual grant total: In 1992/93, the fund had assets of £4.77 million and an income of £771,000. Grants (and loans) to individuals for relief-in-need totalled £888,000.

Applications: On a form available from the correspondent. Applications can be submitted directly by the individual, through a social worker or other welfare agency, via the company by which the applicant was employed, or a local insurance institute.

Correspondent: The Secretary, 20 Aldermanbury, London EC2V 7HY (071-606 3763).

The Insurance Orphans' Fund

Eligibility: Life members of the Insurance Orphans' Fund (or their spouses) where member is unable to provide for his/her family due to disability or death, and where the children are of school age.

Types of grants: Quarterly grants to assist with education and maintenance of school age children. The usual minimum award is £240.

Annual grant total: In 1992/93, the fund had assets of £5.87 million and an income of £375,000. Relief-in-need grants to 24 individuals totalled £26,000 and £349,000 was transferred to the Insurance Benevolent Fund (see entry above).

Applications: On a form available from the correspondent. Applications can be submitted directly by the individual, through a social worker or other welfare agency, via the company by which the applicant was employed, or a local insurance institute.

Correspondent: The Secretary, 20 Aldermanbury, London EC2V 7HY (071-606 3763).

The International Dance Teachers' Association Benevolent Fund

Eligibility: Members and retired members of the association, other dancers, former dancers, teachers or former teachers of dance, employees or former employees of the association, and their dependants.

Types of grants: One-off grants only. "Grants are made of a benevolent nature for people in need during times of crisis or ill health. Grants are not for the purpose of developing career training or prospects."

Annual grant total: Up to £2,000 in 10 grants.

● **Occupational charities**

Applications: In writing to the correspondent.

Correspondent: The General Secretary, 76 Bennett Road, Brighton BN2 5JL (0273-685652).

The Joint Industrial Council & the Match Manufacturing Industry Charitable Fund

Eligibility: People who are or have been involved in the manufacture of matches, and their dependants.

Types of grants: Christmas grants (£10) and one-off grants according to need (usually £50). Recent one-off grants have included help towards winter clothing, moving to sheltered accommodation and home security after a burglary.

Annual grant total: In 1992, the trust had assets of £52,000 and an income of £6,000. Up to 10 one-off grants of £50 and 765 Christmas grants of £10 to pensioners totalled just over £8,000.

Applications: In writing to the correspondent, directly by the individual. Applications are considered throughout the year.

Correspondent: The Secretary (Personnel Manager), c/o Bryant & May Ltd, Mersey Works, Speke Road, Garston, Liverpool L19 2PH (051-494 9555).

The King George's Pension Fund for Actors & Actresses

Eligibility: See below.

Types of grants: Annual grants to British actors and actresses who (a) have rendered such service to the profession as to merit recognition and (b) through altered circumstances are in need. No grants to people under 60, or to people who have been an actor or actress for fewer than 15 years.

Annual grant total: In 1993, the trust gave 35 grants of £2,000 totalling £70,000.

Applications: Usually in writing to the correspondent through an actors' charity or benevolent fund - NOT usually through citizen's advice bureaux or other general welfare organisations.

Correspondent: E Oliver, Secretary, 14-16 Regent Street, London SW1Y 4PS (071-839 4311).

The Bonno Krull Fund

Eligibility: Those who are working or who have worked as shipbrokers or in shipping.

Types of grants: Pensions and one-off grants according to need. This trust is mainly used as a last resort for those who have not been eligible for funding from the other trusts or benevolent funds supporting the industry.

Annual grant total: The trust can distribute between £8,000 and £10,000 each year. Recently only about three people have been given allowances of up to £10 per week.

Applications: In writing to the correspondent.

Correspondent: D A Painter, Charities Secretary, c/o Baltic Exchange, 14-20 St Mary Axe, London EC3A 8BH (071-623 5501).

The Leather & Hides Trades' Benevolent Institution

Eligibility: People who work or have worked in the leather trade (ie. in the production of leather or in the handling of hide and skin), and their dependants. Applicants are usually over 60; people under 60 are considered in exceptional circumstances.

Types of grants: Annuities of £300 a year (paid quarterly) plus bonuses at Christmas and in summer. Also, one-off grants to annuitants and others for special needs, and help towards shortfall in nursing home fees.

Annual grant total: £63,000 in 1992. There are about 95 regular annuitants.

Applications: On a form available from the correspondent. Applications can be submitted directly by the individual, through a welfare agency or other appropriate third party. They are considered in February, June and October.

Correspondent: Mrs Gwenyth M Stapleton, Secretary, 60 Wickham Hill, Hurstpierpoint, Hassocks, West Sussex BN6 9NP (0273-843488).

The Library Association Benevolent Fund

Eligibility: Librarians and their dependants who are in need.

Types of grants: Usually one-off grants according to need.

Annual grant total: In 1992, the trust had an income of £14,000. Grants to individuals for relief of need totalled £22,000.

Applications: In writing to the correspondent. Applications should be made directly or through a friend or relative.

Correspondent: Eric Winter, Secretary, 7 Ridgmount Street, London WC1E 7AE (071-636 7543).

The Lighthouse Club Benevolent Fund

Eligibility: People, or families of people, who are working in the construction industry and allied trades. Nobody over 65 years of age will be supported.

Types of grants: One-off or recurrent grants for those in need through accident, disability or ill-health, or to families of people who had a fatal accident in the construction industry. The maximum grant is £100 per month.

Annual grant total: In 1993, 273 recurrent and one-off grants were given totalling £252,000.

Applications: In writing to the correspondent. The fund has 20 honorary welfare officers in the UK and Ireland to liaise with beneficiaries.

Correspondent: Roy Williams, Administrator, Hazeley, 7 Hampton Hill, Wellington, Telford, Shropshire TF1 2EP (0952-244643).

The Liverpool Governesses' Benevolent Institution

Eligibility: Women in need who are or have been governesses or schoolmistresses, or other women engaged in the education or care of the young. The trust operates nationally but has a preference for those born or who lived in Merseyside, or who have connections with the area.

Types of grants: Mainly pensions of about £60 to £180 per quarter, but some one-off grants (maximum £500) are available.

Annual grant total: In 1993, the trust had an income of about £4,000 and gave grants of around £6,000.

Applications: By letter to the correspondent.

Correspondent: P F Davies, Treasurer, Rathbone Bros & Co, Port of Liverpool Building, 4th Floor, Pier Head, Liverpool L3 1NW (051-236 8674).

Other information: The trust has not supported any new applicants for about three years. Details of new applicants, or people needing more help than this trust can give, are passed to the Liverpool Merchants Guild (see separate entry in this Guide).

The Lloyd's Benevolent Fund

Eligibility: Those who work or have worked in the Lloyd's insurance market, and their dependants, anywhere in the world.

Occupational charities

Types of grants: Grants are usually recurrent to help with normal household expenses, one-off bills and nursing home fees. No help for medical expenses, property maintenance or school fees.

Annual grant total: In 1993, the trust had an income of £282,000 and gave 72 grants totalling £243,000 (an average of £3,900 each).

Applications: On a form available from the correspondent. Applications can be submitted by the individual through a social worker, citizen's advice bureau or other welfare agency, or through a previous employer. They are considered throughout the year.

Correspondent: R G Domney, Secretary, c/o Lloyd's, 1 Lime Street, London EC3M 7HA (071-623 7100 ext. 6453).

The London Shipowners' & Shipbrokers' Benevolent Society

Eligibility: Shipowners and shipbrokers and their dependants.

Types of grants: One-off and recurrent grants according to need.

Annual grant total: In 1993, 10 people received regular grants totalling £28,000. Six additional grants were made to meet unexpected items of expense totalling £4,100.

Applications: On a form available from the correspondent.

Correspondent: Doug Painter, Secretary, 14-20 St Mary Axe, London EC3A 8BH (071-623 5501).

The Magic Circle Benevolent Fund

Eligibility: Members/former members of the Magic Circle and their dependants.

Types of grants: One-off and recurrent grants according to need.

Annual grant total: The fund's income was £4,000 in 1990/91, the most up-to-date information provided by the fund.

Applications: In writing to the correspondent.

Correspondent: The Secretary, c/o The Victory Services Club, 61 Springfield Avenue, Kempston, Bedford MK42 8JB (0234-851607).

The Manufacturing Confectioners' Commercial Travellers' Association Benevolent Fund

Eligibility: Members of the association and their partners.

Types of grants: Christmas and other one-off grants.

Annual grant total: In 1993, grants to individuals totalled £2,655. The fund also gave £400 to the Commercial Travellers Benevolent Institute and £1,800 to the Confectioners' Benevolent Fund (see separate entries).

Applications: Through the local branch or direct to the correspondent.

Correspondent: Antony Franklin, Hon. General Treasurer, 38 Park View Road, London NW10 1AL (081-452 5517).

The Marine Society

Eligibility: Professional seafarers, active and retired, and their immediate dependants.

Types of grants: One-off grants and loans; no recurrent grants. Interest-free loans rather than grants are given where the need is short-term and the applicant expects to be earning again.

Annual grant total: In 1992, the trust had assets of £6 million and an income of £1.23 million. Total expenditure was £1.77 million. Relief-in-need grants to individuals totalled £97,000 (64 grants).

Applications: To the correspondent including reasons for the application and a statement of current income.

Correspondent: The General Secretary, 202 Lambeth Road, London SE1 7JW (071-261 9535).

The Market Research Benevolent Association

Eligibility: People who are or have been engaged in market research, and their dependants.

Types of grants: Generally one-off grants. Loans are also made.

Annual grant total: About £16,000.

Applications: On a form available from the correspondent.

Correspondent: Mrs Gill Wareing, Secretary, 6 Walkfield Drive, Epsom Downs, Surrey KT18 5UF (0737-354369).

The Master Tailors' Benevolent Association

Eligibility: Master tailors who have been in business on their own account for at least 10 years; occasionally their widows and children born in the UK or Eire. The term "master tailor" is defined as a bona fide employer of workmen, trading on his own account or in partnership, or as a director of a private limited company.

Types of grants: Recurrent grants paid quarterly and renewed annually.

Annual grant total: £18,000 in 28 grants.

Applications: On a form available from the correspondent.

Correspondent: C H R Garner, General Secretary, 35 Dewlands, Godstone, Surrey RH9 8BS.

The Merchant Taylors' Company

Eligibility: Primarily members of the company and their dependants. Also people who are or have been involved in the tailoring trade.

Types of grants: One-off and recurrent grants according to need.

Annual grant total: £123,000 in 1992. This includes grants to organisations.

Applications: In writing to the correspondent.

Correspondent: Capt D A Wallis, Clerk, Merchant Taylors' Hall, 30 Threadneedle Street, London EC2R 8AP (071-588 7606).

The Methodist Local Preachers Mutual Aid Association

Eligibility: Accredited Methodist (or Wesleyan Reform) Local Preachers, their widows/widowers and dependants living in the UK.

Types of grants: One-off grants (usually between £50 and £250) and weekly payments (up to £10 a week) according to need. The trust does not make loans.

Annual grant total: In 1993, the trust had assets of £3.56 million and an income of £1.56 million. The trust's total expenditure was £1.63 million, of which £333,000 was given in 140 grants to individuals.

Applications: On a form available from the correspondent which should be submitted through the LPMA branch officer. Applications should include details of weekly income and expenditure and capital resources and are usually considered in March and September.

Correspondent: Derek Bolton, General Secretary, Head Office, Chorleywood Close, Rickmansworth, Hertfordshire WD3 4EG (0923-775856).

Other information: The association also has five residential care homes.

The Metropolitan Police Civil Staff Welfare Fund

Eligibility: Past and present members of the Metropolitan Police civil staff, their

Occupational charities

families and dependants, who through poverty, hardship or distress are in need.

Types of grants: Present members are helped mainly by loans, together with welfare counselling. The loan is repaid by regular deductions from pay at source. For former members non-repayable grants may be available.

Annual grant total: No fixed limit.

Applications: In writing to the correspondent.

Correspondent: Chief Welfare Officer, Civil Staff Welfare Branch, Metropolitan Police Service, 67-73 Buckingham Gate, London SW1E 6BE.

The Metropolitan Police Combined Benevolent Fund

Eligibility: Metropolitan Police officers, cadets, ex-officers, their widows and orphans.

Types of grants: Generally one-off grants according to need.

Annual grant total: In 1992, the fund had assets of £467,000 and an income of £756,000; total expenditure was £720,000, of which £360,000 was in 321 relief-in-need grants. This was distributed as follows: the Metropolitan Police Widows Fund gave £156,000 in grants to widows; the Metropolitan Police Special Widows Fund gave £12,000 in grants; and the Metropolitan & City Police Relief Fund gave £191,000 to or on behalf of police officers in cases of illness or other special circumstances.

Applications: In writing to the correspondent directly by the individual. Applications are considered throughout the year.

Correspondent: A A Smith, Secretary, 2 Bessborough Street, London SW1V 2JF (071-230 8032).

The Morden College

Eligibility: Men and women aged over 50 years who have either been engaged in a trade, business or profession as principals or reached a position of authority or seniority in employment, and who through accident, misfortune, disability or infirmity have been prevented from continuing to follow their former calling and are in reduced material circumstances. Spouses, widows and widowers and dependent children are also eligible. Applicants for accommodation must be in "reasonably satisfactory general health".

Types of grants: Quarterly allowances of up to £125 and occasional one-off grants. The main concern of the college is to provide accommodation for eligible beneficiaries.

Annual grant total: £22,000 in 57 grants in 1993.

Applications: On a form available from the correspondent.

Correspondent: The Clerk, 19 St Germans Place, London SE3 0PW (071-858 3365).

The Junius S Morgan Benevolent Fund for Nurses

Eligibility: Practising and former members of the nursing profession.

Types of grants: Grants can be made to help with general household bills, mortgage arrears in certain circumstances, home furnishings, appliances, television licences and rentals etc.. Recurrent grants are up to £10 a week. Where the applicant is a home-owner, grants will be given up to a maximum of £750. Above this figure, the fund would give a loan, secured by way of a mortgage on the applicant's property, for which interest is payable. No grants for education, residential/nursing home fees, private medical health care or to anyone with no connection with the nursing profession.

Annual grant total: In 1991, the trust had assets of £515,000 generating an income of £70,000. Grants to individuals totalled £50,000 (over 100 grants).

Applications: On a form available from the correspondent. Applications can be submitted by the individual, through a social worker, citizen's advice bureau or other welfare agency, or by a friend, relative or other concerned person. They are considered throughout the year. Applications should give full financial details (including DSS and other benefits) and list other charities approached.

Correspondent: David Roberts, Secretary, Burdett House, 15 Buckingham Street, London WC2N 6ED (071-839 6785).

The John Murdoch Trust

Eligibility: Needy bachelors and widowers who, either as amateurs or professionals, have pursued science in any of its branches, and who are at least 55 years old.

Types of grants: Yearly allowances of about £1,000 to £2,000.

Annual grant total: No information available.

Applications: Considered as they are received.

Correspondent: The Secretary, c/o The Royal Bank of Scotland plc, Private Trust & Taxation Office, 2 Festival Square, Edinburgh EH3 9SU (031-523 2648).

Other information: This entry is repeated in the National and general charities section of the book.

The Musicians Benevolent Fund

Eligibility: Members and former members of the society and their dependants in need through illness, old age or some misfortune, generally from the UK or Ireland. People in other countries are occasionally supported but they must have been born in the UK. Applicants must have been a professional musician in this country for most of their working life. The household must not possess more than £15,000 capital or savings.

Types of grants: One-off grants, usually to applicants of working age. Regular payments and nursing home top up fees, etc. are usually given to pensioners or people who are chronically sick. The maximum award is £5,200 in any one year (usually as a nursing home top up). The fund may suggest a loan where the applicant has sufficient property to act as security.

Annual grant total: In 1992, the fund had an income of £2.6 million and spent £2.3 million, of which, £964,000 was given in 7,555 relief-in-need grants to 900 beneficiaries. The cost of running the two residential homes amounted to £643,000.

Applications: On a form available from the correspondent including two referees. Applications should be submitted by the individual or through a social worker, citizen's advice bureau or other welfare agency, for consideration throughout the year.

Correspondent: Mrs M A Taylor, Head of Casework, 16 Ogle Street, London W1P 7LG (071-636 4481).

Other information: The fund also runs two residential homes for its pensioners and arranges holidays for beneficiaries.

The Musicians' Social & Benevolent Council

Eligibility: Musicians who are or were members of the London branches of the Musicians' Union who are facing sickness or distress.

Types of grants: Monthly £10 grants to old musicians in distress (Musicians Union London Branch Members). Sickness grants to working or retired members of the profession (usually a one-

Occupational charities

off payment up to a maximum of £150). NO grants for educational purposes.

Annual grant total: About £19,000 in 600 grants.

Applications: In writing to the correspondent, including the musicians union branch and membership number. Applications should be submitted directly by the individual or by spouse or friend.

Correspondent: P Cameron, Hon. Secretary, 194 Muswell Hill Road, London N10 3NG (081-444 0246).

The Mylne Trust

Eligibility: Protestants who are/have been involved in evangelistic work including past and present missionaries, married ordinands with dependent children (who are given priority) and other Christian workers at the trustees' discretion.

Types of grants: Annual and one-off grants.

Annual grant total: In 1992/93, the trust had assets of £799,000 with an income of £64,000. Grants to individuals totalled £67,000.

Applications: On a form available from the correspondent to be submitted directly by the individual including a passport size photograph of the applicant certified as a true likeness. Applications are considered each month.

Correspondent: The Secretary, Messrs Bells, Potter & Kempson, 11 South Street, Farnham, Surrey GU9 7QX (0252-733733).

Other information: This entry is repeated in the National and general charities section of the book.

The National Advertising Benevolent Society

Eligibility: Those who work or have worked in advertising and related industries, and their dependants.

Types of grants: One-off and recurrent grants according to need. Welfare advice is available through a NABS helpline.

Annual grant total: About £300,000 in about 580 grants.

Applications: On a form available from the correspondent.

Correspondent: Mrs D Larkin, Director, 199-205 Old Marylebone Road, London NW1 3QP (071-723 8028).

Other information: The society also provides sheltered housing, residential care and nursing accommodation.

The National Association of Cooperative Officials' Benevolent Fund

Eligibility: Members and retired members of the association and their families; also widows and children of deceased members.

Types of grants: Generally one-off grants up to a maximum of about £500, but occasional recurrent grants are given for the relief of educational and financial hardship. All applications are means-tested.

Annual grant total: In 1992, 12 grants totalling £4,000 were given.

Applications: Through area offices or direct to head office.

Correspondent: The General Secretary, Coronation House, Arndale Centre, Manchester M4 2HW (061-834 6029).

The National Association of Master Bakers

Eligibility: Master bakers from England or Wales (whether members of the association or not) and their families who are in need.

Types of grants: Pensions, one-off grants and loans according to need. No grants for business debt or towards nursing home fees. Recent grants have included help with household expenses (eg. telephone, gas), purchase or loan of equipment (eg. stair lifts, wheelchairs, smoke detectors), grants in case of special hardship (eg. to pay off loans, funeral costs) and Christmas food hampers. Recurrent grants are usually for £5 a week and are paid quarterly.

About 150 individuals receive help; some receive more than one grant.

Annual grant total: In 1993, the fund had assets of £564,000 and an income of £52,000. It gave £61,000 in grants.

Applications: On a form available from the correspondent, which can be submitted by the individual or through a recognised referral agency (social worker, citizen's advice bureau, doctor etc.) and are considered every month.

Correspondent: Ms Cindy Honour, 21 Baldock Street, Ware, Hertfordshire SG12 9DH (0920-468061).

The National Association of Schoolmasters Union of Women Teachers Benevolent Fund

Eligibility: Members/former members of the association and their dependants.

Types of grants: One-off and recurrent grants and interest-free loans according to need. Recently grants/loans have been given to terminally ill members to visit relatives and secure possession of their home, to buy a converted vehicle for a paralysed member, and a monthly grant to a member's widow with no occupational pension.

No grants/loans for private health care/treatment, private school fees or costs incurred through legal action, or when state benefit entitlements would be reduced as a result.

Annual grant total: In 1992, the fund had an income of £202,000; relief-in-need grants totalled £79,000 (133 grants).

Applications: On a form available from the correspondent. Forms should be filled in by the secretary of the local association. Applications are considered each month except August.

Correspondent: Jerry Bartlett, Benevolence Officer, Hillscourt Education Centre, Rose Hill, Rednal, Birmingham B45 8RS (021-453 6150).

The National Benevolent Society of Watch & Clock Makers

Eligibility: People working in any branch of the watch and clock trade, and their widows and dependants.

Types of grants: Grants of £300 a year paid quarterly. There is a Christmas gift, winter fuel gift paid in early spring and two other gifts paid at the start of the summer and early autumn. Recipients will receive all four grants; otherwise one-off grants will be towards television licences, fuel bills etc..

Annual grant total: In 1993, 250 people received grants of £300 (total £75,000).

Applications: On a form available from the correspondent.

Correspondent: B J Botting, Secretary, 1st Floor, St Dunstans House, Carey Lane, London EC2V 8AA (071-606 4337).

The National British & Irish Millers' Benevolent Society

Eligibility: Members of the Incorporated National Association of British and Irish Millers, master millers and other flour milling employees from the UK, their widows and, in certain special cases, their dependants.

Types of grants: Recipients are usually retired ex-flour milling employees who are suffering hardship or need. Donations and grants are awarded annually following a review of each individual's

Occupational charities

circumstances. Christmas cash gifts and hampers are also given, as is help with heating bills.

Annual grant total: The following entry was in the previous edition of this Guide. The correspondent stated that the figures are comparable but in 1993, about £20,000 was given in grants.

"Nearly £18,000 to 28 recipients in 1991, distributed as follows: £2,300 in grants (6 payments ranging from £50 to £800); £7,600 in donations (20 grants ranging from £100 to £800, but generally £200 to £400); £2,700 in Christmas gifts (27 grants of £100, mostly to existing beneficiaries); £3,000 in heating payments and Christmas hampers worth £2,310."

Applications: On a form available from the correspondent.

Correspondent: P H Neill, Hon. Secretary, 21 Arlington Street, London SW1A 1RN (071-493 2521).

The National Caravan Council Ltd

Eligibility: People who work or have worked in caravan retail or manufacture, or on caravan sites, and their dependants.

Types of grants: Usually one-off grants, but occasionally recurrent grants may be given. Grants are usually towards redecoration, education or special equipment such as a computer for people who are housebound or with disabilities.

Annual grant total: In 1993, the fund had capital of £160,000 and an income of £9,000. Eight relief-in-need grants to individuals totalled £10,000.

Applications: In writing to the correspondent.

Correspondent: M A Stuart, Catherine House, Victoria Road, Aldershot, Hampshire GU11 1SS (0252-318251).

The National Dairymen's Benevolent Institution

Eligibility: People working or who have worked in the dairy trade in the UK for at least 10 years, and their dependants.

Types of grants: Quarterly grants of £40 if the applicant has not subscribed to this organisation; up to £60 if a subscriber. Monthly grants of up to £50 if towards nursing home fees. One-off payments up to £500 for special items. Recent examples include grants towards respite care; roof repairs; telephone installation; wheelchairs; accommodation/household costs; support while partner is in hospital; house repairs and car insurance.

Those receiving a grant are also offered a free two week holiday at the organisation's holiday home in Worthing. Remaining vacancies are offered to trade pensioners at £52 per week (low season) or £67 (high season). The trust also rents half-board rooms at hotels in Blackpool and Scarborough which will cost £75 or £85 per week. The institution's clients are offered single or double flats (at £38 or £33 per week respectively) by Barham Court Housing Association, closely associated with the dairy trade. The housing association pays water rates, council tax and television licences on behalf of residents.

Annual grant total: In 1992/93, the trust had assets of £1.2 million and an income of £113,000. Total expenditure was £156,000. Relief-in-need grants to individuals totalled £63,000 including 266 monthly grants (minimum £40 per quarter).

Applications: On a form available from the correspondent, submitted directly by the individual or through a social worker or other welfare agency. If the application is for monthly assistance, original certificates of birth, marriage and death are required. If the application is for a one-off grant a note (estimate/bills) of the cost of item to be purchased is required with notification if funds are available from any other source. Applications are considered in January, March, may, July, September and November.

Correspondent: Mrs T Scott, 9 New Parade, Worthing, West Sussex BN11 2BQ (0903-213065).

The National Federation of Fish Friers Benevolent Fund

Eligibility: Members or former members of the federation, living in the UK, and their dependants.

Types of grants: One-off grants only for necessities, including convalescent holidays in the UK (up to £150 per week for two people for two weeks).

No grants for debts due to poor business practice or convalescence outside the UK.

Annual grant total: In 1993, the trust had assets of £90,000 producing an income of £5,000. Six grants were given to individuals and totalled £3,000.

Applications: On a form available from the correspondent. Applications can be submitted by the individual or through a recognised referral agency (social worker, citizen's advice bureau or AFF Association/branch etc.) and are considered monthly.

Correspondent: J A Parrington, General Secretary, New Federation House, 4 Greenwood Mount, Leeds LS6 4LQ (0532-307044).

The National Federation of Retail Newsagents Convalescence Fund

Eligibility: Members of the federation and their dependants. Other people in the retail newsagents trade who are not members of the federation are not eligible.

Types of grants: Grants are given for relief-in-need, including convalescent holidays (maximum of £150 per week for no more than six weeks in any five-year period).

Annual grant total: In 1992, the trust had an income of £34,000. Grants ranging from £195 to £950 were given to individuals and totalled £34,000.

Applications: On an application form available from the correspondent. Applications should be submitted directly by the individual and are considered at any time. They should include confirmation of federation fees paid and confirmation from a doctor of the need for convalescence.

Correspondent: The Administrative & Personnel Manager, Yeoman House, Sekforde Street, Clerkenwell Green, London EC1R 0HD (071-253 4225).

The National Federation of Sub-Postmasters Benevolent Fund

Eligibility: (a) Serving or retired sub-postmasters and sub-mistresses.

(b) Serving or retired full-time employees of the NFSP.

(c) The widows, widowers and children of any of the aforementioned people.

Types of grants: Temporary assistance in cases of financial need resulting from:(a) Breakdown in health.(b) Death of husband, wife, father or mother.(c) Domestic distress.(d) Any exceptional cases which may be brought to notice.

The average recurring grant is £17.50 per week; the average one-off grant is £400.

Annual grant total: In 1992, the fund had assets of £650,000 and an income of £94,000. Total expenditure was £87,000 including £58,000 in 71 relief-in-need grants to individuals.

Applications: On a form available from the correspondent, submitted directly by the individual or any third party acting on his/her behalf. Applications are considered in January, March, June and October, but emergency cases are dealt with as they arise.

Correspondent: Colin Baker, Secretary, Evelyn House, 22 Windlesham Gardens,

Shoreham-by-Sea, West Sussex BN43 5AZ (0273-452324).

The National Grocers' Benevolent Fund

Eligibility: Those who have spent 15 years of their adult working life (after the age of 18) in the grocery, provision and off-licence industries, and their dependants living in the UK. This includes food manufacturing, wholesaling and retailing in all its aspects and the retail off-licence trade.

Types of grants: Allowances of £7 a week plus two annual bonuses of £76 on 1st July and £80 on 1st December, totalling the DSS disregard of £520 a year.

Emergency grants for specific financial problems. These are usually up to £100, but can be more in serious emergencies.

Annual grant total: £620,000 in 1990/91 including 1,200 weekly allowances, plus 63 emergency payments totalling £6,400. The correspondent has confirmed the entry, but has declined to update the financial information.

Applications: On a form available from the correspondent.

Correspondent: The Director General, 17 Farnborough Street, Farnborough, Hampshire GU14 8AG (0252-515946).

The National Health Service Pensioners' Trust

Eligibility: People in need who have worked in the National Health Service (or the equivalent caring services before 1948).

Types of grants: One-off grants usually for £100 to £200 according to need.

Annual grant total: £75,000 to £90,000.

Applications: On a form available from the correspondent.

Correspondent: F S Jackson, Director, 14 Palace Court, London W2 4HT (071-229 9734).

The National Union of Journalists Provident Fund

Eligibility: Members of the NUJ who are sick and disabled and dependants of deceased or former NUJ members, living in the UK or Ireland (with a preference for widows and orphans).

Types of grants: One-off and recurrent grants according to need.

Annual grant total: £155,000 in grants in 1993.

Applications: In writing to the correspondent, by the individual or through the local NUJ branch. Applications are considered throughout the year.

Correspondent: Gerald Sanctuary, Acorn House, 314-320 Gray's Inn Road, London WC1X 8DP (071-833 2766).

Other information: This was formerly the NUJ Widows & Orphans Fund, but its work has been extended by Charity Commission schemes in 1982 and 1984. Under these schemes, when the fund cannot usefully apply its funds to widows, orphans or other dependants, it can give help to members of the union who are in need, or to former members (for at least 12 consecutive months), unless they left the union by expulsion.

The Newspaper Press Fund

Eligibility: Member journalists and their widows and dependants. Limited help to non-members and their families.

Types of grants: One-off grants, typically £250 but to a usual maximum of £2,500. Weekly allowances of up to £20 a week. NO grants to students unless they are dependants of members.

Annual grant total: In 1993, £210,000 was given to 298 recipients (including one-off Christmas gifts).

Applications: In writing to the correspondent, including full supporting financial details.

Correspondent: Peter Evans, Director & Secretary, Dickens House, 35 Wathan Road, Dorking, Surrey RH4 1JY (0306-887511/889366).

Other information: The fund also runs residential homes in Dorking for members and their dependants.

The Newsvendors' Benevolent Institution

Eligibility: Retired people and their dependants, and those who cannot work through ill health, who have been engaged in the distribution and sale of newspapers and magazines in the UK for at least 10 years.

Types of grants: Regular monthly benefits; one-off grants; amenity grants for telephones, television licences, holidays; possible help with shortfall on residential and nursing home fees; grants for orphaned children.

Annual grant total: About £170,000 in 1993.

Applications: On a form available from the correspondent. Applications can be submitted directly by the individual, through a social worker or other welfare agency, or through Old Ben area committees or pension fund managers. Applications are considered every two months from January.

Correspondent: Mrs Betty Davidson, Welfare Officer, PO Box 306, Dunmow, Essex CM6 1HY (0371-874198).

The 1930 Fund for District Nurses

Eligibility: Fully qualified nurses either working or who have worked as district nurses in the community.

Types of grants: One-off and recurrent grants according to need. Weekly grants are £5; one-off grants are up to £300.

Annual grant total: In 1992/93, the trust had assets of £871,000 and an income of £59,000. Grants of £250 each were given to about 200 people and totalled £48,000.

Applications: On a form available from the correspondent. Applications can be submitted directly by the individual, through a social worker, citizen's advice bureau, other welfare agency or third party. Applications are considered throughout the year and should include details of nursing experience.

Correspondent: Miss B A Whitfield, Secretary, 1a Winders Road, Battersea, London SW11 3HE (071-924 2201).

The Evelyn Norris Trust

Eligibility: Members of the concert or theatrical profession who are in need.

Types of grants: One-off grants according to need, ranging from £100 to £300. Grants have been given towards a recuperative holiday, convalescence, heating bills, cars for disabled people, wheelchairs and furniture.

Annual grant total: In 1992, the trust had an income of £22,000. 70 grants to individuals totalled £24,000.

Applications: On a form available from the correspondent. Applications are considered each month.

Correspondent: The Secretary, Guild House, Upper St Martin's Lane, London WC2H 9EG (071-379 6000).

The Northern Police Orphans' Trust

Eligibility: People with at least one parent who was a member of a police force in northern England, or associated with the police, and who is now dead or incapacitated.

Types of grants: One-off and recurrent grants according to need.

Annual grant total: About £18,000 in 75 grants.

● **Occupational charities**

Applications: Applications should be submitted via the police force in which the parent served.

Correspondent: A Outhwaite, St Andrews, Harlow Moor Road, Harrogate, North Yorkshire HG2 0AD (0423-504448).

The NUMAST Welfare Fund (formerly the Mercantile Marine Association)

Eligibility: Seafarers, former seafarers and their dependants. The union manages a number of different funds mainly for the welfare of former seafarers all of which have slightly different eligibility qualifications. In most cases of need or distress, the sufferer will be eligible for help from at least one of these. Applicants should normally be over 50 but exceptions are made, for example in cases of ill-health.

Types of grants: Regular grants or pensions in the region of £260 a year. One-off hardship grants range from £80 to around £500.

Annual grant total: About £143,000 a year in grants to 560 regular beneficiaries, and 168 one-off grants.

Applications: On a form available from the correspondent, submitted directly by the individual or through a social worker, citizen's advice bureau or other welfare agency, or through a third party (eg. family, doctor or union official). Applications are considered monthly, but hardship grants can be considered immediately.

Correspondent: D R Bond, Deputy General Secretary, Nautilus House, Mariners Park, Wallasey, Merseyside L45 7PH (051-639 8454).

The Nurses Fund for Nurses

Eligibility: Poor and elderly or disabled nurses whether fully or specially trained.

Types of grants: One-off grants towards for example fuel bills, telephone rental and installation and convalescent holidays and help with short fall in nursing home fees. Grants range from £4 a week for nursing home fees up to £300 for a single grant.

No grants to dependants of the above, or to auxiliary nurses or towards debts such as credit cards, overdrafts or catalogues.

Annual grant total: In 1993, the trust had an income of £59,000. 379 grants totalled £40,000.

Applications: On a form available from the correspondent. Applications are considered every six weeks.

Correspondent: The Secretary, 1a Winders Road, London SW11 3HE (071-738 0004).

The Tim O'Leary Special Fund

Eligibility: Former registered dock workers who are in need.

Types of grants: A single cheque payment to each qualifying beneficiary around December each year.

Annual grant total: In 1992/93, the trust had assets of £1.8 million and an income of £133,400. Grants to 5,659 individuals totalled £353,000.

Applications: On a form available from the correspondent. Applications should be made through the local TGWU Committee. They are considered in August/September.

Correspondent: M Hartop, Secretary, Briarcliff House, Kingsmead, Farnborough, Hants GU14 7TE (0252-373020).

The Oilseed, Oil & Feedingstuffs Trades Benevolent Association

Eligibility: Members of the association and their dependants.

Types of grants: One-off and recurrent grants according to need.

Annual grant total: In 1993, £26,000 was given in 26 regular grants in 1993 and £4,000 in seven one-off grants. Three grants were also given towards education totalling £3,500.

Applications: On a form available from the correspondent.

Correspondent: Doug Painter, Secretary, 14-20 St Mary Axe, London EC3A 8BH (071-623 5501).

The Overseas Service Pensioners' Benevolent Society

Eligibility: Members of the Overseas Service Pensioners' Association and pensioners eligible for membership, or anyone who has served in the overseas civil service, and their dependants.

Types of grants: Grants of about £600 to £700 a year, mostly paid quarterly to meet basic personal living expenses, but sometimes for specific needs which cannot be met otherwise.

Annual grant total: In 1992, the trust had assets of just over £300,000 and an income of £77,000. About 130 relief-in-need grants totalled £68,000.

Applications: On a form available from the correspondent. Applications can be submitted directly by the individual or through a close relative or legal representative. They are considered at any time, but the committee normally meets three times a year in March, June and November.

Correspondent: D F B Le Breton, Secretary, 138 High Street, Tonbridge, Kent TN9 1AX (0732-363836).

The Pawnbrokers' Charitable Institution

Eligibility: Pawnbrokers who have been employed for at least five years, their widows, widowers and children who are convalescent, disabled or otherwise infirm or in need of financial assistance.

Types of grants: Annual grants and regular allowances. Recurrent grants generally of £520 a year are paid monthly (for those on Income Support) and grants of over £1,000 are available to meet emergency needs.

Annual grant total: About £40,000 in 1993.

Applications: On a form available from the correspondent.

Correspondent: Mrs K Way, Secretary, 184 Crofton Lane, Orpington, Kent BR6 0BW (0689-838528).

The Pension Fund of the Incorporated Society of Authors, Playwrights & Composers

Eligibility: Authors in need.

Types of grants: Pensions.

Annual grant total: In 1992, the trust had an income of £22,000, of which £12,000 was given in pensions.

Applications: In writing to the correspondent. Applicants must be over 65 and have been members of the Society of Authors for at least 10 years. Vacancies are announced from time to time in *The Author*.

Correspondent: The General Secretary, 84 Drayton Gardens, London SW10 9SB (071-373 6642).

The Performing Right Society Members' Fund

Eligibility: Composers, authors and publishers of music who are or were members of the society, and their dependants.

Types of grants: Regular monetary assistance to elderly members or

Occupational charities

dependants whose income has proved inadequate to maintain basic living standards.

Temporary assistance by way of a loan to meet an unexpected financial crisis.

Emergency assistance by way of outright money grants for financial difficulties caused by serious illness or accident.

Help also to elderly members towards holidays, telephone and television rental, television licence or insurances.

Annual grant total: In 1992, the trust's income was £196,000; grants to individuals totalled £162,000 (over 100 grants).

Applications: On a form available from the correspondent. Applications can be submitted by the individual, through a social worker, citizen's advice bureau or other welfare agency, or by next of kin or associate. They are considered on the third Wednesday of each month.

Correspondent: The Secretary, 29-33 Berners Street, London W1P 3DB (071-580 5544).

The PGA European Tour Benevolent Fund

Eligibility: Members and former members of the PGA European Tour and other people whose main livelihood is or has been earned by providing services to professional golf, and their dependants.

Types of grants: One-off or recurrent grants according to need.

Annual grant total: About £16,000 in 1992.

Applications: In writing to the correspondent.

Correspondent: The Secretary, Wentworth Drive, Virginia Water, Surrey GU25 4LX (0344-842881).

The Pharmaceutical Society's Benevolent Fund

Eligibility: Pharmacists, former pharmacists or their dependants in need.

Types of grants: One-off grants can range from £50 to £4,500 in exceptional circumstances. Grants can be towards telephone rental/installation, television licence, boiler repairs etc.. Recurrent grants would usually be £5 or £10 a week paid quarterly to help with general living expenses.

Annual grant total: In 1993, the fund gave regular allowances to about 200 people and about 80 one-off grants. The trust spends about £150,000 a year, not all of which is given in grants to individuals in need.

Applications: In writing to the correspondent.

Correspondent: J Ferguson, Secretary, 1 Lambeth High Street, London SE1 7JN (071-735 9141).

The H T Pickles Benevolent Fund

Eligibility: Members of the Vehicle Builders' and Repairers' Association, and their dependants. (See below).

Types of grants: £50 paid twice a year to 17 beneficiaries. This list of beneficiaries has not altered for a number of years.

Annual grant total: £1,700 in 1993 to 17 beneficiaries.

Applications: Direct to the correspondent or via branches of the association.

Correspondent: The Fund Administrator, The Vehicle Builders' & Repairers' Association Ltd, Belmont House, 102 Finkle Lane, Gildersome, Leeds LS27 7TW (0532-538333).

Other information: This fund is becoming a limited company and broadening its scope to include the staff of members of the association.

The Police Dependants' Trust

Eligibility: (a) Dependants of current police officers or former police officers who died from injuries received in the execution of duty. (b) Police officers or former police officers incapacitated as a result of injury received in the execution of duty, and/or their dependants.

Types of grants: Mainly regular allowances of between £850 and £1,500 a year for general maintenance. One-off grants of £2,000 to £12,000 usually towards medical expenses, special equipment, adapted vehicles or towards wheelchair accessibility, repairs or redecoration to homes, for emergency needs and for holidays.

Annual grant total: In 1991/92, grants totalled £936,000. The trust gave 108 one-off and 296 recurrent grants.

Applications: Through the Chief Police Officer for the area where the applicant lives. Each application is accompanied by a report made by a local officer experienced in welfare matters, following a visit to the applicant's home. Details of income level and need should be included in an application. Urgent cases can be dealt with rapidly.

Correspondent: Peter Cripps, Room T1083, 50 Queen Anne's Gate, London SW1H 9AT (071-273 2921).

Other information: The trust also gave £500,000 to a police convalescence home.

The Pottery & Glass Trade Benevolent Institution

Eligibility: People employed in retail, wholesale or manufacturing aspects of china or glass.

Types of grants: Allowances up to £10 a week; one-off grants up to £100.

Annual grant total: £15,000 to £18,000 in 75 to 100 grants.

Applications: On a form available from the correspondent.

Correspondent: Mrs P Smith, Admin. Secretary, 63 Stanley Hill Avenue, Amersham, Bucks HB7 9BA (0494-722458).

The Printers' Charitable Corporation

Eligibility: Aged, poor or distressed people who are or were either printers or employed in the printing or allied trades (eg. ink-making, paper-making, the warehousing of ink, paper, books or printing materials or the manufacture of typesetting, foundry or printing machinery). Also the needy widows/widowers and children of deceased members.

Types of grants: Both one-off and recurrent grants (including grants for convalescence and holidays) and contributions towards residential care and nursing home fees for the elderly.

Annual grant total: About £300,000. There are over 1,000 regular beneficiaries.

Applications: An application form is available on written request from the correspondent.

Correspondent: The Director, Victoria House, Harestone Valley Road, Caterham, Surrey CR3 6HY (0883-345331).

Other information: The corporation provides sheltered homes for the elderly at Basildon and Bletchley plus a nursing home at Bletchley. It also advises pensioners on their statutory entitlements.

The Professional Classes Aid Council

Eligibility: People of professional background who have no specific fund to turn to when in distress. Grants are also given for the welfare of children of the above.

Types of grants: Weekly allowances and one-off gifts according to need.

Occupational charities

Annual grant total: In 1992, the trust had assets of £859,000 and an income of £277,000. Total expenditure was £252,000. Relief-in-need grants of £50 to £500 a year (up to £10 per week) were given to 600 individuals. About £70,000 was given for educational purposes.

Applications: On a form available from the correspondent. Applications can be submitted by the individual or by other third parties for consideration throughout the year except August.

Correspondent: The Secretary, 10 St Christopher's Place, London W1M 6HY (071-935 0641).

Other information: The Professional Classes Aid Council is operated alongside the Guild of Aid for Gentlepeople. See separate entry.

The Professional Footballers Association Accident Fund

Eligibility: Members or former members of the association, who have been forced to retire from the game through injury, and former players requiring medical help and their dependants.

Types of grants: One-off grants for specific needs. Grants could be up to a maximum of £2,400 in 1993/94.

Annual grant total: In 1992/93, the fund had assets of £1.8 million and an income of £1.3 million. Expenditure totalled £467,000, of which only £49,000 was paid out to members and £62,000 was paid in medical fees. £244,000 was also contributed to Football/Premier League clubs towards the costs of medical insurance cover for professionals and youth trainees.

Applications: On a form available from the correspondent.

Correspondent: The Secretary, 2 Oxford Court, Bishopsgate, Manchester M2 3WQ (061-236 0575).

The Professional Footballers Association Benevolent Fund

Eligibility: Members or former members of the association and their dependants.

Types of grants: One-off grants for specific needs. Grants could be up to a maximum of £2,400 in 1993/94.

Annual grant total: In 1992/93, the fund had assets of £1.5 million and an income of £1 million. Expenditure totalled £300,000, of which £122,000 was paid to 168 beneficiaries. Sizable loans were also paid to a number of teams to help with temporary cash flow problems to protect players' wages.

Applications: On a form available from the correspondent.

Correspondent: The Secretary, 2 Oxford Court, Bishopsgate, Manchester M2 3WQ (061-236 0575).

The Provision Trade Benevolent Institution

Eligibility: People in need in the provision trade, and their dependants. Applicants are normally retired and must have been employed in the trade for at least 10 years.

Types of grants: One-off grants and pensions according to need.

Annual grant total: £33,000 in 1994.

Applications: In writing to the correspondent.

Correspondent: Alan Chandler, Secretary, 17 Clerkenwell Green, London EC1R 0DP (071-253 2114).

Other information: This trust was founded as the Cheesemonger's Benevolent Institution in 1835 "for pensionary relief of indigent or incapacitated members of the Provision Trade and their widows".

The Pyncombe Charity

Eligibility: Serving clergymen in the Church of England and their dependants who are in need.

Types of grants: One-off or recurrent grants according to need for cases of serious illness for the applicant or immediate family.

Annual grant total: In 1991, the trust had an income of £13,000, it is not known how much of this was given in grants to individuals.

Applications: On a form available from the correspondent. Applications should be made through the diocesan bishop and are considered in May.

Correspondent: I L Billinge, Secretary, The Old Rectory, Crowcombe, Taunton, Somerset TA4 4AA (0278-452978).

The Queen's Nursing Institute

Eligibility: Holders of the district nurse qualification who are elderly, retired or severely disabled.

Types of grants: One-off and recurrent grants to help with household expenses, essential equipment, television rental, telephone installation and rental, and help towards provision of specialist aids and equipment and respite breaks. No help towards debt repayment, rent or mortgage arrears.

Annual grant total: In 1993, the trust had an income of £90,000, all of which was given in grants to individuals. 800 individuals received grants ranging from £100 to £520.

Applications: On a form available from the correspondent, including a cost guide and letter of support. Applications can be submitted by the individual, through a recognised referral agency (social worker, citizen's advice bureau or doctor or from other charitable sources) and are considered in January, April, July and October.

Correspondent: Mrs Maureen Proctor, Welfare Adviser, 3 Albemarle Way, Clerkenwell, London EC1V 4JB (071-490 4227).

Other information: The institute also administers the Edith Cavell & Nation's Fund for Nurses (see separate entry).

The Railway Benevolent Institution

Eligibility: Railway employees (active or retired) or their dependants. Assistance does not depend on membership of the RBI, but in general members receive larger grants than non-members.

Types of grants: Annuities (from £100 to £240 a year) are generally available to members of the RBI, but there are a limited number for non-members.

Special Benevolent Grants are available to all active and retired railway employees in particular need, whether RBI members or not. They help with the cost of convalescent treatment, equipment for disabled people and funeral expenses.

Residential Care Grants help with the shortfall between residential/nursing home fees and available income.

There is also help to children of railway families where there is particular financial hardship, special care required for disabled children, help for orphans etc..

Annual grant total: About £200,000 in about 1,300 grants.

Applications: On a form available from the correspondent, submitted by the individual, a direct relative or through a social worker, citizen's advice bureau or other welfare agency. Applications are considered monthly.

Correspondent: R B Boiling, Director, 67 Ashbourne Road, Derby DE22 3FS (0332-363067).

Occupational charities

The Referees Association Members Benevolent Fund

Eligibility: Members or former members of the association and their dependants who are in need, in England, Northern Ireland and Wales.

Types of grants: One-off emergency grants.

Annual grant total: In 1992/93, the trust had an income of £16,000, and gave 15 grants totalling £7,250.

Applications: On a form available from the correspondent. Applications should be made through a council member. They are considered at any time.

Correspondent: The General Secretary, 1 Westhill Road, Coundon, Coventry CV6 2AD (0203-601701).

The Rendlesham Benevolent Fund

Eligibility: National hunt trainers and jockeys, and their dependants, who due to old age or illness are in need.

Types of grants: There are two levels of quarterly allowances (currently of £65 and £100); one-off grants for urgent needs (ranging from £200 to £460), occasionally including funeral costs.

Annual grant total: £22,000 in 1991, including £12,000 in allowances and £10,000 in donations (52 grants in all).

Applications: On a form available from the correspondent to be considered throughout the year. Applications can be submitted directly by the individual or through a social worker, citizen's advice bureau or other welfare agency.

Correspondent: Mrs P Lewis, The Jockey Club Charitable Trust, 121 High Street, Newmarket, Suffolk CB8 9AJ (0638-560763).

The Rev Dr George Richards Charity

Eligibility: Church of England clergy who through sickness or infirmity have become incapable of performing their duties. Widows and other dependants can also be helped.

Types of grants: Both one-off grants and annual pensions, usually around £500.

Annual grant total: About £17,000.

Applications: On a form available from the correspondent. Applications should be submitted directly by the individual. They are considered in June and November.

Correspondent: D J Newman, Secretary, 51 Pole Barn Lane, Frinton-on-Sea, Essex CO13 9NQ (0255-676509).

RMT (National Union of Rail, Maritime & Transport Workers) Orphan Fund

Eligibility: Children under 18 of deceased members of the union. See other information.

Types of grants: An award, paid quarterly, is made when a member has died and left children under 16, or under 18 and still in full-time education. It is paid until the child leaves school or reaches 18 years of age, whichever is sooner, or the parent remarries. The award is £5 a week per child up to 16 and £7.50 a week per child up to 18 and still in full-time education. An additional allowance of £2.50 a week may be paid to guardians of orphaned children up to the age of 16.

Annual grant total: In 1990, the fund had assets of £1.4 million and an income of £324,000. Relief-in-need grants totalled £181,000 to 627 individuals.

Applications: Through the local union branch.

Correspondent: J Knapp, Unity House, Euston Road, London NW1 2BL (071-387 4771).

Other information: The union is restructuring its financial arrangements to cope with ever increasing demands. For the foreseeable future support will only be given to appeals directly related to transport or which involve another trade union in dispute.

The Road Haulage Association Benevolent Fund

Eligibility: Members, former members, employees and former employees of members, and their dependants.

Types of grants: One-off or recurrent grants according to need.

Annual grant total: No information available.

Applications: On a form available from the correspondent, which can be submitted directly by the individual or through a social worker, citizen's advice bureau or other welfare agency or third party. Applications are considered throughout the year.

Correspondent: The Secretary, Roadway House, 35 Monument Hill, Weybridge, Surrey KT13 8RN (0932-841515).

The Royal Agricultural Benevolent Institution

Eligibility: Retired or disabled farmers and their families in need, and British subjects living in England and Wales who have cultivated farm holdings as their only means of support. Farm managers and their dependants may also be considered, but no grants to farm foremen or farm-workers.

There is an emergency fund available for working farmers.

Types of grants: One-off grants according to need and regular allowances of £312 a year (paid quarterly) plus a Christmas and winter bonus if funds permit for applicants over 60 (or earlier if suffering from permanent ill health or disability). Grants towards meeting the fees of nursing homes and rest homes.

Annual grant total: £638,000 in 1993 to over 1,000 beneifciaries.

Applications: On the Preliminary Enquiry Form available from the correspondent.

Correspondent: I M Andrews, Welfare Secretary, Shaw House, 27 West Way, Oxford OX2 0QH (0865-724931).

The Royal Alfred Seafarers' Society

Eligibility: *The Samaritan Fund:* Applicants must have served in British merchants ships for a reasonable period or have had to leave for medical reasons. Those who gave up seafaring early in their lives do not qualify but the fund tries to help those who left the sea because of urgent family needs.

The Widows' Benevolent Fund: A widow's late husband must have served continuously in British merchant ships for a reasonable period and have left the sea because of ill health or died whilst serving.

The War Fund: The applicant must be in need as a result of war service in British merchant ships. Those injured, widows of those who died, and physically disabled war orphans can be helped.

Types of grants: One-off and recurrent grants (up to £260 a year) according to need. No grants to top up fees for nursing homes. About 800 grants are given each year.

Grants can be given for "virtually any expenditure required to maintain people in reasonable comfort and safety in their own homes", including household needs, assistance with debts, top-up for respite or convalescent care and medical equipment.

Occupational charities

Permanent nursing or residential care costs are not supported and loans are never given.

Annual grant total: The society's assets in 1992 were £3.9 million and it's income £1.7 million. 781 relief-in-need grants totalled £184,000 broken down as follows:

Samaritan Fund	£70,000
Widows Fund	£90,000
War Fund	£24,000

Applications: On a form available from the correspondent, to be submitted by the individual or through a social worker, citizen's advice bureau or other welfare agency. Applications can be considered at any time and should include proof of qualifying merchant navy service and details of savings and income and expenditure.

Correspondent: A R Quinton, General Secretary, Weston Acres, Woodmansterne Lane, Banstead, Surrey SM7 3HB (0737-352231).

Other information: The main activity of the society is the operation of two homes and a sheltered housing scheme for retired seafarers and those connected with the seafaring industry. Applications for accommodation from those with Royal Navy service are also accepted.

The Royal Ballet Benevolent Fund

Eligibility: Members/former members of repertory ballet and dance companies (workers may also be eligible), and in special cases dependants of such people after their death.

Types of grants: Regular grants of up to £10 per week towards general living expenses are usually for elderly people. Grants to younger people are usually towards illness or injury. One-off grants can also be given, many of which may be to help people whose company has closed/is closing down. Generally no grants towards education.

Annual grant total: About £50,000 in 1993.

Applications: On a form available from the correspondent.

Correspondent: Peter Wilson, Secretary, 45 Floral Street, London WC2E 9DD (081-643 4470).

The Royal College of Midwives Benevolent Fund

Eligibility: Midwives, former midwives and student midwives in England, Wales and Northern Ireland. Dependants of the above are not eligible.

Types of grants: Usually one-off grants for emergency or other unexpected needs (typically £50 to £200); occasionally regular allowances where needed.

Annual grant total: About £5,000 in 50 to 70 grants.

Applications: On a form available from the correspondent.

Correspondent: The Secretary, The Royal College of Midwives, 15 Mansfield Street, London W1M 0BE (071-580 6523).

The Royal Institution of Chartered Surveyors Benevolent Fund

Eligibility: Members/former members of the Royal Institution of Chartered Surveyors, and their dependants.

Types of grants: One-off and recurrent grants can be given towards holidays, telephone, insurances, travel, community care, residential and nursing care, aids and equipment and household items. No grants for business debts.

Annual grant total: In 1992, the trust had assets of £3.8 million and an income of £710,000. Total expenditure was £702,000 of which grants to individuals totalled £300,000.

Applications: In writing to the correspondent. The fund will then arrange for a local steward to visit the applicant and complete the application form, which are considered throughout the year.

Correspondent: The Chief Executive, 1st Floor, Tavistock House North, Tavistock Square, London WC1H 9RJ (071-387 0578).

Other information: The fund offers confidential advice and information to members of the profession and their dependants on a range of social welfare, financial, employment and property-related matters.

The Royal Institution of Naval Architects Benevolent Fund

Eligibility: Members and their dependants.

Types of grants: Grants according to need.

Annual grant total: In 1992, the fund had assets of £273,000 and an income of £26,000. Relief-in-need grants to individuals totalled £11,000.

Applications: In writing to the correspondent.

Correspondent: The Secretary, 10 Upper Belgrave Street, London SW1X 8BQ (071-235 4622).

The Royal Literary Fund

Eligibility: Authors of published work of literary merit, or their dependants. The authors must have written in English.

Types of grants: Most grants are outright grants which means there can be no re-application within 3 years. Pensions run for 5 years. In special circumstances the trust gives interim grants which allow re-application after one year. Dependants receive single one-off grants. The trust does not make loans.

Annual grant total: In 1992/93, the trust had assets of £4.4 million and an income of £686,000. Grants to individuals totalled £349,000 including 75 major grants and 37 pension payments.

Applications: On a form available from the correspondent. Applications are considered every month except September and can be submitted directly by the individual or through a third party (welfare agency, social worker etc.). Applicants are asked to supply copies of their published work which is then read by two members of the committee who decide on the question of literary merit.

Correspondent: Mrs Fiona Clark, Secretary, 144 Temple Chambers, Temple Avenue, London EC4Y 0DA (071-353 7150).

The Royal Liverpool Seamen's Orphan Institution

Eligibility: The dependant children of deceased British merchant seamen.

Types of grants: Regular allowances, paid monthly, for maintenance and clothing. Grants vary but are typically £110 a month for the first child, less for the second and third child. Grants are reviewed annually.

Annual grant total: £346,000, but not all for individuals in need.

Applications: On a form available from the correspondent, considered at any time.

Correspondent: L Dodd, Secretary, 21 Oriel Chambers, 14 Water Street, Liverpool L2 8TD (051-227 3417).

The Royal Medical Benevolent Fund

Eligibility: Medical graduates and their dependants.

Types of grants: All types of grant can be considered, and loans can sometimes be offered against security.

Occupational charities

Annual grant total: About £680,000 in about 660 grants.

Applications: Considered monthly.

Correspondent: The Senior Caseworker, 24 King's Road, Wimbledon, London SW19 8QN or FREEPOST, London SW19 8BR (081-540 9194).

Other information: Voluntary visitors liaise between beneficiaries and the office.

The Royal Medical Foundation of Epsom College

Eligibility: Members of the medical profession and their dependants.

Types of grants: Pensions of about £10 per week for members of the profession and their widows. Grants also towards nursing home fees.

Annual grant total: About £245,000 in 93 grants, most of which was for educational purposes. Pensions to 23 dependants and 9 grants towards nursing home fees for doctors totalled £40,000.

Applications: In writing to the correspondent.

Correspondent: The Secretary to the Council, Epsom College, Epsom, Surrey KT17 4JQ (0372-728861).

Other information: "Epsom College was founded in 1855 as the Royal Medical Benevolent College to provide pensions for doctors and their widows, a school for sons of doctors and pecuniary assistance to doctors and their dependants in need."

It is now self supporting from fees. The foundation now provides assistance to doctors and their dependants in need from the remaining funds which have been added to over the years by donations, gifts, bequests, legacies and endowed funds."

The Royal Metal Trades Benevolent Society

Eligibility: People who were employed in any capacity, in hardware, hosewares, DIY, garden or builders merchants enterprises, and their spouse or widow/widower. Beneficiaries are typically over 60.

Types of grants: In 1992, 30 people were granted annual awards of either £450 (single person) or £520 (for a couple). 14 of these were to meet a shortfall in nursing/residential home fees. In total, 26 couples and 109 single people were receiving grants. Occasional one-off grants are also given for all kinds of need. At present children are not eligible for grants.

Annual grant total: £71,000 in 1992, almost all in annual awards (to 140 pensioners), but also about £4,000 on Christmas hampers for pensioners and £1,500 in grants (mainly towards heating/enery bills).

Applications: On a form available from the correspondent, making full disclosure of income, expenses and state of health, and including supporting recommendations from two subscribers to the society. The applicant may be visited by the board while the case is under review.

Correspondent: A Whittle, Secretary, 1 Totteridge Avenue, High Wycombe, Buckinghamshire HP13 6XG (0494-530430).

The Royal National Mission to Deep Sea Fishermen

Eligibility: Fishermen and their dependants, suffering unforeseen tragedy or hardship.

Types of grants: Immediate one-off payments to widows of fishermen lost at sea. There are also other individual grants to alleviate cases of hardship (eg. provision of basic furniture for impoverished elderly fishermen). Grants are almost always one-off.

Annual grant total: Over 500 grants totalling £30,000 in 1993.

Applications: Through any of the 20 local offices in fishing ports around the coast or the head office below. Contact the local Superintendent (look in the phone book under the Royal National Mission to Deep Sea Fishermen or under the Fishermen's Mission). There is an application form. Applications can also be submitted through a social worker, welfare agency, parish priest or directly by the individual. Proof of sea service will be required.

Correspondent: Bernard Clampton, Mission Secretary, 43 Nottingham Place, London W1M 4BX (071-487 5101).

Other information: The charity also acts as agents for other grant making charities to seafarers such as the Shipwrecked Mariners Society (see separate entry).

The Royal Opera House Benevolent Fund

Eligibility: Any person who had been permanently employed by the Royal Opera House, or their dependants.

Types of grants: Recurrent grants of £10 per week plus extra payments towards winter fuel. The fund is moving more towards making one-off payments with a usual minimum of £100 towards the purchase of a television/licence, for decoration or towards winter bills etc..

Annual grant total: About 70 to 80 people apply, of whom about 50 are supported. Grants total between £90,000 and £100,000.

Applications: Can be submitted by the individual on a form available from the correspondent.

Correspondent: Joyce Ryley, Secretary, Royal Opera House, Covent Garden, London WC2E 9DD (071-240 1200 ext. 128).

The Royal Seamen's Pension Fund

Eligibility: Masters and seamen (including women) of pensionable age or permanently unfit who (a) have had a minimum of 20 years (15 for women) sea service in the British Merchant Navy (or were only prevented from serving 20 years because they were medically discharged) and (b) little income other than the state pension.

Types of grants: Pensions of £312 a year paid quarterly; Christmas and birthday bonuses.

Annual grant total: About £500,000 to 1,300 beneficiaries. There are about 50 new awards each year.

Applications: On a form available from the fund.

Correspondent: D C Barker, Secretary, 65 High Street, Ewell, Epsom, Surrey KT17 1RX (081-393 5873).

The Royal Society of Chemistry Benevolent Fund

Eligibility: Members or their dependants.

Types of grants: Regular allowances, one-off grants, holiday and Christmas gifts, and crisis payments.

Annual grant total: Over £40,000 in about 100 grants, but only a part of this is for relief in need.

Applications: In writing to the correspondent, requesting an application form.

Correspondent: The Secretary to the Committee, Thomas Graham House, Science Park, Milton Road, Cambridge CB4 4WF (0223-420066).

The Royal Society of Musicians

Eligibility: Professional musicians, their widows and orphans, who are in need through accident, illness, old age or

Occupational charities

bereavement. Distress caused by lack of employment cannot be helped.

Types of grants: One-off grants of up to £3,000 (usually around £1,000) to relieve sickness, illness or bereavement and monthly grants, reviewed every 3 months towards nursing/residential care.

Annual grant total: In 1993, 18 people were being supported. Most grants were for about £1,000 but monthly grants of £200 to £2,500 were also paid. Grants totalled over £40,000 to individual members. There may have been over £80,000 paid to non-members.

Applications: To the correspondent. Enquiries from welfare organisations such as citizen's advice bureaux, social workers etc. are welcomed but it is preferred if applications are supported by a member of the society. Except in the case of emergencies, grants are discussed at meetings held on the first Sunday of each month except August.

Correspondent: Mrs Marjorie Gleed, Secretary, 10 Stratford Place, London W1N 9AE (071-629 6137).

Other information: Office hours are 11.00 am to 4.00 pm.

The Royal Theatrical Fund

Eligibility: Any person in need who has professionally practised or contributed to the theatrical arts (on stage, radio, films or television or any other medium by which such arts may be presented in future) and the relief of needy families or dependants of such people or such deceased people.

Types of grants: 1. Monthly allowances totalling £48,000 in 1992/93.

2. One-off grants, typically £250 but a maximum of £3,000, totalling £106,000. Bills are preferably paid straight to the company concerned. The fund reserves the right to pay the grants in installments. Applicants can re-apply annually.

3. Help with shortfall in nursing home fees or home care nursing/residential home fees, totalling £68,000. The fund shares these costs with other charities where necessary.

Grants are not given for students or re-training schemes, theatre projects or to other (non-theatrical) charities.

Annual grant total: In 1992/93, the trust had assets of £3 million and an income of £268,000. Total expenditure was £331,000 including 245 relief-in-need grants to individuals totalling £222,000.

Applications: On a form available from the correspondent which must be signed by the individual or legal representative. Applications are considered on the second Wednesday of each month except August.

Correspondent: Mrs R M Oliver, Secretary, 11 Garrick Street, London WC2E 9AR (071-836 3322).

The Royal United Kingdom Beneficent Association (RUKBA)

Eligibility: Elderly and infirm people in need who come from a professional background and live in the British Isles, particularly those "who have served their generation in a professional capacity, in devoted service to others or in one of many humanitarian causes. They need to be over pensionable age, or be over 40 and unable to work through infirmity. In addition, their assessed income needs to be below the limits set by RUKBA's committee. These levels are revised regularly and are currently £5,295 for a single person and £9,002 for a married couple."

Types of grants: Annuities, which are granted for life (unless there is an unexpected and considerable improvement in their circumstances) and are up to a maximum of £1,152 a year, are the main form of help.

The association does not give one-off grants.

Annual grant total: £4,296,000 to about 4,950 regular beneficiaries in 1993. Over 600 new annuities were awarded in 1993.

Applications: In the first instance the applicant should write to the correspondent describing their occupational background and giving a brief description of their circumstances. Arrangements will then be made for the applicant to be visited by one of the association's 700 honorary secretaries. Applications are considered bi-monthly.

Applications can also be made from people in residential/nursing homes who are unable to meet the balance of "reasonable" fees. In such cases, the income limit is not necessarily applied but capital resources have to be reduced to £3,000 before a case can be considered.

Correspondent: The Applicants Officer, 6 Avonmore Road, London W14 8RL (071-602 6274; fax 071-371 1807).

Other information: RUKBA has four residential and nursing homes with 181 beds at present and has 77 flats and bungalows for disabled elderly people. This entry is repeated in the National and general charities section of the book.

The Rugby Football Union Charitable Fund

Eligibility: People injured while participating in any sport and dependants of any person killed while participating in any sport. Preference is given to people who have participated in amateur sport.

The trustees are particularly concerned to help people who have suffered spinal injuries and as a consequence are paralysed and facing life in a wheelchair.

Types of grants: Usually one-off grants.

Annual grant total: £35,000 to £40,000.

Applications: In writing to the correspondent.

Correspondent: Michael J Christie, 41 Station Road, North Harrow, Middlesex HA2 7SX (081-863 6366).

The Rural, Agricultural & Allied Workers' Benevolent Fund

Eligibility: Members of the organisation (now a trade group within the Transport and General Workers Union).

Types of grants: Usually one-off grants of about £30. Occasional discretionary grants for other amounts.

Annual grant total: £7,000 to £8,000 in about 250 grants.

Applications: In writing to the correspondent.

Correspondent: Barry Leathwood, National Secretary, Transport House, Smith Square, Westminster, London SW1P 3JP (071-828 7788).

The Sailors' Families Society

Eligibility: Seafarers or their dependants (usually in a one-parent situation) bringing up children under the age of 18.

Types of grants: Yearly allowances of £520 (paid in monthly instalments); one-off grants to help with children's holidays and other needs. Families of seafarers not eligible for regular support may be considered for one-off emergency grants.

Annual grant total: About £200,000 to about 240 families.

Applications: In writing to the correspondent.

Correspondent: The Welfare Officer, Newland Homes, Cottingham Road, Hull HU6 7RJ (0482-42331).

Other information: The society also has a residential home for children at Newland, Hull. Accommodation for aged seafarers or their widows is available at the same

Occupational charities

site. Accommodation for aged seafarers is also available at South Shields.

The Schoolmistresses & Governesses Benevolent Institution

Eligibility: Applicants must be either over 70 or infirm, and must have been employed for the major part of their working lives as:

(a) Governesses, schoolmistresses from the private sector of education, or teachers or lecturers in universities or colleges.

(b) Self-employed teachers of language, music, dancing, art etc..

(c) Actively employed in an administrative capacity in the care and welfare of children/students in private schools, universities, colleges (eg. bursars, matrons etc.).

Applicants must normally be British subjects, but this can be waived in certain circumstances.

Types of grants: All types of help including annuities, one-off grants for special needs (including telephone, colour television, various household crises, etc.), loans and help with holidays.

No grants for education or mid-career retraining.

Annual grant total: About £110,000 in about 100 grants.

Applications: In writing to the correspondent.

Correspondent: L I Baggott, SGBI Office, Queen Mary House, Manor Park Road, Chislehurst, Kent BR7 5PY (081-468 7997).

Other information: The institution arranges annual visits to its beneficiaries. It also runs a residential home in Kent which will accept, in addition to teachers, applications from women with comparable professions or careers.

The Scientific Relief Fund

Eligibility: Scientists or their families in distress in the British Commonwealth and the Republic of Ireland.

Types of grants: Generally one-off grants according to need up to £2,000 a year towards nursing at home, secretarial expenses, a computer or other piece of equipment such as a microscope to enable them to continue with their research at home.

Annual grant total: The fund's income is about £35,000. It gave nine grants in 1993.

Applications: Through an officer of any nationally recognised society within the beneficial area.

Correspondent: The Secretary, 6 Carlton House Terrace, London SW1Y 5AG (071-839 5561).

Other information: The correspondent states: "we receive a lot of applications from musicians - we cannot support musicians".

The Seamen's Hospital Society

Eligibility: The objects of the trust are: "the relief of seamen of all nations in the Port of London or other Ports in Great Britain or Northern Ireland to which seafaring people resort and their dependants who from sickness, misfortune or age are in need of assistance". As such the society can give relief in need grants to anybody who earns their living from the sea, including deep sea fishermen and their dependants.

Types of grants: One-off and recurrent grants according to need. There is a preference for applications of a medical or welfare nature. Recurrent grants are usually for about £35 a month to help with general living expenses. One-off grants can be up to £300 towards council tax, fuel charges, cookers washing machines, clothing or medical equipment such as pain relief machines or nebulizers etc.. Larger grants need approval by the committee. Grants are also given to organisations helping the above. No grants to Royal Navy personnel.

Annual grant total: In 1992, £33,000 was given in grants to over 100 individuals in need and £104,000 to organisations.

Applications: In writing to the correspondent giving full details of sea service. Applicants must be seamen with long service except where accident or illness interrupted intended long-term service.

Correspondent: The General Secretary, 29 King William Walk, Greenwich, London SE10 9HX (081-858 3696).

Other information: The society says it is "also interested in availability of medical services to seafarers. The Dreadnought Unit within St Thomas' Hospital provides free top priority facilities to seafarers and we give this unit every support. We also liaise with other maritime charities who provide residential accommodation for retired seafarers. The allocation of grants to individuals is, therefore, an expanding area of our work."

The Second Post Office Relief Fund

Eligibility: Dependants of Post Office members who were disabled or killed by enemy action during World War II.

Types of grants: Allowances range from £260 a year to £1,500 a year. The applicant must require financial assistance in line with the definition of need as exercised by the Department of Social Security.

Emergency grants are made for medical needs and special diets for diabetics and in extreme cases for relief following for example flood or fire damage to the applicant's home.

Annual grant total: In 1990, the trust had assets of £397,000 and an income of £31,000. Relief-in-need grants to 46 individuals totalled £37,000. In 1992, the trust had an income of £66,000; it is not known how much was given to individuals in need.

Applications: In writing to the correspondent through a social worker, citizen's advice bureau or other welfare agency.

Correspondent: D W Branch, Secretary, Room 505, 80-86 Old Street, London EC1V 9PP (071-320 7350).

Other information: This entry has not been confirmed by the trust.

The Sewing Machine Trade Benevolent Fund

Eligibility: Members or former members of the Sewing Machine Trade Association, the partners and employees of such members, and their dependants.

Types of grants: One-off and recurrent grants according to need.

Annual grant total: The trust's income is about £1,800.

Applications: In writing to the correspondent.

Correspondent: P H Treby, Trustee, 12 Warwick Close, Hertford SG13 8JT (0992-582934).

The Shipwrecked Mariners' Society

Eligibility: Fishermen, merchant seamen, their widows and dependants, especially elderly, sick or chronically disabled people.

Types of grants: Activities are not confined to shipwreck relief. Relief of distress amongst the seafaring community includes:

(a) Immediate financial aid to the dependants of seamen lost at sea;

Occupational charities

(b) Assistance to seamen shipwrecked on the coasts of the British Isles;

(c) Financial aid to needy seamen and their widows and orphans, including regular grants to seamen or their widows;

(d) Other objects for the benefit and welfare of seafarers. Awards are made for skill and gallantry in preventing loss of life at sea.

Annual grant total: Over £750,000 in over 4,000 grants.

Applications: On the society's appropriate application form, signed by the local honorary agent.

Correspondent: Captain J E Dykes, General Secretary, 1 North Pallant, Chichester, West Sussex PO19 1TL (0243-787761).

Other information: There is a Scottish office for the society: Beveridge & Kellas, Hon. Agents, 52 Leith Walk, Edinburgh EH6 5HB (031-554 6321).

The Silverwood Trust

Eligibility: Christian missionaries in need through illness or retirement.

Types of grants: One-off or small recurrent grants according to need.

Annual grant total: In 1993, the trust had an income of £7,000. It is not known how much was given in grants to individuals in need.

Applications: In writing to the correspondent.

Correspondent: J N Shergold, Trustee, Ashdown, The Drive, Belmont, Sutton, Surrey SM2 7DH.

The Sydney Simmons Pension Fund

Eligibility: People in need who are or have been employed in flooring manufacture, distribution and retail, and allied trades.

Types of grants: One-off and recurrent grants according to need. Grants have been given for travel expenses, furniture, clothing, books, tools, fees for examinations and recuperative holidays.

Annual grant total: In 1992, the trust had an income of £5,000.

Applications: In writing to the correspondent detailing the specific need and the association with the trade.

Correspondent: G D Inglesant, Sunnyway Cottage, Seale Lane, Puttenham, Guildford, Surrey GU3 1AX (0483-810545).

Henry Smith's Charity Alfriston Estate

Eligibility: Clergy in need within the UK.

Types of grants: Christmas gifts.

Annual grant total: The charity only has a small endowment of its own (generating an income of about £5,000). Most of the charity's income comes from a transfer each year from the Henry Smith (Kensington Estate) Charity (£630,000 in 1992).

Applications: On a form available from the correspondent available during September and October.

Correspondent: B T McGeough, 5 Chancery Lane, London EC4A 1BU.

The Social Workers' Benevolent Trust

Eligibility: Qualified social workers and those who have been engaged in professional social work, and their dependants.

Types of grants: One-off grants only, typically £50 to £500. Grants are not normally given for income maintenance nor for treatment or care outside the NHS. No grants for fees or basic maintenance to social workers in training.

Annual grant total: About £10,000 in about 60 grants.

Applications: In writing to the correspondent.

Correspondent: The Hon. Secretary, 16 Kent Street, Birmingham B5 6RD (021-622 3911).

The Society of Chiropodists Benevolent Fund

Eligibility: Members/former members of the society or one of its constituent bodies, and their dependants.

Types of grants: One-off and recurrent grants or loans according to need. Grants range from £100 to £500.

Annual grant total: In 1992, the fund had assets of £230,000 and an income of £16,000. 30 relief-in-need grants totalled £3,300.

Applications: On a form available from the correspondent. Applications are considered in March, June, October and December.

Correspondent: J Trouncer, Hon. Secretary, 53 Welbeck Street, London W1M 7HE (071-486 3381).

The Society of Licensed Victuallers

Eligibility: Members of the society and their widows or widowers, who are in need.

Types of grants: Pensions paid quarterly and occasional one-off grants.

Annual grant total: £100,000 in over 200 grants in 1993.

Applications: In writing to the correspondent.

Correspondent: The Chief Executive, Heatherley, London Road, Ascot, Berkshire SL5 8DR (0344-884440).

Other information: Help is also given with the education of children of members at Licensed Victuallers Schools. This amounted to £1,355,000 in 1993.

The Society of Motor Manufacturers & Traders Charitable Trust Fund

Eligibility: People in need who were senior executives in the motor industry, and their dependants.

Types of grants: One-off and recurrent grants according to need.

Annual grant total: £39,000 in 1993 to 19 beneficiaries.

Applications: In writing to the correspondent.

Correspondent: The Hon. Secretary, Forbes House, Halkin Street, London SW1X 7DS (071-235 7000).

The Society of Radiographers Benevolent Fund

Eligibility: Radiographers and their dependants in need, with a possible preference for those who are sick, elderly or incapacitated.

Types of grants: One-off grants of £250 upwards.

Annual grant total: In 1992/93, the trust had an income of £4,275. Eight grants to individuals totalled £3,250.

Applications: In writing to the correspondent. Applications can be submitted directly by the individual or through a third party such as a colleague or relative.

Correspondent: B Macey, Secretary, 14 Upper Wimpole Street, London W1M 8BN (071-935 5726).

The Society for the Relief of Necessitous Protestant Ministers (formerly the Ministers' Relief Society)

Eligibility: Protestant ministers "who are of good repute and who hold and proclaim the doctrines of free and sovereign grace", their widows and dependants.

Types of grants: One-off and recurrent grants according to need.

Annual grant total: About £14,000 in 1990.

Applications: On a form available from the correspondent.

Correspondent: A Lathey, 8 Marston Avenue, Chessington, Surrey KT9 2HF (0372-379441).

The Society for the Relief of Poor Clergymen

Eligibility: Evangelical ordained ministers and accredited lay workers and their dependants in the Church of England and the Church in Wales.

Types of grants: Mainly for bereavement, illness, removals (where other grants are insufficient to cover costs), NOT for educational purposes or towards normal travelling expenses.

Annual grant total: About £17,000 in about 60 grants ranging from £50 to £500.

Applications: On a form available from the correspondent. The committee meets twice yearly (normally in March and October).

Correspondent: The Hon. Secretary, c/o CPAS, Athena Drive, Tachbrook Park, Warwick CV34 6NG (0926-334242).

The Society for Relief of Widows & Orphans of Medical Men

Eligibility: Widows, widowers or orphans of any doctor who was at the time of his/her death and for the preceding two years a member of the society. In certain circumstances members and their dependants may also be eligible.

Types of grants: One-off and recurrent grants according to need.

Annual grant total: In 1991, the trust had assets of over £1.3 million generating an income of about £90,000; it gave over £26,000 in grants (£14,000 in general and half-yearly payments, £2,000 at Easter, £5,000 at Michaelmas and £5,000 at Christmas), and had a surplus of £58,000.

Applications: In writing to the correspondent. Applications can be submitted directly by the individual or through a third party. They are considered at quarterly meetings of the committee.

Correspondent: The Secretary, 11 Chandos Street, Cavendish Square, London W1M 9DE (071-935 8752).

The Society of Schoolmasters

Eligibility: Masters of any independent or maintained school who have 10 years of continuous service; also their widows and orphans.

Types of grants: One-off and quarterly grants of £260 a year according to need.

Annual grant total: In 1991, the trust had assets of £22,000 and an income of £6,000. 10 relief-in-need grants totalled £3,000.

Applications: On a form available from the correspondent. Applications can be submitted directly by the individual or through a social worker, citizen's advice bureau or other welfare agency. They are considered in March, June and November.

Correspondent: Mrs M S Freeburn, Secretary, 29 Corrib Court, Fox Lane, Palmer's Green, London N13 4BG (081-882 6825).

Other information: This entry has not been confirmed by the trust.

The Solicitors' Benevolent Association

Eligibility: Past or present solicitors in England and Wales, and their dependants.

Types of grants: To supplement state and local authority benefits by outright grants or interest-free loans, and to assist with general living expenses such as heating and lighting bills and television rental.

Annual grant total: £610,000 in direct grants and over £120,000 in interest-free loans, to 450 individuals.

Applications: On a form available from the correspondent. Applications can be submitted directly by the individual or through directors or local representatives of the benevolent association.

Correspondent: Cdr A H Lorimer, Secretary, 1 Jaggard Way, Wandsworth Common, London SW12 8SG (081-675 6440).

The Jack Solomons' Charity Fund

Eligibility: Ex-boxers and their dependants in need.

Types of grants: One-off grants according to need.

Annual grant total: About £4,000.

Applications: In writing to the correspondent.

Correspondent: M Frith, Trustee, 101 Borough High Street, London Bridge, London SE1 1NL (071-407 0781).

The Stable Lads Welfare Trust

Eligibility: Past and present stable lads and apprentices, who are or have been employed in the racing industry and are in need.

Types of grants: One-off grants are given for general welfare, holidays and short-term care. Loans are also made.

Annual grant total: In 1992, the trust had an income of £190,000. It is not known how much was given for the relief-in-need of individuals.

Applications: In writing to the correspondent including the applicant's employment history in the racing industry. Applications can be submitted directly by the individual or through a social worker, citizen's advice bureau or other welfare agency. They are considered throughout the year.

Correspondent: Mrs P Lewis, Executive Secretary, 121 High Street, Newmarket, Suffolk CB8 9AJ (0638-560763).

The Staines Trust

Eligibility: Former civil servants employed by the governments of British or former British possessions overseas or by the government of the Anglo-Egyptian Sudan, and their dependants.

Types of grants: Quarterly allowances and special payments towards urgent needs. There are currently 60 beneficiaries.

Annual grant total: About £30,000.

Applications: Trustees meet twice yearly, but qualifying applications are considered at any time.

Correspondent: F G Finch, Chairman, 23 Frobisher Court, Sydenham Rise, London SE23 3XH.

The Stock Exchange Benevolent Fund

Eligibility: Ex-members of the stock exchange and their female dependants. In exceptional circumstances, existing members and children of education age of ex-members.

Types of grants: Annual grants paid quarterly; maximum grant £10,000.

Occupational charities

Beneficiaries are regularly visited and their situations reviewed. There is a strict capital ceiling above which help cannot be given; otherwise the fund is extremely flexible financially and in its advisory services.

Annual grant total: About £300,000 to £350,000

Applications: In writing to the correspondent at any time.

Correspondent: The Secretary, The Stock Exchange Benevolent Fund, The Stock Exchange, London EC2N 1HP (071-797 1092/3120).

The Stock Exchange Clerks Fund

Eligibility: Past or present employees of the Stock Exchange Council or of a member firm of the Stock Exchange, and past or present members of the fund. Also, the widow/widower and children (whether infants or not) of the above.

Types of grants: One-off and recurrent grants according to need. Recurrent grants usually range from £260 a year to £520 a year.

Annual grant total: In 1992, the fund had assets of £835,000 and an income of £114,000; 39 grants to individuals totalled £28,000.

Applications: In writing to the correspondent.

Correspondent: A V Barnard, Secretary, The Stock Exchange Clerks Fund, The Stock Exchange, London EC2N 1HP (071-588 2355).

The Tailors' Benevolent Institute

Eligibility: Tailors, tailoresses and their near relatives who were employed in the bespoke (made to measure) tailoring trade. Preference to past and present members of the institute but help can be given to other eligible applicants.

Types of grants: Typically one-off grants of about £50 or allowances of £10 a week.

Annual grant total: About £100,000 in about 100 grants.

Applications: On a form available from the correspondent, preferably through a social worker but applications submitted directly by the individual or through another third party will be considered.

Correspondent: F G Watson, 1 Fairfield Close, Bosham, Chichester, West Sussex PO18 8JQ (0243-572609).

The Tancred's Charities

Eligibility: Clergymen or present or former commissioned officers in the Armed Forces, being poor and members of the Church of England or Church in Wales and over 50 years of age.

Types of grants: Annual pensions of £1,200 a year paid quarterly to 14 beneficiaries.

Annual grant total: About £17,000 in 1993.

Applications: In writing to the correspondent. However, current pensions account for all available income and no new awards can be made. People whose application is accepted will be added to the waiting list; those in greatest need are placed at the top.

Correspondent: Mrs B S R Watson, Clerk, 4 John Carpenter Street, London EC4Y 0NH (071-405 7878).

Other information: The charities also give help to some specified categories of intending doctors, clergymen and barristers, but they must have attended Christ College or Gonville & Quc Caius College, Cambridge.

The Teachers' Benevolent Fund

Eligibility: Serving and retired teachers (regardless of teacher union affiliation) and their dependants in England, Wales, Channel Islands and Isle of Man.

Types of grants: Welfare grants/loans. Recurrent grants are £5 a week paid quarterly or half yearly.

Annual grant total: £313,000 in about 1,200 grants in 1993.

Applications: Fund application forms should be submitted to local TBF committees. They will then be forwarded for a decision by the national council.

Correspondent: The Managing Secretary, Hamilton House, Mabledon Place, London WC1H 9BE (071-465 0499).

Other information: The fund owns three residential/nursing homes and shares in the ownership of a fourth (total provision for 190 residents). Its housing association maintains seven sheltered housing centres nationally providing accommodation for 300 teachers/dependants. In Greater London there are tenancies available for about 170 serving teachers/dependants. The Housing Association can be contacted on 071-404 3838.

The Textile Benevolent Fund

Eligibility: People in need who are working or have worked in the textile trade (that is anyone who manufactures, wholesales or retails textiles). Beneficiaries tend to be retired.

Types of grants: Single grants or weekly allowances according to need. The fund also has five holiday centres where places are subsidised or free if warranted, (under 16's are not accepted in the holiday centres).

Annual grant total: £35,000 in 200 grants.

Applications: In writing to the correspondent, preferably from the applicant's last employer or a welfare agency, but applications can be made direct.

Correspondent: Sandra Tullet, Secretary, 72a Lee High Road, Lewisham, London SE13 5PT (081-852 7239).

Other information: The Textile Benevolent Association was founded in 1858 as the General Porters Benevolent Association. It gave grants to needy people in banks and warehouses. In the 20th century it changed to helping textile workers through its connection with textile warehouses.

The Theatrical Ladies Guild of Charity

Eligibility: Anyone who has worked in the live theatre or on stage (back stage and front of house staff as well as actors and actresses), and their dependants.

Types of grants: Small regular grants (paid quarterly) and one-off grants, for example for telephone installation or nursing home fees, but covering a wide range of need.

Annual grant total: In 1992, the trust's income was £51,000. Expenditure totalled £33,000 including £14,000 in 37 grants to individuals.

Applications: On a form available from the correspondent. Applications can be submitted directly by the individual or through a third party. They are considered every month except August.

Correspondent: Miss Karen Nichols, Secretary, 49 Endell Street, London WC2H 9AJ (071-497 3030).

The Thornton Fund

Eligibility: Ministers/students of the Unitarian church and their families in need.

Types of grants: Grants, ranging from £350 to £1,500, to supplement low stipends, educational costs and for other needs.

Occupational charities

Annual grant total: In 1992, the trust had assets of £186,000 and an income of £14,500. Total expenditure was £14,500 including £4,650 in education grants.

Applications: In writing to the correspondent.

Correspondent: S A Woolven, Ironstones, 20 Regent Avenue, Lytham St Anne's, Lancashire FY8 4AB.

The Timber Trades Benevolent Society

Eligibility: People engaged in the timber trade in the UK for at least 15 years, excluding furniture manufacturing and local carpenters, joiners and tradesmen servicing the building trade.

Types of grants: Regular allowances, occasional grants and various payments to third parties (eg. telephone or television rentals, television licences and hampers). Grants range from £250 to £400 and are generally made for house repairs/car expenses (where the car is a necessity rather than a luxury). Help also towards holidays, particularly where there is a need for convalescence and for medical treatment in exceptional cases.

Annual grant total: About £165,000 a year. There are currently over 270 beneficiaries.

Applications: In writing to the correspondent. When an approach/enquiry is made, this is referred to the appropriate local district. A local representative of TTBS then visits the applicant and completes an application form. Applications are considered in February, May, July, September and November.

Correspondent: Mrs P M Glover, General Manager, Old Station Road, Hampton-in-Arden, Solihull, West Midlands B92 OHB (0675-443119).

The Michael Tippett Musical Foundation

Eligibility: Musicians and composers who are in need.

Types of grants: One-off grants in special circumstances.

Annual grant total: In 1992/93, the foundation's grants totalled £24,000 mostly applied to musical projects. There were two grants to individuals totalling £500.

Applications: In writing to the correspondent.

Correspondent: Miss G Rhydderch, Secretary, 1 Dean Farrar Street, London SW1H 0DY.

The Tobacco Trade Benevolent Association

Eligibility: Those who have been engaged in the manufacture, wholesale or retail sections of the tobacco industry and their dependants, in need.

Types of grants: Regular assistance and one-off grants, including Christmas gifts, holiday and winter grants.

Annual grant total: £184,400 in 1992/93.

Applications: In writing to the correspondent.

Correspondent: Messrs Crane & Partners, Admin. Secretaries, Rutland House, 44 Masons Hill, Bromley, Kent BR2 9EQ (081-464 0131).

The Trained Nurses Annuity Fund

Eligibility: Nurses aged 40 or over who are disabled and have done at least seven years service.

Types of grants: Annuities. Each year beneficiaries send a short report explaining whether financial circumstances have changed and whether they are still in need of assistance.

Annual grant total: About £20,000.

Applications: On a form available from the correspondent. These should normally be submitted by doctors or social workers along with a doctor's certificate or by the individual. They are considered in July and December.

Correspondent: Royal British Nurses Association, 94 Upper Tollington Park, London N4 4NB (071-272 6821).

The Transport Benevolent Fund

Eligibility: Employees and former employees of the public transport industry in London and the south east of England.

Types of grants: Most grants are given for long-term sickness or disability (for assistance not covered by the NHS). Grants are usually a maximum of £150, and most are one-off.

Annual grant total: £125,000 in 1992

Applications: On a form available from the correspondent. Applications are considered throughout the year.

Correspondent: Chris Godbold, Chief Executive, Walkden House, 10 Melton Street, Euston, London NW1 2EB (071-387 3479).

Other information: The Transport Benevolent Fund includes the London Transport War Comforts Fund Association. This makes grants to employees of London Transport (or their predecessors) and their widows and dependants, plus other employees of London Transport who are in need because of World War II. It has an annual grant total of about £5,000.

The Trinity House Charities

Eligibility: Former Merchant Navy Officers over 60 who have served at least 15 years in UK or Commonwealth vessels, their wives, widows and unmarried daughters.

Types of grants: Regular allowances of £286 a year. One-off grants of up to £520, but generally £200 to £300.

Annual grant total: £23,000 in 126 grants.

Applications: To the correspondent, who will issue the relevant forms.

Correspondent: The General Manager, Corporate Department, The Corporation of Trinity House, Trinity House, Tower Hill, London EC3N 4DH (071-480 6601).

Other information: The Corporation administers almshouses at Walmer, Kent; several charitable trusts, mainly for needy master mariners and their widows and dependants; a special fund to kit boys going to sea; educational grants; and on behalf of King George's Fund for Sailors makes grants of up to £280 a year to Merchant Navy deck, engineer and radio officers.

In April 1989, the Trinity House Scholarship Cadet Training Scheme (Marine Training for future Merchant Navy Officers) was formally launched. Further details can be found in *The Educational Grants Directory*.

The UK Atomic Energy Authority Benevolent Fund

Eligibility: Past, present and future members of the non-industrial staff of British Nuclear Fuels plc, the Atomic Energy Authority and Amersham International plc, their families and dependants.

Types of grants: Single and continuing (including weekly) grants and allowances. Grants given for most purposes, except where this would affect state benefits. Applicants do not need to have been a subscriber to the fund. Loans against property and for serving officers are possible.

Grants are given for or towards furniture, disability aids (stair lifts, wheelchairs, alarms etc.), holidays, Christmas grants, television licences and sets, repairs, fuel bills (to prevent disconnection),

● **Occupational charities**

telephone bills, removal costs, debts (in some cases), minor repairs and child minding.

Grants are not given for private health care (excluding convalescence and residential home fees).

Annual grant total: £97,000 in grants/loans in 1992/93.

Applications: In writing to the correspondent directly by the individual, through a social worker or other welfare agency or through local case worker or site welfare officer.

Correspondent: Miss Marie Sims, c/o Room D337, British Nuclear Fuels plc, Risley, Warrington, Cheshire WA3 6AS (0925-823000 ext. 288).

The UNISON Welfare Fund (National & Local Government Officers Association)

Eligibility: UNISON members and their dependants, whether working or not.

Types of grants: One-off according to need. Grants can be £5,000 to £10,000 in exceptional cases, but are more likely to be £250 to £750 towards a washing machine, dryer, cooker or towards mechanical needs for people with disabilities or towards fuel bills for those who are housebound.

Annual grant total: In 1993, about 2,300 grants were given totalling £950,000.

Applications: To the welfare secretary or the retired members secretary of the local UNISON branch, as appropriate. If necessary, the correspondent below can supply the relevant local contact.

Correspondent: The Welfare Section, 1 Mabledon Place, London WC1H 9AJ (071-388 8402).

Other information: The fund has convalescent homes (for working and retired members needing recuperation after illness) and residential homes for the elderly. Application forms from the branch. Convalescent Centres Hotline: 071-388 8408.

The United Law Clerks Society

Eligibility: People employed in the legal profession in any capacity in England and Wales, and their dependants.

Types of grants: One-off and recurrent grants according to need. Recurrent grants are usually for £5 to £10 a week, but can be for up to £720 a year. One-off grants can be for up to £500 or £600 a year towards cookers, roof repairs, special chairs/beds etc.. No grants for students.

Annual grant total: In 1993, 20 to 25 recurrent grants and six one-off grants were given and totalled about £30,000.

Applications: On a form available from the correspondent.

Correspondent: c/o Messrs Church Adams Tatham & Co, Chatham Court, Lesbourne Road, Reigate, Surrey RH2 7FN (0737-240111).

The Veterinary Benevolent Fund

Eligibility: Members and former members of the Royal College of Veterinary Surgeons, registered veterinary practitioners and their dependants.

Types of grants: Regular monthly grants, limited to £10 a week for those on Income Support (who are also eligible for re-imbursement of the cost of telephone rental, television rental and licence, car insurance and licence).

Occasional one-off gifts for example to help elderly or disabled applicants or children. In 1991, grants ranged from £200 to £5,000.

Annual grant total: In 1991, the trust had assets of £1.3 million generating an income of £163,000. 61 relief-in-need grants to individuals totalled £68,000.

Applications: On a form available from the correspondent. Applications can be made directly by the individual, through a social worker, citizen's advice bureau or other welfare agency, or through a third party eg. a relative or colleague.

Correspondent: Mrs Seabrook, Secretary, 7 Mansfield Street, London SW1 (071-580 8799).

Other information: The fund also owns four bungalows near Christchurch, Dorset for occupation by elderly veterinary surgeons or their dependant relatives.

The Widows' Fund of the Three Denominations

Eligibility: Widows of ministers of Presbyterian, Independent (eg. Congregational and United Reformed) and Baptist churches who are over 50 years of age and who have less than £2,250 a year above state benefits.

Types of grants: At present regular grants of £65 in May and £65 at Christmas. Urgent cases can be considered for help on a small scale. Priority for widows whose husbands were members or subscribers at the time of their death or whose congregations contributed regularly and directly to the fund.

Annual grant total: About £11,000 to 120 recipients.

Applications: On the fund's application form, signed by the local minister.

Correspondent: Rev Geoffrey Satchell, 26 Southdown Road, Loughborough, Leicestershire LE11 2TE (0509-265949).

The Wine & Spirits Trades' Benevolent Society

Eligibility: People who have worked for some years, directly or indirectly, in the buying, selling, producing or distributing of wines and spirits, and their dependants. No grants currently to people who have worked in pubs and hotels as they have their own trade charities.

Types of grants: Recurrent grants of £9 and £10 a week (ie. up to the DSS disregard level). Grants are also given towards the cost of television licences and major expense items when needed. Grants may also be given for help with moving expenses, motor wheelchairs, furnishings and electrical goods.

Annual grant total: In 1992, the trust's income was £616,000; grants to individuals in need totalled £103,000 (282 grants).

Applications: On a form available from the correspondent. Applications can be submitted directly by the individual, through a welfare agency or through relatives and friends. They are considered throughout the year.

Correspondent: The Chief Executive, Five Kings House, 1 Queen Street Place, London EC4R 1QS (071-248 1343).

Other information: The society also has two residential estates and a care home.

The Wine Trade Foundation

Eligibility: People who are or were employed in the wine and spirit and ancilliary trades in the UK and Republic of Ireland, and their dependants.

Types of grants: One-off and recurrent grants according to need.

Annual grant total: According to the Charity Commission the trust had an income of £25,500 in 1991. It is not known how much was given in grants to individuals in need.

Applications: In writing to the correspondent.

Occupational charities

Correspondent: M Hasslacher, Trustee, Broomwood, Kettlewell Hill, Woking, Surrey GU21 4JJ (071-495 4748).

The Worshipful Company of Farriers Charitable Trust

Eligibility: Registered farriers, their widows and dependants who are in need.

Types of grants: Probably one-off or recurrent grants according to need.

Annual grant total: 20 to 30 grants totalling between £3,000 and £5,000.

Applications: Applications should be made either through a member of the company or direct to the Treasurer, J G Barsham, Adversane House, Adversane, Nr Billinghurst, Sussex RH14 9YN.

Correspondent: H W Ellis, Clerk & Registrar, White Garth, 37 The Uplands, Loughton, Essex IG10 1NQ (081-508 6242).

The Worshipful Company of Insurers Charitable Trust Fund

Eligibility: For the relief of poverty of members of the business of insurers or any other recognised business or profession, those dependent on them and in particular members of the company and their dependants.

Types of grants: Probably one-off and recurrent grants according to need.

Annual grant total: In 1991, the trust had an income of £97,000. It is not known how much was given in education grants to individuals.

Applications: In writing to the correspondent.

Correspondent: V D Webb, Hon. Secretary, 20 Aldermanbury, London EC2V 7HY (071-606 3835).

The Worshipful Company of Launderers Benevolent Trust

Eligibility: Elderly and infirm members of the company and their dependants.

Types of grants: Grants can be paid annually (towards fuel bills); bi-annually (fuel bills and a summer grant - maximum £75), or monthly (towards general living expenses - up to £10 a week).

Annual grant total: In 1991/92, the trust had an income of £11,000. £5,000 was given in grants to individuals in need, £4,000 was given to organisations.

Applications: In writing to the correspondent.

Correspondent: Michael Bennett, Hon. Clerk, Glaziers Hall, 9 Montague Close, London Bridge, London SE1 9DD (071-403 3300).

The Worshipful Company of Plaisterers Charitable Trust

Eligibility: People in need, especially those who are or have been a liveryman or freeman of the company, and their dependants.

Types of grants: One-off and recurrent grants according to need.

Annual grant total: £8,500 in 1992/93.

Applications: In writing to the correspondent.

Correspondent: Henry Mott, Trustee, Plaisterers' Hall, No. 1 London Wall, London EC2Y 5JU (071-606 1361/7908).

Charities administered by the Worshipful Company of Tallow Chandlers

Eligibility: People in need who have a connection with the company.

Types of grants: One-off grants according to need.

Annual grant total: No information available.

Applications: In writing to the correspondent.

Correspondent: The Clerk, The Tallow Chandlers Co., 1 Vintners Place, Upper Thames Street, London EC4V 3BB (071-248 4726).

Service and ex-service charities

The service and ex-service charities are a most important source of help for people in need, both for those who served in the forces themselves and equally importantly for their widows/widowers and dependants.

However, the service and ex-service charities do not only help war veterans. Usually anyone who served in the forces as a regular or for their national service is also eligible for help, although some charities exclude those who did national service only.

These charities are exceptionally well organised. Much of this is due to the work of SSAFA/FHS (the Soldiers', Sailors' & Airmen's Families Association/Forces Help Society). SSAFA/FHS are legally separate charities but they work very closely together. They have an extensive network of trained caseworkers around the country who act on behalf of SSAFA/FHS and other service charities.

There is an application form which is used by many service and ex-service charities. This form should not be filled in by the applicant, rather by a trained caseworker at the applicant's home. The completed application form is sent to the appropriate service, regimental or corps benevolent fund (and, where appropriate, copies may be sent to other relevant funds, both service and non-service).

Although many service benevolent funds rely on trained SSAFA/FHS volunteer caseworkers to prepare application forms, some do have their own volunteers who can complete the form. However, these may not be spread so comprehensively around the country. Alternatively, some funds ask applicants to write to a central correspondent. In such cases, applicants may like to follow the guidelines in the article "How to make an application" earlier in this Guide. Most entries in this section state whether the applicant should apply direct to the trust or through a caseworker. If in doubt, the applicant should ring up the trust concerned or the local SSAFA/FHS office (see below).

Some people may prefer to approach their or their former spouse's regimental or corps association. Each corps has its own entry in this Guide; the regimental associations are listed at the end of this section. Many of them have their own charitable funds and volunteers, especially in their own recruiting areas. In other cases they will work through one of the volunteer networks mentioned above. Again, if in doubt or difficulty, the applicant should ring up the regimental/corps association or the local SSAFA/FHS office.

Local SSAFA/FHS offices can generally be found in the local telephone directories (usually under Soldiers', Sailors' & Airmen's Families Association rather than SSAFA) or advertised in such places as the local citizen's advice bureau, doctor's waiting rooms, libraries etc.. In case of difficulty applicants can contact the Central Office Welfare Department as follows: The Welfare Department, SSAFA/FHS, 19 Queen Elizabeth Street, London SE1 2LP (071-403 8783).

The Airborne Forces Security Fund

Eligibility: Serving and former members of all ranks of the Parachute Regiment, the Glider Regiment and other units of airborne forces, and their dependants.

Types of grants: Grants according to need.

Annual grant total: In 1992, the fund's income was £460,000; it gave £196,000 in respect of the Falklands War, over £117,000 in grants in aid, and £1,700 in special donations. About 720 grants were made.

Applications: Through SSAFA Form 9 Report.

Correspondent: Major C M Steggles, Controller, Browning Barracks, Aldershot, Hants GU11 2BY (0252-20772).

The Aircrew Association Charitable Fund

Eligibility: People qualified to be members of the association (but need not necessarily be members) and their dependants in need.

Types of grants: Immediate single payments for emergency needs.

Annual grant total: £5,150 in 1992/93.

Applications: In writing to the correspondent.

Correspondent: Graham S Watson, Hon. Secretary, 26 Mosse Gardens, Fishbourne, Chichester, West Sussex PO19 3PG (0243-533837).

The Army Benevolent Fund

Eligibility: People or dependants of people who are serving or who have served in the British Army and are in real need.

Types of grants: All types of emergency grant. Also £5 weekly allowances for those over retirement age.

Service and ex-service charities

Annual grant total: In 1992/93, the trust had assets of £16.7 million and an income of £4 million, £3.3 million of which was given in grants to individuals and organisations. Grants increased to over £7 million after donations from other corps and regiments were taken into account. Almost 26,000 individuals received grants along with a number of organisations supporting ex-service people. Almost £300,000 was spent on topping up residential and nursing home fees (by far the biggest single item of expenditure). Interest free loans to help ex-soldiers with the transition to civilian life totalled almost £140,000.

Applications: The fund does not deal directly with individual cases, which should be referred initially to the appropriate corps or regimental association, which are listed at the end of this section. (Enquiries about the appropriate association can be made to the Army Benevolent Fund.) See also, in particular, the entries for SSAFA, the Royal British Legion and the Forces Help Society.

Correspondent: The Controller, 41 Queen's Gate, South Kensington, London SW7 5HR (071-584 5235 Grants Dept.).

The Army Catering Corps Association Benevolent Fund

Eligibility: Members and former members of the Army Catering Corps and their dependants.

Types of grants: One-off and recurrent grants according to need. Grants are given towards clothing and essential household goods such as cookers or heaters. Help is also given with fuel or water rates to prevent disconnection, telephones for invalids, or car tax where this is the only form of transport.

Grants will not be given for funeral expenses, building or maintenance work, garden maintenance or business problems (ie. bankruptcy). Loans are not given.

Annual grant total: 416 grants totalling about £50,000 in 1993.

Applications: On an application form available from the correspondent. Applications are considered weekly and should be submitted through SSAFA, the Royal British Legion or another forces welfare organisation.

Correspondent: Lt Col B S Dyson, Controller of Funds, ACCA - RHQ the RLC, Dettingen House, Princess Royal Barracks, Blackdown, Camberley, Surrey GU16 6RW (0252-340893).

The Association of Jewish Ex-Servicemen & Women

Eligibility: Jewish ex-servicemen and women and their spouses or widows.

Types of grants: Grants are usually made to people on Income Support and housing benefit and are divided about equally between regular allowances and one-off grants. Most grants are paid direct to the client, although some go through SSAFA or Jewish Care or are made direct to the supplier of the required goods or services. A welfare clinic is held on Wednesday evenings at the address below.

Annual grant total: Over £45,000 in over 300 grants.

Applications: In writing to the correspondent.

Correspondent: The Honorary Welfare Secretary, Ajex House, East Bank, Stamford Hill, London N16 5RT (081-800 2844).

The Association of Royal Navy Officers

Eligibility: Officers and retired officers of the Royal Navy, Royal Marines, WRNS, QARNNS and their Reserves, who have joined and are members of the association, and their dependants.

Types of grants: Generally one-off grants.

Annual grant total: In 1993, the trust had assets of £1.8 million and an income of £90,000. Total expenditure was £50,000 including £41,000 in over 100 relief-in-need grants to individuals.

Applications: In writing to the correspondent.

Correspondent: Lt Cdr I M P Coombes, 70 Porchester Terrace, Bayswater, London W2 3TP (071-402 5231).

The ATS & WRAC Benevolent Funds

Eligibility: Former members of the Auxiliary Territorial Service and the Women's Royal Army Corps. Also former members of the QMAAC (Queen Mary's Auxiliary Army Corps - 1914/1918 War).

Types of grants: One-off grants to meet emergency needs and regular annuities. In 1992/93, the largest categories of grant aid were for debts, household appliances, furniture and furnishings, clothing and house repairs. The fund gives very wide-ranging help from beds and bedding to funeral expenses, public transport costs and help with rent and rates.

Annual grant total: £146,000 in 1993. There are 1,100 cases a year, of which about half are new cases.

Applications: Most cases are investigated by an honorary representative of SSAFA. The grants committee meets every fortnight to consider requests over £200; cases recommending grants of less than £200 are dealt with by the Joint Secretaries of the fund outside the grants committee.

Correspondent: Mrs A H S Matthews, Case Secretary, ATS & WRAC Benevolent Funds, PO Box 212, Guildford, Surrey GU2 6ZD (0252-355562).

The British Commonwealth Ex-Services League

Eligibility: Ex-servicemen of the crown, their widows or dependants, who are living outside the UK. There are 52 member organisations in 46 countries.

Types of grants: All types of help can be considered. Grants are one-off, renewable on application. Grants are generally for medically related costs such as hearing aids, wheelchairs, artificial limbs, food or repairs to homes wrecked by floods or hurricanes etc.. Grants usually range from £40 to £260 per year.

Annual grant total: £450,000 is distributed by the league, about £270,000 of which is distributed on behalf of other service charities such as the Army Benevolent Fund and King George's Fund for Sailors.

Applications: Considered daily on receipt of applications from BCEL member organisations or British Embassies/High Commissions, but not directly from individuals.

Correspondent: The Secretary-General, 48 Pall Mall, London SW1Y 5JG (071-973 0633).

Other information: The league has members or representatives in most parts of the world through whom former servicemen or their dependants living abroad can seek help. The local British Embassy or High Commission can normally supply the relevant local contact. In a Commonwealth country the local ex-service association will probably be affiliated to the league.

The British Limbless Ex-Servicemen's Association (BLESMA)

Eligibility: Limbless ex-servicemen who are eligible for membership of the association, and their dependants.

Types of grants: One-off and recurrent grants according to need. Grants typically include direct financial support in cases

Service and ex-service charities

of need (usually £100 to £350); grants for aids for disabled people; assistance with gardening and decorating costs; adaptations for vehicles needed by amputees; continuing assistance to widows and members not in receipt of a war widow's pension (up to £10 a week to widows). No loans are given.

Annual grant total: In 1992, the trust had assets of £11.3 million and an income of £1.5 million. The total expenditure was £1.7 million. Grants were given to 578 individuals-in-need and totalled £161,000.

Applications: On a form available from the correspondent. Applications should be made through the local branch of the British Limbless Ex-Servicemen's Association (BLESMA) or the War Pensions Welfare Service. They are considered twice monthly.

Correspondent: R R Holland, General Secretary, 185-187 High Road, Chadwell Heath, Romford, Essex RM6 6NA (081-590 1124).

The Burma Star Association

Eligibility: Holders of the Burma Star, their widows and dependants.

Types of grants: One-off grants only; usual maximum £500. Grants are to relieve immediate need such as debts due to the cost of fuel or use of telephone; to help with convalescent holidays or to supplement fees for residential homes. The trust combines with other charities to buy expensive equipment such as wheelchairs or stairlifts.

The trust does not give pensions or loans.

Annual grant total: In 1993, the trust gave over 1,000 grants of up to £500 totalling over £150,000.

Applications: Applications can be made by the individual or through a third party such as citizen's advice bureau, welfare agency etc. and should be submitted direct to the correspondent or to the correspondent via branches of the association or other ex-service organisations. Grants are made through branches of the association, SSAFA or other ex-service organisations after investigation and completion of application form giving full particulars of circumstances and eligibility (including service particulars verifying the award of the Burma Star).

Correspondent: Mrs R D Patrick, National Welfare Secretary, 4 Lower Belgrave Street, London SW1W 0LA (071-823 4283).

The Commandos' Benevolent Fund

Eligibility: Army commandos who served in the 2nd World War, and their dependants.

Types of grants: One-off and recurrent grants according to need. The usual minimum award is £300.

Annual grant total: In 1992, the trust had an income of £79,000, not all of which was given in grants to individuals.

Applications: In writing to the correspondent directly by the individual or through a social worker, citizen's advice bureau or other welfare agency. Applications are considered as soon as possible after receipt.

Correspondent: The Honorary Secretary, 190 Hammersmith Road, London W6 7DL (081-746 3491).

Other information: This entry has not been confirmed, but the contact address is correct according to the SSAFA 1994 Handbook.

The Ex-Services Mental Welfare Society

Eligibility: People with mental illness who are ex-service personnel of HM Services or the Merchant Navy; all ranks.

Types of grants: One-off grants according to need.

Annual grant total: About £50,000.

Applications: In writing to the correspondent.

Correspondent: The Assistant Director (Welfare), Broadway House, The Broadway, Wimbledon SW19 1RL (081-543 6333).

The Forces Help Society & Lord Roberts Workshops

Eligibility: Men and women serving, or who have served at any time, in the Armed Forces of the Crown (not including officers) including the Nursing Services, those called up under the National Service Acts, and men of the Merchant Navy who are or have been employed on ships working under Admiralty Charter. Also members of the Territorial Army and Naval and Air Force Reserves who have been engaged in active service or have completed one year's satisfactory service, and former members who completed three years satisfactory service, or suffered injury leading to medical discharge during their service, and their dependants.

Types of grants: Grants are made for special needs. The Forces Help Society's (FHS) casework and grant-making activities are fully integrated with those of SSAFA (see separate entry) and are administered from SSAFA Central Office, 19 Queen Elizabeth Street, London SE1 2LP. However, a distinction is still made between "FHS cases" - usually those of single ex-service men and women - and "SSAFA" cases, usually those involving dependants. FHS pays the cost of FHS cases, and the number of grants and grant total given below refers to these cases.

Annual grant total: About £272,000 in 1992. The 16,000 grants made include money disbursed on behalf of other charities, particularly service and regimental benevolent funds.

Applications: Applications for grants should normally be made through the joint SSAFA/FHS network of volunteers. For further details of how to apply, please see the separate SSAFA entry.

Correspondent: The Comptroller & Secretary, 122 Brompton Road, London SW3 1JE (071-589 3243/4/5).

Other information: FHS maintains two residential homes, in Surrey and the Isle of Wight, for disabled and elderly ex-service personnel. The Surrey home now provides full residential care, in modern single rooms, for ex-service men and women needing such care. Fees are at the level of the Income Support obtainable from local authorities. Eligible men and women can be accepted from any part of the UK. Towards the end of 1994 there will be similar residential care accommodation at the Isle of Wight home for a small number of men and women. At present the home can accept men only, sharing two and four-bed rooms, and reasonably independent.

FHS also maintains cottage homes for ex-service men or women and their spouses, some purpose-built for severely disabled people, for which residents pay no rent but make a modest maintenance payment. There are also short-stay apartments in the Isle of Wight providing recuperation and respite holidays for disabled ex-service men and women and their carers.

For all of these forms of help, applications should be made to the correspondent. Correspondence relating to grants should go either to the Honorary Secretary of the local SSAFA/FHS branch or to SSAFA Central Office as above.

Greenwich Hospital

Eligibility: Members and former members of the Royal Navy and Royal Marines and their dependants.

Service and ex-service charities

Types of grants: Pensions of £7 a week to:

(a) Elderly retired officers of Royal Navy or Royal Marines and to ratings, who by reason of age or ill health are unable to contribute to their own support.

(b) Elderly widows of Royal Navy or Marine Petty Officers and ratings who served at least 22 years or died or were invalided out whilst serving for pension.

The charity also gives educational grants (see *The Educational Grants Directory*).

Applications may also be made for a Jellicoe Annuity by elderly and retired Royal Navy or Marines and their widows, who had served less than pensionable service and are in need. They must be on Income Support.

Annual grant total: £400,000 in about 1,600 grants in 1992/93.

Applications: In writing to the correspondent. Applications will then be reviewed by the Royal Naval Benevolent Trust or SSAFA.

Applications for Jellicoe Annuities should be made to the Grant's Secretary of The Royal Naval Benevolent Trust (see separate entry) who administer the annuities on behalf of Greenwich Hospital.

Correspondent: The Director, 40 Queen Anne's Gate, London SW1H 9AP (071-396 0150).

Other information: Greenwich Hospital is a charity responsible to the Admiralty Board and is not registered with the Charity Commission. Its endowment is valued at £102 million. Its main functions are supporting the Royal Hospital School near Ipswich (an independent boarding school for the children and grandchildren of seafarers) through meeting the cost of fees, building sheltered housing for elderly naval families, and granting pensions and bursaries to those in need.

The Hampshire & Isle of Wight Military Aid Fund (1903)

Eligibility: Any person recruited into any Hampshire army unit and his/her dependants.

Types of grants: One-off and recurrent grants according to need.

Annual grant total: £30,000 in 125 grants.

Applications: Normally through the local branch of SSAFA.

Correspondent: The Secretary, Serle's House, Southgate Street, Winchester SO23 9EG (0962-852933).

The Household Cavalry Central Charitable Fund

Eligibility: Past or present members of the Household Cavalry and their wives, widows and dependants.

Types of grants: One-off and recurrent grants according to need.

Annual grant total: About £40,000.

Applications: In writing to the correspondent directly by the individual. Applications are then followed up in the usual way by SSAFA.

Correspondent: The Regimental Secretary of either The Life Guards or The Blues & Royals, Combermere Barracks, Windsor, Berkshire SL4 3DN (0753-868222).

The Household Division Queen's Silver Jubilee Trust

Eligibility: Physically and/or mentally disabled children of officers, warrant officers, non commissioned officers and soldiers of the Household Division, and other such children. Applicants must have been born while their fathers were serving in or who have died having served in the Household Division.

Types of grants: Grants "to assist in the care, upbringing, maintenance and education" of such children.

Annual grant total: £3,000 in 6 to 8 grants.

Applications: To the headquarters of the regiment concerned. In some cases SSAFA will be asked to investigate and make recommendations on grants.

Correspondent: Lt Col D N Thornewill, Household Division Funds, Block 7, Wellington Barracks, Birdcage Walk, London SW1E 6HQ (071-930 4466 [ask for Assistant Regimental Adjutant of the regiment concerned]).

The Kinlock Bequest

Eligibility: Scottish servicemen who have served in the navy, army or airforce, who have become disabled through no fault of their own, and who are in need. There is a preference for those who were wounded in the service of their country.

Types of grants: Weekly allowances of about £10.

Annual grant total: In 1993, the trust gave up to 12 recurrent grants of up to £10 per week.

Applications: In writing to the correspondent. Proof that the applicant is Scottish is needed.

Correspondent: Wing Commander Alan Robertson, The Royal Scottish Corporation, 37 King Street, Covent Garden, London WC2E 8JS (071-240 3718).

Other information: The correspondent also administers The St Andrew's Scottish Soldiers Club Fund and the Royal Scottish Corporation (see separate entries in this Guide).

Lloyd's Patriotic Fund

Eligibility: Ex-servicemen and women (Royal Navy, Army, Royal Marines and Fleet Air Arm, but excluding Royal Air Force personnel) and their dependants.

Types of grants: Special one-off grants for emergency needs from £75 to £100 towards fuel bills, winter clothing, electric wheelchairs etc.. Regular grants are generally £312 a year for people in nursing homes.

Annual grant total: About £70,000 in 400 to 600 grants.

Applications: Through SSAFA or any other services welfare agency.

Correspondent: Miss B A Lowden, Secretary, Lloyd's Building, 1 Lime Street, London EC3M 7HA (071-327 5558).

Other information: Educational grants are also made for officers' children (see *The Educational Grants Directory*).

The Metcalfe Shannon Trust

Eligibility: Canadian ex-servicemen and their dependants who are in need.

Types of grants: One-off grants according to need.

Annual grant total: £7,000 in 1992.

Applications: In writing to the correspondent.

Correspondent: Mrs J I Morton, Secretary, Canadian High Commission, Macdonald House, Grosvenor Square, London W1X 0AB (071-258 6339).

The Nash Charity

Eligibility: Wounded or disabled ex-service personnel.

Types of grants: Grants are usually paid through social services, citizen's advice bureaux or other welfare agencies to purchase specific items that are needed.

Annual grant total: In 1993, the charity gave £10,000 in grants, of which about £2,000 was to individuals.

Applications: In writing to the correspondent.

Correspondent: The Secretary, Messrs Peachey & Co, Arundel House, Arundel Street, London WC2R 3ED (071-836 2994).

Service and ex-service charities

The Navy Special Fund

Eligibility: Relief of temporary hardship or distress to people who are serving/have served in the Royal Navy, Royal Marines, Queen Alexandra's Royal Naval Nursing Service and Women's Royal Naval Service, and their dependants.

Types of grants: Cash grants and loans.

Annual grant total: £13,000 (average annual total of grants and loans).

Applications: Applications should be made initially to the Royal Naval Benevolent Trust (see separate entry).

Correspondent: Lt Cdr C L Prior, Hon. Secretary, Ministry of Defence DGNPS, Old Admiralty Building, Room 308A ABS, Spring Gardens, London SW1A 2BE (071-218 7720).

The "Not Forgotten" Association

Eligibility: Disabled ex-service men and women. Applicants must have served in the Armed Forces of the Crown (or Merchant Navy during hostilities). The Polish forces of 1939-45 may be eligible in some circumstances. The association cannot help widows (unless they are themselves ex-members of the forces).

Types of grants: The association does not give financial grants direct to applicants, rather it gives help in kind in the following areas:

Televisions for those with restricted mobility or who are otherwise largely housebound. Video equipment or radios can sometimes be made available and licences may be provided for those in need;

Holidays (accompanied by carers if required) and day outings to events and places of interest;

Entertainments at ex-service residential homes.

The association does not give cash grants, but in certain cases cheques may be sent to individual applicants for holidays or to office holders of bona fide ex-service organisations. The association does not have the resources to undertake case work.

Wives, widows and families of the above are NOT supported.

Annual grant total: In 1993, the association provided 1,400 television sets, 1,700 licences and 600 holidays. 6,500 people attended the outings and entertainments. 2,400 gifts were provided for residents of service homes (this has now ceased). The association's total expenditure was £560,000.

Applications: If applicants are war disabled and are in receipt of a War Disability Pension, they should approach their DSS Welfare Office. All other disabled ex-service personnel should first approach SSAFA or the Forces Help Society (see separate entries). These agencies will complete the common application form on behalf of the applicant and then make the appropriate recommendation to the association.

Correspondent: Lt Col D G Martin, Director, 5 Grosvenor Crescent, London SW1X 7EH (071-235 1951/2162).

The Officers' Association & the Officers' Families Fund

Eligibility: Anyone, male or female, who has held a Commission in HM Forces, their widows and dependants. Officers on the active list will normally be helped only with resettlement and employment. Ex-RAF officers will be referred to the Royal Air Force Benevolent Fund.

Types of grants: One-off and recurrent grants. "The bulk of our relief work continues to be the provision of a small annual grant to elderly ex-officers or their dependants who are trying to cope on very small pensions and state benefits. In addition to the standard grant the association helps with a wide spectrum of problems ranging from telephone bills to buying disability aids outside the scope of the NHS." Help also with residential care and nursing home fees, and very limited assistance with education.

Annual grant total: £325,000 to ex-officers and £575,000 to widows and dependants in 1992/93.

Applications: In writing to the correspondent. The association has a wide network of honorary representatives throughout the UK who will normally visit the applicant.

Correspondent: The General Secretary, The Officers Association, 48 Pall Mall, London SW1Y 5JY (071-930 0125).

For applicants in Scotland: See entry for the Officers' Association (Scottish Branch) in the Scotland general section of the book.

For applicants in Eire, contact: Captain D J Mooney, 26 South Frederick Street, Dublin 2.

Other information: The association has a residential home at Bishopsteignton, south Devon, for ex-officers (male and female) over the age of 65 who do not need special care. It also provides a series of advice leaflets on finding accommodation in residential care or nursing homes, how to get financial assistance, and how to find short-term convalescence accommodation and sheltered accommodation for elderly disabled people.

It also has an employment department to help ex-officers up to the age of 60 find suitable employment. It helps not only those just leaving the services but also those who have just lost their civilian jobs.

The Polish Air Force Association Benevolent Fund

Eligibility: Ex-servicemen of the Polish Air Force who fought during World War II under British command, and its members settled in the West.

Types of grants: Grants of £50 to £60 paid two or three times a year according to need. Grants are to supplement applicants income.

Annual grant total: Bewteen £30,000 and £35,000.

Applications: In writing to the correspondent.

Correspondent: The Secretary, 14 Collingham Gardens, London SW5 0HT (071-373 1085).

The Polish Soldiers Assistance Fund

Eligibility: People in need who are former Polish comrades-in-arms who were prisoners of war, soldiers' families both inside and outside Poland, Polish children, former Polish combatants, widows and orphans or war invalids.

Types of grants: One-off or recurrent grants according to need, ranging from £25 to £75.

Annual grant total: In 1992/93, the trust had an income of £100,000. Grants to individuals totalled £99,500.

Applications: In writing to the correspondent.

Correspondent: Mrs Teresa Affeltowicz, Administrator, 240 King Street, London W6 0RF (081-741 1911).

The Queen Adelaide Naval Fund

Eligibility: The orphan daughters of officers of the Royal Navy and the Royal Marines (an orphan daughter may be a person of any age whose father is dead, and who is unmarried or a widow).

Types of grants: One-off grants according to need (but typically £400) and assistance with nursing/residential home fees. Occasional help with boarding school fees. (See Other information below.)

Service and ex-service charities

Annual grant total: About £25,000 in 17 grants in 1992.

Applications: Considered three times a year, in March, July and November. Emergency cases can be considered by the chairman between these meetings. Applications should be submitted directly to the correspondent.

Correspondent: Commander D A P Stephens, 86 Cottenham Park Road, Wimbledon, London SW20 0TB.

Other information: This fund was established in 1850 in memory of Queen Adelaide, widow of King William IV. There are special arrangements whereby eligible girls can have subsidised places as Queen Adelaide pupils at the Royal Naval School, Haslemere. The fund is operated jointly with the Admiral of the Fleet Sir Frederick Richards Memorial Fund (see separate entry).

Admiral of the Fleet Sir Frederick Richards Memorial Fund

Eligibility: Officers of the Royal Navy and the Royal Marines, serving or retired, and their widows and children (especially for education).

Types of grants: Most grants are one-off with amounts varying according to need, but typically about £500. In a few cases, small pensions are awarded to elderly beneficiaries. Assistance is also given with residential/nursing home fees.

Annual grant total: £20,000 in 28 grants in 1992.

Applications: Applications are considered three times a year, in March, July and November. Emergency cases can be considered by the chairman between these meetings. Submit applications directly to the correspondent.

Correspondent: Commander D A P Stephens, 86 Cottenham Park Road, Wimbledon, London SW20 0TB.

Other information: This fund was established in 1915 in memory of this outstanding naval administrator who was First Sea Lord from 1893 to 1899. It is operated jointly with the Queen Adelaide Naval Fund (see separate entry).

The Royal Air Force Benevolent Fund

Eligibility: Past and present members of the Royal Air Force (and Women's Royal Air Force) and their dependants. Post-war (1949 to 1960) National Servicemen are excluded, other than those disabled during their period of National Service.

Types of grants: All types of assistance can be considered. In 1992, grants were given as follows:

Housing trust, house purchases, mortgages, repair & decoration	£1,700,000
Maintenance & immediate needs	£1,900,000
Debts (including rent/rates) during illness	£389,000
Education (including school clothing)	£506,000
Furniture, removals, clothing, bedding	£333,000
Medical, dental, rehabilitation, convalescence etc.	£2,900,000

The fund gave 9,700 grants to serving and ex-RAF personnel (total £2.6 million); 5,088 grants to disabled people (total £2.2 million); 3,023 grants to widows (total £2.5 million); 569 grants to children/dependants (£506,000).

Annual grant total: In 1992, the fund had assets of £68 million with an income of £10.6 million. £7.8 million was given in over 18,000 relief-in-need grants to individuals and £432,000 in 140 education grants.

Applications: Can be made direct or through the Royal Air Forces Association, SSAFA or the Forces Help Society or other ex-service welfare agencies. An application form is sent to eligible applicants. Applications are considered weekly.

Correspondent: The Director Welfare, 67 Portland Place, London W1N 4AR (071-580 8343).

Other information: The fund maintains a residential and convalescent home in Sussex and a residential home in Aberdeenshire.

The Royal Air Forces Association

Eligibility: Peace time ex-National Service airmen (1st January 1949 to 18th November 1960) and their dependants.

Types of grants: All types of emergency grants (generally £50 to £250) and loans. No weekly allowances. Grants typically are for gas and electricity bills, removal costs, clothing, bedding, electrical goods, furniture and the costs of transport to hospital for treatment or visiting. Help may be given with nursing/respite care costs in certain cases.

Annual grant total: £2.5 million was disbursed in 1988 - this figure includes grants given directly by the Royal Air Forces Association and on behalf of the Royal Air Force Benevolent Fund (see separate entry). Over 15,000 cases were investigated in 1988, this rose to 40,000 cases in 1993. We were unable to obtain more up to date financial information.

Applications: Through local Branch Honorary Welfare Officers of the Royal Air Forces Association (the association has over 600 such officers based in its local branches); SSAFA and the Forces Help Society also refer applications to the association where appropriate. There is an application form. Applications must include confirmation of RAF service.

Correspondent: Brenda McLaren, Chief Welfare Officer, 43 Grove Park Road, London W4 3RX (081-994 8504).

The Royal Armoured Corps War Memorial Benevolent Fund

Eligibility: Ex-members of the disbanded wartime regiments of the Royal Armoured Corps, and their dependants.

Types of grants: One-off grants to those in need through no fault of their own. Grants have been given for rent, gas, electricity and water rates arrears; clothing; buying a nebulizer; towards wheelchairs and stairlifts, and convalescent holidays (up to 14 days maximum).

No loans. No grants for poll tax arrears or payment of community charge, funeral expenses, HP debt or bank loans, holidays (apart from the above), nursing or residential home fees, or requests to supplement a state pension with ongoing support.

Annual grant total: £19,000 in 127 grants in 1992/93.

Applications: On a form available from the correspondent, to be submitted through SSAFA. Applications are considered at any time. The name of the individual regiment in which the applicant served must be included. To enter "RAC" is not sufficient as all existing armoured regiments have their own regimental funds.

Correspondent: Major R Clooney, Secretary, c/o RHQ RTR, Bovington, Dorset BH20 6JA (0929-403331).

Other information: The Royal Armoured Corps is taken to include all cavalry, yeomanry, Royal Tank Regiment, reconnaissance corps, numbered RAC regiments and miscellaneous units of the RAC.

Service and ex-service charities

The Royal Army Medical Corps Charitable Funds

Eligibility: Members/former members of the Royal Army Medical Corps (who had full-time service) and their dependants.

Types of grants: One-off and recurrent grants according to need.

Annual grant total: £90,000 in 400 grants.

Applications: Only through SSAFA or similar ex-services welfare agency.

Correspondent: The Secretary, RHQ, RAMC Training Centre, Keogh Barracks, Ash Vale, Aldershot, Hants GU12 5RQ (0252-377394).

The Royal Army Service Corps & Royal Corps of Transport Benevolent Fund

Eligibility: Past and present members of the two corps and their dependants, excluding children over 18.

Types of grants: One-off and recurrent grants according to need. Grants range from £50 to £250. No grants for repayment of general debts or loans with finance companies, banks, credit card companies or individuals.

Annual grant total: £155,000 in 951 grants in 1993.

Applications: On a form (SSAFA/FHS Form 9) usually through SSAFA (never directly by the individual).

Correspondent: Lt Col R E Wills, RASC/RCT Association, Dettingen House, Princess Royal Barracks, Deepcut, Camberley, Surrey GU16 6RW (0252-340898).

The Royal Artillery Charitable Fund

Eligibility: Past or present members of all ranks of the Royal Artillery, their families and dependants, and the families and any dependants of any deceased member.

Types of grants: Both one-off grants and regular allowances. One-off grants, typically of about £100, are mainly for such essentials as bedding, clothing or furniture, or paying unexpected bills for heating or house repairs.

Annual grant total: £564,000 in 1993.

Applications: In writing to the correspondent. Applications will then be investigated by SSAFA, through whom applications can also be made.

Correspondent: The Welfare Secretary, Artillery House, Old Royal Military Academy, Woolwich, London SE18 4DN (081-319 4052).

The Royal British Legion

Eligibility: Serving and ex-serving members of the armed forces and their wives, widows, children and other dependants in England, Wales and Ireland (for Scotland see the entry for the Earl Haig Fund [Scotland] in the Scotland general section of the book).

Types of grants: 1. *Local assistance* - of up to £260 in any one year to buy food, clothing, bedding or fuel. Decision made in conjunction with the area organiser.

2. *Winter heating for the elderly* - applicable during the winter months, during or after a period of very bad weather. Cheques are lodged with the gas or electricity authority as credit against the next bill. The limit is £75 in any one year. Authority given through area organiser.

3. *Individual grants* - for the purchase of necessary goods or the payment of debts not covered in (1) above. Up to £250 can be approved by the County Field Officers; more than this has to be approved by head office.

4. *The permanently incapacitated and widows scheme* - regular allowances of £5 a week to certain people at Income Support level of income and in extra need ie. through ill health. Headquarters approval is needed.

5. *Holidays for severely disabled people* - to give a fortnight's holiday to those who are too sick or disabled to stay at the British Legion's own home. Headquarters approval is needed.

6. *Hospital and housebound visiting* - grants of £3.50 a month for each person visited to encourage Legion members to visit long-term inmates of hospitals or other institutions, and the housebound.

Annual grant total: £2,645,000.

Applications: To the benevolent department in London, or to any local branch or area office who can contact County Field Officers. A local telephone number for an initial enquiry can usually be found in any telephone directory.

Correspondent: The Secretary, The Benevolent Department, 48 Pall Mall, London SW1Y 5JY (071-973 0633).

Other information: The Royal British Legion, one of the largest providers of charitable help for individuals in the country, is financed mainly by gifts from individuals, especially through its annual Poppy Day collection.

The Legion provides a comprehensive service for advising and helping all ex-servicemen and women and their dependants (though for ex-service women, wives, widows and dependants, see also the following entry for the Royal British Legion Womens Section). Direct financial assistance is but one aspect of this work. There are over 3,000 branches of the Legion, all of which can act as centres for organising whatever help the circumstances may require. The support of the Legion is available to all who served in the forces, whether in war or peace-time, as regulars or national-servicemen. This means that most people over the age of about 60 may be eligible for help, either in their own right or through their spouse.

Most charities for ex-servicemen and women co-operate together in their work and the British Legion may also be approached through other service organisations, and vice versa.

Besides the above activities, the Legion provides convalescent holidays for those who are sick and disabled; residential care for the elderly; advice and assistance about claims for war disability or war widows' pensions; a training scheme for driving London taxis; arranges visits to overseas war graves; gives interest free loans to the unemployed to start small businesses; and, through associated companies, provides sheltered accommodation for the elderly and employment for the disabled.

There is also a Property Repair Loan Scheme aimed at retired applicants or those who are disabled and cannot work to enable major property repairs to be completed. The maximum loan is £5,000 and interest is charged at 5% a year.

The Royal British Legion Women's Section

Eligibility: Ex-servicewomen, the widows of ex-servicemen and the dependant children of ex-service personnel in England, Wales and Northern Ireland (for Scotland see the entry for the Earl Haig Fund [Scotland] in the Scotland general section of the book).

Types of grants: Emergency grants and weekly allowances (at present £4 a week). Grants are given for necessary items such as heating bills, clothing, bedding and certain household items. Weekly allowances are not given to people in nursing or residential homes.

Annual grant total: Over £300,000 in over 1,200 grants.

Applications: May be made direct to the correspondent or to a local representative of the Women's Section. These can be contacted through the area offices of the Legion.

Correspondent: Miss J H Green, National Secretary, 48 Pall Mall, London SW1Y 5JY (071-973 0633).

Service and ex-service charities

Other information: The Women's Section is an autonomous organisation within the Royal British Legion, concentrating on the needs of widows and ex-servicewomen. It works in close association with the Legion but has its own funds and its own local case workers.

The Royal Electrical & Mechanical Engineers Corps Benevolent Fund

Eligibility: Those who are serving or who have served in the corps, and their immediate dependants.

Types of grants: Generally one-off grants. Recurrent grants to individuals are only made for nursing home fees and a very limited number of supplementary allowances (which are paid by the Army Benevolent Fund). Nursing home fees are limited to £10 a week per individual (total expenditure on nursing home fees must not exceed £12,000 a year). Other grants are limited to £1,000 a case. No grants for funeral expenses, headstones, cars or non-essentials, and very rarely for property improvements.

Annual grant total: £85,000 in about 667 grants (out of 967 applications).

Applications: Generally on a form available from the correspondent or the local branch of SSAFA/FHS. Grants are only made through a third party (eg. SSAFA/FHS), and applications made direct will be referred to a welfare agency for investigation. Applications are screened immediately on receipt and are either rejected on sight, referred back for more information or to a committee which meets on alternate Tuesdays. Grants of under £200 can be paid immediately on receipt of a suitable application.

Correspondent: The Secretary, REME Benevolent Fund, REME Corps Secretariat, Isaac Newton Road, Arborfield, Reading, Berkshire RG2 9LN (0734-763219).

The Royal Naval Benevolent Society

Eligibility: Officers, both active service and retired, of the Royal Navy and the Royal Marines, of the equivalent rank of Sub-Lieutenant RN and above, and their widows, children, mothers and sisters. There are no age limits.

Types of grants: Block grants to augment inadequate incomes or to meet specific unforeseen expenses. Grants have been given to help repair houses, towards car maintenance, removal costs and nursing home fees. Education grants are usually given to complete a particular stage of a child's education (not school fees).

The maximum grant for a member of the society or his dependant is £2,400 a year (in 1993) paid in two six-monthly grants. The maximum grant for an officer who is not a member (or his dependant) is £800 a year paid in two six-monthly grants of £400.

Annual grant total: In 1991/92, the society had assets of £1.75 million and an income of £149,000. Relief-in-need grants to individuals totalled £93,000. There are currently 60 recipients, the majority of whom receive two awards a year.

Applications: On a form available from the correspondent. Applications are considered quarterly in January, April, July and October.

Correspondent: Cdr P F J Moore, Secretary, 1 Fleet Street, London EC4Y 1BD (071 353-4080 ext. 471).

Other information: The society was founded on 16th May, 1739 by a group of naval officers suffering from unreasonable treatment by the Admiralty. The benevolent function of the society emerged later and become its sole purpose in 1791.

The Royal Naval Benevolent Trust

Eligibility: Serving and ex-serving men of the Royal Navy and Royal Marines (not officers) and their dependants.

Types of grants: One-off and recurrent grants according to need. Grants can be to contribute directly or indirectly through other organisations to the maintenance of families and dependants in need and to assist men leaving the service to gain employment.

Annual grant total: £1.3 million in grants in 1992/93, of which £993,000 was given in one-off grants and £326,000 in annuities.

Applications: May be made personally or by letter direct to the correspondent or through a voluntary agency. Applications are considered twice-weekly.

Correspondent: The Grants Secretary, Castaway House, 311 Twyford Avenue, Portsmouth, Hampshire PO2 8PE (0705-660296).

Other information: The trust pays 1,000 annuities of up to £7 a week to elderly beneficiaries. These are called Jellicoe (Greenwich Hospital) Annuities. They cost about £348,000 a year. Most of the balance is in individual grants.

In its 1992/93 Report, the trust comments as follows: "The very wide discretionary powers of the Grants Committee are such that there are but few cases of genuine distress to which the committee is unable to bring prompt relief. Once a need is known to exist and the applicant is deemed to be eligible to benefit and deserving of help, the trust's aim is to provide assistance at a sufficiently high level to enable the beneficiary to make a fresh start with a reasonable prospect of avoiding a further set-back ... often, however, no such satisfactory solution is possible. [Many] face the prospect of long-term unemployment or low living standards and there is little that can be done to improve their lot. Occasional grants can be made to meet exceptional circumstances but frequently recurring applications have to be discouraged because ... the trust's resources cannot be stretched to permit a regular supplementation of income."

The trust also runs a residential home for 38 elderly ex-naval men (not women) in Gillingham, Kent.

The Royal Naval Reserve (V) Benevolent Fund

Eligibility: Members or former members of the Royal Naval Volunteer Reserve, Women's Royal Naval Volunteer Reserve, Royal Naval Reserve and the Women's Royal Naval Reserve, who are serving or have served as a rating. The fund also caters for wives, widows and young children of the above.

Types of grants: One-off grants only, ranging from £50 to £350. Grants have been given for gas, electricity, removal expenses (ie. to be near children/following divorce), clothing, travel to visit sick relatives or for treatment, essential furniture and domestic equipment, and help on bereavement.

Annual grant total: The trust has assets of £62,500 and an income of £6,000. 20 relief-in-need grants to individuals totalled £3,560.

Applications: In writing to the correspondent directly by the individual or through the local reserve division, SSAFA or Royal Naval Benevolent Trust, who investigate applications.

Correspondent: Captain R K Sard, Secretary, Wisteria Cottage, Lee Street, Hookwood, Horley, Surrey RH6 8HD (0293-774776).

Service and ex-service charities

The Royal Navy & Royal Marine Branch & Special Duties Officers' Benevolent Fund

Eligibility: Branch Officers of the Royal Navy and Royal Marines (up to and including officers who received the rank of Lieutenant on retiring, and Special Duties Officers, active and retired, not above the rank of Lieutenant) and their dependants, in cases of illness and other causes of distress.

Types of grants: Grants generally to widows on limited incomes. Nearly 60% of those assisted were over 75 years of age. Most find it increasingly difficult to make ends meet when increases to their pensions fail to match cost of living increases. Grants typically for lighting, heating, rates and telephone charges, and increasingly for eye tests/glasses. Small education grants are also made to children of single-parent families.

The fund does not make loans, although: "The repair and replacement of essential household aids and, for the owner occupier, structural repairs and maintenance, can sometimes require the award of exceptional grants in excess of the maximum Council and Managing Trustees grants".

Annual grant total: In 1992/93, the trust had assets of £89,000 and an income of about £8,000. Grants received from King George's Fund for Sailors (£34,500) and First of June Royal Naval Officers Fund (£12,000) enabled the trust to make 333 grants to 150 people totalling £50,000.

Applications: On a form available from the correspondent, including details of rank, service and income and outgoings. Applications should be submitted directly by the individual and are considered monthly.

Correspondent: Lt Cdr L W Truscott, Hon. General Secretary, 12 The Causeway, Downend, Fareham, Hampshire PO16 8RN (0329-232901).

The Royal Patriotic Fund Corporation

Eligibility: Widows, orphans and dependants of officers and men of the armed forces. Applicants are usually but not categorically over 60.

Types of grants: Quarterly allowances and one-off grants to meet specific needs. The corporation also provides televisions and/or licences. Grants range from £50 to £250.

Annual grant total: In 1992, the corporation had assets of £2.9 million and an income of £360,000. £321,000 was given in about 850 relief-in-need grants.

Applications: Normally through services welfare organisations, social services departments or a similar body. Applications are considered weekly.

Correspondent: The Secretary, Golden Cross House, Duncannon Street, London WC2 4JR (071-930 9370).

The Royal Pioneer Corps Association

Eligibility: Serving Pioneer Services RLC and ex-serving Pioneers and their dependants in need.

Types of grants: Grants for a wide range of needs. Commonly help with clothing and bedding, electricity, gas/fuel bills, household items and mobility. The fund received 717 applications in 1992.

Annual grant total: £86,000 in 1992. A large percentage of grants are made from the Army Benevolent Fund.

Applications: Requests are followed up by SSAFA, the Forces Help Society, the Royal British Legion, the War Pensions Welfare Service or a similar body.

Correspondent: Major G F Crook, Secretary, 51 St George's Drive, London SW1V 4DE (071-834 0415).

The Royal Signals Association Benevolent Fund

Eligibility: Members and former members of the Royal Signals, regular or territorial volunteer reserve, and their dependants.

Types of grants: One-off and recurrent grants according to need. Grants are given towards fuel and lighting costs, funeral expenses, domestic and medical appliances, convalescence, nursing home top-up fees, supplementary and Christmas allowances. No loans.

Annual grant total: £267,000 in about 1,100 grants in 1992.

Applications: Normally through SSAFA, the Forces Help Society or other organisations, but may be submitted direct. Applications are considered as required.

Correspondent: The Welfare Secretary, RHQ Royal Signals, 56 Regency Street, London SW1P 4AD (071-414 8432/630 0801).

St Andrew's Scottish Soldiers Club Fund

Eligibility: Scottish soldiers in need with preference firstly for those from Aldershot Garrison; secondly for all Scottish soldiers serving in the UK, and thereafter serving and former Scottish soldiers' dependants elsewhere.

Types of grants: One-off and recurrent grants according to need.

Annual grant total: In 1993, grants were given to 15 individuals totalling £4,600.

Applications: In writing to the correspondent.

Correspondent: Wing Cmdr Alan Robertson, The Royal Scottish Corporation, 37 King Street, Covent Garden, London WC2E 8JS (071-240 3718).

Other information: The correspondent also administers the Kinlock Bequest and the Royal Scottish Corporation (see separate entries).

Saint Dunstan's

Eligibility: Registered war blinded men and women, and others who lose their sight in peacetime when serving with the armed forces or as a result of that service. "The basic criteria for acceptance have been the granting by the Ministry of a war pension and, of course, to be registered, or be eligible for full registration, as a blind person with a recommendation from our ophthalmic surgeons for enrolment." Also the wife, widow or child of a war blinded person. Some assistance can be given to members of the emergency services (police, fire service and ambulance drivers) who lose their sight on duty.

Types of grants: Grants according to need. There are currently 966 St Dunstaners, all receiving regular support, and 629 widows. There were 37 pensioners added to the list in 1992/93.

Annual grant total: The 1993 accounts show a total of £7.1 million for "Services rendered to blinded men and women of HM forces and Home Defence Services". This consists of training and settling in occupations (£187,000); general welfare including grants for the relief of financial and family difficulties, supply of appliances designed for the use of the blind and the provision of technical and welfare visiting services (£1.6 million); upkeep of training, convalescent and holiday homes (£4.6 million); and repairs and maintenance costs of beneficiaries' dwellings. A further £320,000 was given in assistance to St Dunstaners' widows.

Applications: On a form available from the correspondent.

Correspondent: W C Weisblatt, 12-14 Harcourt Street, London W1A 4XB (071-723 5021).

Service and ex-service charities/Army regimental associations

Other information: Saint Dunstan's is a full scale welfare agency caring for all aspects of its beneficiaries' needs.

The St John & Red Cross Joint Committee

Eligibility: War disabled ex-service men and women and ex-officers (primarily those disabled in the 1st and 2nd World Wars and subsequent recognised conflicts eg. Korea, but other ex-service personnel in receipt of War Disability Pensions will be considered). Also eligible are widows of war disability pensioners, sick and elderly ex-members of the nursing services of HM Forces, and officers and members of VAD's of the Red Cross and St John Ambulance who gave service to the wounded in war.

Types of grants: Grants according to need.

Annual grant total: £200,000 in 1992/93. It gave 729 grants to pensioners, 466 to widows and 124 to nurses.

Applications: Applications are made through the War Pensioners Welfare Service or other welfare organisations.

Correspondent: R Aspinall, Deputy Secretary, 5 Grosvenor Crescent, London SW1X 7EH (071-235 7131).

The Soldiers', Sailors' & Airmen's Families Association (SSAFA)

Eligibility: The families and dependants of serving or former service men and women.

Types of grants: Financial help is normally available to meet a specific and immediate problem. SSAFA caseworkers always visit clients and either help directly or through other organisations.

Annual grant total: £5.5 million in 1992, of which £395,000 was from SSAFA funds, the remainder being distributed on behalf of other charities. 82,300 grants were given in total.

Applications: Contact should normally be made by letter direct to the honorary secretary of the local branch. The appropriate address can usually be obtained from the citizen's advice bureau, the local telephone directory (under Soldiers', Sailors' & Airmen's Families Association) and most main post offices. In case of difficulty, the local address can be obtained from the central office below.

Correspondent: The Director of Welfare (but for applications see above), Queen Elizabeth the Queen Mother House, 19 Queen Elizabeth Street, London SE1 2LP (071-403 8783).

Other information: SSAFA operates throughout the British Isles and in garrisons and stations overseas. It is devoted to the welfare of the families of service and ex-service men and women. Its representatives act as sympathetic, knowledgeable and confidential friends to families with problems and difficulties, however personal and varied, and make financial grants when needed.

Families and other dependants of all service and ex-service men and women are eligible for assistance from SSAFA. All SSAFA branches are empowered to give immediate help without reference to higher committees. Also, because of their unique coverage of the UK and Ireland, they act as agents for service and other associated funds. There are about 7,000 voluntary workers in the UK.

SSAFA works in close collaboration with the Forces Help Society (see separate entry) with whom 80,000 cases and visits were undertaken in 1992.

The Victory (Ex-Services) Benevolent Trust Fund

Eligibility: Ex-servicemen and women and their dependants.

Types of grants: One-off grants only. The trust says that its policy is to assist with initial financial grants pending the larger benevolent funds taking over the account. Grants range from £20 to £80.

Annual grant total: In 1992/93, the trust had assets of £40,000 and an income of £7,000. £6,300 was given in relief-in-need grants to individuals.

Applications: On the common form available for use by service/ex-service organisations, usually through SSAFA, Royal British Legion or War Pensioners Welfare Department of the DSS.

Correspondent: The Secretary, 63-79 Seymour Street, London W2 2HF (071-723 4474).

The WRNS Benevolent Trust

Eligibility: Serving members of the WRNS (Women's Royal Naval Service) and former members of the WRNS who served after September 1939 (excluding those, and dependants of those, who deserted). Also, dependants of the above in need.

Types of grants: One-off grants for debts, clothes, furnishings, removals, kitchen equipment, household repairs and equipment such as wheelchairs and special medical equipment. One-off grants range from £15 to £500. A weekly maintenance grant of £5 is paid quarterly to people over 70 on low income.

Amenity grants amounting to £95 a year to single parents on low income.

No grants to pay off credit cards, bank loans or reimburse people for bills already paid. No loans are made, nor grants to those with savings well above £3,000.

Annual grant total: In 1992, the trust had assets of £896,000 and an income of £234,000. Total expenditure was £157,000 including £118,000 in 613 grants to individuals.

Applications: On a form available from the correspondent. Applications can be submitted directly by the individual or through a social worker, citizen's advice bureau, SSAFA or other welfare agency. They are considered every two weeks throughout the year.

Correspondent: Mrs J Y Ellis, General Secretary, 311 Twyford Avenue, Portsmouth, Hampshire PO2 8PE (0705-655301).

Army Regimental Associations

Adjutant-General's Corps Inst & Assn
Adjutant-General's Corps Depot, Worthy Down, Winchester, Hants SO21 2RG (0962-887435).

Airborne Forces Security Fund
Browning Barracks, Aldershot, Hants GU11 2BU (0252-20772 or 347620).

Argyll & Sutherland Highlanders' Regimental Assn
The Castle, Stirling FK8 1EH (0786-72881 ext. 8274 or 0786-75165).

Army Air Corps Fund (post Sept 1957)
Headquarters Director, Army Air Corps, Middle Wallop, Stockbridge, Hants SO20 8DY (0264-384426).

Army Air Corps (Parachute Regiment & Glider Pilot Regiment) pre 1957
See Airborne Forces Security Fund.

Army Benevolent Fund
41 Queen's Gate, South Kensington, London SW7 5HR (071-584 5235).

Army Catering Corps Assn
Dettingen House, Princess Royal Barracks, Deepcut, Camberley, Surrey GU16 6RW (0252-24431 ext. 5834).

Army regimental associations

Army Commandos Ben. Fund
190 Hammersmith Road, London
W6 7DL (081-746 3491).

Army Cycle Corps
c/o Forces Help Society (see separate entry).

Army Physical Training Corps Assn
Army School of PT, HQ & Depot APTC, Queen's Avenue, Aldershot, Hants GU11 2LB (0252-347131).

Artists' Rifles Aid Fund
c/o Artists' Rifles Regimental Assn, 'B' Block, Duke of York's HQ, London SW3 4SE (071-930 4466).

ATS & WRAC Benevolent Funds
PO Box 212, Guildford, Surrey GU2 6ZD (0252-355562).

Ayrshire Yeomanry (ECO) Yeomanry Charitable Trust
2 Barns Street, Ayr KA7 1XD (0292-264091).

Bedfordshire & Herts Regiment Assn
Blenheim House, Eagle Way, Warley, Brentwood CM13 3BN (0277-213051).

Berkshire Regiment
See Duke of Edinburgh's Royal Regiment.

Berks & Westminster Dragoons Assn
See Westminster Dragoons Assn.

Black Horse Assn (7th Dragoon Guards)
See Royal Dragoon Guards Ben. Fund.

Black Watch Assn
Balhousie Castle, Perth PH1 5HS (0738-23214).

Blues & Royals Assn
Combermere Barracks, Windsor, Berks SL4 3DN (0753-868222 ext. 5297).

Border Regimental Benevolent Fund
See The King's Own Royal Border RA.

Brecknockshire Regiment
See Royal Regiment of Wales Benevolent Fund

Buckinghamshire, Berkshire & Oxfordshire Yeomanry & Artillery Trust
c/o Parrott & Coales, 14 Bourbon Street, Aylesbury, Bucks HP20 2RS (0296-82244).

Buffs Benevolent Fund
See Queen's Own Buffs.

Cameronians (Scottish Rifles) Regimental Assn
c/o Regimental HQ, The King's Own Scottish Borderers, The Barracks, Berwick-on-Tweed TD15 1DG (0289-307426).

Cheshire Regiment Assn
RHQ, The 22nd Cheshire Regiment, The Castle, Chester CH1 2DN (0244-327617).

Cheshire Yeomanry Assn Ben. Fund
L J Curry, Bowend, 3 Larchfields, Saughall, Chester CH1 6BU (0244-881037).

City of Glasgow Regiment
See Royal Highland Fusiliers.

Coldstream Guards Assn
RHQ Coldstream Guards, Wellington Barracks, Birdcage Walk, London SW1E 6HQ (071-930 4466 ext. 3263/3245).

Commandos
See Army Commandos.

Connaught Rangers Assn
c/o Forces Help Society (see separate entry).

County of London Yeomanry (3rd/4th) (Sharpshooters)
See Yeomanry Benevolent Fund.

Derbyshire Yeomanry Old Comrades Assn
50 Whitehurst Street, Allenton, Derby DE2 8LE (0332-43045).

Devonshire & Dorset Regiment Assn
Wyvern Barracks, Exeter, Devon EX2 6AE (0392-218178 ext. 34/35).

Devonshire Regiment Old Comrades' Assn
See Devonshire & Dorset Regiment Assn.

Dorset Regiment Old Comrades Assn
See Devonshire & Dorset Regiment Assn.

Dragoon Guards
1st The Queen's Dragoon Guards Regimental Assn Ben. Fund, Maindy Barracks, Whitchurch Road, Cardiff CF4 3YE (0222-227611 ext. 213).
  1st King's (see 1st Queen's Dragoon Guards (above).
  2nd (Queen's Bays) (see 1st Queen's Dragoon Guards (above).
  3rd Carabiniers (Prince of Wales's Dragoon Guards) (see Royal Scots Dragoon Guards).
  4th/7th (see Royal Dragoon Guards Benevolent Fund).
  5th Royal Inniskilling Dragoon Guards Assn (see Royal Scots Dragoon Guards).
  1st Royal (see Blues and Royals).
  2nd Royal Scots Greys (see Royal Scots Dragoon Guards).
  3rd Dragoon Guards (see Royals Scots Dragoon Guards).
  6th Dragoon Guards (see Royal Scots Dragoon Guards).
  22nd (see Royal Armoured Corps War Memorial Fund).
  25th Dragoon Guards (see Royal Scots Dragoon Guards).
  Westminster Dragoons (see Berkshire and Westminster Dragoons).

Duke of Albany's Seaforth Highlanders
See Seaforth Highlanders.

Duke of Cambridge's Own Middlesex Regiment
See Middlesex Regiment.

Duke of Cornwall's Light Infantry Assn
Light Infantry Office (Cornwall), The Keep, Victoria Barracks, Bodmin, Cornwall PL31 1EG (0208-72810).

Duke of Edinburgh's Royal Regiment Assn (Berkshire & Wiltshire)
The Wardrobe, 58 The Close, Salisbury, Wilts SP1 2EX (0722-414536).

Duke of Wellington's (West Riding) Regimental Assn
Wellesley Park, Highroad Well, Halifax, West Yorks HX2 0BA (0422-361671).

Durham Light Infantry Charitable Fund
Light Infantry Office, Elvet Waterside, Durham DH1 3BW (091-386 5496).

East Anglian Regiments
See Royal Anglian Regiment.

East Kent Regiment
See Queen's Own Buffs.

East Lancashire Regiment Ben. Fund
RHQ, The Queen's Lancashire Regiment, Fulwood Barracks, Preston PR2 4AA (0772-716543 ext. 2362).

East Surrey Regiment
See Queen's Royal Surrey Regiment.

East Yorkshire Regimental Assn
See Prince of Wales's Own (W&E Yorks) RA.

Essex Regiment Assn
RHQ, Royal Anglian Regiment, Blenheim House, Eagle Way, Warley, Brentwood, Essex CM13 3BN (0277-213051).

Fife & Forfar Yeomanry Assn
5 Fairhill Crescent, Perth PH1 1RR (0738-28224).

Fusiliers Aid Society
RHQ, The Royal Regiment of Fusiliers, HM Tower of London, London EC3N 4AB (071-709 0765 ext. 291).

Glasgow Regiment
See Royal Highland Fusiliers.

Glider Pilot Regimental Assn Ben. Fund
3A London Road, Hindhead, Surrey GU26 6AB (0428-605448).

Gloucestershire Regimental Assn
Custom House, 31 Commercial Road, Gloucester GL1 2HE (0452-22682).

Gordon Highlanders' Assn
c/o RHQ Gordon Highlanders, Viewfield Road, Aberdeen AB1 7XH (0224-313387).

Green Howards Benevolent Fund
RHQ The Green Howards, Trinity Church Square, Richmond, North Yorkshire DL10 4QN (0748-822133).

Green Jackets 1st, 2nd, 3rd, 43rd & 52nd
See Rifleman's Aid Society.

Grenadier Guards Assn
RHQ Grenadier Guards, Wellington Barracks, Birdcage Walk, London SW1E 6HQ (071-222 4309 or 930 4466 ext. 3285).

Gurkha Welfare Trusts
c/o LO Brigade of Gurkhas, MOD, Archway North (Room 9), Old Admiralty Building, Spring Gardens, London SW1A 2BE (071-218 9000 ext. 0017).

Hampshire & Isle of Wight Military Aid Fund (1903)
Serles House, Southgate Street, Winchester SO23 9EG (0962-852933).

Highland Light Infantry
See Royal Highland Fusiliers.

Hon. Artillery Company Ben. Fund
Armoury House, City Road, London EC1Y 2BQ (071-606 4644).

Hussars:
  3rd King's Own (see Queen's Royal Hussars).
  4th Queen's Own Hussars Regimental Assn, Turnpike Cottage,

Army regimental associations

Compton Chamberlayne, Salisbury, Wilts SP3 5DH (072270-614).

7th Queen's Own (see Queen's Royal Hussars).

8th King's Royal Irish (see Queen's Royal Irish Hussars).

King's Royal Hussars Welfare Fund, c/o Home Headquarters (North), Fulwood Barracks, Preston PR2 4AA (0772-651420).

10th (Prince of Wales's Own) (see Royal Hussars (PWO) Ben. Fund).

11th (Prince Albert's Own) (see Royal Hussars (PWO) Ben. Fund).

13th/18th Royal (Queen Mary's Own) Aid Fund, 3 Tower Street, York YO1 1SB (0904-642037).

14th/20th King's Hussars Regimental Assn, Fulwood Barracks, Fulwood, Preston PR2 4AA (0772-716543 ext. 2310).

15th/19th King's Royal Hussars Regimental Assn, Fenham Barracks, Newcastle-upon-Tyne NE2 4NP (091-261 1046 ext. 3140).

Queen's Royal Irish Hussars (& 8th Hussars) Assn, Regent's Park Barracks, Albany Street, London, NW1 4AL (071-387 3471 ext. 17).

19th Royal Hussars Assn (see 15/19th King's Royal Hussars).

Imperial Yeomanry
See Yeomanry Benevolent Fund.

Inns of Court Regimental Assn
10 Stone Buildings, Lincoln's Inn, London WC2 3TG (071-831 6727).

Intelligence Corps Assn
c/o The Intelligence Centre, Templar Barracks, Ashford, Kent TN23 3HH (0233-625251 ext. 3208).

Irish Guards Assn
RHQ Irish Guards, Wellington Barracks, Birdcage Walk, London SW1E 6HQ (071-930 4466 ext. 3295).

King's Own Royal Border Regimental Assn
The Castle, Carlisle, Cumbria CA3 8UR (0228-21275 ext. 8240).

King's Own Royal Regiment
See King's Own Royal Border Regimental Assn.

King's Own Scottish Borderers Assn
RHQ The Barracks, Berwick-on-Tweed TD15 1DG (0289-307426).

King's Own Yorkshire Light Infantry Regimental Assn
Light Infantry Office (Yorkshire), Minden House, Wakefield Road, Pontefract, West Yorks WF8 4ES (0977-703181).

King's & Manchester Regiments' Assn (Liverpool Branch)
RHQ The King's Regiment, Graeme House, Derby Square, Liverpool L2 7SD (051-236 6363).

King's & Manchester Regiments' Assn (Manchester Branch)
TA Centre, Ardwick Green, Manchester M12 6HD (061-273 6191).

King's Royal Rifle Corps
See Rifleman's Aid Society.

King's Shropshire & Herefordshire Light Infantry Assn
Light Infantry Office (Shropshire & Herefordshire), Copthorne Barracks, Copthorne, Shrewsbury SY3 8LZ (0743-236060 ext. 2425/2430).

Labour Corps
c/o Forces Help Society (see separate entry).

Lancs Fusiliers' Compassionate Fund
The Lancashire HQ, The Royal Regiment of Fusiliers, Wellington Barracks, Bury, Lancs BL8 2PL (061-761 2680).

Lancashire Regiment (Prince of Wales's Volunteers) Regimental Assn
RHQ (Increment), c/o RHQ The Queen's Lancashire Regiment, Fulwood Barracks, Preston PR2 4AA (0772-716543 ext. 2362).

Lancers:
   9th/12th Royal Lancers (Prince of Wales's & 27th Lancers) Regimental Assn, TA Centre, Saffron Road, Wigston, Leicestershire LE8 2TU (0533-785425).
   16th/5th Queen's Royal Lancers Assn & Ben. Fund, Home Headquarters, Kitchener House, Lammascote Road, Stafford ST16 3TA (0952-674517).
   17th/21st Lancers Regimental Assn Ben. Fund, Regimental Secretary, 17th/21st Lancers, Prince William of Gloucester Barracks, Grantham NG31 7TJ (0476-67413 ext. 3252).
   27th (see 9th/12th Royal, above).

Leicestershire Regiment
See Royal Leicestershire Regiment.

Leinster Regiment
For those resident in UK: c/o Forces Help Society (see separate entry).

Light Dragoons Charitable Trust
OC Home HQ, The Light Dragoons, Fenham Barracks, Newcastle-upon-Tyne NE2 4NP (091-261 1046 ext. 3140).

Life Guards Assn
Household Cavalry Mounted Regiment, Combermere Barracks, Windsor, Berks SL4 3DN (0753-868222 ext. 5204).

Light Infantry Benevolent Assn
RHQ The Light Infantry, Peninsula Barracks, Romsey Road, Winchester, Hants SO23 8TS (0962-864176 ext. 5129).

Lincolnshire Regiment
HQ Royal Anglian Regiment, Sobraon Barracks, Lincoln LN1 3PY (0522-525444).

Liverpool Regiment
See King's & Manchester Regiments Assn.

London Irish Rifles Benevolent Fund
Duke of York's Headquarters, King's Road, Chelsea, London SW3 4SP (071-930 4466 ext. 406).

London Regiment
c/o Forces Help Society (see separate entry).

London Scottish Regiment Ben. Fund
D Henderson, 95 Horseferry Road, London SW1P 2DX (071-630 1639).

Lothian & Border Regimental Assn (1st Lothians & Border Yeomanry, 2nd Lothians & Border Horse)
c/o Royal Armoured Corps War Memorial Ben. Fund, HQ RAC Centre, Bovington Camp, Wareham, Dorset BH20 6JA (0929-462721 ext. 331).

Lovat Scouts Regimental Assn
Flat 4, Beechlawn, 20 Culduthel Road, Inverness IV2 4AJ (0463-230001).

Loyal Regiment (North Lancashire) Regimental & Old Comrades' Assn
Fulwood Barracks, Preston PR2 4AA (0772-716543 ext. 2362).

Machine Gun Corps Old Comrades Assn
140 The Hornbeams, Harlow, Essex CM20 1PJ (0279-428332). For Heavy Branch Machine Gun Corps, see Royal Tank Regiment Assn & Benevolent Fund.

Manchester Regiment Aid Society & Benevolent Fund
TA Centre, Ardwick Green North, Manchester M12 6HD (061-273 6191).

Mercian Volunteers Assn
Wolseley House, Fallings Park, Wolverhampton WV10 9QR (0902-731842/731426/733760).

Middlesex Regiment (Duke of Cambridge's Own) Regimental Assn
The Secretary, 38 Traps Lane, New Malden, Surrey KT3 4SA (081-949 7605).

Military Police
See Royal Military Police.

Military Provost Staff Corps Assn
RHQ, MPSC, Berechurch Hall Camp, Colchester, Essex CO2 9NU (0206-575121 ext. 3494).

Monmouthshire Regiment
See Royal Regiment of Wales Benevolent Fund.

Norfolk Regiment
See Royal Norfolk Regiment.

Northamptonshire Regimental Assn
Gibraltar Barracks, Barrack Road, Northampton NN1 3RE (0604-35412).

Northamptonshire Yeomanry Assn
1st & 2nd Regiments, 228 Kettering Road, Northampton NN2 7DT (0604-713592).

North Lancashire Regiment
See Loyal Regiment.

North Staffordshire Regiment
See Staffordshire Regiment.

Nottinghamshire & Derbyshire Regiment
See Worcestershire & Sherwood Foresters.

"Old Contemptibles"
c/o Forces Help Society (see separate entry).

Oxfordshire & Buckinghamshire Light Infantry Regimental Assn
See Riflemen's Aid Society.

Army regimental associations

Parachute Regiment
See Airborne Forces Security Fund.

Post Office Rifles
c/o Forces Help Society (see separate entry).

Prince of Wales Leinster Regiment
c/o Royal British Legion Ireland (Southern) Area, 3 Crosthwaite Terrace, Clarinda Park West, Dun Laoghaire, Co. Dublin.

Prince of Wales's Own (West & East Yorkshire) Regimental Assn
RHQ PWO, 3 Tower Street, York YO1 1SB (0904-642038 or 659811 ext. 2310).

Princess Louise's Kensington Regimental Assn
A E Easton, 190 Hammersmith Road, London W6 7DJ (081-200 7264).

Queen Alexandra's Royal Army Nursing Corps Assn
Regimental Headquarters, QARANC, QARANC Training Centre, Royal Pavilion, Farnborough Road, Aldershot, Hants GU11 1PZ (0252-347316).

Queen's Bays (2nd Dragoon Guards)
See Dragoon Guards.

Queen's Bodyguard
See Yeoman of the Guard and Yeoman Warders.

Queen's Dragoon Guards
See Dragoons.

Queen's Lancashire Regiment Assn
Fulwood Barracks, Preston PR2 4AA (0772-716543 ext. 2362/2426).

Queen's Own Buffs, The Royal Kent Regiment Benevolent Fund
RHQ The Queen's Regiment, Howe Barracks, Canterbury, Kent CT1 1JU (0227-763434 ext. 4252).

Queen's Own Cameron Highlanders' Regimental Assn
Cameron Barracks, Inverness IV2 3XD (0463-224380).

Queen's Own Highlanders' (Seaforth & Camerons) Regimental Assn
Cameron Barracks, Inverness IV2 3XD (0463-224380).

Queen's Own Hussars Aid Society
28 Jury Street, Warwick CV34 4EW (0926-492035) *(incorporates 3rd King's Own Hussars Ben. Fund & 7th Queen's Own Hussars Aid Society)*.

Queen's Own Royal West Kent Regiment Compassionate Fund
See Queen's Own Buffs.

Queen's Own Yorkshire Dragoons
See Yeomanry Benevolent Fund.

Queen's Regimental Assn
Howe Barracks, Canterbury, Kent CT1 1JU (0227-763434 ext. 4251/2).

Queen's Royal Irish Hussars
Regent's Park Barracks, Albany Street, London NW1 4AL (071-873 6716/7).

Queen's Royal Regiment (West Surrey)
See Queen's Royal Surrey Regiment.

Queen's Royal Surrey Regiment Regimental Assn
Howe Barracks, Canterbury, Kent CT1 1JU (0227-763434 ext. 4253).

Reconnaisance Corps
See Royal Armoured Corps.

Rifle Brigade
See Rifleman's Aid Society.

Rifleman's Aid Society
Peninsula Barracks, Romsey Road, Winchester SO23 8TS (0962-864176 ext. 5128) *(includes Royal Green Jackets, 43rd/52nd Oxf & Bucks Light Infantry, King's Royal Rifle Corps, Rifle Brigade)*.

Ross-Shire Buffs, Duke of Albany's Seaforth Highlanders
See Seaforth Highlanders.

Royal Anglian Regiment Assn
The Keep, Gibraltar Barracks, Bury St Edmunds IP33 3RN (0284-752394/5).

Royal Armoured Corps War Memorial Benevolent Fund
HQ RAC Centre, Bovington Camp, Wareham, Dorset BH20 6JA (0929-462721 ext. 3331).

Royal Army Chaplain's Department Assn
Bagshot Park, Bagshot, Surrey GU19 5PL (0276-71717 ext. 2845).

Royal Army Dental Corps Assn
HQ Royal Army Dental Corps Training Centre, Evelyn Wood's Road, Aldershot, Hants GU11 2LS (0252-347782).

Royal Army Educational Corps Assn
Old Military Academy, Building 318, Academy Road, Woolwich, London SE18 4JJ (081-781 5921).

Royal Army Medical Corps Charitable Funds & Assn
RAMC Training Centre and RHQ, Keogh Barracks, Ash Vale, Aldershot GU12 5RQ (0252-377394).

Royal Army Ordnance Corps Charitable Trust
Dettingen House, Princess Royal Barracks, Deepcut, Camberley, Surrey GU16 6RW (0252-340514).

Royal Army Pay Corps Regimental Assn
Corps Headquarters, RAPC Worthy Down, Winchester, Hants SO21 2RG (0962-887436).

Royal Army Service Corps & Royal Corps of Transport Ben. Funds
Dettingen House, Princess Royal Barracks, Deepcut, Camberley, Surrey GU16 6RW (0252-340898).

Royal Army Veterinary Corps Assn RAVC Soldier Ben. Fund
RHQ RAVC, Doncaster Lodge, Defence Animal Centre, Melton Mowbray, Leics LE13 0SL (0664-63281 ext. 45).

Royal Artillery Charitable Fund
Artillery House, Old Royal Military Academy, London SE18 4DN (081-319 4052).

Royal Berkshire Regiment Old Comrades' Assn
See Duke of Edinburgh's Royal Regt Assn (Berks & Wilts).

4th/7th Royal Dragoon Guards Benevolent Fund
Home HQ, 4/7th RDG, 3 Tower Street, York YO1 1SB (0904-659811).

Royal Dublin Fusiliers
c/o Forces Help Society (see separate entry).

Royal Dublin Fusiliers Old Comrades Assn
c/o Royal British Legion Ireland (Southern) Area, 3 Crosthwaite Terrace, Clarinda Park West, Dun Laoghaire, Co Dublin.

Royal East Kent Regiment
See Queen's Own Buffs.

Royal Electrical & Mechanical Engineers Assn & Benevolent Fund
Isaac Newton Road, Arborfield, Reading, Berks RG2 9LN (0734-763219).

Royal Engineers Assn
RHQ Royal Engineers, Brompton Barracks, Chatham ME4 4UG (0634-847005).

Royal Fusiliers Aid Society
City of London HQ, Royal Regiment of Fusiliers, HM Tower of London, London EC3N 4AB (071-709 0765 ext. 5606).

Royal Gloucestershire Hussars
See Yeomanry Benevolent Fund.

Royal Green Jackets
See Rifleman's Aid Society.

Royal Hampshire Regiment Comrades' Assn
Serles House, Southgate Street, Winchester SO23 9EG (0962-863658).

Royal Highland Fusiliers Regimental Benevolent Assn
518 Sauchiehall Street, Glasgow G2 3LW (041-332 0961/5639).

Royal Horse Guards (Blues) Comrades' Assn
See Blues and Royals Assn.

Royal Hussars (Prince of Wales's Own) Old Comrades' Assn & Ben. Fund
Peninsular Barracks, Winchester SO23 8TS (0962-863751 or 885522 ext. 5140).

5th Royal Inniskilling Dragoon Guards Assn
See Royal Dragoon Guards.

Royal Inniskilling Fusiliers Assn
c/o Regimental Office Royal Irish Rangers, The Castle, Enniskillen, Co Fermanagh BT74 7HL (0365-323142).

Royal Irish Fusiliers (Princess Victoria's) Regimental Assn
c/o Regimental Office, Royal Irish Rangers, Sovereign's House, The Mall, Armagh BT61 9DL (0861-522911).

Royal Irish Rangers Assn
RHQ The Royal Irish Rangers, 5 Waring Street, Belfast BT1 2EW (0232-232086).

Army regimental associations

Royal Irish Regiment & South Irish Horse Old Comrades' Assn
c/o Royal Irish Rangers Assn, 5 Waring Street, Belfast BT1 2EW (0232-232086).

Royal Irish Rifles
c/o Royal Irish Rangers Assn, 5 Waring Street, Belfast BT1 2EW (0232-232086).

Royal Leicestershire Regiment Royal Tigers Assn
TA Centre, Ulverscroft Road, Leicester LE4 6BY (0533-22749).

Royal Lincolnshire Regiment Assn
Sobraon Barracks, Lincoln LN1 3PY (0522-25444).

Royal Logistical Corps Assn
Dettingen House, Princess Royal Barracks, Deepcut, Camberley, Surrey GU16 6RW (0252-24431 ext. 5834).

Royal Military Academy Sandhurst Band
c/o Forces Help Society (see separate entry).

Royal Military Police Central Ben. Fund
RHQ RMP, Roussillon Barracks, Chichester PO19 4BN (0243-786311 ext. 238).

Royal Munster Fusiliers Charitable Fund
c/o Forces Help Society (see separate entry).

Royal Norfolk Regimental Assn
HQ Royal Anglian Regiment, Britannia Barracks, Norwich, Norfolk NR1 4HJ (0603-628455).

Royal Northumberland Fusiliers Aid Society & Regimental Assn
TA Centre, Fenkle Street, Alnwick, Northumberland NE66 1HW (0665-510211).

Royal Pioneer Corps Benevolent Assn
51 St George's Drive, London SW1V 4DE (071-834 0415).

Royal Regiment of Fusiliers
See Fusiliers Aid Society.

Royal Regiment of Wales (24th/41st Foot Benevolent Fund)
The Barracks, Cardiff CF4 3YE (0222-227611 ext. 8215).

Royal Scots Ben. Society
Royal Scots Club, 30 Abercrombie Place, Edinburgh EH3 6QE (031-556 4270).

Royal Scots Dragoon Guards' Assn (Carabiniers & Greys)
Home HQ, Royal Scots Dragoon Guards, The Castle, Edinburgh EH1 2YT (031-310 5100).

Royal Scots Fusiliers Benevolent Assn
See Royal Highland Fusiliers.

Royal Scots Greys (2nd Dragoons)
See Royal Scots Dragoon Guards.

Royal Signals Assn
RHQ Royal Signals, 56 Regency Street, London SW1P 4AD (071-930 4466 ext. 8432).

Royal Sussex Regimental Assn
Roussillon Barracks, Chichester, W Sussex PO19 4BL (0243-786311 ext. 4240).

Royal Tank Regiment Assn & Benevolent Fund
HQ RAC Centre, Bovington Camp, Wareham BH20 6JA (0929-462721 ext. 3331).

Royal Tigers' Assn
See Royal Leicestershire Regiment.

Royal Ulster Rifles Assn
c/o Royal Irish Rangers Assn, 5 Waring Street, Belfast BT1 2EW (0232-232086).

Royal Warwickshire Regimental Assn
RHQ St John's House, Warwick CV34 4NF (0926-491653).

Royal Welsh Fusiliers Comrades' Assn
Hightown Barracks, Wrexham, Clwyd LL13 8RD (0978-264521).

Royal West Kent Regiment
See Queen's Own Buffs.

Scots Guards Assn
Wellington Barracks, Birdcage Walk, London SW1E 6HQ (071-414 3321).

Scottish Rifles
See Cameronians (Scottish Rifles).

Seaforth Highlanders' Regimental Assn
Cameron Barracks, Inverness IV2 3XD (0463-224380 ext. 139: 9-11 am Tues & Fri).

Sharpshooters Yeomanry Assn
See Yeomanry Benevolent Fund.

Sherwood Foresters
See Worcestershire & Sherwood Foresters Regimental Assn

Sherwood Rangers Yeomanry Regimental Assn
24 Low Pavement, Nottingham NG1 7ED (0602-507121).

Signals
See Royal Signals.

Small Arms School Corps Comrades' Assn
School of Infantry, Warminster, Wilts BA12 0DJ (0985-214000 ext. 2487).

Somerset Light Infantry Regimental Assn
Light Infantry Office Somerset, 14 Mount Street, Taunton, Somerset TA1 3QE (0823-333434 ext. 663/665).

South Lancashire Regiment (Prince of Wales's Volunteers)
c/o RHQ The Queen's Lancashire Regiment, Fulwood Barracks, Preston PR2 4AA (0772-716543 ext. 2362/2426).

South Staffordshire Regiment
See Staffordshire Regiment.

South Wales' Borderers
See Royal Regiment of Wales Benevolent Fund.

Special Air Service Regimental Assn (Ben. Fund SAS)
Centre Block, Duke of York's HQ, Chelsea, London SW3 4SP (071-930 4466 ext. 5317).

Staffordshire Regiment (Prince of Wales's) Regimental Assn
Whittington Barracks, Lichfield, Staffs WS14 9PY (0543-433333 ext. 3229/3263).

Staffordshire Yeomanry
See Yeomanry Benevolent Fund.

Suffolk Regiment Assoc & Royal Anglian Regiment Assn (Norfolk, Suffolk & Cambs Branch)
Britannia Barracks, Norwich NR1 4HJ (0603-628455).

Sussex Regiment
See Royal Sussex Regiment.

Ulster Defence Regiment Ben. Fund
RHQ Royal Irish Regiment, St Patricks Barracks, BFPO 808 (0266-661388).

Welsh Regiment Ben. Fund
See Royal Regiment of Wales Benevolent Fund.

Welsh Guards Assn & Benevolent Fund
Maindy Barracks, Whitchurch Road, Cardiff CF4 3YE (0222-227611 ext. 8219).

West Kent Regiment
See Queen's Own Buffs.

Westminster Dragoons Benevolence Sub-Committee (inc the Berkshire & Westminster Dragoons)
2 Amherst Road, Sevenoaks, Kent TN13 3LS (0732-458877).

West Riding Regiment
See Duke of Wellington's.

West Surrey Regiment
See Queen's Royal Surrey Regiment.

West Yorkshire Regimental Assn.
See Prince of Wales's Own (West & East Yorkshire) Regimental Assn.

Wiltshire Regiment Old Comrades' Assn
See Duke of Edinburgh's Royal Regt Assn (Berks & Wilts).

Women's Royal Army Corps Benevolent Fund
See ATS and WRAC Ben. Funds.

Worcestershire Regiments' Assn
TA Centre, Silver Street, Worcester WR1 2DB (0905-23835).

Yeoman of the Guard - Queen's Bodyguard
St James's Palace, London SW1 (071-930 3643).

Yeoman Warders The Constable's Fund
The Resident Governor, HM Tower of London, London EC3N 4AB (071-709 0765).

Yeomanry Benevolent Fund
10 Stone Buildings, Lincoln's Inn, London WC2A 3TG (071-831 6727). (This fund covers all Yeomanry Regiments).

York & Lancaster Regimental Assn
Endcliffe Hall, Endcliffe Vale Road, Sheffield S10 3EU (0742-663242 ext. 150).

Yorkshire Hussars Regimental Assn
See Yeomanry Benevolent Fund.

Yorkshire Regiment (Alexandra, Princess of Wales's Own)
See Green Howards.

Sickness and disability charities

There are many charities for people with illnesses or disabilities. The full entries in this section are only for those which give financial help from their own resources. There are many others which do not have a large enough income to do this but may be the starting point for getting financial help. For this reason we have also printed at the end of this section a list of organisations which provide advice and support.

The section starts with an index to direct the reader to the charities which cater for the disability concerned. The index is arranged in alphabetical order of sickness or disability. The entries are then arranged alphabetically.

Local disability charities, such as the Metropolitan Society for the Blind, are not included in this section but are listed in the relevant local section of the book.

Index of sickness and disability funds

AIDS/HIV
Body Positive
Crusaid
Paul Flynn Memorial Fund
Terrence Higgins Trust
Jewish AIDS Trust
Macfarlane Trust
Positively Partners & Positively Children

Alzheimer's Disease
Alzheimer's Disease Society

Arthritis
Arthritis Care

Asthma
Queen Alexandra Sanatorium Fund & Allied Funds

Blindness/partial sight
Action for Blind People
Electronic Aids for the Blind
Gardner's Trust for the Blind
Guide Dogs for the Blind Association
Jewish Care
Royal Blind Pension Society of the UK
Royal National Institute for the Blind

Brittle Bones
Brittle Bone Society

Cancer
Cancer & Leukaemia in Childhood Trust (CLIC)
Cancer Relief Macmillan Fund
Children's Leukeamia Appeal
Ada Oliver Will Trust
Malcolm Sargent Cancer Fund for Children
Tenovus Cancer Appeal

Cerebral Palsy
Spastics Society Personal Services Fund

Children with disabilities generally
Les Evans Holiday Fund for Sick & Handicapped Children
Family Fund
Handicapped Children's Aid Committee
Jewels for Children
National Foundation for Incurably Sick Children
Research Education & Aid for Children with Potentially Terminal Illness

Convalescence
See Disability/convalescence/ill health generally

Cystic Fibrosis
Cystic Fibrosis Trust

Deafness
Hearing Dogs for the Deaf
National Deaf Children's Society

Deaf-blind
National Deaf-Blind League
Sense, the National Deaf-Blind & Rubella Association

Diabetes
British Diabetic Association

Disability/convalescence/ill health generally
Frederick Andrew Convalescent Trust
Percy Bilton Charity Limited
Margaret Champney Rest & Holiday Fund
Alfred de Rothschild Charity
Independent Living (1993) Fund
Invalids at Home
Jewish Care
Medical Aid Trust
Mobility Trust
Motability
Florence Nightingale Aid-in-Sickness Trust
Betty Rhodes Fund
Rosslyn Park Injury Trust Fund
Victoria Convalescent Trust Fund
Wireless for the Bedridden

Sickness and disability charities

Eczema
National Eczema Society

Epilepsy
British Epilepsy Association

Friedreich's Ataxia
Ataxia Group

Haemophilia
Haemophilia Society

Huntington's Disease
Huntington's Disease Association

Hydrocephalus
Association for Spina Bifida & Hydrocephalus (ASBAH)

Kidney Disease
British Kidney Patient Association

Leukaemia
Cancer & Leukaemia in Childhood Trust (CLIC)
Leukaemia Care Society

Liver disease
Ben Hardwick Memorial Fund *(for children)*

Mental health generally
Matthew Trust

Motor Neurone Disease
Motor Neurone Disease Association

Mucopolysaccharide Diseases
Society for Mucopolysaccharide Diseases

Multiple Sclerosis
Multiple Sclerosis Society of Great Britain

Muscular Dystrophy
Joseph Patrick Memorial Trust

Neurological illness
Chartered Society of Queen Square

Non-Hodkins Lymphoma
David Jenkinson Memorial Fund

Parkinson's Disease
Parkinson's Disease Society

Polio
British Polio Fellowship

Rheumatism
Ada Oliver Will Trust

Spina Bifida
Association for Spina Bifida & Hydrocephalus (ASBAH)

Spinal Muscular Atrophy
Jennifer Trust for Spinal Muscular Atrophy

Stroke illness
Stroke Association

Tuberculosis
Margaret de Sousa Deiro Fund

Action for Blind People

Eligibility: Registered blind or partially sighted people living in the UK who are in financial need.

Types of grants: Low income grants are made to boost income generally or meet specific bills eg. telephone and heating costs. These can be applied for each year. Special grants up to £400 are given for cookers, furniture, washing machines, refrigerators, computer equipment, beds, medical equipment, repairs/decoration, telephone installation, household bills, clothing, holidays and expenses related to children.

No grants towards nursing home fees and for conditions other than visual impairment (eg. supplying wheelchairs and hearing aids). A welfare benefit check is carried out on all new application forms and the referring agent advised if there appears to be any unclaimed entitlement to benefit.

Annual grant total: £500,000 in 3,000 grants to individuals.

Applications: On a form available from the correspondent. Applications can be submitted monthly through a social worker, citizen's advice bureau or other welfare agency.

Correspondent: The Grants Officer, 14-16 Verney Road, London SE16 3DZ (071-732 8771).

Other information: The organisation also has sheltered accommodation and employment, holiday hotels, and an information and advice service. A number of booklets and fact sheets are available from the address above.

Alzheimer's Disease Society

Eligibility: People with Alzheimer's disease and related disorders, and their carers, who live in England, Northern Ireland and Wales.

Types of grants: Generally one-off grants for much needed household items or to cover a specific aspect of respite care. Grants are restricted to £500 per application and £2,500 a month.

Annual grant total: In 1993, the trust had an income of £2.6 million; expenditure totalled £2.3 million. Grants ranging from £100 to £500 were given to individuals and totalled £35,000.

Applications: On a form available from the correspondent. Applications can be submitted at any time by a social worker, citizen's advice bureau or welfare agency on the individual's behalf.

Correspondent: Clive Evers, Assistant Director, Gordon House, 10 Greencoat Place, London SW1P 1PH (071-306 0606).

Sickness and disability charities

The Frederick Andrew Convalescent Trust

Eligibility: Broadly, professional women who are working or retired.

Types of grants: One-off grants for convalescence only. Grants range from £150 to £500.

Annual grant total: The trust's income is £50,000 to £60,000, with a total expenditure of £50,000. £40,000 of this is given to individuals.

Applications: On a form available from the correspondent. Applications are considered throughout the year and can be submitted by the individual or through a recognised referral agency (social worker, citizen's advice bureau or doctor etc.). Applications must be countersigned by a doctor.

Correspondent: C T Prichard, Andrew & Co, St Swithin's Square, Lincoln LN2 1HB (0522-512123).

Other information: This entry is repeated in the National and general charities section of the book.

Arthritis Care

Eligibility: People with arthritis (and occasionally their carers).

Types of grants: Help for people with arthritis (or their carers) to relieve the direct or indirect effects of the condition. Grants are one-off for £100 to £200 for single items, but can be larger in exceptional circumstances. There is a scholarship fund for people of all ages to continue or resume their studies. No grants are given towards holidays, bills or arrears, nursing home fees or private medical treatment.

Annual grant total: £126,000.

Applications: On a form available from the correspondent.

Correspondent: The Grants Officer, 18 Stephenson Way, London NW1 2HD (071-916 1500).

Other information: Arthritis Care also runs a number of hotels and self-catering units for members of the organisation.

The Association for Spina Bifida & Hydrocephalus (ASBAH)

Eligibility: People with spina bifida and/or hydrocephalus and their families or carers, living in England, Wales and Northern Ireland.

Types of grants: One-off grants towards the cost of wheelchairs, driving assessments, hospital visiting, household items (particularly helping young people to move into independent accommodation), holidays, car adaptations, funeral expenses and occasional "special items". No loans or help towards the cost of pilgrimages.

Annual grant total: In 1990/91, the association had assets of £954,500 and an income of almost £1.6 million. £53,000 was given in 200 to 250 relief-in-need grants.

Applications: In writing to the correspondent directly by the individual or by a social worker, citizen's advice bureau or similar third party. Applications should include details of any other agencies approached and the outcome; whether the individual has spina bifida, hydrocephalus or both; whether the family know ASBAH has been contacted if the referral is by a third party, and when the amount requested is large, whether any other funds have been raised and how much. Applications are considered throughout the year.

Correspondent: Andrew Russell, Executive Director, ASBAH House, 42 Park Road, Peterborough PE1 2UQ (0733-555988).

Other information: ASBAH provides advisory and other specialised services. There are local associations in most parts of the country.

Ataxia

Eligibility: Subscribed members of the Friedreich's Ataxia Group who have Friedreich's Ataxia or Cerebellar Ataxia, living in the UK.

Types of grants: One-off grants usually between £100 and £500 for welfare needs (eg. holidays, respite care, computers). Larger amounts are considered for more expensive items of equipment (eg. electric wheelchairs, scooters).

The group does not make loans, on-going payments of any kind or pay off debts.

Annual grant total: £30,000 to individuals in need.

Applications: On a form available from the correspondent. Applications can be submitted throughout the year directly by the individual, or by a welfare agency, parent, spouse or friend

Correspondent: Susan Grice, Services Co-ordinator or Chrissie Porter, Copse Edge, Thursley Road, Elstead, Godalming, Surrey GU8 6DJ (0252-702864).

Other information: The annual subscription fee is £10. The fund also finances medical research.

The Percy Bilton Charity Limited

Eligibility: 1. Elderly people.

2. Disabled/handicapped people: both children and adults whether in a family unit or living alone.

3. People suffering from a medical illness where treatment is required either by hospital or in cases of genuine illness being dealt with by a doctor. Guidance notes are available upon receipt of an sae.

Types of grants: Grants are usually between £20 and £1,000. Christmas hampers are also given.

The trust states: "Whilst the following list gives the more general requests for assistance, it is by no means complete. Therefore more unusual requests will be considered provided they do not fall outside current criteria given below:

Laundry equipment, transport, aids and adaptations, certain visiting expenses, the purchase of heating equipment, bedding, general items of clothing, telephone installations (not rental), refrigerators, furniture and furnishings, holidays (only if an applicant has not taken a holiday within the last two years)."

The trust will not consider any of the following:

- General cases of hardship falling outside the stated criteria above.
- Requests for foreign holidays or visits.
- Educational grants.
- Debts of any kind, including gas, electricity and rent arrears.
- Television and car licences.
- Nursing fees.
- Funeral expenses.
- Applications found to be requesting re-imbursements of any nature.
- Requests for school uniforms.
- Continuing donations over a specified period.

Annual grant total: About £140,000 in 800 grants together with about 3,500 Christmas hampers.

Applications: "Applications are received only from social workers in social services departments and hospitals.

Applications must include the following information before they can be processed:

- Full name and address of applicant, including names and ages of children.
- Status, whether married/divorced/single parent etc.
- Income of applicant.
- Brief history to present day.

Sickness and disability charities

- Requirement and an estimation of the cost.
- If any other charities or organisations have been approached please state.
- Please quote amounts received from statutory sources (ie. DSS) or other charitable funding within the past six months.
- Please state clearly the name of the authority to which the cheque should be made payable in the event of a grant being issued."

Correspondent: Mrs J A Beasley, Bilton House, Uxbridge Road, London W5 2TL (081-579 2829).

Other information: This entry is repeated in the National and general charities section of the book.

Body Positive

Eligibility: People with HIV/AIDS.

Types of grants: Grants of £50 to £100 per year to any one applicant, paid in two instalments. Grants are usually towards domestic appliances, household goods and bills. No grants are available for travel, holidays or funeral expenses.

Annual grant total: In 1993, about 1,000 people received £50 twice a year. Grants totalled £100,000.

Applications: In writing to the correspondent at any time including a letter from a doctor, social worker, carer or clinic stating (i) that the applicant is HIV positive and (ii) whether or not a previous application to the Small Grants Fund has been made. Applications can be submitted directly by the individual, or by a social worker, citizen's advice bureau or similar third party. Decisions can take up to 10 working days but can be quicker if all the necessary information is included; the fund may contact an applicant for further information. Grants are normally given in the form of cheques, usually made out to the creditor if issued for payment of a bill. If cash is required, the applicant should state this in the letter.

Correspondent: D Elavia, Small Grants Fund, 51b Philbeach Gardens, Earls Court, London SW5 9EB (071-835 1045).

The British Diabetic Association

Eligibility: Diabetics and their families in the UK especially, though not solely, where financial difficulties are the result of the diabetes.

Types of grants: One-off grants (up to £100) for welfare needs. "Most of the people we have helped are suffering form real poverty eg. an elderly couple, both diabetic and with additional disability due to diabetes, unable to pay fuel bills; and a number of deserted insulin dependent mothers with young children whose telephones have been cut off because of their inability to pay the bill." No grants for the cost of food or nursing home fees.

Annual grant total: In 1993, the trust gave grants totalling £28,000.

Applications: On a form available from the correspondent. Applications should be submitted by a social worker or other welfare agency or diabetes specialist nurse and are considered every week.

Correspondent: The Samaritan Fund Administrator, 10 Queen Anne Street, London W1M 0BD (071-323 1531).

Other information: The British Diabetic Association was founded in 1934 as the first self-help organisation in Britain. Current membership is 112,000 and there are nearly 400 voluntary groups throughout Britain. The association also spends a large amount, £220,000 in 1990, on group educational holidays for diabetic children, and £2 million on medical research.

The British Epilepsy Association

Eligibility: Children aged 7-16 years who have difficulty in controlling epilepsy.

Types of grants: One-off grants for children to have holidays away from their carers to provide respite care. Grants range between £300 and £500.

Annual grant total: £5,000 in 10 grants to individuals in 1991. The trust is unable to give any grants at all in 1994, but has not yet made any decision for 1995.

Applications: On a form available from the correspondent. Applications should be submitted by a social worker, citizen's advice bureau or other welfare agency, to be considered between January and June.

Correspondent: The Director of Information & Training, Anstey House, 40 Hanover Square, Leeds LS3 1BE (0532-439393).

The British Kidney Patient Association

Eligibility: Renal patients in Britain, whether on dialysis or not.

Types of grants: One-off and recurrent grants for all kinds of need caused by the condition, including fares for hospital visits.

Annual grant total: About 1,200 grants totalling £214,000, some of which were given to individuals for educational purposes.

Applications: Via a social worker or medical staff.

Correspondent: Mrs Elizabeth Ward, BKPA, Bordon, Hampshire GU35 9JZ (0420-472021/2).

Other information: The association also runs two holiday dialysis centres, in Jersey and Hampshire, where dialysis facilities are available free of charge.

The British Polio Fellowship

Eligibility: People disabled through poliomyelitis (polio) living in the UK and Eire.

Types of grants: One-off grants according to need including help with household items, holidays, home improvements, mobility and disablity aids. The fellowship aims to alleviate all kinds of need among polio sufferers, not merely financial ones.

Annual grant total: In 1992, almost £400,000 was given in nearly 3,000 grants.

Applications: On a form available from the correspondent. Applications should be submitted by the individual or by an appropriate third party on their behalf.

Correspondent: The Welfare Department, Bell Close, West End Road, Ruislip, Middlesex HA4 6LP (0895-639453).

Other information: The fellowship's Welfare Department also provides support through (a) information on a wide range of issues affecting people disabled through polio and (b) advocacy/liaison with other agencies. The fellowship has over 50 local branches or groups, its own holiday accommodation and runs indoor and outdoor sports championships.

The Brittle Bone Society

Eligibility: Children and others with oteogenesis imperfecta (brittle bones).

Types of grants: Grants for specialised equipment and other welfare needs.

Annual grant total: In 1992/93, the trust had an income of £216,000. Total expenditure was £170,000, with £2,500 given in 12 grants to individuals in need.

Applications: Applications should be in writing by the individual or through a recognised referral agency (social worker, citizen's advice bureau, doctor etc.).

Correspondent: Mrs Margaret Grant, Hon. Secretary, 112 City Road, Dundee DD2 2PW (0382-817771).

● **Sickness and disability charities**

The Cancer & Leukaemia in Childhood Trust (CLIC)

Eligibility: Children and young people up to the age of 22 with leukaemia or other forms of cancer, and families in financial need as a result of their child's illness.

Types of grants: One-off grants of £100 to £3,000 for transport to provide treatment, welfare and research. Grants can also be given for medical equipment and clinical support. No loans.

Annual grant total: In 1992, the trust had an income of £1.4 million. £37,500 was disbursed in 147 grants to individuals.

Applications: In writing by a social worker, health professional or similar third party on behalf of the individual. Application forms are available from the correspondent, but are not always required. Applications should include details of the total cost of the service or item and payment terms (one-off or instalments), clearly defined reasons for the application and receipts or costings where appropriate.

Correspondent: Felicity Hanley, Executive Assistant, 3 Nugent Hill, Cotham, Bristol BS6 5TD (0272-248844).

The Cancer Relief Macmillan Fund

Eligibility: Individuals over the age of 21 who are on low income and have cancer or are suffering from the effects of cancer.

Types of grants: Generally one-off grants between £50 and £500 for a wide range of goods or services including clothing, bedding, telephone installation, heating bills, fares for treatment and visits etc.. No grants for funeral expenses, medical equipment or structural work.

Annual grant total: In 1992, the fund had an income of £30 million. Over £3 million was given in 20,000 grants to individuals.

Applications: Through social workers, community nurses and other professional field workers on a form available from the correspondent. A medical certificate should be enclosed with the application.

Correspondent: The Manager, Patient Welfare Department, 15-19 Britten Street, London SW3 3TZ (071-351-7811).

Other information: Grants to patients are only one feature of the fund's work. Others include funding Macmillan Nurses (who provide advice and support on symptom control and pain relief), Macmillan buildings for in-patient and day care, and financing an education programme for professionals in palliative care. The fund also gives grants to four associated charities.

The Margaret Champney Rest & Holiday Fund

Eligibility: Adults in need of a recuperative holiday (especially those tired out by nursing or long hours of work, continued worry, or suffering from nervous breakdown), for whom a period of rest would be beneficial and who would be helped thereby to renew their own health and strength. There may be a preference for those whose exhaustion is due to their intensive care of others.

Types of grants: Generally one-off grants for the above.

Annual grant total: About 100 grants totalling £10,000.

Applications: Through a social worker, community nurse or other welfare agency. No forms are issued, but details of need, recommended solution and applicant's weekly income and expenditure must be given. A preliminary telephone call may be useful. Office hours are 9 am to 1 pm, 2 pm to 4 pm, Tuesdays to Fridays only.

Correspondent: The General Manager, 2a Church Walk, Colchester, Essex CO1 1NS (0206-573738).

Other information: This entry is included under the heading The Ogilvie Charities in the National and general charities section of the book.

The Chartered Society of Queen Square

Eligibility: People in need who have incurable neurological illness or needy indivudals who have such people in their care.

Types of grants: One-off grants (including payments for recuperative holidays). Grants range from £100 to £250 and have been given for debts, furniture, telephone installation etc. and towards computers, wheelchairs and vehicles.

Annual grant total: £128,000 in 1992, of which £76,000 was in pensions and £52,000 in one-off grants.

Applications: On a form available from the correspondent. Applications must be made through a social worker as the society will not deal directly with the individual. They are considered in February, May, August and November.

Correspondent: Mrs O G Rodger, Secretary, 11 Queen Court, Queen Square, London WC1N 3BA (071-837 4858).

Other information: The award of new pensions is temporarily suspended owing to current financial constraints.

Children's Leukeamia Appeal

Eligibility: Children in need who have Leukaemia (and other such life threatening diseases).

Types of grants: For the relief of poverty and distress of the children and their families. Grants can also be given towards holidays for the above and towards their education.

Annual grant total: In 1992, the trust had an income of £102,000. It is not known how much was given for the relief-in-need of individuals.

Applications: In writing to the correspondent.

Correspondent: Carole Tesrowski, Trustee/Treasurer, 979 Penistone Road, Sheffield, Yorkshire S6 2DH (0742-852209).

Crusaid

Eligibility: People with symptomatic HIV disease/AIDS.

Types of grants: Grants towards telephone bills (maximum £60) and other domestic bills (eg. gas, electricity etc.). Household equipment such as refrigerators and cookers are available on loan. Help also towards the costs of respite care and alternative treatments, where statutory funding is not available.

No grants for holiday expenses, air fares or funeral costs. The correspondent states: "people residing in the UK on student/tourist visas or those awaiting results of immigration/residency status who have no recourse to public funding are NOT eligible for support". The trust receives about 20 such enquiries each week.

Annual grant total: £260,000 in 150 to 200 grants a month in 1993.

Applications: Applications should be made through a social worker. Evidence of diagnosis will be required. All information is in the strictest confidence.

Correspondent: Jane Young, Hardship Administrator, 1 Walcott Street, London SW1P 2NG (071-834 7566).

The Cystic Fibrosis Trust

Eligibility: People with cystic fibrosis.

Types of grants: One-off grants for urgent needs where a grant will have an immediate effect. The trust is reluctant to make grants for significant debts or to meet on-going costs.

Annual grant total: No information available.

Applications: On a form available from the correspondent. Applications can be

Sickness and disability charities

submitted directly by the individual or through a social worker or other professional.

Correspondent: *FASS Co-ordinator England*, Alexandra House, 5 Blyth Road, Bromley, Kent BR1 3RS (081-464 7211).

FASS Co-ordinator Wales, Debra Winstanley, Cystic Fibrosis Trust, WCVA, Llys Ifor, Crescent Road, Caerphilly CF8 1XL (0228-852751).

FASS Co-ordinator Scotland, Joyce Hubbert, Cystic Fibrosis Trust, CAVOC House, 241 Brandon Street, Motherwell ML1 1RS (0698-275469).

The Alfred de Rothschild Charity

Eligibility: People unable to pay in full for medical treatment of a special nature.

Types of grants: Generally one-off grants; typically £300, usual maximum £500.

Annual grant total: £9,000 given in about 20 grants.

Applications: In writing to the correspondent.

Correspondent: The Administrator, 57 Elm Park Mansions, Park Walk, London SW10 0AP.

Other information: This entry is repeated in the National and general charities section of the book. This entry has not been confirmed by the trust, but the address is accurate according to the latest information on file at the Charity Commission.

The Margaret de Sousa Deiro Fund

Eligibility: Gentlewomen with tuberculosis or other diseases.

Types of grants: "Grants are restricted to extra comforts, warm clothing, nourishment, heating and convalescent holidays (these are only accepted through hospital social workers requesting convalescent holidays for patients). No grants for debts, hire-purchase, property alteration/repair/furnishing." Generally one-off grants between £100 and £300 depending on circumstances.

Annual grant total: About 200 grants totalling £48,000.

Applications: In writing from local authority/hospital social workers setting out full name, address, age, total income and the type of illness of the applicant, and the purpose of the grant.

Correspondent: The Secretaries, c/o Messrs Field Fisher Waterhouse, 41 Vine Street, London EC3N 2AA (071-481 4841).

Electronic Aids for the Blind

Eligibility: Children and adults who are registered blind or partially sighted.

Types of grants: Grants towards the cost of specialist electronic equipment for blind and visually impaired people where there are no statutory or personal resources available to meet the need.

Annual grant total: About 100 grants totalling £20,000 in 1991/92.

Applications: On a form available from the correspondent.

Correspondent: The Administrator, Suite 4b, 73-75 High Street, Chislehurst, Kent BR7 7AG (081-295 3636).

Other information: This trust is also involved with projects providing hi-tech equipment for establishments where a number of visually impaired users can benefit eg. schools, resource centres, rehabilitation centres.

The Les Evans Holiday Fund for Sick & Handicapped Children

Eligibility: Children up to the age of 15 with a chronic illness or severe physical disability.

Types of grants: The trust does not give cash grants, rather provides Disneyworld holidays.

Annual grant total: See below.

Applications: In writing to the correspondent. The trust states that owing to the "ravages of the recession our income has been severely affected, to such a point that we have no alternative but to temporarily suspend processing further applicants. We have in hand a recovery programme but it will take a considerable while before we are back on an even keel."

Correspondent: L N Evans, 12a High Street, Brentwood, Essex CM14 4AB.

Other information: This entry has not been confirmed by the trust, but the address is correct according to the latest information on file at the Charity Commission.

The Family Fund

Eligibility: Families with a very severely disabled child under 16 years of age.

Types of grants: "The object is to complement not replace existing services and resources in meeting certain special needs. Help given includes laundry equipment, family holidays, outings, driving lessons, clothing, bedding, recreational and other items." Also see Other information below.

Annual grant total: In 1993, the trust supported over 50,000 families, with grants totalling £14 million. About 7,500 families were new applicants. About two thirds of children on the fund's register have a problem with incontinence; a similar number received a grant for laundry equipment. The trust is currently in touch with over 65,000 families.

Applications: "Applications can be made by the parents of a very severely disabled child or, with parental consent, from professionals. They should give the child's full name, age, address and details of the disability and the request." See Other information below.

Correspondent: The Managing Director, PO Box 50, York YO1 2ZX (0904-621115).

Other information: "Independently administered by the Joseph Rowntree Foundation, the money for the fund comes from the government. Decisions and policy rest with the staff at York, but the fund's own visiting social workers throughout the UK visit families to discuss their needs, obtain the information necessary, establish eligibility and, if possible, make a grant.

"For a successful application it must be shown that the child is very severely disabled within the definitions laid down by the fund's medical advisers; next that the family's economic circumstances justify help from the fund, and lastly that the request is within the scope of the fund's guidelines.

"Decisions about the severity of disablement are based on a detailed description of the child's functioning in all areas and, if necessary, on a report from the doctor most familiar with the child's problems.

"A statement of income is not requested, but each grant has to be justified in the light of the family's circumstances. The fund would not expect to help parents with a high income who could reasonably be expected to be able to afford the modest needs with which the fund is concerned.

"The help given relates to the basic needs posed by the child's disability and not available from existing services: laundry equipment to cope with incontinence; family holidays to relieve the stress; outings when holidays prove too difficult to face; driving lessons, if the mother would then have access to a car; clothing and bedding when the disablement causes extra wear and tear; recreational equipment if justified by the disability; a fridge/freezer to cope with diet problems arising from the disability - and any other items."

Sickness and disability charities

Paul Flynn Memorial Fund

Eligibility: People who have hearing difficulties and who have HIV/AIDS.

Types of grants: Help with installing telephone lines with a minicom facility. Minicoms and textphones are also loaned to the immediate family. Grants are given for chairlifts, help with heating/telephone bills, breaks away from home, travel to support groups, childcare for mothers with HIV/AIDS and hearing difficulties. Grants do not exceed £300 and are not recurrent. No grants to people with hearing difficulties who do not have HIV/AIDS, or towards communication support services or course fees.

Annual grant total: In 1992, the trust had assets of £2,500 and an income of £1,400. Four relief-in-need grants of £300 were given to individuals.

Applications: In writing to the correspondent at any time, either submitted directly by the individual or through social services departments, HIV/AIDS organisations, a member of the AIDS Ahead Volunteer Group or another organisation for people with hearing difficulties.

Correspondent: Peter Jackson, British Deaf Association, Health Promotion Services, Unit 17, Macon Court, Herald Drive, Crewe, Cheshire CW1 1EA (0270-250736).

Other information: The trust is linked with the British Deaf Association.

The Gardner's Trust for the Blind

Eligibility: Registered blind or partially sighted people in need who live in England or Wales.

Types of grants: Pensions, maintenance and training grants to meet specific needs. No grants for holidays, residential or nursing home fees or for loan repayments.

Annual grant total: In 1993, the trust gave 175 one-off grants (maximum of £300, but generally £200 to £250) totalling nearly £32,000. About 60% of the grants were given for educational purposes. Pensions of £5 a week were paid quarterly to 139 people and totalled about £34,000.

Applications: On a form available from the correspondent. Applications should be submitted by a social worker, citizen's advice bureau or other welfare agency. They are considered in March, June, September and December.

Correspondent: B D Essex, Secretary, Suite 118, Canada House, 272 Field End Road, Eastcote, Middlesex HA4 9NA (081-866 4400).

The Guide Dogs for the Blind Association

Eligibility: Blind people aged 16 or over who normally live in the UK and are fit enough to use and care for a dog.

Types of grants: The association provides guide dogs to blind people at a nominal charge of 50p to the recipient. The recipient will also be invited to spend three to four weeks at a training centre to learn to handle the guide dog safely and effectively. Some training can be carried out in the applicant's home area in special circumstances. The association offers a feeding allowance, pays vet's bills and can sometimes help with any other costs associated with owning a guide dog (eg. providing a fenced run etc.).

Annual grant total: 700 to 800 dogs a year (including dogs for new applicants and as replacements).

Applications: Application forms are available from GDBA regional training centres or via the address below and can be completed by the individual or by a third party on their behalf. Medical and social worker's reports will also be requested before an applicant can be informally interviewed to confirm his or her suitability for training.

Correspondent: Hillfields, Burghfield, Reading, Berkshire RG7 3YG (0734-835555).

Other information: The association can also offer Orientation and Mobility training, especially where this may lead to guide dog ownership. A leaflet "Independence" is available in large print, braille and tape versions from regional centres or the above address. Also available is a cassette tape "Applying for a Guide Dog", a 30 minute radio style programme about getting and living with a guide dog.

The Haemophilia Society

Eligibility: People with haemophilia.

Types of grants: One-off grants, average £150, up to a maximum of £700. Grants have been given for telephone installation (not on-going costs), household items such as bed linen, shoes and occasionally holidays, but can be given for any need arising from haemophilia.

Annual grant total: About 100 grants totalling about £19,000.

Applications: On a form available from the correspondent. Applications should be submitted by a representative from a haemophilia centre.

Correspondent: Susan Archer, Registrar, 123 Westminster Bridge Road, London SE1 7HR (071-928 2020).

The Handicapped Children's Aid Committee

Eligibility: Disabled children, under 19, who live in London and the home counties.

Types of grants: The committee provides equipment or clothing etc. but NOT cash grants.

Annual grant total: About £300,000.

Applications: To the correspondent via a social worker or medical staff. Applications can be made direct by individuals, but must be backed up with medical recommendations.

Correspondent: J S Bonn, 15 Phillimore Gardens, London NW10 3LL (071-286 4214).

Other information: The committee supplies equipment etc. for schools, hospitals and clubs for disabled children, as well as for individuals. Please note that in no case does the committee make any grants in cash. All equipment, clothing etc. is purchased by the committee and supplied by them to the recipient.

The Ben Hardwick Memorial Fund

Eligibility: Children under the age of 18 who have primary liver disease.

Types of grants: One-off grants between £50 and £200 for low income families to help with costs which are the direct result of the child's illness, such as hospital travelling costs or telephone bills.

Annual grant total: Varies according to donations; in 1993, 30 relief-in-need grants totalled £6,500.

Applications: By letter to the correspondent with brief details of family circumstances. Applications should be submitted by a social worker, citizen's advice bureau or other welfare agency, and will be considered at any time.

Correspondent: Mrs Anne Auber, 12 Nassau Road, Barnes, London SW13 9QE (081-741 8499).

Hearing Dogs for the Deaf

Eligibility: 1. People over the age of 18 who have a severe, profound or total hearing loss.

2. Where there is a real need for help with sounds and the person lives alone or spends a lot of time alone or with another deaf or disabled person(s).

3. No other dogs live in the house.

4. There is a genuine like of dogs and the dog will be properly cared for both physically and financially which includes

providing regular exercise and grooming, suitable food and medical care.

There may be exceptions to some of these guidelines and if in doubt contact should be made with the training centre, for example;

Where there is an elderly pet dog an application for a hearing dog may still be persued.

If the person works, sometimes arrangements can be made for the dog to accompany them.

Where a person has another disability in addition to being deaf such as partial sight or the need for a wheelchair they can still apply for a hearing dog.

Types of grants: The charity provides dogs trained to respond to household sounds eg. a telephone, a baby crying, or a doorbell. The dog alerts the owner by touch and leads them to the source of the sound. Dogs are provided free of charge to deaf recipients who also get some free veterinary services, help with feeding costs and transport concessions for their dog. Anyone who is given a dog will receive a week residential training at one of the purpose built training centres in Oxfordshire or Yorkshire and will receive follow up visits and support in the home.

Annual grant total: Over 55 dogs a year are currently being trained.

Applications: On a form available from the correspondent. Applications are considered throughout the year, and can be submitted directly by the individual or by a social worker, hearing therapist, citizen's advice bureau or other welfare agency.

Correspondent: The Director General, Training Centre, London Road (A 40), Lewknor, Oxford OX9 5RY (0844-353898).

The Terrence Higgins Trust (Trust No 1 Fund)

Eligibility: People with HIV/AIDS, who face difficulty or extra expenditure because of their HIV status.

Types of grants: One-off grants, ranging from £50 to £350, for items or services which cannot reasonably be afforded on current income, are not available from other sources and will improve the quality of life. Examples include gas, electricity, telephone and water bill payments, clothing, beds and bedding and respite care. Electrical items such as a fridge or fridge/freezer, washing machine, tumble dryer or microwave may be provided on a loan basis.

No grants for funerals, travel outside the UK, council tax or mortgage or rent arrears.

Annual grant total: £180,000 in 1,700 grants.

Applications: On an application form to be submitted by a social worker, welfare rights worker, health adviser or buddy. A diagnosis letter from a consultant or doctor should be enclosed.

Correspondent: Paul Funning, 52-54 Grays Inn Road, London WC1X 8JU (071-831 0330).

The Huntington's Disease Association

Eligibility: People with Huntington's disease, their immediate families and those at risk, who live in England or Wales.

Types of grants: One-off grants only, typically up to £300, although each application is considered on merit. Recent grants have been for clothing, furniture, domestic equipment (eg. washing machines and cookers), telephone installation, respite care and holidays, car repairs and driving lessons. No grants towards nursing home or day care fees, courses, rent or season tickets. No loans.

Annual grant total: 50 grants totalling £8,800 in 1990/91.

Applications: On a form available from the correspondent. Applications should be submitted by a social worker, citizen's advice bureau or other welfare agency, although application can be made directly by the individual or by a friend, teacher or voluntary worker. Requests are processed monthly although urgent cases will be considered as soon as possible.

Correspondent: Margaret Catling, Manager of Family Services, 108 Battersea High Street, London SW11 3HP (071-223 7000).

The Independent Living (1993) Fund

Eligibility: People between 16 and 65 years of age currently receiving the maximum Disability Living Allowance care component rate. Applicants must not have savings over £8,000 and should be living alone or with another person who is unable to provide sufficient care, or be planning to move out of residential care.

Types of grants: Payments are up to £300, provided the local authority firstly agrees to provide a minimum of £200 worth of services per week. They are towards the cost of buying in care to enable the applicant to continue living at home. Help is for people with ongoing needs, not short-term illness. Beneficiaries also have to be capable of living independently in the community for at least six months.

Annual grant total: 1993/94 was the 1993 Fund's first year of operation. The budget was £4 million. Only about £500,000 of this was spent. The remaining money could not be held over for the following year, so £3.5 million was returned to the Treasury. The underspend appears to be due to much tougher new criteria for applicants and local authorities. Local authorities have to provide the applicant with at least £200 worth of services each week; many social service departments appear to find this too high. Almost half of the country's local authorities have not made any applications to the fund. The budget for 1994/95 will be £11 million for new claimants and on-going support for previous beneficiaries. The ILF Director predicts that the underspend will not be repeated. The average payment by the fund is about £170 per person per week.

Applications: On a form available from the local authority social work department or the correspondent. Applicants are visited at home by one of the fund's social workers together with the local authority social worker to agree a joint care package to a maximum level of £500 per week.

Correspondent: ILF (1993), PO Box 183, Nottingham NG8 3RD (0602-290423).

Other information: The old Independent Living Fund has now been split into two separate funds: (i) the Independent Living (extension) Fund which continues to administer payments to the 21,500 existing clients. No new names can be added to this list, and (ii) the Independent Living (1993) Fund which deals with all new claimants since 1993. In the previous entry of this Guide we stated: "Over 12,000 grants are given annually from the fund's income awarded by the government. There will be £97 million available for disbursement in 1992/93, before the responsibility for new applicants is handed over to local authorities in April 1993".

Invalids at Home

Eligibility: People who are severely ill or permanently disabled and who live at home or who wish to do so. Preference to those with very severe disabilities and to those living on or just above Income Support level, or on very low incomes.

Types of grants: One-off grants to help with specific additional costs of living at home with a disability, including equipment and emergencies. Grants range between £25 and £400 and priority is given for items directly related to needs arising from the disability or illness such as heating bills, wheelchairs and stair lifts. The trust can only make a grant if

Sickness and disability charities

adequate statutory provision is not available. No grants for medical treatment. Awards are seldom made for telephone rental, televisions or holidays and only one grant per person will be given in any one year. No grants to groups of people, organisations or anyone living in institutional care.

Annual grant total: In 1992/93, the trust had an income of £152,000. Although almost 1,000 grants were given totalling £118,000; about 400 applicants had to be refused, mainly due to lack of funds.

Applications: Applications by letter should be made by a social worker, occupational therapist, health visitor or similar professional person, or voluntary agency. Applications are considered throughout the year.

Correspondent: Mrs S E Lomas, 17 Lapstone Gardens, Kenton, Harrow HA3 0EB (081-907 1706).

Other information: In their annual report the trustees state: "increasing numbers of requests for help are being channelled to the voluntary sector and unfortunately although Invalids at Home has increased its income it has not been able to meet this growing need thus more and more applications are having to be turned down".

The David Jenkinson Memorial Fund

Eligibility: Children under 21, who are suffering from non-Hodgkins lymphoma disease, and their families who are in need. Children suffering from any other form of cancerous disease may be helped if there is no assistance available from other organisations.

Types of grants: Usually one-off grants towards mortgage arrears or outstanding bills etc.. Recuperative holidays are also provided for the child and family.

Annual grant total: In 1992/93, the trust had an income of £30,000, some of which is used for research or provision of computers to hospitals.

Applications: In writing to the correspondent, including financial information and details of the illness.

Correspondent: D Jenkinson, General Secretary, 173 Hainault Road, Romford, Essex RM5 3DD (0708-750981).

The Jennifer Trust for Spinal Muscular Atrophy

Eligibility: People with spinal muscular atrophy.

Types of grants: One-off grants ranging from £50 to £1,000. Grants have been given towards equipment to facilitate independent living such as electric wheelchairs, seating, bathing aids and electric beds. Grants are also given for the maintenance service/repair of such equipment, funeral costs and holidays in the UK.

Annual grant total: In 1992, the trust had an income of £94,000. Grants to 20 individuals totalled £11,700. The trust also supports research into spinal muscular atrophy.

Applications: On a form available from the correspondent, together with a supporting letter from an involved professional. Applications can be submitted directly by the individual, through a social worker, citizen's advice bureau, other welfare agency or parent/guardian. They are considered in February, May, August and November.

Correspondent: Mrs Anita Macaulay, Director, 11 Ash Tree Close, Wellesbourne, Warwick CV35 9SA (0789-842377).

Jewels for Children

Eligibility: Individual severely disabled or seriously ill children up to the age of 18 living in the UK.

Types of grants: One-off grants for special equipment or modest financial help for any item of direct benefit to children for whom such help is not available elsewhere. Grants range between £50 and £500.

Annual grant total: Depends on donations of jewellery, which are auctioned to raise funds for the charity. In 1993, the trust's income was £9,500 of which over £5,000 was given in around 25 grants to individuals. The trust gives half its income each year to ChildLine.

Applications: By letter to the correspondent through a social worker, citizen's advice bureau or other welfare agency,

Correspondent: Mrs Anne Auber, 12 Nassau Road, Barnes, London SW13 9QE (081-741 8499).

Jewish AIDS Trust

Eligibility: Jewish people with HIV/AIDS.

Types of grants: One-off grants towards gas, electricity, television licences and other household bills. Respite care can ONLY be paid direct to recognised respite centres eg. Bethany. Grants cannot be given for rent or mortgage arrears, debt and loan repayments, credit card repayments and luxury items. The trust cannot give cash loans or emergency cash payments.

Annual grant total: No information available.

Applications: Forms available from the correspondent. All referrals must be through a professional person ie. social worker, health visitor etc; buddies or befrienders are not considered appropriate. A referral must accompany every application and be on headed paper including client's name, date of birth, detailed breakdown of weekly income, details and nature of request, name, position and signature of referrer and details of whom the cheque should be made payable to. First applications require symptomatic proof of diagnosis from the applicant's doctor.

Correspondent: Rosalind Collin, HIV Education Unit, Colindale Hospital, Colindale Avenue, London NW9 5HG (081-200 0369).

Jewish Care

Eligibility: Registered blind or partially sighted Jewish people plus severely physically disabled Jewish people under pensionable age.

Types of grants: Jewish Care (includes the former Jewish Welfare Board, Jewish Blind Society and the Jewish Home and Hospital at Tottenham) is the largest Jewish social work agency, providing a range of services, both domiciliary and residential. Financial assistance is not a normal part of the board's work, though some such expenditures are inevitably associated with its social work service. (See also the Egerton Fund at the same address.) One-off grants only to alleviate hardship (eg. a gadget or equipment to improve independence).

Annual grant total: "Small".

Applications: In writing to the correspondent either direct by the individual or through a social worker.

Correspondent: The Director of Social Services, 221 Golders Green Road, London NW11 9DQ (081-458 3282).

Other information: This entry is repeated in the National and general charities section of the book.

The Leukaemia Care Society

Eligibility: People with leukaemia and allied blood disorders.

Types of grants: One-off and recurrent grants according to need. The trust also runs a holiday scheme.

Annual grant total: £90,000 in 1990/91, the most up-to-date information provided by the society.

Sickness and disability charities

Applications: In writing to the correspondent.

Correspondent: The Director, 14 Kingfisher Court, Venny Bridge, Pinhoe, Exeter, Devon EX4 8JN (0392-464848).

The Macfarlane Trust

Eligibility: People with haemophilia who have been infected with HIV through blood products, and their dependants. No other people are eligible. The trust is in contact with those known to have haemophilia and to be HIV positive through infected blood products, and therefore any further eligibility to register with the trust seems unlikely.

Annual grant total: About £2.1 million.

Applications: Procedures will be notified to people registering with the trust.

Correspondent: The Administrator, PO Box 627, London SW1H 0QG (071-233 0342).

The Matthew Trust

Eligibility: Patients and former patients at special hospitals: mentally ill people in prisons and those discharged; victims of aggression; one parent families and those who are socially disadvantaged with mental health problems; people who are mentally ill generally. There is a preference for those who have been treated under a Mental Health Act Order.

Types of grants: (a) *For patients from special hospitals:* financial assistance with rehabilitation, legal and taxation advice, medical/psychiatric specialist counselling, clothing for work purposes, private fees for educational and professional courses, equipment for accommodation.

(b) *For patients in special hospitals and regional secure units and prisoners with mental health conditions:* assistance with fees for educational courses; where appropriate, legal assistance for mental health review tribunals and independent psychiatric reports; financial assistance to families of patients and prisoners and counselling.

(c) *For victims of violent crimes:* payment for private counselling sessions, installation of telephones, installation of security equipment to the home, cash grants.

(d) *Individuals who are socially disadvantaged with mental health problems:* grants to assist financial difficulties given mainly to keep the family in tact, plus counselling, liaison with local authorities and government departments.

Grants range from £50 to £1,000.

Annual grant total: In 1992/93, the trust had an income of £94,000, of which 12% to 15% (about £12,000) is given in grants. About 140 grants of £20 to £700 were distributed.

Applications: On a form available from the correspondent submitted through a social worker, citizen's advice bureau or other probation service, mental health teams; also from other voluntary organisations and statutory bodies including a declaration that all other sources have been exhausted first.

Correspondent: Peter Thompson, Director, PO Box 604, London SW6 3AG (071-736 5976)(FAX 071-731 6961).

The Medical Aid Trust

Eligibility: See below.

Types of grants: Grants for people (mainly children) who need medical or hospital treatment but are unable to obtain the specialised therapy through the NHS. The vast majority of people helped are from outside the UK. The trust pays the hospital or medical staff directly.

Annual grant total: About £10,000.

Applications: In writing to the correspondent. Applications must include a referral letter from a consultant physician or surgeon.

Correspondent: J J Rosner, 3 Rookwood Road, London N16 6SP (081-802 0700).

Other information: The correspondent states: "We receive about 50 letters a week, 90% of which are totally inappropriate - most are for relief in need or for complementary medicine, which are not supported".

Mobility Trust

Eligibility: See below.

Types of grants: The trust will consider any person with any disability in the UK. It helps physically or mentally disabled people to obtain greater mobility of mind or body. It does this by "loaning in perpetuity, or until such time as the recipient has no further use for it, a piece of equipment, aid or technological device". See Applications below.

No cash is given, the trust purchases equipment on behalf of individuals such as wheelchairs (powered, sports etc.), scooters, communication equipment such as computers, software, printers, voice synthesisers etc. and very occasionally chair lifts.

No help for people on mobility allowance unless it is being used for a motor vehicle and they need some specialist equipment such as a wheelchair. No Motability deposits - applicant should use their own local or specialist charity for this.

Annual grant total: This figure varies according to the number of applicants and the trust's success in fundraising. In 1992/93, the trust's income was £235,000, of which about £200,000 was spent on equipment such as mobility aids and communication devices, insurance and repairs to equipment.

Applications: *Powered/manual wheelchairs:* No application is considered without an assessment from an occupational therapist or physiotherapist as to the best type of chair, make, model, price and adaptations (if any). If an applicant is in receipt of mobility allowance they should, unless otherwise stated, apply to Motability (see separate entry).

Computers/communication aids: One of the trust's consultants visits any potential applicant and then submits a report.

The trust insures any equipment loaned for the first year against fire, theft or accident and in the second year expects the recipient to take over and to include parts in the insurance.

All applications must be countersigned by a social worker or responsible professional.

Correspondent: Peter Mahon, Director, 4 Hughes Mews, 143a Chatham Road, London SW11 6HJ (071-924 3597 [24 hour answerphone]).

Other information: "All staff are voluntary, funding is raised from the public and companies we receive no government funding whatsoever." The trust has an information service and runs seminars and workshops throughout the country on issues around disability.

Motability

Eligibility: Disabled people receiving the higher rate mobility component of the Disability Living Allowance or the War Pensioner's Mobility Supplement.

Types of grants: Motability provides cars and powered wheelchairs to the above at low cost (through favourable terms negotiated with the manufacturers, banks and insurance companies) either on hire or hire purchase. It has its own charitable fund and Mobility Equipment Fund to help those who cannot afford the car or the adaptations they need.

Annual grant total: Over 4,000 grants totalling about £4,000,000 in 1992/93.

Applications: On a form available from the correspondent.

Correspondent: The Grants Section, Gate House, Westgate, Harlow, Essex CM20 1HR (0279-635666).

Sickness and disability charities

The Motor Neurone Disease Association

Eligibility: People with motor neurone disease, living in the UK.

Types of grants: Limited financial assistance to meet care needs of beneficiaries, including contributions towards nursing home fees and top-up grants for equipment.

Annual grant total: No information available.

Applications: Forms available from the correspondent. Forms should be submitted by a MNDA Regional Care Adviser.

Correspondent: Philip Wood, PO Box 246, Northampton NN1 2PR (0604-250505).

The Multiple Sclerosis Society of Great Britain

Eligibility: People with multiple sclerosis and their families living in the UK.

Types of grants: Grants for "Any legitimate expenditure where funding is not available from statutory sources and where need can be demonstrated". One-off grants up to £500 at the Welfare Administrator's discretion, and up to £2,000 on the decision of the Welfare Committee. Grants are typically for mobility equipment, respite care, home alterations, special equipment and furniture.

No grants for holidays, education, insurance, mortgage/rent or legal costs.

Annual grant total: About 1,000 grants totalling £600,000 from headquarters.

Applications: Through local branches of the society (addresses in the local telephone book) or the correspondent below. Supporting documentation to prove the legitimacy of the expenditure should be included from a social worker, health professional or occupational therapist.

Correspondent: Welfare Grants Officer, 25 Effie Road, Fulham, London SW6 1EE (071-736 6267).

Other information: "The above relates only to HQ expenditure; there are 350 branches who have their own funds and make their own grants. HQ can only consider applications which have the recommendation of the local branch and assessments are made locally in the first instance. Where possible applications should be made to these local branches. HQ funds are available as a 'top up' for such branch grants."

The National Deaf Children's Society

Eligibility: Deaf children and their families.

Types of grants: The society has a children's equipment fund and a Blue Peter Lend An Aid Service for deaf children. Holiday and welfare grants are also given and there is a scholarship fund for teachers of deaf children. Training and research grants for students and/or professionals training or working with deaf children are available occasionally.

Annual grant total: 200 grants totalling about £150,000.

Applications: Application forms are available but not necessary, except for research grants. Support from social workers, teachers of deaf people, health visitors etc. is usually necessary.

Correspondent: The Family Services Officer, 24 Wakefield Road, Rothwell Haigh, Leeds LS26 0SF (0532-823458 voice and text).

The National Deaf-Blind League

Eligibility: Deaf-blind people in need who live in the UK.

Types of grants: One-off grants according to need including towards holidays, limited Christmas grants and for specialist equipment.

Annual grant total: In 1993, the trust had assets of £785,000, generating an income of £338,000. Grants were given to 23 individuals and totalled £700.

Applications: In writing to the correspondent stating what the grant is for. Applications can be submitted by the individual or through a recognised referral agency (social worker, citizen's advice bureau or doctor etc.) and are considered each month.

Correspondent: The Chief Executive, 18 Rainbow Court, Paston Ridings, Peterborough PE4 7UP (0733-573511).

The National Eczema Society

Eligibility: People with eczema and their families.

Types of grants: One-off grants up to £150 towards buying a washing machine, cotton bedding, cotton clothing or shoes.

Annual grant total: £1,500 allocated to the Welfare Fund for 1994. Up to 30 grants could be given.

Applications: Applications must be made through a social worker, health visitor or doctor to whom the cheque is paid. For further information and an application form send a large sae.

Correspondent: Mrs Christina Funnell, 4 Tavistock Place, London WC1H 9RA (071-388 4097).

Other information: The society has a network of local contacts and provides up-to-date information on all aspects of eczema, its management and treatment. Together with the National Asthma Campaign NES organises holidays for children, teenagers and young adults with eczema, asthma or both.

The National Foundation for Incurably Sick Children

Eligibility: See below.

Types of grants: The trust's objects include: "Relief of financial distress of parents of children with terminal or incurable diseases or of deceased children".

Annual grant total: No information available.

Applications: In writing to the correspondent.

Correspondent: Miss A Entwhistle, Trustee, 100 West Hill, London SW15 2UT.

Other information: This entry has not been confirmed by the trust, but is accurate according to the latest information on file at the Charity Commission.

The Florence Nightingale Aid-in-Sickness Trust

Eligibility: People who are sick, convalescent, disabled or infirm.

Types of grants: One-off grants according to need; grants have ranged from a few pounds to over £1,000. Grants are NOT given for computers, debts, holidays or powered wheelchairs, motor cars or adaptations.

Annual grant total: 1,500 grants totalling £200,000 in 1992/93.

Applications: By letter from a qualified third party, eg. social worker, occupational therapist, doctor.

Correspondent: The Administrator, 5 Grosvenor Crescent, London SW1X 7EH (071-235 2369).

The Ada Oliver Will Trust

Eligibility: People with cancer or rheumatism.

Types of grants: Monthly and one-off grants up to £150 for any kind of need, including settling rent arrears, nursing

Sickness and disability charities

home fees where there is a shortfall, and necessities. No grants towards holidays.

Annual grant total: In 1993, £5,400 was given in 14 monthly grants all to existing beneficiaries. No new beneficiaries have been added to the list for a number of years.

Applications: On a form available from the correspondent and including details of income, family and dependants. Applications can be submitted throughout the year by a social worker, citizen's advice bureau or other welfare agency on behalf of the individual.

Correspondent: Marshalls Solicitors, 102 High Street, Godalming, Surrey GU7 1DS (0483-416101).

The Parkinson's Disease Society

Eligibility: People with Parkinson's disease.

Types of grants: One-off grants only, up to a usual maximum of £250. Grants are towards medical equipment, household items, holidays, telephones, recliner chairs etc..

Annual grant total: In 1993, the trust had a distributable income (for individuals) of £20,000, all of which was given in grants to 500 individuals.

Applications: On a form available from the correspondent. Applications can be submitted by the individual or through a recognised referral agency (social worker, citizen's advice bureau or doctor etc.) and are considered throughout the year. Where possible applicants will be visited by the society.

Correspondent: Miss Evelyn Goodchild, 22 Upper Woburn Place, London WC1H 0RA (071-383 3513 or 0485-600499).

The Joseph Patrick Memorial Trust

Eligibility: People with muscular dystrophy or associated neuromuscular conditions.

Types of grants: Grants are provided towards the cost of equipment not provided by statutory bodies.

No recurrent grants, loans or help with the purchase of vehicles.

Annual grant total: In 1992, the trust had assets of £616,000 and an income of £352,000. Total expenditure was £423,000, of which £145,000 was given in grants to individuals.

Applications: On a form available from the correspondent. Applications can be submitted by the individual or through a recognised referral agency (social worker, citizen's advice bureau, muscular dystrophy group, doctor, occupational therapist, physiotherapist etc.) and are considered monthly.

Correspondent: The Grants Administrator, 7-11 Prescott Place, London SW4 6BS (071-720 8055).

Other information: As all administrative costs are paid by a private family trust, all donations to the Welfare Grants Trust are available in full to applicants.

Positively Partners & Positively Children

Eligibility: Children aged 18 or under who are HIV positive.

Types of grants: Grants of £50 per child are specifically for the child's needs and are given towards expenses for which grants are unavailable elsewhere, such as Christmas presents, holidays etc..

Annual grant total: We were unable to obtain financial details, but the correspondent stated: "The fund is often low as it is reliant on fundraising".

Applications: In writing to the correspondent enclosing a letter of diagnosis and the child's birth certificate.

Correspondent: Maggie Woonton/Maureen Borras, Jan Rebane Centre, 14 Thornton Street, London SW9 0BL (071-738 7333).

The Queen Alexandra Sanatorium Fund & Allied Funds

Eligibility: Children with asthma receiving treatment in Alpine climates.

Types of grants: Grants for board, lodging, medical treatment and other needs.

Annual grant total: The funds had an income of £19,000 in 1992.

Applications: In writing to the correspondent.

Correspondent: The Secretary, c/o The Stroke Association, CHSA House, Whitecross Street, London EC1Y 8JJ (071-490 7999).

Research Education & Aid for Children with Potentially Terminal Illness

Eligibility: Children with potentially terminal illnesses.

Types of grants: One-off or recurrent grants according to need. Grants can be for equipment/facilities to help with the care and treatment of the children, and to help with funeral costs.

Annual grant total: No information available.

Applications: In writing to the correspondent.

Correspondent: REACT, 73 Whitehall Park Road, Chiswick, London W4 3NB (081-995 8188).

The Betty Rhodes Fund

Eligibility: People in need who are sick, disabled or infirm, who require care (nursing, housekeeping, cooking or otherwise) in their own home, and/or equipment necessitated by their condition.

Types of grants: Mainly one-off grants. 44 grants were given in 1992, up to a maximum of £300. Grants include provision of care while awaiting award of DSS provision, towards respite for a carer and towards equipment to enable care to be given. No grants for those in residential care away from their own home.

Annual grant total: In 1992, the trust had an income of £15,000. Grants to individuals totalled £14,000.

Applications: In writing to the correspondent. Applications must be made by a social worker, care manager or other person who is working with the client. They are considered at any time and decisions about grants can be made quickly, usually within a few days.

Correspondent: Mrs E Burnham, Secretary, 36 Manor Way, Worcester Park, Surrey KT4 7PH.

The Rosslyn Park Injury Trust Fund

Eligibility: People who are sick or disabled through a sports injury (amateur sports).

Types of grants: One-off grants according to need.

Annual grant total: About £5,000.

Applications: In writing to the correspondent.

Correspondent: Brian St J C Carr, Trustee, 6 Dyers Buildings, Holborn, London EC1N 2JT (071-831 6981).

The Royal Blind Pension Society of the UK

Eligibility: Registered blind and partially sighted people.

Types of grants: Pensions of £160 a year, paid in quarterly instalments. An

Sickness and disability charities

applicant should have a maximum disposable income of £70 per person in the household a week ie. money available after rent/mortgage and council tax has been paid.

Annual grant total: About £40,000 to around 300 pensioners.

Applications: On a form available from the correspondent. Applications should be submitted by a social worker, citizen's advice bureau or similar welfare agency on the individual's behalf. They are considered each month.

Correspondent: Mrs Jackie Low, 14-16 Verney Road, London SE16 3DZ (071-732 8771).

Royal National Institute for the Blind

Eligibility: Registered blind and partially sighted people in exceptional need.

Types of grants: One-off and recurrent grants according to need. Grants average about £250. No grants for recreational needs, nursing home fees, the costs of medical treatment, telephone installation or repeatedly accruing debts.

Annual grant total: £80,000 to individuals in need.

Applications: Normally through an officer of the local authority social services department or local voluntary society. Application forms available from the correspondent.

Correspondent: The Grants & Information Officer, 224 Great Portland Street, London W1N 6AA (071-388 1266).

Other information: The RNIB provides over 60 services for blind and partially sighted people. Financial and other assistance is also available from the wide range of local charities for blind people, almost all of which work in close co-operation with the RNIB.

The Malcolm Sargent Cancer Fund for Children

Eligibility: Young people living in the UK up to the age of 21 who have cancer, leukaemia or Hodgkin's disease.

Types of grants: One-off and recurrent grants for travel expenses, heating bills, holidays, clothing, computers, toys, hobbies, water rates, community charge, mortgage or rent and furniture. No grants for research and treatment costs or headstones or memorials.

Annual grant total: In 1992/93, £1,057,000 was given in grants to children. This was broken down geographically as follows:

England	£921,500
Scotland	£75,100
Northern Ireland	£32,700
Channel Islands	£4,300

Applications: On a form available from the correspondent. Applications can be submitted at any time by the individual or by a third party on their behalf such as a medical social worker, health visitor or doctor. The trust funds 45 social workers based at various hospitals throughout the country (list available from the correspondent). Most applications come through these social workers working with the families.

Correspondent: Miss Sylvia Darley, General Administrator, 14 Abingdon Road, London W8 6AF (071-937 4548).

Other information: The trust also runs two holiday homes in Essex and Ayrshire and are hoping for a third.

Sense, the National Deaf-Blind & Rubella Association

Eligibility: People who are deaf-blind, deaf or blind with another disability, and their families.

Types of grants: One-off emergency grants only, in exceptional circumstances. Grants are generally £50.

Annual grant total: £1,000.

Applications: In writing to the correspondent.

Correspondent: Derry Newton, Services Department, 11-13 Clifton Terrace, Finsbury Park, London N4 3SR (071-272 7774).

Other information: Sense provides a complete range of support and welfare services for people with dual sensory impairments, or a sensory impairment and another disability (and their families) including holidays.

The Society for Mucopolysaccharide Diseases

Eligibility: People suffering from mucopolysaccharide diseases and their families.

Types of grants: One-off grants and loans up to £100 towards funeral costs, travel, equipment, holidays and the society's conference costs. No grants towards arrears.

Annual grant total: In 1992/93, grants to individuals totalled £6,200.

Applications: In writing to the correspondent including a statement of income and expenditure and the specific need. Applications can be submitted directly by the individual or through a social worker, citizen's advice bureau, other welfare agency or other third party. They are considered in January, April, July and October.

Correspondent: Mrs C Lavery, Director, 55 Hill Avenue, Amersham, Bucks HP6 5BX (0494-434156).

The Spastics Society - Personal Services Fund

Eligibility: Children and adults with cerebral palsy, and their families. Priority will be given to those on income support or low incomes; those where unemployment or redundancy has affected them and families; where the degree of disability creates a particularly heavy financial demand; single parents; those with ageing carers under stress; after a particularly stressful period or where more than one person has a disability.

Types of grants: All types of help can be considered, sometimes in association with a local group of the society. Grants are usually towards domestic equipment, household debts, housing adaptations, aids and equipment, motor vehicle adaptations, transport, respite care, visits to Peto (UK), Bobath or similar therapy centres, holidays and summer schools. Other requests will be considered. Only one grant for specific items can be given in any one year per household. Grants of up to £250 can be agreed by the chairman and one other. Larger grants need the approval of the board. Emergency action can be taken by the chairman.

Annual grant total: No information available.

Applications: Normally through the social work offices of the society, which can be found in most telephone books, or from the office below. Applications are considered in January, May, July and October.

Correspondent: The Personal Services Fund, 16 Fitzroy Square, London W1P 5HQ (071-387 9571).

Other information: The society provides an extensive range of welfare services for people with cerebral palsy throughout the country. Financial grants are a very small part of its activities.

The Stroke Association

Eligibility: People who have had a stroke.

Types of grants: One-off grants usually for amounts between £10 and £200. Help is given towards medical aids, fuel bills, essential household items, holidays in special circumstances, hospital visiting,

Sickness and disability charities/Advice organisations

telephone installation in special circumstances and clothing. The normal procedure for payment is through the local authority, health authority or hospital, not the patient.

No grants for telephone bills (except in exceptional circumstances), structural alterations, motor expenses, nursing home fees or holidays outside the UK.

Annual grant total: In 1991/92, £58,000 was given in 460 grants to individuals.

Applications: On a form available from the correspondent to be completed only by social workers, citizen's advice bureaux, occupational therapists, speech therapists or similar health professionals on the individual's behalf. Applications are considered monthly and must be supported by a doctor's letter confirming the stroke.

Correspondent: The Welfare Secretary, CHSA House, 123-127 Whitecross Street, London EC1Y 8JJ (071-490 7999).

Other information: The Stroke Association was previously known as the Chest, Heart and Stroke Association.

The Tenovus Cancer Appeal

Eligibility: People with cancer and their dependants. Applicants must live in Wales or southern England.

Types of grants: One-off grants of £50 to £100. Help is given towards replacing domestic appliances, costs incurred travelling to and from hospital and clothing. No grants for funeral expenses.

Annual grant total: About £12,000 in around 150 grants in 1993.

Applications: In writing from doctors or social workers only, for immediate consideration.

Correspondent: The Organising Secretary, 11 Whitchurch Road, Cardiff CF4 3JN (0222-621433/621543).

The Victoria Convalescent Trust Fund

Eligibility: People in need.

Types of grants: Grants towards the cost of convalescent or recuperative holidays. Grants are paid direct to registered convalescence or nursing homes.

Annual grant total: About £50,000 in 250 to 300 grants.

Applications: Only accepted from those responsible for the medical treatment, **not** the individual.

Correspondent: A C Winter, Chairman, 62 Wilson Street, London EC2A 2BU.

Wireless for the Bedridden

Eligibility: Housebound invalids and housebound elderly people who are unable to afford a television or radio set.

Types of grants: Radio and television (black and white or colour) sets are available, as may be help with the initial television licence fee.

Annual grant total: In 1993, 200 radios and 700 television sets were given.

Applications: On the official application form available from the correspondent and supported by a sponsor from an appropriate welfare agency. Applications are considered weekly.

Correspondent: The Secretary, 159a High Street, Hornchurch, Essex RM11 3YB (0708-621101).

Other information: This entry is repeated in the National and general charities section of the book.

Advice organisations

The following list gives the names, addresses and telephone numbers of voluntary organisations which offer advice and support to disabled people and others with specific needs. They are arranged in alphabetical order of the illness or disability.

Some of these organisations have their own financial resources available for people in need; where they do have such resources they and their policies are described separately earlier in the section. We have marked them in this list with an asterisk (*).

Some organisations have local branches, details of which will be available from the head offices given below.

It would help the organisations listed if any request for information included a stamped addressed envelope.

Albinos
Albino Fellowship, 16 Neward Crescent, Preswick, Ayrshire KA9 2JB (0292-70336).

Alcohol
ACCEPT, ACCEPT Clinic, 724 Fulham Road, London SW6 5SE (071-371 7477).
Al-Anon Family Groups (for relatives and families of people with a drink problem), 61 Great Dover Street, London SE1 4YF (071-403 0888).
Alcohol Concern, Waterbridge House, 32–36 Loman Street, London SE1 0EE (071-928 7377).
Alcohol Counselling & Prevention Service, 34 Electric Lane, London SW9 8JT (071-737 3570).
Alcohol Recovery Project, 68 Newington Causeway, London SE1 6DF (071-403 3369).
Alcoholics Anonymous, General Service Office, PO Box 1, Stonebow House, Stonebow, York YO1 2NJ (0904-644026).

Libra Trust, Rick Evans, 19 Lansdowne Place, Lewes, E Sussex BN7 2JU (0273-480012).
Turning Point, New Loom House, 101 Back Church Lane, London E1 1LU (071-702 2300).

Ageing
Age Concern England, Astral House, 1268 London Road, Norbury, London SW16 4ER (081-679 8000).
Counsel & Care for the Elderly, Lower Ground Floor, Twyman House, 16 Bonny Street, London NW1 9PG (071-485 1550).

AIDS/HIV
Aids Ahead, Unit 17, Nacon Court, Herald Drive, Crewe, Cheshire CW1 1EA (0270-250736 [voice]; 0270-250743 [text only]).
* Body Positive, 51b Philbeach Gardens, Earls Court, London SW5 9EB (071-835 1045).

Advice organisations

* Terrence Higgins Trust, 52–54 Grays Inn Road, London WC1X 8JU (071-831 0330).
National Aids Helpline, PO Box 1577, London NW1 3DW (080- 567123).

Allergy
Food & Chemical Allergy Association, 27 Ferringham Lane, Ferring-by-Sea, West Sussex BN12 5NB (0903-241178).

Alzheimer's Disease
* Alzheimer's Disease Society, 158–160 Balham High Road, London SW12 9BN (081-675 6657).

Angelmann (Happy Puppet) Syndrome
Angelmann (Happy Puppet) Syndrome Support Group, Mrs S Woolven, 15 Place Crescent, Waterlooville, Hampshire PO7 5UR (0705-264224).

Ankylosing Spondylitis
National Ankylosing Spondylitis Society (NASS), 5 Grosvenor Crescent, London SW1X 7ER (071-235 9585).

Apert Syndrome
Apert Syndrome Support Group, Mrs P Walker, Fullers Barn, The Green, Loughton, Milton Keynes, Bucks MK5 8AW (0908-608557).

Arthritis/Rheumatic Diseases
* Arthritis Care, 18 Stephenson Way, London NW1 2HD (071-916 1500).
Arthritis & Rheumatism Council, Copeman House, St Mary's Court, St Mary's Gate, Castlefield, Derbyshire S41 7TD (0246-558033).

Arthrogryposis
Arthrogryposis Group (TAG), 1 The Oaks, Common Mead Lane, Gillingham, Dorset SP8 4SW (0747-822655).

Asthma
National Asthma Campaign, Providence House, Providence Place, London N1 0NT (071-226 2260).

Autism
National Autistic Society, 276 Willesden Lane, London NW2 5RB (081-451 1114).

Back Pain
National Back Pain Association, 31–33 Park Road, Teddington, Middlesex TW11 0AB (081-977 5474).

Behcet's Syndrome
Behcet's Syndrome Society, 3 Church Close, Lambourn, Newbury, Berkshire RG16 7PU (0488-71116).

Birthmarks
Naevus Support Group, 58 Necton Road, Wheathamstead, St Albans, Herts AL4 8AU (0582-832853).

Blindness/Partial Sight
British Retinitis Pigmentosa Society, PO Box 350, Bucks MK18 5AL (0280-860363).
International Glaucoma Association, c/o King's College Hospital, London SE5 9RS (071-274 6222 ext 2934).
* Jewish Care, 221 Golders Green Road, London NW11 9DQ (081-458 3282).
* National Deaf-Blind League, 18 Rainbow Court, Paston Ridings, Peterborough PE4 7UP (0733-573511).
National Federation of the Blind of the United Kingdom, Unity House, Smyth Street, Westgate, Wakefield, West Yorkshire WF1 1ER (0924-291313).
National League of the Blind & Disabled, 2 Tenterden Road, Tottenham, London N17 8BE (081-808 6030).
Partially Sighted Society, Queen's Road, Doncaster DN1 2NX (0302-368998).
Royal National Institute for the Blind, 224 Great Portland Street, London W1N 6AA (071-388 1266).

Bowel Disorders
British Colostomy Association, 15 Station Road, Reading RG1 1LG (0734-391537).
National Advisory Service for Parents of Children with a Stoma (NASPCS), 51 Anderson Drive, Darvel, Ayrshire KA17 0DE (0560-322024).
National Association for Colitis & Crohn's Disease (NACC), 98a London Road, St Albans, Herts AL1 1NX (0727-844296).

Brain Injury
British Institute for Brain-Injured Children, Knowle Hall, Knowle, Bridgwater TA7 8PT (0278-684060).

Brittle Bones
* Brittle Bone Society, 112 City Road, Dundee DD2 2PW (0382-817771).

Burns
British Burn Association, Dr J Kearney, Regional Burns Centre, Pinderfields Hospital, Wakefield, West Yorkshire WF1 4DG (0924-201688).

Cancer
Action Cancer, 127 Marlborough Park South, Belfast BT9 6HW (0232-661081).
BACUP, 121–123 Charterhouse Street, London EC1M 6AA (071-613 2121).
Cancer Care Society, 21 Zetland Road, Redland, Bristol, Avon BS6 7AH (0272-427419).
* Cancer Relief Macmillan Fund, 15–19 Britten Street, London SW3 3TZ (071-351 7811).
Cancerlink, 17 Britannia Street, London WC1X 9JN (071-833 2451).
* CLIC Trust (Cancer & Leukaemia in Childhood Trust), CLIC Annexe, 3 Nugent Hill, Cotham, Bristol BS6 5TD (0272-248844).
Marie Curie Foundation, 28 Belgrave Square, London SW1X 8QG (071-235 3325).
* Tenovous Cancer Information Centre, 11 Whitchurch Road, Cardiff CF4 3JN (0222-621433).
Tak Tent Cancer Support, 4th Floor, G Block, Western Infirmary, Glasgow G11 6NT (041-334 6699).

Cerebral Palsy
International Cerebral Palsy Society, 5a Netherhall Gardens, London NW3 5RN (081-995 5721).
* The Spastics Society, 12 Park Crescent, London W1N 4EQ (071-636 5020).

Chest/Lungs
British Lung Foundation, 8 Peterborough Mews, London SW6 3BL (071-371 7704).

Cleft Lip/Palate Disorder
Cleft Lip & Palate Association (CLAPA), 1 Eastwood Gardens, Kenton, Newcastle-upon-Tyne, NE3 3DQ (091-285 9396).

CMT
CMT International UK, c/o 121 Lavernock Road, Penarth, South Glamorgan CF64 3QG (0222-709537).

Coeliac Disease
Coeliac Society, PO Box 220, High Wycombe, Bucks HP11 2HY (0494- 437278).

Crohn's Disease
Crohn's in Childhood Research Appeal (CICRA), Parkgate House, 356 West Barnes Lane, Motspur Park, Surrey KT3 6NB (081-949 6209).
National Association for Colitis & Crohn's Disease (NACC), 98a London Road, St Albans, Herts AL1 1NX.

Cystic Fibrosis
Cystic Fibrosis Research Trust, Alexandra House, 5 Blyth Road, Bromley, Kent BR1 3RS (081-464 7211).

Cystic Hygroma
Cystic Hygroma & Lymphangioma Support Group, Villa Fontane, Church Road, Worth, Crawley, West Sussex RH10 7RS (0293-883901).

Advice organisations

Deafness/Hearing Difficulties
British Deaf Association, 38 Victoria Place, Carlisle CA1 1HU (0228-48844).
* National Deaf Children's Society, 45 Hereford Road, London W2 5AH (071-229 9272).
* National Deaf-Blind League, 18 Rainbow Court, Paston Ridings, Peterborough PE4 7UP (0733-573511).
Royal National Institute for the Deaf, 105 Gower Street, London WC1E 6AH (071-387 8033).
Tinnitus Helpline: 0345-090210.
* Sense, 11–13 Clifton Terrace, Finsbury Park, London N4 3SR (071-272 7774).

Depression
Depressives Anonymous, 36 Chestnut Avenue, Beverley, North Humberside HU17 9QU (0482-860619).
Manic Depression Fellowship Ltd, 8–10 High Street, Kingston-upon-Thames, Surrey KT1 1EY (081-974 6550).

Diabetes
* British Diabetic Association, 10 Queen Anne Street, London W1M 0BD (071-323 1531).
National Diabetes Foundation, 177a Tennison Road, London SE25 5NF (081-656 5467).

Disability (General)
Action Research, Vincent House, North Parade, Horsham, West Sussex RH12 2DA (0403-210406)
Carematch Residential Care Consortium Computer Service, 286 Camden Road, London N7 0BJ (071-609 9966).
Disability Alliance, Universal House, 88–94 Wentworth Street, London (071-247 8776/8673).
Disability Law, 16 Princeton Street, London WC1R 4BB (071-831 8031).
Disabled Drivers' Association, Ashwellthorpe, Norwich, Norfolk NR16 1EX (050-841449).
Disabled Housing Trust, Norfolk Lodge, Oakenfield, Burgess Hill, West Sussex RH15 8SJ (0444-247892).
Disabled Living Foundation, 380–384 Harrow Road, London W9 2HU (071-289 6111).
Disabled Living Services, Redbank House, 4 St Chad's Street, Cheetham, Manchester M8 8QA (061-832 3678).
Disablement Income Group (DIG), Millmead Business Centre, Millmead Road, London N17 9QU.
Invalid Children's Aid Association (ICAN), Barbican City Gate, 1–3 Dufferin Street, London EC1Y 8NA (071-374 4422).
Mobility Information Service, National Mobility Centre, Unit 2a, Atcham Estate, Shrewsbury SY4 4UG (0743-761889).
National League of the Blind & Disabled, 2 Tenterden Road, Tottenham, London N17 8BE (081-808 6030).
PHAB UK (Physically Handicapped & Able Bodied), PHAB Centre, Bushland Road, Northampton NN3 2NS (0604-785233).
Queen Elizabeth's Foundation for the Disabled, Leatherhead Court, Woodlands Road, Leatherhead, Surrey KT22 0BN (0372-842204).
Royal Association for Disability & Rehabilitation (RADAR), 25 Mortimer Street, London W1N 8AB (071-637 5400).

Disfigurement
Disfigurement Guidance Centre, PO Box 7, Cupar, Fife K115 4PF (0337-870281).
Let's Face It, 10 Wood End, Crowthorne, Berkshire RG11 6DQ (0344-774405).

Down's Syndrome
Down's Syndrome Association, 155 Mitcham Road, Tooting, London SW17 9PG (081-682 4001).

Drugs
Association for the Prevention of Addiction, 37–39 Great Guildford Street, London SE1 0ES (071-620 1919).
Drugline Ltd, 9a Brockley Cross, London SE4 2AB (081-692 4975).
Libra Trust (see alcohol).
Narcotics Anonymous, PO Box 1980, London N19 3LS (071-272 9040 or Helpline: 071-498 9005 midday to 8pm).
Standing Conference on Drug Abuse, 1–4 Hatton Place, Hatton Garden, London EC1N 8ND (071-430 2341).
Turning Point, New Loom House, 101 Back Church Lane, London E1 1LU (071-702 2300).

Dyslexia
British Dyslexia Association, 98 London Road, Reading, Berkshire RG1 5AU (0734-668271).
Defining Dyslexia, 132 High Street, Ruislip, Middlesex HA4 8LL (081-868 6810).
Dyslexia Institute (Dyslexia Foundation Ltd), 133 Gresham Road, Staines, Middlesex TW18 2AJ (0784-463851).

Dysphasia (See Speech/Language Difficulties)

Dyspraxia
Dyspraxia Trust, Administrator, PO Box 30, Hitchin, Hertfordshire SG5 1UU (0462-454986).

Dystonia
Dystonia Society, Omnibus Workspace, 39–41 North Road, London N7 9DP (071-700 4594).

Eating Disorders
Anorexics Anonymous, 24 Westmorland Road, Barnes, London SW13 (081-748 3994).
Anorexic Family Aid & National Information Centre, Sackville Place, 44 Magdalen Street, Norwich NR3 1JE (0603-621414).
BANISH (Bulimia & Anorexia Nervosa Intermediate Self-Help), Jenny Ceasar, 27 Lawrence Avenue, Lytham St Annes, Lancashire FY8 3LG (0253-726829).
Eating Disorders Association, Sackville Place, 44 Magdalene Street, Norwich Norfolk NR3 1JU (0603-621414).
Feed-Back, 19 Powell Street, Sheffield S3 7NW (0742-756501).

Ectodermal Dysplasia
Ectodermal Dysplasia Suport Group, 37 Cambridge Close, Haverhill, Suffolk CB9 9HP.

Eczema
* National Eczema Society, 4 Tavistock Place, London, WC1H 9RA (071-388 4097).

Endometriosis
Endometriosis Society, 65 Holmdene Avenue, London SE24 9LD (071-737 4764 evenings).

Epidermolysis Bullosa
DEBRA (Dystrophic Epidermolysis Bullosa Research Association), Debra House, 13 Wellington Business Park, Dukes Ride, Crowthorne, Berkshire RG11 6LS (0344-771961).

Epilepsy
* British Epilepsy Association, Anstey House, 40 Hanover Square, Leeds LS3 1BE (0532-439393).

Friedreich's Ataxia
* Friedreich's Ataxia Group, Copse Edge, Thursley Road, Elstead, Godalming, Surrey GU8 6DJ (0252-702864).

German Measles (See Rubella)

Gilles de la Tourette Syndrome
Tourette Syndrome (UK) Association, 169 Wickham Street, Welling, Kent DA16 3BS (081-304 5446).

Glaucoma (See Blindness/Partial Sight)

Guillain Barre Syndrome
Guillain Barre Syndrome Support Group, Foxley, Holdingham Sleaford, Lincolnshire NG34 8NR (0529-304615).

● **Advice organisations**

Haemophilia
* Haemophilia Society, 123 Westminster Bridge Road, London SE1 7HR (071-928 2020).

Head Injury
Headway, 7 King Edward Court, King Edward Street, Nottingham NG1 1EW (0602-240800).

Heart Attacks/Heart Disease (General)
British Heart Foundation, 14 Fitzhardinge Street, London W1H 4DH (071-935 0185).
* The Stroke Association, CHSA House, 123–127 Whitecross Street, London EC1Y 8JJ (071-490 7999).
Heart to Heart, PO Box 7, High Street, Pershore, Worcestershire WR10 1AA.

Hernia
Diaphragmatic Hernia Support Association (DHSA), 36 Langley Drive, Bridewell, Ashford, Kent TN23 2UF.

Herpes
Herpes Association, 41 North Road, London N7 9DP (071-609 9061)

Hodgkin's Disease
Hodgkin's Disease Association, PO Box 275, Haddenham, Aylesbury, Bucks HP17 8JJ (0844-291500).

Huntington's Chorea
* Huntington's Disease Association, 108 Battersea High Street, London SW11 3HP (071-223 7000).

Illeostomy
IA - The Illeostomy International Pouch Support Group, Amblehurst House, PO Box 23, Mansfield NG18 4TT (0623-28099).

Incontinence
Association for Continence Advice, The Basement, 2 Doughty Street, London WC2N 2PH (071-404 6821).

Infantile Hypercalcaemia
Infantile Hypercalcaemia Foundation Ltd, 37 Mulberry Green, Old Harlow, Essex CM17 0EY (0279-427214).

Infertility
Child, PO Box 154, Hounslow, Middlesex TW5 0EZ.

Kidney Disease
* British Kidney Patient Association, Bordon, Hampshire GU35 9JZ (0420-472021/2).

National Federation of Kidney Patients' Associations, 6 Stanley Street, Worksop, Notts S81 7HX (0909-487795).

Leukaemia
* CLIC (Cancer & Leukaemia in Childhood), CLIC Annexe, 3 Nugent Hill, Cotham, Bristol BS6 5TD (0272-248844).
* Leukaemia Care Society, 14 Kingfisher Court, Venney Bridge, Pinhoe, Exeter, Devon EX4 8JN (0392-464848).

Limb Disorder
British Limbless Ex-Servicemen's Association (BLESMA), 185–187 High Road, Chadwell Heath, Romford, Essex RM6 6NA (081-590 1124) (see Service & ex-service charities).
The Limbless Association, 31 The Mall, Ealing, London W5 2PX (081-579 1758).
REACH (The Association for Children with Hand or Arm Deficiency), 13 Park Terrace, Crimchard, Chard, Somerset TA20 1LA (0460-61578).
STEPS (A National Association for Families of Children with Congenital Abnormalities of the Lower Limbs), 15 Statham Close, Lymm, Cheshire WA13 9NN (0925-757525).

Lowe's Syndrome
Lowe's Syndrome Association, 29 Gleneagles Drive, Penwortham, Preston, Lancashire PR1 0JT (0772-745070).

Lungs *(See Chest/Lungs)*

Lupus
Lupus Group, Arthritis Care, 18 Stephenson Way, London NW1 2HD (071-916 1500).

Mastectomy
Mastectomy Cancer Care, 15–19 Britten Street, London SW3 3TZ (071-867 8275).

Medical Accidents
Action for Victims of Medical Accidents, Bank Chambers, 1 London Road, Forest Hill, London SE23 3TP (081-291 2793).

Meniere's Disease
Meniere's Society, 98 Maybury Road, Woking, Surrey GU21 5HX (0483-740597).

Meningitis
National Meningitis Trust, Fern House, Bath Road, Stroud, Gloucestershire GL5 3TJ (0453-751738).

Mental Handicap
CARE, 9 Weir Road, Kibworth, Leicester LE8 0LQ (0533-793225).

In Touch, 10 Norman Road, Sale, Cheshire M33 3DF (061-905 2440).
MENCAP, Mencap National Centre, 123 Golden Lane, London EC1Y 0RT (071-454 0454).

Mental Health
MIND (National Association for Mental Health), Granta House, 15–19 The Broadway, Stratford, London E15 4BQ (081-519 2122).

Migraine
British Migraine Association, 178a High Road, West Byfleet, Surrey KT14 7ED (0932-352468).
Migraine Trust, 45 Great Ormond Street, London WC1N 3HZ (071-278 2676).

Motor Neurone Disease
* Motor Neurone Disease Association, PO Box 246, Northampton NN1 2PR (0604-250505).

Multiple Sclerosis
* Multiple Sclerosis Society of Great Britain & Northern Ireland, 25 Effie Road, Fulham, London SW6 1EE (071-736 6267).

Muscular Dystrophy
Muscular Dystrophy Group of Great Britain & Northern Ireland, 7–11 Prescot Place, London SW4 6BS (071-720 8055).

Myalgic Encephalomyelitis (ME)
Myalgic Encephalomyelitis Association, Stanhope House, High Street, Stanford-le-Hope, Essex SS17 0HA.

Myasthenia Gravis
Myasthenia Gravis Association, Keynes House, 77 Nottingham Road, Derby DE1 3QS (0332-290219).

Myotonic Dystrophy
Myotonic Dystrophy Support Group, c/o 175a Carlton Hill, Carlton, Nottingham NG4 1GZ (0602-870080).

Narcolepsy
Narcolepsy Association UK (UKAN), South Hall, High Street, Farningham, Kent DA4 0DE (0322-863056).

Neurofibromatosis
The Neurofibromatosis Association, 120 London Road, Kingston-upon-Thames, Surrey KT2 6QJ (081-547 1636 or 081-974 8707).

Noonan Syndrome
Noonan Syndrome Society, 12d Low Street, Cheslyn Hay, Nr Walsall, Staffordshire WS6 7DS (0922-415500).

Advice organisations

Opitz Kaveggia Syndrome
International F G Syndrome Support Group, 66 Ford Road, Dagenham, Essex RN10 9JR (081-592 3406).

Osteoporosis
National Osteoporosis Society, PO Box 10, Radstock, Bath, Avon BA3 3YB (0761-432472).

Paget's Disease
National Association for the Relief of Paget's Disease, Room B, 304 CSB, Hope Hospital, Salford M6 8HD.

Parkinson's Disease
* Parkinson's Disease Society, 22 Upper Woburn Place, London WC1H 0RA (071-383 3513).

Phobias
Action on Phobias, 8–9 The Avenue, Eastbourne, Sussex BN21 3YA.

Poliomyelitis
British Polio Fellowship, Bell Close, West End Road, Ruislip, Middlesex HA4 6LP (0895-675515).

Pre-Eclampsia
Pre-Eclampsia Society, Eaton Lodge, 8 Southend Road, Hockley, Essex SS5 4QQ (0702-205088).

Pre-Menstrual Syndrome
Women's Nutritional Advisory Service, PO Box 268, Lewes, East Sussex BN7 2QN (0273-487366).

Psoriasis
Psoriasis Association, Milton House, 7 Milton Street, Northampton NN2 7JG (0604-711129).

Raynaud's Disease
Raynaud's Scleroderma Association, 112 Crewe Road, Alsager, Cheshire ST7 2JA (0270-872776).

Restricted Growth
Restricted Growth Association (RGA), 103 St Thomas Avenue, Hayling Island, Hampshire PO11 0EU (0705-461813).

Rett Syndrome
United Kingdom Rett Syndrome Association, Hartspool, Golden Valley, Castlemorton, Malvern, Worcestershire WR13 6AA.

Reye's Syndrome
Mrs Gillian Denney, National Reye's Syndrome Foundation of UK, 15 Nicholas Gardens, Pyrford, Woking, Surrey GU22 8SD (0932-346843).

Rheumatic Diseases (See Arthritis/ Rheumatism Diseases)

Rubella
* Sense, 11–13 Clifton Terrace, Finsbury Park, London N4 3SR (071-272 7774).

Sarcoidosis
Sarcoidosis Association UK, 19 Ashurst Close, Blackbrook, St Helens, Merseyside WA11 9DN (0744-28020).

Schizophrenia
National Schizophrenia Fellowship, 28 Castle Street, Kingston-upon-Thames, Surrey KT1 1SS (081-547 3937).
SANE, 2nd Floor, 199–205 Old Marylebone Road, London NW1 5QP (071-724 8000 Helpline).

Sickle Cell Disease
Sickle Cell Society (SCS), Station Road, Harlesden, London NW10 4BU (081-961 7795).

Sjogren's Syndrome
British Sjogren's Syndrome Association (BSSA), 20 Kingston Way, Nailsea, Bristol BS19 2RL.

Solvent Abuse
Re-Solv, 30a High Street, Stone, Staffs ST15 8AW (0785-817885).

Sotos Syndrome
Sotos Syndrome Support Group, c/o Child Growth Foundation, 2 Mayfield Avenue, London W4 1PW (081-944 7625).

Spastics (See Cerebral Palsy)

Speech & Language Difficulties
Action for Dysphasic Adults (ADA), 1 Royal Street, London SE1 7LL (071-261 9572).
Association for All Speech-Impaired Children (AFASIC), 347 Central Markets, Smithfield, London EC1A 9NH (071-236 3632).
Association for Stammerers, 15 Oldford Road, London E2 9PJ (081-983 1003).
Royal Association in Aid of Deaf People, 27 Old Oak Road, Acton, London W3 7HN (081-743 6187).

Spina Bifida
* Association for Spina Bifida & Hydrocephalus, 42 Park Road, Peterborough PE1 2UQ (0733-555988).

Spinal Injuries
Spinal Injuries Association, Newpoint House, 76 St James' Lane, Muswell Hill, London N10 3DF (081-444 2121).

Stroke
* Stroke, CHSA House, 123–127 Whitecross Street, London EC1Y 8JJ (071-490 7999).

Thalassaemia
UK Thalassaemia Society, 107 Nightingale Lane, London N8 7QY (081-348 0437).

Thrombocytopenia with Absent Radii
Thrombocytopenia with Absent Radii (TAR) Support Group, 13 Friarside, Witton Gilbert, Durham DH7 6RY.

Tinnitus
British Tinnitus Association, 14–18 West Bar Green, Sheffield S1 2DA.
See also Royal National Institute for the Deaf under Deafness/Hearing difficulties.

Toxoplasmosis
Toxoplasmosis Trust, 61–71 Collier Street, London N1 9BE (071-713 0663).

Tracheo-Oesophageal Fistula
Aid for Children with Tracheostomies, 215a Perry Street, Billericay, Essex CM12 0NZ.
TOFs, St George's Centre, 91 Victoria Road, Netherfield, Nottingham NG4 2NN (0602-400694).

Traquillizers
Life Without Tranquillizers, Lynmouth, Devon EX35 6EE.
TRANX (UK) Ltd, National Tranquillizer Advice Centre, 25a Masons Avenue, Wealdstone, Harrow HA3 5AH.

Tuberous Sclerosis
Tuberous Sclerosis Association, Little Barnsley Farm, Catshill, Bromsgrove, Worcestershire B61 0NQ (0527-871898).

Turner Syndrome
Turner Syndrome Society, c/o Child Growth Foundation, 2 Mayfield Avenue, London W4 1PW (081-994 7625).

Urostomy
Urostomy Association, Buckland, Beaumont Park, Danbury, Essex CM3 4DE (0245-224294).

Vaccine Damage (See Medical Accidents)

Williams Syndrome
Infantile Hypercalcaemia Foundation Ltd, Mulberry Cottage, 37 Mulberry Green, Old Harlow, Essex CM17 0EY (0279-427214).

Local charities

This section lists local charities giving grants to individuals in need. The information in the entry applies only to relief-in-need payments and concentrates on what the charity actually does rather than what its trust deed allows it to do. It does not give a complete picture of the charity's work. All the charities listed have a grant making potential of £500 a year for individuals; most are spending considerably more than this.

Regional classification

We have divided Britain into nine geographical regions. The charities in each region are divided as follows:

- Firstly the charities which apply to the whole region, or to at least two counties in the region.
- Each region is sub-divided into counties. The entries which apply to the **whole county** (or to at least **two towns** within it) appear first.
- The rest of the charities in the county are listed in **alphabetical order of parish, district, town or city**.

To be sure of identifying every relevant local charity, look first at the entries for the **parish, district, town** or **city** in which you live. Next, look at the entries for the **county** in which you live. The charities which apply to more than one county can be located by looking under the **regional headings**, for example the North West.

For example, if you live in Liverpool, firstly establish which region Merseyside is in by looking at the map. Then, having established that Merseyside is in region 5, look at the list below and see which page the entries for Merseyside are on. Then, look under the heading for Liverpool to see if there are any relevant charities benefiting the city. Next, check the charities which apply to Merseyside generally. Finally, check under the heading for the North West generally.

1. Northern Ireland *page 94*

2. Scotland *page 96*
Borders *page 103*
Central *page 103*
Dumfries & Galloway *page 104*
Fife *page 105*
Grampian *page 106*
Highlands *page 109*
Lothian *page 110*
Shetland *page 114*
Strathclyde *page 114*
Tayside *page 116*
Western Isles *page 118*

3. Wales *page 119*
Clwyd *page 120*
Dyfed *page 121*
Gwent *page 121*
Gwynedd *page 122*
Mid-Glamorgan *page 123*
Powys *page 123*
South Glamorgan *page 124*
West Glamorgan *page 125*

4. North East *page 126*
Cleveland *page 128*
Durham *page 129*
Humberside *page 129*
North Yorkshire *page 132*
Northumberland *page 135*
South Yorkshire *page 136*
Tyne & Wear *page 137*
West Yorkshire *page 140*

5. North West *page 147*
Cheshire *page 148*
Cumbria *page 151*
Greater Manchester *page 152*
Lancashire *page 157*
Merseyside *page 160*

6. Midlands *page 165*
Derbyshire *page 167*
Hereford & Worcester *page 169*
Leicestershire *page 172*
Lincolnshire *page 174*
Northamptonshire *page 178*
Nottinghamshire *page 182*
Shropshire *page 186*
Staffordshire *page 188*
Warwickshire *page 190*
West Midlands *page 195*

7. South West *page 203*
Avon *page 204*
Cornwall *page 206*
Devon *page 207*
Dorset *page 213*
Gloucestershire *page 215*
Somerset *page 217*
Wiltshire *page 218*

8. South East *page 221*
Bedfordshire *page 222*
Berkshire *page 223*
Buckinghamshire *page 224*
Cambridgeshire *page 226*
East Sussex *page 229*
Essex *page 230*
Hampshire *page 232*
Hertfordshire *page 235*
Kent *page 236*
Norfolk *page 239*
Oxfordshire *page 245*
Suffolk *page 247*
Surrey *page 250*
West Sussex *page 260*

9. London *page 261*

Local charities

93

1. Northern Ireland

The Belfast Association for the Blind

Eligibility: Registered blind people living in Northern Ireland.

Types of grants: Christmas grants to retired blind employees of Belfast Workshops for the Blind, and grants towards the installation of telephones. Grants are also given to hospitals registered in Northern Ireland towards equipment for cure or relief of blindness. Partially sighted people are not supported.

Annual grant total: No information available.

Applications: In writing through a social worker or from the secretary of an organisation. Applications are considered throughout the year.

Correspondent: J Sherman, Hon. Secretary, c/o 11 Clonmore Park, Harmony Hill, Lambeg, Lisburn, County Antrim BT27 4EU (0846-662947).

The Belfast Central Mission

Eligibility: People in need.

Types of grants: Small one-off grants for "assessed social need"; summer holidays for elderly people, their carers and children.

Annual grant total: No information available.

Applications: Via the Mission's own social work staff or a board social worker. Direct applications are also considered.

Correspondent: B Sharpe, Director of Social Work, Belfast Central Mission, Grosvenor Hall, Glengall Street, Belfast BT12 5AD (0232-241917).

The Children's Community Holidays

Eligibility: Needy or deprived children of any denomination who live in Northern Ireland.

Types of grants: About 300 grants a year towards holidays.

Annual grant total: In 1992/93, the trust had an income of £173,000. Total expenditure was £170,000 of which £18,000 was given in grants to individuals.

Applications: On a form included in a holiday brochure available from the correspondent in the spring of each year.

Correspondent: The Secretary, 3 Blackwater Road, Mallusk, Newtownabbey BT36 8TZ.

The Church of Ireland Retirement Trust

Eligibility: Retiring clergy and clergy widows in need.

Types of grants: Financial assistance to buy a home and occasionally small grants towards renovation of homes.

Annual grant total: No information available.

Applications: In writing to the correspondent.

Correspondent: The Chairman, 27 Lisburn Road, Belfast BT9 7AA.

The Ian Gow Memorial Fund

Eligibility: Young people aged 16 to 30 and natives of Northern Ireland.

Types of grants: Awards usually of £500, though larger grants will be considered in exceptional circumstances. One-off grants are given for education/training where public funds are not available; to help individuals with a disability; and to provide help through a personal crisis. The fund will not normally consider support for assistance beyond third level education ie. postgraduate or research work.

Annual grant total: In 1993, the trust had assets of £400,000 producing an income of £40,000. Total expenditure was £50,000. Grants of between £50 and £500 were given to 1,000 individuals and totalled £45,000.

Applications: On a form available from the correspondent. Applications should be submitted directly by the individual or if necessary through a social worker, citizen's advice bureau or other welfare agency. They are usually considered in the second week of March, June, September and December.

Correspondent: The Director, Voluntary Service Belfast, 70-72 Lisburn Road, Belfast BT9 6AF (0232-329499).

The Londonderry Methodist City Mission

Eligibility: People in need.

Types of grants: One-off grants for necessities and some help at Christmas and holiday time.

Annual grant total: No information available.

Applications: By personal application or through a referral by a minister of religion, social worker or citizen's advice bureau.

Correspondent: Rev K Best, 11 Clearwater, Londonderry BT47 1BE (0504-42644).

The Methodist Child Care Society

Eligibility: Children from families under stress and/or hardship due to a variety of factors eg. single parents who have lost their partner through death, separation or divorce and families where there is a loss of income through illness or unemployment. Applicants should be members of the Methodist Church in Ireland. The maximum age for benefit is normally 18, but can be extended if the young person is going into further education without a source of income.

Types of grants: Quarterly payments plus occasional one-off payments.

Northern Ireland

Annual grant total: In 1993, the trust had assets of £250,000 and an income of £43,000. £42,000 was given in relief-in-need grants to individuals.

Applications: On a form available from the correspondent. Applications can only be considered when submitted by the superintendent of a Methodist Circuit and passed by the circuit quarterly meeting. They are considered in January, March, June and September.

Correspondent: Joseph Edgar, Knockbracken House, 19 Knockbracken Road South, Belfast BT8 8AA (0232-812612).

The Newtownabbey Methodist Mission

Eligibility: Socially deprived children, adults, families and elderly people who live in Northern Ireland, especially the Rathcoole Estate and Greater Belfast.

Types of grants: Grants for holidays and outings, one-off grants for food, clothing, fuel and bills throughout the year, and food/toy parcels at Christmas.

Annual grant total: About £10,000 to around 400 people, including cash grants of about £5,000 and the value of holidays for 120 children.

Applications: By personal application or through a referral by a minister of religion, social worker or citizen's advice bureau.

Correspondent: A Porter, Administrator, 35a Rathcoole Drive, Newtownabbey, Co Antrim BT37 9AQ (0232-852546).

Other information: The mission can offer counselling to people in need.

The Northern Ireland Children's Holiday Schemes

Eligibility: Underprivileged children aged between 9 and 18 living in Northern Ireland.

Types of grants: Grants are NOT given. Community Relations Residentials are organised and paid for by the scheme. Beneficiaries are equally drawn from both sections of the community and nominated by local community contacts.

Annual grant total: About 330 children attend the Residentials.

Applications: In writing to the correspondent by the community contact. Applications are considered in March/April.

Correspondent: The Director, 547 Antrim Road, Belfast BT15 3BU (0232-370373).

The Presbyterian Old Age Fund, Women's Fund & Indigent Ladies Fund

Eligibility: Needy, elderly or infirm members of the Presbyterian Church who live in any part of Ireland.

Types of grants: Recurrent grants of up to £100 paid quarterly plus a Christmas gift. The Women's Fund and Indigent Ladies Fund are administered with the Old Age Fund but give mainly one-off emergency grants according to need.

Annual grant total: Over 180 people throughout the whole of Ireland receive nearly £65,000 in grants.

Applications: In writing through a minister to the correspondent.

Correspondent: The Secretary, Church House, Fisherwick Place, Belfast BT1 6DW (0232-322284).

The Presbyterian Orphan Society

Eligibility: Children under 21, usually of single parents, living in Ireland. The applicant should have a Presbyterian church connection and must be selected by the age of 19.

Types of grants: One-off and recurrent grants according to need. The usual award is £435 for one child, one adult.

Annual grant total: In 1992, the society had assets of £2.5 million and an income of £411,000. Grants to about 1,000 individuals totalled £336,000

Applications: Applications are made by Presbyterian clergy on a form available from the correspondent. They are considered in April and October. Applications are means tested.

Correspondent: W P Gray, Church House, Fisherwick Place, Belfast BT1 6DW (0232-323737).

The Protestant Orphan Society for the Counties of Antrim & Down (Inc)

Eligibility: Orphan children who live in the counties of Antrim or Down and who are members of the Church of Ireland.

Types of grants: An annual grant of £300 with holiday and Christmas bonuses of £10 each; also one-off bereavement grants of £400 to a family on the death of a parent.

Annual grant total: About £65,000 in 200 to 250 grants.

Applications: Through the clergyman of the parish in which the individual lives.

Correspondent: T N Wilson, Executive Secretary, Church of Ireland House, 12 Talbot Street, Belfast BT1 2QH (0232-322268).

The Retired Ministers' House Fund

Eligibility: Retired full-time ministers and servants of the Presbyterian Church in Ireland.

Types of grants: Provision of rented accommodation and loans. No grants.

Annual grant total: About £110,000.

Applications: In writing to the correspondent.

Correspondent: The Secretary, Church House, Fisherwick Place, Belfast BT1 6DW (0232-322284).

The RUC Benevolent Fund

Eligibility: Members and ex-members of the Royal Ulster Constabulary and their dependants in need.

Types of grants: One-off or recurrent grants according to need, up to £500.

Annual grant total: £800,000 in about 300 grants/loans and other disbursements.

Applications: In writing to the correspondent.

Correspondent: The Secretary, Police Federation for Northern Ireland, RUC Garnerville, Garnerville Road, Belfast BT4 2NX (0232-760831).

The Society for the Orphans of Ministers & Missionaries of the Presbyterian Church in Northern Ireland

Eligibility: Orphan children of ministers and missionaries of the Presbyterian Church in Ireland. Beneficiaries must be under 25.

Types of grants: One-off and recurrent grants according to need.

Annual grant total: In 1992, the trust had assets of £356,000 and an income of £30,000. 12 grants to individuals totalled £25,000.

Applications: On a form available from the correspondent. Applications should be submitted directly by the individual and are considered in April and October.

Correspondent: Paul Gray, Church House, Fisherwick Place, Belfast BT1 6DW (0232-323737).

● **Belfast**

The Belfast Sick Poor Fund

Eligibility: People in need who live in Belfast, with preference given to ill or disabled people. Applicants should be living at home.

Types of grants: One-off grants up to £300 for necessities and comforts. Grants towards special diets or other essentials for illness or disability have priority. No grants towards holidays.

Annual grant total: About £2,000.

Applications: By letter to the correspondent through a social worker, citizen's advice bureau or other welfare agency. Applications are considered continuously.

Correspondent: The Administrator, c/o Bryson House, 28 Bedford Street, Belfast BT2 7FE (0232-325835).

Other information: The fund states that demands from professional referrers already far out-strip available resources.

The Sunshine Society

Eligibility: People who live in the Eastern Health and Social Services Board area (ie. the Greater Belfast area) and are in exceptional need of a holiday.

Types of grants: Grants up to £150 towards the cost of holidays (to be taken in Northern Ireland only).

Annual grant total: About £2,000.

Applications: Via professional workers only.

Correspondent: The Administrator, c/o Bryson House, 28 Bedford Street, Belfast BT2 7FE (0232-325835).

Other information: The society states that demands from professional referers for cases of desperate need already far outstrip available resources.

2. Scotland

The Adamson Trust

Eligibility: Disabled children aged 16 and under.

Types of grants: Grants to help with the cost of holidays.

Annual grant total: £25,000 in 300 grants.

Applications: Applications should be made through a social work department or a medical authority and should not come direct from parents.

Correspondent: Messrs Drysdale, Anderson WS, 14 Comrie Street, Crieff, Tayside PH7 4AZ (0764-655151).

The Aged Christian Friend Society of Scotland

Eligibility: Christians in need living in Scotland who are over 60 years of age.

Types of grants: About 43 pensions of £50 to £200 a year.

Annual grant total: In 1993, relief-in-need grants to individuals totalled £6,000.

Applications: In writing to the correspondent. The society prefers any application to be put forward by a church or similar body and for that body to make a contribution to the cost of the pension.

Correspondent: Brodies WS, 15 Atholl Crescent, Edinburgh EH3 8HA (031-228 3777).

Applicants living in the Glasgow area should apply to: Marcharg, Houston, MacFarlane & Co, 36 Renfield Street, Glasgow G2 1BD (041-204 1537).

The Airth Benefaction Trust

Eligibility: People in need.

Types of grants: Grants of £115 paid in November.

Annual grant total: £5,750. A maximum of 50 grants are given each year.

Applications: On an application form available from the correspondent. These should be returned not later than 30th September. Accepted applicants are invited to re-apply each year.

Correspondent: Mrs Fiona Marshall, Administrator, Henderson Boyd Jackson, 19 Ainslie Place, Edinburgh EH3 6AU (031-226 6881).

The Association for the Relief of Incurables in Glasgow & the West of Scotland

Eligibility: People in financial need who are suffering from incurable diseases and are living at home. Applicants must be living in the West of Scotland, from Dumfries to John O'Groats.

Types of grants: Pensions of £307 a year paid quarterly. One-off grants totalling no more than £300 per person, for specific needs such as telephone installation, washing machines and cookers.

Annual grant total: Over £108,000 in 1993 (353 pensions).

Applications: Applications must be made through social workers or welfare agencies.

Correspondent: Messrs Montgomerie & Co, Apsley House, 29 Wellington Street, Glasgow G2 6JA (041-221-8004).

The Benevolent Fund for Nurses in Scotland

Eligibility: Trained nurses or midwives who have trained in Scotland and/or held professional posts there.

Types of grants: One-off and quarterly grants to applicants with limited income owing to illness or disability, or in the case of retired nurses, those with little or no superannuation pension.

Annual grant total: Over £17,000 in 1985, the most recent year for which information is available.

Applications: Application forms, available from the correspondent, can be submitted by the individual or through a recognised referral agency (social worker,

Scotland

citizen's advice bureau, doctor etc.) and are considered as they are received.

Correspondent: Mrs M C Plenderleith, Crianon, 3 Ailsa View, Stewarton, Ayrshire KA3 5HF (0560-485080).

The Benevolent Society of the Licensed Trade of Scotland

Eligibility: Members of the society and people who have been employed in the licensed trade in Scotland for at least three years.

Types of grants: One-off and recurrent grants according to need. One-off grants are up to a maximum of £200.

Annual grant total: £150,000 in 300 grants.

Applications: On a form available from the correspondent. Applications can also be made through a social worker, citizen's advice bureau or other welfare agency.

Correspondent: George McCulloch, Secretary, 79 West Regent Street, Glasgow G2 2AW (041-353 3596).

The Biggart Trust

Eligibility: People in need, with preference for people related to the founders and their descendants.

Types of grants: One-off or recurrent grants according to need.

Annual grant total: Not known, but paid in a lump sum or by instalments.

Applications: In writing to the correspondent.

Correspondent: C Mitchell Biggart, Taylor & Ireland, 307 West George Street, Glasgow G2 4LB (041-221 7206).

The Blackwood Trust

Eligibility: Disabled people in Scotland.

Types of grants: Generally one-off grants for specific purposes (eg. buying capital items such as wheelchairs, clothing or furniture). Grants range from £100 to £300 and are often only part of the cost. No grants towards holidays.

Annual grant total: £11,000 in 1992 in 84 grants.

Applications: Through a social worker, doctor or similar third party. Applications should include full details of the applicant's personal situation including finance and the purpose of the grant. The trustees meet four/five times a year.

Correspondent: G G Calderwood, 30 Bramdean Rise, Edinburgh EH10 6JR (031-447 4472).

The Blyth Benevolent Trust

Eligibility: Women aged over 60 and in need. Preference is given to blind or partially sighted people with the surname Bell or Blyth, and who live in or are connected with Newport-on-Tay, Fife or Dundee.

Types of grants: Annuities paid twice a year and a Christmas bonus, amounting to about £60 per beneficiary.

Annual grant total: About £1,800 to about 30 individuals.

Applications: In writing to the correspondent.

Correspondent: Mrs Pamela M M Bowman, Secretary, 27 Bank Street, Dundee DD1 1RP (0382-322267).

The Buchanan Society

Eligibility: People with the following surnames: Buchanan, McAuslan (any spelling), McWattie, and Risk.

Types of grants: Pensions of £420 for elderly people in need; scholarships of £420 to encourage able young people to remain in school after the age of 16, and bursaries for students in severe financial difficulties.

Annual grant total: About £17,000 in pensions (40 beneficiaries), about £13,000 in scholarships (30 beneficiaries), and a growing number of bursaries.

Applications: On application to the correspondent.

Correspondent: Mrs Fiona Risk, Secretary, 18 Iddesleigh Avenue, Milngavie, Glasgow G62 8NT (041-956 1939).

Other information: The Buchanan Society is the oldest Clan Society in Scotland having been founded in 1725.

The Challenger Children's Fund

Eligibility: Physically disabled children under 18 who live in Scotland.

Types of grants: About 200 one-off and recurrent grants totalling £16,000, for maintenance, education, clothing and general welfare. Grants are given in May and November.

Annual grant total: No information available.

Applications: Directly from parents or through a social worker or other welfare agency.

Correspondent: The Chairman, Cunningham Unit, Astley Ainslie Hospital, 133 Grange Loan, Edinburgh EH9 2HL (031-447 7095).

The Church of Scotland Ministers' Orphan Fund

Eligibility: Orphaned children under 21 of former ministers of the Church of Scotland.

Types of grants: Recurrent grants of less than £700. Grants must be applied for annually.

Annual grant total: Under 20 grants totalling about £5,000.

Applications: On a form available from the correspondent.

Correspondent: E Hubbard, Treasurer, 121 George Street, Edinburgh EH2 4YN (031-225 5722).

The Commercial Travellers of Scotland Benevolent Fund for Widows & Orphans

Eligibility: Widows and orphans of commercial travellers in Scotland.

Types of grants: One-off grants for emergencies, telephone, home repairs/alterations, smoke and personal alarms; annual grants paid quarterly for general financial need. Grants are between £120 and £200 a year. The trust also makes donations of Christmas parcels and summer days out.

Annual grant total: About £11,000 in 1992/93.

Applications: In writing to the correspondent. Applications are considered quarterly.

Correspondent: A R C Alexander, Manager, 23 Beech Avenue, Newton, Mearns, Glasgow G77 5PP (041-639 2603).

The Craigcrook Mortification

Eligibility: People over 60 and in need who were born in Scotland and have lived there for most of their lives.

Types of grants: Annual pensions.

Annual grant total: About £15,000 in about 50 grants of £300.

Applications: In writing to the correspondent. Applications should be supported by a member of the clergy.

Correspondent: R Graeme Thom, Clerk, 17 Melville Street, Edinburgh EH3 7PH (031-226 6281).

Other information: The trust has limited capacity to take on new applicants.

Scotland

The Alastair Crerar Trust for Single Poor

Eligibility: Single people on low incomes aged 16 or over.

Types of grants: Help towards holiday accommodation, Christmas meals, theatre and cinema outings, bus trips, household necessities etc.. Grants are rarely over £300.

Annual grant total: £6,000 in 26 grants 1990/91.

Applications: In writing to the correspondent who has stated that "the trust receives more applications than it can cope with".

Correspondent: Michael I D Sturrock, Secretary, 43 York Place, Edinburgh EH1 3HT (031-556 7951).

Other information: The purpose of the trust is to support individuals or groups who, having a Christian conviction, will utilise such financial provision to add to the quality of life of such single people.

The Marie Curie Memorial Foundation

Eligibility: Cancer patients in Scotland being nursed in their own homes.

Types of grants: Small one-off grants to meet a patient's needs arising as a result of their illness. Typically these grants will be for bedding, clothing and dietary needs. Grants range from £20 to £80. No grants to pay household bills or accrued debts.

Annual grant total: About £9,000 in 200 grants.

Applications: On a form available only from health care professionals and social workers. Grants are seldom made directly to patients but through statutory bodies such as social work departments.

Correspondent: Mrs C McGilvray, Nursing Co-ordinator, 21 Rutland Street, Edinburgh EH1 2AE (031-229 8332).

The Disablement Income Group Scotland

Eligibility: Chronically disabled people who live in Scotland.

Types of grants: One-off grants of up to £100 per year according to need.

Annual grant total: No grants have been made for two years, although funds are available.

Applications: In writing to the correspondent, including details of weekly income/expenditure. Applications with a supporting letter from a social worker, doctor, clergyman etc. are preferred.

Correspondent: The General Secretary, 5 Quayside Street, Edinburgh EH6 6EJ (031-555 2811).

The Educational Institute of Scotland Benevolent Fund

Eligibility: Members of the institute, their widows and dependants in need. Limited funds are available for non-members who have been teachers or governesses, and their widows and dependants.

Types of grants: One-off and recurrent grants according to need.

Annual grant total: In 1992/93, about £58,000 in 90 grants of up to £1,100.

Applications: On a form available from local Association Benevolent Fund correspondents or from the correspondent below. Meetings are normally held in February, April, June, September and November.

Correspondent: The Secretary, 46 Moray Place, Edinburgh EH3 6BH (031-225 6244).

The Faculty of Advocates 1985 Charitable Trust

Eligibility: 1. Widows, widowers, children or former dependants of deceased members of the Faculty of Advocates.

2. Members of the Faculty who are unable to practice by reason of ill health.

Types of grants: Single grants, annuities or loans appropriate to the circumstances.

Annual grant total: No information available.

Applications: In writing to the correspondent.

Correspondent: J W Macpherson, Bursar, Advocate's Library, Parliament House, Edinburgh EH1 1RF (031-226 5071).

The Glasgow Society of Sons of Ministers of the Church of Scotland

Eligibility: Children of deceased ministers of the Church of Scotland who are in need whether at school, college, university or otherwise.

Types of grants: Emergency grants payable at any time and annual grants payable at the end of March. The maximum grant is £1,500 per annum.

Annual grant total: No information available.

Applications: On a form available from the correspondent, including full details of income, capital and eligibility. Applications are usually considered in February. Emergency applications will be considered at all times.

Correspondent: G D M Reid, Secretary, 48 St Vincent Street, Glasgow G2 5HS (041-221 8012).

The Glasgow & West of Scotland Society for the Blind

Eligibility: Registered visually impaired people in Strathclyde and Dumfries & Galloway.

Types of grants: About 50 one-off grants for heating, clothing, aids and appliances. The average grant is £200. The society works in close co-operation with regional social work departments.

Annual grant total: £10,000.

Applications: Applications must be made via the social work department in the appropriate region.

Correspondent: Dr A Foster, Executive Officer, 2 Queens Crescent, Glasgow G4 9BW (041-332 4632).

Other information: The society also considers applications from groups or organisations of visually impaired people to support recreational and developmental activities aimed at increasing the independence of blind people.

The Governesses' Benevolent Society of Scotland

Eligibility: Elderly governesses in need.

Types of grants: Grants are given to elderly governesses in temporary difficulties through poverty or ill-health, and to contribute, in cases of poverty, towards the cost of a deferred annuity or life assurance for governesses.

Annual grant total: In 1991, the trust had assets of £215,000 with an income of £42,500. £18,000 was given in 8 relief-in-need grants to individuals.

Applications: On a form available from the correspondent, to be submitted directly by the individual and certified by a clergyman. Applications are usually considered in April/May but new applications can be considered as received.

Correspondent: G Sharp, Grant Thornton, 1-4 Atholl Crescent, Edinburgh EH3 8LQ (031-229 9181).

Scotland

The Grand Lodge of Antient, Free & Accepted Masons of Scotland

Eligibility: Members and their dependants, and the widows and dependants of deceased members.

Types of grants: One-off and recurrent grants according to need.

Annual grant total: About £180,000.

Applications: On a form available from the correspondent, or by direct approach to the local lodge.

Correspondent: Arthur O Hazel, Grand Secretary, Freemasons Hall, 96 George Street, Edinburgh EH2 3DH (031-225 5304).

The Earl Haig Fund (Scotland)

Eligibility: Serving and ex-serving members of the Armed Forces in Scotland and their widows/widowers and dependants.

Types of grants: Annual grants for food vouchers and clothing and small financial grants. Grants range from £25 to £520; about 4,500 grants are made.

Annual grant total: In 1990/91, the fund's assets totalled £4,600,000 with an income of £1,248,000. Expenditure totalled £1,165,000 including £390,000 in relief-in-need grants to individuals.

Applications: On a form available from the correspondent. Applications should be submitted through a social worker, citizen's advice bureau, other welfare agencies, the fund's own case workers or other ex-service charity case workers.

Correspondent: Brigadier R W Riddle, General Secretary, New Haig House, Logie Green Road, Edinburgh EH7 4HR (031-557 2782).

Other information: The Earl Haig Fund (Scotland) is in many respects the Scottish equivalent of the Benevolence Department of the Royal British Legion in the rest of Britain. Like the Legion it runs the Poppy Day Appeal, which is a major source of income to help those in distress. There is, however, also a Royal British Legion, Scotland, which has a separate entry. The two organisations share the same premises and work closely together.

The Douglas Hay Trust

Eligibility: Physically disabled children in Scotland, under 18.

Types of grants: Probably one-off and recurrent grants according to need.

Annual grant total: No information available.

Applications: In writing to the correspondent.

Correspondent: L R S Mackenzie, Tigh na H'ath, Dulnain Bridge, Morayshire PH26 3NU (0479-851266).

The Law Society of Scotland Benevolent Fund

Eligibility: Members and former members of the society and their dependants.

Types of grants: One-off and recurrent grants according to need.

Annual grant total: No information available.

Applications: In writing to the correspondent.

Correspondent: The Secretary, 26 Drumsheugh Gardens, Edinburgh EH3 7YR (031-226 7411).

The Andrew & Mary Elizabeth Little Charitable Trust

Eligibility: People in need who live in Scotland, with a preference for people living in the city of Glasgow.

Types of grants: One-off grants according to need, plus annuities of £400 per year.

Annual grant total: About £70,000.

Applications: Applications, in writing to the correspondent, should generally be made through social work departments, doctors or similar third parties and be supported by a confirmatory letter by a responsible person.

Correspondent: Messrs Wilson, Chalmers & Hendry, 33a Gordon Street, Glasgow G1 3PH (041-248 7761).

The Lyall Bequest

Eligibility: Ministers of the Church of Scotland.

Types of grants: Grants are given for the following:

1. Towards the cost of holiday accommodation at any hotel or boarding house in St Andrews to any minister and his wife at the rate of £50 a week each for up to two weeks a year.

2. Towards the travel expenses of ministers or charges situated over 100 miles from St Andrews and their wives who are attending the University of St Andrews Summer School of Theology.

3. Towards the cost of sickness and convalescence not covered by the NHS or otherwise.

Annual grant total: £1,300.

Applications: In writing to the correspondent.

Correspondent: Miss E L Calderwood, Secretary, c/o Pagan Osborne, 83 Market Street, St Andrews, Fife KY16 9PD (0334-75001).

The McLaren Fund for Indigent Ladies

Eligibility: Scottish widows/unmarried women (preferably over 40) and widows/unmarried daughters of commissioned officers in certain Scottish regiments.

Types of grants: Regular yearly allowances only of £260 a year. Between 130 and 150 grants are made each year.

Annual grant total: About £48,000.

Applications: On a form available from the correspondent. Considered twice yearly, in July and December.

Correspondent: J G Robinson, Secretary, Apsley House, 29 Wellington Street, Glasgow G2 6JA (041-221 8004).

The Annie Ramsay McLean Trust for the Elderly

Eligibility: Elderly people in Fife and Tayside. No specific age restriction applies; those of state pensionable age are generally considered eligible.

Types of grants: No restrictions apply. Grants may be awarded for house furnishings, medical aids, holidays, maintenance in nursing homes, temporary home nursing or clothing.

Annual grant total: No information available.

Applications: In writing to the correspondent.

Correspondent: Messrs Carlton Gilruth (Ref. CFSW), 30 Whitehall Street, Dundee DD1 4AL (0382-200111).

The Nurses Memorial to King Edward VII Edinburgh Committee

Eligibility: Nurses in Scotland who are retired, ill or otherwise in need. Retired nurses are given priority.

Types of grants: One-off grants to a maximum of about £400. Recurrent grants paid monthly. Help is given towards accommodation charges, domestic bills and inadequate income.

Annual grant total: About £15,000.

Applications: Details of present financial and other circumstances are required on a

● **Scotland**

form available from the correspondent. The information given should be confirmed by a social worker, health visitor, doctor or similar professional.

Correspondent: Mr Sweet, Clunie & Scott Chartered Accountants, 13 Alva Street, Edinburgh EH2 4PH (031-225 3973).

The Officers' Association (Scottish Branch)

Eligibility: Ex-officers (including the women's and nursing services) and their widows/widowers and dependants who are in distress, and ex-officers of all ages seeking employment.

Types of grants: Normally annual grants in four quarterly payments. One-off grants are investigated and dealt with as they arise. About 250 grants are made.

Annual grant total: In 1992/93, the trust had assets of £2.3 million with an income of over £200,000. £265,000 was given in relief-in-need grants to individuals.

Applications: On a form available from the correspondent, submitted through SSAFA, a social worker, citizen's advice bureau or other suitable agency, or Officer's Association case workers.

Correspondent: Lt Col J S D Robertson, Deputy General Secretary, Haig House, 1 Fitzroy Place, Glasgow G3 7RJ (041-221 8141).

The Royal British Legion Scotland

Eligibility: Serving and ex-serving members of the Armed Forces in Scotland and their widows/widowers or dependants.

Types of grants: Grants according to need; most types of assistance can be considered. The maximum grant is usually £200.

Annual grant total: In 1990/91, the trust had assets of £830,000 with an income of £300,000. Total expenditure was £285,000 including £49,000 in about 2,200 relief-in-need grants to individuals.

Applications: To the national headquarters or to any local branch (usually to be found in the local telephone book).

Correspondent: Brigadier R W Riddle, General Secretary, New Haig House, Logie Green Road, Edinburgh EH7 4HR (031-557 2782).

Other information: This charity works in close association with the Earl Haig Fund (Scotland), with which it shares offices and premises.

The Royal College of Midwives' Scottish Board

Eligibility: Midwives and former midwives in Scotland, and their dependants.

Types of grants: Grants of £125 a year paid quarterly.

Annual grant total: £500.

Applications: Write to the correspondent requesting an application form.

Correspondent: Mrs Patricia Purton, Secretary of the Benevolent Fund, 37 Frederick Street, Edinburgh EH2 1EP (031-225 1633).

The Royal Incorporation of Architects in Scotland

Eligibility: Architects and their dependants.

Types of grants: Probably small one-off grants.

Annual grant total: No information available.

Applications: In writing to the correspondent.

Correspondent: The Secretary to the Benevolent Fund, 15 Rutland Square, Edinburgh EH1 2BE (031-229 7205).

The Royal Scottish Agricultural Benevolent Institution

Eligibility: Elderly and/or disabled farmers (including aquaculture, horticulture, estate work and forestry), tenants or managers and their dependants. Applicants must normally live in Scotland.

Types of grants: 317 annual beneficiaries each received £520 in 1992/93, and all television licence fees were paid. One-off grants towards television licence fees, telephone and telephone alarm installation costs, debt and minor building repairs etc. were given to 14 individuals.

Annual grant total: In 1992/93, the trust had assets of £2.7 million with an income of £419,000. £180,000 was given in relief-in-need grants to individuals.

Applications: Write to or telephone the correspondent for an application form. Applications through referrals by local representatives, welfare organisations or social service departments are also welcomed. They are considered at any time.

Correspondent: Ian Purves-Hume, Director, South Bungalow, Ingliston, Edinburgh EH28 8NB (031-333 1023).

The Royal Society for Home Relief to Incurables, Edinburgh (General Fund)

Eligibility: Adult people throughout Scotland under retirement age, who have earned a livelihood (or been a housewife) and are no longer able to do so because of incurable illness.

Types of grants: A grant is given quarterly (totalling £276 per year) to help provide extra comforts. 331 grants were made in 1992. The fund is not in a position to consider isolated requests to meet single emergencies.

Annual grant total: Since the last edition of this Guide the General Fund has amalgamated with the Dunlop Fund. In 1992, the trust had assets of £1.8 million with an income of £114,000. Grants to individuals totalled over £91,000.

Applications: On a form available from the correspondent. Applications are considered in January, April, July and October.

Correspondent: Scott-Moncrieff, 17 Melville Street, Edinburgh EH3 7PH (031-226 6281).

The Royal Society for the Relief of Indigent Gentlewomen of Scotland

Eligibility: Spinsters and widows over 50 years of age of Scottish birth or background, who have (or whose husband or father had) a professional/business background. Applicants' income must be limited, currently under £5,400 a year, with capital below £8,000. Applicants need not live in Scotland.

Types of grants: Regular yearly allowances of £520 (subject to DSS regulations) and up to about £900 including other benefits. Occasional one-off grants have been given for holidays, telephone installation and rental, television licences, nursing costs and property maintenance.

Annual grant total: In 1992/93, the trust had assets of £6 million with an income of £754,000. Grants to 864 individuals totalled £665,000.

Applications: On a form available from the correspondent submitted directly by the individual or through a social worker, citizen's advice bureau or other welfare agency or third party. Applications are considered in May and November so completed forms must be received by 31st March and 30th September.

Correspondent: G F Goddard, Secretary, 14 Rutland Square, Edinburgh EH1 2BD (031-229 2308).

Scotland

The Sailors' Orphan Society of Scotland

Eligibility: Needy children of deceased Scottish seafarers.

Types of grants: About 200 recurrent grants of about £5 per week, paid monthly, for necessities and maintenance.

Annual grant total: About £40,000 to £50,000.

Applications: In writing to the correspondent.

Correspondent: A Thomson, Secretary, Cumbrae House, 15 Carlton Court, Glasgow G5 9JP (041-429 2181).

The Scottish Chartered Accountants' Benevolent Association

Eligibility: Members of the Institute of Chartered Accountants of Scotland, and their dependants.

Types of grants: Generally one-off grants or quarterly allowances. Occasional loans are also available.

Annual grant total: £71,500 in 45 grants.

Applications: In writing to the correspondent.

Correspondent: R Linton, Hon. Secretary, 142 St Vincent Street, Glasgow G2 5LB (041-248 6976).

The Scottish Cinematograph Trade Benevolent Fund

Eligibility: People in need who are or have been involved in the cinema trade, and their dependants.

Types of grants: One-off grants or recurrent grants of under £10 a week paid quarterly.

Annual grant total: £24,000 in 1990.

Applications: In writing to the correspondent.

Correspondent: The Secretary, c/o Ernst & Young, George House, 50 George Square, Glasgow G2 1RR (041-552 3456).

The Scottish Grocers' Federation Benevolent Fund

Eligibility: Past members or employees of the grocery trade in need who live in Scotland.

Types of grants: One-off or recurrent grants (up to £520 a year) according to need.

Annual grant total: About £12,000.

Applications: On a form available from the correspondent. Applicants are then visited to assess the most appropriate form of help.

Correspondent: Lawrie Dewar, Secretary, Federation House, 3 Loaning Road, Edinburgh EH7 6JE (031-652 2482).

The Scottish Hide & Leather Trades Provident & Benevolent Society

Eligibility: Members, officials and employees of the society, or their dependants, who are in need.

Types of grants: Pensions, one-off and recurrent grants according to need.

Annual grant total: £5,000 to £6,000.

Applications: In writing to the correspondent.

Correspondent: D A R Ballantine, Secretary, c/o Mitchells Roberton, George House, 36 North Hanover Street, Glasgow G1 2AD (041-552 3422).

The Scottish Law Agents Society Benevolent Fund

Eligibility: Scottish Law Agents or Scottish Law Society members, their spouses or dependants.

Types of grants: Pensions paid twice yearly on June 1st and December 1st, generally to adult and elderly dependants of solicitors who practised in Scotland and have died. Occasional help is given to practising solicitors who are in need. Grants range from £100 to £750.

Annual grant total: 28 grants totalling £15,000 in 1991.

Applications: In writing to the correspondent, including financial details. Applications are usually considered in June and December.

Correspondent: R M Sinclair, Secretary, 3 Albyn Place, Edinburgh EH2 4NQ.

Scottish Mining Disasters Relief Fund

Eligibility: People in need as the result of any accident in the coal mining industry in Scotland.

Types of grants: The trust gives a grants of £2,000 to women made widows as a result of a fatal mine accident. It can also give grants for other needs associated with the mining industry and is currently trying to widen the scope of its grant giving.

Annual grant total: £4,000 in 1993.

Applications: In writing to the correspondent.

Correspondent: I McWhir, Secretary, c/o British Coal Corporation, Castlebridge Access, Gartlove, Nr Alloa FK10 3PZ (0259-730134).

The Scottish Musicians' Benevolent Fund

Eligibility: Scottish professional musicians (and their dependants) who are in need, ill or convalescing.

Types of grants: Regular monthly allowances, typically £30 a month, and one-off grants at Christmas (typically £40) and all kinds of financial need. Recipients do not have to be members of a trade union or other professional organisation.

Annual grant total: In 1993, the fund had an income of £44,000. £20,000 was given in relief-in-need grants to individuals.

Applications: To the correspondent at any time. There is a quick response in emergencies.

Correspondent: Lesley Paterson, Hon. Secretary, c/o National Youth Orchestra of Scotland, 13 Somerset Place, Glasgow G3 7JT (041-353 1335).

The Scottish National Institution for the War-Blinded

Eligibility: People blinded or with visual impairment due to service with the Armed Forces, and their widows and dependants. Applicants should live in Scotland.

Types of grants: Mainly regular monthly grants for aftercare and workshop allowances. A few hardship grants are given.

Annual grant total: In 1992/93, the institution had assets of £29 million with an income of £1.65 million. Grants totalled £1.45 million.

Applications: Through the Workshops and After-Care Department. Telephone 031-333 1369.

Correspondent: (See above for applications.) J B M Munro, Secretary, PO Box 500, Gillespie Crescent, Edinburgh EH10 4HZ (031-229 1456).

Scottish Secondary Teachers' Association Benevolent Fund

Eligibility: Members and retired members of the association and in certain circumstances their dependants who are in need.

Types of grants: Recurrent grants usually during a period of long-term illness. One-off grants can also be given.

Annual grant total: £3,000 to £4,000.

Scotland

Applications: In writing to the correspondent, but most applications are received through the member representative in the school.

Correspondent: General Secretary, 15 Dundas Street, Edinburgh EH3 6QG (031-556 5919).

The Scottish Trust for the Physically Disabled

Eligibility: Physically disabled people who live in Scotland.

Types of grants: One-off grants enabling people to adapt houses or cars. The trust only considers giving a grant where the money is not available or not wholly available from statutory sources.

Annual grant total: About £30,000.

Applications: In writing to the correspondent. All applications must be supported by a letter from the local authority stating why the grant is necessary and why the authority cannot meet the cost.

Correspondent: D R M Gregory, Director, 77 Craigmount Brae, Edinburgh EH12 8YL (031-317 7227).

The Scottish Women's Land Army Welfare & Benevolent Fund

Eligibility: Former members of the Scottish Women's Land Army who have had an association with Scottish agriculture or forestry.

Types of grants: One-off grants to cope with illness and other types of financial need.

Annual grant total: About £1,100 in 1992/93. Severely limited funds.

Applications: Through referral from social services departments, welfare organisations, doctors or other professional people such as lawyers or bankers, or direct to the correspondent.

Correspondent: Ian Purves-Hume, Director, c/o RSABI, South Bungalow, Ingliston, Edinburgh EH28 8NB (031-333 1023).

The Show Business Benevolent Fund (Scotland)

Eligibility: Members of the Show Business Association (Scotland), over 60 years old, their children and other dependants in need. People cannot become members after the age of 50. Grants to non-members who are or who have been connected with the entertainment profession can be made from the W F Frame Benevolent Fund.

Types of grants: Weekly grants (maximum £10 a week) and monthly cash grants (maximum £15 a month), to help towards clothing, fuel, funeral expenses and other needs. Christmas and New Year (£30 to £40) and Easter (about £100) gifts are also given to up to around 20 people. The trust also sends about 20 members to Blackpool for an all expenses paid holiday.

Annual grant total: 11 individuals receive weekly grants, 3 receive monthly grants and about 20 receive one-off payments totalling about £8,000. The Blackpool trip costs an additional £7,000.

Applications: In writing to the correspondent. Considered monthly.

Correspondent: Mrs Findley, Wright, Johnston & Mackensie, 12 St Vincent Place, Glasgow G1 2EQ (041-248 3434).

Dr J R Sibbald's Trust

Eligibility: People living in Scotland who are suffering from an incurable disease and who are in financial need.

Types of grants: Currently 18 pensions of not more than £100 a year payable in two instalments in May and November. Occasional one-off grants are given in exceptional circumstances.

Annual grant total: In 1992/93, the trust had assets of £42,000 with an income of £5,800. £2,900 was given in 23 relief-in-need grants to individuals.

Applications: On a form available from the correspondent. Applications should be accompanied by a certificate from a surgeon or physician giving full details of the disease and that in their opinion it is incurable. As much background information about the applicant as is possible is also required which can be a letter from a social worker or friend describing the family circumstances and giving other personal information. Applications are considered annually in December but can be made at any time.

Correspondent: H J Stevens, Brodies WS, 15 Atholl Crescent, Edinburgh EH3 8HA (031-228 3777).

The Society at Aberdeen for the Benefit of Children of Deceased Clergymen of the Church of Scotland & Professors of the Universities of Scotland

Eligibility: Children of deceased ministers of the Church of Scotland or professors of Scottish universities.

Types of grants: One-off and recurrent grants according to need.

Annual grant total: No information available.

Applications: On a form available from the correspondent, but an "intelligently written letter of claim setting out the applicant's circumstances may be sufficient". Information given should include name of deceased, applicant's general family circumstances (capital and income), employment or field of study and any other relevant information. Applications are considered in April/May each year, but emergency grants can be considered at any time.

Correspondent: I M S Park, Paull & Williamsons Solicitors, Investment House, 6 Union Row, Aberdeen AB9 8DQ.

Other information: This entry has not been confirmed by the trust.

The Society for Benefit of Sons & Daughters of the Clergy of the Church of Scotland

Eligibility: 1. Unmarried or widowed daughters and unmarried sisters, over 40, of ordained ministers of the Church of Scotland. Preference is given to the elderly and infirm.

2. Ministers with children at secondary school and university.

Types of grants: 1. Annual pension.

2. One-off or recurrent grants according to need.

Annual grant total: 1. £6,000; 2. About £15,000.

Applications: In writing to the correspondent.

Correspondent: R Graeme Thom, Secretary, Scott-Moncrieff, Chartered Accountants, 17 Melville Street, Edinburgh EH3 7PH (031-266 6281).

The Society for Welfare & Teaching of the Blind

Eligibility: Registered blind and partially sighted people in Edinburgh and south east Scotland.

Types of grants: Mainly one-off grants according to need, though recurrent grants may occasionally be made. Grants can be to a maximum of about £130 towards children's activity holidays, to subsidise outings, to repair household equipment etc.. Christmas gifts of £5 each or pensions (£40 to £60 paid twice a year) are occasionally given.

Annual grant total: In 1993, grants totalled £31,000, of which £18,000 was to provide subsidised holidays, £4,500 in

Christmas gifts leaving £8,500 for relief in need grants to individuals.

Applications: In writing to the correspondent usually through a social worker.

Correspondent: The Director, 4 Coates Crescent, Edinburgh EH3 7AP (031-225 6381).

The Stead Benefaction Trust

Eligibility: People born in Scotland who are suffering from an incurable disease.

Types of grants: A grant of £75 paid in May.

Annual grant total: £750. A maximum of 10 grants are given each year.

Applications: On a form available from the correspondent, to be returned not later than 31st March. Accepted applicants are invited to reapply each year.

Correspondent: Mrs Fiona Marshall, Administrator, Henderson Boyd Jackson, 19 Ainslie Place, Edinburgh EH3 6AU (031-226 6881).

The Miss M O Taylor's Trust

Eligibility: "For the relief of impoverished authors, actors and actresses, artists and musicians of sufficient standing to deserve the title, ie. they must have had some measure of success in the profession they have adopted and must have earned money in it."

Types of grants: Generally recurrent grants according to need.

Annual grant total: About £800 in 8 or 10 grants.

Applications: In writing to the correspondent.

Correspondent: Messrs Geoghegan & Co, 6 St Colme Street, Edinburgh EH3 6AD (031-225 4681).

Other information: The trust is in the process of trying to pass its funds, about £25,000, onto the relevant drama, arts and music academies to ensure that the money gets to the individuals who need it, as the trust has found it difficult to allocate all its funds. The correspondent should be able to give more details.

The Third Inglis Property Trust

Eligibility: People in need.

Types of grants: One-off and recurrent grants according to need.

Annual grant total: No information available.

Applications: On a form available from the correspondent.

Correspondent: H R Galbraith, Rothesay House, 134 Douglas Street, Glasgow G2 4HF (041-331 1333).

Borders

The Blackstock Trust

Eligibility: Elderly or sick people living in the counties of Roxburgh, Berwick or Selkirk.

Types of grants: Financial assistance with accommodation, maintenance or welfare, and the provision of amenities for individuals in need. Grants may also be made to organisations in Scotland providing for the care and attention of elderly, sick or disabled people.

Annual grant total: About £20,000.

Applications: In writing to the correspondent.

Correspondent: William Windram, Secretary, Messrs Pike & Chapman, 36 Bank Street, Galashiels TD1 1ER (0896-2379).

Charities Administered by Berwickshire District Council

Correspondent: The correspondent for all the following is: D W Dewar, Director of Finance, Berwickshire District Council, 8 Newtown Street, Duns, Berwickshire TD11 3DU (0361-82600).

Applications: In writing to the correspondent.

(i) Black's Bequest

Eligibility: People in need who live in Coldstream and Coldstream Newton.

Types of grants: One-off grants according to need.

Annual grant total: £850 in 1992/93.

(ii) The MacWatt Bequest

Eligibility: People in need who live in the former burgh of Duns.

Types of grants: Grants for coal and food.

Annual grant total: Generally 2 or 3 grants of £200 to £300 each.

(iii) The Watson Bequest

Eligibility: People in need who live in Cranshaws.

Types of grants: Probably one-off and recurrent grants according to need.

Annual grant total: No information available.

● **Galashiels**

The R S Hayward Trust

Eligibility: People in need who have been employed in Galashiels for at least 10 years, and have retired or become incapacitated, either permanently or temporarily, from work, and their wives or widows.

Types of grants: One-off and recurrent grants according to need.

Annual grant total: No information available.

Applications: In writing to the correspondent.

Correspondent: The Secretary, c/o Pike & Chapman, Solicitors, Bank Street, Galashiels, Selkirkshire TD1 1ER (0896-2379).

● **Roxburgh**

The Roxburghshire Landward Benevolent Trust

Eligibility: People in need who live in the landward area of the former Roxburgh County Council.

Types of grants: Grants to help with heating expenditure relating to home illness, travel to hospital, equipment such as wheelchairs etc.. Grants range from £10 to £300.

Annual grant total: £5,000 in 1993.

Applications: In writing to the correspondent. Applications can be submitted directly by the individual or through a third party. They are considered throughout the year.

Correspondent: Alastair Turnbull, c/o Messrs Taits, 10 The Square, Kelso TD5 7HJ (0573-224311).

Central

● **Alloa**

The Spittal Bequest

Eligibility: People in need who have lived in Alloa for at least 10 years immediately before receiving benefit.

Types of grants: One-off and recurrent grants according to need.

Central/Dumfries & Galloway

Annual grant total: No information available.

Applications: On a form available from the correspondent.

Correspondent: The Chief Executive, Clackmannan District Council, Greenfield, Alloa FK10 2AD (0259-722160).

● Clackmannan

The Clackmannan District Charitable Trust

Eligibility: People in need who live in the area administered by the Clackmannan District Council, and have either lived there at least 12 consecutive months immediately before receiving benefit, or have had three years' continuous residence in the district at any period and six months immediately before receiving benefit. People eligible for the Spittal Trust (see above entry) should not apply to the Clackmannan District Charitable Trust.

Types of grants: One-off and recurrent grants according to need.

Annual grant total: No information available.

Applications: On a form available from the correspondent.

Correspondent: The Chief Executive, Clackmannan District Council, Greenfield, Alloa FK10 2AD (0259-722160).

● Denny

The Shanks Bequest

Eligibility: People in need who live in Denny.

Types of grants: Probably one-off and recurrent grants according to need.

Annual grant total: No information available.

Applications: In writing to the correspondent.

Correspondent: The Director of Finance, Falkirk District Council, Municipal Buildings, Falkirk FK1 5RS (0324-24911).

Other information: Falkirk District Council also administers other small trusts for individuals in need who live in the Falkirk area. Further details from the correspondent above.

● Dunblane

The Dunblane Coal Fund

Eligibility: People in need (especially elderly people) who live in Dunblane.

Types of grants: Vouchers for coal or stamps for electric heating costs. £10 vouchers are also given at Christmas.

Annual grant total: Probably about £1,000. In 1991, there were 53 beneficiaries.

Applications: In writing to the correspondent.

Correspondent: Mrs Jean Thompson, Hon. Clerk, c/o Registrar's Office, Municipal Buildings, Dunblane FK15 0AA (0786-822214).

Dumfries & Galloway

The Holywood Trust

Eligibility: Disadvantaged/needy young people aged 15 to 19 (up to 25 in some instances) and living in the Dumfries and Galloway region. Some preventative work is also undertaken with under 15s.

Types of grants: One-off and recurrent grants according to need. The trust is particularly keen to provide grants to young people who produce proposals aimed at setting up self-help activities which contribute to their personal development, to help other young people and benefit the wider community.

Annual grant total: £70,000 in 1992/93, of which £30,000 was given in 142 grants to individuals. It is not known how much of this was for relief-in-need purposes.

Applications: In writing to the correspondent, directly by the individual or through a third party such as a social worker or citizen's advice bureau. Applications are considered every six/eight weeks.

Applications should include:
(a) Who you are.
(b) What you want to do or develop.
(c) What you have achieved to date.
(d) Why you need the trust's assistance.
(e) How you propose to use the experience or develop the project.
(f) Who else you have approached and what their likely response will be.
(g) An income/expenditure statement for your project.

Correspondent: Peter Robertson, Director, Mount St Michael, Crays Road, Dumfries DG1 4UT (0387-69176/7).

● Annandale & Eskdale

Charities Administered by Annandale & Eskdale District Council

Correspondent: The correspondent for all the following is: Annandale & Eskdale District Council, District Council Chambers, High Street, Annan DG12 6AQ (04612-3311).

(i) The Samuel Elliot Bequest

Eligibility: People, particularly the elderly, who are in need and live in the burgh of Lockerbie and the parishes of Dryfesdale and Johnstone.

Types of grants: Probably one-off and recurrent grants according to need.

Annual grant total: In 1991/92, the trust had assets of £15,000 with an income of £1,330. Expenditure totalled £1,460.

Applications: On a form available from the correspondent. Applications should be submitted directly by the individual and are considered throughout the year.

(ii) George Hunter Trust

Eligibility: People in need who live in Lochmaben.

Types of grants: Recurrent grants for Sunday school prizes, school dictionaries, garden competitions and the general welfare of the local community.

Annual grant total: In 1992, the trust had assets of £5,600 generating an income of £1,300. Total expenditure was £1,060.

Applications: Directly by the individual on a form available from the correspondent.

(iii) Lockerbie Trust

Eligibility: People in need who live in Lockerbie.

Types of grants: One-off grants to individuals, groups, societies etc.. Annual payments are only considered in exceptional circumstances. The availability of grants from other sources will be taken into account in assessing applications.

Annual grant total: In 1992/93, the trust had assets of £268,800 generating an income of £17,400. Total expenditure was £860.

Applications: Applications, on a form available from the correspondent, can be submitted by the individual, through a recognised referral agency (eg. social worker, citizen's advice bureau or doctor) or other third party, and are considered throughout the year.

Kirkbean

The James McKune Mortification

Eligibility: People in need who are natives of the parish of Kirkbean and still live there, or people who have lived for at least 20 years in the parish.

Types of grants: Annual pensions of £30.

Annual grant total: In 1993, the trust had an income of £700. Eight grants to individuals totalled £240.

Applications: On a form available from the correspondent. Applications should be submitted directly by the individual and are considered in March.

Correspondent: George Fazakerley, Secretary, Coniston, Carsethorn, Dumfries DG2 8DS (0387-88662).

Nithsdale

The Nithsdale District Charities

Eligibility: People in need who live in the area administered by Nithsdale District Council.

Types of grants: The council administers a number of very small trusts. The largest has a grant total of £400.

Annual grant total: See above.

Applications: In writing to the correspondent.

Correspondent: The Chief Executive, Nithsdale District Council, Municipal Chambers, Dumfries DG1 2AD (0387-53166).

Wigtown

The Henry Macdonald Fund

Eligibility: Mothers and young children who live in Stranraer.

Types of grants: Probably one-off and recurrent grants according to need. Grants are given through the Social Work Department of the Dumfries and Galloway Regional Council.

Annual grant total: £9,500.

Applications: In writing to the correspondent.

Correspondent: The Chief Executive, Wigtown District Council, Sun Street, Stranraer DG9 7JJ (0776-702151).

Other information: The council administers a number of other very small trusts for various places in the district including Dr David Matthew's Bequest, The James Lees & James McClandish Bequests, Agnes McMeekan's Bequest, and The John Agnew Simpson Fund.

Fife

Cupar

The Bruce Charitable Trust

Eligibility: People in need who live in the burgh of Cupar.

Types of grants: Grants to poor, elderly, infirm or distressed people in the burgh of Cupar. Grants are also given to organisations.

Annual grant total: About £8,000.

Applications: In writing to the correspondent.

Correspondent: Miss E L Calderwood, Secretary, c/o Pagan Osborne, 83 Market Street, St Andrews KY16 9PD (0334-75001).

Dunfermline

Charities Administered by Dunfermline District Council

Eligibility: The beneficial area differs from charity to charity, the largest of which are the McGregor Bequest and the Wildridge Memorial Fund. The majority refer only to Dunfermline, but smaller ones exist for Aberdour, Lochgelly and Tulliallan.

Types of grants: Generally one-off grants, many of which are restricted to elderly people and include help in the form of coal and groceries.

Annual grant total: In 1992/93, the charities' combined income totalled about £3,400 of which about £2,220 was given out in grants. Over £1,400 of this is limited to Dunfermline.

Applications: In writing to the correspondent.

Correspondent: Dunfermline District Council, Central Services, 15 East Port, Dunfermline KY12 7LF (0383-728291).

Kirkcaldy

The Kirkcaldy Charitable Trust

Eligibility: Poor, sick, disabled and elderly people living in the former royal burgh of Kirkcaldy.

Types of grants: One-off grants only for emergencies, heating/fuel, clothing, aids/appliances and food. 35 to 40 grants are made ranging from £10 to £250.

Annual grant total: £2,500.

Applications: Made through the social work department. The trust requires evidence of Social Fund refusal before considering giving a grant.

Correspondent: J McDonald, Community Development Manager, Fife Regional Council, Fyfe House, North Street, Glenrothes, Fife KY7 5LT (0592-754411).

Moonzie

The Moonzie Parish Trust

Eligibility: People in need who live in the parish of Moonzie.

Types of grants: Pensions paid annually.

Annual grant total: The trust has an income of about £700. It also gives grants to organisations.

Applications: In writing to the correspondent.

Correspondent: The Trustees, c/o Messrs Rollo, Davidson & McFarlane, 67 Crossgate, Cupar, Fife KY15 5AS (0334-54081).

Other information: The same correspondent administers two smaller trusts, Dr Guland's Bequest and the Charles Skinner Trust. The former is restricted to people, particularly the elderly, who are in need and who live in the parish of Falkland, and the latter to people over 65 years of age in need who live in Dairsie.

North East Fife

Charities Administered by North East Fife District Council

Eligibility: Elderly residents in the North East Fife area.

Types of grants: Distributions are made each year from various charitable bequests at Christmas.

Annual grant total: No information available.

Applications: In writing to the correspondent.

Correspondent: The Chief Executive, North East Fife District Council, County Buildings, St Catherine Street, Cupar, Fife KY15 4TA (0334-53722).

● Fife/Grampian

● **St Andrews**

The Fleming Bequest

Eligibility: Poor, elderly, infirm or distressed people living in the parish of St Andrews and St Leonards in the town of St Andrews.

Types of grants: About 50 one-off and recurrent grants between £75 and £200.

Annual grant total: £3,500.

Applications: In writing to the correspondent through a social worker, citizen's advice bureau or other welfare agency. Applications are considered at any time, but particularly in May or November.

Correspondent: Janet Hunter, Messrs Pagan, Osborne, Grace & Calders, 83 Market Street, St Andrews, Fife KY16 9NX (0334-75001).

The Macdonald Bequest

Eligibility: Young people in need who live in the city of St Andrews or in the parish of St Andrews and St Leonards.

Types of grants: Grants are given towards the cost of holidays or convalescence at home or elsewhere for those suffering or recovering from illness.

Annual grant total: £700.

Applications: In writing to the correspondent.

Correspondent: Miss E L Calderwood, Secretary, c/o Pagan Osborne, 83 Market Street, St Andrews, Fife KY16 9PD (0334-75001).

Other information: The trust also gives grants towards Christmas parties, entertainment and treats for young people under 14 and to youth organisations in the area of benefit.

Mrs Simpson's Charity

Eligibility: People in need who live in the parishes of St Andrews and St Leonards in the city of St Andrews.

Types of grants: One-off or recurrent grants according to need.

Annual grant total: No information available.

Applications: In writing to the correspondent.

Correspondent: Miss E L Calderwood, Secretary, Pagan Osborne, 83 Market Street, St Andrews, Fife KY16 9PD (0334-75001).

The St Andrews Welfare Trust

Eligibility: People in need who live within a 3 or 4 mile radius of St Andrews.

Types of grants: One-off and recurrent grants according to need up to a maximum of £200. About 20 grants are made each year. Grants are given (a) towards expenses incurred during sickness and convalescence in so far as the expenses are outside the provisions of the National Health Service and applicants cannot meet such expenses; (b) to elderly people in special circumstances of need, and (c) to young people who are in special need. Grants are also given to local organisations for eligible people.

Annual grant total: About £4,000, mainly paid through the social work department to low income families.

Applications: In writing to the correspondent through a social worker, citizen's advice bureau or other welfare agency. Applications are considered throughout the year.

Correspondent: Mrs Janet Hunter, Messrs Pagan Osborne, 83 Market Street, St Andrews, Fife KY16 9PD (0334-75001).

Grampian

Charities Administered by Grampian Regional Council

Eligibility: Residents within the Grampian region.

Types of grants: The council administers a number of small trusts. No further details available.

Annual grant total: No information available.

Applications: In writing to the correspondent.

Correspondent: The Chief Executive, Grampian Regional Council, Woodhill House, Ashgrove Road West, Aberdeen AB9 2LU (0224-682222).

The George Jamieson Fund

Eligibility: Needy widows and single women who live in the city of Aberdeen or the counties of Aberdeen and Kincardine.

Types of grants: 30 grants of £300 a year payable half yearly in May and November.

Annual grant total: £7,500.

Applications: Considered two or three times a year.

Correspondent: Messrs Wilsone & Duffus, 7 Golden Square, Aberdeen AB9 8EP (0224-641065).

● **Aberdeen**

The Aberdeen Disabled Person's Trust

Eligibility: Severely disabled people who live in the city of Aberdeen.

Types of grants: One-off grants for aids/appliances (washing machines, mattresses etc.); special clothing and items no longer available through DSS; convalescence/holidays; home repairs/alterations, including telephone installation. Grants rarely cover the full cost of the need, but the trust often joins other charities in raising the sum required eg. for electric wheelchairs. The trust also has a fully equipped flat which is available to disabled people/families on holiday in Aberdeen.

Annual grant total: In 1993, the trust had assets of £30,000 and an income of £3,400. Grants of £100 to £250 were given to 18 people totalling £2,300.

Applications: Applications must be in writing and submitted through a social worker, citizen's advice bureau or other welfare agency.

Correspondent: A McKenzie, 52 Beaconsfield Place, Aberdeen AB2 4AJ (0224-643176).

The Aberdeen Widows' & Spinsters' Benevolent Fund

Eligibility: Widows and unmarried women over 60 years of age who live in the city or county of Aberdeen; in cases of special need and where surplus income is available, those between 40 and 60 are considered.

Types of grants: Generally yearly allowances of up to £100 payable twice yearly in June and December.

Annual grant total: No information available.

Applications: On a form available from the correspondent. However, the correspondent states: "we are oversubscribed and cannot consider new applications at the moment".

Correspondent: Messrs Ledingham Chalmers, 1 Golden Square, Aberdeen AB9 8BH (0224-647344).

The James Allan of Mid-Beltie (Widows' Fund)

Eligibility: Needy widows, usually elderly, who live in Aberdeen.

Grampian

Types of grants: Recurrent yearly allowances only; at present grants are £220 a year.

Annual grant total: In 1993, the trust had assets of £150,000 and an income of £34,000 of which £12,700 was given to 60 widows.

Applications: To the correspondent; applications are considered at six-monthly intervals.

Correspondent: Adam Cochran, Solicitors, 6 Bon Accord Square, Aberdeen AB9 1XU (0224-588913).

The George, James & Alexander Chalmers Trust

Eligibility: Women living in Aberdeen who have fallen on hard times as a result of misfortune and not through any fault of their own.

Types of grants: Annuities are currently £400 a year, payable by half-yearly instalments in June and December. Up to 70 annuities are given.

Annual grant total: Up to £18,000.

Applications: On a form available from the correspondent.

Correspondent: J C Chisholm, Clerk, Factor, 2 Bon Accord Crescent, Aberdeen AB1 2DH (0224-587261).

The Gordon Cheyne Trust Fund

Eligibility: Widows and daughters of deceased merchants, shopkeepers and other businessmen, who are natives of Aberdeen or who have lived there for at least 25 years.

Types of grants: Annual allowances paid twice-yearly in May and November.

Annual grant total: No information available.

Applications: On a form available from the correspondent.

Correspondent: Messrs Ledingham Chalmers, 1 Golden Square, Aberdeen AB9 8BH (0224-647344).

The Crisis Fund of Voluntary Service Aberdeen

Eligibility: People in need who live in Aberdeen.

Types of grants: About 700 one-off grants each year according to need; typically £30.

Annual grant total: About £20,000.

Applications: By interview with Voluntary Service Aberdeen's social work team, or through a social worker or other professional welfare agency on an application form available from the correspondent.

Correspondent: Voluntary Service Aberdeen, 38 Castle Street, Aberdeen AB1 1AB (0224-586395).

The Donald Trust

Eligibility: People in need who "belong to" the city or county of Aberdeen. "Advanced age, lack of health, inability to work, high character and former industry are strong recommendations."

Types of grants: Annual allowances paid twice-yearly in May and November.

Annual grant total: No information available.

Applications: On a form available from the correspondent.

Correspondent: Messrs Ledingham Chalmers, 1 Golden Square, Aberdeen AB9 8BH (0224-647344).

The Forbes Fund

Eligibility: Burgesses of Guild of the city of Aberdeen and their dependants; widows or daughters of deceased merchants, shopkeepers and businessmen who have lived in Aberdeen for at least 25 years and who are in need.

Types of grants: Annual allowances paid twice-yearly in June and December.

Annual grant total: No information available.

Applications: On a form available from the correspondent.

Correspondent: Messrs Ledingham Chalmers, 1 Golden Square, Aberdeen AB9 8BH (0224-647344).

The Fuel Fund of Voluntary Service Aberdeen

Eligibility: People living in Aberdeen who need help in maintaining a warm home, particularly elderly and disabled people.

Types of grants: About 350 one-off grants typically of £20.

Annual grant total: £8,000.

Applications: By interview with Voluntary Service Aberdeen's social work team, or on an application form available from the correspondent, to be submitted through a social worker or other professional welfare agency.

Correspondent: Voluntary Service Aberdeen, 38 Castle Street, Aberdeen AB1 1AB (0224-586395).

The Henry John Jopp Fund

Eligibility: Widowed or single women in need living in Aberdeen.

Types of grants: Pensions of £300 a year payable in half-yearly instalments in May and November.

Annual grant total: About £13,000 in over 40 pensions.

Applications: On a form available from the correspondent.

Correspondent: Messrs Wilsone & Duffus, 7 Golden Square, Aberdeen AB9 8EP (0224-641065).

The Matilda Murray Trust

Eligibility: People in need who have lived in Old Aberdeen for at least the five years before the date of application.

Types of grants: Annual grants only of £100 to £150.

Annual grant total: About £3,500 in 30 grants.

Applications: On a form available from the correspondent. Applications must be submitted by mid-October for consideration in November and grants are distributed in December.

Correspondent: E Grant MacKenzie, Solicitor, Stronarchs, 12 Carden Place, Aberdeen AB9 1FW (0224-643573).

The Shepherd Fund

Eligibility: Needy widows or daughters of deceased merchants, shopkeepers or other businessmen who have lived in Aberdeen for at least 25 years.

Types of grants: £320 a year payable half-yearly in March and September. Currently 17 beneficiaries.

Annual grant total: About £4,400.

Applications: On a form available from the correspondent.

Correspondent: Mr Esslemant, Messrs Wilsone & Duffus, 7 Golden Square, Aberdeen AB9 8EP (0224-641065).

The James Sim of Cornhill Trust

Eligibility: Merchants, shopkeepers and businessmen who were either born in Aberdeen or who carried on business there, and their dependants.

Types of grants: Annual allowances paid half-yearly in June and December.

Annual grant total: No information available.

Applications: On a form available from the correspondent.

Grampian

Correspondent: Messrs Ledingham Chalmers, 1 Golden Square, Aberdeen AB9 8BH (0224-647344).

The Sutherland Bequest

Eligibility: Needy widows or widowers who live in Aberdeen and have children of school age; adult and elderly people who have had treatment in a mental hospital or who are mentally disabled and who are in financial need.

Types of grants: Grants paid twice-yearly. Amounts vary according to need. About 25 grants per year.

Annual grant total: About £2,500.

Applications: On a form available from the correspondent. Applications must be submitted before the end of March.

Correspondent: Voluntary Service Aberdeen, 38 Castle Street, Aberdeen AB1 1AB (0224-586395).

Miss Jessie Ann Thomson's Trust

Eligibility: Indigent gentlewomen living in the city of Aberdeen. Preference to women whose maiden name is Thomson or Middleton. In practice beneficiaries tend to be elderly.

Types of grants: One-off or recurrent grants according to need, up to £280 a year.

Annual grant total: £4,800 in 18 grants in 1992.

Applications: In writing to the correspondent; considered in January or February.

Correspondent: Adam Cochran, Solicitors, 6 Bon Accord Square, Aberdeen AB9 1XU (0224-588913).

Banff & Buchan

The Banff & Buchan District Charities

Eligibility: People who live in the area administered by the Banff and Buchan District Council.

Types of grants: One-off and recurrent grants according to need. No loans are given. Grants are also given to organisations.

Annual grant total: In 1993/94, the trust gave grants totalling £12,800.

Applications: In writing to the correspondent and including a financial statement or profit and loss account for groups or organisations.

Correspondent: The Chief Executive, Council HQ, St Leonards, Sandyhill Road, Banff AB45 1BH (0261-813200).

The McRobert Mortification - Gamrie & Forglen

Eligibility: Residents over 60 of the parishes of Gamrie and Forglen in the Banff and Buchan district.

Types of grants: Recurrent grants.

Annual grant total: No information available.

Applications: On a form available from the correspondent.

Correspondent: Messrs Alexander George & Co, 24 Shore Street, Macduff, Banffshire AB44 1TX (0261-832201).

Gordon

The Gordon District Charities

Eligibility: People in need who live in the area administered by Gordon District Council.

Types of grants: One-off and recurrent grants according to need. The council administers a number of funds details of which are available from the correspondent.

Annual grant total: No information available.

Applications: In writing to the correspondent.

Correspondent: The Chief Executive, Gordon House, Blackhall Road, Inverurie, Aberdeenshire AB5 9WA (0467-620981).

Macduff

The Simpson Trust

Eligibility: People in need who live in the burgh of Macduff, although in practice elderly people living on their own who are in need.

Types of grants: Annuities ranging from £60 to £100, usually paid in two instalments in December and June.

Annual grant total: £4,000 in 43 grants in 1992/93.

Applications: On a form available from the correspondent. When there are vacancies in the list of annuitants, applications are invited through the local press.

Correspondent: Messrs Alexander George & Co, 24 Shore Street, Macduff, Banffshire AB44 1TX (0261-832201).

Moray

Charities Administered by Moray District Council

Correspondent: The correspondent for all the following is: The Director of Finance, Moray District Council, District Headquarters, Elgin, Moray IV30 1BX (0343-543451).

(i) The Auchray Fund

Eligibility: Elderly and infirm people who were in business in the burgh of Elgin and who are now in financial need.

Types of grants: Help with council house rent. Four grants per year.

Annual grant total: About £2,300.

Applications: Grants are advertised in the local press. Applications must be supported by a magistrate.

Other information: The council administers another 17 trusts for the benefit of residents of Elgin and surrounding area, most of which are very small. Further details can be obtained from the correspondent.

(ii) The Forres Poor Fund & Others

Eligibility: People in need who live in Forres.

Types of grants: One-off and recurrent grants given once and twice a year.

Applications: Applications to the correspondent following an advertisement in a local paper. Cases are considered by a local councillor. Applicants are nominated by a local councillor for the Jonathon & Robert Anderson Funds when a vacancy arises.

Other information: The council administers other trusts including the Forres Poor Fund, the Dick & Smith Fund, the Jonathon & Robert Anderson Funds and various smaller funds.

(iii) The Keith Coal Funds & the Keith Poor Funds

Eligibility: People in need who live in Keith.

Types of grants: One-off payments and grants for coal. About 200 grants per year.

Annual grant total: About £800.

Applications: To the correspondent following advertisements in the local paper. Cases will be considered by a local councillor.

(iv) The Keith Nursing Funds

Eligibility: Sick, infirm or elderly people who live in Keith.

Grampian/Highlands

Types of grants: Grants towards the cost of food, clothing and other essential home comforts, medicines, treatment and medical appliances, where no money is available from the National Health Scheme. Three grants per year.

Annual grant total: £600.

Applications: In writing to the correspondent.

(v) Other trusts

The council also administers various small charities (under £500 grant total) for residents of the following areas: Kirkmichael, Inveravon, Mortlach, Keith and Aberlour; Dufftown; Lossiemouth; the parishes of Boharm, Deskford, Dibble, Knockando, Rothes and Speymouth, and the burgh of Cullen. Further details are available from the correspondent.

● Peterhead

The Peterhead Coal Fund

Eligibility: People in need who live in the parish of Peterhead.

Types of grants: Four or five bags of coal to those coal-using households who are on the lowest levels of income. It is distributed in December and January.

Annual grant total: About £2,000.

Applications: In writing to the correspondent.

Correspondent: David Taylor, Hon. Secretary, 28 Broad Street, Peterhead, Aberdeenshire AB42 6BY (0779-476384).

Highlands

The Argyll Naval Fund

Eligibility: Parents or guardians of young people who have been awarded Reserved Cadetship or scholarships in the Royal Navy. Applicants must have some connection with the Highlands of Scotland.

Types of grants: Regular yearly allowances of up to £150 for those in need.

Annual grant total: Over £2,000.

Applications: Entrance examinations for the Royal Navy are conducted at HMS Gosport, Hants, by the Admiralty Interview Board through whom prospective applicants should register their interest.

Correspondent: The Treasurer, RHASS, Ingliston, Newbridge, Midlothian EH28 8NF (031-333 2444 ext. 209).

The Howard Doris Trust

Eligibility: People in need who live in the districts of Lochcarron and South West Ross.

Types of grants: Usually one-off grants.

Annual grant total: The trust's annual income is £30,000, but probably only a small proportion of this is given in grants to individuals.

Applications: In writing to the correspondent.

Correspondent: Andrew M C Dalgleish, Solicitor, Brodies WS, 15 Atholl Crescent, Edinburgh EH3 8HA (031-228 3777).

● Caithness

The Julie Wheatcroft Trust

Eligibility: Children in Caithness whose medical conditions require treatment in the south.

Types of grants: Financial assistance and advice to enable parents to remain with their children while undergoing treatment.

Annual grant total: No information available.

Applications: To the correspondent by telephone or in writing.

Correspondent: c/o Dr Gordon Shepherd, Riverbank, Janet Street, Thurso KW14 7AR (0847-63321).

● Inverness

The Dr Forbes (Inverness) Trust

Eligibility: People in need who live in the former burgh of Inverness.

Types of grants: Generally one-off grants to help with the cost of medical treatment, electrical equipment, convalescence, food, clothing and travel expenses to visit sick relatives in the same area. Help has also been given with holidays for people who from a medical point of view would benefit.

Annual grant total: In 1992/93, the trust had assets of £120,000. Total expenditure was £7,500. Grants up to a maximum of £1,000 were given to 45 individuals and totalled £9,000.

Applications: Applications, on a form available from the correspondent, can be submitted by the individual, through a recognised referral agency (eg. social worker, citizen's advice bureau or doctor) or other third party, and are considered throughout the year. Application forms must be signed by the applicant's general medical practitioner. Supporting letters help the application.

Correspondent: J H S Stewart, Secretary & Treasurer, Munro & Noble Solicitors, 26 Church Street, Inverness IV1 1HX (0463-221727).

Charities Administered by Inverness District Council

Applications: Forms are available from the local district councillor for each ward, community councils and the library and should be submitted by the start of December each year. The exact date is advertised locally.

Correspondent: The correspondent for all the following is: The Director of Administration, Inverness District Council, Town House, Inverness IV1 1JJ (0463-23911).

(i) The Inverness Benevolent Fund & Seasonal Comforts Scheme

Eligibility: Pensioners who live within the boundaries of the old burgh area of Inverness. Applicants must not have a wage-earning member of the family living with them, must have no other source of income other than state pension apart from supplementary benefit or rent/community charge rebate, and be the sole claimant in the household.

Types of grants: One-off grants.

Annual grant total: No information available.

(ii) The Inverness District Benevolent Fund & Seasonal Comforts Scheme

Eligibility: Pensioners who live in Inverness district, but outside the boundaries of the old burgh area of Inverness. Applicants must fulfil the criteria stated in (i) above.

Types of grants: One-off grants.

Annual grant total: No information available.

(iii) Other trusts

The council administers various smaller charities for residents of Inverness with a combined annual income of about £3,000. Further details from the correspondent.

● Ross & Cromarty

The Ross & Cromarty District Charities

Eligibility: People in need who live in the area administered by Ross and Cromarty District Council.

● Highlands/Lothian

Types of grants: Probably one-off and recurrent grants according to need.

Annual grant total: No information available.

Applications: In writing to the correspondent.

Correspondent: The Chief Executive, Council Offices, Ross & Cromarty District Council, Dingwall IV15 9QN (0349-63381).

Lothian

The Avenel Trust

Eligibility: Children in need under 18 living in the area covered by Lothian Regional Council Social Work Department and Lothian Health Board.

Types of grants: Small one-off grants for safety items such as fireguards and safety gates, also for shoes and clothing, bedding, cots and pushchairs.

Grants are not given for holidays or household furnishings.

Annual grant total: £7,500 in 137 grants in 1992.

Applications: Applications should be submitted through a recognised referral agency (eg. social worker, health visitor or doctor). They are considered every two months.

Correspondent: Mrs Fiona Kelly, Hon. Secretary, 1 Midmar Gardens, Edinburgh EH1 6DY (031-447 6805).

The Capital Charitable Trust

Eligibility: People in extreme need who live in Edinburgh and the Lothians.

Types of grants: One-off and recurrent grants according to need.

Annual grant total: Grants of up to £20 were given to 750 individuals and totalled £13,000.

Applications: Through social workers, not direct from individuals.

Correspondent: S Y Marshall, Aitken Nairn WS, 7 Abercromby Place, Edinburgh EH3 6LA (031-556 6644).

The Robert Christie Bequest Fund

Eligibility: People over 60 who live in Edinburgh or Midlothian and who are suffering from an acutely painful disease.

Types of grants: Yearly allowances of up to £500.

Annual grant total: No information available.

Applications: In writing to the correspondent.

Correspondent: Messrs J & R A Robertson, WS, 15 Great Stuart Street, Edinburgh EH3 7TS (031-225 5095).

The Edinburgh Cripple Aid Society

Eligibility: Physically disabled people living in Edinburgh and the Lothians.

Types of grants: Grants to help with heating, bedding, holidays, telephone installations and similar needs. These grants should not replace statutory provision, rather they should be seen as supplementary. Grants are not awarded retrospectively.

Annual grant total: About £5,000 given towards holidays and £8,000 in other welfare grants.

Applications: Applications should be made through social workers, health visitors and doctors. They are considered monthly.

Correspondent: Mrs J Morag McLafferty, Company Secretary, Cunningham Unit, Astley Ainslie Hospital, 133 Grange Loan, Edinburgh EH9 2HL (031-668 3371).

The Edinburgh Merchants Company Endowment Trust

Eligibility: People in need over the age of 55 who are unable to work (certified on medical grounds) and who live in Midlothian. Preference is given to people with the name Gillespie, Gibb or Heriot or who were connected with the building trade in Edinburgh.

Types of grants: Probably one-off and recurrent grants according to need.

Annual grant total: £93,000, but some of this is spent on providing accommodation.

Applications: On a form available from the correspondent.

Correspondent: R H Wilson, Secretary, Merchants' Hall, 22 Hanover Street, Edinburgh EH2 2EP (031-225 7202).

Charities Administered by Edinburgh Voluntary Organisations' Council (EVCO)

Applications: All the following trusts are administered by the EVCO. Some cover the whole Lothian region, some are more restricted, particularly to Edinburgh, please check the eligibility criteria carefully.

Applications must be submitted through a recognised referral agency (eg. social worker, citizen's advice bureau or doctor); those received either directly from individuals or from outside the grant area will not be accepted. Applications for grants of over £200 are considered quarterly in March, June, October and December.

Applications should be made in writing on a form available from the correspondent.

Correspondent: Trust Fund Administrator, Edinburgh Voluntary Organisations' Council, Ainslie House, 11 St Colme Street, Edinburgh EH3 6AG (031-225 4606).

(i) Thomas Barclay Bequest

Eligibility: People in need living in Edinburgh and Lothian.

Types of grants: One-off grants according to need.

Annual grant total: In 1992/93, grants totalled £1,100 and ranged between £30 and £50.

(ii) Miss Beveridge's Trust

Eligibility: Children/young people who live in the Edinburgh area (generally taken to be Lothian).

Types of grants: One-off grants according to need. (Grants are also made to organisations working with children.)

Annual grant total: In 1992/93, grants totalled £62,000. It is not known how much of this went to individuals in need, but grants to organisations ranged between £500 and £1,000.

(iii) Buccleuch Place Trust

Eligibility: Elderly people in need who live in Edinburgh and Lothian.

Types of grants: One-off grants according to need, ranging from £200 to £500.

Annual grant total: In 1992/93, grants totalled £6,700. 50 to 60% of this went directly to people in need with the remainder given to charitable organisations providing services to elderly people.

(iv) Edinburgh Coal Fund

Eligibility: Elderly people who live in the Edinburgh area and cannot heat their home properly. No applications from outside Edinburgh will be considered or acknowledged.

Types of grants: One-off grants between £20 and £30 for heating/fuel.

Annual grant total: About £1,300 in 60 grants.

(v) Edinburgh Discharged Prisoners Aid Society

Eligibility: Ex-offenders and their families living in the Edinburgh and Lothian area.

Types of grants: One-off grants according to need, but especially to help in the process of rehabilitation.

Annual grant total: In 1992/93, grants totalled £1,600 and ranged between £25 and £50.

(vi) New Town Dispensary Trust

Eligibility: Young women who live in the Lothian area.

Types of grants: One-off grants according to need, especially towards maternity costs for those who do not qualify for state benefits.

Annual grant total: In 1992/93, grants totalled £1,200 and ranged between £30 and £50.

(vii) Ponton House Association

Eligibility: Young people who live in the Edinburgh area and are in need but where there are also other extenuating circumstances such as physical or mental disability.

Types of grants: One-off grants according to need.

Annual grant total: £2,500 in 1993.

(viii) Quiller Bequest

Eligibility: People who live in Edinburgh and Lothian.

Types of grants: One-off grants according to need with a preference for older people.

Annual grant total: In 1992/93, grants totalled £960 and ranged between £15 and £20.

(ix) Joseph Thomson Mortification

Eligibility: People in need who live in the Edinburgh and Lothian area.

Types of grants: One-off grants between £25 and £50 for emergency relief where all possibility of statutory funding has been exhausted.

Annual grant total: £3,000 in 1992/93.

(x) William Thyne Trust

Eligibility: People in need living in Edinburgh.

Types of grants: One-off grants according to need, ranging from £50 to £100.

Annual grant total: In 1992/93, grants totalled £49,000. About £7,000 was given in 75 grants to individuals in need. (The Edinburgh Council of Social Services received 50% of the trust's income as a grant.)

The Leith Aged Mariners Fund

Eligibility: Needy elderly mariners (or those who had some connection with the sea) and their widows, currently living in or connected with Leith or Edinburgh (and not receiving assistance from other seafaring charities).

Types of grants: Regular yearly allowances of £260.

Annual grant total: £30,000 to 115 beneficiaries.

Applications: Application forms are available from and should be returned to: The Master, Trinity House of Leith, 99 Kirkgate, Leith, Edinburgh EH6 6BJ (031-554 3289).

Correspondent: Tods Murray WS, Solicitors, 66 Queen Street, Edinburgh EH2 4NE (031-226 4771).

The Leith Benevolent Association

Eligibility: Residents of Leith, Newhaven or Granton who are in distress and where no other help is available.

Types of grants: One-off grants, usually between £15 and £25, according to need.

Annual grant total: £700.

Applications: Applications by post only, with a reference from a responsible person or agency (eg. social work department or citizen's advice bureau), considered at any time.

Correspondent: J Bowers, Administrator, 38 Constitution Street, Leith, Edinburgh EH6 6RS (031-554 7208).

Other information: The association runs two residential care homes for the elderly within the voluntary sector.

The William Brown Nimmo Charitable Trust

Eligibility: Women in need aged over 50 who were born and permanently live in Leith or Edinburgh and who are on a small income.

Types of grants: Annual grants, currently £53 paid in November.

Annual grant total: £26,500. The trust usually accepts 30 to 40 new beneficiaries a year, but this is dependent on available income and existing beneficiaries failing to requalify for a grant.

Applications: On a form only available from 1st June from the correspondent. They should be returned by 31st July. Applicants are visited.

Correspondent: Mrs Fiona D Marshall, Secretary, Henderson Boyd Jackson, 19 Ainslie Place, Edinburgh EH3 6AU (031-226 6881).

● Bo'ness

The Anderson Bequest

Eligibility: People in need who live in Bo'ness.

Types of grants: Annual grants.

Annual grant total: In 1991, £9,000 out of an net income of £20,000 was allocated to individuals in need.

Applications: In writing to the correspondent.

Correspondent: J W Johnston, 7 Register Street, Bo'ness, West Lothian EH51 9AE (0506-822112).

● Edinburgh

The Alexander Mortification Fund

Eligibility: People in need over 50 years old. Preference is given to the relatives of Mr James Alexander Knockhill (who died in 1696) and to people with the surname (or maiden name) of Alexander. Other applicants must live in Edinburgh.

Types of grants: Regular allowances of £102 a year (paid in six equal instalments) and a one-off grant of £20 for funeral costs where there is insufficient in the estate to meet the costs.

Annual grant total: In 1994, the trust had assets of £221,000 producing an income of £23,500. Grants of £102 were given to 198 individuals and totalled £21,000.

Applications: Applications, invited twice a year by advertisement, can be submitted by the individual or through a recognised referral agency (eg. social worker, citizen's advice bureau or doctor) and are considered in January and July. Emergency applications cannot be considered.

Correspondent: The Trinity Hospital Visitor, 247 High Street, Edinburgh EH1 1YJ (031-225 2424 ext. 4332 or 031-529 4332 both pm only).

Lothian

The Corstorphine & Cramond Bequests

Eligibility: Applicants must (a) be over 55 or, on account of incurable disease, permanently incapacitated; (b) have lived within the boundaries of the former parishes of Corstorphine and Cramond for at least five years; (c) be of good character and in necessitous circumstances which are not accounted for by their own improvidence or misconduct.

Types of grants: One-off or recurrent grants according to need.

Annual grant total: In 1993/94, the trust had assets of £170,000 generating an income of £20,000. Expenditure totalled £20,000. Grants of about £100 were given to 100 individuals and totalled £10,000.

Applications: In writing to the correspondent.

Correspondent: D Dolan, Department of Administration, City Chambers, High Street, Edinburgh EH1 1YJ (031-529 4237).

The Edinburgh Children's Holiday Fund

Eligibility: Children and families in need who live in the Edinburgh area.

Types of grants: Grants to help with the costs of holidays ranging from £100 to £400.

Annual grant total: In 1992/93, the trust had assets of £730,000 with an income of £50,000. £4,400 was given in 17 relief-in-need grants to individual families.

Applications: On a form available from the correspondent, to be submitted through a social worker, citizen's advice bureau or other welfare agency. Applications are usually considered in May and December.

Correspondent: Ernst & Young, 10 George Street, Edinburgh EH2 2DZ (031-226 6400).

Other information: The trust mainly makes grants to organisations who arrange holidays and outings for children and families in need. Also to social workers and health visitors to finance holidays for individuals and families recommended by them.

The Edinburgh Medical Missionary Society Hawthornbrae Trust

Eligibility: People in need who live in Edinburgh.

Types of grants: Grants to help with the cost of a convalescent holiday.

Annual grant total: About £7,500.

Applications: Applications must be supported by a general practitioner.

Correspondent: F M Aitken, Executive Secretary, 7 Washington Lane, Edinburgh EH11 2HA.

The Edinburgh Royal Infirmary Samaritan Society

Eligibility: Needy families and dependants of patients in the Edinburgh Royal Infirmary, the City Hospital, the Royal Hospital for Sick Children and such other hospitals in Edinburgh as the council may from time to time decide.

Types of grants: Specific sums of money for clothing, travel expenses or other help for patients while in these hospitals or on leaving (eg. grants for travel expenses for members of families visiting or accompanying patients). About 280 grants are made annually, ranging from £5 to £50.

Annual grant total: £8,250 to individuals in 1991/92.

Applications: Through a medical social worker on an application form.

Correspondent: Mrs Sheila Somerville, 23 Morningside Place, Edinburgh EH10 5ES (031-447 1618).

The Edinburgh Society for Relief of Indigent Old Men

Eligibility: Elderly men of good character resident in Edinburgh who usually have no pension apart from old age pension, have capital of £3,000 or less and are experiencing hardship or disability. (Under exceptional circumstances, men under 65 will be considered.)

Types of grants: Monthly payment of £40.

Annual grant total: About £25,000 to 54 individuals

Applications: In writing to the correspondent.

Correspondent: R J Elliot, Secretary, Lindsays WS, 11 Atholl Crescent, Edinburgh EH3 8HE (031-229 1212).

The Indigent Old Women's Society

Eligibility: Widows and unmarried women over 60 years old who live in Edinburgh.

Types of grants: Regular allowances of £17 a month to help with fuel/heating costs.

Annual grant total: In 1993, the trust had an income of £13,000. Allowances were paid to 85 individuals and totalled £14,000.

Applications: In writing at any time. Applications should be made through a third party (social worker, citizen's advice bureau, friend etc.) and are considered monthly.

Correspondent: Miss Eileen Kerr, Hon. Secretary, 15 Belgrave Place, Edinburgh EH4 3AW (031-332 8867).

The Johnstone Wright Fund

Eligibility: Needy unmarried or widowed ladies (a) who were born in Scotland, (b) are "connected with Edinburgh" and (c) are "of the professional classes".

Types of grants: Grants paid half-yearly in May and November, although some receive additional amounts.

Annual grant total: No information available.

Applications: In writing to the correspondent.

Correspondent: Messrs Morton Fraser Milligan, 15-19 York Place, Edinburgh EH1 3EL (031-556 8444).

The John McGibbon Fund

Eligibility: Governesses, female day-school teachers and women in business over 50 who live in Edinburgh. Applicants must also be of Scottish birth and the daughters of deceased businessmen, master tradesmen or professional men in the city of Edinburgh. Younger applicants who are incapacitated and unable to work may be considered if a medical certificate is supplied.

Types of grants: Regular allowances of £102 a year (paid in six equal instalments); small one-off grants for funeral costs up to £20 when the estate is insufficient to cover costs.

Annual grant total: In 1993/94, £26,400 was given in 258 grants.

Applications: On a form available from the correspondent. Applications are considered in January and July; emergency applications cannot be considered. They can be submitted directly by the individual or through a third party, but only with the individual's knowledge.

Correspondent: The Trinity Hospital Visitor, 247 High Street, Edinburgh EH1 1YJ (031-225 2424 ext. 4332).

Lothian

The Police Aided Clothing Scheme of Edinburgh

Eligibility: Children and in exceptional cases adults in need who live in the area administered by Edinburgh District Council (the city of Edinburgh and a small area bordering the west side of the city).

Types of grants: Clothing and footwear to children and fuel vouchers to elderly people at Christmas. All children receive a pair of shoes and socks; outer garments may be available depending on family circumstances and the availability of funds.

Annual grant total: Varies considerably from about 400 children a year to over 1,000. In 1993, about 925 children were helped.

Applications: Either from the family direct or through a social worker or similar third party. All applicants are visited in their homes by a police officer in uniform.

Correspondent: The Force Custodian, Lothian & Borders Police Headquarters, Fettes Avenue, Edinburgh EH4 1RB (031-311 3131).

The Sir James Steel's Trust

Eligibility: Joiners, masons and other workers connected with the building trade, and their widows and daughters. Applicants must be over 50 and live in Edinburgh and district. Younger applicants are only accepted if they suffer from an incurable physical condition.

Types of grants: Regular allowances of £102 a year (paid in six equal instalments). Small one-off grants are given towards funeral costs where the estate is insufficient.

Annual grant total: In 1993/94, the trust had assets of £362,000 and an income of £42,000. Grants to 352 individuals totalled £36,000.

Applications: On a form available from the correspondent. Applications can be submitted directly by the individual or through a third party (with the individual's knowledge). They are considered in January and July.

Correspondent: The Trinity Hospital Visitor, 247 High Street, Edinburgh EH1 1YJ (031-225 2424 ext. 4332).

The John Wilson Bequest

Eligibility: "Men over 60 years of age resident in the Edinburgh area who have been in a fairly good position in life."

Types of grants: Yearly allowances of £400.

Annual grant total: No information available.

Applications: In writing to the correspondent.

Correspondent: Messrs J & R A Robertson, WS, 15 Great Stuart Street, Edinburgh EH3 7TS (031-225 5095).

● Leith

Miss Jane Campbell Fraser's Trust

Eligibility: Elderly people living in Leith.

Types of grants: Probably one-off and recurrent grants according to need.

Annual grant total: About £1,800.

Applications: In writing to the correspondent.

Correspondent: A Anderson, Partner, Wallace & Menzies, 21 Westgate, North Berwick EH39 4AE (0620-2641).

The John Reid Mortification Fund

Eligibility: People in need who live in the former burgh of Leith.

Types of grants: Annual award of £12.

Annual grant total: £1,416 in 118 grants in 1993/94.

Applications: On a form available form the correspondent. Applications should be submitted directly by the individual and are considered in November.

Correspondent: D Dolan, Department of Administration, Edinburgh District Council, City Chambers, High Street, Edinburgh EH1 1YJ (031-529 4121).

● Midlothian

Charities Administered by Midlothian District Council

There are various trusts administered by the Council. Most of them are small (under £500) and so do not warrant individual entries in this Guide. However, together they are large enough to be included. The following entry gives basic details about the trusts; further information is available from the correspondent or from Dalkeith & Penicuik Citizen's Advice Bureau.

Applications: All applications should be in writing to the correspondent.

Correspondent: The District Secretary, Midlothian District Council, Midlothian House, Buccleuch Street, Dalkeith EH22 1DN (031-663 2881 ext. 2432).

(i) The Ainslie, Sir Samuel Chisholm & Fraser Hogg Bequests

Eligibility: Poor people who live in the parish of Dalkeith.

Types of grants: Grants paid twice yearly.

(ii) The Cockpen, Lasswade & Falconer Bequest

Eligibility: People in need who live in the formal burghal areas of Bonnyrigg and Lasswade, and in the immediately surrounding district.

Types of grants: One-off and recurrent grants generally for medical or convalescent expenses not covered by the National Health Service. Applications should be made through doctors or district nurses.

(iii) The John & Margaret Haig Bequest

Eligibility: People in need over 70 who live in the former burghal area of Bonnyrigg.

Types of grants: Usually coal or groceries.

(iv) The Earl of Stair Bequest

Eligibility: People in need who live in the parish of Cranston.

Types of grants: Logs for the poor.

(v) The Tod Bequest

Eligibility: People in need who live in Loanhead or Polton.

Types of grants: One-off and recurrent grants according to need.

(vi) The Mrs E W Yorston Bequest

Eligibility: Poor young people belonging to the former burghal area of Lasswade who have suffered from infectious diseases.

Types of grants: Grants to help with the cost of a suitable rest in the country or at a convalescent home. Grants are one-off or recurrent according to need.

● West Lothian

Captain & Mrs White's Loan Fund

Eligibility: Applicants must (a) be born of a Scots father and Scots mother; (b) have lived in Whitburn for at least 10 years; (c) be aged 65 years or over and not receiving any unearned income, and (d) have no children who can give financial support. Preference will be given to

Lothian/Shetland Isles/Strathclyde

relatives of Captain White up to the rank of first cousin inclusive.

Types of grants: Grants are advertised and paid once a year just before Christmas.

Annual grant total: £600 in 194 grants.

Applications: On a form available from the Area Office, Whitburn. Further information available from the address below.

Correspondent: The Director of Finance, West Lothian District Council, District Headquarters, South Bridge Street, Bathgate, West Lothian EH48 1TS (0506-53631).

The James Wood Bequest and the James Wood & Christina Shaw Bequest

Eligibility: People in need who live in Armadale and Blackridge/Torphichen.

Types of grants: About 100 one-off grants at Christmas.

Annual grant total: About £650.

Applications: For the James Wood Bequest application forms are available from the the Director of Finance at the address below. (Previous recipients will be sent a form automatically.)

For the James Wood and Christina Shaw Bequest forms are available from the District Council, Armadale Area Office, East Main Street, Armadale.

Correspondent: The Director of Finance, West Lothian District Council, District Headquarters, South Bridge Street, Bathgate, West Lothian EH48 1TS (0506-53631).

Shetland Isles

The Gilbertson Trust

Eligibility: Natives of Lerwick and the Shetland Islands who are in need.

Types of grants: Recurrent grants.

Annual grant total: In 1992/93, the trust had assets of £49,000 with an income of £3,400. Pensions of £20 were given to 62 individuals and totalled £1,200.

Applications: Should be submitted through a recognised referral agency (eg. social worker, citizen's advice bureau or doctor) or other third party such as a councillor, and are considered in May.

Correspondent: Director of Finance, Breiwick House, 15 South Road, Lerwick, Shetland ZE1 0RB (0595-3535).

Strathclyde

The Oban & District Trust for the Disabled

Eligibility: Disabled people in need who live in Oban and North Argyll.

Types of grants: One-off grants towards the cost of appliances/apparatus which makes life easier, such as a telephone or washing machine. Grants range from £25 to £300.

Annual grant total: £500 in five grants in 1993.

Applications: In writing to the correspondent. Applications should be made through a social worker, citizen's advice bureau, doctor or welfare agency. They are considered throughout the year.

Correspondent: Mrs E C Clunie, Hon. Treasurer, Duavon, Craigard Road, Oban, Argyll PA34 5DS (0631-62534).

Semple Fund for Cancer Relief & Research, Mairi

Eligibility: People who live in West Kintyre and the island of Gigha and who are suffering from any type of cancer.

Types of grants: Provision of equipment and/or nursing help in the home, and grants for travelling to cancer treatment centres for patients or relatives.

Annual grant total: £5,000, not all of which is available for individuals.

Applications: In writing to the correspondent.

Correspondent: Margaret Park, Treasurer, 1 Muasdale, Tarbert, Argyll PA29 6XE (0583-2265).

The Strathblane & Strathendrick District Welfare Fund

Eligibility: Pensioners in need who live in the Strathblane and Strathendrick district.

Types of grants: Heating vouchers of £10 at Christmas.

Annual grant total: About £600.

Applications: In writing to the correspondent.

Correspondent: Irene Cameron, Area Officer, District Office, 32 Buchanan Street, Balfron, Glasgow G63 0LX (0360-440315).

● **Argyll & Bute**

The Argyll & Bute District Charities

Eligibility: People in need who live in the area administered by Argyll and Bute District Council.

Types of grants: Probably one-off and recurrent grants according to need.

Annual grant total: No information available.

Applications: In writing to the correspondent.

Correspondent: The Department of Finance, Kilmory, Lochgilphead, Argyll PA31 8RT (0546-602127).

The Glasgow Bute Benevolent Society

Eligibility: "Indigent persons belonging to Bute, particularly as are of advanced age and responsibility of character." The length of time a person has lived in Bute and how long they have been connected with Bute are taken into consideration.

Types of grants: The society does not award grants as such; suitable applicants are admitted to the Society's Roll of Pensioners and receive a pension payable half-yearly in May and November and a Christmas bonus payment. The half-yearly pension is currently about £50; the value of the bonus depends on income available.

Annual grant total: £8,500 in 1992.

Applications: On a form available from the correspondent, with supporting recommendation by a minister of religion, doctor, solicitor or other responsible person. Applications are considered in April, June and October.

Correspondent: Alex Donaldson, Secretary, McLeish Thomson & Co, 29 St Vincent Place, Glasgow G1 2DT (041-248 4134).

● **Arran**

The Dr Robert Jamieson Bequest Fund

Eligibility: Elderly people living in Arran who are in need.

Types of grants: Generally one-off grants for groceries and such like.

Annual grant total: No information available.

Applications: In writing to the correspondent.

Correspondent: Arran Council for Voluntary Service, Park Terrace, Lamlash, Isle of Arran KA27 8NB (0770-600611).

Barrhead

The Janet Hamilton Memorial Fund

Eligibility: People who are chronically sick or disabled and living in the former burgh of Barrhead.

Types of grants: Recurrent grants only.

Annual grant total: £3,400 in 1992/93 in about 250 grants. Grants in 1993/94 were for £8 per applicant.

Applications: Directly by the individual on a form available from the correspondent. Applications are considered in June.

Correspondent: The Director of Finance, Renfrew District Council, Municipal Buildings, Cotton Street, Paisley PA1 1BU (041-889 5400).

Glasgow

The Fife, Kinross & Clackmannan Charitable Society

Eligibility: People living in Glasgow who are in need and have connections by birth or ancestry with the former counties of Fife, Kinross and Clackmannan.

Types of grants: Annual pensions or single grants towards heating bills etc..

Annual grant total: No information available.

Applications: In writing to the correspondent.

Correspondent: J Smillie, General Secretary, City of Glasgow Society of Social Service, 30 George Square, Glasgow G2 1EG (041-248 3535).

Charities Administered by City of Glasgow Society of Social Service

Various trusts are administered by the society, but we have been unable to obtain any financail information. All give one-off or recurrent grants according to need, except (ii) see below.

Applications: In writing to the correspondent.

Correspondent: J Smillie, General Secretary, City of Glasgow Society of Social Service, 30 George Square, Glasgow G2 1EG (041-248 3535).

(i) The Glasgow Angus & Mearns Benevolent Society

Eligibility: Life members of the Society and their dependants, together with people who live in Glasgow and the surrounding area who are connected with the counties of Angus and Mearns by birth or by marriage.

(ii) The Glasgow Benevolent Society

Eligibility: People in need who live in Glasgow.

Types of grants: One-off grants through the society's almoners who are usually representatives of churches of Protestant denominations and various missions.

(iii) The Glasgow Dumbartonshire Benevolent Association

Eligibility: People born in the county of Dumbarton or their children living in and around Glasgow.

(iv) The Glasgow Dumfriesshire Society

Eligibility: People in need who live in Glasgow.

(v) The Glasgow Kilmarnock Society

Eligibility: "Honest and industrious" people who live in Glasgow but were born in or around Kilmarnock.

(vi) The Frances Lipton Memorial Fund

Eligibility: "Poor working class mothers and their children under 16 years old and physically or mentally disabled young people between 16 and 21 years old who are substantially dependant on their parents. Motherless children are excluded." Applicants must live within the city of Glasgow.

Charities Administered by Glasgow District Council

Eligibility: People in need who live in Glasgow. There are a number of trusts administered by the council (including Buchanan's Mortification, Coulter's Mortification, The Dorcas Relief Fund, Hamilton's Trust & Govan's Mortification, Mitchell's Mortification, Robertson's Trust, Mrs Esther Ross's Bequest and The Stevenson Bequest). Some have specific eligibility requirements but in practice the trusts are administered as one fund.

Types of grants: Regular allowances, pensions and one-off grants.

Annual grant total: About £15,000.

Applications: In writing to the correspondent at any time.

Correspondent: The Town Clerk, City Chambers, Glasgow G1 2DU (041-227 4540).

The Glasgow Jewish Welfare Board

Eligibility: Jewish people in need living in Glasgow.

Types of grants: One-off grants, monthly allowances and loans are all considered.

Annual grant total: No information available.

Applications: In writing to the correspondent.

Correspondent: Miss Z Endlar, Administrative Officer, 49 Coplaw Street, Glasgow G42 7JE (041-423 8916).

Other information: The board also helps with friendship clubs, housing, clothing, meals-on-wheels, counselling etc.. A small proportion of the grant total is given for education purposes.

The City of Glasgow Native Benevolent Association

Eligibility: "Worthy citizens, their widows and families, who from reverses of fortune are in need of assistance."

Types of grants: Grants for heating, lighting, television, telephone or Christmas gifts. Grants range from £130 to £520. The basic grant is £280 (ie. Christmas gift of £140 and summer gift of £140). Adjusted payments can be made for heating, telephone and holidays.

Annual grant total: In 1992/93, the trust had assets of £246,000 producing an income of £29,000. Relief-in-need grants totalling £22,000 were given to 39 individuals.

Applications: In writing to the correspondent. Applications are considered in April, September and October.

Correspondent: Robert F Frame, Hon. Secretary, 1 Royal Bank Place, Glasgow G1 3AA (041-221 6551).

The Glasgow Seamen's Friend Society

Eligibility: Widows of seamen living in Glasgow.

Types of grants: Quarterly grants ranging from £130 to £260 a year.

Annual grant total: £21,000 in 1993.

Applications: Applications on a form available from the correspondent can be submitted by the individual, through a recognised referral agency (eg. social worker, citizen's advice bureau or doctor)

Strathclyde/Tayside

or other third party, and are considered in January, April, July and October.

Consideration will not be given to applications which do not specifically comply with the eligibility requirements.

Correspondent: A B Hunter, Secretary, 10 Longbank Road, Ayr KA7 4SA (0292-262326).

The Ure Elder Fund for Widows

Eligibility: Widows in need who live in Glasgow, particularly Govan.

Types of grants: In 1992, about 25 widows received a twice-yearly payment of £60 plus a Christmas bonus of £90, totalling £210.

Annual grant total: In 1992, the trust had assets of £107,000 generating an income of £9,800. 80 grants totalled £5,500.

Applications: On a form available from the correspondent. Applications can be submitted directly by the individual or through a third party, They are considered in April and October.

Correspondent: Mrs E M Kerr, McGrigor Donald, Solicitors, Pacific House, 70 Wellington Street, Glasgow G2 6SB (041-248 6677).

● Gourock

The Gourock Coal & Benevolent Fund

Eligibility: People in need who live in Gourock.

Types of grants: Help with heating and lighting bills.

Annual grant total: About £3,000.

Applications: In writing to the correspondent, or to any minister or parish priest in the town, or the local branch of the WRVS.

Correspondent: D M Blair, Hon. Secretary, Royal Bank Buildings, Gourock PA19 1PA (0475-31266).

● Inverclyde

The Lady Alice Shaw-Stewart Memorial Fund

Eligibility: See below.

Types of grants: Help with female cases recommended by the probation officer firstly in the burgh of Greenock, then in the Inverclyde district.

Annual grant total: In 1993, the trust had an income of almost £17,000. No grants have been given in recent years.

Applications: In writing to the correspondent.

Correspondent: The Director of Finance, Inverclyde District Council, Municipal Buildings, Greenock PA15 1JA (0475-724400).

Other information: The council administers a number of other small trusts for people living in Greenock, Gourock, Inverkip and Kilmalcolm.

● Kyle & Carrick

Kyle & Carrick District Trusts

Eligibility: Residents of the area administered by the Kyle and Carrick District Council who are in need or distress. Mainly elderly people who have lived in Ayr for a number of years.

Types of grants: Mostly regular yearly allowances of £10 to £15 paid in May/June. Very few grants for emergency cases.

Annual grant total: About £8,000.

Applications: In writing to the correspondent.

Correspondent: The Director of Support Services, Kyle & Carrick District Council, Burns House, Burns Statue Square, Ayr KA7 1UP (0292-281511).

Other information: A scheme is in preparation to group various trusts administered by the council into one fund which will be able to help in emergencies.

● Paisley

Paisley's Former Town Council Charitable Funds

Eligibility: People in need who are over 80 years of age and live in Paisley. People aged 70-79 are also eligible if they have lived in Paisley for at least 30 years and if their income does not exceed the basic state retirement pension plus 33%. Anybody aged 70-79 will be discounted if they have members of the family living with them unless these members of the family have no income or their income is invalidity benefit.

Types of grants: One-off grants of £3 to about 1,100 recipients.

Annual grant total: £3,300.

Applications: On a form available from the correspondent in November each year.

Correspondent: The Director of Finance, Renfrew District Council, Municipal Buildings, Cotton Street, Paisley PA1 1BU (041-889 5400).

Tayside

The Neil Gow Charitable Trust

Eligibility: People in need who live in the district of Perth and Kinross or immediate neighbourhood.

Types of grants: Annuities.

Annual grant total: Over £10,000.

Applications: In writing to the correspondent.

Correspondent: Miller Hendry, Solicitors, 10 Blackfriars Street, Perth PH1 5NS (0738-37311).

The Jamieson Charity

Eligibility: Elderly people living in Arbroath or Arbirlot who are in need.

Types of grants: Grants at Whitsunday and Christmas each year; special grants for emergency needs at other times.

Annual grant total: No information available.

Applications: In writing to the correspondent.

Correspondent: G McNicol, Thorntons WS, Brothockbank House, Arbroath, Angus DD11 1NJ (0241-872683).

The Gertrude Muriel Pattullo Trusts for Handicapped Boys & Girls

Eligibility: Physically disabled boys and girls (generally under 18) in the city of Dundee and county of Angus.

Types of grants: General welfare including (a) provision of medical services not obtainable under the National Health Service; (b) financial assistance for holidays, and (c) grants to buy clothing.

Annual grant total: No information available.

Applications: In writing to the correspondent, detailing the circumstances of the proposed beneficiary and the nature and cost of assistance required.

Correspondent: Messrs Carlton Gilruth (Ref. SW), M30 Whitehall Street, Dundee DD1 4AL (0382-200111).

Tayside

The Gertrude Muriel Pattullo Trust for the Elderly

Eligibility: Elderly people (ie. generally those of state pensionable age) in the city of Dundee and county of Angus.

Types of grants: General welfare including (a) help for people in reduced circumstances, particularly those with a physical disability; (b) financial provision in respect of admission to a residential home or similar; (c) provision of medical services not obtainable under National Health Service facilities; (d) financial provision for home nursing in appropriate cases; (e) provision of accommodation, furnishings, clothing and other necessities, and (f) provision of holidays.

Annual grant total: No information available.

Applications: In writing to the correspondent, detailing the circumstances of the proposed beneficiary and the nature and cost of assistance required.

Correspondent: Messrs Carlton Gilruth (Ref. SW), M30 Whitehall Street, Dundee DD1 4AL (0382-200111).

● Angus

Charities Administered by Angus District Council

Eligibility: People in need who live in the burghs of Arbroath (especially those people who have an association with the sea), Brechin and Forfar. Also people in need who live in the Landward parish of Forfar (Lunanhead, Kingsmuir etc.), the parish of Carnoustie and Kirriemuir.

Types of grants: One-off grants generally of £30 upwards.

Annual grant total: The combined grant totals of these charities is about £10,000.

Applications: On a form available from the correspondent. Applications can be submitted directly by the individual or through a recognised referral agency (social worker, citizen's advice bureau or doctor etc.) and are usually considered in February or November.

Correspondent: The Chief Executive, Angus District Council, County Buildings, Market Street, Forfar DD8 4HF (0307-465101).

Other information: This entry includes the following charities: Brechin Charitable Funds, Arbroath Charitable Funds, Forfar Charitable Funds, Forfar Landward Charities, Carnoustie Charitable Funds and Kirriemuir Charitable Funds.

● Arbroath

The Colvill Trust

Eligibility: Elderly people living in Arbroath.

Types of grants: Pensions of £100 to about 75 people each year, paid in May and November.

Annual grant total: About £7,500.

Applications: On a form available from the correspondent.

Correspondent: Thorntons WS, Brothockbank House, Arbroath, Angus DD11 1NJ (0241-72683).

Other information: The charity also has a special fund which gives one-off grants to people in need in Arbroath. These grants are made at the discretion of the trustees usually after recommendation from a doctor or social services.

Gibson's Charity

Eligibility: Elderly people living in Arbroath.

Types of grants: Yearly allowances of £50 paid in May and November to a maximum of 60 beneficiaries.

Annual grant total: About £3,000.

Applications: In writing to the correspondent and referred by doctors and social workers.

Correspondent: G McNicol, Thorntons WS, Brothockbank House, Arbroath, Angus DD11 1NJ (0241-872683).

● Brechin

The Brechin Victoria Nursing Association

Eligibility: People who are sick, infirm, poor or distressed and live in the district of Brechin.

Types of grants: One-off or recurrent grants according to need for the provision of medical and surgical equipment and/or assistance, and the supply of comforts and necessities. Also help to people requiring but unable to employ a private nurse. Grants usually range from £50 to £100.

Annual grant total: Not known.

Applications: Applications should be submitted through a recognised referral agency (eg. social worker, health visitor or doctor).

Correspondent: I A McFatridge, Ferguson & Will, Secretaries, 24 Swan Street, Brechin, Angus DD9 6EJ (0356-622289).

The Mrs Marie Dargie Trust

Eligibility: Pensioners living within the city boundaries of Brechin.

Types of grants: Probably one-off or recurrent grants according to need.

Annual grant total: Not known.

Applications: In writing to the correspondent.

Correspondent: David H Will, Trustee, Ferguson & Will, 24 Swan Street, Brechin, Angus DD9 6EJ (0356-622289).

● Dundee

The Broughty Ferry Benevolent Fund

Eligibility: People in need living in Broughty Ferry, preferably not in residential care.

Types of grants: Payments totalling about £110 are made to individuals twice each year. There are about 35 beneficiaries on an approved list usually made up by church ministers.

Annual grant total: About £4,000.

Applications: In writing to the correspondent.

Correspondent: The Clerk, Thorntons WS, 11 Whitehall Street, Dundee DD1 4AE (0382-29111).

The City of Dundee District Charities

Eligibility: People in need who live in the area administered by the City of Dundee District Council.

Types of grants: The main trust is the Hospital Fund & Johnston Bequest from which around 800 pensioners receive £40 each totalling about £30,000.

Annual grant total: See above.

Applications: In writing to the correspondent. For the main trust each local councillor nominates one person to receive a grant, funds permiting.

Correspondent: The Director of Finance, City of Dundee District Council, 8 City Square, Dundee DD1 3BG (0382-23141 ext. 4222).

The Dundee Indigent Sick Society

Eligibility: People who live in Dundee and who are sick or infirm and in financial need.

Types of grants: One-off grants up to a maximum of £50 per year.

Tayside/Western Isles

Annual grant total: In 1993, grants to individuals totalled £1,500.

Applications: In writing to the correspondent.

Correspondent: D N Gordon, Secretary, 30 Whitehall Street, Dundee DD1 4AL (0382-200111).

The Misses Elizabeth & Agnes Lindsay Fund

Eligibility: Elderly, deserving, unmarried women aged 55 years or over who have been dependent on their own industry and are not in receipt of an old age pension. They must be natives of Dundee and living there, or born elsewhere but living in Dundee for at least 10 years preceding their application.

Types of grants: One-off or recurrent grants according to need.

Annual grant total: No information available.

Applications: In writing to the correspondent.

Correspondent: Miss Dron, Messrs Carlton Gilruth, 30 Whitehall Street, Dundee DD1 4AL (0382-200111).

The Ouchterlony Old Men's Indigent Society

Eligibility: Deserving and indigent old men (generally over 60) belonging to or born in Dundee or neighbourhood.

Types of grants: 16 beneficiaries receive £50 each in May and November each year.

Annual grant total: £1,600 in 1993.

Applications: In writing to the correspondent.

Correspondent: Mrs Stewart, Thorntons WS, 11 Whitehall Street, Dundee DD1 4AE (0382-29111).

The Peter Benevolent Fund

Eligibility: Indigent gentlewomen who live in Dundee and Broughty Ferry.

Types of grants: £110 per year to each individual.

Annual grant total: No information available.

Applications: On a form available from the correspondent.

Correspondent: Mr Steven, Rollo, Steven & Bond, Solicitors, 21 Dock Street, Dundee DD1 3DS (0382-24624).

Mrs Margaret T Petrie's Mortification

Eligibility: Elderly, infirm and indigent people belonging to, or settled in, Dundee.

Types of grants: Payments of £95 are made twice yearly to 26 beneficiaries.

Annual grant total: About £2,500.

Applications: In writing to the correspondent.

Correspondent: Thorntons WS, 11 Whitehall Street, Dundee DD1 4AE (0382-29111).

The Mair Robertson Benevolent Fund

Eligibility: Indigent gentlewomen who live in Dundee, Blairgowrie and Broughty Ferry.

Types of grants: £100 per year payable in June and December to about 15 beneficiaries.

Annual grant total: About £1,500 in 1993.

Applications: On a form available from the correspondent.

Correspondent: Mr Steven, Rollo Steven & Bond Solicitors, 21 Dock Street, Dundee DD1 3DS (0382-24624).

The Hanna & Margaret Thomson Trust

Eligibility: People who are war wounded from the Second World War or their spouses. Applicants must live in Dundee and be in need.

Types of grants: £150 is paid twice yearly to about 65 people at present.

Annual grant total: About £16,000.

Applications: In writing to the correspondent.

Correspondent: Mr McDonald, Thorntons WS, 11 Whitehall Street, Dundee DD1 4AE (0382-29111).

Montrose

The St Cyrus Benevolent Fund

Eligibility: Sick, needy and infirm people who live in the parish of St Cyrus, Montrose.

Types of grants: Cash grants are not given, but assistance is given with payment of utility accounts, essential medical equipment etc. on a one-off basis.

Annual grant total: About £1,000.

Applications: In writing to the correspondent. Recommendation by minister, doctor, nurse or similar is essential. Applications are considered at any time.

Correspondent: c/o Scott Alexander, Solicitors, Queen's Close, 113 High Street, Montrose, Tayside.

Perth

King James VI Hospital Fund

Eligibility: People in need aged over 60 who are members of the church and live in Perth.

Types of grants: Weekly grants.

Annual grant total: Over £5,000 to individuals.

Applications: In writing to the correspondent.

Correspondent: George Maitland, Hospital Master-Clerk, King James VI Hospital, Perth PH2 8HP (0738-24660).

The Perth Indigent Old Men's Society

Eligibility: Men over 55 who are in need and live in Perth.

Types of grants: Help with gas and electricity heating costs and vouchers for groceries, clothing and footwear.

Annual grant total: About £10,000.

Applications: In writing to the correspondent to be considered in November each year.

Correspondent: J S M Craig, Hon. Secretary, Lynedoch House, 31 Barossa Place, Perth PH1 5HH (0738-27111).

Western Isles

The William MacKenzie Trust

Eligibility: Elderly and infirm people who live in the old burgh of Stornoway.

Types of grants: One-off or recurrent grants according to need.

Annual grant total: No information available.

Applications: In writing to the correspondent.

Correspondent: R H MacLeod, Chairman, 26 Lewis Street, Stornaway, Isle of Lewis (0851-702335).

3. Wales

The Cancer Help Society (Wales)

Eligibility: People with cancer who live in Wales.

Types of grants: Usually one-off grants of about £50 (eg. for travel expenses to cancer centres).

Annual grant total: About £2,000.

Applications: In writing or in person to the correspondent.

Correspondent: H Lloyd Hamlyn, Secretary, 1 Alexander Place, Sirhowy, Tredegar, Gwent NP2 4QA.

Other information: This entry has not been confirmed by the trust.

The Care & Action Trust for Children with Handicaps

Eligibility: Families of children with disabilities who live in Wales (including Monmouthshire), with a preference for those whose disability is a result of brain damage.

Types of grants: One-off and recurrent grants ranging from £50 to £1,000 towards treatment and equipment. Occasional grants towards holidays.

Annual grant total: £11,500 in 53 grants in 1991/92.

Applications: In writing to the correspondent directly by the individual. Applications are considered at any time.

Correspondent: T J England, 18 Tawe Business Village, Phoenix Way, Enterprise Park, Swansea SA7 9LA (0792-790077).

The Corwen College Pension Charity

Eligibility: Needy widows of clergymen of the Church in Wales whose husband held office in the district of Merionydd in Gwynedd or the communities of Betws, Gwerfil Goch, Corwen Gwyddeldern, Llandrillo, Llangar and Llansantffraid Glyndyfrdwy (all in Clwyd).

Types of grants: Pensions only.

Annual grant total: £2,450 in 10 grants in 1992.

Applications: In writing to the correspondent.

Correspondent: The Clerk, The Diocese of St Asaph, Diocesan Office, St Asaph, Clwyd LL17 ORD (0745-582245).

The Gresford Colliery Disaster Relief Fund

Eligibility: Needy widows, children or other dependants of the victims of the Gresford Colliery Disaster (22/9/34).

Types of grants: One-off and regular allowances.

Annual grant total: Over £11,000.

Applications: In writing to the correspondent.

Correspondent: T V R Roberts, Trustee, 41 Grosvenor Road, Wrexham LL11 1BU.

Other information: This entry has not been confirmed by the trust.

The James Edward Harris Trust

Eligibility: People in need who live in south Wales. Preference for elderly people in need of regular assistance.

Types of grants: Regular annuities and occasional one-off grants.

Annual grant total: In 1993, the trust had an income of £10,500. Pensions of up to £800 a year were given to 10 individuals and totalled £5,000.

Applications: Applications (for regular annuities only) should be made on a form available from the correspondent either directly by the individual, through a recognised referral agency (eg. social worker, citizen's advice bureau or doctor) or third party. Applications are considered in January, April, July and October.

Correspondent: R M H Read, Llanmaes, St Fagans, Cardiff CF5 6DU (0222-553511).

The North Wales Fund for Needy Psychiatric Patients

Eligibility: People with mental illness who live in Clwyd and Gwynedd.

Types of grants: One-off grants only ranging from £25 to £150 (eg. for clothes, furniture, holidays and learning courses). No grants for the payment of debts.

Annual grant total: In 1990, the trust had an income of £3,300. £2,800 was given in 34 relief-in need grants to individuals.

Applications: In writing to the correspondent, through a social worker or any health professional, including details of income and other possible grant sources. Applications are considered throughout the year.

Correspondent: Mrs K M Hemsley, Clerk, North Wales Hospital, Denbigh, Clwyd LL16 5SS (0745-812871).

The North Wales Police Benevolent Fund

Eligibility: See below.

Types of grants: "To relieve, in conditions of need, members of the North Wales Police Force and former members of this and previous forces amalgamated within constituent forces, and their families and immediate dependants."

Annual grant total: The fund gives around £4,000 in Christmas grants to widows and children and about £900 in other grants to individuals. More than 200 people were supported in 1993.

Applications: In writing to the correspondent.

Correspondent: The Fund Treasurer, Chief Constable's Office, Glan-y-Don, Colwyn Bay LL29 8AW (0492-517171).

Wales/Clwyd

The North Wales Society for the Blind

Eligibility: Blind and partially sighted people who live in the Colwyn, Glyndwr or Wrexham Maelor districts in Clwyd; anywhere in Gwynedd, and Montgomery in Powys.

Types of grants: Grants for necessities, comforts, equipment, fares and other needs.

Annual grant total: £29,000 in 1992/93.

Applications: On a form available from the correspondent. Applications should be submitted through a social worker and are considered monthly. "All other sources should be explored before making an application."

Correspondent: G C Williams, Director, 325 High Street, Bangor, Gwynedd LL57 1YB (0248-353604).

The South Wales Association for Spina Bifida & Hydrocephalus

Eligibility: People who have spina bifida and hydrocephalus and live in south Wales.

Types of grants: Grants for general welfare, holidays and leisure purposes. Other grants specifically for those 16 years or older, including car adaptions. There is also a holiday caravan available.

Annual grant total: About £2,000 to £3,000.

Applications: In writing to the correspondent.

Correspondent: Mrs Brenda Sharp, Hon. Secretary, 4 Lakeside, Barry, South Glamorgan CF62 6SS (0446-735714).

The South Wales Constabulary Benevolent Fund

Eligibility: In practice members and retired members of the South Wales Constabulary, and their dependants.

Types of grants: Grants for those who are sick, convalescent, disabled, infirm or otherwise in need.

Annual grant total: In 1992, £15,000 was given in 35 grants.

Applications: In writing to the correspondent.

Correspondent: The Chief Constable, South Wales Constabulary, Police Headquarters, Bridgend, Mid-Glamorgan CF31 3SU (0656-655555).

The Welsh Rugby Union Charitable Trust

Eligibility: Amateur sportsmen and sportswomen, mainly of rugby union football, who have sports injuries, and their dependants in need.

Types of grants: One-off grants for necessities, comforts and other needs.

Annual grant total: £50,000 to £60,000.

Applications: In writing to the correspondent.

Correspondent: Edward Jones, Hon. Secretary, Welsh Rugby Union Headquarters, Cardiff Arms Park, PO Box 22, Cardiff CF1 1JL.

The Widows', Orphans' & Dependants' Society of the Church in Wales

Eligibility: See below.

Types of grants: One-off and recurrent grants for "the charitable relief by pecuniary or other assistance of necessitous persons who are the widows, orphans or dependants of deceased clergy of the Church in Wales".

Annual grant total: £32,000 in 100 grants.

Applications: In writing to the correspondent.

Correspondent: G Ellis, 39 Cathedral Road, Cardiff CF1 9XF (0222-231638).

Clwyd

The Evan & Catherine Roberts Charity

Eligibility: People in need who are over 60 and live within a 40-mile radius of Old Colwyn. Preference for members of the Methodist church.

Types of grants: Probably one-off or recurrent grants according to need.

Annual grant total: In 1991, the trust had an income of £8,200. It is not known how much was given in grants to individuals in need.

Applications: In writing to the correspondent.

Correspondent: J Haines Davies, 24 Cadwgan Road, Old Colwyn, Clwyd LL29 9PY (0492-515463).

The Ruabon & District Relief-in-Need Charity

Eligibility: People in need who live in Wrexham Maelor and the Community Council Districts of Cefn Mawr, Penycae, Rhosllanerchrugog (including Johnstown) and Ruabon.

Types of grants: One-off and recurrent grants according to need. Grants can be towards installation of telephone, heating costs, children's clothing, cookers, electric wheelchairs, clothing for adults in hospital and travel costs of hospital visits or for university students.

Annual grant total: In 1992, the trust had assets of £41,000 and an income of £2,000. Grants ranging from £25 to £200 were given to 24 individuals totalling £1,600.

Applications: In writing to the correspondent.

Correspondent: J R Fenner, Secretary, Cyncoed, 65 Albert Grove, Ruabon, Wrexham, Clwyd LL14 6AF (0978-820102).

Elizabeth Williams' Charity

Eligibility: People in need who live in the communities of St Asaph, Bodelwyddan, Cefn (in the district of Colwyn) and Waen. There is a preference for pensioners, blind people and children.

Types of grants: One-off grants and small pensions according to need, generally of £10 to £50 but can be for up to £100.

Annual grant total: In 1992, the trust had an income of about £5,000 and gave grants totalling £3,500 to £4,000.

Applications: In writing to the correspondent.

Correspondent: F Cripps, Flat 6, The Old Palace, High Street, St Asaph, Clwyd LL17 0RQ (0745-584744).

Other information: This trust has been amalgamated with the St Asaph Relief-in-Need Charity.

The Wrexham & District Relief-in-Need Charity

Eligibility: People in need who live in the former borough of Wrexham and the communities of Abenbury, Bersham, Bieston, Broughton, Brymbo, Esclusham Above, Esclusham Below, Gresford, Gwersyllt and Minera in Clwyd.

Types of grants: One-off or recurrent grants according to need, from £50 upwards.

Annual grant total: In 1993, the trust had an income of £8,440. Expenditure totalled £4,200. 33 grants to individuals totalled £3,750.

Applications: In writing to the correspondent. Applications should be submitted directly by the individual and are considered in November.

Correspondent: P J Blore, Clerk, 49 Norfolk Road, Borras Park, Wrexham, Clwyd LL12 7RT (0978-356901).

Denbigh

The Freeman Evans St Davids Day Denbigh Charity

Eligibility: Elderly, poor and chronically sick and disabled people who live in the former borough of Denbigh.

Types of grants: Probably one-off and recurrent grants according to need.

Annual grant total: No information available, although in 1986 the charity estimated its annual income to be £10,000.

Applications: In writing to the correspondent.

Correspondent: Rev William Hugh Pritchard, Blaen Ddol, Ruthin Road, Denbigh, Clwyd.

Other information: This entry has not been confirmed by the trust.

Dyfed

Abergwili

The Abergwili Relief-in-Need Charity

Eligibility: People in need who live in the parish of Abergwili.

Types of grants: Cash grants.

Annual grant total: In 1993, the trust had assets of £1,400 and an income of £500. No grants were given.

Applications: In writing to the correspondent by the individual or the parent/guardian.

Correspondent: H Wynne Evans, Hon. Secretary, 4 Plas Penwern, Johnstown, Carmarthen, Dyfed SA31 3PN (0267-231555).

Ammanford Cum Betws

The Linnecar Trust

Eligibility: Registered blind people who live in the parish of Ammanford Cum Betws.

Types of grants: One-off grants in cases where other sources of help have been exhausted. Grants have recently been given towards computer equipment, sports/leisure/craft equipment, household equipment and holidays.

Annual grant total: In 1993, the trust gave 45 grants of between £150 and £800 totalling £3,900.

Applications: Applications, on a form available from the correspondent, can be submitted by the individual, through a recognised referral agency (eg. social worker, citizen's advice bureau or doctor) or other third party, and are considered throughout the year. Applications directly from individuals must be supported by a professional worker in the field.

Correspondent: c/o Wales Council for the Blind, Shand House, 20 Newport Road, Cardiff CF2 1YB (0222-473954).

Haverfordwest

The Trustees for the Freemen of the Borough & County of the Town of Haverfordwest

Eligibility: Hereditary freemen of Haverfordwest aged 18 years and over.

Types of grants: One-off and recurrent grants according to need.

Annual grant total: £1,800 in 1982/83, the most recent year for which information is available.

Applications: Freemen must be enrolled by the chairman of the local authority. The honour is hereditary being passed down through the male line only.

Correspondent: Messrs R K Lucas & Son, 9 Victoria Place, Haverfordwest, Dyfed SA61 2JX (0437-762538).

William Vawer's Charity

Eligibility: People in need who live in the town of Haverfordwest.

Types of grants: Pensions to existing pensioners. Other grants to those in need, hardship or distress, especially freemen.

Annual grant total: In 1986/87, the trust's income was £8,000. £2,000 was given in grants, leaving a surplus for the year of £5,600. No more recent information is available.

Applications: In writing to the correspondent.

Correspondent: Messrs R K Lucas & Son, 9 Victoria Place, Haverfordwest, Dyfed SA61 2JX (0437-762538).

Pembroke

The William Sanders Charity

Eligibility: "Poor and deserving spinsters" who live within a five-mile radius of St John's parish in Pembroke.

Types of grants: Christmas gifts of £10 to £25.

Annual grant total: No information available.

Applications: In writing to the correspondent.

Correspondent: The Vicar, The Vicarage, Church Street, Pembroke Dock, Dyfed SA72 6AR (0646-682943).

Tenby

The Tenby Relief-in-Need & Pensions Charity

Eligibility: Pensioners in need who live in the community of Tenby.

Types of grants: Monthly pensions of £12 only.

Annual grant total: About 200 pensions totalling abround £28,000.

Applications: In writing to the correspondent.

Correspondent: Clive Mathias, Clerk, County Chambers, Pentre Road, St Clears, Carmathen SA33 4AA (0994-231044).

Gwent

The Gwent Charitable Fund

Eligibility: People who live in Gwent and who are sick, infirm or mentally disabled. Priority is given to members of the fund and their dependants.

Types of grants: One-off and recurrent grants according to need.

Annual grant total: About £7,500 in about 100 grants.

Applications: In writing to the correspondent. Applications are considered on November 30th each year.

Correspondent: Mrs Anne Dyer, 13 Cardiff Road, Newport, Gwent NP9 2EH (0633-266152).

Chepstow

The John Bowsher's Charity for Bachelors

Eligibility: Bachelors over the age of 65 who are in need and live in Chepstow.

Types of grants: One-off grants to supplement low income.

Gwent/Gwynedd

Annual grant total: In 1992, the trust had an income of £550 which was given in five grants.

Applications: Directly by the individual in writing to the correspondent. Applications are considered in May.

Correspondent: Mrs A M Harris, Secretary, 25 Mount Way, Chepstow, Gwent NP6 5NF (0291-620980).

Cwmbran

The Girling (Cwmbran) Trust

Eligibility: People in need who live in the former urban area of Cwmbran.

Types of grants: One-off and recurrent grants and loans according to need.

Annual grant total: The trust has an income of about £50,000. At least half is given to individuals; the remainder is given to organisations in Cwmbran.

Applications: In writing to the correspondent.

Correspondent: Ken Maddox, Grange Works, Cwmbran, Gwent NP44 3XU (0633-834040).

Llandenny

The Llandenny Charities

Eligibility: People over 65 and in need who live in the parish of Llandenny.

Types of grants: Grants for those in need, especially grants for medical equipment, coal, oil and bread. Small book grants may also be available for students.

Annual grant total: In 1992, the trust had an income of £800. Grants of between £25 and £30 totalled £1,000.

Applications: Directly by the individual in writing to the correspondent, or through a trustee. Applications are usually considered in January.

Correspondent: W J Hampshire, Rock Farm, Llandenny, Usk, Gwent NP5 1DL (0291-690750).

Monmouth

The Monmouth Charity

Eligibility: People in need who live in Monmouth and neighbourhood.

Types of grants: One-off grants.

Annual grant total: The trust can make grants to individuals and organisations. No figures available.

Applications: The trust advertises in the local press once a year and applications should be made in response to this advertisement. Emergency grants can be considered at any time.

Correspondent: T P Williams, Ambleside, 17a Monkswell Road, Monmouth NP5 3PF (0600-712653).

Frederick William Smith's Charity

Eligibility: Widows in need who live in the community of Monmouth.

Types of grants: Generally one-off grants of £40 towards winter heating costs.

Annual grant total: In 1993, 15 grants were given totalling £600.

Applications: In writing to the correspondent for consideration in January.

Correspondent: Rev Julian F Gray, St Thomas's Vicarage, Overmonnow, Monmouth, Gwent NP5 3ES (0600-712869).

Other information: The smaller Monmouth Relief-in-Need Charity (about £80 in 1991) is also administered by the correspondent above.

Trevethin

The Charities of Thomas Williams & Charles Price

Eligibility: People in need who live in Trevethin.

Types of grants: Blankets and grants of money according to need.

Annual grant total: No information available.

Applications: In writing to the correspondent.

Correspondent: Rev B R Pippen, Trevethin Vicarage, Pontypool, Gwent NP4 8JF (0495-762228).

Gwynedd

The Gwynedd Children's Heart Association

Eligibility: Children up to 18 who live in Gwynedd and who are suffering from congenital heart disease.

Types of grants: Emergency financial help with hospital stays and travel. Grants range from £10 to £50.

Annual grant total: In 1992/93, the trust had an income of £8,800. Total expenditure was £2,000. Grants of between £10 and £50 totalled £270. £6,000 was used to buy equipment.

Applications: In writing to the correspondent, preferably through a social worker, although parents can also apply.

Correspondent: Mrs Olwen Williams, Secretary, Cloona, Llanfachraeth, Holyhead LL65 4YR (0407-740594).

Anglesey

The John Theodore Wood Charity

Eligibility: Pensioners in need, especially married couples, who live in the county of Anglesey.

Types of grants: One-off or recurrent grants according to need.

Annual grant total: £3,000 to £4,000 in 15 to 20 grants.

Applications: In writing to the correspondent.

Correspondent: Mrs Brenda Randall, Clerk, Gwynedd Voluntary Service Office, 27 High Street, Llangefni, Anglesey LL77 7NA (0248-722288).

Blaenau Ffestiniog

The Freeman Evans St David's Day Ffestiniog Charity

Eligibility: Elderly, disabled, chronically sick or poor people who live in the districts of Blaenau Ffestiniog and Llan Ffestiniog as they were on March 31st 1974.

Types of grants: One-off grants according to need. Grants have recently been given towards stair-lifts and "mechanical perambulators".

Annual grant total: No information available.

Applications: Applications can be submitted by the individual, through a recognised referral agency (eg. social worker, citizen's advice bureau or doctor) or other third party, and are considered in April and October. Urgent cases are dealt with immediately if the need arises.

Correspondent: Elwyn Hughes, Council Office, Blaenau Ffestiniog, Gwynedd LL41 3ES (0766-831338).

Mid-Glamorgan

The Mid-Glamorgan County Blind Welfare Association

Eligibility: Blind people living in Mid-Glamorgan (excluding the borough of Merthyr Tydfil).

Types of grants: One-off grants for special needs.

Annual grant total: About £2,300.

Applications: In writing to the correspondent.

Correspondent: A G Williams, Director, Social Services Department, Mid-Glamorgan County Council Office, Greyfriars Road, Cardiff CF1 3LL (0222-820431).

The Norris Charity

Eligibility: People in need who live in Penarth, Cogan and Llandough.

Types of grants: One-off heating grants for widows.

Annual grant total: The trust's income is about £2,000, but not all of this is given in grants to individuals.

Applications: On a form available from the correspondent. Applications are considered in February, April, June, September and November.

Correspondent: Mrs J A Morrison, 12 Beechwood Drive, Penarth, South Glamorgan CF6 2QZ (0222-712412).

The Rhondda Blind Welfare Society

Eligibility: Blind people in financial need who live in the Rhondda valleys.

Types of grants: One-off grants for yearly outings, holidays, Christmas gifts and other needs.

Annual grant total: About £2,000.

Applications: In writing to the correspondent.

Correspondent: T Stanley Hughes, 3 Illtyd Street, Treorchy, Mid-Glamorgan.

Other information: This is the most up to date information at the Charity Commission. The entry has not been confirmed by the trust.

● Laleston

The Laleston Relief-in-Sickness Charity

Eligibility: People who live in the civil parish of Laleston and who are sick, convalescing, disabled or infirm.

Types of grants: One-off and recurrent grants according to need.

Annual grant total: No information available.

Applications: In writing to the correspondent.

Correspondent: T Lardeau-Randall, 3 Heol-y-Onnen, Brynitirion Hill, Brigend, Mid-Glamorgan (0656-56506).

● Maerdy

The Maerdy Children's Welfare Fund

Eligibility: Children under 17, living in the electoral ward of Maerdy Rhonda.

Types of grants: Primarily grants towards urgently required equipment. Grants have also been given towards travel expenses in cases where children's parents have to be present at hospital.

Annual grant total: £1,400 in 10 grants in 1992/93.

Applications: In writing to the correspondent. Consultation takes place between the chairman and the local senior doctor before any equipment is bought.

Correspondent: John A Lewis, Chairman, 15 Station Terrace, Maerdy, Ferndale, Rhondda, Mid-Glamorgan CF43 4BE (0443-755281).

● Merthyr Tydfil

The Lord Buckland Trust

Eligibility: People over 30 years of age who were either born in the old county borough of Merthyr Tydfil or who have lived there for at least 10 years.

Types of grants: "Distress payments" (presumably one-off payments for emergencies) and Christmas grants.

Annual grant total: £8,000 in distress payments and £4,000 in Christmas grants in 1987. We have not been able to obtain more up-to-date figures.

Applications: In writing to the correspondent.

Correspondent: W E Healey, Chairman, 13 Stables Court, Dowlais, Merthyr Tydfil CF48 3AG (0685-723085).

The Mendicants, Merthyr Tydfil

Eligibility: People in need who live in the borough of Merthyr Tydfil.

Types of grants: One-off grants towards medical equipment not available on the NHS (providing it is recommended by a medical authority); Christmas parcels; holidays for children aged 10 to 14 whose parents are caught in the poverty trap; telephone help line for disabled people; help with domestic equipment eg. cookers, refrigerators, washing machines, bedding/beds, quite often to invalids and unmarried mothers. In 1993, 153 grants were given ranging from £25 to £500.

Annual grant total: In 1993, the trust had an income of £10,000. Grants to individuals totalled £6,250. £5,800 is already committed for 1994.

Applications: In writing to the correspondent, including information on other sources of income. Applications can be submitted directly by the individual or through a social worker, citizen's advice bureau or other welfare agency. They are considered monthly on the third Monday.

Correspondent: L A Goodwin, 1 York Close, Shirley Gardens, Heolgerrig, Merthyr Tydfil, Mid Glamorgan C48 1SL (0685-385831).

● Rhymney

The Rhymney Trust

Eligibility: People in need who live in Rhymney.

Types of grants: Probably one-off and recurrent grants according to need.

Annual grant total: The trust had an income of £3,200 in 1990/91.

Applications: In writing to the correspondent.

Correspondent: The Solicitor to the Council (IGM/L1442), Rhymney Valley District Council, Ystrad Fawr, Ystrad Mynach, Hengoed, Mid-Glamorgan CF8 7SF (0443-815588).

Powys

The Garthgwynion Charities

Eligibility: People in need who live in the parishes of Isygarreg and Uwchygarreg and Machynlleth.

Types of grants: One-off grants according to need.

Powys/South Glamorgan

Annual grant total: The charities had an income of £32,000 in 1989/90, but only a small part of this is given to individuals. We have been unable to obtain more recent information.

Applications: In writing to the correspondent. Applications are considered quarterly in March, June, September and December.

Correspondent: The Secretary, 13 Osborne Close, Hanworth, Middlesex TW13 6SR (081-890 0469).

Brecknock

The Brecknock Association for the Welfare of the Blind

Eligibility: Blind and partially-sighted people living in Brecknock.

Types of grants: One-off grants at Christmas and for special equipment/special needs eg. cooker, talking book and college fees.

Annual grant total: About £2,000.

Applications: In writing to the correspondent.

Correspondent: W G Phillips, Hon. Secretary, Springfield, Pendre Close, Brecon, Powys LD3 9EL (0874-622292).

The Brecknock Welfare Trust

Eligibility: People who are in conditions of need, hardship or distress and who live in the town of Brecon.

Types of grants: One-off grants according to need.

Annual grant total: About £1,000.

Applications: In writing to the correspondent. Applications can be submitted by the individual or through a recognised referral agency (social worker, citizen's advice bureaux or doctor etc.).

Correspondent: W G Phillips, Town Clerk, Brecon Town Council, Guild Hall, Brecon, Powys LD3 7AL (0874-622884 am only).

Llanidloes

The Llanidloes & District Community Nurses' Comforts Fund Committee

Eligibility: People in need living in and around Llanidloes who are sick, disabled, housebound or infirm and who are being nursed at home.

Types of grants: One-off grants for medical aids and necessities such as purchase of disposable sheets and payment towards special telephones to Age Concern etc. as recommended by the community nurses.

Annual grant total: In 1993, the trust had an income of £5,000 and gave grants of £5 to £200 totalling £1,300.

Applications: In writing to the correspondent usually through community nurses, to be considered throughout the year.

Correspondent: Mrs M Edwards, 23 Hafren Terrace, Llanidloes, Powys SY18 6AT (0686-412621).

The Llanidloes Relief-in-Need Charity

Eligibility: People in need who live in the communities of Llanidloes and Llanidloes Without.

Types of grants: One-off grants for fuel, equipment for disabled people and to families and students in need.

Annual grant total: About £1,700 in 36 grants, although not all this was given to individuals.

Applications: In writing to the correspondent. Applications should be made through social service, doctors, citizen's advice bureaux or churches.

Correspondent: Mrs G M Thomas, Clerk, Nant Afallen, Llanidloes, Powys SY18 6EU (05512-2331).

Llanwog

The Caersws Community Care Fund

Eligibility: People who are patients of a hospital or medical practice in the community of Llanwog.

Types of grants: One-off and recurrent grants according to need.

Annual grant total: About £1,500.

Applications: In writing to the correspondent.

Correspondent: Susan Rosser, Tregeiriog, Caersws, Powys SY17 5HJ (0686-688732).

Montgomery

The Montgomery Welfare Fund

Eligibility: People in need who live in the parish of Montgomery.

Types of grants: Annual grants. Very occasional one-off grants up to £100 can also be made.

Annual grant total: £900 in 36 grants of £25 in 1991.

Applications: In writing to the correspondent directly by the individual, including a brief note of financial circumstances and income. Applications are usually considered in December.

Correspondent: Rev Barry Letson, The Rectory, Montgomery, Powys SY15 6PT (0686-668243).

South Glamorgan

The Llandough LATCH

Eligibility: All children referred to the Oncology Unit of the Llandough Hospital, South Glamorgan.

Types of grants: One-off grants for necessities, travel expenses and holidays.

Annual grant total: No information available.

Applications: In writing to the correspondent, usually through a social worker.

Correspondent: Mrs Coles, Secretary, c/o LATCH Office, Llandough Hospital, Llandough, Cardiff CF6 1XX (0222-711711).

Cardiff

The Bequest of Miss Marjorie Williams

Eligibility: People in need and over the age of 50 who have lived in Cardiff for at least 25 years.

Types of grants: One-off grants ranging from £100 to £200.

Annual grant total: In 1992/93, the trust's income was £2,000 to £3,000.

Applications: Applications on a form available from the correspondent should generally be submitted by the individual through a recognised referral agency (eg. social worker, citizen's advice bureau or doctor).

Correspondent: The Director of Administrative & Legal Services, City Hall, Cardiff CF1 3ND (0222-822063).

The Cardiff Caledonian Society

Eligibility: People of Scottish nationality and their families, who live in Cardiff or the surrounding district and are in need.

Types of grants: Relief payments to meet gas and electricity bills, monthly rental payments and cost of living expenses.

Annual grant total: In 1993, the trust had an income of £3,400. Expenditure amounted to £3,200. Grants ranging from £10 to £500 were given to 16 individuals and totalled £1,300.

Applications: Directly by the individual in writing to the correspondent. Applications are considered throughout the year.

Correspondent: P Stuart, St Valery, 12 Windsor Road, Radyr, Cardiff CF4 8BP (0222-842706).

The Cardiff Charity of Special Relief

Eligibility: People in need who live in the city of Cardiff.

Types of grants: One-off grants. No grants for educational purposes.

Annual grant total: About £600.

Applications: Applications, on a form available from the correspondent, can be submitted by the individual, through a recognised referral agency (eg. social worker, citizen's advice bureau or doctor) or other third party. Evidence of special distress must be shown.

Correspondent: The Director of Administrative & Legal Services, City Hall, Cardiff CF1 3ND (0222-822000).

The Poor's Charity of Margaret Evans

Eligibility: People in need who live in the ecclesiastical parish of St Margaret's, Roath as constituted on 5th January 1911.

Types of grants: One-off grants as Christmas gifts and heating allowances.

Annual grant total: The charity's income was £3,800 in 1990.

Applications: In writing to the correspondent.

Correspondent: R M Oxenham, 5 Melrose Avenue, Penylan, Cardiff CF3 7AR.

Other information: This entry has not been confirmed by the trust.

● **St Andrews Major**

The Dinas Powis Relief-in-Sickness Fund

Eligibility: People in need who live in St Andrews Major.

Types of grants: Usually one-off grants.

Annual grant total: The charity has an income of about £400.

Applications: In writing to the correspondent.

Correspondent: The Rector, St Andrews Church Rectory, Lettons Way, Dinas Powis, Nr Cardiff CF64 4BY.

West Glamorgan

Local Aid for Children & Community Special Needs

Eligibility: People with special needs/learning difficulties under 50 years of age who live in West Glamorgan.

Types of grants: One-off grants ranging from £50 to £1,000 for specialist equipment such as a specialist bed, chair and bike.

Annual grant total: In 1992/93, the trust had an income of £31,500. 30 relief-in-need grants totalled £9,100.

Applications: In writing to the correspondent, including confirmation that the amount requested is not available from statutory sources. Applications should be submitted through a social worker, citizen's advice bureau or other welfare agency or professional. They are considered bi-monthly.

Correspondent: Mrs D Inger, Chairperson, 9 Linden Avenue, Westcross, Swansea SA3 5LE (0792-405041).

The West Glamorgan County Blind Welfare Association

Eligibility: Registered blind people who live in West Glamorgan.

Types of grants: One-off grants for special items for blind people (eg. RNIB aids) and towards computer/technical equipment.

Annual grant total: About £20,000.

Applications: In writing to the correspondent.

Correspondent: Miss Blackmore, Hon. Secretary, Director of Social Services, West Glamorgan County Council, County Hall, Oystermouth Road, Swansea SA1 3SW (0792-471243).

● **Neath**

The Neath Nursing Association

Eligibility: Former nurses of the association and people in need who live in Neath.

Types of grants: One-off grants for necessities and comforts.

Annual grant total: About £1,000.

Applications: In writing to the correspondent.

Correspondent: Mr Walters, Treasurer, c/o Lloyds Bank plc, 5 Windsor Road, Neath, West Glamorgan SA11 1LS (0639-635136).

● **Swansea**

The Swansea & District Friends of the Blind

Eligibility: Blind people living in Swansea.

Types of grants: One-off grants, especially at Christmas and Easter.

Annual grant total: About £5,000.

Applications: In writing to the correspondent.

Correspondent: Evan Lewis, 3 Delbeche Street, Swansea.

Other information: This entry has not been confirmed by the trust.

4. North East

The Joseph Brough Benevolent Association

Eligibility: People in need who live in Tyne & Wear, Durham and Northumberland.

Types of grants: One-off grants of between £50 and £100. Priority is given to families with young children. Grants have helped towards the cost of cookers, washers etc. and to assist with rent/council tax arrears, but other applications are considered.

No grants to buy toys or clothing.

Annual grant total: About £24,000 in about 360 grants.

Applications: Application forms are available from the correspondent and should be sent through a local social services department or other welfare agency such as probation or Victim Support. Grants are considered in the month of receipt.

Correspondent: F Lumsden, Tyne & Wear Foundation, Mea House, Ellison Place, Newcastle-Upon-Tyne NE1 8XS (091-222 0945).

Lord Crewe's Charity

Eligibility: Widows and other dependants of deceased clergy of the old diocese of Durham (ie. the modern counties of Durham, Northumberland and Tyne & Wear) who are in need.

Types of grants: Probably one-off and recurrent grants according to need.

Annual grant total: In 1985, the most recent year for which information is available, the charity's income was £203,000. It spent £53,000 on the upkeep of its estate leaving a net income available for distribution of about £150,000. £5,000 was given in grants to clergy and their families, £50,000 was allocated to the dioceses of Durham and Newcastle (presumably in support of parishes there), and the total expenditure was £60,000. This left about £90,000 unallocated for the year.

The only figure we have been able to update is the income for 1992 which was £319,000 (according to the Charity Commission).

Applications: On a form available from the correspondent.

Correspondent: F S Gibbs, Clerk, The Chapter Office, The College, Durham DH1 3EH (091-386 4266).

Other information: This entry has not been confirmed by the trust. There is also a Lord Crewe's Durham Educational Foundation which gives grants to boys and girls living in Durham, for educational purposes. For details see the companion *The Educational Grants Directory*.

The Hadrian Trust

Eligibility: People in need who live within the boundaries of the old counties of Tyne & Wear, Northumberland and Durham.

Types of grants: One-off grants according to need ranging from £100 to £400, but generally of around £250.

Annual grant total: About £155,000 in 1993, including about £7,000 in grants to about 30 individuals.

Applications: In writing to the correspondent stating the individual's full circumstances. Applications are considered quarterly. Individuals can apply directly to the correspondent, but nearly all successful applications are made through a social worker, probation officer and sometimes through the Council for Voluntary Service or other welfare agency.

Correspondent: J Parker, Stanford & Lambert, Alliance House, Hood Street, Newcastle-upon-Tyne NE1 6LD (091-232 6226).

The Hospital of God

Eligibility: People in need who live in and around Cleveland, Durham, Sunderland, Northumberland and Tyne & Wear.

Types of grants: One-off grants for items and services including household items, clothing and telephone installation. Grants are not usually made for holidays, rent arrears or other debts.

Annual grant total: £125,000 in 1993/94 including £29,000 to individuals.

Applications: Applications are ONLY considered when they originate from Social Service offices and the dioceses of Durham and Newcastle with which the charity has established arrangements. Applications from clergy must come via the Archdeacons of Auckland and Northumberland.

Correspondent: G Leggatt-Chidgey, Estate Office, Greatham Hospital, Greatham, Hartlepool TS25 2HS (0429-870247).

The Rose Joicey Fund

Eligibility: Needy families or individuals who live in the counties of Durham, Northumberland and Tyne & Wear.

Types of grants: One-off grants only ranging from £50 to £200. Priority for grants is given to groups or organisations which organise holidays for the needy. Requests from individuals will only be considered if made by a proper social work agency. Preference will be given to cases of hardship involving the sickness or disability of a family member.

Annual grant total: £3,200 in 25 grants in 1992/93.

Applications: By letter to the correspondent stating the costs, amount sought and other sources approached.

Correspondent: C Lamb, c/o Newcastle Council for Voluntary Service, Mea House, Ellison Place, Newcastle-Upon-Tyne NE1 8XS (091-232 7445).

The North Eastern Prison After Care Society

Eligibility: People who live in Northumberland, Durham, Tyne & Wear, Cleveland and North Yorkshire who are suffering or who have suffered a legal restriction on their liberty, and their families, and who are in need.

Types of grants: Most of the society's income is given to projects which help groups of people. Small grants to individuals are made for: rehabilitative purposes (eg. educational or training equipment, or tools); support of an isolated person through a prison sentence (eg. for radios or hobby material); a prisoner's family in need (eg. towards children's clothing, a cooker, a washing machine); in relation to accommodation problems either for families or for a released prisoner (such as help with rent arrears, payment of a housing bond or for essential furniture). Grants range from £10 to £100. Only one-off grants are given.

Annual grant total: In 1991, the society had an income of £24,000. Expenditure totalled £18,000, including £8,000 in relief-in-need grants to individuals. About 200 grants were made.

Applications: Practically all applications are made through the probation service on the society's application form. They are usually considered in March, June, September and December.

Correspondent: Mrs R Cranfield, 22 Old Elvet, Durham DH1 3HW.

The North-East Area Mineworkers' Convalescent Fund

Eligibility: Workers or their spouses who are/were employed in the mining industry (above or below ground) in County Durham, Northumberland or Tyne & Wear, and who need rest to regain their health.

Types of grants: For women, the fund provides a period of rest at an establishment in Richmond, North Yorkshire. Medical treatment is not provided and applicants should not be more than 72 years of age in the year of application and not be confined to a wheelchair.

For men, a period of rest is provided at an establishment in Blackpool. Medical treatment is not provided.

Annual grant total: About £232,000 was given in supporting the three schemes in 1992. Over 1,300 people were assisted in 1991.

Applications: On a form available from the correspondent.

Correspondent: The Coal Industry Social Welfare Organisation, 6 Berwick Road, Gateshead, Tyne & Wear NE8 4DP (091-477 7242).

The Northern Counties' Charity for the Incapacitated

Eligibility: People who are totally and permanently incapacitated owing to an incurable or chronic disease, to accident or to deformity, and who live in the north of England. There is a preference for people living in Bolton and Greater Manchester.

Types of grants: Regular monthly allowances of £5 to £10 a week, paid quarterly to about 10 beneficiaries. Gifts in kind such as shoes and/or a bonus can also be paid to existing beneficiaries when money is available.

Annual grant total: Over £5,000 in 1993.

Applications: On a form available from the correspondent. Applications should be submitted directly by the individual if this is possible, otherwise through a social worker, citizen's advice bureau or other welfare agency. Applications are considered three or four times a year.

Correspondent: The Clerk, 1 Westminster Drive, Cheadle Hulme, Cheadle, Cheshire SK8 7QX (061-440 9407).

Other information: This entry is repeated in the North West section of the book.

The Northern Counties Orphans' Benevolent Society

Eligibility: Children in need through sickness, disability or other causes with a preference for those who live in the counties of Cleveland, Durham, Tyne & Wear, Northumberland and Cumbria. There is a preference for orphaned children.

Types of grants: Both one-off and recurrent grants for education and clothing. In 1993, "Assistance took the form of grants towards school fees, the cost of school clothing and equipment and, in a limited number of cases, the provision of special equipment of an educational or physical nature for disabled children. In almost every case, the need for assistance arises through the premature death of the major wage earner, or the break up of the family unit. Applications are treated in strict confidence and the financial circumstances of each applicant are fully and carefully considered by the trustees before an award is made."

Annual grant total: £44,000 in 36 grants to individuals for education and relief in need in 1993.

Applications: In writing to the correspondent.

Correspondent: J M Davison, Secretary, 27 Portland Terrace, Newcastle-upon-Tyne NE2 1QP (091-281 1292).

Other information: This entry is repeated in the Cumbria section of the book.

The Sir John Priestman Charity Trust

Eligibility: Clergy and their families in need who live in the historic counties of Durham and York (especially the county borough of Sunderland).

Types of grants: One-off or recurrent grants according to need. Grants range from £50 to £1,000.

Annual grant total: In 1990/91, the trust had assets of £1.5 million and an income of £220,000. 18 grants to individuals totalled £10,500.

Applications: In writing to the correspondent.

Correspondent: R W Farr, McKenzie Bell, 19 John Street, Sunderland SR1 1JG.

Other information: The trust also assists organisations serving County Durham (especially the Sunderland area) and helps maintain Church of England churches and buildings in the above area. This entry has not been confirmed by the trust.

The Rycroft Children's Fund

Eligibility: Children in need who live in Cheshire, Derbyshire, Greater Manchester, Lancashire, Staffordshire, South and West Yorkshire. There is a preference for children living in the cities of Manchester and Salford and the borough of Trafford. Applicants should be aged 18 or under.

Types of grants: One-off and recurrent grants according to need. No grants for further or higher education.

Annual grant total: About £25,000 is given for relief-in-need in about 20 grants.

Applications: On a form available from the correspondent.

Correspondent: Christopher Lees-Jones, Chairman, Hermitage Farm, Holmes Chapel, Cheshire CW4 8DP (0477-532875).

Other information: This entry is repeated in the North West general and Midlands general sections of the book.

North East/Cleveland

The Society for the Relief of Widows & Orphans of Shipwrecked Mariners

Eligibility: Widows and children of seafarers who die at sea. Applicants should live on the coast of Northumberland or in an area of three miles on either side of the River Tyne.

Types of grants: One-off and recurrent grants according to need.

Annual grant total: About £2,000.

Applications: In writing to the correspondent. No applications have been received recently.

Correspondent: Mrs Wilson, Messrs Hadaway & Hadaway, 58 Howard Street, North Shields, Tyne & Wear NE30 1AL (091-257 0382).

Other information: Unallocated income is transferred to the Tyne Mariners Benevolent Institution. See entry in the Tyne & Wear section of the book.

The West Riding Distress Fund

Eligibility: People in need who live in the area of the former county of the West Riding of Yorkshire. When the trust deed was written the former county of West Riding did NOT include the county boroughs of Barnsley, Bradford, Dewsbury, Doncaster, Halifax, Huddersfield, Leeds, Rotherham, Sheffield, Wakefield and York.

Types of grants: One-off grants only, usually £30 to £150, for bedding, clothing, food, fuel, furniture or comforts or aids for the sick (including holidays, travel expenses to hospital etc. for the sick person and their relatives).

Annual grant total: £2,560 in about 20 grants in 1992.

Applications: No direct applications from individuals. All requests must come through social services departments.

Correspondent: M Mulligan, North Yorkshire County Council, County Hall, Northallerton, North Yorkshire DL7 8AD (0609-780780 ext. 2858)

The Yorkshire County Bowling Association Benevolent Fund

Eligibility: Bowlers and their dependants from Yorkshire County EBA Clubs who are in need.

Types of grants: Christmas grants of £60.

Annual grant total: In 1993, the fund had an income of £2,000. 25 relief-in-need grants totalled £1,600.

Applications: On a form available from the correspondent submitted by club secretaries. Applications are usually considered in November.

Correspondent: B H Reeve, 53 Hull Road, Cottingham HU16 4PN.

Cleveland

The King Edward VII & Sister Purvis Convalescent Fund

Eligibility: People in need who are sick, convalescing, disabled or infirm and who live in Middlesbrough, the South Bank or Grangetown.

Types of grants: One-off grants to help with fees for applicants in convalescent homes, rail and bus fares, the provision of some services and equipment.

Annual grant total: Over £1,000 a year given in about 12 grants.

Applications: On a form available from the correspondent. Applications can be submitted directly by the individual, through a welfare agency or via a friend, relation or other suitable third party. Applications should include details of the applicant's medical condition and a doctor's signature. They are considered twice a year in April/May and September/October.

Correspondent: The Borough Secretary, Middlesbrough Borough Council, PO Box 99a, Municipal Buildings, Middlesbrough, Cleveland TS1 2QQ (0642-263526).

The Teesside Emergency Relief Fund

Eligibility: People in need who live in the former county borough of Teesside.

Types of grants: One-off grants for necessities and services.

Annual grant total: Over £1,000. About 30 applications are made each year, only half of which receive a grant of between £100 and £250.

Applications: On a form available from the correspondent. Applications should preferably be submitted through a welfare agency.

Correspondent: The Town Clerk, Stockton Borough Council, Municipal Buildings, Church Road, Stockton, Cleveland TS18 1LD (0642-248155).

Other information: This trust now includes the Mayor of Teesside Clothing Fund.

● Hartlepool

The Furness Seamen's Pension Fund

Eligibility: Seamen in need who are 50 or over and live in the borough of Hartlepool or the former county borough of West Hartlepool, or who had their permanent residence there during their sea service. All applicants must have served as deep-seamen for at least 15 years and with some part of the sea service in vessels registered in Hartlepool, West Hartlepool or the Port of Hartlepool, or vessels trading to/from any of these ports.

Types of grants: Regular allowances only.

Annual grant total: About £10,000 to about 65 pensioners.

Applications: On a form available from the correspondent.

Correspondent: Mr Williams, Secretary, c/o Clark Whitehill, 40 Victoria Road, Hartlepool, Cleveland TS26 8DD (0429-234414).

● Middlesbrough

The Sir Hugh & Lady Bell Memorial Fund

Eligibility: Needy or invalid iron and steel workers or their families who live in the Middlesbrough area.

Types of grants: Usually one-off grants of about £100.

Annual grant total: £4,000 in about 30 grants.

Applications: In writing to the correspondent or through social workers.

Correspondent: The Clerk, Outhwaite Sutcliffe & Howard, 50 Albert Road, Middlesbrough, Cleveland TS1 1PE (0642-247633).

The Lady Crosthwaite Bequest Fund

Eligibility: Old age pensioners in need who live in the former county borough of Middlesbrough.

Types of grants: Small grants at Christmas via the social services and community councils, together with one-off lump sums to organisations.

Annual grant total: In 1993, the trust had an income of £8,000 of which £2,000 was given in grants to individuals.

Applications: Applications must be made in writing to the correspondent through the social services.

Cleveland/Durham/Humberside

Correspondent: The Borough Treasurer, Middlesbrough Borough Council, PO Box 99, Middlesbrough, Cleveland TS1 2QH (0642-245432).

Stockton-on-Tees

The Speck Walker Annuity Fund

Eligibility: Spinsters and widows over the age of 25 who live in the parish of Stockton-on-Tees or in the North Riding of the county of York.

Types of grants: Grants of up to £50 a quarter.

Annual grant total: In 1990, the trust gave 35 grants of £50 per quarter (£7,000).

Applications: In writing to the correspondent.

Correspondent: Mrs Smith, Archers Solicitors, 24 Yarm Road, Stockton-on-Tees, Cleveland TS18 3NB (0642-673431).

Other information: This entry is repeated in the North Yorkshire section of the book.

Durham

The Ferryhill Station, Mainsforth & Bishop Middleham Aid-in-Sickness Charity

Eligibility: People in need who live in Chilton Lane, Ferryhill Station, Mainsforth and Bishop Middleham.

Types of grants: One-off and recurrent grants according to need.

Annual grant total: About £1,000 in about 15 grants.

Applications: In writing to the correspondent.

Correspondent: Mrs Gladys Courtney, Nevilla, Mainsforth Village, Ferry Hill, County Durham (0740-651328).

The Hamsterley Poors' Land & Stock Charity

Eligibility: People in need who live in Hamsterley, Bedburn, Woodland, Copley and Butterknowle.

Types of grants: One-off and recurrent grants according to need.

Annual grant total: In 1993, the trust had assets of £70,000 and an income of £1,000. Grants of between £15 and £30 were given to 46 people totalling £690.

Applications: "Applications by word of mouth (or in writing) to any trustee or the secretary, for consideration in June or December."

Correspondent: Mrs D Brainbridge, Secretary, West Hoppyland, Hamsterley, Bishop Auckland, Co Durham DL13 3MP (0388-488617).

The Hilton & Dawson Charity

Eligibility: People who live in Teesdale in County Durham, and Caldwell Eppleby, Melsonby, Middleton Tyas, Barton, Reeth and the upper part of Swaledale, all in North Yorkshire, and are unable to support themselves financially.

Types of grants: Regular yearly allowances only, at present limited to £60 per year paid quarterly by cheque.

Annual grant total: About £2,000 in around 30 grants.

Applications: On a form available from the correspondent.

Correspondent: Mrs I Appleton, Whitkirk, Winston, Nr Darlington, County Durham (0325-730423).

Other information: This entry is repeated in the North Yorkshire section of the book.

The Sedgefield & District Relief-in-Need Charity, Thomas Cooper's Charity, Howle Hope Estate, the Sedgefield Poor Fund

Eligibility: People in need who live in the parishes of Bradbury, Mordon, Sedgefield and Fishburn in County Durham.

Types of grants: One-off grants for household goods, medical equipment, holidays for sick and disabled people, and a Christmas "dole" to elderly people living alone. No loans.

Annual grant total: In 1993, expenditure totalled £19,000 including £6,000 in 280 grants to individuals.

Applications: On a form available from the correspondent. Applications can be submitted directly by the individual or through a welfare agency or other third party. They are considered as they arise.

Correspondent: R Smeeton, Clerk, 13 North Park Road, Sedgefield, Stockton-on-Tees, Cleveland TS21 2AP (0740-620009).

Other information: Grants are also given to other voluntary organisations with similar objectives.

Darlington

The Thomas Metcalfe Barron Charity

Eligibility: Communicant members of the Church of England who have lived in the borough of Darlington for at least five years.

Types of grants: One-off grants and pensions up to a maximum of £1 a week according to need.

Annual grant total: The total income for the trust in 1992 was about £500 but grants to individuals in need totalled £720. There were 24 grants of £30.

Applications: In writing to the correspondent.

Correspondent: The Director of Central Services, Town Hall, Darlington, Durham DL1 5QX (0325-380651).

Middleton

The Ralph Gowland Trust

Eligibility: People over the age of 60 who are in need and who live in the parish of Middleton in Teesdale.

Types of grants: One-off and recurrent grants according to need.

Annual grant total: This trust was registered in December 1988. No further information available.

Applications: In writing to the correspondent.

Correspondent: Ronald Corner, Hyland View, Alston Road, Middleton-in-Teesdale, Barnard Castle, County Durham DL12 0UU.

Humberside

The Hesselwood Children's Trust (Hull Seamen's & General Orphanage)

Eligibility: People under 25 and in need who live in, or have family connections with, the county of Humberside or north Lincoln. Students who have come to Humberside to study are not eligible.

Types of grants: One-off and recurrent grants according to need. Grants have been given for specified short periods of time at special schools, holiday funding for individuals and youth organisations in the UK and abroad, and for musical instruments and special equipment or alterations for disabled children.

Humberside

Annual grant total: In 1993, the trust's income was £67,500. Grants totalled £64,000, but not all of this went to individuals.

Applications: In writing to the correspondent giving financial details of the applicant/parent(s), the grant required, and why parents cannot provide the money. If possible, a contact telephone number should be quoted. Applications are considered in March, July and October.

Correspondent: Mrs J A Roberts, Secretary, Poplar Farm, Garton, Aldbrough, North Humberside HU11 4QB (0964-527898).

Other information: This entry is repeated in the Lincolnshire section of the book.

The Ethel Maude Townend Charity

Eligibility: People in need who live in Hull and the area formerly known as the East Riding of the county of York. Applicants should have been in the medical, nursing or legal professions, ministers of religion, accountants, architects and other professions generally; also their widows/widowers.

Types of grants: Usually weekly payments plus a Christmas bonus. Also one-off grants eg. to pay a registration fee to enable a nurse to take up employment, to pay an outstanding telephone account, to buy a top loading washer for a nurse suffering back injury, and to pay for roof repairs.

Annual grant total: About £6,000 in 1992; about 20 annuitants.

Applications: On a form available from the correspondent following an advertisement.

Correspondent: Chas H Spooner, Secretary, 100 Eastfield Road, Hull HU4 6DY (0482-561470).

The Robert Towries Charity

Eligibility: People in need who live in the parishes of Aldbrough and West Newton, and have done so for two years.

Types of grants: Recurrent grants.

Annual grant total: In 1992/93, the trust had an income of £6,600. Expenditure totalled £3,100 and 158 grants totalled £1,900.

Applications: In writing to the correspondent. Applications should be submitted directly by the individual and are considered at any time.

Correspondent: Mrs P M Auty, 6 Willow Grove, Headlands Park, Aldbrough, Humberside HU11 4SH (0964-527553).

● Barmby-on-the-Marsh

The Garlthorpe Charity

Eligibility: People in need who live in the parish of Barmby-on-the-Marsh.

Types of grants: One-off grants only.

Annual grant total: About £3,000.

Applications: Directly by the individual in writing to the correspondent. Applications are considered in July and December.

Correspondent: Roger Beattie, Clerk, 1 Vicar Lane, Howden, Goole, North Humberside DN14 7BP (0430-430209).

● Barrow-on-Humber

The Beeton, Barrick & Beck Relief-in-Need Charity

Eligibility: People in need who live in the parish of Barrow-on-Humber.

Types of grants: Christmas vouchers and one-off grants eg. immediate relief following a house fire and travel costs to hospital.

Annual grant total: In 1992, the trust had an income of £2,300. About 150 Christmas vouchers of £12 were given and about 10 one-off grants of £50 to £100.

Applications: In writing to the correspondent by September/October.

Correspondent: T J Clark, Low Farm, Wold Road, Barrow-upon-Humber, South Humberside (0469-530438).

● Barton-upon-Humber

The Barton-upon-Humber Relief-in-Sickness Fund

Eligibility: People who are sick or disabled and who live in the parish of Barton-upon-Humber.

Types of grants: Discretionary grants are given for all kinds of need, but usually for fuel and equipment.

Annual grant total: £1,250 made up of 50 grants of £25. The trust has not updated these figures since the last edition of this Guide.

Applications: In writing to the correspondent.

Correspondent: H K Ready, Keith Ready & Co, Market Place, Barton-upon-Humber DN18 5DA (0652-32215).

The Charity of John Tripp (Blue Coat)

Eligibility: People in need who live in Barton-upon-Humber.

Types of grants: One-off grants only. Typically £25, up to a maximum of £200.

Annual grant total: About £2,000 in about 50 grants.

Applications: By letter to the correspondent. Unless urgent they are considered each November.

Correspondent: H K Ready, Keith Ready & Co, Market Place, Barton-upon-Humber DN18 5DA (0652-632215).

● Bridlington

The Bridlington Charity Trustees

Eligibility: People in need who live in the parish of Bridlington.

Types of grants: Recurrent grants ranging from £7 to £100 for purchase of fuel (gas, coal, electricity) during winter, payment is made direct to the suppliers.

No loans or grants for meals or paid help.

Annual grant total: In 1992, the trust had an income of £34,000. Relief-in-need grants totalled £32,000 (326 grants).

Applications: On a form available from the correspondent. Applications can be submitted directly by the individual or through a social worker, citizen's advice bureau or other welfare agency. They are considered 8/9 times a year.

Correspondent: S Greenheld, 15 Kingston Crescent, Bridlington, North Humberside YO15 3NL (0262-676648).

● Grimsby

The Grimsby Fishermen's Dependants' Fund

Eligibility: Widows, children and parents of Grimsby fishermen lost at sea, or dying ashore while still on ships articles.

Types of grants: Regular allowances of £9 a week for widows, £8 a week for additional relatives. Extra quarterly grants are available at the trustees' discretion.

Annual grant total: In 1991/92, the trust had assets of £350,000 with an income of £50,000. £30,000 was given in 35 relief-in-need grants to individuals.

Applications: Applications on a form available from the correspondent or from the Port Missioner can be submitted

Humberside

directly by the individual or through a social worker, citizen's advice bureau or other welfare agency.

Correspondent: D G Allen, Charities Administrator, Rinovia Buildings, Faringdon Road, Fish Docks, Grimsby DN31 3TE (0472-347914).

Other information: Most claims are initiated by the Port Missioner who visits the family of any deceased fisherman and helps with the completion of the form. Applications may also be made directly to the correspondent.

The Mayor of Great Grimsby's Fund

Eligibility: People in need who live in the borough of Great Grimsby.

Types of grants: One-off grants for urgent needs; grants are typically from £75 to £100.

Annual grant total: About £1,000 in about 10 grants.

Applications: By letter to the mayor.

Correspondent: The Mayor's Secretary, Town Clerk's Department, Town Hall Square, Great Grimsby DN31 1HU (0472-242000 ext. 1450).

● Hull

The Charity of Leonard Chamberlain

Eligibility: People in need who live in the urban district of Selby in North Yorkshire and the city of Kingston-upon-Hull in Humberside.

Types of grants: Probably one-off and recurrent grants according to need.

Annual grant total: The trust had an income of £1,200 in 1991.

Applications: In writing to the correspondent.

Correspondent: Mrs C Caley, Secretary, 8 Posterngate, Hull HU1 2JN (0482-228213).

Other information: This entry is repeated in the North Yorkshire section of the book.

The Hull Aid in Sickness Trust

Eligibility: People in need who live in the city and county of Kingston-upon-Hull and who are sick, disabled, infirm or convalescent.

Types of grants: One-off grants to a usual maximum of £100 for all kinds of need, clothing, bedding, heating and dietary foods etc. but not for rates, taxes, other public charges or outstanding debts. Grants are one-off but applicants can re-apply for on-going expenses.

Annual grant total: In 1993, the trust gave £13,600 in 121 grants, mostly to individuals. There was a surplus of £1,900 of income over expenditure.

Applications: By letter to the correspondent. The trustees require a doctor's certificate and details of all household income.

Correspondent: D J Batty, Clerk to the Trustees, 15 Mead Walk, Anlaby Park, Hull HU4 6XL (0482-509697).

The Hull Fisherman's Trust Fund

Eligibility: Needy relatives of:
1. Deceased fishermen who sailed on a Hull fishing vessel, or
2. Disabled fishermen who served on a Hull fishing vessel.

Types of grants: Regular weekly allowances only.

Annual grant total: About £90,000 in about 550 grants.

Applications: To the correspondent.

Correspondent: R Brooks, Chairman, Marr Building, St Andrews Dock, Hull HU3 4PN (0482-27873).

The Charity of Miss Eliza Clubley Middleton

Eligibility: Poor women of the Catholic faith who live in the Hull area.

Types of grants: Grants are distributed twice a year, at Christmas and in summer.

Annual grant total: About £10,000.

Applications: A list of current beneficiaries is circulated to all local priests each year. They then recommend any additions or note changes in circumstances.

Correspondent: Messrs Rollit, Farell & Bladon Solicitors, Wilberforce Court, High Street, Hull HU1 1YJ (0482-23239).

The National Amalgamated Stevedores & Dockers Union Building & Benevolent Fund

Eligibility: Retired former members of the National Amalgamated Stevedores and Dockers Union, operating in Hull.

Types of grants: Grants are paid twice yearly (£20 in July and £30 in December). About 60 grants were given in 1993.

Annual grant total: The grant total of £3,100 is derived from the leasing of a social club to the Post Office.

Applications: In writing to the correspondent.

Correspondent: Mr Atkinson, Clerk, Williamson Solicitors, Manor Street, Hull HU1 1YX (0482-23834).

The Joseph Rank Benevolent Fund

Eligibility: Women aged 60 or over and men aged 65 or over (married or single) who are in receipt of a pension. Applicants must have lived in Hull (or within two miles of the city boundary) for at least 10 of the 15 years before application.

Types of grants: About 1,000 monthly allowances of £7 a month for single people and £14 a month for married couples. Priority is given to pensioners on Income Support.

Annual grant total: In 1993, the trust had assets of £2 million and an income of £116,500. Grants totalled £79,000, of which £2,000 was given to organisations in the Hull area.

Applications: By attending the office. There is a waiting list.

Correspondent: C West, Clerk, Suite 4, The Avenue, Bishop Lane, Hull HU1 1NP (0482-225542).

The Wilmington Trust

Eligibility: People who live in Kingston-upon-Hull (east of the River Hull).

Types of grants: One-off grants ranging from £50 to £100 in the form of Christmas hampers and help with holidays and emergencies. Weekly allowances may be made for a limited period.

Annual grant total: In 1992/93, the trust spent £5,500, of which £5,000 was given in grants of £50 to £100 to 60 individuals.

Applications: On a form available from the correspondent for consideration in March or October. Applications can be submitted directly by the individual or through a social worker, citizen's advice bureau or other welfare agency, or through clergy.

Correspondent: Miss S Outram, Clerk, 58 Church Street, Sutton on Hull, North Humberside HU7 4TL (0482-709699).

● Nafferton & Wansford

The Poors' Estate Charity & Others

Eligibility: Elderly people in need who live alone in the parish of All Saints, Nafferton, with St Mary the Virgin, Wansford.

● Humberside/North Yorkshire

Types of grants: Grants are usually £12 before Christmas and £15 after Christmas to help about 150 people with fuel bills, or direct assistance with goods or services. Some grants are for educational purposes.

No retrospective grants.

Annual grant total: Over £2,000 in 1992/93.

Applications: In writing to the correspondent.

Correspondent: Mrs Margaret Buckton, South Cattleholmes, Wansford, Driffield, East Yorkshire YO25 8NW (0377-254293).

● **Ottringham**

The Ottringham Charities

Eligibility: People in hardship and/or distress who live in the parish of Ottringham.

Types of grants: Normally one-off grants, but recurrent grants or loans might be considered.

Annual grant total: £1,000 in 7 grants in 1992/93.

Applications: In writing to the correspondent either directly by the individual or through a guardian or caseworker. Applications are considered throughout the year.

Correspondent: J Doerner, 34 South Side Villas, Ottringham, Hull HU12 0DT (0964-623900).

North Yorkshire

The Aldborough, Boroughbridge & District Relief-in-Sickness Fund

Eligibility: People who are sick, mentally/physically disabled or infirm and live in the parishes of Ellenthorpe, Humberton, Kirkby Hill, Langthorpe, Marton-le-Moor, Milby, Skelton, Boroughbridge, Roecliffe and Westwick. No-one else can be considered.

Types of grants: One-off grants in kind (eg. beds, pillows, coal etc.).

Annual grant total: Under £1,000.

Applications: Applications should be in writing and can be submitted by the individual or through a recognised referral agency (social worker, citizen's advice bureau or doctor etc.).

Correspondent: G Craggs, Fishergate, Boroughbridge, York YO5 9AL (0423-322221).

The Mrs E L Blakeley Marillier Annuity Fund

Eligibility: Ladies over 55 who are in reduced circumstances and are not of the Roman Catholic faith or members of the Salvation Army. Preference is given to women from the counties of York and Devon and in particular the towns of Scarborough and Torbay.

Types of grants: Annuities ranging from £100 to £520.

Annual grant total: In 1990/91, the trust had an income of £19,000; annuities totalled £13,000.

Applications: In writing to the correspondent. The trustees are actively looking for new annuitants.

Correspondent: Mr James, Messrs Hooper & Wollen, Carlton House, Torquay, Devon TQ1 1BS.

Other information: This entry is repeated in the Devon section of the book.

The Susannah Fearnsides Charity

Eligibility: People in need who have carried on the business of a farmer in the former county of York, or a dependant or former spouse of a farmer.

Types of grants: Under a new scheme the trust will continue to award pensions each year, usually not exceeding £150 and subject to an annual review. This will enable the trust to consider giving help either through one-off cash grants or by providing items, services or facilities. In future more of the trust's income may be allocated to one-off grants than to pensions.

Help has recently been given with fuel costs, carpeting and a television set.

Annual grant total: In 1992, the trust had assets of £29,900 generating an income of £2,800. Total expenditure was £2,400. Grants of between £100 and £150 were given to eight individuals and totalled £1,500.

Applications: Applications can be submitted by the individual or through a recognised referral agency (eg. social worker, citizen's advice bureau or doctor) on a form available from the correspondent following an annual public notice in the local press. Trustees meet twice-yearly in March and October.

Correspondent: C N Hobson, Clerk, 26-28 Lairgate, Beverley, Humberside HU17 8ER (0482-882278).

The Olive & Norman Field Charity

Eligibility: People who are sick, convalescent, disabled or infirm and their carers. Preference will be given to children or adults who live in the area of the North Riding of the former county of York.

Types of grants: Usually one-off grants according to need. Grants are not usually given to clear debt.

Annual grant total: In 1992, the trust had an income of £22,000. It is not known how much was given in grants to individuals in need.

Applications: Applications, on a form available from the correspondent, can be submitted by the individual, through a recognised referral agency (eg. social worker, citizen's advice bureau or doctor) or other third party, and are considered every two months.

Correspondent: The Secretary, c/o The British Red Cross Society (North Yorkshire Branch), 62 Thirsk Road, Northallerton, North Yorkshire DL6 1PN (0609-772186).

The Goldsborough Poor's Charity

Eligibility: People over 70 who live, or used to live, in Goldsborough, Flaxby or Coneythorpe.

Types of grants: Recurrent cash grants of between £40 and £50 to supplement pensions or low incomes. Distribution takes place half-yearly in June and December.

Annual grant total: In 1993, the trust had assets of £24,800 producing an income of £1,500. Grants to 14 individuals totalled £1,100.

Applications: In writing to the correspondent. Applications are considered in May and November following discussions by the four trustees acquainted with people who live in the villages.

Correspondent: J L Clarkson, 25 Princess Mead, Goldsborough, Knaresborough, North Yorkshire HG5 8NP (0423-865102).

The Harrogate Good Samaritan Fund

Eligibility: People in need aged 55 or over who live within a 10 mile radius of Harrogate and are members of a Protestant church.

Types of grants: One-off grants towards eg. hospital visits, holidays, telephone installations for housebound people and winter heating. Quarterly grants as

North Yorkshire

agreed and reviewed at each trustees meeting.

Annual grant total: In 1992, the trust had an income of £12,700. Total expenditure was £11,400 including £8,850 in grants to individuals. 25 to 30 quarterly grants are given and about 35 occasional grants.

Applications: On a form available from and submitted through the correspondent or through the minister of the relevant local church. Trustees meet in February, May, August and November.

Correspondent: Mrs F K Reid, 16 Larkfield Drive, Harrogate HG2 0BX (0423-567915).

The Hilton & Dawson Charity

Eligibility: People who live in Teesdale in County Durham, and Caldwell Eppleby, Melsonby, Middleton Tyas, Barton, Reeth and the upper part of Swaledale, all in North Yorkshire, and are unable to support themselves financially.

Types of grants: Regular yearly allowances only, at present limited to £60 per year paid quarterly by cheque.

Annual grant total: About £2,000 in around 30 grants.

Applications: On a form available from the correspondent.

Correspondent: Mrs I Appleton, Whitkirk, Winston, Nr Darlington, County Durham (0325-730423)

Other information: This entry is repeated in the Durham section of the book.

Reverend Matthew Hutchinson's Charity (Gilling & Richmond)

Eligibility: People who live in the parishes of (i) Gilling or (ii) Richmond.

Types of grants: For the relief of need, hardship or distress, or the payment/provision of items, services or facilities.

Annual grant total: (i) £3,000; (ii) £1,000.

Applications: Applications, in writing, can be submitted directly by the individual, through a recognised referral agency (eg. social worker, citizen's advice bureau or doctor) or other third party, and are considered in March and November.

Correspondent: Mrs B D Beatham, 10 High Garth, Richmond, North Yorkshire D10 4DG (0784-824193).

The Rector & Four & Twenty of Bedale

Eligibility: People who are elderly and/or infirm and/or in need who live in the parishes of Aiskew, Bedale, Burrill, Cowling, Crakehall, Firby, Langthorne and Rand Grange.

Types of grants: One-off or recurrent grants according to need ranging from £15 to £500.

Annual grant total: In 1992/93, the trust had an income of £8,000. Grants to individuals in need totalled £7,000 in about 200 grants.

Applications: In writing to the correspondent. Applications should be submitted by a social worker, citizen's advice bureau or other welfare agency. They are considered quarterly.

Correspondent: R A Crinall, Crakehall Lodge, Crakehall, Bedale, North Yorkshire DL8 1HT (0677-423547).

● **Carperby**

The Carperby Poor's Land Charity

Eligibility: People in need who live in the parish of Carperby-cum-Thoresby.

Types of grants: One-off and quarterly grants to those in need.

Annual grant total: In 1992, the trust had assets of £16,000 generating an income of £1,300. Grants ranging from £36 to £51 were given to 32 individuals and totalled £1,300.

Applications: In writing to the correspondent.

Correspondent: E R D Johnson, Messrs Johnsons Solicitors, Market Place, Hawes, North Yorkshire DL8 3QS (0969-667000).

● **Craven**

The Cotton Districts' Convalescent Fund

Eligibility: People who are convalescing or who have a severe/incurable illness or disability and who live in the district of Craven. See entry in the North West general section of the book.

● **Danby**

Joseph Ford's Trust

Eligibility: People in need who live within the old Danby parish boundary.

Types of grants: One-off or recurrent grants according to need.

Annual grant total: About £2,500.

Applications: In writing to the correspondent or any trustee, at any time.

Correspondent: M F Holborn, National Westminster Bank plc, 4 High Street, Castleton, Whitby, North Yorkshire YO21 2DA (0287-660314).

● **Gargrave**

The Gargrave Poor's Land Charity

Eligibility: People in need who live in Gargrave.

Types of grants: One-off grants.

Annual grant total: About £3,500.

Applications: In writing to the correspondent or any trustee.

Correspondent: J H Maud, 19 Neville Road, Gargrave, North Yorkshire BD23 3RE.

● **Knaresborough**

The Knaresborough Relief-in-Need Charity

Eligibility: People in need who live in the parish of Knaresborough, with a preference for people who have lived there for at least five years.

Types of grants: About 40 one-off grants ranging from £18 to £1,000 towards items such as a cooker and television licence. Also about 290 Christmas grants of £20.

Annual grant total: £13,000 to £15,000.

Applications: In writing to the correspondent.

Correspondent: P R Harris, The Chequers, Boroughbridge Road, Knaresborough, North Yorkshire HG5 0LX (0423-863086).

● **Lothersdale**

The Raygill Trust

Eligibility: People who live in the ecclesiastical parish of Lothersdale.

Types of grants: One-off or recurrent grants according to need.

Annual grant total: £4,000.

Applications: In writing to the correspondent. Applications can be submitted directly by the individual and are considered throughout the year.

Correspondent: Colin L Clarkson, 6-14 Devonshire Street, Keighley, West Yorkshire BD21 2AY (0535-667731).

North Yorkshire

Northallerton

The Grace Gardner Trust

Eligibility: Elderly people who live within the boundary of Northallerton Town Council.

Types of grants: One-off grants according to need. The trust makes contributions towards various activities such as providing transport to the library once a fortnight.

Annual grant total: In 1993, the trust had assets of £70,000 generating an income of £5,000. Total expenditure was £5,000. Grants totalled between £4,000 and £5,000.

Applications: Applications in writing can be submitted by the individual, through a recognised referral agency (eg. social worker, citizen's advice bureau or doctor) or other third party, to be considered throughout the year.

Correspondent: Mrs Sheila Gibbins, c/o Town Hall, High Street, Northallerton, North Yorkshire DL6 2RL (0609-776718).

Scarborough

The Scarborough Municipal Charities

Eligibility: People in need who are of retirement age and live in Scarborough.

Types of grants: One-off grants ranging from £25 to £185.

Annual grant total: The trust has an income of about £2,500. Grants to individuals for relief-in-need and education total about £2,000. Surplus money is used for the upkeep of almshouses.

Applications: In writing to the correspondent.

Correspondent: W Temple, Accountant, 59–61 Falsgrave Road, Scarborough, North Yorkshire YO12 5EA (0723-362362).

Selby

The Charity of Leonard Chamberlain

Eligibility: People in need who live in the urban district of Selby in North Yorkshire and the city of Kingston-upon-Hull in Humberside.

Types of grants: Probably one-off and recurrent grants according to need.

Annual grant total: The trust had an income of £1,200 in 1991.

Applications: In writing to the correspondent.

Correspondent: Mrs C Caley, Secretary, 8 Posterngate, Hull HU1 2JN (0482-228213).

Other information: This entry is repeated in the Humberside section of the book.

West Witton

The Smorthwaite Charity

Eligibility: Elderly people in need who live in West Witton. Applicants must be at least 70 if born in the parish or at least 75 if born elsewhere.

Types of grants: "£100 is given to any applicants who meet the criteria."

Annual grant total: In 1992/93, the trust had an income of £7,500. Grants to 27 individuals in need totalled £2,270.

Applications: In writing to the correspondent directly by the individual. They are considered in July/August.

Correspondent: T W Hooley, Thistlebout, West Witton, Leyburn, North Yorkshire DL8 4LY (0748-822991).

York

The Arlish & Chambers Charity

Eligibility: People in need who live in York.

Types of grants: One-off grants and recurrent grants of between £100 and £500.

Annual grant total: About £4,500 in 1992/93, most of which was given to local organisations.

Applications: In writing to the correspondent.

Correspondent: R Watson, Messrs Crombie Wilkinson, Clifford House, 19 Clifford Street, York YO1 1RJ (0904-624185).

The Merchant Taylors' Charity

Eligibility: "Decayed tailors" in need who live in the city of York and its suburbs.

Types of grants: One-off grants.

Annual grant total: About £1,000.

Applications: In writing to the correspondent.

Correspondent: R M Pontefract, Elvington Hall, York YO4 5AA (0904-608218).

The Micklegate Strays Charity

Eligibility: Freemen of the city of York and their dependants living in the Micklegate Strays ward. (This area is now defined as the whole of that part of the city of York to the west of the River Ouse.)

Types of grants: Pensions and medical grants.

Annual grant total: In 1993, the charity had £1,000 available income; they paid 46 pensions of £20 and 3 £25 medical grants.

Applications: On a form available from the correspondent.

Correspondent: C Sanderson, Clerk, 17 Middlethorpe Drive, Dringhouses, York YO2 2NG (0904-706330).

The Speck Walker Annuity Fund

Eligibility: Spinsters and widows over the age of 25 who live in the parish of Stockton-on-Tees or in the city of York.

Types of grants: Grants of up to £50 a quarter.

Annual grant total: In 1990, the trust gave 35 grants of £50 per quarter (£7,000).

Applications: In writing to the correspondent.

Correspondent: Mrs Smith, Archers Solicitors, 24 Yarm Road, Stockton-on-Tees, Cleveland TS18 3NB (0642-673431).

Other information: This entry is repeated in the Cleveland section of the book.

The Charity of St Michael-le-Belfry

Eligibility: People in need who live in York, with priority for those living in the parish of St Michael-le-Belfry.

Types of grants: Generally pensions of £800 a year paid quarterly, and one-off payments for special needs.

Annual grant total: £10,700 in 1993.

Applications: In writing to the correspondent, including evidence of financial circumstances.

Correspondent: C C Goodway, Clerk, Grays Solicitors, Duncombe Place, York YO1 2DY (0904-634771).

The Robert Winterscale Charity

Eligibility: People in need who live in the Wasmagate area of York.

Types of grants: Pensions to about six beneficiaries.

North Yorkshire/Northumberland

Annual grant total: About £500.

Applications: In writing to the correspondent.

Correspondent: Mrs J A Bartram, Messrs Crombie Wilkinson, 6 Park Street, Selby, York YO8 0PW (0757-708957).

Jane Wright's Charity

Eligibility: People in need who live in the city of York.

Types of grants: One-off and recurrent grants according to need.

Annual grant total: About £24,500 in 1992/93.

Applications: Applications must be made direct or via recognised welfare agencies. Applications are considered within a few days.

Correspondent: P E Baines, Clerk, 18 St Saviourgate, York YO1 2NS (0904-655555).

The York Children's Trust

Eligibility: Children and young people under the age of 25 who are in need and live in the greater York area.

Types of grants: Generally one-off grants, but the trustees also give consideration to recurrent grants and loans.

Annual grant total: The trust's income is about £57,000; it is not known how much is given in grants to individuals.

Applications: On a form available from the correspondent preferably submitted through an established welfare or educational agency, though direct application is possible. Applications are considered in January, April, July and October.

Correspondent: H G Sherriff, Secretary, 23 Muncastergate, York YO3 9JX (0904-423382).

The York City Charities

Eligibility: People in need who live in York.

Types of grants: One-off grants towards clothing, fuel and television licenses etc..

Annual grant total: In 1992, the trust had an income of £1,100. Total expenditure was £1,600, of which £550 was given in grants of £25 to £100 to 12 individuals.

Applications: In writing to the correspondent by recognised welfare agencies or by the individual. Applications are considered any time.

Correspondent: Mrs A C Bell, 41 Avenue Road, York.

The York Dispensary Sick Poor Fund & the Purey Cust Fund

Eligibility: People in need who live in York and surrounding districts.

Types of grants: Usually one-off grants for specific needs such as clothing, domestic equipment or holidays.

Annual grant total: About £9,000 given in 60 to 65 grants.

Applications: Preferably through social services or a similar welfare agency, though direct application is possible.

Correspondent: Gale Smith, Customer Relations Manager, Yearsley House, Huntingdon Road, York YO3 9DU (0904-631391).

The York Fund for Women & Girls

Eligibility: Young women and girls who live in York and who are in need.

Types of grants: Generally one-off grants, between £25 and £50.

Annual grant total: About £1,000 in 20 grants in 1992.

Applications: Only from recognised agencies on behalf of individuals. Applications considered within a few days.

Correspondent: Colin Stroud, Clerk, c/o York Council for Voluntary Service, 10 Priory Street, York YO1 1EZ (0904-621133).

Northumberland

The John Routledge Hunter Memorial Fund

Eligibility: Men who live in Northumberland and Whitley Bay (now in North Tyneside) who have (or recently have had) chest, lung or catarrhal complaints.

Types of grants: Total cost of a three week recuperative holiday in a hotel in Worthing, Sussex (including rail travel expenses). The usual grant is £425. Holidays are taken between Easter and September. 26 grants were given in 1990.

Annual grant total: In 1990, the trust had assets of £225,000 and an income of £12,000. Expenditure totalled £11,000.

Applications: On a form available from the correspondent. Applications should be submitted directly by the individual and are considered from January to June.

Correspondent: Norman Robson, Dickinson Dees (Solicitors), Cross House, Westgate Road, Newcastle-upon-Tyne NE99 1SB (091-261 1911).

Other information: This entry is repeated in the Tyne & Wear section of the book.

● **Alnwick**

The Alnwick & District Relief-in-Sickness Fund

Eligibility: People who live in and around Alnwick who are sick, convalescing, disabled or infirm.

Types of grants: Grants of fuel; cash grants of about £20 to 20 people, plus three grants a year totalling £500.

Annual grant total: £900 in 1991.

Applications: By referral from health visitors, nurses, ministers etc.. Direct applications are not encouraged.

Correspondent: Mrs A White, 33 Swansfield Park Road, Alnwick, Northumberland NE66 1AT (0665-602718).

● **Berwick-upon-Tweed**

The Berwick-upon-Tweed Guild of Freemen

Eligibility: Freemen and their widows who live in Berwick-upon-Tweed.

Types of grants: Probably one-off and recurrent grants according to need.

Annual grant total: £7,000 in 1990/91.

Applications: In writing to the correspondent.

Correspondent: K M Anderson, 22 Windsor Crescent, Berwick-upon-Tweed, Northumberland TD15 1NT.

The Jane Turner Fleming Charity

Eligibility: Daughters of freemen of Berwick-upon-Tweed who are widows or spinsters over the age of 21, or orphaned children of the above freemen who are under 21.

Types of grants: Deserving cases are granted an annuity, usually for life and paid quarterly. The amount (currently £200 a year) is set at the annual meeting of the charity in November. The senior annuitant receives an additional Christmas bonus of £50.

Annual grant total: About £2,400 (12 annuities).

Applications: On a form available from the correspondent.

Northumberland/South Yorkshire

Correspondent: K M Anderson, Secretary, 22 Windsor Crescent, Berwick-upon-Tweed, Northumberland TD15 1NT (0289-307367/330289).

● Dudley

The Dudley Annitsford Aged People's Treat Fund

Eligibility: Elderly people in need who live in Dudley.

Types of grants: Probably one-off and recurrent grants according to need.

Annual grant total: Over £3,000.

Applications: In writing to the correspondent.

Correspondent: J B Grieves, 77 Weetslade Crescent, Dudley, Tyne & Wear NE23 7LL.

Other information: This entry has not been confirmed by the trust.

● Morpeth

The Mary Hollon Annuity & Relief-in-Need Fund

Eligibility: Poor and deserving people over 60, with 15 years' residence in Morpeth (including Buller's Green) immediately before election.

Types of grants: Quarterly annuities of £2.50 and an allowance in December in lieu of meat and coal, currently £30. Also a liberal meat tea on November 5th each year, the anniversary of Mr & Mrs Hollon's wedding.

Annual grant total: About £4,000 to about 100 annuitants.

Applications: On a form obtainable from the council after public advertisement (usually two/three times a year).

Correspondent: T S Fairhurst, Borough Treasurer, Castle Morpeth Borough Council, Financial Services Department, The Kylins, Loansdean, Morpeth, Northumberland NE61 2EQ (0670-514351).

The Morpeth Dispensary

Eligibility: Sick poor people in need who live in and around Morpeth.

Types of grants: Grants range from £25 to £300. Recent grants have included milk and eggs to a beneficiary on a weekly basis, telephone reconnection charges, a contribution to a sports wheel-chair, decoration materials, repair of cooker, gas refills for heater, microwave cooker, bedding, holiday, fridge, carpets, vouchers for groceries at Christmas.

Annual grant total: £2,185 in 1992.

Applications: In writing to the correspondent. Money is not given directly to the applicant but through an agency such as social services.

Correspondent: M A Gaunt, 15 Bridge Street, Morpeth, Northumberland NE61 1NX (0670-512336).

● Wansbeck

The Wansbeck Appeal Trust Fund

Eligibility: People in need who live in the administrative area of Wansbeck District Council. Preference for people who are disabled, elderly or sick and for the relief of hardship. Other people in need at the discretion of the trustees if funds are available.

Types of grants: Varies from year to year.

Annual grant total: £1,000 in about 10 grants.

Applications: In writing by the individual or through a social worker, citizen's advice bureau or other welfare agency direct to the correspondent.

Correspondent: A G White, Chief Executive, Wansbeck District Council, Town Hall, Ashington, Northumberland NE63 8RX (0670-814444).

Other information: Relief of need is only at the discretion of the trustees who may vary the objects from time to time.

South Yorkshire

The Brampton Bierlow Welfare Trust

Eligibility: People in need who live in Brampton Bierlow and West Melton, and those parts of Wentworth and Elscar within the ancient parish of Brampton Bierlow.

Types of grants: One-off grants from £100 to £250 for necessities and comforts.

Annual grant total: In 1993, one-off grants plus 400 Christmas grocery vouchers of £6 were given to individuals in need.

Applications: Applications in writing to the correspondent can be submitted by the individual, through a recognised referral agency (eg. social worker, citizen's advice bureau or doctor) or other third party, and are considered at any time, but usually in January, April, July and October.

Correspondent: Ian McDonald, Newman & Bond, 35 Church Street, Barnsley S70 2AP (0226-289336).

The Cooper & Lancaster Annuities

Eligibility: Women in need who live in Barnsley, Worsborough Dale and Worsborough Bridge.

Types of grants: 12 recipients of regular grants only, paid quarterly.

Annual grant total: About £600.

Applications: In writing to the correspondent.

Correspondent: Messrs Newman & Bond, Solicitors, 35 Church Street, Barnsley S70 2AP (0226-289336).

The George & Clara Ann Hall Charity

Eligibility: Widows and spinsters over the age of 45 who have lived in the city of Sheffield or the township and chapelry of Bradfield for the past five years.

Types of grants: Annuities of £75 paid twice yearly.

Annual grant total: £1,800 in 1993.

Applications: On a form available from the correspondent.

Correspondent: Nick Warren, Director, c/o Voluntary Action Sheffield, 69 Division Street, Sheffield S1 4GE (0742-755138).

The Hounsfield Pension

Eligibility: People in need, normally widows at least 50 years old, who live in South Yorkshire, are members of the Church of England and have never received parochial relief or public assistance.

Types of grants: Regular allowances of £500 a year paid in two instalments.

Annual grant total: About £6,000 to about 12 recipients.

Applications: On a form available from the correspondent.

Correspondent: M P W Lee, Clerk, c/o Dibb, Lupton & Broomhead, Solicitors, Fountain Precinct, Balm Green, Sheffield S1 1RZ (0742-760351).

The Sheffield West Riding Charitable Society Trust

Eligibility: Needy clergymen of the Church of England in the diocese of Sheffield. Also their widows, orphans or distressed families, and people keeping house, or who have kept house, for clergymen of the Church of England or their families.

Types of grants: One-off and recurrent grants according to need.

Annual grant total: About £6,000.

Applications: Applicants should apply to the correspondent.

Correspondent: Canon R Thomson, 34 Kingwell Road, Ward Green, Worborough, Barnsley S70 4HF (0226-203553).

● Aston-cum-Aughton

The Aston-cum-Aughton Charity Estate

Eligibility: People in need who live in the parish of Aston-cum-Aughton.

Types of grants: One-off and recurrent grants according to need.

Annual grant total: In 1991, the trust had an income of £10,000. Grants to individuals and groups totalled £7,730.

Applications: In writing to the correspondent.

Correspondent: R Vollum, Clerk, 2 Thoresby Close, Aston, Sheffield S31 0EJ (0742-872178).

● Barnsley

The Barnsley Prisoner of War Fund

Eligibility: Needy ex-servicemen and women (not necessarily ex-prisoners-of-war) living in the Barnsley Metropolitan area and their dependants.

Types of grants: One-off grants only of between £100 and £500.

Annual grant total: In 1993, grants totalling around £4,500 were made to 50 individuals.

Applications: In writing to the correspondent or through local branches of forces welfare agencies.

Correspondent: Mr Loach, Borough Secretary, Committee Section, Barnsley Borough Council, The Town Hall, Barnsley S70 2TA (0226-770770).

The Barnsley Tradesmen's Benevolent Institution

Eligibility: Merchants and traders, their widows and unmarried daughters, who are in need and who have lived in the old borough of Barnsley for at least seven years.

Types of grants: Usually £30 per month. There are currently three beneficiaries.

Annual grant total: About £1,100. A further £300 was distributed as electricity stamps in October and January.

Applications: On a form available from the correspondent.

Correspondent: D B Richards & Co, 29 Church Street, Barnsley S70 2AL (0226-243261).

● Beighton

Beighton Relief-in-Need Charity

Eligibility: People in need who live in the former parish of Beighton.

Types of grants: One-off and recurrent grants according to need. Fuel grants of £15 are given to elderly people and grants have also been given towards the cost of a wheelchair, holidays for families and visits to hospital.

Annual grant total: In 1993, the trust had an income of £14,000. 489 grants totalling £9,300 were given to individuals and a further £4,400 to groups.

Applications: In writing to the correspondent. Applications can be submitted directly by the individual or through a social worker, citizen's advice bureau, other welfare agency or a third party such as a relative, neighbour or trustee.

Correspondent: R Purdy, Secretary, 48 Queens Road, Beighton, Sheffield S19 6AW (0742-690846).

● Cantley

The Cantley Poors' Land

Eligibility: People in need who live in the ancient parish of Cantley (which now includes the areas known as Bessacarr and the Cantley Estates, together with the villages of Old Cantley and Branton).

Types of grants: "Both one-off and recurrent grants. No maximum award but regard paid to current funds and number of applicants. Aim is to relieve immediate need as far as other commitments allow."

Annual grant total: £25,000 in over 400 grants in 1993, most of which was given to individuals in need.

Applications: On a form available from the correspondent (not via a third party).

Correspondent: Mrs M Jackson, Clerk, 30 Selhurst Crescent, Bessacar, Doncaster DN4 6EF (0302-530566).

● Darton

The Fountain Nursing Trust

Eligibility: People in need who live in the former urban district of Darton.

Types of grants: One-off or recurrent grants according to need.

Annual grant total: In 1991, the trust had an income of £540 and gave two grants totalling £100.

Applications: In writing to the correspondent.

Correspondent: A Oxley, 35 Church Street, Barnsley, South Yorkshire S20 2AP (0226-289336).

● Doncaster

The John William Chapman Charitable Trust

Eligibility: People in need who live in the metropolitan borough of Doncaster. Preference is given to elderly or disabled people, single parents, discharged prisoners and families with children.

Types of grants: One-off grants in kind, not cash. No assistance given in connection with education, debt, fuel bills, or building work on council or rented property.

Annual grant total: £30,000.

Applications: On a form available from the correspondent. Applications must be completed/signed by the individual concerned and are considered monthly.

Correspondent: The Visitor, JWCCT, Community House, 7 Netherhall Road, Doncaster, South Yorkshire DN1 2PH.

● Rotherham

The Feoffees of the Common Lands of Rotherham

Eligibility: People in need over the age of 80 who live in the borough of Rotherham.

Types of grants: One-off grants at Christmas.

Annual grant total: Over £4,000.

Applications: Applications to the correspondent taken during the first full week of September.

Correspondent: W B Copley, Secretary, Thornbank, 38 Moorgate Road, Rotherham, South Yorkshire S60 2BU (0709-371360).

South Yorkshire/Tyne & Wear

The Rotherham Borough Co-ordinating Committee for the Blind & Partially Sighted

Eligibility: People in need who are blind or visually impaired and who live in the borough of Rotherham.

Types of grants: Yearly holidays, day trips, Christmas grants, television licences, guide dogs and other special equipment.

Annual grant total: About £10,000, but the trust receives extra financial help from other trusts.

Applications: In writing to the correspondent, usually from social services staff who know of all registered blind people.

Correspondent: P Lesley, c/o Director of Social Services, Rotherham Borough Council, Civic Building, Walker Place, Rotherham S65 1UF (0709-382121 ext. 3962).

Other information: There are about 1,450 people registered as visually impaired in the area; 95% are invited on the day trips and given Christmas gifts.

The Stoddart Samaritan Fund

Eligibility: People aged 16 or over who have been ill and are in need of convalescence to help them recover and return to work. Applicants should be either living or working within a 4-mile radius of Rotherham Town Hall.

Types of grants: One-off grants only.

Annual grant total: Over £4,000.

Applications: Applications should be made through a doctor.

Correspondent: Peter Wright, Secretary, 7 Melrose Grove, Rotherham, South Yorkshire S60 3NA (0709-376448).

● Sheffield

The Fisher Institution

Eligibility: Needy women over 45 living in and around Sheffield who are believers in the Unity of God (Unitarian) or are members of the Roman Catholic Church.

Types of grants: Regular yearly allowances of £90.

Annual grant total: In 1993, the trust had assets of £20,000 producing an income of £2,000. Grants of around £90 were given to 21 individuals and totalled £1,900.

Applications: Applications, on a form available from the correspondent, can be submitted by the individual, through a recognised referral agency (eg. social worker, citizen's advice bureau or doctor) or other third party (eg. Roman Catholic priest, Unitarian minister or trustee) and are considered in March. Details of income and capital must be included.

Correspondent: Mrs K Woodhouse, 38 Tom Lane, Sheffield S10 3PB (0742-303027).

Sir George Franklin's Pension Charity

Eligibility: People in need aged 50 and over who live in the city of Sheffield.

Types of grants: Annual allowances of £200.

Annual grant total: About £2,000.

Applications: Vacancies arise infrequently and are publicised locally. Applications should only be made in response to this publicity. Speculative applications will not be successful.

Correspondent: R H M Plews, Clerk, Pannell Kerr Forster, Knowle House, 4 Norfolk Park Road, Sheffield S2 3QE (0742-767991).

The Zachary Merton & George Woofindin Convalescent Trust

Eligibility: People in need who live in the cities of Sheffield and Lincoln.

Types of grants: Convalescence only.

Annual grant total: About £40,000.

Applications: In writing to the correspondent by the 31st March or 30th September.

Correspondent: M P W Lee, Clerk, Dibb Lupton & Broomhead Solicitors, Fountain Precinct, Balm Green, Sheffield S1 1RZ (0742-760351).

Other information: This entry is repeated in the Lincolnshire section of the book.

The Samuel Roberts Trust

Eligibility: Poor and infirm widows and single women of good character at least 65 years of age who do not have an income of more than £2 per week from other sources and who live in Sheffield.

Types of grants: Pensions of £80 a year. There is also a hardship fund for payments (usually £20 to £50) to elderly women who have been through an emergency eg. burglary.

Annual grant total: About £3,000 to under 100 people in 1993.

Applications: In writing to the correspondent through a social worker, citizen's advice bureau or other welfare agency. Applications are considered throughout the year.

Correspondent: Pat Stabler, Hon. Treasurer, Voluntary Action Sheffield, 69 Division Street, Sheffield S1 4GE (0742-755138).

The John Walsh Fund

Eligibility: People in need who have been employed in the retail trade for at least 20 years; preference is given to those who live in Sheffield.

Types of grants: One-off and recurrent grants according to need.

Annual grant total: About £2,400 in about 30 grants of £5 to £10 a week.

Applications: On a form available from the correspondent.

Correspondent: R Lesirge, Chief Executive, The Cottage Homes, Marshall Estate, Hammers Lane, London NW7 4EE (081-959 7071).

Wither's Pension

Eligibility: Women in need who are single or widowed and who live in the ancient parish of Sheffield.

Types of grants: 19 yearly allowances of £150 (£75 paid in April and October).

Annual grant total: £2,800.

Applications: Considered in October of each year.

Correspondent: Michael L Chadwick, Secretary, The Annexe, The Manor House, 260 Ecclesall Road South, Sheffield S11 9UZ.

Tyne & Wear

The Abbott Memorial Trust

Eligibility: Children up to the age of 18 who are in need and who live in Newcastle-upon-Tyne or Gateshead.

Types of grants: One-off grants, usually up to £150, for all types of need. The trust has helped many children from one-parent families.

Grants are not usually given to relieve debts.

Annual grant total: Up to £4,500. Between 15 and 20 grants are made in each area.

Applications: Must be made through the relevant social services department (see below). Applications are considered monthly.

Tyne & Wear

Correspondent: The Principal Officer (Health & Community), Social Services Department, Civic Centre, Newcastle or Gateshead.

For applications north of the Tyne contact: Newcastle (091-232 8520).

For applications south of the Tyne contact: Gateshead (091-477 1011).

The Cathedral Nursing Society Charitable Trust

Eligibility: Retired nurses and sick and elderly poor people who live in the diocese of Newcastle.

Types of grants: One-off grants only.

Annual grant total: £1,000 in 1991.

Applications: In writing to the correspondent.

Correspondent: N T Garbutt, Clifton House, Morpeth, Northumberland NE61 6DQ (091-201 3800).

The Charlton Bequest & Dispensary Trust

Eligibility: People who are sick or poor and live in the former county borough of Tynemouth, now part of North Tyneside County Borough.

Types of grants: One-off grants.

Annual grant total: In 1992/93, the trust had an income of £25,500. Most of this is used maintaining two houses for elderly people. Three grants were given to individuals.

Applications: In writing to the correspondent.

Correspondent: A Galley, Hon. Chairman, 18 Mast Lane, Cullercoats, North Shields NE30 3DE (091-252 5823).

Other information: This trust was formed from the County Borough of Tynemouth Nursing Association and the North Shields & Tynemouth Dispensary.

The South Shields Indigent Sick Society

Eligibility: People in need who are sick, convalescent, disabled or infirm and who live in South Shields parliamentary constituency.

Types of grants: One-off and recurrent grants according to need.

Annual grant total: Income of £2,500.

Applications: In writing to the correspondent.

Correspondent: B W Lee, 36 The General's Wood, Washington, Tyne & Wear (091-4160 732).

The Tyne Mariners' Benevolent Institution/Society of Widows & Orphans

Eligibility: Elderly merchant seamen who live in Tyneside (about five miles either side of the River Tyne), and their widows. Applicants must either be (a) at least 63 years old and have served at least 21 years at sea, or (b) under the age of 63, but unable to work owing to ill-health, or (c) be widows of such people.

Types of grants: Yearly allowances only of £240 (paid monthly), plus some bonuses.

Annual grant total: About £90,000 given in 500 to 600 grants.

Applications: Application forms available from the correspondent.

Correspondent: Messrs Hadaway & Hadaway, 58 Howard Street, North Shields, Tyne & Wear NE30 1AL (091-257 0382).

Other information: The institution also administers the Master Mariners Homes in Tynemouth which provides 30 flats for beneficiaries of the institution.

● Gateshead

The Davidson Charity Trust

Eligibility: People in need who live in the metropolitan borough of Gateshead.

Types of grants: One-off grants only.

Annual grant total: About £5,000.

Applications: In writing to the correspondent.

Correspondent: R D Hurst, Rhodeferns, 741 Durham Road, Gateshead, Tyne & Wear NE9 (091-487 7004).

● Newcastle-upon-Tyne

The Arnison Fund

Eligibility: People who are sick and live in the Newcastle-upon-Tyne area.

Types of grants: One-off grants for travel to and from hospital and for necessities not provided by the National Health Service.

Annual grant total: About £700.

Applications: In writing to the correspondent.

Correspondent: K J Hilton, c/o Tyne & Wear Foundation, Mea House, Ellison Place, Newcastle-upon-Tyne NE1 8XS (091-261 4111).

The Town Moor Money Charity & Robert Bell Harrison's Legacy

Eligibility: Freemen of Newcastle-upon-Tyne and their widows and daughters who are in need.

Types of grants: One-off and recurrent grants according to need, up to a maximum of £120. Grants are means tested and paid in June and December.

Annual grant total: About 250 people received grants totalling £25,000 in 1993.

Applications: In writing to the correspondent for consideration in May and November.

Correspondent: Mrs Ansell, Clerk, Moor Bank Lodge, Claremont Road, Newcastle-upon-Tyne NE2 4NL (091-261 5970).

● Sunderland

The Mayor's Fund for Necessitous Children

Eligibility: Children in need who live in the city of Sunderland.

Types of grants: About £25 grants for provision of footwear.

Annual grant total: About 500 to 600 grants totalling £12,500 to £15,000 in 1992/93.

Applications: By letter to the correspondent.

Correspondent: The City Education Officer, Pupil & Student Services, Civic Centre, PO Box 101, Sunderland SR2 7DN (091-567 6161 ext. 2233).

● Usworth

The Robinson Memorial Gift

Eligibility: Widows and elderly people who are in need and who live in the ecclesiastical parish of Holy Trinity, Usworth.

Types of grants: One-off and recurrent grants according to need. Grants are generally £30 to £50 but can be up to £150 in special circumstances.

Annual grant total: According to the Charity Commission the trust had an income of £3,700 in 1993.

Applications: In writing to the correspondent.

Correspondent: J A Siggens, Clerk, Audel-Glen, 70 Manor Park, Washington, Tyne & Wear NE37 2BS (091-416 2401).

Wallsend

The Wallsend Charitable Trust (also known as the Victor Mann Trust)

Eligibility: People on state benefit who live in the former borough of Wallsend. (There is a preference for people of pensionable age.)

Types of grants: One-off grants only to help meet extra requirements. The trust will not help with continuing costs such as residential care or telephone rentals and will not help a person whose income is significantly above state benefit levels.

Annual grant total: About £30,000, but not all of this is given to individuals.

Applications: In writing to the correspondent. Applications are considered quarterly.

Correspondent: Fred Lilley, Secretary, Assesment Fund, Social Services, Great Lime Road, West Moor, Newcastle-upon-Tyne NE12 (091-268 2567).

Whitley Bay

The John Routledge Hunter Memorial Fund

Eligibility: Men who live in Northumberland and Whitley Bay (now in North Tyneside) who have (or recently have had) chest, lung or catarrhal complaints.

Types of grants: Total cost of a three week recuperative holiday in a hotel in Worthing, Sussex (including rail travel expenses). The usual grant is £425. Holidays are taken between Easter and September. 26 grants were given in 1990.

Annual grant total: Expenditure totalled £11,000 in 1990.

Applications: On a form available from the correspondent. Applications should be submitted directly by the individual and are considered from January to June.

Correspondent: Norman Robson, Dickinson Dees, Solicitors, Cross House, Westgate Road, Newcastle-upon-Tyne NE99 1SB (091-261 1911).

Other information: This entry is repeated in the Northumberland section of the book.

West Yorkshire

The Calverley Charity

Eligibility: People in need who live in the parishes of Calverley, Farsley and Thornbury.

Types of grants: One-off grants, generally of £3 and £5. The trustees meet once a year and at Christmas £700 is distributed between people over the age of 70 irrespective of need. Trustees have their own ways of choosing beneficiaries, but applications are considered.

Annual grant total: About £1,000.

Applications: In writing to the correspondent.

Correspondent: P Rogerson, Chief Legal Officer, Leeds City Council, Civic Hall, Leeds LS1 1UR (0532-474536).

The Charities Fund

Eligibility: Needy, sick and elderly people who live in West Yorkshire.

Types of grants: One-off and recurrent grants according to need.

Annual grant total: £123,000 in 1991, but only a small proportion of this went to individuals.

Applications: "Through the organiser or similar person within an organisation or hospital."

Correspondent: G A Clarkson, Secretary, c/o Sovereign Health Care, PO Box 86, 72 Vicar Lane, Bradford, West Yorkshire BD1 5AL (0274-729472).

The Emmandjay Charitable Trust

Eligibility: People in need who live in West Yorkshire.

Types of grants: Generally one-off grants, but can be spread up to three years.

Annual grant total: £140,000 in 1991/92 in 300 to 400 grants, but only a portion of this was given directly to individuals.

Applications: In writing to the correspondent.

Correspondent: C T P Horne, PO Box 31, Bradford, West Yorkshire BD1 5NH.

The Leeds Jewish Welfare Board

Eligibility: Jewish people who live in Leeds or West Yorkshire.

Types of grants: One-off grants for items and services, including counselling and meals-on-wheels. A number of festivities are organised for holidays and at Passover.

Annual grant total: In 1991, about £261,000, of which about £10,000 was given to 320 individuals in need.

Applications: Applications for help can be made at any time by individuals, welfare agencies, friends or relatives. The board can respond quickly in urgent cases.

Correspondent: Pippa Landey, Social Work Manager, 311 Stonegate Road, Leeds LS17 6AZ (0532-684211).

The Lucy Lund Holiday Grants

Eligibility: Present or former teachers only (especially women teachers living in West Yorkshire), who need a recuperative holiday. No grants to dependants or to students.

Types of grants: Grants for recuperative holidays.

Annual grant total: Around 26 grants up to a maximum of £60, totalling £1,400.

Applications: On a form available from the correspondent by post only.

Correspondent: The Honorary Secretary, 17 Westover Road, Warton, Carnforth, Lancashire LA5 9QT.

The Printers' Community Fund

Eligibility: People in need who live in Leeds and Bradford.

Types of grants: About 50 one-off and recurrent grants according to need. The normal maximum grant is £100. In addition 80 people who have been ill for a long period (about six months) receive Christmas grants of £25.

Annual grant total: £2,000.

Applications: Applications should be made on behalf of the individual by a welfare agency. All applicants should first approach statutory and other sources of help. Any support given by the fund will seek to provide long term benefit. A visit will be made to any intended recipient. Application forms are available from the correspondent. Trustees meet on the last Thursday of every month.

Correspondent: D J Juniper, Hon. Secretary, 21 Chelwood Crescent, Leeds LS8 2AQ (0532-663228).

Other information: The fund's income came from an annual fundraising event which has now stopped. The fund is now spending the last of its remaining capital.

The Sir Titus Salt's Charity

Eligibility: People in need who are over the age of 75 and who live in Shipley, Baildon, Saltaire, Nab Wood and Wrose.

Types of grants: Food vouchers of £2.50 paid once a year, available from Shipley Town Hall. The trust can make grants or loans up to about £250 towards the supply of special foods or medicines, medical comforts, shoes and domestic help. No suitable applications for these one-off grants have been received recently.

Annual grant total: About £4,000 in about 1,500 food vouchers.

Applications: Applications considered November/December each year. "All applications will receive the grant if they are of the correct age and live in the grant area."

Correspondent: N Free, Chairman, 192 Leeds Road, Shipley, West Yorkshire BD18 1BX.

● Baildon

The Butterfield Trust

Eligibility: People in need who live in the parish of Baildon.

Types of grants: One-off grants for emergencies.

Annual grant total: £1,500.

Applications: In writing to the correspondent. Decisions can be made immediately.

Correspondent: Rev John Nowell, The Vicarage, Browgate, Baildon, West Yorkshire BD17 6BY (0274-594941).

● Batley

The Batley Town Mission

Eligibility: People in need who live in the former borough of Batley.

Types of grants: One-off grants up to about £100, or providing or paying for items, services or facilities calculated to relieve sick, elderly or needy people.

Annual grant total: £4,000.

Applications: Applications can only be made through social workers or other welfare agencies on forms available from the correspondent.

Correspondent: The Secretary, The Batley Town Mission, Oakwood House, Upper Batley, Batley, West Yorkshire WF17 0AL.

● Bingley

The Bingley Diamond Jubilee Relief-in-Sickness Charity

Eligibility: People who live in the parish of Bingley as constituted on 14th February 1898 who are sick, convalescent, disabled or infirm.

Types of grants: Emergency payments or annual grants according to need.

Annual grant total: About £1,000.

Applications: In writing to the correspondent. Annual grants are considered at the trustees meeting in early February. A sub-committee of trustees can deal promptly with emergency payments.

Correspondent: Roger Bamforth, Clerk, Weatherhead & Butcher, Solicitors, 120 Main Street, Bingley BD16 2JJ (0274-562322).

The Samuel Sunderland Relief-in-Need Charity

Eligibility: Residents of the former parish of Bingley as constituted on 14th February 1898, who are in need, hardship or distress.

Types of grants: Emergency payments and annual grants.

Annual grant total: About £3,000.

Applications: In writing to the correspondent.

Correspondent: Roger Bamforth, Clerk, Weatherhead & Butcher Solicitors, 120 Main Street, Bingley BD16 2JJ (0274-562322).

● Bradford

The City of Bradford Fund for the Disabled

Eligibility: Physically disabled people of any age who live in the city of Bradford metropolitan area.

Types of grants: Applicants must be in need through lack of finance or insufficient benefits to be able to afford extra essential items, or who have through unusual circumstances large bills which they cannot meet. Preference for one-off grants covering a range of needs eg. nebulisers, aids, equipment, and help with holidays. Grants generally up to £100.

Annual grant total: In 1993, the trust had an income of £1,300. 21 grants ranged from £50 to £100 and totalled £1,150.

Applications: Applications can be submitted through a recognised referral agency (social worker, citizen's advice bureau or doctor) and are considered quarterly from March onwards.

Correspondent: The Honorary Secretary, Social Services, Community Development, Olicana House, Chapel Street, Bradford BD1 5RE (0274-757965).

Other information: Grant applications for medical equipment must be supported by a doctor's note. Holiday grants will only be paid direct to the accommodation address. Applications should therefore be made well in advance of the holiday date.

The Bradford & District Wool Association Benevolent Fund

Eligibility: Former workers who have worked in offices in the wool trade in Bradford and district or their spouses, who are in need.

Types of grants: Normally fuel vouchers and cash grants. Special cases (eg. the need for an invalid chair) are considered.

Annual grant total: No information available.

Applications: In writing to the correspondent either directly by the individual or through a relative or friend. Applications are considered at any time.

Correspondent: G W Bryson, Chairman, Committee of London Wool Brokers, Oakwood House, City Road, Bradford BD8 8JY (0274-725865).

The Bradford Gentlewomen's Pension Fund

Eligibility: Women in need who are over the age of 50, live in Bradford and whose fathers, mothers or husbands have been members of the landed, professional, commercial or farming classes.

Types of grants: Regular allowances only.

Annual grant total: About £2,000.

Applications: In writing to the correspondent.

Correspondent: M Chappell, 56 Carr Lane, Windhill, Shipley, Bradford BD18 2LD (0274-585301).

The Bradford Jewish Benevolent Society

Eligibility: Jewish people who live in the city and district of Bradford or originate from there.

Types of grants: One-off or recurrent grants according to need. Grants have been given for funeral costs and to send children on holiday.

West Yorkshire

Annual grant total: In 1990, the trust had an income of £2,900. Expenditure totalled £1,800 including grants of £1,300 all to organisations.

Applications: In writing to the correspondent. Applications can be considered at any time.

Correspondent: L Solity, 7 Castlemoor Road, Baildon, Shipley, West Yorkshire.

The Bradford Spinsters' Endowment Fund

Eligibility: Women over the age of 60 who have lived in Bradford for at least seven years. They must not be in work.

Types of grants: Pensions of £40 a quarter, plus a £60 Christmas grant.

Annual grant total: £3,000.

Applications: In writing to the correspondent. Applicants will be visited before an award is made.

Correspondent: P Wainwright, Trust Administrator, Lilycroft, Heaton Road, Bradford BD8 8QY (0274-543022).

The Children's Charity Circle

Eligibility: Children in need under 16 who live in Bradford.

Types of grants: Cash grants for clothes, bedding, prams and pushchairs. Generally no grants for holidays.

Annual grant total: £2,500 to £3,000 to individuals.

Applications: In writing to the correspondent. The circle meets on the first Wednesday of each month and can make quick decisions in urgent cases.

Correspondent: Mrs Christine Hopkinson, 17 The Grove, Moorhead, Shipley, West Yorkshire BD18 4LD (0274-583615).

The Moser Benevolent Trust Fund

Eligibility: People in need who are over 60 and have lived or worked in the former county borough of Bradford for at least three years before their application.

Types of grants: Usually £1.50 given four times a year.

Annual grant total: About £4,000

Applications: In writing to the correspondent.

Correspondent: The Clerk, c/o Stokes & Co, Chartered Accountants, 10 Eldon Place, Bradford BD1 3AZ (0274-740502).

The Viscount Mountgarret Permanent Trust

Eligibility: People in need who live within the three constitual boundaries of Bradford North, South & West ie. pre-1974 city of Bradford. Preference for people of pensionable age but, any individual in need will be considered.

Types of grants: One-off grants to help buy furniture, gas/electric appliances etc.. Although geared towards helping the elderly, the trust considers giving assistance to younger mentally disturbed people who have been placed in the community. "Samaritan" payments of up to £10 are made to people through the social services. Grants to groups dealing with the welfare of the elderly are also considered.

Annual grant total: In 1993, the trust had an income of £2,725. Grants ranging from £5 to £50 (£100 on occasions) were given to 81 individuals and totalled £5,665.

Applications: Applications can be submitted through a recognised referral agency (social worker, citizen's advice bureau, doctor etc.) or the Royal British Legion, and are considered immediately. Applications should be accompanied by details of the individual's finances, physical condition and age, and whether or not they are an ex-service man/woman.

Correspondent: P France, Deputy Chairman, Bradford Association for the Elderly, 40a Piccadilly, Bradford BD1 3NN (0274-720225).

Bramley

The Bramley Poors' Allotment & Other Charities

Eligibility: People in need, especially poor and sick people, who live in the ancient township of Bramley.

Types of grants: One-off grants (generally up to £200) for necessities (including holidays).

Annual grant total: £3,000.

Applications: Applications can be submitted by the individual or through a recognised referral agency (social worker, citizen's advice bureau or doctor).

Correspondent: Len Barnett, 31 St Oswald's Terrace, Guisley, Leeds LS20 9BD (0943-876033).

Calderdale

The Cotton Districts' Convalescent Fund

Eligibility: People who are convalescing or who have a severe/incurable illness or disability and who live in the district of Calderdale. See entry in the North West general section of the book.

Dewsbury

Dewsbury & District Sick Poor Fund

Eligibility: People who live in the county borough of Dewsbury and the ecclesiastical parish of Hanging Heaton.

Types of grants: One-off grants only.

Annual grant total: £8,000.

Applications: In writing to the correspondent.

Correspondent: W S Harrison, Secretary, Greenways, 18 Oxford Road, Dewsbury, West Yorkshire WF13 4JT (0924-466658).

The Whittuck Charity

Eligibility: People in need who live in the former county borough of Dewsbury (as constituted on 1st April 1974). There is a preference for people who are sick, convalescent or disabled.

Types of grants: Grants for clothing, holidays, household equipment and other items, services or facilities to relieve suffering or assist the recovery of sick, disabled or infirm people, where help is not readily available from other sources. In 1991, 177 grants were made ranging from £50 to £250. Grants can also be given to organisations.

Annual grant total: In 1991, the trust's income was £1,700. Relief-in-need grants to individuals totalled £2,600.

Applications: On a form available from the correspondent. Applications can be submitted directly by the individual or through a social worker, citizen's advice bureau or other welfare agency or a third party such as parents, spouses or doctors. They are considered throughout the year.

Correspondent: G Swain, Clerk, 27 Union Street, Dewsbury, West Yorkshire WF13 1AY (0924-455391).

Golcar

The Herbert Whitwam Trust

Eligibility: People in need who live in the township of Golcar (as constituted in July 1932).

Types of grants: Usually Christmas grants, but grants can be given at other times.

Annual grant total: About £1,000.

Applications: In writing to the Vicar of Golcar.

Correspondent: Eric Lord, Bank Chambers, Market Street, Huddersfield HD1 2EW (0484-534431).

Halifax

The Samuel Watson Batty Trust

Eligibility: People in need over the age of 65 who live in Halifax. There is a preference for people living in King Cross.

Types of grants: One-off grants for television rental, hairdressing, comforts and necessities and small Christmas gifts. Grants usually range from £5 to £50. The trust also supports crime prevention, fixing safety grills and intercom systems.

Annual grant total: Not more than £1,500 including about 120 Christmas gifts and about 80 one-off grants.

Applications: In writing to the correspondent. The trustees meet in March and September.

Correspondent: Jackie Stark, Director, Calderdale Council for Voluntary Service, 32 Clare Road, Halifax HX1 2HX (0422-363341).

Mary Farrar's Benevolent Trust Fund

Eligibility: Respectable women of limited means who are not less than 55 years of age. They should be natives of, or have lived in, the ancient parish of Halifax (the current metropolitan borough of Calderdale and Fixby in the metropolitan borough of Kirklees) for at least five consecutive years.

Types of grants: Annual pensions paid quarterly from 1st January (at present £30 a quarter) plus an annual bonus (£30 in 1993). Grants are not given to people in residential care.

Annual grant total: £6,500.

Applications: Applications, on a form available from the correspondent, can be submitted by the individual, through a recognised referral agency (eg. social worker, citizen's advice bureau or doctor) or other third party such as a relative, friend or minister of religion. Applications are considered in March, June, September and December.

Correspondent: Peter Haley, P Haley & Co, Chartered Accountants, Poverty Hall, Lower Ellistones, Greetland, Halifax HX4 8NG (0422-376690).

The Goodall Trust

Eligibility: Widows and spinsters in need who live in the parishes of St Jude and All Saints, Halifax (the ancient township of Skircoat).

Types of grants: One-off or recurrent grants according to need.

Annual grant total: In 1992, the trust had an income of £2,150. Grants of between £100 and £175 were given to 15 individuals and totalled £1,950.

Applications: On a form available from the correspondent, to be submitted prior to the annual meeting of the trustees in October. Advertisements are placed in the local press and parish magazines.

Correspondent: C R Woodward, 11 Fountain Street, Halifax HX1 1LU (0422-362737).

The Halifax Society for the Blind

Eligibility: Blind and partially sighted people who live in and around Halifax.

Types of grants: One-off and recurrent grants of cash or equipment according to need. A visiting scheme, three afternoon centres, vacations at a holiday home for members and their guides, and a resource centre are organised.

Annual grant total: £10,000 to £20,000.

Applications: In writing to the correspondent, either directly or through a welfare agency. The committee meets monthly and can act rapidly in urgent cases.

Correspondent: Jackie Mitchell, Secretary, 3 Wards End, Halifax HX1 1DD (0422-52383).

The Halifax Tradesmen's Benevolent Institution

Eligibility: People in need aged 60 or over, who live in the parish of Halifax and who were manufacturers, merchants, tradesmen, professional men or self-employed, or others and their widows or unmarried daughters. Applicants should have no other income than a pension and have savings below £3,000.

Types of grants: Quartely allowances only, at present of £200 a year plus a Christmas grant of £60.

Annual grant total: 69 grants totalled £18,800 in 1992/93.

Applications: In writing to the correspondent including details of residence, savings, income and business history. Applications are considered in September and February.

Correspondent: J K Allen, 3 Wards End, Halifax HX1 1DB (0422-365858).

The Charity of Ann Holt

Eligibility: Single women over the age of 50 and in need who have lived in Halifax for at least five years.

Types of grants: Pensions, currently £74 a year, paid in quarterly instalments until the recipient dies, moves out of the area or moves into a residential home. About 110 grants are given.

Annual grant total: £7,500 to £8,000.

Applications: Directly by the individual in writing to the correspondent.

Correspondent: Jackie Stark, Director, Calderdale Council for Voluntary Service, 32 Clare Road, Halifax HX1 2HX (0422-363341).

Heckmondwike

The Heckmondwike & District Fund for the Needy Sick

Eligibility: People in need who are sick and live in and around Heckmondwike.

Types of grants: Usually one-off grants of about £100.

Annual grant total: About £1,800.

Applications: In writing to the correspondent or personal attendance at the Midland Bank Chambers. Most claimants are referred by welfare organisations or head teachers etc.. The trustees can act promptly with urgent cases.

Correspondent: J E Pilkington, Clerk, Redferns Solicitors, Midland Bank Chambers, Heckmondwike, West Yorkshire WF16 0HZ (0924-403745).

Horbury

The St Leonards Hospital Charity

Eligibility: People in need, hardship or distress who live in the former urban district of Horbury.

Types of grants: One-off grants according to need. In the past the charity has helped with the provision of night nurses for terminally ill people, equipment for disabled people, and cash payments for specific items.

West Yorkshire

Annual grant total: About £4,500 in 9 grants ranging from £100 to £1,500 in 1993.

Applications: In writing to the correspondent. Applications can be submitted directly by the individual or through a third party. They are considered at any time and the trustees can act quickly in urgent cases.

Correspondent: The Vicar, St Peter's Vicarage, Northgate, Horbury, Wakefield, West Yorkshire WF4 6AS (0924-273477).

Horton

The John Ashton & Ellis Smethurst Charities

Eligibility: People in need who are over 65 and live in the ancient township of Horton.

Types of grants: Grants paid twice yearly on the 21st June and 21st December. Priority is given to people aged over 65 and living alone. Consideration is also given to those people on a state pension who also receive income support and/or have partial or complete exemption from council tax, and have a limited additional income not exceeding £75 per month.

Annual grant total: In 1993, the trust had an income of £2,000. Grants ranging from £7 to £18 were given to 190 individuals and totalled about £1,900.

Applications: On a form available from Bradford Council's Social Directorate Office, Paternoster Lane, Bradford BD7. Applications should be submitted directly by the individual and are considered in May and November.

Correspondent: C Richardson, Secretary, 262 Poplar Grove, Bradford BD7 4HU (0274-571098).

Huddersfield

The Beaumont & Jessop Relief-in-Need Charity

Eligibility: People in need who are over 65 and live in the ancient township of Honley (in Huddersfield).

Types of grants: One-off and recurrent grants according to need. Grants generally up to £100.

Annual grant total: About £1,850.

Applications: In writing to the correspondent. Applicants should contact the parish vicar, or the minister of the United Reformed Church/Methodist United Church. Referrals can be made by local doctors, clergy or health service workers.

Correspondent: Mrs Rachael Booth, Secretary, 3 High Street, Honley, Huddersfield (0484-661766).

The Charles Brook Convalescent Fund

Eligibility: People in need who live within the old Huddersfield Health Authority catchment area.

Types of grants: One-off grants for medical comforts, items essential to live independently and convalescent holidays. No loans or help with the payment of bills.

Annual grant total: In 1992/93, the trust had an income of £12,000. Grants up to £150 were given to 70 individuals and totalled £9,500.

Applications: Applications, on a form available from the correspondent, must be submitted through a social worker and include details of weekly income/ expenditure and family situation.

Correspondent: Mrs J L Hobson, 22 Osprey Drive, Netherton, Huddersfield HD4 7LG.

The Henry Percy Dugdale Charity

Eligibility: People in need who live in the county borough of Huddersfield (comprising the urban districts of Colne Valley, Kirkburton, Meltham and Holmfirth).

Types of grants: One-off and recurrent grants according to need. Assistance may be given with gas and electricity accounts. Currently about 110 grants of £10 per week and about 100 single payments.

Annual grant total: The trust in 1993 had assets of £805,000 giving an income of £65,000. The total amount given to individuals in need was £78,000.

Applications: Applications must be made through a sponsor (eg. social worker, vicar, citizen's advice bureau).

Correspondent: T J Green, Clerk, 72 New North Road, Huddersfield HD1 5NW (0484-538121).

The Huddersfield Orphan Home Endowment

Eligibility: Children who live in the former county borough of Huddersfield.

Types of grants: Towards holidays for needy children.

Annual grant total: £4,000 in 1992/93.

Applications: Trustees meet twice yearly (usually in May and November) and applications, made through schools, social workers or a welfare agency should be made in time for the May meeting.

Correspondent: The Chief Education Officer, Kirklees Metropolitan Council, Oldgate House, 2 Oldgate, Huddersfield HD1 6QW (0484-422133 ext. 6514).

Leeds

The Bramhope Trust

Eligibility: Organisations and people in need within the parish of Bramhope.

Types of grants: "We do not give grants, we give a gift which we hope is of such an amount that this is given once only." These are mainly given to organisations although small sums of money are occasionally available to individuals following special activity appeals eg. Operation Raleigh, the International Guide or Scout Jamboree. The minimum grant is about £50. The maximum amount varied.

Annual grant total: In 1993, the trust had a total expenditure of about £15,000. The amount given to individuals varies.

Applications: In writing to the correspondent directly by the individual or through a third party.

Correspondent: Mrs Anne Schofield, Wharfe Croft, 51 Breary Lane East, Bramhope, Leeds LS16 9EU.

The Chapel Allerton & Potternewton Relief-in-Need Charity

Eligibility: People who live in the parish boundaries of Chapel Allerton and Potternewton.

Types of grants: One-off grants to assist with arrears of fuel bills, rent (where housing benefit is not available); telephone (where required by sick/ housebound people); to replace cookers beyond repair; and to provide food in emergencies when social security is not available. No grants for furniture as there are two local furniture stores organised by churches.

Annual grant total: In 1992, the trust had assets of £24,000 producing an income of £1,100. Grants up to £100 were given to 17 individuals and totalled £1,200.

Applications: In writing to either correspondent at any time. Applications can also be made through the Chapeltown Citizen's Advice Bureau, social services department, probation officers etc.. Trustees meet in March and

West Yorkshire

September but applications can be dealt with at any time according to need.

Correspondent: C T Keighley, 44 Stainburn Crescent, Leeds LS17 6NS (0532-686949), or the Vicar of Chapel Allerton, St Matthew's Vicarage, Wood Lane, Leeds LS7 3QF (0532-683072).

The Community Shop

Eligibility: People in need who live in or near Leeds.

Types of grants: The Community Shop is a charity shop and distributes its profits to local charities, groups and individuals in need, particularly people in vulnerable situations (eg. people with physical or mental disabilities, homeless people, victims of violence, families in distress, the chronically ill and elderly people in general). Grants are one-off ranging from £25 to £250. Recent grants have been given towards an automatic washing machine for a 16 year old caring for a chronically ill relative, a swing for a child with severe learning difficulties, and a teletext television for a deaf person.

Annual grant total: In 1993, the shop had an income of £48,000 of which £40,000 was given to individuals in need.

Applications: Applications on behalf of individuals should be made in writing through a social worker or similar welfare agency, and are usually dealt with within 2/3 weeks of receipt. Full details with reference to the criteria should be given and details of who cheques should be made payable to. The shop is at 14 to 16, Green Road, Meanwood.

Correspondent: Mrs Teresa Felton, 1 St Helen's Lane, Adel, Leeds LS16 8AB (0532-671718).

The Harrison & Potter Trust (incorporating Josias Jenkinson Relief-in-Need Charity)

Eligibility: People in need who live in Leeds.

Types of grants: One-off grants ranging from £100 to £200 for items or services eg. gas, electricity, rent, clothing, holidays and for particular items of furniture (excluding washing machines). Grants have also been made for essential repairs to owner occupied properties. No grants are available for rates or taxes.

Annual grant total: In 1992, the trust's income was £225,000. Total expenditure was £55,000 including £12,600 in relief-in-need grants.

Applications: In writing to the correspondent supported by a detailed breakdown of income and expenditure. Applicants should indicate other charities approached. They should be submitted through a citizen's advice bureau, social worker or other welfare agency and are considered throughout the year.

Correspondent: Miss A S Duchart, Clerk, 117 The Headrow, Leeds LS1 5JX (0532-439301).

Other information: The trust owns and operates two housing schemes for elderly people in Leeds. Eligible applicants must be within DSS income/capital limits and under the terms of the scheme preference must be given to women. Suitable applicants are eligible for grants to meet removal costs, furnishings etc..

Kirke's Charity

Eligibility: People in need who live in the ancient parish of Adel comprising Arthington, Cookridge and Ireland Wood. There must be evidence of real need/poverty.

Types of grants: One-off grants only generally up to about £200 but occasionally up to £2,000.

Annual grant total: In 1990/91, the trust's income was £6,600. Relief-in-need grants totalled £5,600 (10 grants).

Applications: In writing to the correspondent. Applications can be submitted directly by the individual or through a social worker, citizen's advice bureau or other welfare agency or third party. There is a quick response in emergencies. Other applications are considered in January and June.

Correspondent: D B Livett, 16 Dunstarn Drive, Adel, Leeds L16 8EH (0532-673436).

The Leeds Benevolent Society for Single Ladies

Eligibility: Unmarried women in need who are over 60 and live in the Leeds Metropolitan area.

Types of grants: Mainly regular allowances of about £5 per week paid quarterly.

Annual grant total: About £20,000.

Applications: In writing, or by telephone, to the correspondent. The applicant will be visited to assess the case.

Correspondent: Miss H I Savage, Treasurer, 4 Grove Wood, Grove Lane, Headingley, Leeds LS6 4AD (0532-785079).

The Leeds District Aid-in-Sickness Fund

Eligibility: People who live in the city of Leeds and are in need through unexpected illness or accident.

Types of grants: One-off grants only, up to £100. In exceptional circumstances larger grants may be given.

Annual grant total: About £2,000 in about 70 grants.

Applications: Applications must be made in writing on behalf of the applicant by a social worker, welfare agency, doctor, teacher or similar third party. It should include details of the illness, the applicant's income and expenditure and the purpose of the grant.

Correspondent: Miss E Loach, 88 Wynford Avenue, Leeds LS16 6JW (0532-674843).

The Leeds Family Holiday Fund

Eligibility: Families living in the Leeds metropolitan area for whom a holiday would be beneficial (especially children, the elderly, infirm, sick or those suffering from physical or mental illness and poor people).

Types of grants: One-off grants ranging from £80 to £150 to help with the cost of a holiday. Grants are given to families making their own holiday arrangements through the help of the referring agency. The trust liaises with two organisations which arrange holidays for one-parent families and with PHAB, but families can choose whatever type of holiday they prefer. The trust also organises a week's holiday for 12 families, providing accommodation. Help can also be given with fares for visiting relatives.

No grants to families who have received help from the trust in the preceding five years.

Annual grant total: In 1993, the trust had an income of £14,000. Grants of between £80 and £150 were given to 110 families (303 children) totalling £13,000.

Applications: Applications should always be submitted via social workers, health visitors or other welfare agencies and are considered in January. Details should be included of when the family last had a holiday, health problems and names and ages of children.

Correspondent: Mrs E Windross, 2 Burnt Side Road, Moor Top, New Farnley, Leeds LS12 5HX (0532-854435).

West Yorkshire

The Leeds Poors' Estate

Eligibility: People in need, particularly the young and the elderly, who live within the pre-1974 boundary of Leeds.

Types of grants: Grants to help towards the cost of heating, lighting, food etc. and small grants of not over £100 for essential items.

Annual grant total: The trust has an income of about £5,000 and paid about 50 grants of £50 to £100, leaving about £1,000 unallocated.

Applications: In writing to the correspondent. Applications should be short, sufficient to enable the trustees to confirm that the application falls within the scope of the charity. An application form will then be sent, which should be returned through welfare agencies eg. citizen's advice bureau, social services or vicars. Applications should be returned to the trustees by 1st of December, March, June and September.

Correspondent: W M Wrigley, Dibb, Lupton, Broomhead, 117 The Headrow, Leeds LS1 5JX (0532-439301).

The Leeds Tradesmen's Trust

Eligibility: People over 50 who have carried on business, practised a profession or been a tradesperson for at least five years (either consecutively or in total) and who, during that time, have lived in Leeds or whose business premises (rented or owned) were in the city of Leeds. Widows and unmarried daughters of the former are also eligible.

Types of grants: Quarterly pensions of £10 to £360 a year, plus Christmas grants and spring fuel grants only to those already receiving a pension.

Annual grant total: The trust had assets of over £300,000 and an income of £43,000. It distributed over £25,000 in 1992, which left a surplus for the year of £7,000. Nearly £19,000 was given in about 100 pensions; £4,500 was allocated to special grants; £700 for cash grants and gifts in kind, and £1,800 was for outings.

Applications: In writing to the correspondent, including details of the business or professional addresses, length of time spent there and financial position. Applications are considered monthly. All applicants are visited by the assistant secretary.

Correspondent: Sidney Brown, Assistant Secretary, Centenary House, North Street, Leeds LS2 8AY (0532-460560).

Other information: The 1992 annual report states they have helped over 2,200 people and "in these 149 years, over £500,000 have been disbursed and it is a sad reflection that the present and future needs appear to be as great as ever".

The Metcalfe Smith Trust

Eligibility: People in need who are sick and live in Leeds.

Types of grants: Grants are given via welfare agencies to individuals who are sick, disabled, convalescing or infirm. Grants are unlikely to exceed £50.

Annual grant total: About £1,000.

Applications: Applications should only be made by a social worker or similar third party and will be dealt with as received.

Correspondent: John Kaye, Director, Voluntary Action Leeds, 34 Lupton Street, Leeds LS10 2QW (0532-700777).

Other information: The major part of the trust's income is given to organisations working with people with a disability or providing convalescent facilities. A small part of its income is made available to Voluntary Action Leeds for emergency payments to individuals as above.

● Lees

The William & Sarah Midgley Charity

Eligibility: People over 65 who are in need and live in Lees.

Types of grants: One off grants and gifts at Christmas. Over 15 grants a year ranging from £10 to £100.

Annual grant total: About £1,000.

Applications: In writing to the correspondent.

Correspondent: Gordons Wright & Wright, 6–14 Devonshire Street, Keighley, West Yorkshire BD21 2AY.

● Morley

The Morley Guild of Help

Eligibility: People in need who live in the borough of Morley.

Types of grants: One-off or recurrent grants according to need.

Annual grant total: £700.

Applications: In writing to the correspondent.

Correspondent: R A Akeroyd, 72 Springbank Road, Gildersome, Morley, Leeds LS27 7DT (0532-525392).

● Sandal Magna

The Henry & Ada Chalker Trust

Eligibility: People in need who live in Sandal Magna. There is no age restriction but most beneficiaries are pensioners.

Types of grants: The normal level of help is £10 a year to each beneficiary.

Annual grant total: In 1993, the trust had assets of £26,000 generating an income of £1,800. Grants of £10 were given to 125 individuals and totalled £1,250.

Applications: Directly by the individual on a form available from the correspondent. Applications are considered throughout the year but grants are not issued until December.

Correspondent: Greaves, Atter & Beaumont, 67 Westgate, Wakefield, West Yorkshire WF1 1BP (0924-291234).

The Sandal Magna Relief-in-Need Charity

Eligibility: People in need who live in the old parish of Sandal Magna (this includes Sandal, Walton, Crigglestone, Painthorpe and West Bretton).

Types of grants: One-off grants of about £50 to 20 to 25 individuals.

Annual grant total: £1,000 to £1,500.

Applications: In writing to the correspondent. Trustees meet quarterly; urgent cases can be dealt with rapidly.

Correspondent: M J Perry, Clerk, 20 The Balk, Walton, Wakefield WF2 6JU (0924-363511).

● Todmorden

The Todmorden Needy Sick Fund

Eligibility: People in need who live in the former borough of Todmorden.

Types of grants: Food vouchers. Television licence fees are paid for first and second world war families.

Annual grant total: £4,000.

Applications: In writing to the correspondent through a welfare agency or similar. Applications are dealt with at monthly meetings.

Correspondent: A S Marshall, 50 Claremont Place, Stansfield Road, Todmorden OL14 5DX (0706-812235).

The Todmorden War Memorial Fund

Eligibility: First and second World War veterans, their dependants and others who are sick and in need and live in Todmorden.

Types of grants: One-off grants (typically £70) and recurrent grants according to need.

Annual grant total: £2,000 in 100 grants.

Applications: A visitors report must be submitted, including social services recommendations.

Correspondent: A S Marshall, Chairman, 50 Claremont Place, Stansfield Road, Todmorden OL14 5DX (0706-812235).

● **Wakefield**

The Brotherton Charity Fund

Eligibility: People in need over 60 who have lived in Wakefield for at least 15 years continuously or 25 years in broken periods.

Types of grants: Pensions of £3 a calendar month, £4 in April (to commemorate the birthdays of Lord Brotherton and Mrs Eva Greaves) and £5 extra at Christmas.

Annual grant total: £2,900 in 65 grants.

Applications: When vacancies arise an advert is placed in the Wakefield Express and a waiting list is then drawn up.

Correspondent: K Sykes, PO Box 25, 11 Market Street, Wakefield WF1 1DD (0924-372827).

The Clayton, Taylor & Foster Charity

Eligibility: People in need who live in the area administered by Wakefield Metropolitan District Council.

Types of grants: Grants of £10, paid three times a year in March, September and December, to people over 60 and in need. Very occasionally, grants may be given to people under 60 in urgent need.

Annual grant total: In 1993, the trust had an income of £2,600. 55 grants of £30 a year totalled £1,650.

Applications: For pension applicants aged over 60 a form is available from the correspondent. Other individuals should apply directly in writing. Trustees meet in March and September.

Correspondent: K Butcher, 27 Greenfield Avenue, Osset, West Yorkshire WF5 0EW (0924-261402).

The Sanderson's Women's Pension Fund

Eligibility: Women in need who live in the diocese of Wakefield.

Types of grants: One-off and recurrent grants according to need.

Annual grant total: £3,000 in 1993.

Applications: On a form available from the correspondent. The trustees meet three times a year; for grants of £100 or under decisions can be made quickly.

Correspondent: Ken Duce, Clerk, 43 Davis Avenue, Tonnville, Castleford WF10 3RG (0977-553607).

The Stanley St Peter Relief-in-Sickness Fund

Eligibility: Residents of the ecclesiastical parish of St Peter, Stanley.

Types of grants: Relief of need for sick, convalescent, infirm or disabled people.

Annual grant total: £1,000.

Applications: In writing to the correspondent. Trustees meet quarterly but can act quickly in urgent cases.

Correspondent: The Vicar, The Vicarage, 379 Aberford Road, Stanley, Wakefield WF3 4HE.

Other information: This entry has not been confirmed by the trust.

5. North West

The Cotton Districts' Convalescent Fund

Eligibility: People who are convalescing or who have a severe/incurable illness or disability and who live in Lancashire, Greater Manchester or the districts of Craven in North Yorkshire, High Peak in Derbyshire, Macclesfield and Warrington in Cheshire, and Calderdale in West Yorkshire.

Types of grants: One-off grants towards the establishment costs of a week's convalescent holiday. The grant is made direct to the establishment not to the beneficiary.

Annual grant total: £30,000 in 350 grants 1993.

Applications: On forms available from the correspondent. Applications may be submitted directly by the individual or through a social worker, citizen's advice bureau or other welfare agency.

Correspondent: John Bardsley, Secretary, J B Lever & Co, Bow Chambers, 8 Tib Lane, Manchester M2 4JB (061-832 3074).

The Diocesan Institutions of Chester, Manchester, Liverpool & Blackburn

Eligibility: Widows and orphans of clergy whose last official post was in the archdeaconries of Blackburn, Chester, Liverpool, Macclesfield, Manchester, Rochdale or Warrington.

Types of grants: One-off or recurrent grants according to need.

Annual grant total: No information available.

Applications: In writing to the correspondent.

Correspondent: Canon J O Colling, Hon. Secretary, The Rectory, Warrington WA1 2TL (0925-635020).

Other information: This entry has not been confirmed by the trust.

The Grant, Bagshaw, Rogers & Tidswell Fund

Eligibility: Elderly people in need who live or were born in Liverpool, the Wirral,

North West/Cheshire

Ellesmere Port or Chester and who have not been able to provide adequately for their declining years.

Types of grants: Pensions, currently of £140 per person, paid twice yearly.

Annual grant total: Grants totalling £14,000 were given to 50 individuals.

Applications: On a form available from the correspondent. Applications should be returned by 31st March and 30th October for consideration in April and November respectively.

Correspondent: Barrie Marsh, Secretary, Mace & Jones, Drury House, 19 Water Street, Liverpool L2 0RP (051-236 8989).

The Gregson Memorial Annuities

Eligibility: Female domestic servants who have worked for at least 10 years in one service in or within 10 miles of Liverpool, Southport or Chester or in or within five miles of Malpas, Cheshire, and cannot now work for health reasons.

Also, governesses, gentlewomen, widows and unmarried daughters or sisters of clergymen, physicians, lawyers or merchants. These applicants must be born within 10 miles of Liverpool, Southport or Chester, or within five miles of Malpas, be over 50 and members of the Church of England. They must be of limited means and have lived for at least seven years, since the age of 21, in one of the areas mentioned above. No grants to women whose husband is alive.

Types of grants: Annuities of £220 a year, payable in two equal six-monthly instalments in advance in March and September.

Annual grant total: £1,320 in six annuities.

Applications: Applications in writing to the correspondent are considered throughout the year.

Correspondent: Lace Mawer, Solicitors, Reference RM/818.1, Castle Chambers, 43 Castle Street, Liverpool L2 9SU (051-236 2002).

The North West Police Benevolent Fund

Eligibility: Serving officers and pensioners of Cheshire County Constabulary, Greater Manchester and Merseyside Police Forces and amalgamated forces of those areas. Also their dependants.

Types of grants: Grants and loans for convalescence and medical equipment (but not for private health care) and financial help for cases of need arising from unforeseen circumstances.

Annual grant total: No information available.

Applications: On a form available from the correspondent. Applications are usually made through a force welfare officer or a member of the management committee. They are considered each month except August.

Correspondent: The Hon. Secretary, Progress House, Broadstone Hall Road South, Reddish, Stockport SK5 7DE (061-480 2216).

The Northern Counties' Charity for the Incapacitated

Eligibility: People who are totally and permanently incapacitated owing to an incurable or chronic disease, to accident or to deformity, and who live in the north of England. There is a preference for people living in Bolton and Greater Manchester.

Types of grants: Regular monthly allowances of £5 to £10 a week, paid quarterly to about 10 beneficiaries. Gifts in kind such as shoes and/or a bonus can also be paid to existing beneficiaries when money is available.

Annual grant total: Over £5,000 in 1993.

Applications: On a form available from the correspondent. Applications should be submitted directly by the individual if this is possible, otherwise through a social worker, citizen's advice bureau or other welfare agency. Applications are considered three or four times a year.

Correspondent: The Clerk, 1 Westminster Drive, Cheadle Hulme, Cheadle, Cheshire SK8 7QX (061-440 9407).

Other information: This entry is repeated in the North West section of the book.

The James Parrott Charity

Eligibility: People in need who live in the South Shore area of Blackpool and the boroughs of Manchester and Salford.

Types of grants: Monthly allowances of £4 per person per week. One-off grants are only paid in exceptional circumstances.

Annual grant total: Over £2,000 in about 16 allowances.

Applications: For applicants living in South Shore, Blackpool, applications should be processed through Blackpool Council for Voluntary Service. For applicants living in Salford and Manchester, applications should be processed through the FWA.

Correspondent: J W M McKie, Secretary, Messrs Coopers & Lybrand, Abacus Court, 6 Minshull Street, Manchester M1 3ED (061-236 9191).

The Rycroft Children's Fund

Eligibility: Children in need who live in Cheshire, Derbyshire, Greater Manchester, Lancashire, Staffordshire, South and West Yorkshire. There is a preference for children living in the cities of Manchester and Salford and the borough of Trafford. Applicants should be aged 18 or under.

Types of grants: One-off and recurrent grants according to need. No grants for further or higher education.

Annual grant total: Of the £30,000 given in grants about £25,000 is given for relief-in-need in about 20 grants.

Applications: On a form available from the correspondent.

Correspondent: Christopher Lees-Jones, Chairman, Hermitage Farm, Holmes Chapel, Cheshire CW4 8DP (0477-532875.)

Other information: This entry is repeated in the North East general and Midlands general sections of the book.

Cheshire

The Lady Forester Trust

Eligibility: Primarily people who live in Shropshire who are sick, disabled, convalescent or infirm, followed by people who live in the surrounding areas of Cheshire and Staffordshire.

Types of grants: One-off grants for medical equipment or nursing care not otherwise available on the NHS. No grants for building repairs/alterations.

Annual grant total: £112,000 in 1992.

Applications: On a form available from the correspondent. Applications should be made through a social worker, citizen's advice bureau, doctor, specialist or other welfare agency and are considered throughout the year.

Correspondent: The Administrator, Willey Park, Broseley, Shropshire TF12 5JJ (0952-884318).

Other information: This entry is repeated in the Midlands section of the book.

John Holford's Charity

Eligibility: People in need who live in the parishes of Clutton and Middlewich, the borough of Congleton and that part of

Astbury which lies outside the borough of Congleton.

Types of grants: One-off and recurrent grants ranging from £100 to £2,500.

Annual grant total: In 1993, the trust had an income of about £30,000.

Applications: In writing to the correspondent.

Correspondent: Messrs Birch Cullimore, Friars, White Friars, Chester CH1 1XS (0244-321066).

The Wrenbury Consolidated Charities

Eligibility: People in need who live in the parishes of Chorley, Sound, Broomhall, Newhall, Wrenbury, Woodcott and Dodcott-cum-Wilkesley.

Types of grants: Payments on St Marks (25th April) and St Thomas (21st December) days to pensioners and one-off grants for necessities.

Annual grant total: Around £8,000 in about 120 grants.

Applications: In writing to the correspondent. The vicar of Wrenbury and the parish council can give details of the six nominated trustees who can help with applications.

Correspondent: Mrs M H Goodwin, The Royals, Aston, Nr Nantwich, Cheshire CW5 8DJ (0270-780262).

● Chester

The Chester Parochial Relief-in-Need Charity

Eligibility: People in need who live in the city of Chester, with preference given to the area of the ecclesiastical parish called the Chester Team Parish in Cheshire.

Types of grants: One-off and recurrent grants ranging from £50 to £500.

Annual grant total: Probably about £1,000.

Applications: Applications should be made through a recognised referral agency (eg. social worker, citizen's advice bureau or doctor).

Correspondent: Messrs Birch Cullimore, Friars, Whitefriars, Chester CH1 1XS (0244-321066).

The Chester Sick Poor Fund

Eligibility: People who live in and around the city of Chester and who are in need through sickness or ill-health (especially women after having given birth).

Types of grants: One-off grants for necessities and comforts eg. bedding, clothing and heating; also for convalescence, including necessary transport.

Annual grant total: In 1990/91, the trust's income was £2,800. Expenditure totalled £1,140 including £900 to individuals.

Applications: In writing to the correspondent. Applications are usually submitted through Chester Council of Voluntary Service or a social worker through Chester/Halton NHS Trust.

Correspondent: D G Mason, Messrs Birch Cullimore, Friars, Whitefriars, Chester CH1 1XS (0244-321066).

● Congleton

The Congleton Municipal Charities

Eligibility: People in need who live in the borough of Congleton.

Types of grants: One-off or recurrent grants according to need.

Annual grant total: The annual income of the trust is about £20,000 but not all of this is available for individual relief-in-need purposes.

Applications: In writing to the correspondent.

Correspondent: D A Daniel, 8-10 West Street, Congleton, Cheshire CW12 1JS (0260-272777).

The William Barlow Skelland Charity for the Poor

Eligibility: People in need who live in the borough of Congleton.

Types of grants: Usually one-off grants. In 1993, the trust had an income of over £500, but only gave 3 grants of £50 each.

Annual grant total: About £150 in 1993.

Applications: In writing to the correspondent.

Correspondent: The Director of Corporate Resources, Congleton Borough Council, Market Square, Congleton, Cheshire CW12 1EX (0260-274821).

● Crewe

The Webb Relief-in-Sickness Fund

Eligibility: People who live in Crewe who are sick, convalescing, disabled or infirm.

Types of grants: One-off grants only.

Annual grant total: About £1,000.

Applications: In writing to the correspondent.

Correspondent: D Roberts, Staff Officer, ABB Transportation Ltd, West Street, Crewe CW1 3JB (0270-538732).

● Lymm

The Lymn Relief-in-Sickness Fund No. 1

Eligibility: People in need of all ages who are sick or infirm and live in the district of Lymn in the borough of Warrington.

Types of grants: Normally one-off grants according to need.

Annual grant total: About £500.

Applications: Applications in writing by a social worker, welfare officer, voluntary organisation or similar third party on behalf of the individual.

Correspondent: The Director, Warrington Council for Voluntary Service, 5 Hanover Street, Warrington WA1 1LZ (0925-30239).

● Macclesfield

The Macclesfield Relief-in-Sickness Fund

Eligibility: People in need who live in Macclesfield and who have a chronic illness.

Types of grants: One-off grants only for necessary items eg. washing machine, telephone installation, removals and donations towards computers or specialist wheelchair.

Annual grant total: About £1,500.

Applications: Preferably through a local social services office or other welfare agencies.

Correspondent: The Secretary, Macclesfield Council of Voluntary Service, 81 Park Lane, Macclesfield, Cheshire SK11 6TX (0625-428301).

● Mottram St Andrew

The Mottram St Andrew United Charities

Eligibility: People in need who live in the parish of Mottram St Andrew including Newton.

Types of grants: One-off grants ranging from £50 to £100 reviewed annually; recurrent grants according to need. Recent grants have included expenses for

Cheshire

hospital visits, death grants to the surviving spouse and Christmas bonuses to pensioners.

Annual grant total: In 1993, the trust had assets of £80,000 and an income of £4,300. 50 relief-in-need grants totalled £2,000.

Applications: In writing to the correspondent or to individual trustees. Applications should be submitted by the individual or a friend. They are considered in November.

Correspondent: J D Carr, Thornlea, Oak Road, Mottram St Andrew, Macclesfield, Cheshire SK10 4RA (0625-829634).

Runcorn

The Runcorn General War Relief Fund

Eligibility: People in need who live in the former urban district of Runcorn. There is a preference for people in need as a result of service in World War II.

Types of grants: One-off grants for items such as cookers or beds.

Annual grant total: About £3,500.

Applications: On a form available from the correspondent.

Correspondent: Greg Yeomans, Secretary, Halton Borough Council, Kingsway, Widnes, Cheshire WA8 7QF (051-424 2061).

Warrington

The Charity of Letitia Beaumont

Eligibility: People in need who live in the borough of Warrington and the parish of Moore.

Types of grants: Regular allowances probably of £26 to £156 a year.

Annual grant total: About £1,000.

Applications: In writing to the correspondent.

Correspondent: Miss N J Herbert, Messrs Robert Davies & Co, 21 Bold Street, Warrington WA1 1DF (0925-50161).

The Joseph Monk Christmas Gift Trust

Eligibility: People in need of all ages who live in the borough of Warrington.

Types of grants: One-off grants for warm bedding or clothing at Christmas (generally between £10 and £30). Grants are in the form of vouchers exchangeable at specified shops.

Annual grant total: £700 to £800 in 50 to 60 grants.

Applications: On a form available from the correspondent. Applications should be submitted through a social worker, welfare officer, voluntary organisation or a similar third party.

Correspondent: The Director, Warrington Council for Voluntary Service, 5 Hanover Street, Warrington, Cheshire WA1 1LZ (0925-30239).

The Joseph & Lucy Monk's Trust

Eligibility: People in need who live in the borough of Warrington and Moore or a radius of three miles from the borough.

Types of grants: Regular allowances of £26 to £52 a year.

Annual grant total: About £1,000.

Applications: In writing to the correspondent.

Correspondent: Miss N J Herbert, Messrs Robert Davies & Co, 21 Bold Street, Warrington WA1 1DF (0925-50161).

The Police-Aided Children's Relief-in-Need Fund

Eligibility: Children in need who live in the borough of Warrington.

Types of grants: Grants to help with the cost of clothing and footwear.

Annual grant total: About £7,500 in about 210 grants (normal maximum £40 per child; £60 when over 10).

Applications: Via welfare agencies.

Correspondent: Peter Warburton, Hon. Clerk, Warrington Borough Council, Town Hall, Sankey Street, Warrington WA1 1UH (0925-442110).

The Warrington Children's Summer Camp

Eligibility: Children in need who live in the borough of Warrington.

Types of grants: Grants to help with the cost of holidays.

Annual grant total: About £1,600 in about 80 grants (normal maximum £25 a child).

Applications: Via the education department or other welfare agencies.

Correspondent: H M M Roberts, Hon. Clerk, Warrington Borough Council, Town Hall, Sankey Street, Warrington WA1 1UH (0925-444400).

The Warrington Sick & Disabled Trust

Eligibility: People in need, especially those who are disabled or infirm, who live in a six-mile radius of the Nurses' Home at 21 Arpley Street, Warrington.

Types of grants: One-off grants for holidays, Christmas parcels and other needs.

Annual grant total: Over £1,000.

Applications: In writing to the correspondent.

Correspondent: J B Naylor, Chairman, Ridgway Greenall Solicitors, 21 Palmyra Square, Warrington WA1 1BW (0925-54221).

The Clara Westgarth Trust

Eligibility: Elderly people over 60 who are in need and live in the borough of Warrington.

Types of grants: One-off grants ranging from £10 to £400. Grants are given to enable elderly people to live as independently as possible, such as for equipment or service provision, where this is not available from statutory sources.

Annual grant total: In 1992/93, the trust had an income of £7,000. Expenditure totalled £9,800 of which £2,900 was given in grants to individuals.

Applications: In writing to the correspondent. Applications must be submitted through a social worker, citizen's advice bureau, health service, charitable body or other welfare agency. They are considered throughout the year.

Correspondent: R Valerie Dabbs, Secretary, Warrington Council of Voluntary Service, 5 Hanover Street, Warrington, Cheshire WA1 1LZ (0925-30239).

Widnes

The Knight's House Charity

Eligibility: People in need who live in Widnes as far as Hale Village.

Types of grants: One-off grants for a cooker, bed, washing machine, clothing etc..

Annual grant total: About £3,000.

Applications: On a form available from the correspondent.

Correspondent: The Chief Executive's Department, Municipal Buildings, Kingsway, Widnes, Cheshire WA8 7QF (051-424 2061).

Wilmslow

The Lindow Workhouse Charity

Eligibility: People in need who live in the ancient parish of Wilmslow.

Types of grants: One-off grants to help with fuel bills, funeral expenses and property repairs.

Annual grant total: 30 to 40 grants totalled £3,000 in 1993.

Applications: In writing to the correspondent for consideration in July and December.

Correspondent: Grp Capt J Buckley, Clerk, 10 Summerfield Place, Wilmslow, Cheshire SK9 1NE (0625-531227).

The Wilmslow Aid Trust

Eligibility: People in need, especially sick or disabled people, who live in the urban district of Wilmslow and neighbourhood.

Types of grants: One-off grants including furniture, bedding, comforts, food, fuel, medical aids, recuperative holidays and domestic help. Grants range from £5 to £200. Recent grants have included bedding/children's beds after a house fire; fridge/freezers to single parents; removal costs due to bankruptcy; heating system repairs; furniture, clothing, and decorating materials.

Annual grant total: In 1992/93, the trust had an income of £2,700. £2,600 was given in 74 grants.

Applications: Through a welfare agency or in writing to the correspondent including address, income and statement of what is needed and why.

Correspondent: Dr A R Anderson, 2 Fulmards Close, Wilmslow, Cheshire SK9 2EB (0625-535634).

Wybunbury

The Wybunbury United Charities

Eligibility: People in need who live in the 18 townships of the ancient parish of Wybunbury as it was in the 1600s and 1700s. The townships are Basford, Batherton, Blakenhall, Bridgemere, Chorlton, Checkley-cum-Wrinehill, Doddington, Hatherton, Hough, Hunsterson, Lea, Rope, Shavington-cum-Gresty, Stapeley, Walgherton, Weston, Willaston and Wybunbury.

Types of grants: The three administering trustees for each township are responsible for distribution of grants. Some make annual payments to individuals in need but funds are also kept in most townships to cover emergency payments for accidents, bereavement or sudden distress.

Annual grant total: In 1994, the trust had assets of £46,500 and an income of £4,400, all of which was spent.

Applications: By direct application to one of your townships's three administering trustees, one of which will be the vicar.

Correspondent: Clement Bishop, 88 Dig Lane, Wybunbury, Nantwich, Cheshire CW5 7EY (0270-841774).

Cumbria

The Barrow-Thornbarrow Charity

Eligibility: People in need who are sick, convalescent, disabled or infirm, and who live in the former county of Westmorland, the former county borough of Barrow, the former rural districts of Sedbergh and North Lonsdale, or the former urban districts of Dalton-in-Furness, Grange and Ulverston.

Types of grants: One-off and recurrent grants according to need.

Annual grant total: About £10,000 to £12,000 in 1993.

Applications: In writing to the correspondent including details of the applicant's circumstances. Applications can be submitted directly by the individual or through a social worker, citizen's advice bureau or other welfare agency. They are considered in January, April, July and October, although applications can be considered between meetings in an emergency.

Correspondent: Rev J Johnston, 8 Sedbergh Drive, Kendal, Cumbria LA9 6BJ (0539-725422).

The Cumbria Constabulary Benevolent Fund

Eligibility: Members and former members of the Cumbria Constabulary in need, and their widows and dependants.

Types of grants: One-off cash grants.

Annual grant total: Over £1,000.

Applications: In writing to the correspondent.

Correspondent: The Welfare Officer, Police Headquarters, Carleton Hall, Penrith, Cumbria CA10 2AU (0768-64411 ext. 7086).

The Cumbria Miners' Welfare Trust Fund

Eligibility: Miners and their families who are in need and live or work in Cumbria.

Types of grants: Grants are given mainly to miners' welfare schemes in the Cumbria area, but individuals may also apply. Mineworkers who have taken up other employment since leaving the industry are excluded from applying. No recurrent grants are made.

Annual grant total: In 1992, the trust had an income of £48,000 and a total expenditure of £9,500 leaving a surplus of £38,000. Individual relief-in-need grants totalled £663.

Applications: In writing to the correspondent either directly by the individual, through the union or via a CISWO social worker. Applications are considered each month.

Correspondent: Miss A L Taylor, c/o CISWO, 142 Queen's Road, Penkhull, Stoke-on-Trent ST4 7LH (0782-744996).

The Jane Fisher Trust

Eligibility: People in need over 50 who have lived in the the townships of Ulverston and Osmotherly, and the parish of Pennington for at least 20 years. There is no age restriction for disabled residents needing assistance.

Types of grants: Monthly payments of £13 to 32 beneficiaries. No lump sum payments have been made for many years.

Annual grant total: In 1992/93, the trust had assets of £75,000 with an income of £7,600. Expenditure totalled £6,800.

Applications: On a form available from the correspondent. Applications can be submitted directly by the individual or through a social worker, citizen's advice bureau or other welfare agency. They are considered when they are received.

Correspondent: S J Marsden, 9 Benson Street, Ulverston, Cumbria LA12 7AU (0229-583576).

The Northern Counties Orphans' Benevolent Society

Eligibility: Children in need through sickness, disability or other causes with a preference for those who live in the counties of Cleveland, Durham, Tyne & Wear, Northumberland and Cumbria. There is a preference for orphaned children.

Types of grants: Both one-off and recurrent grants for education and clothing. In 1993, "Assistance took the form of grants towards school fees, the

Cumbria/Greater Manchester

cost of school clothing and equipment and, in a limited number of cases, the provision of special equipment of an educational or physical nature for disabled children. In almost every case, the need for assistance arises through the premature death of the major wage earner, or the break up of the family unit. Applications are treated in strict confidence and the financial circumstances of each applicant are fully and carefully considered by the trustees before an award is made."

Annual grant total: £44,000 in 36 grants to individuals for education and relief in need in 1993.

Applications: In writing to the correspondent.

Correspondent: J M Davison, Secretary, 27 Portland Terrace, Newcastle-upon-Tyne NE2 1QP (091-281 1292).

Other information: This entry is repeated in the North East section of the book.

● Ambleside

The Ambleside Welfare Charity

Eligibility: People in need, especially those who are ill, who live in the parish of Ambleside.

Types of grants: One-off and recurrent grants according to need. (Help also to local relatives for hospital visits.)

Annual grant total: About £5,000 in at least 100 grants.

Applications: In writing to the correspondent.

Correspondent: A G Burrows, 28 Greenbank Road, Ambleside, Cumbria LA22 9BG (0539-432491).

The Agnes Backhouse & Dorothy Barrow Annuity Trusts

Eligibility: Unmarried women (widows and spinsters) aged over 50 who live in the parish of Ambleside.

Types of grants: The trusts give individual grants of £20 and £30 according to need.

Annual grant total: About £3,900 in 1992/93.

Applications: In writing to the correspondent.

Correspondent: N C Davenport, Gatey, Heelis & Co, Solicitors, Planetree House, Rydal Road, Ambleside, Cumbria LA22 9AP (0539-433131).

Other information: People currently who fit the above criteria should be receiving a grant, whether rich or poor. The trustees hope to merge the two charities and slightly alter their constitution so that the money can go to those in most need. People receiving payments will probably continue to do so.

● Carlisle

The Carlisle Sick Poor Fund

Eligibility: Sick people in need who live in and around the city of Carlisle.

Types of grants: One-off grants for necessities.

Annual grant total: About £4,000.

Applications: In writing to the correspondent.

Correspondent: Atkinson Ritson & Lightfoot Solicitors, 15 Fisher Street, Carlisle, Cumbria CA3 8RW (0228-25221).

● Cockermouth

The Cockermouth Relief-in-Need Charity

Eligibility: People in need who live in Cockermouth.

Types of grants: One-off grants according to need.

Annual grant total: £1,300.

Applications: In writing to the correspondent.

Correspondent: The Rector, The Rectory, Lorton Road, Cockermouth, Cumbria CA13 9DU.

● Crosby Ravensworth

The Crosby Ravensworth Relief-in-Need Charities

Eligibility: People in need who have lived in the ancient parish of Crosby Ravensworth for at least 12 months. Preference is given to elderly people.

Types of grants: One-off and recurrent grants. Help has recently been given with television licences, fuel, and to people unable to work owing to ill-health.

Annual grant total: In 1993, the trust had an income of £4,000. Grants ranging from £30 to £50 were given to 78 individuals and totalled £2,200.

Applications: In writing to the correspondent directly by the individual or via a trustee. Applications are considered in February, May, and October.

Correspondent: G G Bowness, Ravenseat, Crosby Ravensworth, Penrith, Cumbria CA10 3JB (0931-715382).

● Kirkby Lonsdale

The Kirkby Lonsdale Relief-in-Need Charity

Eligibility: People in need who live in Kirkby Lonsdale.

Types of grants: £20 to £25 grants usually given just before Christmas.

Annual grant total: In 1993, the trust had an income of £800. Grants to 33 individuals totalled £760.

Applications: In writing to the correspondent. Applications are considered in November/December.

Correspondent: D A Donald, Orchard House, Kirkby Lonsdale LA6 2BA (0524-271250).

● Workington

The Bowness Trust

Eligibility: People in need who live in Workington and who live at home (not in institutions).

Types of grants: One-off grants only.

Annual grant total: About £1,000.

Applications: In writing to the correspondent.

Correspondent: Messrs Milburn Kerr & Co, Oxford House, 19 Oxford Street, Workington, Cumbria CA14 2AW (0900-67363).

Greater Manchester

The Barnes Samaritan Charity

Eligibility: People living in the beneficial area who are convalescing, who have a severe/incurable disease, or are disabled or infirm, and who are living in their own homes. The beneficial area is Manchester and the former hundred of Salford, which covers the area approximately bordered by the lines Horwich to Flixton in the west, Flixton to Denton in the south, Denton to Todmorden in the east and Todmorden to Horwich in the north.

Types of grants: Monthly grants not exceeding £25 a month as long as the need continues. Applicants must be able to demonstrate an on-going, rather than temporary, shortage of income.

Greater Manchester

Annual grant total: £9,300 in about 31 grants in 1993.

Applications: On forms available from the correspondent. Applications can be submitted directly by the individual or through a social worker, citizen's advice bureau or other welfare agency. They are considered on one day in most months of the year.

Correspondent: John Bardsley, Secretary, J B Lever & Co, Bow Chambers, 8 Tib Lane, Manchester M2 4JB (061-832 3074).

The James Bayne Charitable Trust

Eligibility: People in need who live in Greater Manchester.

Types of grants: One-off grants ranging from £100 to £500.

Annual grant total: In 1990/91, the trust had assets of £65,000 and an income of £6,650. Relief-in-need grants to individuals totalled £8,900 (15 grants). The trust did not update this information.

Applications: In writing to the correspondent. Applications should be submitted through a social worker, citizen's advice bureau or other welfare agency. They are considered on receipt.

Correspondent: W M Cliff, Cooper Lancaster Brewers, 14 Wood Street, Bolton, Lancashire BL1 1DZ (0204-31573).

J T Blair's Charity

Eligibility: People in need, especially the elderly, who live in Manchester and Salford.

Types of grants: Weekly pensions of up to £5, paid at four weekly intervals. Additional grants are made to recipients under unusual circumstances.

Annual grant total: About £13,000 in about 60 grants.

Applications: On a form available from the correspondent. The trustees meet twice a year but there are facilities for emergency decisions. All recipients are visited on a regular basis as appropriate.

Correspondent: The Trust Administrator, FWA, Gaddum House, 6 Great Jackson Street, Manchester M15 4AX (061-834 6069).

The Lawrence Brownlow Charity

Eligibility: People in need who live in the ancient townships of Tonge, Haulgh and Darcy Lever in Greater Manchester.

Types of grants: One-off grants for gas, electricity, fuel, footwear, clothing and food.

Annual grant total: No information available, but about 300 grants are given.

Applications: In writing to the correspondent. Applicants are visited by the trustees.

Correspondent: Patrick Shorten, Secretary, Bolton Guild of Help (Inc.), Scott House, 27 Silverwell Street, Bolton BL1 1PP (0204-24858).

The Gratrix Charity

Eligibility: People within a 15-mile radius of the Manchester Exchange who work as (or formerly worked as) plumbers, glaziers, brass workers, lead workers or gas fitters; also their dependants, widows or orphans.

Types of grants: Weekly pensions of up to £3 paid at four weekly intervals.

Annual grant total: About £2,000 in about 20 grants.

Applications: No new applications have been accepted for the last few years. It was previously administered by other trustees who paid smaller grants. The present trustees aim to make more realistic payments. When this is achieved the charity will then consider new applicants. Grants as well as pensions will then be considered.

Correspondent: Miss M W Harrison, Secretary, FWA, Gaddum House, 6 Great Jackson Street, Manchester M15 4AX (061-834 6069).

The Manchester District Nursing Institution Fund

Eligibility: People in need who are sick, disabled or infirm and live in the cities of Manchester and Salford and the borough of Trafford.

Types of grants: One-off grants according to need. "It is important that the request relates to the need of the applicant only and does not constitute a general poverty condition of the family."

Annual grant total: About £19,000 in about 220 grants in 1993.

Applications: On a form available from the correspondent.

Correspondent: The Trust Administrator, FWA, Gaddum House, 6 Great Jackson Street, Manchester M15 4AX (061-834 6069).

The Manchester Jewish Soup Kitchen

Eligibility: Poor, elderly and housebound people who live in Greater Manchester.

Types of grants: Food distribution only.

Annual grant total: Food to the value of £18,000 to over 200 beneficiaries.

Applications: In writing to the correspondent direct or through a hospital, social worker, member of the clergy, doctor or other welfare agency.

Correspondent: Mrs D Phillips, Rita Glickman House, Ravensway, Prestwhich, Manchester M25 8EX (061-795 4930).

The Manchester Jews Benevolent Society

Eligibility: Jewish people in need who live in Greater Manchester.

Types of grants: One-off or recurrent grants according to need.

Annual grant total: No information available.

Applications: Application should be made in person at the address below on Sunday mornings.

Correspondent: The Secretary, Levi House, Bury Old Road, Manchester M8 6FX (061-740 4089).

The Mellor Fund

Eligibility: People in need who live in Radcliffe, Whitefield and Unsworth.

Types of grants: Usually one-off grants.

Annual grant total: Income of £4,000 in 1992.

Applications: In writing to the correspondent or via welfare agencies.

Correspondent: Miss D Glover, 297 Bury New Road, Whitefield, Manchester M25 7SE.

Other information: This entry has not been confirmed by the trust, but the correspondent is correct according to the Charity Commission.

The Swiss Relief Society

Eligibility: Swiss people in need who live in Manchester and neighbourhood (either Swiss nationals or dual nationals).

Types of grants: One-off, recurrent grants or loans according to need.

Annual grant total: In 1992, the trust had an income of £1,860. Five grants totalled £1,900.

Applications: In writing to the correspondent either directly by the individual or through the Consulate General of Switzerland, Sunley Tower, Piccadilly Plaza, Manchester M1 4BT.

Correspondent: P A Senn, President, Cloud Park Farm, Dial Lane, Congleton, Cheshire CW12 3QJ (0260-272407).

Greater Manchester

Bolton

The Bolton & District Nursing Association

Eligibility: People who are sick, disabled convalescing or infirm and live in Bolton.

Types of grants: One-off grants for items and services.

Annual grant total: £1,600 in about 20 grants.

Applications: In writing to the correspondent.

Correspondent: Patrick Shorten, Secretary, Bolton Guild of Help (Inc.), Scott House, 27 Silverwell Street, Bolton BL1 1PP (0204-24858).

The Bolton Poor Protection Society

Eligibility: People in need who live in the former county borough of Bolton.

Types of grants: One-off grants for emergencies and all kinds of need.

Annual grant total: In 1993, grants totalled around £1,100. Of these, 17 averaged £18.50 and 25 were for between £20 and £72.

Applications: Applications on a form available from the correspondent.

Correspondent: Patrick Shorten, Secretary, Bolton Guild of Help (Inc.), Scott House, 27 Silverwell Street, Bolton BL1 1PP (0204-24858).

The Louisa Alice Kay Fund

Eligibility: People in need who live in Bolton.

Types of grants: One-off grants for emergencies and all kinds of need.

Annual grant total: £36,000 in about 450 grants.

Applications: In writing to the correspondent.

Correspondent: Patrick Shorten, Secretary, Bolton Guild of Help (Inc.), Scott House, 27 Silverwell Street, Bolton BL1 1PP (0204-24858).

Bury

The Bury Relief-in-Sickness Fund

Eligibility: People who live in the borough of Bury and who are sick, convalescent, disabled or infirm.

Types of grants: One-off grants for convalescence and necessities in the home (not telephone installation).

Annual grant total: About £2,000.

Applications: In writing to the correspondent. Applications should be made through a social worker, citizen's advice bureau or other welfare agency.

Correspondent: Mrs J P Fraser, Secretary, 245 Brandlesholme Road, Bury, Lancashire (061-764 4947).

Dukinfield

The Emma Rowland Fund

Eligibility: People in need who have lived most of their lives in Dukinfield and are over pensionable age.

Types of grants: Pensions only, paid quarterly.

Annual grant total: About £1,000 to 45 pensioners in 1993.

Applications: On a form available from the correspondent.

Correspondent: C W Viney, D G Birtwistle & Co Accountants, 13b Hyde Road, Denton, Manchester M34 3AF (061-320 6994).

Golborne

The Golborne Charities

Eligibility: People in need who live in the parish of Golborne as it was in 1892.

Types of grants: One-off and recurrent grants between £25 and £50 usually cash payments, but occasionally in kind, eg. food, bedding, clothing and shoes. Also help with hospital travel and necessary holidays.

Annual grant total: In 1992/93, about £3,590 was given to 112 individuals.

Applications: In writing to the correspondent through a social worker, citizen's advice bureau or other welfare agency or through the trustees, teachers, doctors, clergy, health visitors etc.. Applications are considered throughout the year.

Correspondent: The Secretary, 1 Northfield Court, Golborne, Warrington WA3 3EW (0942-725846).

Heywood

The Heywood Charities

Eligibility: Disabled ex-servicemen and their dependants who live in Heywood.

Types of grants: Grants for relief-in-need and towards the cost of holidays.

Annual grant total: No information available.

Applications: Where possible applications should be submitted through a voluntary agency or similar.

Correspondent: David Broome, Committee Services Manager, PO Box 15, Town Hall, Rochdale OL16 1AB (0706-47474).

The Heywood Relief-in-Need Trust Fund

Eligibility: People in need who live in the former municipal borough of Heywood.

Types of grants: One-off grants ranging from £50 to £400 particularly to help with fuel arrears, clothing and furniture. Grants have also been given towards baby clothing for single parents and for telephone installation.

Annual grant total: In 1991/92, the trust's income was £6,900. £5,000 was given in about 40 relief-in-need grants.

Applications: On a form available from the correspondent. Applications should preferably be supported by a social worker, health visitor or similar professional. Applications are considered in January, March, May, July, September and November.

Correspondent: The Chief Executive, Rochdale Metropolitan Borough Council, PO Box 15, Town Hall, Rochdale OL16 1AB (0706-47474 ext. 4708).

Manchester

The Dr Garrett Memorial Trust

Eligibility: People in need who live in Manchester.

Types of grants: Grants towards the cost of convalescence or holidays.

Annual grant total: No information available.

Applications: Application forms available from the correspondent must be completed by social workers or other welfare agencies.

Correspondent: The Trust Administrator, FWA, Gaddum House, 6 Great Jackson Street, Manchester M15 4AX (061-834 6069).

The Lord Mayor's Family Holiday Fund

Eligibility: People in need who live in the city of Manchester.

Types of grants: One-off grants to provide or assist in providing holidays for families in need.

Greater Manchester

Annual grant total: In 1991, grants totalled £12,000, but this varies from year to year. We have been unable to obtain a more up-to-date total.

Applications: In writing to the correspondent through a social services department. Applications are considered throughout the year.

Correspondent: The Honorary Treasury, Lord Mayor's Suite, Town Hall, Albert Square, Manchester M60 2LA.

Other information: This entry has not been confirmed by the trust.

The Dean of Manchester Crossland Fund

Eligibility: People in need who live in the city of Manchester.

Types of grants: One-off grants, usually of £40 to £60, for general need.

Annual grant total: About £5,000.

Applications: In writing to the correspondent, through organisations such as probation services, social services, citizen's advice bureaux etc..

Correspondent: The Dean of Manchester, The Cathedral, Manchester M3 1SX (061-833 2220).

The Manchester Relief-in-Need & Children's Relief-in-Need Charities

Eligibility: People in need who live in the city of Manchester and are over 25 (Relief-in-Need) or under 25 (Children's Relief-in-Need).

Types of grants: One-off grants only for emergencies, heating/fuel, clothing, sickness, aids/appliances, convalescence, holidays, travel, home repairs/alteration, funeral costs and general necessities. Grants up to £200, but typically £75.

Annual grant total: The combined grant total for the two trusts in 1991 was about £50,000 given in 660 grants.

Applications: Application forms must be completed by social workers or other welfare agencies. Forms are available from the correspondent.

Correspondent: The Trust Administrator, FWA, Gaddum House, 6 Great Jackson Street, Manchester M15 4AX (061-834 6069).

● **Middleton**

The Middleton Relief-in-Need Charity

Eligibility: People in need who live in the former borough of Middleton. Sometimes grants will be paid to people living immediately outside the area.

Types of grants: One-off grants (typically £50) for emergencies eg. travel expenses to visit people in hospital or similar institutions, fuel bills, television licence fees, arrears, holidays for deprived families, general household necessities.

Annual grant total: £1,500 in 20 grants.

Applications: Made by individual application and through social workers, health visitors, victim support schemes and citizen's advice bureaux.

Correspondent: Mrs Fiona Shepherd, Committee Services Section, PO Box 15, Metropolitan Borough of Rochdale, Town Hall, Rochdale OL16 1AB (0706-47474 ext. 4717).

● **Oldham**

The Charity of Arthur Vernon Davies for the Poor Parishioners of Shaw

Eligibility: People in conditions of hardship, distress or need who live in the ecclesiastical parishes of St James, East Crompton; St Mary, High Crompton and Holy Trinity, Shaw.

Types of grants: One off grants only.

Annual grant total: Around £2,500 in about 20 grants.

Applications: On a form available from the correspondent.

Correspondent: The Legal Services Department, PO Box 33, Civic Centre, West Street, Oldham OL1 1UL (061-678 4714).

The Sarah Lees Relief Trust

Eligibility: People living in Oldham who are sick, convalescent, disabled or infirm.

Types of grants: One-off grants.

Annual grant total: About £10,000 in 1990/91.

Applications: Through a social worker, citizen's advice bureau or other recognised welfare agency.

Correspondent: Mrs Julia Mercer, Moorlands, 6 The Park, Grasscroft, Oldham OL4 4ES.

The Oldham Distress Fund

Eligibility: People in need who live in the borough of Oldham.

Types of grants: One-off grants up to £100.

Annual grant total: About £1,800 in about 50 grants.

Applications: On a form available from the correspondent.

Correspondent: The Legal Services Department, PO Box 33, Civic Centre, West Street, Oldham OL1 1UL (061-678 4710).

The Oldham United Charities

Eligibility: People in need who live in the borough of Oldham.

Types of grants: One-off grants normally of £50 or over usually towards medical needs eg. wheelchairs, holidays for people who are sick or disabled, washing machines for people who are incontinent. Some grants are given to students towards educational expenses. Grants are also given to local organisations.

Annual grant total: About £4,000 was given in 1993, about £1,500 of which was given to individuals for relief-in-need.

Applications: In writing to the correspondent. Trustees meet quarterly in May, November, August and February.

Correspondent: B McKown, c/o Mills McKown, 85 Union Street, Oldham OL1 1PF (061-624 9977).

● **Ramsbottom**

The Ramsbottom Aid-in-Sickness Fund

Eligibility: People in need who are sick, convalescent, disabled or infirm and who live in the former urban district of Ramsbottom, now partly in Lancashire and partly in Greater Manchester.

Types of grants: Grants are in the form of vouchers worth about £40 for fuel, bedding, clothing, television licences, convalescence, Christmas parcels, food and medical needs.

Annual grant total: In 1993, around £2,000 was given, of which about £600 to £700 was distributed in Christmas parcels.

Applications: In writing to the correspondent. Applicants are usually referred to the correspondent by doctors, nurses, health visitors or social workers.

Greater Manchester

Correspondent: Mrs E M Waite, Secretary, 9 Park Avenue, Ramsbottom, Bury BL0 0DA (0706-822082).

Other information: This entry is repeated in the Lancashire section of the book.

● Rochdale

The Rochdale Fund for Relief-in-Sickness

Eligibility: People living in Rochdale who are sick, convalescent, disabled or infirm. This is not a charity for relief of poverty.

Types of grants: One-off grants only, usually of £50 to £500 but also larger payments of £1,000 to £5,000 for specialist equipment eg. electric bed or wheelchair, specialist computer etc..

Annual grant total: About £15,000 in between 30 and 40 grants.

Applications: In writing to the correspondent.

Correspondent: Ms S M Stoney, Clerk, Messrs Jackson Stoney & Co, The Old Parsonage, 2 St Mary's Gate, Rochdale OL16 1AP (0706-44187/47094).

The Rochdale United & Ladies Charities

Eligibility: People in need who live in the ancient parish of Rochdale (the former county of Rochdale, Castleton, Wardle, Whitworth, Littleborough, Todmorden and Saddleworth). The United Charity is a general charity for people in need; the Ladies Charity is particularly for women, especially those who are pregnant or who have recently given birth.

Types of grants: One-off grants of £50 to £250. Grants have been given towards furniture, bedding, clothing, food, fuel and heating appliances; tools, books, fees or travelling expenses; a recuperative holiday for people long deprived of such; special food, medical or other aids; washing machines and freezers, and televisions or radios for lonely people.

The trust cannot commit itself to renew or repeat a grant on a further occasion.

Annual grant total: In 1991/92, the combined expenditure of the two charities was £4,850. Relief-in-need grants to individuals totalled £1,600 (25 grants) made up of £1,400 from the United Charity and £200 from the Ladies Charity.

Applications: On a form available from the correspondent usually supported by social workers, victim support schemes, health visitors or citizen's advice bureau. The trustees meet four times a year.

Correspondent: Moira Brown, Corporate Services Department, PO Box 15, Town Hall, Rochdale OL16 1AB (0706-47474 ext. 4713).

The Charity of Harold Shawcross

Eligibility: Sick people in need who live in and around Rochdale.

Types of grants: One-off and recurrent grants according to need.

Annual grant total: In 1992/93, the trusts disposable income was £650.

Applications: In writing to the correspondent. Preference for applications supported by a social worker or similar.

Correspondent: C Fletcher, Director of Social Services, Metropolitan Borough of Rochdale, Municipal Offices, Smith Street, Rochdale OL16 1YQ (0706-47474).

● Royton

The Royton Sick & Needy Fund

Eligibility: People in need who live in the district of Royton.

Types of grants: Supply of special food and medicines, medical comforts, extra bedding, fuel, and medical and surgical appliances; provision of domestic help; cash grants to obtain the benefits above or to defray the expenses of convalescence, obtaining change of air, special protection or treatment including the expense of any necessary transport.

Grants are not given towards council tax.

Annual grant total: About £750 in about 8 grants.

Applications: On a form available from the correspondent.

Correspondent: The Legal Services Department, PO Box 33, Civic Centre, West Street, Oldham OL1 1UL (061-678 4714).

● Salford

The Booth Charities

Eligibility: Elderly people in need who must be retired, over 60, on a basic pension and live in the city of Salford.

Types of grants: Regular allowances mainly of heating stamps.

Annual grant total: The charities' income was £300,000 in 1992. £117,000 was given in regular allowances of £1.50 to £2 a week in heating stamps to 1,500 individuals (the rest is given to organisations). No one-off grants are made but this could change in the future.

Applications: On a form available from the correspondent.

Correspondent: R Spence, Messrs Taylor, Kirkman & Mainprice, Midwood Hall, 1 Eccles Old Road, Salford, Manchester M6 7AE (061-736 2989).

The City of Salford Relief-in-Distress Fund

Eligibility: People in need who live in the city of Salford.

Types of grants: One-off grants of £50 to £100 for emergencies, heating/fuel, clothing, aids/appliances, convalescence/holidays and travel.

Annual grant total: About £2,000.

Applications: On a form available from the correspondent, usually made by a social worker on behalf of individuals.

Correspondent: The Director of Social Services, c/o Anti-Poverty Unit, 1st Floor, 12 Station Road, Swinton M27.

● Stockport

Sir Ralph Pendlebury's Charity for Orphans & the Elderly

Eligibility: Orphans in need who have lived (or whose parents have lived) in the borough of Stockport for at least two years. The charity also gives small pensions to the elderly in need.

Types of grants: One-off grants for clothes, holidays and other needs, as well as regular allowances of £5 to £6 a week.

Annual grant total: Grants to individuals for relief-in-need and education totalled over £8,000 in 1993.

Applications: In writing to the correspondent.

Correspondent: J C G Pickering, PO Box 60, Wilmslow, Cheshire SK9 1QX (0625-586300).

Stockport Sick Poor Nursing Association

Eligibility: People in need who are sick or infirm and who live in the old county borough of Stockport.

Types of grants: One-off grants only.

Annual grant total: About £5,000.

Applications: In writing to the correspondent through social services or a welfare agency. Direct applications from individuals are not accepted.

Correspondent: Mrs Gwen Jackson, Secretary, 11 Heathfield Road, Davenport, Stockport, Cheshire SK2 6JL (061-480 2915).

● Tameside

The Mayor of Tameside's Distress Fund

Eligibility: People who live in the borough of Tameside and are deprived of the basic necessities of life.

Types of grants: One-off grants generally of about £50 to £200.

Annual grant total: No information available.

Applications: By letter (or telephone in an emergency) including details of income, expenditure, reason for and amount of request and other organisations approached. Applications are usually made through a social worker or similar third party, but can be made directly.

Correspondent: Simon Smith, Committee Administration, Tameside Metropolitan Borough Council, Council Offices, Wellington Road, Ashton-under-Lyne, Lancashire OL6 6DL (061-342 8355).

● Wigan

The Wigan Town Relief-in-Need Charity

Eligibility: People in need who live in the county borough of Wigan.

Types of grants: One-off grants ranging from £15 to £150.

Annual grant total: In 1991, the trust's income was £7,400. Relief-in-need grants to individuals totalled £500 (11 grants).

Applications: In writing to the correspondent. Applications can be submitted directly by the individual or through a social worker, citizen's advice bureau or other welfare agency. They are considered in May and November.

Correspondent: William R Linton, Clerk, Healds Solicitors, Moot Hall Chambers, 8 Wallgate, Wigan WN1 1JE (0942-41511).

Lancashire

The Baines Charity

Eligibility: People in need who live in the ancient townships of Carleton, Hardhorn-with-Newton, Marton, Poulton-le-Fylde and Thornton-Cleveleys.

Types of grants: One-off Christmas grants between £20 and £50. No other grants given.

Annual grant total: About £7,000.

Applications: On a form available from the correspondent. Applications should be submitted by 31st October each year.

Correspondent: W S Haworth, Messrs Hamer, Park & Haworth, 71 Adelaide Street, Blackpool FY1 4LQ (0253-21531).

The Blackpool, Fylde & Wyre Society for the Blind

Eligibility: People who are blind/visually impaired and live in Blackpool, Fylde and Wyre.

Types of grants: One-off grants to relieve difficulties arising from visual impairment.

Annual grant total: In 1992/93, the trust had assets of £1.5 million and an income of almost £200,000. Grants ranging from £10 to £250 were given totalling £2,500.

Applications: On a form available from the correspondent to be submitted through a society welfare officer. Applications are considered throughout the year.

Correspondent: The Chief Executive, Clifton Road, Marton, Blackpool FY4 4QZ (0253-792600).

The Chronicle Cinderella Fund

Eligibility: Disadvantaged children under 18 who live in Lancashire.

Types of grants: Help with the cost of holidays. Grants are given to organisations running holidays for disadvantaged children, to individual children to allow them to go on group holidays, and to children and mothers for family holidays on referral from agencies.

Annual grant total: The trust had an income of £9,000 in 1993. It is not known how much was given in grants to individuals in need.

Applications: Usually referred by child guidance clinics, special school support units or other welfare agencies or voluntary bodies. Applications are considered in March, June, September and December. Direct applications are not considered.

Correspondent: Richard Davey, Clerk, Community Council of Lancashire, 15 Victoria Road, Fulwood, Preston PL2 4PS (0772-718710).

The Foxton Dispensary

Eligibility: People who are sick and in need who live in Blackpool and Poulton-le-Fylde.

Types of grants: Grants to help with heating bills or for food.

Annual grant total: No information available.

Applications: In writing to the correspondent through doctors, health visitors or social services departments.

Correspondent: W S Haworth, Clerk, Messrs Hamer, Park & Haworth, 71 Adelaide Street, Blackpool FY1 4LQ (0253-21531).

The Goosnargh & Whittingham United Charity

Eligibility: People in need who live in the parishes of Goosnargh, Whittingham and part of Barton.

Types of grants: Grants or provision of services.

Annual grant total: In 1992, the trust had an income of £6,000.

Applications: In writing to the correspondent.

Correspondent: L Howarth, Clerk, 30 Greengate, Hutton, Preston PR4 5FH (0772-613322).

The Harris Charity

Eligibility: People in need under 25 who live in Lancashire, with preference for the Preston district.

Types of grants: One-off or recurrent grants according to need.

Annual grant total: The trust had an income of £116,000 in 1992/93. Expenditure totalled £133,000 but not all of this is available for individuals.

Applications: On a form available from the correspondent. The trustees advertise in the local press in March and September for applications. Following the closing dates of June and December, successful applicants are notified in July and January respectively.

Correspondent: P R Metcalf, Secretary, Richard House, 9 Winckley Square, Preston PR1 3HP (0772-821021).

Lancashire

Lancashire County Nursing Trust

Eligibility: (i) Retired nurses, who are in need and have been employed by Lancashire County Nursing Association.

(ii) People in need who are sick and live in the old county of Lancashire.

One-fifth of the income is for the benefit of retired nurses; the remaining income to be distributed as the trustees think fit to sick and needy people.

Types of grants: One-off and recurrent grants according to need.

Annual grant total: In 1991, the trust had an income of £12,000. It is not known how much was given in grants to individuals.

Applications: In writing to the correspondent.

Correspondent: Mrs S A Gill, Secretary, 12 Southfield Drive, New Longton, Preston PR4 4XD (0772-613390).

Peter Lathom's Charity

Eligibility: Elderly people in need living in Bickerstaffe, Bispham and Mawdesley, Burscough, Croston, Dalton and Parbold, Newburgh and Lathom, Ormskirk, Rufford, Scarisbrick, Skelmersdale, Ulnes Walton and Eccleston, Welch Whittle, Heskin and Wrightington.

Types of grants: One-off grants at Christmas.

Annual grant total: The trust's income is about £13,000, but not all of this is given to elderly people.

Applications: On a form available from the correspondent.

Correspondent: Mr Byron, Clerk, 15 Railway Road, Ormskirk, Lancashire L39 2DW (0695-575271).

The Skelton Swindells Trust

Eligibility: Women in need who live in Lancashire, usually those not supported by a partner.

Types of grants: One-off grants usually between £50 to £250 for heating, furnishings, special equipment, provision of services etc..

Annual grant total: About £2,000.

Applications: On a form available from the correspondent, via the social services department or other statutory or voluntary agencies. Applications are considered quarterly.

Correspondent: Mrs Jill Rouse, Secretary, c/o Community Council of Lancashire, 15 Victoria Road, Fulwood, Preston PR2 4PS (0772-718710).

● Blackburn

The Irving Trust to Relieve Distress

Eligibility: People in need who live in the borough of Blackburn. There may be a preference for elderly people.

Types of grants: One-off gifts in kind generally to the value of £25 to £275.

Annual grant total: The trust had an income of £3,200 in 1990. No more recent information is available.

Applications: In writing to the correspondent.

Correspondent: Peter Smith, Clerk, 60 Cornelian Street, Blackburn BB1 9AW (0254-57054).

● Blackpool

The Blackpool Ladies' Sick Poor Association

Eligibility: People in need who live in Blackpool.

Types of grants: One-off grants for necessities, convalescent holidays and towards paying bills. Help has recently been given in the form of food vouchers, cookers and prams. No cash grant.

Annual grant total: Over £12,000.

Applications: Via health visitors, social workers or the Town Hall in Blackpool.

Correspondent: Mrs Jones, Chairwoman, c/o Blackpool Borough Council, Municipal Buildings, Corporation Street, Blackpool FY1 1AD.

The Mayor of Blackpool's Welfare Services Fund

Eligibility: Ex-service men and women who lived in Blackpool and enlisted from there during World War II, and who live in Blackpool at the time of application.

Types of grants: One-off grants for emergencies, heating/fuel, clothing, aids/appliances, travel, home repairs/alterations and funeral costs. No fixed limit on grants to ex-service personnel; the maximum grant to widows is £300.

Annual grant total: Four grants totalling £1,100 in 1993.

Applications: On a form available from the correspondent. Applications can be submitted directly by the individual or through a social worker, citizen's advice bureau or other welfare agency.

Correspondent: Major A H Pendleton, Welfare Officer, 108 Worcester Road, Blackpool FY3 9SZ (0253-62773).

● Caton with Littledale

The Cottam Charities

Eligibility: People in need who are at least 50 and have lived in Caton with Littledale for at least five years.

Types of grants: One-off grants according to need.

Annual grant total: About £10,000 in 1993.

Applications: In writing to the correspondent. Grants are awarded in December. Applicants must reapply each year.

Correspondent: Mr Harris, Messrs Swainson, Son & Reynolds, 21 Castle Hill, Lancaster LA1 1YN (0524-32471).

● Darwen

The W M & B W Lloyd Trust

Eligibility: People in need who live in Darwen.

Types of grants: 20 to 30 one-off grants up to a maximum of £250 only for necessities. Help is usually given to groups rather than to individuals.

Annual grant total: £42,000, but not all of this is given to individuals.

Applications: In writing to the correspondent, including financial information and the type of help being sought.

Correspondent: The Secretary, The Lloyd Charity Committee, 10 Borough Road, Darwen, Lancashire BB3 1PL (0254-702111).

Other information: Although the charity can only give direct help to individuals in Darwen, organisations in the Blackburn area can also be helped. Education is given priority, although social amenities and medical needs are also considered.

● Esprick

The Charity of Mary Hankinson

Eligibility: People in need who live in the hamlet of Esprick.

Types of grants: Probably one-off and recurrent grants according to need.

Annual grant total: About £3,000.

Applications: In writing to the correspondent.

Correspondent: D J Kirkham, Clerk, Pendle View, Fleetwood Road, Esprick, Preston PR4 3HJ (0253-836234).

Lancashire

Fleetwood

The Fleetwood Fishing Industry Benevolent Fund

Eligibility: People directly employed in all sections of the fishing industry of Fleetwood, and their dependants.

Types of grants: Recurrent grants paid quarterly and one-off grants according to need.

Annual grant total: £16,000 in 1993.

Applications: In writing to the correspondent.

Correspondent: Mrs J Porter, c/o Wyre Fish Dock Management, Southgate Lodge, Denham Way, Fleetwood Docks, Fleetwood, Lancashire FY7 6NB (0253-778226).

Hyndburn

The Accrington Relief-in-Need Charity & Others

Eligibility: People in need over 65 who are on state benefits and live in the area administered by Hyndburn Borough Council.

Types of grants: One-off grants for emergencies, heating/fuel, clothing, sickness, aids/appliances, convalescence/holidays, travel and funeral costs.

Annual grant total: About £3,500 in 350 grants.

Applications: Trustees advertise in the local press then normally consider applications between October and November of each year, but there is a quick response for emergency cases.

Correspondent: The Chief Executive, Borough Treasurer's Department, Town Hall, The Broadway, Accrington, Lancashire BB5 1PQ (0254-233521).

Lancaster

The James Bond Charity

Eligibility: People who live in the city of Lancaster and a 10-mile radius around and have chest diseases, especially tuberculosis.

Types of grants: Probably one-off and recurrent grants according to need.

Annual grant total: About £3,000.

Applications: Via doctors or social workers; applications are considered four times a year at a meeting of trustees.

Correspondent: W Pearson, Town Clerk, Lancaster City Council, Town Hall, Lancaster LA1 1PJ (0524-582070).

The Gibson, Simpson & Brockbank Annuities Trust

Eligibility: Unmarried women or widows who are 50 or over, in need, and live in the district of Lancaster.

Types of grants: Regular yearly allowances. No grants where the applicant's income is over £150 per year, excluding her old age pension.

Annual grant total: About £2,000 (10 to 15 people receive quarterly payments of £37.50).

Applications: On a form available from the correspondent.

Correspondent: W J Harris, Messrs Swainson, Son & Reynolds, Solicitors, 21 Castle Hill, Lancaster LA1 1YW (0524-32471).

The Lancaster Charity

Eligibility: People in need who live in the old city of Lancaster and have done so for at least three years, and are at least 60 years old (or under 60 but unable to work to maintain themselves owing to age, accident or infirmity).

Types of grants: £2.50 a week paid monthly to six individuals.

Annual grant total: About £60,000, but nearly all going to almshouses.

Applications: On a form available from the correspondent. Applications are considered when vacancies occur.

Correspondent: P E M Oglethorpe, Clerk, 16 Castle Park, Lancaster LA1 1YG (0524-67171).

Lowton

The Lowton Charities

Eligibility: People in need who live in the parishes of St Luke's and St Mary's in Lowton.

Types of grants: One-off grants at Christmas and emergency one-off grants at any time.

Annual grant total: £8,000 in 1991/92, including £3,500 in Christmas grants. Most of the remainder was given in emergency grants and some educational grants to individuals.

Applications: Usually through the rectors of the parishes or other trustees.

Correspondent: J B Davies, Secretary, 10 Tarvin Close, Lowton, Warrington WA3 2NX (0942-678108).

Lytham St Anne's

The Lytham St Anne's Relief-in-Sickness Charity

Eligibility: People of all ages who are in need through sickness and who live in Lytham St Anne's.

Types of grants: One-off grants eg. towards fuel bills and special beds/chairs. No grants for court fees or funeral costs.

Annual grant total: About £2,000.

Applications: In writing to the correspondent.

Correspondent: Mrs T Woods, Chief Officer, Age Concern, Lytham St Anne's, 7 St George's Road, St Anne's, Lancashire FY8 1BS (0253-725563).

Nelson

The Nelson District Nursing Association Fund

Eligibility: Sick poor people who live in Nelson.

Types of grants: One-off grants according to need.

Annual grant total: In 1992, the trust had an income of £5,000. It is not known how much was given in grants to individuals in need.

Applications: In writing to the correspondent.

Correspondent: The Secretary to the Trustees, c/o Corporate & Financial Services, Borough of Pendle, Town Hall, Market Street, Nelson, Lancashire BB9 7LG (0282-617731).

Preston

The Preston Relief-in-Need & Sickness Charities

Eligibility: People who live in the area administered by Preston Borough Council who are in need through poverty, sickness, disability or convalescence.

Types of grants: One-off grants calculated to reduce need, hardship or distress. Recent examples include provision of washing machines and paying of arrears (gas and telephone).

Annual grant total: With six weeks remaining to the end of the 1993/94 financial year, grants for aid sickness totalled £1,000 and grants for relief-in-need totalled £12,000.

Applications: On an application form submitted through a social worker,

Lancashire/Merseyside

citizen's advice bureau or other welfare agency. Applications are considered every 10 weeks. All statutory entitlements must have have been exhausted.

Correspondent: The Town Clerk, Preston Town Hall, PO Box 10, Lancaster Road, Preston PR1 2RL (0772-266115).

Ramsbottom

The Ramsbottom Aid-in-Sickness Fund

Eligibility: People in need who are sick, convalescent, disabled or infirm and who live in the former urban district of Ramsbottom, now partly in Lancashire and partly in Greater Manchester.

Types of grants: Grants are in the form of vouchers worth about £40 for fuel, bedding, clothing, television licences, convalescence, Christmas parcels, food and medical needs.

Annual grant total: In 1993, around £2,000 was given, of which about £600 to £700 was distributed in Christmas parcels.

Applications: In writing to the correspondent. Applications are usually referred to the correspondent by doctors, nurses, health visitors or social workers.

Correspondent: Mrs E M Waite, Secretary, 9 Park Avenue, Ramsbottom, Bury BL0 0DA (0706-822082).

Other information: This entry is repeated in the Greater Manchester section of the book.

Merseyside

The Conroy Trust

Eligibility: People in need who live (permanently) in the parishes of St Andrew's and Holy Trinity, Bebington and St Mark's, New Ferry. Applications from people outside these areas cannot be considered.

Types of grants: About half the income is distributed as bi-monthly payments to regular beneficiaries. The rest is used to make one-off grants for a special needs. Grants range from £20 to £500.

Annual grant total: About £4,000.

Applications: In writing to the correspondent. Applications are considered in January of each year.

Correspondent: F R Jackson, 2 Norbury Avenue, Bebington, Wirral L63 2HJ (051-608 3090).

The Convalescent & Holiday Fund

Eligibility: People in need who live in Merseyside.

Types of grants: One-off grants up to £100 for holidays and convalescence.

Annual grant total: £1,000.

Applications: On a form available from the correspondent. Applications should be made by a social worker or similar third party on behalf of the individual. They are considered on the third Tuesday of every month except August.

Correspondent: Mrs E Ashcroft, Senior Social Worker, Personal Service Society, 18-28 Seel Street, Liverpool L1 4BE (051-707 0131).

The John Lloyd Corkhill Trust

Eligibility: People with chest complaints who live in the borough of Wirral.

Types of grants: Mostly for equipment (eg. nebulisers). Help is also given towards services and amenities eg. holidays and milk bills, and occasionally to buy domestic appliances eg. fire, washing machine etc..

Annual grant total: About £4,000 in payments usually of £80 to £100.

Applications: Clients are generally referred by their social worker or doctor and have a low income. Supporting medical evidence must be supplied. Applications are considered in June and December.

Correspondent: Mrs Christine Rowlands, 12 Mere Park Road, Greasby, Wirral L49 3GN.

The Echo Goodfellow Fund

Eligibility: People in need as a result of poverty and who live in Merseyside.

Types of grants: One-off and recurrent grants according to need. The annual grant is passed over to Merseyside Council for Voluntary Service who provide food hampers for the elderly at Christmas.

Annual grant total: £4,000 to £6,000.

Applications: In writing to the correspondent.

Correspondent: K R Pye, Trustee, Liverpool Daily Post & Echo, PO Box 48, Old Hall Street, Liverpool L69 3EB.

The Girls' Welfare Fund

Eligibility: Girls and young women (aged 15 to 25) who are in need and live in Merseyside. Applications from other areas will not be acknowledged.

Types of grants: One-off and recurrent grants according to need.

Annual grant total: £5,500 given in grants, not all of which was given for relief-in-need.

Applications: By letter to the correspondent (including all relevant information); considered quarterly.

Correspondent: Mrs S M O'Leary, Hon. Secretary, West Hey, Dawstone Road, Heswall, Merseyside L60 4RP.

Other information: This entry has not been confirmed by the trust.

The trust also gives grants to organisations benefiting girls and young women on Merseyside, and to eligible individuals for leisure, creative activities, sports, arts and education.

The Ladies Aid Fund

Eligibility: Women in need over the age of 40 who live within a 10 mile radius of Liverpool or Southport Town Halls.

Types of grants: One-off and recurrent grants according to need. No grants where there is evidence of debt.

Annual grant total: In 1992, the trust's income was £1,200. £1,100 was given in two relief-in-need grants to individuals.

Applications: On a form available from the correspondent after written detailed enquiry. Applications can be submitted directly by the individual or through a welfare agency. Applications are considered throughout the year.

Correspondent: J N L Packer, Secretary, Nigel Packer & Co, 1st Floor, Royal Liver Building, Pier Head Liverpool L3 1HU (051-471 9888).

The Liverpool Caledonian Association

Eligibility: People of Scottish descent, or their immediate family, who are in need and who live within a 15-mile radius of Liverpool Town Hall.

Types of grants: Up to 10 one-off grants (generally up to £50) and 28 monthly annuities of less than the £5.20.

Annual grant total: In 1991, the trust's income was about £8,000; grants totalled about £6,000. Applicants may telephone or write to the correspondent. Applications are considered at any time and applicants will be visited.

Merseyside

Applications: In writing to the correspondent.

Correspondent: Mr Crichton, Relief Committee Chairman, 18 Stella Precinct, Seaforth, Liverpool L21 3TB (051-920 6409).

The Liverpool Children's Welfare Trust

Eligibility: Children aged 16 or under who live in Merseyside. The trust mainly supports children of single-parent families and of long-term unemployed people.

Types of grants: One-off grants up to £100 for clothing, holidays for mothers and children, days out, bedding, washing machines and other household equipment etc..

No grants for debts, telephone rental or installation, or medical equipment.

Annual grant total: Grants totalled about £6,000 to individuals in need.

Applications: On a form available from the correspondent. Applications are considered on the third Tuesday of every month except August. Applications must be submitted by a social worker or other professional. Direct applications from the client will not be considered.

Correspondent: Mrs E Ashcroft, Senior Social Worker, Personal Service Society, 18–28 Seel Street, Liverpool L1 4BE (051-707 0131).

The Liverpool Customs & Excise Benevolent Society

Eligibility: Present and former Liverpool customs officials who are in need, their widows and other dependants.

Types of grants: One-off grants and loans according to need. Currently an annual payment is made to six widows.

Annual grant total: About £1,000.

Applications: In writing to the correspondent.

Correspondent: The Secretary, Custom House, Cunard Building, Liverpool L3 1DX (051-227 4343).

The Liverpool Ladies Institution

Eligibility: Single women in need who were either born in the city of Liverpool or who live in Merseyside.

Types of grants: Usually £140 a year paid half-yearly in June and December. Also Christmas gifts of £30 and birthday gifts of £10.

Annual grant total: In 1992, the trust had assets of £62,000 and an income of £5,800. 30 relief-in-need grants to individuals totalled £4,900.

Applications: On a form available from the correspondent. Applications should be submitted through a social worker, citizen's advice bureau or other welfare agency. They are considered on receipt.

Correspondent: E W Boon, Wyncote Lodge, 230 Allerton Road, Liverpool L18 6JN (051-724 3889).

The Liverpool Merchants' Guild

Eligibility: Retired, professional, clerical or self-employed people or their dependants who live in or near the city of Liverpool (or who have lived in the city for a continuous period of at least 15 years), are aged 50 or over, and are in need or distress. Women whose husbands are still living are only eligible in exceptional circumstances.

Types of grants: Mainly pensions of up to £10 a week paid half-yearly (that is up to the DSS disregard level). Occasional one-off grants for items of exceptional expenditure eg. telephone bills, repairs, cooker, washing machine etc. for those already in receipt of a pension.

Annual grant total: In 1992, the trust had an income of £705,000 and gave grants to 500 individuals totalling £720,000.

Applications: On a form available from the correspondent, which requires counter-signing by two unrelated referees eg. doctors, clergy, social services, citizen's advice bureau etc.. Applications are considered quarterly.

Correspondent: Moore Stephens, 42 Castle Street, Liverpool L2 7TJ (051-236 9044).

The Liverpool Provision Trade Guild

Eligibility: Members of the guild who are in need and their dependants. If funds permit, benefits can be extended to other members of the provision trade on Merseyside who are in need and their dependants.

Types of grants: Monthly, annually or twice annually dependant on circumstances. Grants range from £250 to £800.

Annual grant total: In 1992, the trust had assets of £80,000 and an income of £9,000. 18 relief-in-need grants totalled £13,000.

Applications: On a form available from the correspondent to be submitted directly by the individual. Applications are considered in May and December.

Correspondent: The Secretary, c/o Macfarlane & Co, 2nd Floor, Cunard Building, Water Street, Liverpool L3 1DS (051-236 6161).

The Liverpool Queen Victoria District Nursing Association (LCSS)

Eligibility: People who are sick or disabled and who live in Merseyside.

Types of grants: One-off grants to enable people to remain in the community. Maximum grant £200 (or £100 if for a holiday). Grants have included help towards buying of a liquidiser for a person who had undergone surgery for cancer of the tongue, and a heater for a person who was severely disabled.

No help is given where this should be provided by the "public purse". No grants for debts or travel to hospital.

Annual grant total: In 1992, the trust's income was £27,000. Grants totalled £23,500 but it is not known how much of this was to individuals in need as the trust also gives grants to organisations and for nurses' education.

Applications: On a form only available from the Community Nursing Services of Merseyside Health Districts (not from the correspondent) via district nurses and health visitors. Applications are considered in mid-January, April/May and September and are to be received by mid-December, 1st April and mid-August.

Correspondent: (Not for applications): The Secretary, Liverpool Council of Social Service, 14 Castle Street, Liverpool L2 0NJ (051-236 7728).

The Liverpool Queen Victoria Nursing Association (PSS)

Eligibility: People who are sick, convalescing, disabled or infirm and who live in Merseyside.

Types of grants: One-off grants up to £100 for bedding, clothing, household equipment and holidays. No grants for medical equipment, telephones or debts.

Annual grant total: About £3,000.

Applications: On a form available from the correspondent. Applications must be made through a social worker, citizen's advice bureau or other welfare agency. Appeals are considered on the third Tuesday of every month except August.

Correspondent: Mrs E Ashcroft, Senior Social Worker, Personal Service Society,

Merseyside

18–28 Seel Street, Liverpool L1 (051-707 0131).

Other information: A larger part of the charity's income is administered by the Liverpool Council of Social Service. See entry above.

The Merseyside Police Orphans' Fund

Eligibility: Children (including adopted children) of retired, deceased or incapacitated members of the Merseyside Police Force.

Types of grants: Allowances of £160 a quarter and a parting gift of £100. Allowances are paid until the child is 16 (unless he/she remains in full-time secondary education).

Annual grant total: About £28,000.

Applications: In writing to the correspondent.

Correspondent: C Pierce, Merseyside Police Headquarters, Canning Place, Liverpool L69 1JD (051-709 6010).

The South Moss Foundation

Eligibility: Children under the age of 18 who live in Merseyside and are in need of care or rehabilitation, particularly as a result of crime, deprivation, maltreatment or neglect, or who are in danger of lapsing into delinquency.

Types of grants: Single payments up to £250 to enable the above to pursue a constructive interest or hobby; enable them to take up education, training or employment opportunities; assist those leaving care or custody to move into their own accommodation. Generally NO grants for holidays or as a substitute for state benefits.

Annual grant total: £1,600 in 1992/93, of which £930 was given in 8 grants to individuals. The foundation's income for 1993/94 is about £6,000.

Applications: Applications should be made on a form available from the correspondent by a social worker, youth worker, probation officer, headteacher or representative of the agency/youth group working with the child concerned. Applications are considered throughout the year and grants are made payable to the agency. A copy of the grant letter or refusal letter is sent to the child concerned.

Correspondent: Linda Lazenby, 21 Brancote Road, Oxton, Birkenhead L43 6TL (051-653 6364).

The Richard Warbrick Charities

Eligibility: Widows in need who live in Merseyside. Applicants must be on Income Support or rent/community charge rebate.

Types of grants: Pensions of £140 a year (£35 quarterly). At least three quarters of the beneficiaries must be widows of seamen of the port or city of Liverpool.

Annual grant total: About £12,000 in 90 grants.

Applications: On a form from Liverpool Parish Church, Our Lady & St Nicholas, Liverpool L2. Applications must be accompanied by the marriage certificate, the husband's death certificate, a letter from a professional who knew the husband to certify that the applicant is the lawful widow, and a testimonial from a minister of religion.

Correspondent: A T R Macfarlane, Macfarlane & Co, 2nd Floor, Cunard Building, Water Street, Liverpool L3 1DS (051-236 6161).

The West Kirby Charities

Eligibility: Elderly people living in Hoylake, Meols, Greasby, Frankby and West Kirby (the old Hoylake urban district).

Types of grants: Pensions of £4 a week and one-off grants for necessities such as help with fuel bills. The grant total is divided almost equally between pensions and special and Christmas payments.

Annual grant total: About £5,500 in 25 pensions and 35 grants.

Applications: On a form available from the correspondent; considered four times a year. Applications for emergency grants can be considered between meetings.

Correspondent: R B Brown, Clerk, 1 Crosshall Street, Liverpool L1 6DH (051-227 1301).

Bebington

The Mayor of Bebington's Benevolent Fund

Eligibility: People in need who live in the former borough of Bebington. Anyone living outside the post codes L63 and L62 will not be considered.

Types of grants: One-off grants and loans for people in extreme poverty or distress, excluding council tax.

Annual grant total: About £1,500.

Applications: In writing to the correspondent. Applications can be submitted directly by the individual or through a social worker, citizen's advice bureau or other welfare agency or third party. They are considered at any time.

Correspondent: Ms M Aitken, 38 Wirral Gardens, Bebington, Wirral L63 3BD (051-334 3469).

Bidston

The Emily Clover Trust

Eligibility: People in need who live within a 10-mile radius of St Oswalds Church, Bidston.

Types of grants: One-off grants only. Preference for small grants to cover family needs and to alleviate hardship and distress.

No grants for relief of rates, taxes or other public funds or for college/school fees, adventure holidays or similar activities.

Annual grant total: In 1992, the trust had assets of £35,000 with a disposable income of £4,000. Grants totalling £4,600 were given to 50 individuals in need.

Applications: In writing to the correspondent; support from a social worker or other welfare agency is useful. Trustees meet three or four times a year, but some grants can be made between meetings.

Correspondent: L F Chettenden, 31 Brookside Crescent, Upton, Wirral L49 4LE (051-677 2119).

Birkenhead

The Birkenhead Relief-in-Sickness Fund

Eligibility: People in need through ill-health who live in the old county borough of Birkenhead.

Types of grants: One-off grants to a usual maximum of £200. Grants are given for items such as clothing, electrical appliances, furniture (eg. beds), travel costs and household items (eg. bedding, towels).

Annual grant total: In 1993, the trust had an income of £1,500. Relief-in-need grants were given to 20 individuals.

Applications: Applications, in writing to the correspondent, can be submitted by the individual, through a recognised referral agency (eg. social worker, citizen's advice bureau or doctor) or other third party, and are considered throughout the year. Potential recipients will be visited.

Correspondent: Mary Worcester, Wirral CVS, 46 Hamilton Square, Birkenhead L41 5AR (051-647 5432).

The Christ Church Fund for Children

Eligibility: Children in need up to the age of 17 whose parents are members of the Church of England and who live in the county borough of Birkenhead. Preference is given to children living in the ecclesiastical parish of Christ Church, Birkenhead.

Types of grants: Any kind of need but typically bedding, furniture, clothing, grocery parcels and trips.

Annual grant total: In 1991/92, the trust had an income of £2,450. Grants of between £10 and £250 were given to 17 individuals and totalled nearly £3,000.

Applications: In writing through a recognised referral agency (eg. social worker, citizen's advice bureau or doctor) or other third party.

Correspondent: Mrs N Corcoran, c/o Christ Church Parish Office, Bessborough Road, Birkenhead L43 5RW.

● **Higher Bebington**

The Thomas Robinson Charity

Eligibility: People in need who live in Higher Bebington.

Types of grants: One-off or recurrent grants according to need.

Annual grant total: £1,800.

Applications: In writing to the correspondent.

Correspondent: Canon Faulkner, The Vicarage, Higher Bebington, Wirral L63 8LX (051-608 4429).

● **Hoylake & West Kirby**

The Hoylake & West Kirby Aid-in-Sickness Fund

Eligibility: People who are sick, convalescent, disabled or infirm who live within a five mile-radius of Hoylake Town Hall.

Types of grants: One-off grants for special need.

Annual grant total: £1,000.

Applications: Must be recommended by doctors, nurses or social services.

Correspondent: N Kidd, Secretary, 22 Madeley Drive, Off Hilbre Road, West Kirby, Wirral L48 3LB (051-625 7975).

● **Huyton with Roby**

The Huyton with Roby Distress Fund

Eligibility: People in need who live in the former urban district of Huyton with Roby (in Knowsley).

Types of grants: One-off grants ranging from £100 to £500 towards the cost of items such as washing machines, carpets and beds. The level of help is based on what would have been provided by the DSS if the applicant had been eligible.

No grants for debts or fuel costs.

Annual grant total: In 1993/94, grants totalling £1,800 were given to 12 individuals.

Applications: In writing to the correspondent through a social worker, citizen's advice bureau or other welfare agency. Applications are considered on receipt.

Correspondent: The Director of Finance, Metropolitan Borough of Knowsley, PO Box 24, Municipal Buildings, Archway Road, Huyton, Merseyside L36 9YZ (051-443 4396).

● **Liverpool**

The William Edmonds Fund

Eligibility: Married women and widows with dependent children who live in the archdiocese of Liverpool.

Types of grants: One-off grants, usually up to £100, for holidays, clothing, household necessities (eg. washing machines, beds/bedding), interior decorating, help to avoid re-possession etc.. Most women helped have several children, are often in poor health and are emotionally stressed and financially impoverished.

Annual grant total: £6,500 in 65 grants.

Applications: On a form available from the correspondent. This must be completed and signed by the applicant, social worker, probation officer or priest in charge of the parish where the woman lives. A professional person must apply on the applicant's behalf; payment is made to this third party. Applications are considered throughout the year.

Correspondent: Dr O McKendrick, Flat 2, 1 Ibbotson's Lane, Liverpool L17 1AL.

The Garston & Grassendale Fund for the Sick & Convalescent

Eligibility: People who are sick and live in the Garston, Grassendale, Springwood and Speke areas of Liverpool.

Types of grants: One-off grants up to £100 towards clothing, bedding, household equipment and holidays. No grants for telephones, medical equipment or debts.

Annual grant total: About £1,500.

Applications: Applications should be submitted through a recognised referral agency (eg. social worker, citizen's advice bureau or doctor) or other third party, and are considered on the third Tuesday of every month except August.

Correspondent: Mrs E Ashcroft, Senior Social Worker, Personal Service Society, 18-28 Seel Street, Liverpool L1 4BE (051-707 0131).

The Liverpool Corn Trade Guild

Eligibility: Members of the guild who are over 60 and in need, and their dependants. If funds permit benefits can be extended to former members and their dependants. Membership is open to anyone employed by any firm engaged in the Liverpool Corn and Feed Trade.

Types of grants: One-off and recurrent grants according to need.

Annual grant total: Grants totalled about £4,700.

Applications: In writing to the correspondent. Applications should be made directly by the individual.

Correspondent: Mrs J Hatch, Secretary, c/o 4th Floor, Royal Seaforth Grain Terminal, Port of Liverpool, Liverpool L21 4PB (051-949 0955).

The Liverpool Cotton Association Ltd Benevolent Fund

Eligibility: Present and former members of the association under 50, and their dependants.

Types of grants: Christmas grants of about £250.

Annual grant total: In 1992/93, the fund had assets of £3,000 with an income of £25. Relief-in-need grants totalled £1,100.

Applications: On a form available form the correspondent. Applications should be made directly by the individual. They are considered in November.

Correspondent: Miss G Ormesher, 620 Cotton Exchange Building, Liverpool L3 9LH (051-236 6041).

The Liverpool Wholesale Fruit & Vegetable Trade Association Benevolent Fund

Merseyside

Eligibility: Members and former members of the association and their families who are in need. Grants may also be given to other agencies or other people who have worked in the fruit trade.

Types of grants: One-off and recurrent grants according to need.

Annual grant total: In 1992/93, the trust had an income of £2,600 of which £2,500 was given in grants to individuals in need.

Applications: In writing to the correspondent.

Correspondent: T J C Dobbin, Secretary, c/o Westmore Brennand, Masons Building, 28 Exchange St East, Liverpool L2 3XS (051-236 0421).

Charities administered by Merseyside Jewish Welfare Council

Eligibility: Poor people of Liverpool of the Jewish faith.

Types of grants: Grants are given for holidays, students, elderly people, one-parent families and children. Both one-off and recurrent grants are given.

Annual grant total: £22,500 in 1990/91.

Applications: By letter or telephone to the correspondent. A social worker may visit if necessary. Applications are considered at any time.

Correspondent: A Hurst, Shifrin House, 433 Smithdown Road, Liverpool L15 3JL (051-733 2292/3).

The Ann Molyneux Charity

Eligibility: Seamen or their widows living in the city of Liverpool. Preference for men who sailed from the city for most of the last five years that they were at sea, and their widows. Applicants must receive Income Support, rent or council tax rebate.

Types of grants: Pensions of £140 a year (£35 paid quarterly).

Annual grant total: About £11,000 in 86 grants.

Applications: On a form available from Liverpool Parish Church, Our Lady & St Nicholas, Liverpool 2. Applications should be accompanied by seamen's books, a testimonial from a minister of religion and details of income. Widows must give evidence of marriage, their husband's death certificate and a reference letter from a professional.

Correspondent: Macfarlane & Co, 2nd Floor, Cunard Building, Water Street, Liverpool L3 1DS (051-236 6161).

The Pritt & Corlett Funds

Eligibility: Solicitors who are in need and have practised in the city of Liverpool or within the area of Liverpool Law Society, and their dependants.

Types of grants: One-off and recurrent grants according to need.

Annual grant total: About £11,500 in about 6 grants.

Applications: On a form available from the correspondent.

Correspondent: R Arden, Liverpool Law Society, Castle Chambers, Liverpool L2 9SH (051-236 6998 – ask for Mrs Wright).

The Elizabeth Stringer Trust

Eligibility: Retired professional non-manual workers over 50 and their dependants who were born within a 10-mile radius of Liverpool town hall or who have lived within that radius for at least five years and have been unable to make provision for their retirement.

Types of grants: Pensions only.

Annual grant total: £2,000.

Applications: On a form available from the correspondent. Applications are considered half yearly.

Correspondent: Moore Stephens, 42 Castle Street, Liverpool L2 7TJ (051-236 9044).

Lydiate

John Goore's Charity

Eligibility: Poor and sick people resident in the ancient township of Lydiate. Applicants must be on the electoral roll or, if they live outside the area, must have lived in Lydiate for a period of five years during the 10 year period immediately preceding the application.

Types of grants: Recurrent grants of £40 distributed in summer and at Christmas to 95 individuals, and one-off grants for special needs as requested to a maximum of £500.

Annual grant total: In 1992/93, the trust had an income of £10,000. Total expenditure was £13,000. Grants totalled about £9,800.

Applications: On a form available from the correspondent. Applications should be made through a social worker, teacher, probation officer, cleric, doctor or other third party.

Correspondent: E R Bostock, 124 Liverpool Road, Lydiate, Merseyside L31 2NB (051-526 4919).

Sefton

The Sefton Association for the Deaf

Eligibility: People living in Sefton who are profoundly deaf or hard of hearing.

Types of grants: One-off or recurrent grants according to need including buying household items, grants towards holidays and respite holidays and help with education needs of deaf children.

Annual grant total: In 1993, the income was £7,600 and expenditure totalled £14,800. Not all of this was given in grants to individuals.

Applications: In writing to the correspondent. Applications should be submitted directly by the individual or through a social worker, citizen's advice bureau or other welfare agency.

Correspondent: Miss Lynn Evans, Secretary, Merseyside Deaf Centre, Queens Drive, West Derby, Liverpool L13 0DJ (051-228 0888).

The Southport & Birkdale Provident Society

Eligibility: People in need who live in the borough of Sefton.

Types of grants: One-off grants only, after social services have confirmed that all other benefits have been fully explored. Grants are not given for education, training experience or personal debts.

Annual grant total: About £22,000 in about 150 grants.

Applications: On a form available from the correspondent, via social services. Applications are considered every two months from January.

Correspondent: The Secretary, Haigh Court, Peel Street, Southport PR8 6JL.

6. Midlands

The Birmingham & Three Counties Trust for Nurses

Eligibility: Elderly nurses and any nurse in distress whether registered or enrolled who have worked or work in Birmingham, Staffordshire, Warwickshire and/or Worcestershire for a reasonable period.

Types of grants: One-off or recurrent grants according to need.

Annual grant total: In 1992/93, the trust had assets of £194,000 producing an income of £22,000. Grants totalled £20,000.

Applications: On a form available from the correspondent. Applications can be submitted directly by the individual or through a social worker, citizen's advice bureau or other welfare agency. They are considered throughout the year.

Correspondent: Wragge & Co, Solicitors, 55 Colmore Row, Birmingham B3 2AS (021-233 1000).

The Charities of Susanna Cole & Others

Eligibility: Quakers in need who live in parts of Worcestershire and most of Warwickshire and are "a member or attender of one of the constituent meetings of the Warwickshire Monthly Meeting of the Society of Friends".

Types of grants: One-off and recurrent grants according to need. Help may be given with domestic running costs, rent or accommodation fees, convalescence, recreation or home help. Preference is given to those with small children and retired people on inadequate pensions.

Annual grant total: In 1992, the trust had assets of £47,500 producing an income of £7,500. Total expenditure was £6,400 of which part was given towards managing Quaker homes for the elderly. Grants of between £150 and £260 were given to 14 individuals and totalled £3,300.

Applications: In writing to the correspondent via overseers of Quaker meetings. Applications are considered early in March and October.

Correspondent: The Secretary, Warwickshire Monthly Meeting Office, Friends Meeting House, 40 Bull Street, Birmingham B3 6AF (021-238 5231).

The Baron Davenport Charity Trust

Eligibility: Needy widows, spinsters and children under 21 whose fathers are dead, who live in the West Midlands, Staffordshire, Warwickshire or Worcestershire.

Types of grants: Recurrent grants, typically £160 a year and up to £200 a year, paid half yearly. One-off grants for all kinds of need eg. telephone installation and occasionally holidays.

Annual grant total: About £300,000 direct grants and allowances to 1,750 beneficiaries, and about £30,000 through local CVSs.

Applications: Except for emergency cases, applications should be made through local authority social services departments or recognised welfare agencies (when they will be considered at six monthly intervals), but direct applications from individuals may also be considered. Applications forms are available from the correspondent and are considered in May and November.

Applications where prompt relief is needed should be addressed to the local Council of Voluntary Service, as listed under their separate entries.

Correspondent: E J Rough, Secretary, 43 Temple Row, Birmingham B2 5JT (021-236 8004).

Other information: The trust and the CVS's regard as fatherless only those whose fathers are dead, so children abandoned by their fathers cannot be helped. Similarly, although "spinster" covers all women who have not married, they seem to prefer elderly women who fit the traditional usage of the term.

For emergency needs, see the separate CVS entries below and in the county sections as follows:

Hereford & Worcester: Malvern; Redditch.

Staffordshire: East Staffordshire; Stafford district; Stoke-on-Trent; Tamworth.

Warwickshire: North Warwickshire; Rugby; Stratford-upon-Avon; Warwick district; Nuneaton and Bedworth.

West Midlands: Birmingham, Coventry, Dudley, Solihull, Walsall, Wolverhampton.

The Baron Davenport Emergency Grant

Eligibility: Needy widows, spinsters and children under 21 whose fathers are dead, who live within the county boundaries of Staffordshire, Warwickshire or Worcestershire.

Types of grants: One-off grants for emergencies only.

Annual grant total: Generally about £2,000.

Applications: On a form available from the correspondent.

Correspondent: Age Concern North Staffordshire, 6 Albion Street, Hanley, Stoke-on-Trent ST1 1QH.

Other information: For information on Baron Davenport's Charity Trust, see entry above.

The Baron Davenport Emergency Grant

Eligibility: Needy widows, spinsters and children under 21 whose fathers are dead. Applicants should not have savings over £1,000. Applicants will have lived within the old county boundaries of Warwickshire for at least 10 years (this includes Coventry).

● **Midlands**

Types of grants: One-off grants for emergencies only, particularly "unexpected domestic expenses, heavy funeral expenses or similar instances where state benefit is not available or undue delay would cause hardship". Grants are normally for £60 to £100.

Annual grant total: About £500 in 1993/94.

Applications: Through a social worker, health professional or other welfare agency.

Correspondent: Helen Aird, Director, Coventry Voluntary Service Council, 58-64 Corporation Street, Coventry CV1 1GF (0203-220381).

Other information: For information on Baron Davenport's Charity Trust, see entry above.

The Maud Elkington Charitable Trust

Eligibility: People in need who live in Northamptonshire and Leicestershire.

Types of grants: One-off and recurrent grants according to need.

Annual grant total: The trust's net income is around £220,000. However, most of its grants go to organisations.

Applications: In writing to the correspondent. Applications should be made through social services, health authorities, welfare agencies and similar third parties.

Correspondent: R Bowder, c/o Messrs Harvey Ingram, 20 New Walk, Leicester LE1 6TX (0533-545454).

Other information: Further information on this trust can be found in *A Guide to the Major Trusts*.

The Estate Charity of Lady Leveson's (or the Foxley Charity)

Eligibility: People in need who live in the parishes of Blakesley, Litchborough and Pattishall in Northamptonshire; Trentham in Staffordshire, and Lilleshall in Shropshire.

Types of grants: Pensions, especially widows, and grants for students.

Annual grant total: In 1986, the most recent year for which information is available, the trust's income was £23,000. Grants were given to "Beauchamp Chapel and Parishes" totalling £8,000. It is not known how many grants were given to individuals. We were unable to obtain more up-to-date information.

Applications: In writing to the appropriate local trustee (see below).

Correspondent: *Blakesley:* Mrs P A Paterson, Quinbury Cottage, Blakesley, Towcester, Northamptonshire.

Lilleshall: N Rozzell, 14a Church Road, Lilleshall, Newport, Shropshire TF10 9HJ.

Pattishall: Miss D Kirton, 5 Birds Hill, Eastcote, Towcester, Northamptonshire.

Trentham: Rev D Marsh, Trentham Vicarage, Trentham Park, Trentham, Stoke-on-Trent ST4 8AE.

The Lady Forester Trust

Eligibility: Primarily people who live in Shropshire who are sick, disabled, convalescent or infirm, followed by people who live in the surrounding areas of Cheshire and Staffordshire.

Types of grants: One-off grants for medical equipment or nursing care not otherwise available on the NHS. No grants for building repairs/alterations.

Annual grant total: £112,000 in 1992.

Applications: On a form available from the correspondent. Applications should be made through a social worker, citizen's advice bureau, doctor, specialist or other welfare agency and are considered throughout the year.

Correspondent: The Administrator, Willey Park, Broseley, Shropshire TF12 5JJ (0952-884318).

Other information: This entry is repeated in the Cheshire section of the book.

Dr Isaac Massey's Charity

Eligibility: Women who have lived in Nottinghamshire, Derbyshire or Lincolnshire for at least 10 years and who are either (a) widows over 50 who have not remarried, or (b) fatherless unmarried daughters of clergymen, professional or business people.

Types of grants: Regular yearly allowances of up to £250.

Annual grant total: About £2,300 in about 9 grants.

Applications: On a form available from the correspondent.

Correspondent: J C Foxon, Blythens Accountants, Haydn House, 309-329 Haydn Road, Sherwood, Nottingham NG5 1HG (0602-607111).

The Oldbury Nurses' Pension Trust Fund

Eligibility: Retired district nurses and midwives in need who have worked in Oldbury or the county of Worcester.

Types of grants: Grants usually between £50 and £500 towards necessities such as washing machines.

Annual grant total: No information available but only four or five grants are made a year.

Applications: In writing to the correspondent.

Correspondent: J C Waites, Trustee, Worcester & District Health Authority, Isaac Maddox House, Shrub Hill Road, Worcester WR4 9RW (0905-763333).

The Persehouse Pensions Fund

Eligibility: Elderly or distressed people belonging to the upper or middle classes of society who were born in the counties of Staffordshire or Worcestershire, or people who have lived in either county for 10 years or more.

Types of grants: Mainly pensions, but occasional one-off grants.

Annual grant total: £7,600 in 10 pensions paid quarterly in 1992/93.

Applications: On a form available from the correspondent.

Correspondent: The Secretary, Clive Wheatley Pinsent & Co Solicitors, 31 Colmore Circus, Birmingham B4 6BH (021-200 1050).

The Royal Leicestershire, Rutland & Wycliffe Society for the Blind

Eligibility: Visually impaired people who live in Leicestershire and Rutland.

Types of grants: 1. Special needs grants which can range from replacement of stolen cash to help with removal costs to household equipment such as a new/safer cooker. Grants from £50 to £150.

2. Grants towards holidays whether they are organised by the individual or a group or organisation. They tend to be £50. Holiday grants will not be given in two successive years, unless under exceptional circumstances.

No grants for electricity, gas, rent or community charge arrears, nor for telephone installation, rental or calls.

Annual grant total: £3,200 in 42 grants in 1992/93.

Applications: On a form available from the correspondent through welfare agencies at any time and decisions are normally made within three weeks.

Correspondent: The Director, Margaret Road, Off Gwendolen Road, Leicester LE5 5FU (0533-490909).

The Rycroft Children's Fund

Eligibility: Children in need who live in Cheshire, Derbyshire, Greater Manchester, Lancashire, Staffordshire, South and West Yorkshire. There is a preference for children living in the cities of Manchester and Salford and the borough of Trafford. Applicants should be aged 18 or under.

Types of grants: One-off and recurrent grants according to need. No grants for further or higher education.

Annual grant total: Of the £30,000 given in grants about £25,000 is given for relief-in-need in about 20 grants.

Applications: On a form available from the correspondent.

Correspondent: Christopher Lees-Jones, Chairman, Hermitage Farm, Holmes Chapel, Cheshire CW4 8DP (0477-532875.)

Other information: This entry is repeated in the North East and North West general sections of the book.

Richard Smedley's Charity

Eligibility: People in need who live in the parishes of Breaston, Dale Abbey, Draycott with Church Wilne, Heanor, Hopwell, Ilkerton, Ockbrook and Risley (all in Derbyshire) and of Awsworth, Bilborough, Brinsley, Greasley and Strelley (all in Nottinghamshire).

Types of grants: Usually one-off grants of £100 to £300 towards items such as washing machines or holidays.

Annual grant total: In 1993, the trust had an income of £5,000, all of which was distributed. In fact, the trust is receiving more applications than it can possibly support.

Applications: In writing to the correspondent normally supported by welfare agencies.

Correspondent: M T E Ward, Clerk, c/o Messrs Robinsons, Market Place, Ilkeston, Derbyshire DE7 5RQ (0602-324101).

The Sir Thomas White's Charity

Eligibility: The trust is for the benefit of Coventry, Leicester, Northampton, Nottingham and Warwick. See below.

Types of grants: In 1993, the trust had an income of about £919,000. After administration and other costs the income available for distribution is dispersed as follows:

Coventry trustees 8/70ths
Leicester trustees 8/70ths
Northampton trustees 8/70ths
Nottingham trustees 8/70ths
Warwick Trustees 8/70ths
Coventry General Charities 24/70ths
Clerk to the Trustees - Coventry General Charities 1/70th
Coventry Stock Charity 4/70ths
Merchant Taylors Company 1/70th

The trustees of Sir Thomas White's Charity simply distribute the money in the above proportions in accordance with the trust deed. Therefore, as Sir Thomas White's Charity does not give grants we have not named the correspondent. Grants are allocated by the recipient trustees and details of the grant-giving policies are given in the following entries in this section:

Coventry - The General Charities of the City of Coventry

Northampton - Thomas White's Loan Fund

There is also an entry for the Merchant Taylors Company in the Occupational section of the book.

There is no entry for Leicester, Nottingham or Warwick in this Guide; the recipient trustees only gives loans for new businesses/tradespeople, details can be found in *The Educational Grants Directory*.

The Anthony & Gwendoline Wylde Memorial Charity

Eligibility: People in need with a preference for residents of Stourbridge (West Midlands) and Kinver (Staffordshire).

Types of grants: One-off grants only.

Annual grant total: In 1993, the trust had assets of about £670,000 and an income of £46,000. It is thought that grants totalled around £60,000 (100 grants).

Applications: In writing to the correspondent. Applications can be submitted directly by the individual or through a social worker, citizen's advice bureau or other welfare agency or through a third party such as a doctor or church minister. They are considered in January, May, July and September.

Correspondent: Mrs P I Gardener, 1 Worcester Street, Stourbridge, West Midlands DY8 1AJ (0384-378821).

Other information: According to the Charity Commission the address is correct, but the entry has not been confirmed by the trust.

Derbyshire

The Burton & South Derbyshire Charity for the Sufferers of Multiple Sclerosis

Eligibility: People with multiple sclerosis living in Burton and south Derbyshire.

Types of grants: Generally recurrent grants towards telephone rental, exercise equipment and naudicelle treatment.

Annual grant total: In 1992/93, grants totalling £6,500 were given to about 100 individuals

Applications: In writing to the correspondent. Applications can be submitted directly by the individual and are considered throughout the year.

Correspondent: J H Osborne, Chairman, 24 Beech Grove, Newhall, Swadlincote, Derbyshire DE11 ONH (0283-216638).

Other information: The charity also provides information on multiple sclerosis. People with multiple sclerosis throughout England can get 10% off the cost of naudicelle. Further information from the correspondent. This entry is repeated in the Staffordshire section of the book.

The Cotton Districts' Convalescent Fund

Eligibility: People who are convalescing or who have a severe/incurable illness or disability and who live in the High Peak district of Derbyshire. See entry at the start of the North West section of the book.

The Dronfield Nightingales

Eligibility: People with terminal illnesses who live in Dronfield and the villages of Homesfield, Barlow, Coal Aston, Unstone and Trowey.

Types of grants: To relieve carers of terminally ill people. Grants are made by meeting the bills of nursing agencies who have been authorised by the charity to attend terminally ill people. Grants range from £200 to £500.

Annual grant total: £3,200 in 21 grants in 1990. No more recent information available.

Applications: By referral from a doctor or nurse attending terminally ill people in their homes.

Correspondent: Mrs A Doxley, Secretary, Hill-Crest, Bole Hill, Calow, Chesterfield, Derbyshire S44 5UZ (0246-235162).

Derbyshire

The Dronfield Relief-in-Need Charity

Eligibility: People in need who live in the ecclesiastical parishes of Dronfield, Holmesfield, Unstone and Woodhouse.

Types of grants: One-off grants according to need.

Annual grant total: About £2,000.

Applications: In writing to the correspondent.

Correspondent: R E Moore, Hounscliffe, Unstone, Nr Sheffield S18 5AA (0246-413434).

The Goldminers OAP Outing & Christmas Fund

Eligibility: People of retirement age who are in need and live in Littlemoor, Dunston and Newbold.

Types of grants: Subsidies of about £40 towards an annual week's holiday for all elderly people in the area, irrespective of need. Gifts of between £2 and £5 to those not going on the holiday.

Annual grant total: About £10,000 was given in 2,000 gifts and around £50,000 in 1,300 holiday subsidies.

Correspondent: W F Whittaker Walters, 33 Thirlmere Road, Newbold, Chesterfield, Derbyshire S41 8EH (0246-271519).

The Margaret Harrison Trust

Eligibility: "Gentlewomen of good character" aged 50 or over who have lived within a 15 mile radius of St Giles Parish Church, Matlock for at least five years.

Types of grants: Pensions.

Annual grant total: The trust had an income of £2,700 in 1989.

Applications: In writing to the correspondent.

Correspondent: Ian Duff, Heny, Loveday & Keighley, Bank Road, Matlock, Derbyshire DE4 3AQ (0629-583142).

The Municipal Charities of Chesterfield

Eligibility: Firstly, elderly and poor people who were born or live in Hasland; then, respectable widows and elderly spinsters in Chesterfield.

Types of grants: One-off grants and regular payments to seven people of about £100 twice a year. These beneficiaries have remained the same for a number of years, but the charity is able to support new applicants.

Annual grant total: £1,400 to £2,000.

Applications: In writing to the correspondent.

Correspondent: D Dolman, Solicitor, 23 West Bars, Chesterfield, Derbyshire S40 1AB (0246-232140).

The Arthur Townrow Pensions Fund

Eligibility: Unmarried women who are in need, of good character and are members of the Church of England or of a Protestant dissenting church that acknowledges the doctrine of the Holy Trinity.

Types of grants: Regular allowances of between £25 and £260 a year. One half of the pensions granted must be paid to women living in Chesterfield, Bolsover and North East Derbyshire. The remaining grants may be paid anywhere in England but only to people over 40. Allowances will not be made to those with an income greater than £3,865 a year.

Annual grant total: £70,000 in about 350 grants.

Applications: In writing to the correspondent.

Correspondent: P I King, Secretary, 24 Gluman Gate, Chesterfield, Derbyshire S40 1UA (0246-208081).

Other information: This entry is repeated in the National and general section of the book.

The Woodthorpe Relief-in-Need Charity

Eligibility: People in need who live in the ancient parishes of Barlborough, Staveley and Unstone.

Types of grants: One-off grants for fuel, washing machines, furnishings etc..

Annual grant total: In 1993, the trust had an income of £2,000. Nearly £1,800 was given in 42 grants of £25 to £50.

Applications: In writing to the correspondent, or contact The Rector of the Parish of Staveley. Applications are considered monthly.

Correspondent: Rev W A Butt, Chairman, 1 Eckington Road, Chesterfield S43 3XZ.

Alfreton

The Alfreton Welfare Trust

Eligibility: People in need who live in the former urban district of Alfreton (ie. the parishes of Alfreton, Ironville, Leabrooks, Riddings, Somercotes and Swanwick).

Types of grants: Grants have included travel expenses to hospital; provision of necessary household items and installation costs; recuperative holidays; relief of sudden distress (eg. theft of pension or purse); telephone installation, and outstanding bills. Support is also given to disabled people (including helping to buy wheelchairs etc.).

Grants are not given to organisations or for educational purposes.

Annual grant total: In 1993, the trust had assets of £15,000 and an income of £2,150. £1,200 was given in 25 grants ranging from £20 to £60.

Applications: In writing to the correspondent directly by the individual. Considered throughout the year.

Correspondent: Mrs U Vessey, Clerk, The Vicarage, Broadway, Swanwick, Derbyshire DE55 1DQ (0773-602684).

Clay Cross

The Eliza Ann Cresswell Memorial

Eligibility: People in any kind of need who live in the former urban district of Clay Cross (now the civil parish of Clay Cross), particularly needy families with young children.

Types of grants: Usually one-off grants in whole or part payment of a particular need eg. heating costs; housing; debts; replacement of bedding and damaged furniture; removal costs; and holidays. The trust does not give cash directly to applicants nor does it usually pay the full amount of a debt unless any repayment is beyond the individual's means.

Annual grant total: In 1992/93, grants totalling £1,875 were made to 16 individuals.

Applications: Grants are given on the recommendation of social workers, health visitors, probation officers, home nurses, doctors, clergy and welfare organisations (eg. citizen's advice bureau), and are paid through these bodies. A description of the person's financial position, the gaps in statutory provision, what contribution the applicant can make towards the need and what help can be given to prevent the need for future applications should be included. Applications are considered throughout the year.

Correspondent: Dr J Hammerton, Correspondent Trustee, Elm Tree, Handley, Clay Cross, Chesterfield S45 9AT (0246-862563).

Derbyshire/Hereford & Worcester

Derby

The Lavender's Charity

Eligibility: People in need who are aged and sick and live in the city of Derby.

Types of grants: One-off grants of £50 to £100 for heating, bedding, clothing etc..

Annual grant total: About £1,000.

Applications: In writing to the correspondent.

Correspondent: The City Secretary, Derby City Council, The Council House, Corporation Street, Derby DE1 2FS (0332-255464).

The Liversage Trust

Eligibility: People in need who live in the city of Derby.

Types of grants: One-off Christmas grants and cash payments for necessities.

Annual grant total: In 1992/93, individual grants of up to £100 totalled about £15,000.

Applications: Applications, on a form available from the correspondent, can be submitted by the individual or through a recognised referral agency (eg. social worker, citizen's advice bureau or doctor), and are considered throughout the year.

Correspondent: R Pike, Clerk, The Board Room, London Road, Derby DE1 2QW (0332-348155).

Glossop

The Mary Ellen Allen Charity

Eligibility: People over 60 who are in need and have lived in the former borough of Glossop (as it was in 1947) for at least five years.

Types of grants: One-off grants for necessities, holidays and comforts.

Annual grant total: About £5,000.

Applications: In writing to the correspondent.

Correspondent: G Jones, 63 Macclesfield Road, Buxton, Derbyshire SK17 9AG (0298-23687).

Ilkeston

The Old Park Ward Age Pensioners Fund

Eligibility: People over 65 who are in need and who live in the Old Park ward of the former borough of Ilkeston.

Types of grants: One-off cash grants, usually £5, at Christmas.

Annual grant total: Over £2,000 in 450 grants in 1993.

Applications: Applicants are required to supply address and date of birth. A register is kept of applicants. Beneficiaries are issued cards which must be presented to enable a grant to be claimed. Applications are considered from January to November.

Correspondent: Miss J Ellson, 16 Chaucer Street, Ilkeston, Derbyshire DE7 5JJ (0602-325053).

Matlock

The Ernest Bailey Charity

Eligibility: People in need who live in Matlock (this includes Darley Dale, Tansley, Matlock Bath and Cromford).

Types of grants: Awarded annually in October. Most applications have been from local groups but applications are sometimes considered from individuals. Each application is considered on its merits.

Annual grant total: No information available.

Applications: On a form available by writing to the correspondent.

Correspondent: The Trustees of the Ernest Bailey Charity, c/o D Wheatcroft, Chief Executive & Treasurer, Derbyshire Dales District Council, Town Hall, Matlock, Derbyshire DE4 3NN (0629-580580).

Sawley

The Sawley Charities

Eligibility: Pensioners who have lived in Sawley for five years or more.

Types of grants: Help with electricity bills in the form of account credits ranging from £6 to £8.

Annual grant total: About £2,800 in 335 grants.

Applications: On a form available from the correspondent to be considered in September.

Correspondent: Mrs Mary Perry, Secretary, 12 Shirley Street, Sawley, Long Eaton, Nottingham NG10 3BN (0602-733963).

Spondon

The Spondon Relief-in-Need Charity

Eligibility: People in need, hardship or distress, who live in Spondon.

Types of grants: The charity itemised its grants for 1993 in a very clear and concise way as follows:

(a) 14 grants via Derbyshire County Council Social Services averaging £209, including grants for mentally and physically disabled people and young mothers, and towards house repairs, washing machine, holidays, baby equipment, carpets, fuel bills, medical equipment, bedding and redecorating. These grants totalled £2,900.

(b) 2 grants via Spondon schools averaging £248, including grants for equipment for children with special needs and for children to attend summer camp. Grants totalled £500 plus an additional £340 float for small items.

(c) 29 grants via direct request for miscellaneous items, many similar to (a). Grants totalled £4,300; average £148.

(d) 108 small grants for Christmas goodwill for families with children and for old people. Grants totalled £2,400; average £22.

Annual grant total: £10,430.

Applications: In writing to the correspondent. Applications must be endorsed by a social worker, doctor, city councillor, clergyman, probation officer, health authority official or headteacher. Trustees meet in February, April, June, September and November.

Correspondent: David A Oddie, Secretary/Treasurer, 37 Huntley Avenue, Spondon, Derby DE21 7DW (0332-662048).

Hereford & Worcester

The Worcestershire Cancer Aid Committee

Eligibility: People with cancer who live in the old county of South Worcestershire.

Types of grants: Grants to help with heating, travel, holidays, extra food and bedding and anything that may help in the nursing and care of the patient. The trust also helps to buy equipment.

No grants towards funeral costs or the installation of a telephone.

Hereford & Worcester

Annual grant total: About £12,000; nearly all this was given in grants to individuals.

Applications: Through doctors, district nurses, health and social workers. Applications are considered every month.

Correspondent: Mrs Catherine Joan Taylor, Hon. Secretary, Glenbeck, Marlbank Road, Welland, Nr Malvern, Worcestershire WR13 6NE (0684-310760).

Hereford

The Hereford Municipal Charities

Eligibility: People in need who live in the city of Hereford.

Types of grants: One-off grants generally of £50 to £100, but up to a maximum of £150.

Annual grant total: In 1993, the trust gave about 175 people grants totalling about £15,000.

Applications: On a form available from the correspondent to be submitted directly by the individual or through a social worker, citizen's advice bureau or other welfare agency. Applications are considered throughout the year, about 15 people receive grants each month.

Correspondent: The Clerk, 145a St Owen Street, Hereford HR1 2JR (0432-354002).

The Hereford Open House Charity Dart League

Eligibility: People who are sick or mentally/physically disabled and who live in the city of Hereford.

Types of grants: One-off and recurrent grants in the form of purchased goods only (not cash) eg. a computer to aid a disabled child with their education. Requests for help towards heating/telephone bills, are not considered.

Annual grant total: In 1992/93, the trust had an income of £2,500. Total expenditure was £3,500. Items costing between £50 and £300 were bought for 5 individuals and totalled £1,600.

Applications: Applications can be submitted directly by the individual, or through a recognised referral agency (eg. social worker, citizen's advice bureau or doctor) and are considered throughout the year.

Correspondent: Keith Scott, 9 Oban Way, Newton Farm Estate, Hereford HR2 7EZ (0432-357303).

The United Charity of All Saints (Relief-in-Need Branch)

Eligibility: People in need who live in the city of Hereford.

Types of grants: One-off grants according to need.

Annual grant total: In 1992/93, the trust had assets of £137,000 and an income of £12,000. Expenditure totalled £4,100 including £1,500 in 16 grants to individuals.

Applications: In writing to the correspondent, either directly by the individual, through a social worker or other welfare agency or a third party. Applications are considered in March, June, September and November.

Correspondent: Gordon J Witts, Clerk, 2 Queenswood Drive, Tupsley, Hereford HR1 1AT (0432-358075).

Kington

The Kington United Charities

Eligibility: People in need who live in Kington.

Types of grants: One-off or recurrent grants according to need.

Annual grant total: In 1992/93, the trust had an income of £3,600. Grants to individuals in need totalled £875.

Applications: In writing to the correspondent.

Correspondent: P R Lambert, Clerk, 32 Duke Street, Kington, Hereford & Worcester HR5 3BW (0544-230325).

Malvern

The Baron Davenport Emergency Fund

Eligibility: Needy widows, spinsters and children under 21 whose fathers are dead, who live in and around Malvern. Applicants must have been living within the old county boundaries of Warwickshire, Worcestershire or Staffordshire for 10 years.

Types of grants: One-off grants (£100 to £250) for emergencies only. Grants have been given towards house repairs, rewiring and funeral expenses, only when state benefit is not available.

Annual grant total: About £2,000.

Applications: On a form available from the correspondent. Applications are usually made through a social worker or other welfare agency. They are considered throughout the year.

Correspondent: The Co-ordinator, Malvern Hills Council of Community Service, Library Buildings, 44 Graham Road, Malvern WR14 2HU (0684-563872).

Other information: For information on Baron Davenport's Charity Trust, see entry in the Midlands general section.

Pershore

The Henry Smith Charity

Eligibility: Elderly people in need who live in Pershore. Priority to elderly and needy people who have lived in the town for several years.

Types of grants: Recurrent and occasional one-off grants to help with heating costs at Christmas.

Annual grant total: In 1992, the trust was allocated £2,750 by Henry Smith's (General Estate) Charity.

Applications: In writing to the correspondent.

Correspondent: M Talbot-Smith, Fairlawns, School Lane, Wick, Pershore, Worcester WR10 3PD (0386-553416).

Redditch

The Baron Davenport Emergency Grant

Eligibility: Needy widows, spinsters and children under 21 whose fathers are dead, who have lived in Redditch for at least 10 years.

Types of grants: One-off grants for emergencies only.

Annual grant total: Probably about £1,000.

Applications: Via social services, citizen's advice bureaux, education departments and other welfare agencies, using the application form available. Applications are considered throughout the year.

Correspondent: Redditch Council for Voluntary Service, Room 1, Ecumenical Centre, 6 Evesham Walk, Redditch B97 4EX (0527-68403/62156).

Other information: For information on Baron Davenport's Charity Trust, see entry in the Midlands general section.

Hereford & Worcester

● Tenbury Wells

The Godson's Charity

Eligibility: People in need who wish to emigrate and who currently live in the London borough of Greenwich; Tenbury Wells in Hereford and Worcester and Shinfield in Berkshire. The majority of applications are received from Greenwich.

Types of grants: One-off grants up to £1,000 for those in need and wishing to emigrate (especially where the applicant has a new job to go to).

Annual grant total: Two grants totalling £1,500 were given in 1992. (The total expenditure of the trust was £3,500.) The trust has assets of £80,000, generating an income of £6,500.

Applications: Directly by the individual on a form available from the correspondent. Details of the proposed destination, occupation, and financial circumstances must be given. Applications are considered as they are received.

Correspondent: Anne Gregory, c/o Teredo Petroleum plc, 13-14 Hanover Street, London W1R 9HG (071-495 5916).

Other information: This entry is repeated in the South East and London sections of the book.

● Worcester

Armchair

Eligibility: People in need who live in Worcester.

Types of grants: The charity provides furniture rather than cash. Electrical goods and bedding are not given.

Annual grant total: In 1990/91, the trust had an income of £23,000 according to the Charity Commission.

Applications: In writing to the correspondent.

Correspondent: Mrs V M Gammon, Chairperson, Hereford & Worcester County Council, Area Office County Buildings, St Marys Street, Worcester WR1 2JQ (0905-765617).

The Mary Hill Trust

Eligibility: People in need who live in Worcester and its immediate surroundings.

Types of grants: One-off grants according to need.

Annual grant total: In 1992, the trust had an income of £7,700; £4,300 was given to individuals.

Applications: In writing to the correspondent.

Correspondent: A G Duncan, Clerk, 16 The Tything, Worcester, Hereford & Worcester WR1 1HD (0905-20361).

The Charity known as the Mayors Fund

Eligibility: People in need who live in the Worcester city boundary.

Types of grants: Usually one-off grants of between £30 and £80.

Annual grant total: About £1,500 in 50 grants in 1991.

Applications: On a form available from the correspondent.

Correspondent: Stephen Taylor, Clerk, The Guildhall, Worcester WR1 2EY (0905-723471).

The Shewringe's Hospital & Robert Goulding's Charities

Eligibility: People in need who live in the city of Worcester.

Types of grants: Mainly recurrent grants to organisations and assistance to individuals by means of a voucher scheme.

Annual grant total: About £8,500 in 35 grants.

Applications: In writing to the correspondent by mid-February.

Correspondent: D M Alexander, 8 Sansome Walk, Worcester WR1 1LW.

The Henry Smith Charity

Eligibility: People in need who live in St John Bedwardine. Priority to elderly and needy people who have lived in the town for several years.

Types of grants: Recurrent and occasional one-off grants.

Annual grant total: About £1,000.

Applications: In writing to the correspondent.

Correspondent: Rev C Pullin, St John's Vicarage, 143 Malvern Road, Worcester WR2 4LN.

The United Charity of Saint Martin

Eligibility: People in need who live in the parish of St Martin, Worcester.

Types of grants: One-off grants only.

Annual grant total: About £3,000.

Applications: Contact the vicar of the church at St Martin.

Correspondent: D R Harrison, 5 Deans Way, Worcester WR1 2JG (0905-612001).

Other information: The correspondent should not be contacted for applications.

The Henry & James Willis Trust

Eligibility: People who are convalescing and who live in the city of Worcester.

Types of grants: One-off grants for up to six weeks at the seaside or a health resort.

Annual grant total: About £5,000 in about 40 grants.

Applications: On a form obtainable from the correspondent. Applications can be submitted directly by the individual and are considered throughout the year. They should include a medical certificate.

Correspondent: John Wagstaff, 26–28 Sansome Walk, Worcester WR1 1LY (0905-25771).

The Worcester Consolidated Municipal Charity

Eligibility: People in need who live in Worcester.

Types of grants: One-off and recurrent grants according to need.

Annual grant total: About £100,000 given in about 300 grants to organisations and individuals for relief-in-need.

Applications: On a form available from the correspondent.

Correspondent: H E Wagstaffe, Clerk, Russell & Hallmark, 3-5 Sansome Place, Worcester, WR1 1UQ (0905-726600).

● Wolverley & Cookley

The Wolverley & Cookley Anne A Mitchell Fund

Eligibility: People in need who are sick or infirm and live in the parish of Wolverley and Cookley.

Types of grants: Probably one-off and recurrent grants according to need.

Annual grant total: In 1992/93, the trust had an income of £9,000. £800 was given in grants to individuals in need.

Applications: In writing to the correspondent.

Correspondent: A J Cowles, Secretary, 9 Fairfield Lane, Wolverley, Kidderminster, Hereford & Worcester DY11 5QH (0562-850725).

Leicestershire

The Ashby-de-la-Zouch Relief-in-Sickness Fund

Eligibility: People in need who live in Ashby-de-la-Zouch and Blackfordby.

Types of grants: One-off grants ranging from £20 to £500 in 1990/91. Grants have included help with transport to hospital, buying a nebuliser for a child, and the cost of a wheelchair.

Annual grant total: £1,100 in 26 grants in 1990/91.

Applications: In writing to the correspondent at any time.

Correspondent: The Secretary, c/o Messrs Crane & Walton, 30 South Street, Ashby-de-la-Zouch, Leicestershire LE5 5BT (0530-414111).

The John Heggs Bates' Charity for Convalescents

Eligibility: People who are convalescing with a preference for those living in Leicestershire.

Types of grants: One-off grants of about £200.

Annual grant total: 36 grants of around £200, totalling £8,000.

Applications: Applications should be through a doctor or a church and are considered each month.

Correspondent: The Clerk, 4-6 New Street, Leicester LE1 5NR (0533-512300).

The J Reginald Corah Foundation Fund

Eligibility: People in need, especially elderly people or employees or former employees of hosiery firms carrying on business in Leicestershire.

Types of grants: Probably one-off and recurrent grants according to need.

Annual grant total: In 1986/87, the trust gave £500 to elderly people and £3,500 to people formerly employed in the hosiery trade (the latter being paid through the Leicester Charity Organisation Society). No more recent information available.

Applications: In writing to the correspondent.

Correspondent: June Harris, Corah plc, PO Box 32, St Johns Street, Leicester LE1 9BB (0533-620811).

The Leslie Corah Memorial Trust

Eligibility: Members of the English working class who are in need.

Types of grants: Probably one-off and recurrent grants according to need.

Annual grant total: £2,200 was given in Christmas parcels in 1982/83, the most recent year for which information is available.

Applications: In writing to the correspondent.

Correspondent: June Harris, Corah plc, PO Box 32, St Johns Street, Leicester LE1 9BB (0533-620811).

Miss Herrick's Annuity Fund & the Herrick Fund for Widows & Single Women Afflicted with Incurable Diseases

Eligibility: In general, people in need who live in Leicestershire.

Specifically for Miss Herrick's Annuity: women members of the Church of England, especially "ladies over 50 years of age who are widows, daughters or sisters of clergymen or of officers in the armed service of the Crown or of professional men or gentlemen"; for the Herrick Fund, widows or single women aged 30 or over who have incurable diseases (except blindness, deafness or insanity).

Types of grants: One-off and recurrent grants according to need. The trust has been giving two grants of about £100 each.

Annual grant total: The combined income was about £800 in 1991.

Applications: In writing to the correspondent.

Correspondent: J Fox-Russell, Clerk, c/o 20 Churchgate, Loughborough LE11 1UD (0509-650572).

The Leicester Charity Organisation

Eligibility: People in need who live in the city of Leicester and the vicinity, which may include the whole of Leicestershire.

Types of grants: One-off grants and occasionally recurrent grants or pensions. The society makes payments from its own funds, administers funds on behalf of other charities, and puts potential beneficiaries into contact with funds and charities which may be able to help. A very wide range of grants is considered from small immediate payments, for example, for food, to larger payments of, for example, £6,500 for a special computer for a handicapped man.

Annual grant total: In 1993, the trust gave nearly 4,200 grants of £100 to £500 totalling £601,000, but not all were for individuals in need.

Applications: Generally through a social worker, health visitor, doctor or welfare agency on an application form.

Correspondent: M A Marvell, Director, 18 Friar Lane, Leicester LE1 5RA (0533-516229).

The Leicester Freemen's Estate

Eligibility: Needy freemen of Leicester and their widows, living in Leicestershire.

Types of grants: Generally one-off grants.

Annual grant total: In 1991, the trust had assets of £1.3 million generating an income of £145,000. Expenditure for the year totalled £74,000, of which £10,000 was given to 41 individuals.

Applications: On a form available from the correspondent. Applications can be submitted directly by the individual and are considered throughout the year.

Correspondent: Mrs I M Spencer, 32 Freemen's Holt, Old Church Street, Aylestone, Leicester LE2 8NH (0533-834017 on Wednesdays and Thursdays between 11am and 2pm).

Other information: The trust also provides accommodation for needy freemen and their widows. Applications should be made to the above address.

The Leicestershire County Nursing Association

Eligibility: Retired district nurses and people who are sick and in need, who live in Leicestershire.

Types of grants: One-off grants ranging from £5 to £550.

Annual grant total: In 1990/91, the trust had an income of £32,500 and expenditure of £25,000. 148 relief-in-need grants to individuals totalled £24,000.

Applications: In writing to the correspondent, directly by the individual in the case of retired district nurses or through Leicester Charity Organisation Society (see separate entry) in other cases. Applications are considered in October and February.

Correspondent: M J Cufflin, Secretary, 19 The Crescent, King Street, Leicester LE1 6RX (0533-541344).

Leicestershire

The Loughborough Welfare Trusts

Eligibility: People in need who live in Loughborough and Hathern.

Types of grants: One-off and recurrent grants according to need.

Annual grant total: About £5,800 given in grants to individuals for relief-in-need and education.

Applications: In writing to the correspondent.

Correspondent: John Fox-Russell, Bird, Wilford & Sale, Solicitors, 20 Churchgate, Loughborough LE11 1UD (0509-650572).

Other information: Since the last edition of this guide this trust has taken over the administration of Miss Herrick's Annuity Fund, the Herrick Fund, the Reg Burton Fund and the Loughborough Community Chest.

The Thomas Stanley Shipman Charitable Trust

Eligibility: People in need who live in Leicestershire.

Types of grants: One-off and recurrent grants according to need.

Annual grant total: In 1992/93, the trust had assets of over £1 million with an income of £79,000. Relief-in-need grants to individuals totalled £64,000.

Applications: In writing to the correspondent, directly by the individual. Applications are considered in April, July, October and December.

Correspondent: A R York, 18 Friar Lane, Leicester LE1 5RA (0533-516229).

● Brooke

Brooke Poor's Land

Eligibility: People in need who live in the parish of Brooke and adjoining parishes.

Types of grants: One-off grants.

Annual grant total: In 1992, the trust had an income of £7,600. It is not known how much was given in grants to individuals in need.

Applications: In writing to the correspondent. Applications can be submitted directly by the individual or through a social worker, citizen's advice bureau or other welfare agency. They are considered at any time.

Correspondent: The Chairman, c/o Priory Farm, Brooke, Oakham, Leics LE15 8DE.

● Leicester

The Leicester Aid-in-Sickness Fund

Eligibility: Sick, poor people who live in the city of Leicester.

Types of grants: Almost entirely one-off grants ranging from £5 to £50.

Annual grant total: In 1992/93, the trust had assets of £155,000 with an income of £18,000. Expenditure totalled £11,000 including £9,000 in relief-in-need grants.

Applications: Leicester Charity Organisation (see separate entry) acts as agent of the trustees for the purpose of considering and administering grants. Applications are considered continually.

Correspondent: R P Harris, Clerk, 23 Friar Lane, Leicester LE1 5QQ (0533-530851).

The Leicester Indigent Old Age Society

Eligibility: Elderly people, 65 or over, in need who live in the city of Leicester.

Types of grants: Pensions only of £80 a year, paid quarterly.

Annual grant total: In 1992, 10 relief-in-need grants totalled £800.

Applications: In writing to the correspondent, through a social worker or other welfare agency.

Correspondent: M A Marvell, 18 Friar Lane, Leicester LE1 5RA (0533-516229).

The Parish Piece Charity

Eligibility: People in need who are over 60 and live in the city of Leicester.

Types of grants: Pensions only.

Annual grant total: Over £4,000 in about 80 pensions.

Applications: In writing to the correspondent or via the Leicester Charity Organisation.

Correspondent: J E Adams, 25 Fernhurst Road, Braunstone, Leicester LE3 2PG (0533-897432).

The St Margaret's Select Vestry

Eligibility: People in need who live in the city of Leicester.

Types of grants: One-off and recurrent grants according to need.

Annual grant total: About £600 in 10 to 20 grants.

Applications: In writing to the correspondent or via the Leicester Charity Organisation.

Correspondent: J E Adams, Clerk, 25 Fernhurst Road, Braunstone, Leicester LE3 2PG (0533-897432).

The Edward Wood Bequest

Eligibility: Gentlewomen (either unmarried or widows) at least 55 years old who have lived in the area administered by Leicester City Council for at least 10 years, and who are members of a Protestant Non-Conformist Church.

Types of grants: Pensions only.

Annual grant total: About £1,000.

Applications: In writing to the correspondent.

Correspondent: M J Cufflin, Secretary, 19 The Crescent, King Street, Leicester LE1 6RX (0533-541344).

● Loughborough

The Reg Burton Fund

Eligibility: See below.

Types of grants: To enable assistants to travel with the disabled people of Loughborough on holiday.

Annual grant total: In 1993, £385 was given in grants. It was anticipated that this would rise above £500 in 1994.

Applications: In writing to the correspondent.

Correspondent: J Fox-Russell, c/o Bird & Wilford Solicitors, 20 Churchgate, Loughborough LE1 1UD (0509-650572).

● Market Harborough

The Market Harborough Town Estate & Bates Charity

Eligibility: People in need who live in the ecclesiastical parish of St Dionysius, Market Harborough.

Types of grants: Pensions and one-off grants.

Annual grant total: About £20,000, including grants to organisations.

Applications: In writing to the correspondent. Applications can be submitted directly by the individual or through a third party.

Correspondent: Miss Amanda E Carter, 51 High Street, Market Harborough, Leicestershire LE16 7AF (0858-467181).

Leicestershire/Lincolnshire

Markfield

The Jane Avery Charity

Eligibility: People in need who live in the parish of Markfield.

Types of grants: Normally one-off grants from £25 to £150. Grants have been given towards the cost of spectacles, cooker, refrigerator and groceries and repair of a washing machine. Expenses for visiting a patient in hospital have also been subsidised.

Annual grant total: In 1993, the trust's income was £700. Expenditure totalled £600 including nine relief-in-need grants.

Applications: In writing to the correspondent. Applications can be submitted directly by the individual or through a social worker, citizen's advice bureau or other welfare agency, or through a third party such as a doctor, minister, neighbour or relative. They can be considered at any time.

Correspondent: G T Willett, Secretary, The Rectory, The Nook, Markfield, Leicestershire LE67 9WE.

Mountsorrel

The Mountsorrel Relief-in-Need Charity

Eligibility: People in need who live in the parish of Mountsorrel.

Types of grants: Grants ranging from £25 to £2,000. They have been given towards invalid chairs, house repairs, essential domestic appliances, emergency telephones, travel costs (eg. for visiting hospitals, day centres etc.), nursing home fees, house decoration and gardening.

Annual grant total: In 1991, the trust had assets of £752,000 and an income of £37,000. Grants to individuals in need totalled £61,000 in 240 grants.

Applications: On a form available from the correspondent. Applications can be submitted directly by the individual or through a social worker, citizen's advice bureau, other welfare agency or family members. They are considered each month.

Correspondent: C Leafe, Clerk, 26 Nicolson Road, Loughborough, Leics LE11 3SD (0509-213563).

Shepshed

The Charity of John Lambert

Eligibility: People in need who live in Shepshed.

Types of grants: One-off grants only.

Annual grant total: £2,000 in 12 grants.

Applications: In writing to the correspondent either directly by the individual or through a social worker, citizen's advice bureau or other welfare agency. Applications are considered in March, June, September and December.

Correspondent: G S Freckelton, 1 Leicester Road, Loughborough, Leicestershire LE11 2AE.

Syston

The H A Taylor Fund

Eligibility: People in need who live in the parish of Syston.

Types of grants: Grants have been given to help with travel, furniture, clothing, fuel, medical treatment, books and fees, a vehicle for a disabled person, telephone and television costs, repairs and redecoration, and a loan to help with getting a job.

Annual grant total: About £15,000 in 66 grants in 1992/93.

Applications: In writing to the correspondent.

Correspondent: Andrew York, Clerk, Leicester Charity Organisation, 18 Friar Lane, Leicester LE1 5RA (0533-516229).

Wigston

The Elizabeth Clarke & Wigston Relief-in-Need Funds

Eligibility: People in need who live in Wigston Magna, Wigston Fields and South Wigston.

Types of grants: One-off grants towards winter/school clothing, safety alarm, special chair, wheelchair, orthopaedic footwear, travel costs for medical treatment, incontinence bedding, spectacles etc.. No grants for rent arrears, rent, community charge, gas/electric payments, on-going assistance of any kind or where trustees feel the need can be met in a better way or through other sources.

Annual grant total: Elizabeth Clarke Relief-in-Need Fund: 9 grants totalling £850 in 1992. Wigston Relief-in-Need Fund: 14 grants totalling £1,750 in 1993.

Applications: In writing to the correspondent, accompanied by a supporting letter from a social worker or other welfare agency if possible. Applications are considered in March, September and November, but exceptions can be made in emergencies.

Correspondent: The Clerk, Bushloe House, Station Road, Wigston, Leicestershire LE18 2DR (0533-888961).

Wymeswold

The Wymeswold Parochial Charities

Eligibility: People in need who live in Wymeswold.

Types of grants: One-off grants only.

Annual grant total: About £1,000.

Applications: In writing to the correspondent.

Correspondent: Mrs P Hubbard, 97 Brook Street, Wymeswold, Loughborough LE12 6TT (0509-880166).

Other information: According to the Charity Commission the address is correct, but the entry has not been confirmed by the trust.

Lincolnshire

The Farmers' Benevolent Institution

Eligibility: People living within a 15 mile radius of Grantham and "having been owners or occupiers of land, but who from losses or other untoward circumstances have become destitute."

Types of grants: Annual payments of £100 in July and a supplementary payment of £200 at Christmas.

Annual grant total: About £3,600 to 10 to 15 beneficiaries.

Applications: In writing to the correspondent.

Correspondent: The Secretary, c/o Duncan & Toplis, 3 Castlegate, Grantham, Lincolnshire NG31 6SF (0476-591200).

The Hesselwood Children's Trust (Hull Seamen's & General Orphanage)

Eligibility: People in need who live in the county of Humberside or North Lincoln.

Types of grants: One-off and recurrent grants according to need. Grants have been given for specified short periods of time at special schools, holiday funding for individuals and youth organisations in the UK and abroad, and for musical instruments and special equipment or alterations for disabled people.

Lincolnshire

Annual grant total: In 1993, the trust's income was £67,500. Grants totalled £64,000, but not all of this went to individuals.

Applications: In writing to the correspondent. Applications are considered in March, July, October and December.

Correspondent: J A Roberts, Secretary, Poplar Farm, Garton, Aldbrough, North Humberside HU11 4QB (0964-527898).

Other information: This entry is repeated in the Humberside section of the book.

Hunstone's Charity

Eligibility: People in need who live in Lincolnshire with preference for "Decayed gentlemen of the family of Edward Hunstone or of the several families of the Gedneys or of Robert Smith or of the Woodliffes and decayed gentlemen living in the county of Lincoln." Particular mention is also made of retired clergymen, members of HM Forces, farmers, farm labourers or anyone connected with land, and disabled people.

Types of grants: In 1992, 32 recipients received £200. This has now been increased to £250 a year, paid in two instalments of £125 in April and October. The assistance will be given as long as the trustees consider necessary or until the death of the recipient.

Annual grant total: In 1992, the trust had an income of £26,000. Grants to individuals totalled £6,400. There was a further £16,000 unallocated for the year.

Applications: On a form available from the correspondent. Applications are considered in May of each year, though can be considered at other times if urgent. Two references are required with each application.

Correspondent: W N Hubbert, Clerk, 143 Eastwood Road, Boston, Lincs PE21 0PW (0205-362781).

The Lincoln General Dispensary Fund

Eligibility: People in need who are sick, convalescent, disabled or infirm and who live in the district of Lincoln.

Types of grants: Grants to alleviate suffering or aid recovery "by providing or paying for items, services or facilities which are calculated to achieve this objective but are not readily available to them from other sources". Recent grants have been given for orthopaedic beds, alarm systems and recuperative holidays. Grants are also given to local organisations. No grants for funeral expenses, property improvements and no recurrent grants.

Annual grant total: In 1993, the trust had assets of £182,000 and an income of £15,000. Grants of £40 to £400 were given to 82 individuals in need totalling nearly £12,000.

Applications: Applications should be made through local social services, area health authority, organisations for the elderly, the church and other caring organisations. Guidance notes for completing the application are available from the correspondent. They are considered throughout the year.

Correspondent: John A Houghton, Secretary, 7 Sturton Road, Saxilby, Lincoln LN1 2PG (0522-702537).

The Lincolnshire Police Charitable Fund

Eligibility: Present and former employees of the Lincolnshire police authorities, their widows, widowers and dependants.

Types of grants: One-off grants and loans according to need.

Annual grant total: In 1990/91, loans totalling £15,000 were given to 21 people, and over £5,000 was given in other grants.

Applications: In writing to the correspondent through a police welfare office.

Correspondent: The Force Welfare Officer, Police Headquarters, PO Box 999, Lincoln LN5 7PH (0522-558015).

The Whitton Trust

Eligibility: People in need who live in Gainsborough and Lincoln.

Types of grants: Probably one-off and recurrent grants according to need.

Annual grant total: No information available.

Applications: In writing to the correspondent.

Correspondent: B Dickinson, Clerk, 5 Gainsborough Road, Blyton, Gainsborough DN21 3NB (0427-628352).

● **Addlethorpe**

The Addlethorpe Parochial Charity

Eligibility: People in need, and people who are sick, convalescing, disabled or infirm who live in the parish of Addlethorpe, or who previously lived in Addlethorpe and now live in an adjoining parish.

Types of grants: One-off and recurrent grants according to need. Most grants were in the form of solid fuel or electricity/gas cheques for £25 three times a year and food parcels at Christmas. Grants were also given for hospital or doctor's visits, funeral expenses, household repairs, clothing for a disabled child and other necessities. Grants range from £20 to £50.

Annual grant total: In 1992/93, the trust had an income of £5,000. Grants to 100 individuals in need totalled £4,800.

Applications: In writing to the correspondent, including details of length of residence in Addlethorpe and the applicant's income.

Correspondent: J Smedley, Secretary, Carinya, Church Lane, Addlethorpe, Skegness, Lincs PE24 4UN (0754-873940).

● **Bardney**

The Kitchings General Charity

Eligibility: People in need who live in the parish of Bardney and the surrounding area.

Types of grants: One-off grants towards holidays for disabled people (mostly at a special home at Sandringham), specialised nursing equipment and funeral expenses.

Annual grant total: In 1992, nine grants to individuals totalled £4,200, a further £9,000 was unallocated.

Applications: In writing to the correspondent. Applications should be submitted directly by the individual or through a third party such as the district nurse. They are considered in May, but urgent cases can be considered at other times.

Correspondent: Mrs J Smith, Secretary, 42 Abbey Road, Bardney, Lincoln LN3 5XA (0526-398505).

● **Dorrington**

The Dorrington Welfare Charity

Eligibility: People in need who live in the parish of Dorrington.

Types of grants: One-off grants only towards, for example, relieving sudden distress; travel expenses to visit family in hospital; heating and lighting costs in cases of real hardship; washing machines for widows with large families; radio or television sets for lonely or housebound people; adaptations to homes of disabled people; and relief of sickness or infirmity.

Lincolnshire

The trust also makes education grants to people under 25.

Annual grant total: £850 in 15 grants in 1992.

Applications: In writing to the correspondent or trustee, directly by the individual. Applications are considered throughout the year (trustees meet in February, July and November). Applications should include a general explanation of assistance required, an estimate of the expenses involved, details of any other assistance received or confirmation that no assistance has been or can be received from the DSS or any other public funds.

Correspondent: Mrs E M Tonge, 57 Main Street, Dorrington, Lincoln LN4 3PX (0526-832377).

Frampton

The Frampton United Charities

Eligibility: People in need over 65, and recently bereaved widows who have lived in the ancient parish of Frampton for at least five years.

Types of grants: Usually recurrent grants ranging from £30 to £135.

Annual grant total: In 1992/93, the trust had an income of £9,000. £5,800 was given in 123 relief-in-need and education grants to individuals.

Applications: In writing to the correspondent. Applications are considered in early October.

Correspondent: R F Barber, The Hollies, West End Road, Frampton, Boston, Lincolnshire PE20 1RG (0205-722746).

Friskney

The Friskney United Charities

Eligibility: People especially elderly people in need who live in Friskney.

Types of grants: About 20 elderly people receive 3 cwt of coal and £2.50 each in December. Other one-off grants are considered. The main purpose of the charity is the running of almshouses.

Annual grant total: In 1992, the trust had an income of £23,000. £500 was given in 20 grants to individuals.

Applications: In writing to the correspondent.

Correspondent: Mrs W J Smith, Secretary, Kentoo, Low Gate, Friskney, Boston, Lincolnshire PE22 8NJ (0754-820291).

Gainsborough

The Gainsborough Dispensary Charity

Eligibility: People in need who live in Gainsborough and Morton.

Types of grants: One-off or recurrent grants according to need.

Annual grant total: In 1993, the trust had an income of £5,800. £6,200 was given to individuals in need.

Applications: In writing to the correspondent.

Correspondent: B E Stonehouse, Clerk, 15 Chestnut Avenue, Gainsborough, Lincolnshire DN21 1EX (0427-613067).

Grantham

The Grantham Aid-in-Sickness Fund

Eligibility: People in need who live in the former borough of Grantham as constituted on 31st March 1974.

Types of grants: Vouchers ranging £5 to £12 to be spent in Greater Nottingham Co-operative Society or on groceries delivered to the door. Cash grants are only given for train or bus fares to visit ill relatives.

Annual grant total: In 1991, the trust's income was £2,800 and expenditure was £1,120. 90 relief-in-need grants totalled £800.

Applications: Trustees, doctors, clerics and other third parties on behalf of individuals apply to the secretary who visits the applicant and reports back to the trustees. Applications are considered in March, June, September and December.

Correspondent: Mrs Marion Adamson, Harlaxton Lodge, 7 Rectory Lane, Harlaxton, Grantham, Lincolnshire NG32 1HD (0476-61261).

Other information: The trust is in the process of handing over its assets to the Grantham Initiative for Terminally Ill.

Kesteven

The Kesteven Children in Need

Eligibility: Children/young people under 18 who live in the Kesteven area.

Types of grants: One-off and recurrent grants ranging from £30 to £70. Recent examples include grants towards clothing, educational holidays, days out, prams/pushchairs, beds/sheets, fireguard, secondhand washing machines, educational toys and playschool fees.

Annual grant total: In 1993, the trust had an income of £2,700. Grants of £10 to £250 were given to 32 individuals totalling £3,500.

Applications: Generally through local social workers, health visitors, teachers and education officers. Information should include the family situation, the age of the children and their special needs. Considered throughout the year.

Correspondent: Maxine Padley, Gaslights, Belton Lane, Great Gonekby, Grantham, Lincolnshire NG31 8NA.

Lincoln

The Lincoln Municipal Relief-in-Need Charities

Eligibility: People in need who live in the city of Lincoln.

Types of grants: One-off grants for all kinds of need except relief with rates, taxes or public funds.

Annual grant total: Grants totalling £12,000 given in relief-in-need and education grants.

Applications: In writing to the correspondent.

Correspondent: M G Bonass, Clerk, McKinnells Solicitors, 188 High Street, Lincoln LN5 7BE (0522-541181).

The Zachary Merton & George Woofindin Convalescent Trust

Eligibility: People in need who live in Sheffield and Lincoln.

Types of grants: Grants for convalescence only.

Annual grant total: About £40,000.

Applications: In writing to the correspondent by 31st March or 30th September.

Correspondent: M P W Lee, Clerk, Dibb Lupton & Broomhead Solicitors, Fountain Precinct, Balm Green, Sheffield S1 1RZ (0742-760351).

Other information: This entry is repeated in the South Yorkshire section of the book.

The Herbert William Sollitt Memorial Trust

Eligibility: Elderly or infirm people and widows or widowers who live in the city of Lincoln.

Lincolnshire

Types of grants: One-off grants of about £50.

Annual grant total: About £1,200 in 1993.

Applications: Applications to be sent to Social Services Section, The Care of The Elderly, Park Street, Lincoln.

Correspondent: Mrs J Smith, Secretary, 24 Sunfield Crescent, Birchwood, Lincoln LN6 0LL (0522-687434).

● Long Sutton

Long Sutton Consolidated Charity

Eligibility: Widows in need who live in the parish of Long Sutton and surrounding district.

Types of grants: One-off and recurrent grants according to need.

Annual grant total: In 1992, the trust had an income of £4,500, it is not known how much of this was given in grants to individuals.

Applications: In writing to the correspondent.

Correspondent: The Clerk, Messrs Mossop & Bowser, Long Sutton, Spalding, Lincs PE12 9JH (0406-363212).

● Moulton

The Moulton Poors' Lands Charity

Eligibility: People in need, generally the elderly, who live in the civil parish of Moulton.

Types of grants: One-off grants only.

Annual grant total: Over £2,000 in about 110 grants of about £20.

Applications: In writing to the correspondent.

Correspondent: R W Lewis, Maples & Son, 23 New Road, Spalding, Lincolnshire PE11 1DH (0775-722261).

● Spalding

The Spalding Relief-in-Need Charity

Eligibility: People in need who live in Spalding, Cowbit, Pinchbeck, Weston and Deeping St Nicholas.

Types of grants: One-off grants according to need.

Annual grant total: Acording to the Charity Commission, the trust had an income of £16,700 in 1992. It is not known how much was given in grants to individuals in need.

Applications: In writing to the correspondent. Applications can be submitted directly by the individual or through a social worker, citizen's advice bureau, other welfare agency or third party. They are considered at any time.

Correspondent: R A Knipe, Solicitor, 12 Broad Street, Spalding, Lincs PE11 1TB (0775-768774).

● Spilsby

The Spilsby Feoffees Charities

Eligibility: People in need who have lived in Spilsby for at least five years.

Types of grants: Grants currently of £9 to £17 a year. No grants to people living permanently in a nursing or rest home.

Annual grant total: £1,700 in 1991, to 98 people.

Applications: In writing to the correspondent. Applications can be submitted directly by the individual and are considered in June and December.

Correspondent: Mrs J Tong, Clerk, Brookfield Willoughly Drive, Spilsby, Lincolnshire PE23 5EX.

● Stamford

Winifrede Browne's Charity

Eligibility: People in need who live in Stamford.

Types of grants: One-off and recurrent grants according to need.

Annual grant total: In 1992, the trust had an income of £6,500. It is not known how much was given in grants to individuals in need.

Applications: In writing to the correspondent.

Correspondent: The Clerk to the Trustees, Messrs Stapleton & Son, 1 Broad Street, Stamford, Lincolnshire PE9 1PD (0780-51226).

● Stickford

The Stickford Relief-in-Need Charity

Eligibility: People in need who live in the parish of Stickford.

Types of grants: Annual Christmas grants of £30 to single people and £45 to couples. One-off grants are also given eg. for funeral expenses, holiday, utility connection, school clothing etc..

Annual grant total: In 1992, the trust had an income of £12,000. Expenditure totalled £6,400 including £2,200 in 28 grants to individuals.

Applications: In writing to the correspondent. Applications should be submitted directly by the individual and are considered all year.

Correspondent: D W Packham, Clerk, Green Roofs, Church Road, Stickford, Boston, Lincolnshire PE22 8EP (0205-480279).

● Surfleet

The Surfleet United Charities (Feoffees)

Eligibility: People in need over 60, who live in the ancient parish of Surfleet.

Types of grants: Normally grants before Christmas each year of £15 (individuals) and £25 (couples). Other one-off grants are given according to need.

Annual grant total: About £1,500 to about 90 applicants.

Applications: In writing to the correspondent. Applications can be submitted directly by the individual or through a third party. They are considered in November.

Correspondent: A L Munton, 76 Pinchbeck Road, Spalding, Lincolnshire PE11 1QF (0775-724407).

● Sutton St James

The Sutton St James United Charities

Eligibility: People in need who live in the parish of Sutton St James.

Types of grants: One-off and recurrent grants according to need, including bereavement grants.

Annual grant total: The charities have an income of about £8,000. This is divided between education and relief-in-need.

Applications: In writing to the correspondent.

Correspondent: K Savage, Clerk, Lenton House, 25 Albert Street, Holbeach, Lincolnshire PE12 7DR (0406-422161).

• Northamptonshire

Northamptonshire

Edmund Arnold's Charity (Poors Branch)

Eligibility: People in need who live in the parish of Nether Heyford, the ancient parish of St Giles in Northampton and the parish of Stony Stratford.

Types of grants: Probably one-off and recurrent grants according to need.

Annual grant total: About £1,260.

Applications: In writing to the correspondent.

Correspondent: Gordon Gee, Clerk, Wilson Browne, Solicitors, 60 Gold Street, Northampton NN1 1RS (0604-28131).

The Valentine Goodman Estate Charity

Eligibility: People in need who live in the parishes of Blaston, Bringhurst, Drayton, East Magna, Hallaton and Medbourne.

Types of grants: One-off or recurrent grants according to need.

Annual grant total: In 1991, the trust had an income of £6,000. It is not known how much was given in grants to individuals in need.

Applications: In writing to the correspondent.

Correspondent: Norman Paske, Secretary, Samuel Rose, The Lodge, Brixworth, Northampton NN6 9BX (0604-882255).

The Northampton Municipal Church Charities

Eligibility: People in need who live in the borough of Northampton.

Types of grants: Cash grants usually not exceeding £225 in any one year.

Annual grant total: In 1992/93, the trust gave £16,000 in annual grants to individuals and £2,200 in Christmas grants. Its income was £92,000, total expenditure was £42,000 leaving a surplus of £50,000. There appears to have been a fairly consistent surplus of income over expenditure in recent years.

Applications: In writing to the correspondent.

Correspondent: Wilson Browne, Solicitors (Ref WGG), 60 Gold Street, Northampton NN1 1RS (0604-28131).

Other information: The charity runs a sheltered housing scheme at St Thomas House in St Giles Street, Northampton. It is warden controlled and has 17 one-bedroomed flats for people over 60. For further information, contact the correspondent.

The Northamptonshire Medical Charity

Eligibility: People in need who have served as medical practitioners in the borough/county of Northampton, or their dependants. Medical charities are also supported.

Types of grants: One-off and recurrent grants according to need.

Annual grant total: In 1992, the trust had an income of £12,500. Grants to five individuals totalled £5,000.

Applications: In writing to the correspondent.

Correspondent: Dr R G Daniels, Secretary, 429 Wellingborough Road, Northampton NN1 4EZ (0604-31256).

Sir Thomas White's Loan Fund

Eligibility: Young men and women aged over 21 years and up to 34 years of age who live in the extended borough of Northampton.

Types of grants: Nine-year interest-free loans for education and new businesses (and household expenses for newly-married couples). The fund was originally set up for the provision of tools for people setting up in a trade or profession.

Annual grant total: About 150 loans of about £800, totalling about £100,000.

Applications: On a form available from 1st December each year following a public notice appearing on the last day of November.

Correspondent: Mrs Duberry, Hewitson, Becke & Shaw, 7 Spencer Parade, Northampton NN1 5AB.

Other information: The fund is administered by the trustees of the Northampton Municipal General Charities.

The Yelvertoft & District Relief in Sickness Fund

Eligibility: People in need who live in the parishes of Yelvertoft, West Haddon, Crick, Winwick, Clay Coton, Elkington and Lilbourne who are sick, convalescent, disabled or infirm.

Types of grants: One-off and recurrent grants according to need. In the past grants have been given to help with hospital visiting and convalescence, and towards treatment costs through the chiropody service. In addition, local visiting nurses have been given equipment to help them in their work and a wheelchair is available on loan.

Annual grant total: In 1992, the trust had an income of £4,800. Grants totalled £3,000.

Applications: In writing to the correspondent. Applications should be submitted directly by the individual or by a close relative or village representative. Each village has appointed a representative and he/she will pass on all requests for help to the trustees in writing. They are considered at any time.

Correspondent: Mrs Anne Drewett, Secretary, The Cottages, West Haddon, Northampton NN6 7AD (0788-510278).

• **Blakesley**

The Blakesley Parochial Charities

Eligibility: People in need who live in Blakesley.

Types of grants: One-off and recurrent grants according to need.

Annual grant total: £2,000 in 1986/87 which was given as follows: £425 to widows; £720 to students; £60 in Christmas gifts; £800 in Christmas grants.

Applications: In writing to the correspondent.

Correspondent: J Curedale, The Walnuts, Blakesley, Towcester, Northants NN12.

Other information: This entry has not been confirmed by the trust, but the address is correct according to the Charity Commission.

• **Brackley**

The Brackley United Feoffee Charity

Eligibility: People in need who live in Brackley.

Types of grants: One-off grants which have helped with buying children's shoes, a washing machine and the provision of supplementary heating. No grants for the relief of rates, taxes etc. but the trust may supplement statutory provision. In 1993, the trust also gave 60 Christmas grants of £15.

Annual grant total: £1,300 in 1991.

Applications: In writing to the correspondent, preferably by the individual. The correspondent states: "When in doubt apply - funds are usually

Northamptonshire

available. Almost any reasonable case succeeds."

Correspondent: Mrs R Hedges, 7 Easthill Close, Brackley, Northants NN13 7BS (0280-702420).

● Braunston

The Braunston Town Lands Charity

Eligibility: People in need who live in Braunston and spend four nights in a hospital.

Types of grants: One-off and recurrent grants. £10 grants for people in local hospitals and £20 to £25 for those further afield. Three widows over 90 years of age receive £25 at Christmas and needy couples £10 to £15. Everybody in hospital or housebound is given a Christmas gift.

Annual grant total: Over £1,000 including £400 in Christmas gifts and £700 in about 80 hospital and housebound grants (plus about £2,300 to local organisations).

Applications: In writing to the correspondent.

Correspondent: Mrs D V Knibbs, 39 Church Road, Braunston, Daventry, Northants NN11 7HG (0788-891008).

● Brington

The Brington Chauntry Estate

Eligibility: People in need who live in the parish of Brington.

Types of grants: One-off and recurrent grants according to need. Paid quarterly, as stated on the parish notice board.

Annual grant total: About £7,000, most of which goes to individuals.

Applications: In writing to "The Clerk". at the address obtained below.

Correspondent: The address is stated on the parish notice board.(Please telephone 0604-770839.)

● Byfield

The Byfield Poors' Allotment

Eligibility: People in need who live in the parish of Byfield.

Types of grants: One-off grants towards fuel payments, buying emergency medi-alarms and specialist medical equipment, transport costs to hospital etc.. Gifts in kind are also given.

Annual grant total: In 1993, the trust had an income of £1,000. Grants ranging from £5 to £20 were given to 51 individuals and totalled £1,500.

Applications: In writing to the correspondent. Applications can be made directly by the individual, through a social worker, citizen's advice bureau, medical centre or other welfare agency or third party such as a relative or neighbour.

Correspondent: Mrs J L Hicks, 1 Edwards Close, Byfield, Daventry, Northants NN11 6XP (0327-61257).

● Chipping Warden

The Reverend W Smart's Charity

Eligibility: People in need who live in the parish of Chipping Warden.

Types of grants: One-off and recurrent grants according to need. Grants can be given to individuals or organisations.

Annual grant total: Generally about £1,000 is given to individuals. In 1993, about £4,000 was given to local churches.

Applications: In writing to the correspondent.

Correspondent: P J Houghton-Brown, Manor Farm, Chipping Warden, Banbury, Oxfordshire OX17 1LH (0295-660238).

● Daventry

The Daventry Consolidated Charity

Eligibility: People in need who live in Daventry.

Types of grants: One-off or recurrent grants according to need.

Annual grant total: About £6,000.

Applications: In writing to the correspondent. Trustees meet twice a year in April and October, but urgent applications can be considered at other times.

Correspondent: A W Tooby, 109 St Augustin Way, Daventry NN11 4EG (0327-71684).

● Desborough

The Town Welfare Committee

Eligibility: People in need who live in Desborough.

Types of grants: One-off and recurrent grants, paid mainly at Christmas.

Annual grant total: Over £1,000 in about 30 grants, plus £2,000 in Coop vouchers.

Applications: In writing to the correspondent.

Correspondent: Mrs A King, 190 Dunkirk Avenue, Desborough, Kettering, Northants NN14 2PP (0536-761872).

● Gayton

The Gayton Relief-in-Need Charity

Eligibility: People in need who live in the parish of Gayton.

Types of grants: Monthly pensions and electricity stamps for the elderly and grants towards funeral costs. Grants range from £5 to £100.

Annual grant total: In 1993, the trust had assets of £40,000 with an income of £4,000. Relief-in-need grants to individuals totalled £3,500.

Applications: In writing to the correspondent.

Correspondent: M J Percival, Clerk, Oxford House, Cliftonville, Northampton NN1 5PN (0604-230400).

● Harpole

The Harpole Parochial Charities

Eligibility: People in need who live in Harpole, with a preference for those over 60.

Types of grants: One-off grants only ranging from £10 to £25.

Annual grant total: Over £1,000 in 90 grants.

Applications: On a form available from the correspondent. Applications can be submitted at any time, but are considered in November.

Correspondent: J Calderwood, 39 Upper High Street, Harpole, Northampton NN7 4DJ.

● Kettering

The Kettering Charities for the Poor

Eligibility: Single/widowed pensioners in need who live in the area of the former borough of Kettering.

Types of grants: Christmas grants of £6.50 to help with fuel costs; usually recurrent.

Northamptonshire

Annual grant total: About £7,000 in about 1,000 grants.

Applications: On a form available from the correspondent which can be obtained after the charity is advertised in local newspapers in November each year. Grants are decided by February/March.

Correspondent: The Chief Executive, Kettering Borough Council, Municipal Offices, Bowling Green Road, Kettering NN15 7QX (0536-410333).

The Stockburn Memorial Trust

Eligibility: Sick poor people who live in the town of Kettering.

Types of grants: One-off and recurrent grants towards heating and medical comforts usually for about £70.

Annual grant total: In 1992, the trust had an income of £5,350 and expenditure of £3,000. This included £2,750 in 39 relief-in-need grants to individuals.

Applications: In writing to the correspondent through a social worker, citizen's advice bureau or other welfare agency. Details should include age, financial situation and health circumstances of the applicant.

Correspondent: R Henman, Clerk, 60 Derwent Crescent, Kettering, Northants NN16 8UJ (0536-81387).

Litchborough

The Litchborough Parochial Charities

Eligibility: People in need who live in Litchborough.

Types of grants: One-off grants only.

Annual grant total: Over £1,000.

Applications: In writing to the correspondent.

Correspondent: A Harvey, The Briars, Farthingstone Road, Litchborough, Towcester, Northamptonshire NN12 8JE.

Other information: This is the most up to date information at the Charity Commission. The entry has not been confirmed by the trust.

Long Buckby

The Long Buckby United Charities

Eligibility: People in need who are over 70 and live in the parish of Long Buckby.

Types of grants: One-off grants at Christmas to all eligible people.

Annual grant total: The income of the trust is about £1,300. The trust has a policy of giving modest grants of £2 to around 360 individuals.

Applications: In writing to the correspondent. Applications should be submitted directly by the individual to be considered in November/December.

Correspondent: J H Williams, 115 East Street, Long Buckby, Northampton NN6 7RB (0327-842468).

Middleton Cheney

The Middleton Cheney United Charities

Eligibility: People in need under pension age who live in Middleton Cheney.

Types of grants: One-off grants only.

Annual grant total: About £1,000 in about 10 grants in 1988.

Applications: In writing to the correspondent.

Correspondent: E V Ward, 128 Main Road, Middleton Cheney, Banbury OX17 2PD.

Other information: This entry has not been confirmed by the trust.

Northampton

The Mary Anne & Ruth Blunt Charity

Eligibility: Unmarried women over 60 who have lived in the borough of Northampton for at least 20 years.

Types of grants: Annuities in four quarterly payments of £7.50 with an additional £5 allowance in December.

Annual grant total: About £2,000 to about 60 annuitants.

Applications: By nomination by one of the trustees.

Correspondent: Hewitson, Becke & Shaw, 7 Spencer Parade, Northampton NN1 5AB (0604-233233).

Other information: The charity is administered by the trustees of the Northampton Municipal General Charities and is shortly to be amalgamated with a number of other small charities.

The John & Anne Camp's Charity

Eligibility: Widows and spinsters of "good character" aged 55 or over who have lived in the parliamentary borough of Northampton for at least 5 years. Preference to people born in the borough or county of Northampton.

Types of grants: Up to 20 annuities paid in quarterly payments of £5 with an additional £5 allowance at Christmas.

Annual grant total: About £500.

Applications: By nomination by one of the trustees.

Correspondent: Mrs Dewsbury, Hewitson, Becke & Shaw, 7 Spencer Parade, Northampton NN1 5AB (0604-233233).

Other information: The charity is administered by the trustees of the Northampton Municipal General Charities and is shortly to be amalgamated with The Mary Anne & Ruth Blunt's Charity.

The Coles & Rice Charity

Eligibility: People in need who are at least 55 years old and live in Northampton.

Types of grants: Recently one-off grants have seldom been made. Most grants are annual pensions of £152 paid in quarterly instalments. Each pensioner also receives a Christmas voucher (£20 in 1991).

Annual grant total: £11,500 in 62 grants in 1991.

Applications: Potential applicants are interviewed by a trustee who helps them to fill in an application form. Applications are considered in March and November.

Correspondent: Simon Bridgens, Clerk, c/o Wilson Browne, 60 Gold Street, Northampton NN1 1RS (0604-28131).

The Henry & Elizabeth Lineham Charity

Eligibility: Women in need, generally widows or spinsters, who are at least 55 and live in Northampton borough.

Types of grants: Annuities by quarterly payments of £78 plus a £25 allowance at Christmas. There were 85 annuitants in 1991, but this may be reduced to 70 payments of £10 a week.

Annual grant total: About £28,500 in 1991.

Applications: Through nomination by one of the trustees.

Correspondent: Mrs Dewsbury, Hewitson Becke & Shaw, 7 Spencer Parade, Northampton NN1 5AB (0604-233233).

Other information: The charity is administered by the trustees of the Northampton Municipal General Charities (see separate entry).

Page's Fund

Eligibility: People in need who live in Northampton. Preference is given to those with a sudden unforeseen drop in income.

Types of grants: One-off and recurrent grants according to need.

Annual grant total: £3,500 for individuals and £10,200 to organisations in 1993.

Applications: In writing to the correspondent.

Correspondent: The Clerk, Wilson Browne, Solicitors (Ref WGG), 60 Gold Street, Northampton NN1 1RS (0604-28131).

The Saint Giles Charity Estate

Eligibility: People in need who live in Northampton with preference to those in the ancient parish of St Giles.

Types of grants: One-off grants up to a maximum of £1,000 and annual payments to a maximum of £200 according to need.

Annual grant total: In 1993, the trust had an income of £80,000, most of which was given to organisations. About £5,000 was given to individuals in need.

Applications: In writing to the correspondent.

Correspondent: John Saynor, Clerk, Wilson Browne Solicitors, 60 Gold Street, Northampton NN1 1RS (0604-28131).

● Old

The Old Parish Charities

Eligibility: People in need who live in the parish of Old, Northamptonshire.

Types of grants: One-off and recurrent grants ranging from £25 to £600. Grants towards education, holidays, Christmas gifts, television rental, hospital visits, funeral expenses etc..

Annual grant total: In 1992, the trust had assets of £1 million and an income of £45,000. 200 relief-in-need grants totalled £16,000.

Applications: On a form available from the correspondent. Applications are considered each month.

Correspondent: R Frankham, 2 Townson Close, Old, Northampton NN6 9RR (0604-781252).

● Pattishall

The Pattishall Parochial Charities

Eligibility: Retired people in need who have lived in Pattishall parish for three years and are householders.

Types of grants: Annual grants of £18 to £60 are paid in December each year and up to 14 of the oldest parishioners receive monthly retirement grants of £5.

Annual grant total: In 1992, the trust had assets of over £6,000 and an income of nearly £2,700. 98 grants totalling £3,300 were given to elderly widows/widowers.

Applications: In writing to the correspondent for consideration in July and December.

Correspondent: Miss D Kirton, 5 Birds Hill Road, Eastcote, Nr Towcester, Northants NN12 8NF (0327 830226).

● Roade

The Roade Feoffees & Chivalls Charity

Eligibility: People in need who live in Roade.

Types of grants: One-off grants ranging from £15 to £100.

Annual grant total: In 1992, the trust's income was £5,500. Expenditure totalled £2,300 of which £1,400 was given to 85 individuals in need.

Applications: In writing to the correspondent. Applications are considered at any time.

Correspondent: A Keniston, Secretary, 18 High Street, Roade, Northampton NN7 2NW (0604-863508).

● Scaldwell

The Scaldwell Charity

Eligibility: People in need who live in the parish of Scaldwell.

Types of grants: One-off and recurrent grants according to need.

Annual grant total: The income in 1992 was £3,800.

Applications: In writing to the correspondent, including details of financial circumstances. Applications are considered in March, July and November.

Correspondent: J C Kearns, Clerk, Wilson Browne, The Manor House, Market Square, Higham Ferrers, Northampton NN9 8BT (0933-410000).

The Scaldwell Relief-in-Need Charity

Eligibility: People in need who live in the parish of Scaldwell only.

Types of grants: One-off grants ranging from £25 to £200.

Annual grant total: In 1992, the trust gave £525 in 18 grants.

Applications: In writing to the correspondent.

Correspondent: A H Nash, Cobbler's Cottage, East End, Scaldwell, Northampton NN6 9LB (0604-880638).

● Silverstone

The Silverstone Poors' Allotment Charity

Eligibility: People in need who live in the parish of Silverstone.

Types of grants: Grants are given as cash or in kind for coal, hospital visiting and travel necessary for treatment etc..

Annual grant total: In 1990/91, the trust had assets of £20,000 with an income of £2,500. 5 relief-in-need grants totalled £870.

Applications: In writing to the correspondent. Applications can be submitted directly by the individual or through a social worker, citizen's advice bureau or other welfare agency, or through a third party such as neighbours or relatives. Applications are considered on receipt.

Correspondent: J Tustian, 11 Towcester Road, Silverstone, Towcester, Northants NN12 8UB (0327-857842).

● Towcester

The Sponne & Bickerstaffe Charity

Eligibility: People in need who live in Towcester.

Types of grants: One-off and recurrent grants according to need.

Annual grant total: About £5,000 in grants to individuals for relief-in-need and education.

Applications: In writing to the correspondent.

Correspondent: Mrs S D Jolly, Clerk, Buckingham Way, Towcester, Northants NN12 7JY (0327-351206).

Northamptonshire/Nottinghamshire

Wappenham

The Wappenham Poors' Land Charity

Eligibility: People in need who live in the ecclesiastical parish of Wappenham.

Types of grants: The trust gives a small standard grant to pensioners in need. Grants also to widows, widowers and people who are sick or disabled and are in need of specific items eg. wheelchairs, orthopaedic beds, home improvements, shower installation, redecoration etc..

Annual grant total: In 1993, the trust had an income of £1,000 all of which was given in 29 grants of £25 to £100.

Applications: In writing to the correspondent for consideration in October and November.

Correspondent: Rev J W Phillips, The Vicarage, Weedon Lois, Towcester, Northants NN12 8PN (0327-860278).

Welton

The Welton Town Lands Trust

Eligibility: People in need who live in Welton.

Types of grants: Grants can be recurrent but usually only one grant is given per household in any year. Grants can also be given for educational purposes.

Annual grant total: About £1,500.

Applications: In writing to the correspondent. "Details of the trust are well publicised within the village."

Correspondent: Joan Morgan, Clerk, Richmond Cottage, High Street, Welton, Daventry, Northants NN11 5JP (0327-704185).

Other information: The trust has stated that there are inaccuracies in this entry, but appeared unwilling to correct them.

Woodford

The Woodford Charity Estate

Eligibility: Pensioners in need who have lived in Woodford for five years.

Types of grants: One-off and recurrent grants ranging from £8 to £12. Some grants may be given towards education.

No grants to people in full-time employment.

Annual grant total: In 1993, the trust had an income of £3,000. Expenditure totalled £1,400 in 164 relief-in-need grants to individuals.

Applications: On a form available from the correspondent. Applications can be submitted directly by the individual or through a social worker, citizen's advice bureau or other welfare agency. They are generally considered in December.

Correspondent: G W Marriott, 28 West Street, Woodford, Kettering NN14 4HZ (0832-732053).

Nottinghamshire

The Beatrice Eveline Bright Trust

Eligibility: Women in need who live within a five-mile radius of the Council House in the city of Nottingham.

Types of grants: Quarterly cash payments ranging from £120 to £1,160 in 1992. Also, payment of telephone/television rentals.

Annual grant total: In 1992, the trust's income was £21,745. £22,000 was given in quarterly payments to 42 people.

Applications: In writing to the correspondent (there is no application form). Applicants are likely to be visited by the trust. Applications can be submitted directly by the individual or through a welfare agency or other third party.

Correspondent: Nelsons, Solicitors, 8 Stanford Street, Nottingham NG1 7BQ (0602-586262).

The Lucy Derbyshire Annuity Fund

Eligibility: People in need who have lived in Nottinghamshire for at least five years.

Types of grants: A yearly allowance of up to £156.

Annual grant total: About £1,000 in six grants in recent years, but now virtually nil owing to lack of applications.

Applications: In writing to the correspondent.

Correspondent: P R Moore, BDO Binder Hamlyn, Accountants, 206 Derby Road, Nottingham NG7 1NQ (0602-415312).

The Mary Dickinson Charity

Eligibility: Widows or the unmarried fatherless daughters of clergymen, gentlemen, professionals or others in trade or agriculture. Applicants must also be members of the Church of England or some other Protestant faith or the Roman Catholic Church, and have lived in Nottinghamshire for at least 10 years.

Types of grants: One-off and recurrent grants according to need.

Annual grant total: About £15,000.

Applications: On a form available from the correspondent.

Correspondent: Alan Wheelhouse, c/o Freeth, Cartwright, Solicitors, Willoughby House, 20 Low Pavement, Nottingham NG1 7EA (0602-506861).

The Francis Butcher Gill's Charity

Eligibility: Unmarried or widowed Christian women (especially members of the Church of England) over the age of 50 and of good standing, who are in need and who live in Nottinghamshire.

Types of grants: Regular allowances and one-off grants at Christmas and Easter.

Annual grant total: About £8,500.

Applications: On a form available from the correspondent.

Correspondent: J Boden, Messrs Dowsons, Solicitors, 13 Weekday Cross, Nottingham NG1 2GG (0602-501087).

Other information: Failing sufficient appropriate applications from Nottinghamshire, eligible applications are considered from Lincolnshire and Derbyshire; in practice, most recent beneficiaries have been from Nottinghamshire.

The Charles Wright Gowthorpe Fund & Clergy Augmentation Fund

Eligibility: The Gowthorpe Fund supports widows and other women in need who live within a 12-mile radius of the Market Square, Nottingham. The Clergy Augmentation Fund generally supports clergymen within the same area.

Types of grants: One-off grants only.

Annual grant total: About £4,000.

Applications: In writing to the correspondent.

Correspondent: The Sub-Manager, Lloyds Bank Financial Services Ltd, Birmingham Area Office, 123 Colmore Row, Birmingham B3 3AE (021-236 2581).

Holidays for Fatherless Children

Eligibility: Children aged 7 to 12 who live in the district of Mansfield and surrounding areas and whose mothers are widows.

Types of grants: Grants towards the cost of a group holiday organised by the charity.

Annual grant total: About £3,500 in about 20 grants of between £150 and £200.

Applications: Holidays are advertised locally at the appropriate time.

Correspondent: Miss McNulty, Flat 8, Nursery Court, Nursery Street, Mansfield, Nottinghamshire NG18 2AJ (0623-25818).

The John William Lamb Charity

Eligibility: People in need who have been living for at least one year within the city of Nottingham, or within 20 miles of the Nottingham Exchange.

Types of grants: Annuities, one-off grants or help in kind as needed.

Annual grant total: Over £18,000.

Applications: In writing to the correspondent.

Correspondent: Evershed Wells & Hind, Solicitors, 14 Fletcher Gate, Nottingham NG1 2FX (0602-506201).

The New Appeals Organisation for the City & County of Nottingham

Eligibility: People in need who live in the city and county of Nottingham.

Types of grants: One-off grants according to need. "The charity only meets needs which cannot be met from any other source." Much of the money is raised for specific projects or people. The trust has a library of equipment for adults and children including electric and sports wheelchairs and computers. No grants for debts or arrears.

Annual grant total: £18,000 in 1987/88, some of which was given in one-off donations and Christmas gifts. This information was not updated by the trust.

Applications: In writing to the correspondent at any time. Applications should ideally be made through a social worker, citizen's advice bureau or other welfare agency.

Correspondent: Mrs S Levin, 13 Huntingdon Drive, The Park, Nottingham NG7 1BW (0602-412180).

The Nottingham Annuity Charity

Eligibility: Spinsters or widows of good character who live in the city of Nottingham or county of Nottinghamshire.

Types of grants: Regular yearly allowances of £208.

Annual grant total: About £15,000 in 72 allowances.

Applications: On a form available from the correspondent to be submitted directly by the individual. Applications are considered in February, May, September and November.

Correspondent: F B Raven, Evershed, Wells & Hind Solicitors, 14 Fletcher Gate, Nottingham NG1 2FX (0602-506201).

The Nottingham Children's Welfare Fund

Eligibility: Children under 18 who live in Nottinghamshire, especially those who have lost either or both of their parents.

Types of grants: One-off grants for almost any purpose where there is a need. Recent awards have been made to buy washing machines, beds, bedding, clothing, buggies, contributions towards the cost of school trips and family holidays, and to young people taking part in overseas projects. Grants range from £50 to £150.

Annual grant total: In 1991/92, the trust had an income of £4,000. £3,900 was given in 42 relief-in-need grants to individuals.

Applications: On a form available from the correspondent preferably through social services, probation service or other welfare agency or third party eg. teacher. Applications are considered in March, June, September and December.

Correspondent: Carol Bebawi, Clerk, c/o Actons, Solicitors, 2 King Street, Nottingham NG1 2AX (0602-476635).

The Nottinghamshire Constabulary Benevolent Fund

Eligibility: Members and former members of the force, their widows and dependants.

Types of grants: One-off and recurrent grants ranging from £15 to over £1,000 according to need.

Annual grant total: £23,000 in 400 to 500 grants in 1991/92.

Applications: In writing to the correspondent.

Correspondent: The Secretary, Force Welfare Office, Sherwood Lodge, Arnold, Nottinghamshire NG5 8PP (0623-672166).

The Nottinghamshire Miners' Welfare Trust Fund

Eligibility: Miners or ex-miners in need living in Nottinghamshire, who are retired or were made redundant and are still unemployed, and their dependants.

Types of grants: Grants, generally one-off, are evenly divided between individuals and organisations connected with the coal mining industry or communities.

Annual grant total: Over £5,000 in 1992, but the trust is expected to grow quite considerably over the next few years.

Applications: In writing to the correspondent.

Correspondent: Patrick Maiden, Coal Industry Social Welfare Organisation, Berry Hill Lane, Mansfield NG18 4JR (0623-25767).

The Perry Trust Gift Fund

Eligibility: In order of preference: (a) people in need who have lived in the city of Nottingham for at least five years; (b) people in need who have lived in Nottinghamshire for at least five years.

Types of grants: One-off and recurrent grants according to need.

Annual grant total: In 1992/93, the trust's income was £17,500. 151 relief-in-need grants totalled £19,000 (£125 each).

Applications: On a form available from the correspondent. Applications are considered in May and November.

Correspondent: Mrs B J Martin, 51 Ringwood Crescent, Wollaton, Nottingham NG8 1HL (0602-281764).

The Mary Elizabeth Siebel Charity

Eligibility: People over 60 years of age who are ill and who live within a radius of 12 miles of Newark Town Hall.

Types of grants: One-off grants ranging from £50 to £2,500. The trust aims to enable applicants to live in their own homes eg. help with the cost of stairlifts, essential home repairs, aids for disabled people, care at home, relief for carers etc..

Annual grant total: In 1993, the trust had an income of £51,000. £50,000 was given in 92 grants to individuals.

Applications: On a form available from the correspondent, which requires the endorsement of the applicant's doctor.

Correspondent: Messrs Tallents Godfrey & Co, 3 Middlegate, Newark, Nottinghamshire NG24 1AQ (0636-71881).

Nottinghamshire

The Charity of Lily Taylor

Eligibility: People in need who live within a radius of 15 miles of the city of Nottingham.

Types of grants: One-off grants for necessities. The charity states that it receives more relevant applications than its resources can meet.

Annual grant total: About £9,000.

Applications: In writing to the correspondent, generally from social workers.

Correspondent: Eversheds Wells & Hind, Solicitors, 14 Fletcher Gate, Nottingham NG1 2FX (0602-506201).

Thomas Underwood's Charity

Eligibility: Spinsters and widows who live in the city or county of Nottingham and who are at least 45 years old.

Types of grants: Regular yearly allowances of £150, paid half-yearly. Allowances are paid for life unless circumstances change. No one-off grants.

Annual grant total: About £2,500 in about 30 allowances.

Applications: On a form available from the correspondent, usually after the recommendation of the trustees "or other similar people who know of people with financial difficulties". Applications are considered at any time, but trustees' meetings are held in June and December.

Correspondent: Miss D Rednall, 1 Rugby Road, Lutterworth, Leicestershire LE17 4BW (0455-554295).

● Balderton

Balderton Parochial Charity

Eligibility: People in need who live in the parish of Balderton.

Types of grants: Christmas grants to widows and widowers and other one-off grants.

Annual grant total: £3,500 to £4,000 in about 300 grants.

Applications: In writing to the correspondent.

Correspondent: A Young, Secretary, 180 London Road, New Balderton, Newark, Notts NG24 3BN (0636-703626).

● Bingham

Bingham United Charities

Eligibility: People in need who live in the parish of Bingham.

Types of grants: One-off grants according to need.

Annual grant total: In 1992/93, the trust had an income of £6,500. Grants to individuals in need totalled £4,500.

Applications: In writing to the correspondent.

Correspondent: B Jones, Secretary, The Court House, Church Street, Bingham, Nottingham NG13 8AL (0949-831445).

● Calverton

The Calverton Jane Pepper & Poor Lands Charity

Eligibility: People in need who live in the parish of Calverton.

Types of grants: One-off/recurrent grants and loans according to need. Help has recently been given to a cancer sufferer, people with cerebral palsy, a women's refuge group, and towards the cost of clothing for disabled children. Loans have been granted to buy mobility chairs and electric scooters.

Annual grant total: In 1993, the trust had an income of £3,700. Grants ranging from £100 to £1,000 were given to 18 individuals and totalled £3,900.

Applications: Applications can be submitted by the individual or through a recognised referral agency (eg. social worker, citizen's advice bureau or doctor) and are considered monthly. Details of the applicants general financial resources must be included.

Correspondent: W Peet, Secretary, 2 Bonner Hill, Calverton, Nottingham NG14 6FR (0602-653293).

● Carlton

The Christopher Johnson & the Green Charity

Eligibility: People in need who live in the parish of Carlton in Lindrick.

Types of grants: One-off grants ranging from £50 to £200. The charity also owns 40 allotments let at a nominal rent of £5 a year and lets two bungalows to elderly people. It also gives £2.50 vouchers to all pensioners at Christmas following an advertisement.

Annual grant total: In 1993, the trust had assets of £33,000 with an income of £3,000. Expenditure totalled £2,100 including £440 in three relief-in-need grants towards a bed, a cot and a washing machine.

Applications: In writing to the correspondent. Most applicants are referred by social services.

Correspondent: H R Parry, Hon. Secretary, 4 Warwick Avenue, Carlton-in-Lindrick, Worksop S81 9BP (0909-730645).

● Coddington

The Coddington United Charities

Eligibility: People in need who live in the parish of Coddington.

Types of grants: Probably one-off and recurrent grants according to need.

Annual grant total: In 1990, the trust had an income of £6,200. It is not known how much was given in grants to individuals.

Applications: In writing to the correspondent.

Correspondent: A F Morrison, Secretary, c/o W H Brown, 17 Market Place, Southwell, Nottinghamshire NG25 0HE (0636-813971).

● Long Bennington

The Lupton & Poor's Land Charity & Grote's Charity

Eligibility: People in need who live in the parish of Long Bennington and Foston.

Types of grants: The trust gives Christmas grants to help with fuel costs, grants towards television licences for housebound people, transport costs for hospital visiting and other one-off and recurrent grants according to need.

Annual grant total: In 1993, the trust had an income of £5,000. All of this was given in about 200 grants to individuals.

Applications: In writing to the correspondent.

Correspondent: Mrs G Baggaley, Trustee, 6 Lilley Street, Long Bennington, Nr Newark, Nottinghamshire NG23 5EJ (0400-81364).

● Mansfield

The Brunts Charity

Eligibility: Elderly people in need who have lived in the former borough of Mansfield (as constituted in 1958) for at least five years at the time of application; women must be at least 60, men at least 65.

Types of grants: Regular allowances only.

Nottinghamshire

Annual grant total: No information available.

Applications: On a form available from the correspondent to be submitted directly by the individual. Applications are considered in February.

Correspondent: D Hale, Clerk, Brunts Chambers, 2 Toothill Lane, Mansfield, Notts NG18 1NG (0623-23055).

Other information: The charity is mainly concerned with running almshouses.

George Henry Francis Payling's Charity

Eligibility: Elderly people in need who live in the former district of Mansfield.

Types of grants: One-off and recurrent grants according to need.

Annual grant total: In 1992, the trust had an income of £6,000. It is not known how much was given in grants to individuals.

Applications: In writing to the correspondent.

Correspondent: D Greaves, Clerk, 2 Toothill Lane, Mansfield, Nottinghamshire NG18 1NJ (0623-23055).

● Newark

The Stuart Goodwin Charity

Eligibility: People aged 60 or over living in the parish of Newark.

Types of grants: A cash gift of £6 and a meal.

Annual grant total: In 1992, the trust had assets of £58,000 with an income of £5,000. Grants were made to 293 individuals.

Applications: On a form published in the local paper in February.

Correspondent: The Branch Manager, Barclays Bank plc, 41 Market Place, Newark, Notts NG24 1EJ (0636-73641).

The Newark Municipal (General) Charities

Eligibility: People in need who live in the borough of Newark.

Types of grants: Christmas gifts and other grants ranging from £100 to £1,000.

Annual grant total: £33,600 in 1993.

Applications: In writing to the correspondent through a social worker, citizen's advice bureau, other welfare agency or third party such as a vicar.

Correspondent: M Gamage, Clerk, 48 Lombard Street, Newark, Nottinghamshire NG24 1XP (0636-640649).

● Nottingham

The Kate Adams Trust

Eligibility: People in need who live in and around the city of Nottingham.

Types of grants: One-off and recurrent grants according to need.

Annual grant total: £2,500.

Applications: Should be submitted in January to March or July to September, quoting reference J01.

Correspondent: P H Jenkins, Messrs Browne & Jacobson, Solicitors, 44 Friar Lane, Nottingham NG1 6EA (0602-500055).

The Endowment Fund

Eligibility: People who have been professionally employed in nursing in Nottingham. Also, other people in need who live in Nottingham.

Types of grants: Payments of £130 a quarter. Payment of telephone and television rentals and licences. The trust also gives one-off grants and loans.

Annual grant total: In 1992, the trust's income was £79,000. Grants to 50 people totalled £69,000.

Applications: In writing to the correspondent (there is no application form). Applicants are likely to be visited by the trust. Applications can be submitted directly by the individual or through a welfare agency or other third party.

Correspondent: Nelsons, Solicitors, 8 Branford Street, Nottingham NG1 7BQ (0602-586262).

The Fifty Fund

Eligibility: People in need who live in and around Nottingham.

Types of grants: Payments of £130 a quarter. Payment of telephone and television rentals and licences. The trust also gives one-off grants and loans.

Annual grant total: In 1992, the trust had assets of £848,000 and an income of £130,000. It gave a total of £110,000 to 100 people.

Applications: Applications, in writing to the correspondent, can be submitted by the individual, through a recognised referral agency (eg. social worker, citizen's advice bureau or doctor) or other third party. Applicants are likely to be visited by a member of the trust.

Correspondent: Nelsons, Solicitors, 8 Stanford Street, Nottingham NG1 7BQ (0602-586262).

The Harper Annuities

Eligibility: Women in need who live or have lived in Nottingham.

Types of grants: Pensions only of £91 a quarter.

Annual grant total: It is thought that the trust has an income of about £20,000. In 1993, the trust gave 27 pensions totalling £10,000.

Applications: In writing to the correspondent.

Correspondent: Miss Blasdale, Secretary, Sharp & Partners, 6 Weekday Cross, Nottingham NG1 2GF (0602-580381).

The Frank Hodson Foundation Ltd

Eligibility: Elderly and other people in need who live in Nottingham.

Types of grants: One-off and recurrent grants according to need.

Annual grant total: About £13,800 in over 50 winter heating grants and about 50 tenants receive rent free flats.

Applications: The correspondent does not wish to receive any new applications.

Correspondent: P R Hannah, Chartered Accountant, 4 Villiers Road, Woodthorpe, Nottingham NG5 4FB (0602-605633).

Other information: The foundation mainly provides rent-free flats for elderly people, especially war widows.

The Nottingham Gordon Memorial Trust for Boys & Girls

Eligibility: Children of school age and below who are in need and who live in the Nottingham area.

Types of grants: Single grants for physical needs such as clothing, beds, basic equipment for disabled children and, in exceptional cases, holidays and educational courses. A few recurrent grants are given, but this is not normal policy. Grants are also given to organisations.

Annual grant total: Over £30,000 in about 250 grants usually of £50 to £100, but not all of these are to individuals.

Applications: On a form available from the correspondent.

Correspondent: Miss Luwenz, Applications Secretary, Calvert's House, Westhorpe, Southwell, Nottinghamshire NG25 0NG (0636-813631).

Nottinghamshire/Shropshire

The Thorpe Trust

Eligibility: Widows and spinsters in need who live in the city of Nottingham. "The recipients must be the widows or fatherless daughters of clergymen, gentlemen or professional people or of people engaged (otherwise than in a menial capacity) in trade or agriculture."

Types of grants: Recurrent grants ranging from £100 to £350.

Annual grant total: In 1992/93, the trust had assets of about £63,000 with an income of £10,250. £11,000 was given in 96 relief-in-need grants to 35 individuals.

Applications: On a form available from the correspondent. Applications can be submitted directly by the individual or through a social worker, citizen's advice bureau or other welfare agency. They are considered in June and December.

Correspondent: C M Shute, Actons Solicitors, 2 King Street, Nottingham NG1 2AX (0602-476635).

● Retford

The East Retford Relief-in-Need Charity

Eligibility: People in need who live in the former borough of Retford.

Types of grants: One-off grants for a wide range of needs including travel costs for hospital visits, furniture, bedding, fuel, heating, clothing, tools, books, special foods, medicines, televisions and radios for lonely people, and laundry costs. Weekly allowances can be given for a limited period as can help towards a recuperative holiday. Grants are usually up to £100.

Annual grant total: In 1993, the trust's income was £2,000; it gave £500 in grants, leaving a surplus of about £1,500.

Applications: In writing to the correspondent including financial details (ie. income and expenditure) and preferably including a supporting statement from a doctor or social services department. Applications are usually considered in December. They can be submitted directly by the individual or through a third party (including trustees or district councillors).

Correspondent: The Director of Professional Services, Bassetlaw District Council, Queen's Buildings, Potter Street, Worksop S80 2AH (0909-475531).

The Sir Stuart & Lady Florence Goodwin Charity

Eligibility: People over 60 and in need who live in the former rural district of East Retford and the Finningly parish of South Yorkshire.

Types of grants: Recurrent grants.

Annual grant total: In 1992/93, the trust had assets of £133,000 producing an income of £10,000. Total expenditure was £8,500. Grants of £5 were given to 1,662 individuals and totalled £8,300.

Applications: Applications in writing to the correspondent via the parish council are considered in March/April.

Correspondent: The Head of Financial Services, Bassetlaw District Council, Queen's Buildings, Potter Street, Worksop, Nottinghamshire S80 2AH (0909-475531 ext. 3268).

The West Gate Benevolent Trust

Eligibility: People in need who live in Retford.

Types of grants: One-off and recurrent grants according to need.

Annual grant total: £730 in 1992/93 in "payment of household bills".

Applications: Through a third party eg. social services or citizen's advice bureau.

Correspondent: J R Waite, Secretary, Meadow View, 16 Durham Grove, Retford, Notts DN22 6ST.

● Southwell

The Southwell Charities for the Poor & Sick Poor

Eligibility: People in need who live in the ancient parish of Southwell.

Types of grants: Probably one-off and recurrent grants according to need.

Annual grant total: £800 in 1985/86, the most recent year for which information is available. This includes payments for fuel.

Applications: In writing to the correspondent.

Correspondent: R G Beckett, Clerk, Zennor, Halam Road, Southwell, Notts NG25 0AH (0636-812291).

● Warsop

The Warsop United Charities

Eligibility: People in need who live in the former urban district of Warsop.

Types of grants: One-off grants for necessities and quarterly grants to about 60 individuals.

Annual grant total: About £3,000.

Applications: In writing to the correspondent.

Correspondent: Mrs D Fritchley, 13 York Terrace, Warsop, Mansfield, Notts NG20 0BJ (0623-843631).

● Wilford

Carter's Charity for the Poor of Wilford

Eligibility: Elderly people in need who live in the ancient parish of Wilford.

Types of grants: Annual grants of £85.

Annual grant total: About £4,000, made up of 46 individual grants of £85 in 1993.

Applications: New annuitants are recommended by the trustees, two of whom are the rectors in the south and north of the parish and another five are members nominated by the city and county councils, one of whom visits elderly and infirm people.

Correspondent: Mrs C M Byers, Pennine House, 8 Stanford Street, Nottingham NG1 7BQ (0602-586262).

Shropshire

The Atherton Trust

Eligibility: Widows, orphans, disabled people and others in need who live in the parishes of Pontesbury and Hanwood and the villages of Annscroft and Hook-a-Gate in the county of Shropshire.

Types of grants: One-off and recurrent grants according to need.

Annual grant total: In 1992/93, the trust's income was £9,600. It spent £16,000, although not all on grants to individuals.

Applications: On a form available from the correspondent.

Correspondent: The Secretary, Messrs Moss & Poulson, Solicitors, 4 Claremont Bank, Shrewsbury S1Y 1RS (0743-350571).

The Ellen Barnes Charitable Trust

Eligibility: People in need who live in Weston Rhyn and adjoining parishes.

Types of grants: The trust's income is mainly used for almshouses and to help their own evangelical church and local schools. One-off grants are considered. An individual recently received £700 to purchase a wheelchair enabling them to continue their education.

Annual grant total: No information available.

Applications: In writing to the correspondent either directly by the individual, through a social worker, citizen's advice bureau or doctor, or other welfare agency. Applications are considered throughout the year.

Correspondent: G A Lewis, Messrs Crampton, Pym & Lewis, 47 Willow Street, Oswestry, Shropshire SY11 1PR (0691-653301).

The Edward's Bequest

Eligibility: Widows and orphans in need who have lived in Pant, Porthywaen and Treflach for at least three years.

Types of grants: Single annual cheques for £10.

Annual grant total: £720 in 72 grants in 1991.

Applications: In writing to the correspondent directly or through a third party (eg. relative or neighbour). Applications should include confirmation of widowhood. Payments are made at two local centres in October.

Correspondent: Rev C I Penberthy, 1 Penygarreg Rise, Pant, Oswestry, Shropshire SY10 8JR (0691-830071).

Dr Gardner's Trust for Nurses

Eligibility: Nursing staff in Shropshire.

Types of grants: One-off grants up to £400 mainly towards convalescent holidays.

Annual grant total: In 1992, the trust's income was £2,700. Expenditure totalled £1,300 in five grants to individuals.

Applications: In writing to the correspondent. Applications can be submitted by the individual, through a recognised referral agency (eg. social worker, citizen's advice bureau or doctor) or other third party, and are considered throughout the year.

Correspondent: J R Riddell, Brookhill, Longmeadow Drive, Abbey Foregate, Shrewsbury SY2 6NA (0743-356553).

The Shrewsbury & District Welfare Society

Eligibility: Post Office employees and their dependants who live in Shrewsbury, Wem, Church Stretton and Craven Arms.

Types of grants: Loans and one-off grants according to need. Recurrent grants may be available for the long term sick.

Annual grant total: In 1990, the trust paid out about £10,000. This included £5,000 in loans, £4,000 in cash grants to staff and £220 in death benefit and funeral donations. The trust also gives grants to local organisations.

Applications: In writing to the correspondent.

Correspondent: M Wills, Chairman, The Sorting Office, Castle Forgate, Shrewsbury SY1 1AA (0743-277300).

The Shrewsbury Municipal Charities

Eligibility: People in need who live in the boroughs of Shrewsbury and Atcham.

Types of grants: One-off grants of £50 to £250.

Annual grant total: £865 in 11 grants in 1992/93, but some of these were for education.

Applications: On a form available from the correspondent. Applications can be submitted directly by the individual or through a third party. They are considered in January, April, July and October.

Correspondent: W Avery, 11 The Wharfage, Ironbridge TF8 7AW.

The Shropshire Welfare Trust

Eligibility: People in need who live in Shropshire.

Types of grants: One-off grants ranging from £20 to £300.

Annual grant total: In 1992, the trust had assets of £244,000 and an income of £16,000. 80 relief-in-need grants to individuals totalled £3,200.

Applications: In writing to the correspondent. Applications can be submitted directly by the individual or through a social worker, citizen's advice bureau or other welfare agency. They are considered throughout the year.

Correspondent: J R Riddell, Brookhill, Longmeadow Drive, Abbey Foregate, Shrewsbury SY2 6NA (0743-356553).

● Alveley

The Arthur Arden Charities & Others

Eligibility: People in need who live in the parish of Alveley.

Types of grants: Probably one-off and recurrent grants according to need.

Annual grant total: In 1985/86, the most recent year for which information is available, "charitable payments and allotment prizes" totalled £5,200, but not all of this may have been given to individuals. The Charity Commission is amending the deeds. The trustees told us they have accumulated quite a surplus over the last few years and have only made a few grants, one to buy a wheelchair. The trust was unwilling to give any more recent information.

Applications: In writing to the correspondent.

Correspondent: Mrs E Briggs, Secretary, The Bite Farm, Trimpley Near Bewdley, Worcester DY12 1NU (0299-403308).

● Farlow

The Farlow James & Williams Charity

Eligibility: People in need who live in the ancient parish of Farlow.

Types of grants: One-off and recurrent grants according to need.

Annual grant total: In 1992/93, the trust had an income of £8,000. Grants to individuals in need totalled £6,000.

Applications: In writing to the correspondent.

Correspondent: Mrs T A Swash, Secretary, Longfield, Oreton, Cleobury Mortimer, Shropshire DY14 0TJ (0746-32605).

● Lilleshall

The Charity of Edith Todd

Eligibility: Pensioners in need who live in Lilleshall.

Types of grants: Pensions of £10 a month with a £10 payment at Christmas.

Annual grant total: About £2,900 in 1992.

Applications: In writing to the correspondent.

Correspondent: Mr Williams, Messrs Liddle & Heane, 60 High Street, Newport, Shropshire TF10 7AH (0952-820028).

● Oswestry

The Oswestry Dispensary Fund

Eligibility: Sick and poor people who live in the borough of Oswestry.

Types of grants: One-off and recurrent grants according to need.

Annual grant total: £900 in 1993.

Applications: In writing to the correspondent.

Shropshire/Staffordshire

● Shrewsbury

The Charities of Peter Langley & Others

Eligibility: People in need who live in the parish of Shrewsbury Holy Cross (the Abbey).

Types of grants: One-off and recurrent grants according to need.

Annual grant total: About £7,000 in 1991/92 to about 50 individuals.

Applications: In writing to the correspondent setting out in full why the trustees should support the application.

Correspondent: K M Vine, 25 Ashley Street, Shrewsbury SY2 5DU (0743-362303).

St Chad's Consolidated Charities

Eligibility: People aged 65 and over who have lived in the ecclesiastical districts of St Chad and St George, Shrewsbury, for not less than five years immediately before their application.

Types of grants: Grants paid in December each year ranging from £22 to £44.

Annual grant total: £400 out of an income of £700.

Applications: In writing to the correspondent. Applications should be submitted directly by the individual and are considered in November.

Correspondent: R B Morgan, 25 Richmond Drive, Copthorne, Shrewsbury SY3 0TN (0743-360145).

Staffordshire

The Baron Davenport Emergency Grant

Eligibility: Needy widows, spinsters and children under 21 whose fathers are dead, who live in the borough of Stafford and neighbouring areas.

Types of grants: One-off grants for emergencies only; applications for help with heating bills are not accepted.

Annual grant total: About £1,000 a year in grants of between £20 and £400.

Applications: Applications can be submitted by the individual, through a recognised referral agency (eg. social worker, citizen's advice bureau or doctor) or other third party.

Correspondent: Mrs Helen Dart, Stafford District Voluntary Services, 131–141 North Walls, Stafford ST16 3AD (0785-45466).

Other information: For information on Baron Davenport's Charity Trust, see entry in the Midlands general section.

The Baron Davenport's Charity Trust Emergency Fund

Eligibility: Needy widows, spinsters and children under 21 whose fathers are dead, who live in east Staffordshire.

Types of grants: One-off grants ranging from £50 to £200 for emergencies only. Help has been given with funeral costs, a much needed holiday/respite, Christmas gifts for children and urgent household repairs. No grants to pay off debts.

Annual grant total: About £2,000.

Applications: In writing to the correspondent at any time. Applications can be submitted directly by the individual or through a social worker, citizen's advice bureau or other welfare agency.

Correspondent: Mrs S Hudson, East Staffordshire Council for Voluntary Service, Voluntary Services Centre, Union Street Car Park, Burton-on-Trent, Staffordshire DE14 1AA (0283-43414).

Other information: For information on Baron Davenport's Charity Trust, see entry in the Midlands general section.

The Heath Memorial Trust Fund

Eligibility: People over 18 and in need who are convalescing and who live in the city of Stoke-on-Trent or North Staffordshire.

Types of grants: One-off grants for a recuperative holiday/convalescence only, up to £30 per person per week; £55 for two people per week; £50 per person for two weeks, and £70 for two people for two weeks. Christmas vouchers, for which applications should not be submitted, are distributed by trustees to eligible people.

Annual grant total: In 1992, the trust had assets of £48,000 generating an income of £5,330. Total expenditure was £4,600. Grants of between £30 and £70 were given to 170 individuals and totalled £4,590.

Applications: On a form available from the correspondent, countersigned by a trustee, local councillor, health visitor, social worker or doctor. Applications are considered throughout the year.

Correspondent: c/o Mrs J Barlow, Stoke-on-Trent City Council, Civic Centre, Glebe Street, Stoke-on-Trent ST4 1RG (0782-744241).

The Edward Malam Convalescent Fund

Eligibility: Adults who are convalescing and who live in the city of Stoke-on-Trent and north Staffordshire.

Types of grants: One-off grants for convalescence only. Maximum grants are as follows: £30 per person per week maximum; £55 for a couple per week; £50 per person for two weeks; £70 for a couple for two weeks.

Annual grant total: In 1992, the trust's income was £4,900. 90 grants were given totalling £4,700.

Applications: On a form available from the correspondent to be signed by a trustee, local councillor, health visitor or doctor when completed. Applications are considered throughout the year.

Correspondent: c/o Mrs J Barlow, Stoke-on-Trent City Council, Civic Centre, Glebe Street, Stoke-on-Trent ST4 1RG (0782-744241).

The North Staffordshire Convalescent & Incurable Fund

Eligibility: People with an incurable disease, and disadvantaged children in need of a holiday. Applicants must live in Staffordshire.

Types of grants: Grants are given towards the cost of holidays.

Annual grant total: About £500.

Applications: In writing to the correspondent.

Correspondent: Mrs V Duke, Secretary, 5 Caroline Close, Werrington, Stoke-on-Trent.

The North Staffordshire Miners Convalescent & Relief Fund

Eligibility: Mineworkers in North Staffordshire and their dependants.

Types of grants: One-off and recurrent grants according to need.

Annual grant total: In 1982/83, the most recent year for which information is available, the trust's income was £3,800;

Correspondent: Richard Lloyd, A W Brown & Lloyd, 37-39 Willow Street, Oswestry, Shropshire SY11 1AQ (0691-659194).

Staffordshire

£500 was given in grants and unspent income for the year totalled £3,000.

Applications: In writing to the correspondent.

Correspondent: L N Dodd, Solicitor, 19 Glebe Street, Stoke-on-Trent ST4 1HL.

Other information: The address has been confirmed by the trust, but we were unable to update the financial information.

Burton-on-Trent

The Burton & South Derbyshire Charity for the Sufferers of Multiple Sclerosis

Eligibility: People with multiple sclerosis living in Burton and south Derbyshire.

Types of grants: Generally recurrent grants towards telephone rental, exercise equipment and naudicelle treatment.

Annual grant total: In 1992/93, grants totalling £6,500 were given to about 100 individuals

Applications: In writing to the correspondent. Applications can be submitted directly by the individual and are considered throughout the year.

Correspondent: J H Osborne, Chairman, 24 Beech Grove, Newhall, Swadlincote, Derbyshire DE11 ONH (0283-216638).

Other information: The charity also provides information on multiple sclerosis. People with multiple sclerosis throughout England can get 10% off the cost of naudicelle. Further information from the correspondent. This entry is repeated in the Staffordshire section of the book.

The Burton-on-Trent Sick Poor Fund

Eligibility: People in need who live in the former county borough of Burton-on-Trent.

Types of grants: Usually one-off grants for the purchase of, for example, chiropody services, grab rails for baths & stairs, hypothermia packs for elderly people and personal alarm systems.

Annual grant total: In 1992, the trust had an income of £5,700. Individual relief-in-need grants totalling £3,000 were given to between 80 and 100 people.

Applications: In writing to the correspondent. Applications can be submitted by the individual or through a recognised referral agency (social worker, citizen's advice bureau or doctor etc.) and are considered at any time. Grants to organisations such hospitals, clinics, doctors' surgeries and churches are also considered.

Correspondent: A Betteridge, Clerk, Messrs Talbot & Co, Solicitors, 148 High Street, Burton-on-Trent DE14 1JY (0283-64716).

Enville

The Enville Poor's Charity

Eligibility: People in need who live in the parish of Enville.

Types of grants: One-off or recurrent grants ranging from £50 to £250. Grants have been given for telephone installation/connection (including an emergency contact line), emergency medical help, optician bills for partially sighted people, special dental treatment, food parcels, clothing and for fuel in winter.

Annual grant total: In 1992/93, the trust's income was £1,600. It gave 2 grants totalling £250.

Applications: On a form available from the correspondent. Applications can be submitted directly by the individual or through a social worker, citizen's advice bureau or other welfare agency, or through the rector of the parish church. They are considered at any time.

Correspondent: J A Gloss, Walls Cottage, Kinver Road, Enville, Staffordshire DY7 5HE (0384-873691).

Leek

The Carr Trust

Eligibility: Elderly people in need who live in Leek.

Types of grants: Beneficiaries receive £10 a month and a Christmas bonus. There are currently about 100 beneficiaries.

Annual grant total: About £12,000.

Applications: A notice about applications appears in the local paper in March each year.

Correspondent: R F Belfield, Clerk, Challinors & Shaw, 10 Derby Street, Leek, Staffordshire ST13 5AW (0538-399332).

Newcastle-under-Lyme

The Newcastle-under-Lyme United Charities

Eligibility: People in need who live in the borough of Newcastle-under-Lyme (as it was before 1974).

Types of grants: Christmas grants, not exceeding £10.

Annual grant total: £4,000 in 400 grants.

Applications: In writing to the correspondent directly by the individual. All applications are "vetted by one of the trustees to verify need" and considered each October.

Correspondent: F R Harley (Ref C54/2), Newcastle-under-Lyme Borough Council, Civic Offices, Mernal Street, Newcastle-under-Lyme, Staffordshire ST5 2AQ (0782-717171).

Stoke-on-Trent

The John Pepper Charity

Eligibility: Elderly people in need who live in Stoke-on-Trent.

Types of grants: £6 recurrent Christmas grants.

Annual grant total: In 1992/93, grants of £6 were given to 172 individuals totalling over £1,000.

Applications: Applications are considered in November/December and should be made through a social worker, citizen's advice bureau or local authority tenancy section housing or health department. Emergency applications cannot be considered.

Correspondent: Mrs J Barlow, Legal, Property & Administrative Services, PO Box 631, Civic Centre, Glebe Street, Stoke-on-Trent ST4 1RG (0782-404617).

The Stoke-on-Trent Children's Holiday Trust Fund

Eligibility: Children aged 5 to 17 who live in Stoke-on-Trent and whose parents are unable to afford a holiday for them.

Types of grants: One-off grants for children only (which includes travel costs and pocket money) for a recuperative holiday. A holiday can be anything from a day at the seaside to two weeks abroad. "The purpose of the grant is to give the child a break from the home environment, away from the pressures of everyday life."

Annual grant total: In 1992, the trust had assets of £65,000 and an income of £7,200. Grants totalled £7,300.

Applications: On a form available from the correspondent. Applications can be submitted directly by the individual or through a teacher, social worker, citizen's advice bureau or other welfare agency. They are considered as received.

Staffordshire/Warwickshire

Correspondent: Mrs J Barlow, Legal Property & Admin Services, PO Box 631, Civic Centre, Glebe Street, Stoke-on-Trent ST4 1RG (0782-404617).

Tamworth

Beardsley's Relief-in-Need Charity

Eligibility: People in need who live in the borough of Tamworth.

Types of grants: One-off grants according to need.

Annual grant total: In 1991/92, the trust had an income of £9,000. It is not known how much was given in grants to individuals in need.

Applications: In writing to the correspondent.

Correspondent: Messrs Argyles, 43 Albert Road, Tamworth, Staffordshire B79 7JZ (0827-56276).

The Baron Davenport Emergency Grant

Eligibility: Needy widows, spinsters and children under 21 whose fathers are dead. Only applicants who have lived in the area of Tamworth for at least 10 years will be considered.

Types of grants: One-off grants for emergencies only. No grants for fuel bills.

Annual grant total: About £2,000.

Applications: Applications through clergy, social services or a similar third party only.

Correspondent: Megan Malpas, Tamworth Community Service Council, Carnegie Centre, Corporation Street, Tamworth, Staffordshire B79 7DN (0827-69000).

Other information: For information on Baron Davenport's Charity Trust, see entry in the Midlands general section.

The Rawlet Trust

Eligibility: People in need who live in the borough of Tamworth.

Types of grants: One-off grants ranging from £90 to £2,000, including help with Home link telephone costs for elderly people.

Annual grant total: In 1992/93, the trust had an income of £15,500. 20 relief in need grants to individuals totalled £6,400.

Applications: In writing to the correspondent. Applications can be submitted directly by the individual or through a social worker, citizen's advice bureau or other welfare agency. They are considered in March, October and December.

Correspondent: Mrs A M Brooks, Clerk, 7 Winterdyne Cottages, Wigginton, Tamworth, Staffs B79 9LB (0827-383623).

The Tamworth Municipal Charities

Eligibility: People in need who live in the borough of Tamworth.

Types of grants: One-off grants.

Annual grant total: £5,300 in 1990, including 12 grants to individuals and grants to organisations.

Applications: In writing to the correspondent.

Correspondent: The Chief Executive, Tamworth Borough Council, Marmion House, Lichfield Street, Tamworth, Staffordshire B79 7BZ (0827-311222).

Trentham

The Edith Emily Todd Trust

Eligibility: People in need who live in the ecclesiastical parish of St Mary and All Saints, Trentham.

Types of grants: One-off and recurrent grants according to need.

Annual grant total: In 1992/93, the trust had an income of £1,000, it is not known how much of this was given in grants to individuals.

Applications: In writing to the correspondent or the vicar/churchwardens.

Correspondent: G C Cooper, Administrator, 5 Fairway, Stoke-on-Trent ST4 8AS (0782-657988).

Tutbury

The Tutbury General Charities

Eligibility: People in need who live in the parish of Tutbury.

Types of grants: One-off and recurrent grants according to need.

Annual grant total: In 1992, the trust had an income of £5,200. It is not known how much was given in grants to individuals in need.

Applications: In writing to the correspondent.

Correspondent: The Clerk, Charity Office, Duke Street, Tutbury, Burton-on-Trent, Staffordshire DE13 9NE.

Warwickshire

The Alcester Wednesday Night Over 70's Fund

Eligibility: People in need who are over 70 and who live in Alcester, Oversley, Arrow, Wixford and Great Alne.

Types of grants: Help mainly during the winter months with £5 cash grants and assistance with coal/wood (usually £10). Help is also given in case of flood or frost (ie. burst pipes etc.). Grants range from £5 to £100.

Annual grant total: £1,400 in about 200 grants in 1991.

Applications: In writing to the correspondent. Applications should be submitted directly by the individual or through committee members. They are considered from January to November.

Correspondent: M J Pick, Secretary, 49 Ten Acres, Kinwarton Road, Alcester, Warwickshire.

Other information: This entry has not been confirmed by the trust.

The Sarah Chamberlayne Charity

Eligibility: Widows/unmarried women who are at least 50 years old; elderly men; physically/visually disabled people of either sex, and children who have lost both parents or children who are mentally/physically disabled or infirm. Applicants must live in Southam and Long Itchington in Warwickshire or Hatfield Broad Oak and Ugely in Essex.

Types of grants: Quarterly annuities of £14 or £15 to 30 individuals.

Annual grant total: About £1,800.

Applications: In writing to the correspondent.

Correspondent: J M P Hathaway, Clerk, Messrs Heath & Blenkinsop, Solicitors, 13 Old Square, Warwick CV34 4RA (0926-492407).

Other information: This entry is repeated in the Essex section of the book.

The Baron Davenport Emergency Grant

Eligibility: Needy widows, spinsters and children under the age of 21 whose fathers are dead. Applicants must live in north Warwickshire.

Types of grants: One-off grants for emergencies only.

Warwickshire

Annual grant total: The income is about £2,000.

Applications: Directly by the individual in writing to the correspondent.

Correspondent: Gower Johnson, General Secretary, North Warwickshire Council for Voluntary Service, Community House, Coleshill Road, Atherstone, Warwickshire CV9 1BN (0827-718080).

Other information: For information on Baron Davenport's Charity Trust, see entry in the Midland general section.

The Baron Davenport Emergency Grant

Eligibility: Needy widows, spinsters and children under 21 whose fathers are dead, who live in Nuneaton and Bedworth.

Types of grants: One-off grants for emergencies only.

Annual grant total: About £1,000 in 1993.

Applications: Applications can be made directly to the correspondent.

Correspondent: Liz Stuart, Nuneaton & Bedworth Council for Voluntary Service, 72 High Street, Nuneaton, Warwickshire CV11 5DA (0203-385765).

Other information: For information on Baron Davenport's Charity Trust, see entry in the Midlands general section.

The Dunchurch & Thurlaston Community Trust

Eligibility: People in need who live in the parishes of Dunchurch and Thurlaston.

Types of grants: One-off grants. For example help has been given towards heating, an orthopaedic chair and an electric wheelchair.

Annual grant total: Between £3,000 and £4,000 to local organisations and individuals.

Applications: In writing to the correspondent.

Correspondent: J F Flint, 24 Barton Road, Rugby CV22 7PT (0788-579579).

The Hatton Consolidated Charities

Eligibility: People in need who live in the parishes of Hatton, Beausale and Shrewley. Applications from outside the above areas will not be considered.

Types of grants: One-off grants in cash or in kind. Grants are also given to students and young people starting work to help buy books and tools.

Annual grant total: About £3,000.

Applications: Apply to the trustees or the correspondent.

Correspondent: Mrs M H Sparks, Clerk, Weare Giffard, 32 Shrewley Common, Warwick CV35 7AP (0926-842533).

The Merevale Sickness Fund

Eligibility: People who are sick, convalescing, physically/mentally disabled or infirm and who live in Merevale, Grendon, Baddesley, Ensor, Bentley or Baxterley.

Types of grants: One-off grants in kind, eg. fruit, flowers and necessities.

Annual grant total: About £1,000 in about 20 grants.

Applications: By telephoning one of the trustees.

Correspondent: H J McCranor, Accountant, Merevale, 89 Brinklow Road, Binley, Coventry CV3 2JB.

Other information: This entry has not been confirmed by the trust, but the correspondent is correct according to the Charity Commission.

The Charity of Lord Redesdale

Eligibility: Members of the Church of England or people in regular attendance at divine service, living in the ancient parishes of Batsford, Bourton-on-the-Hill, Blockley, Great Wolford, Moreton-in-Marsh, Little Wolford and Snowshill. Applicants should be aged 60 or over, or aged 40 or over if disabled in war.

Types of grants: One-off grants according to need.

Annual grant total: £1,500 in 1990.

Applications: In writing to the correspondent.

Correspondent: M Hughes-Hallett, Secretary, Batsford Estate Office, Moreton-in-Marsh, Gloucestershire GL56 9QF (0608-650722).

Other information: This entry is repeated in the Gloucestershire section of the book.

The South Warwickshire Welfare Trust

Eligibility: People in need who live in Warwick district and the former rural district of Southam.

Types of grants: One-off grants for items, services or facilities to alleviate suffering or assist recovery for people who are sick, convalescent, disabled or infirm.

Annual grant total: About £8,000.

Applications: To be made through a social worker, health visitor, doctor, church official or similar third party.

Correspondent: Mrs V Grimmer, Clerk, 4 Northgate Street, Warwick CV34 4SP (0926-491358).

The Warwickshire Constabulary Benevolent Fund

Eligibility: Members and retired members of the fund, their widows or widowers and dependants.

Types of grants: Grants to those in need, including to members attending a police or other convalescent home to help with travel and incidental expenditure during their stay. Loans may also be given to members.

Annual grant total: In 1992, the trust had an income of £11,800 and expenditure of £7,400. Grants totalled £6,400 given in 35 travel grants and 12 other grants.

Applications: On a form available from the correspondent, any member of the management committee or the force welfare department will advise on the application. The committee meets at least four times a year. In urgent cases for grants up to £1,000 a sub-committee may consider the application.

Correspondent: R Allsop, Secretary, Chief Constable's Office, PO Box 4, Leek Wootton, Warwick CV35 7QB (0926-415000).

The Warwickshire Miners Convalescent & Benevolent Fund

Eligibility: Mineworkers and former mineworkers of Warwickshire Miners Association (NUM) and their dependants.

Types of grants: One-off grants from £150 to £300 towards convalescent holidays, hospital visits to spouse (or applicant), electrical appliances such as cookers and vacuum cleaners, carpets, beds and other furniture, wheelchairs, inhalors, electric hoists etc., medical reports for industrial diseases. No death grants or grants to people who have received redundancy pay in the last 10 years.

Annual grant total: In 1992, the trust had assets of £202,000 and an income of £19,000, £18,000 of which was given in grants to 67 individuals.

Applications: In writing to the correspondent. Applications can be submitted directly by the individual or through a social worker, citizen's advice

Warwickshire

bureau or other welfare agency or third party. Applications should include weekly income, medical proof from doctor (if applicable) and are considered at any time.

Correspondent: Barry Keith Daynes, General Secretary, 17 Bulkington Road, Bedworth, Warwickshire CV12 9DP (0203-313181).

Atherstone

The Charity of Priscilla Gent & Others

Eligibility: People in need who live in Atherstone, Warickshire.

Types of grants: One-off grants to individuals and organisations.

Annual grant total: In 1992, the trust had an income of £3,000. Grants totalled £2,400 although it is not known how much of this was given directly to individuals.

Applications: Applications can be submitted by the individual, through a recognised referral agency (eg. social worker, citizen's advice bureau or doctor) or a third party and are considered in May and November. In emergencies, applications will be considered outside these months.

Details of the need and the individual's connection with Atherstone must be clearly stated.

Correspondent: M L R Harris, Clerk, 42 King Street, Seagrave, Loughborough, Leicestershire LE12 7LY (0509-812366).

Baginton

The Lucy Price Relief-in-Need Charity

Eligibility: People in need who are under 25 and live in the parish of Baginton.

Types of grants: Grants according to need made only for the calendar year in which the application is made. All applications for grants spread over more than one year must be submitted annually.

Annual grant total: £38,000 in 1992, including 86 individual grants totalling £27,000.

Applications: On a form available from the correspondent.

Correspondent: R Friend, Clerk, 5 Lythall Close, Radford Semele, Leamington Spa, Warwickshire CV31 1UG.

Barford

The Barford Relief-in-Need Charity

Eligibility: People in need who live in the parish of Barford.

Types of grants: One-off or recurrent grants. Includes Christmas gifts to old and needy people, help in particular financial difficulties, and assistance towards funeral expenses for those recently bereaved. No loans are given.

Annual grant total: In 1993, the trust had assets of £141,000 and an income of £6,900. Grants of £80 to £200 were given to 64 individuals and totalled £5,300.

Applications: In writing to the correspondent directly by the individual. Considered in May and November, but at anytime in an emergency.

Correspondent: Mrs D A Wood, Secretary, South of St Peter's, Church Lane, Barford, Warwickshire CV35 8ES (0926-624342).

Bedworth

The Henry Smith Charity

Eligibility: Elderly people in need who live in Bedworth.

Types of grants: Generally vouchers at Christmas to needy old age pensioners.

Annual grant total: In 1993, the trust had an income of £900 and gave £2 vouchers totalling £1,100.

Applications: In writing to the correspondent for consideration in December.

Correspondent: The Borough Manager, Town Hall, Nuneaton, Warwickshire CV11 5AA (0203-376376 ext. 204)

Coleshill

The Simon Lord Digby Relief-in-Need Charity

Eligibility: People in need who live in the parish of Coleshill.

Types of grants: Grants according to need.

Annual grant total: In 1992, the trust had an income of £4,300. It is not known how much was given in grants to individuals.

Applications: In writing to the correspondent. Applications are decided twice-yearly although decisions can be made more quickly in an emergency.

Correspondent: Mrs Diana Awad, The Vicarage Office, High Street, Coleshill, Warwickshire B46 3BP (0675-462188).

Grandborough

The Grandborough & Sutton Charities

Eligibility: People in need who live in the parish of Grandborough.

Types of grants: Grants range from £20 to £100 and have included help with chiropodists' fees, text books, road tax and telephone installation.

Annual grant total: About £800 in 22 grants in 1990/91.

Applications: In writing to the correspondent.

Correspondent: Mrs P J Wright, Clerk, Quorn Cottage, Grandborough, Rugby CV23 8DH (0788-814728).

Other information: This entry has not been confirmed by the trust.

Kenilworth

The Kenilworth Carnival Comforts Fund

Eligibility: People in need who live in Kenilworth.

Types of grants: Mainly one-off grants of £15 per person or £20 per couple, usually in the form of a grocery voucher redeemable at various shops in Kenilworth.

Annual grant total: In 1993, the trust had an income of £3,300. 190 grants were given totalling £2,500.

Applications: In writing to the correspondent. Applications can be submitted directly by the individual or through a social worker, citizen's advice bureau, other welfare agency or a third party eg. a friend or relative. They are considered monthly.

Correspondent: J A Evans, 7 Queens Road, Kenilworth CV8 1JQ.

The Kenilworth United Charities

Eligibility: People in need who live in the ancient parish of Kenilworth.

Types of grants: Generally grocery vouchers given to one-parent families. Recently one-off grants have also been given towards a washing machine, training in beauty therapy and fire damage.

Warwickshire

Annual grant total: In 1993, the trust had assets of £233,000 and an income of only £8,700. The trust spent £6,800 and gave 200 grants of £40 to £150 totalling £3,500.

Applications: On a form available from the correspondent. Applications are considered quarterly.

Correspondent: H Newall, 73 Rouncil Lane, Kenilworth CV8 1FN.

Other information: The trust also administers four almshouses.

Leamington

The Leamington Fund

Eligibility: People suffering from ill-health who live in the former borough of Leamington Spa and the neighbourhood.

Types of grants: One-off grants only, ranging from £25 to £55, including help with fuel debts, fares for visiting hospitals or sick relatives, children's clothing, and repairs to washing machines.

Annual grant total: The trust gives about 30 grants a year.

Applications: In writing to the correspondent through a social worker, citizen's advice bureau or other welfare agency. Applications are considered throughout the year.

Correspondent: Mrs O Johnson, Clerk, 73 Northumberland Road, Leamington Spa, Warwickshire.

Other information: This entry has not been confirmed by the trust.

Long Lawford

The Long Lawford Pension & Relief-in-Need Charity

Eligibility: For regular grants: people in need who have lived in the parish of Long Lawford for at least five years immediately before an application is made. For one-off grants: people in need who live in the parish of Long Lawford.

Types of grants: One-off and recurrent grants according to need (and eligibility see above).

Annual grant total: About £1,000.

Applications: In writing to the correspondent.

Correspondent: Rev P Watkins, Trustee, The Vicarage, Brook Street, Wolston, Coventry (0203-542722).

Napton-on-the-Hill

The Napton Charities

Eligibility: People in need who live in Napton-on-the-Hill.

Types of grants: Grants are only given towards heating. Grants may be in cash or in coal and logs to the value of £15 to £24.

Annual grant total: £900 to £1,000.

Applications: On a form available from the correspondent.

Correspondent: A Fletcher, Secretary, Endene, Southam Road, Napton-on-the-Hill, Nr Rugby, Warwickshire CV23 8NG (0926-812416).

Nuneaton

The Nuneaton Poors' Piece Charity

Eligibility: People in need who live in the borough of Nuneaton. Preference for those in a position of need due to serious accident, illness or trauma.

Types of grants: One-off and recurrent grants according to need.

Annual grant total: About £1,200 in 1991 to individuals and very occasionally organisations.

Applications: In writing to the correspondent through the social services, citizen's advice bureau or similar welfare agency.

Correspondent: F L Matts, Clerk, 31 Chartwell Close, Nuneaton, Warwickshire CV11 6SL (0203-349401).

Rugby

The Bilton Poors' Land & Other Charities

Eligibility: People in need who live in the ancient parishes of Bilton and New Bilton (now part of Rugby).

Types of grants: One-off grants averaging £50 and a Christmas distribution usually to pensioners.

Annual grant total: £9,000. Christmas grants totalled £3,000, £2,000 was paid to 20 individuals and £4,000 to schools/groups.

Applications: In writing to the correspondent, generally through welfare agencies although individuals can apply direct.

Correspondent: Mrs A J Parker, Clerk, 2 David Road, Bilton, Rugby CV22 7PX (0788-810930).

The Baron Davenport Emergency Grant

Eligibility: Needy widows, spinsters and children under 21 whose fathers are dead, who live in the Rugby area. All applicants must have lived in Warwickshire, Worcestershire or Staffordshire for a number of years.

Types of grants: One-off grants for emergencies only. The CVS has been told that high fuel bills cannot be considered for the emergency grant.

Annual grant total: About £2,000.

Applications: Applications should be made to one of the following, all of whom have copies of the application form (they are considered at any time):

Mrs B Grenet, Citizen's Advice Bureau, 7 Regent Place, Rugby (0788-541000).

N Sandison, Coventry Churches Housing Association, 61 Albert Street, Rugby (0788-579172).

Mrs E Gardner, c/o Age Concern, Claremont, Clifton Road, Rugby (0788-577028).

Pete Morgan, Social Services Department, 10 Craven Road, Rugby (0788-541333).

Correspondent: Rugby Council for Voluntary Service, 20 North Street, Rugby CV21 2AG (0788-574258 between 10am – 2 pm).

Other information: For information on Baron Davenport's Charity Trust, see entry in the Midlands general section.

The Rugby Relief-in-Need Charity

Eligibility: Elderly and sick people in need, who live in the ancient parish of Rugby.

Types of grants: One-off grants only.

Annual grant total: About £1,000.

Applications: In writing to the correspondent.

Correspondent: The Rector, The Rectory, 79 Clifton Road, Rugby CV21 3QG.

Other information: This is the latest information available at the Charity Commission. This entry has not been confirmed by the trust.

The Rugby Welfare Charities

Eligibility: People in need who live in the ancient parish of Rugby, which includes St Andrew's and St Matthew's.

Types of grants: One-off grants, mainly for pensioners though some for general relief-in-need. Grants are usually paid at Christmas.

Warwickshire

Annual grant total: About 100 grants to individuals totalling over £1,000.

Applications: In writing to the correspondent.

Correspondent: Mrs P Redfern, 12 Park Road, Rugby CV21 2QH (0788-543062).

Stratford-upon-Avon

The Baron Davenport Emergency Grant

Eligibility: Needy widows, spinsters and children under 21 whose fathers are dead, who live in Stratford-upon-Avon district.

Types of grants: One-off grants up to a maximum of £200 for emergencies only.

Annual grant total: About £1,000 out of an income of £2,000.

Applications: Applications can be made directly to the correspondent but must include supporting evidence from a third party.

Correspondent: FAO the CVS Executive, Stratford-upon-Avon Council for Voluntary Service, The Hospital, Arden Street, Stratford-upon-Avon CV37 6NW (0789-298115).

Other information: For information on Baron Davenport's Charity Trust, see entry in the Midlands general section.

The Mayor's Fund Society of Stratford-upon-Avon

Eligibility: People in need who live in Stratford-upon-Avon.

Types of grants: Grocery vouchers of £10.

Annual grant total: In 1992/93, the trust gave £1,850 in 185 relief-in-need grants.

Applications: In writing to the correspondent. Applications can be submitted directly by the individual or through a social worker, citizen's advice bureau or other welfare agency. They are considered from September to February.

Correspondent: Trevor Cox, Hon. Secretary, 7 Keats Road, Stratford-upon-Avon CV37 7JL (0789-204730).

The Municipal Charities of Stratford-upon-Avon, Relief-in-Need Charity

Eligibility: People in need who live in Stratford-upon-Avon.

Types of grants: One-off and recurrent grants according to need. Grants tend to be £55 or £65 paid once a year.

Annual grant total: In 1991, the trust's income was £31,000, but some of this is given as education grants. It gave about 250 annual grants totalling £12,500. The surplus of income over expenditure for the year was £17,000. The trust may regularly have a surplus of income over expenditure.

Applications: In writing to the correspondent. Advertisements are also placed in the local press asking for suitable applicants to apply.

Correspondent: Mrs Joan Benningfield, 9 Shottery, Stratford-upon-Avon, Warwickshire CV37 9HA (0789-297899).

Thurlaston

The Poor's Plot Charity

Eligibility: People of any age who are in need and live in Thurlaston.

Types of grants: Most grants are given to pensioners to help with heating costs. The trust has also helped with the cost of lifeline alarm systems and television licences.

Annual grant total: In 1991, the trust had an income of £3,200 and gave grants totalling £1,000.

Applications: In writing to the correspondent.

Correspondent: Mrs K Owen, Clerk, Congreaves, Main Street, Thurlaston, Rugby CV23 9JS (0788-817466).

Warwick

The Baron Davenport Emergency Grant

Eligibility: Needy widows, spinsters and children under 21 whose fathers are dead, who live in and around Warwick.

Types of grants: One-off grants for emergencies only.

Annual grant total: About £2,000.

Applications: Can be made to the correspondent directly or via welfare agencies.

Correspondent: Jean Ball, Warwick District Council for Voluntary Service, 109 Warwick Street, Leamington Spa CV32 4QZ (0926-881151).

Other information: For information on Baron Davenport's Charity Trust, see the entry in the Midlands general section.

The Warwick Municipal Charities - King Henry VIII Charity

Eligibility: People in need who live in the former borough of Warwick.

Types of grants: Mainly one-off grants according to need.

Annual grant total: This charity had assets of £17 million in 1990, generating an income of £991,000. This is one the largest incomes of any local charity in the country. Of the £991,000, £54,000 was spent on administration and the upkeep of properties owned by the charity, leaving £937,000 available for distribution. The money is allocated as follows:

50% to churches in Warwick;
30% to the governors of Kings School, Warwick;
20% to the town of Warwick. This latter sum is distributed in grants to individuals (for both relief-in-need and educational purposes) and organisations in the town.

Of the money allocated to the church, (£95,000) was spent on clergy stipends and clergy housing. The remaining money was given to the following Parochial Church Councils:

The parish of Warwick (£210,000);
The parish of St Michael (£46,000);
The parish of St Paul (£45,000);
The parish of All Saints (£45,000).

It is not known whether these sums allocated to the various PCCs were used for exclusively church purposes, or whether they were in part at least given as grants to individuals in need.

Applications: In writing to the correspondent. Applications are considered in February, April, July, September and November.

Correspondent: P G Butler, Clerk, 12 Euston Place, Leamington Spa, Warwickshire, CV32 4LR (0926-429268).

The Warwick Provident Dispensary

Eligibility: People in need who live in Warwick.

Types of grants: One-off grants for the relief of sickness or infirmity.

Annual grant total: £5,400 in 12 grants in 1991.

Applications: In writing to the correspondent, directly by the individual or through a social worker, citizen's advice bureau, other welfare agency or third party. Applications are considered at all times.

Correspondent: Christopher Houghton, Messrs Moore & Tibbits, 34 High Street, Warwick CV34 4BE (0926-491181).

West Midlands

The Badley Memorial Trust

Eligibility: People in need who live in the former county borough of Dudley (as constituted in 1953) and, in certain cases, the present metropolitan boroughs of Dudley and Sandwell.

Types of grants: Usually one-off grants to relieve people who are sick, convalescent, disabled or infirm. Grants have been made towards medical aids, clothing, beds/bedding, heating appliances, cookers, washing machines, vacuum cleaners, televisions, radios, fuel, and adaptations for disabled people. Grants range from £50 to £1,750. Recurrent grants are only given in exceptional cases.

Annual grant total: In 1992/93, the trust had assets of £592,379 with an income of £41,880. Relief-in-need grants totalled £42,000.

Applications: On a form available from the correspondent to be submitted directly by the individual, through a social worker, citizen's advice bureau, other welfare agency, or a third party eg. a relative. Applications are considered in February, May, August and November.

Correspondent: D Underwood, 23 Water Street, Kingswinford, West Midlands DY6 7QA (0384-277463).

The Beacon Centre for the Blind

Eligibility: People who are registered blind or partially sighted and live in the metropolitan boroughs of Dudley (except Halesowen and Stourbridge), Sandwell and Wolverhampton, and part of the South Staffordshire District Council area.

Types of grants: One-off grants. In 1992/93, grants were given towards socials and outings (£24,000); holidays (£12,000); and talking books and newspapers (£25,000). Some of these grants may have come from the budget for organisations and some for individuals. Grants for specific items of equipment can be given to those who are visually impaired.

Annual grant total: In 1992/93, the trust had assets of over £2 million and an income of almost £1.2 million. The total expenditure was £1.1 million. Most of this is spent maintaining a day centre, residential home and running employment schemes. About 3,000 individuals received nearly £63,000 in relief-in-need grants.

Applications: In writing to the correspondent stating the degree of vision and age of the applicant. Applications can be submitted directly by the individual or through a social worker, citizen's advice bureau or other welfare agency and are considered each month.

Correspondent: David J Bourne, Head of Appeals & Publicity, Wolverhampton Road East, Wolverhampton WV4 6AZ (0902-880111).

The Birmingham Jewish Welfare Board

Eligibility: Jewish people in need living in the West Midlands.

Types of grants: Mainly one-off grants ranging from £10 to £200. Grants are given to a small number of clients at Jewish festivals, for school clothing and occasionally to provide lifeline telephones and cover monitoring charges where there is no family support. There is also a kosher meals on wheels service.

Annual grant total: In 1992/93, expenditure totalled £700,000, but most of this was spent on maintaining two residential homes, a day centre and a full social work service. £1,300 was given in 21 grants to individuals.

Applications: In writing to the Principal Social Worker, including information on length of residence in the area, other applications made and whether or not the applicant is in receipt of Income Support. Applications are considered monthly and may be submitted directly by the individual or through a social worker, citizen's advice bureau or other welfare agency or third party eg. rabbis.

Correspondent: George Greenstone, Director, 1 Rake Way, Birmingham B15 1EG (021-643 2835).

The Birmingham & Midland Cinematograph Trade Benevolent Fund

Eligibility: Individuals and their dependents who are or have been employed for a reasonable period in the cinematograph industry in Birmingham or the Midland counties.

Types of grants: One-off or recurrent grants according to need.

Annual grant total: £3,500.

Applications: In writing to the correspondent or through a member of the Committee of Cinema Proprietors.

Correspondent: K West, Morse Stephens Accountants, Charter House, 165 Newhall Street Birmingham B3 1SW (021-200 3077).

The Thomas Bromwich Charity

Eligibility: People in need living in Handsworth (ie. the ecclesiastical parishes of St Mary, St Andrew, St James, St Michael, St Peter and the Holy Trinity, Birdfield and St Paul, and Hanstead); Great Barr (ie. the ecclesiastical parish of St Margaret), and Perry Barr (ie. the ecclesiastical parishes of St John the Evangelist, Perry Barr, St Luke, Kingstanding, and St Matthews and Perry Beeches).

Types of grants: One-off grants towards telephone installation, school uniform and payment of gas or electricity bills etc..

Annual grant total: In 1991, the trust had assets of £212,000 with an income of £17,000.

Applications: In writing to the correspondent either directly by the individual or through a social worker, citizen's advice bureau or other welfare agency. Applications are considered at any time.

Correspondent: John D Derry, Clerk, Willcox Lane Clutterbuck, 55 Charlotte Street, St Paul's Square, Birmingham B3 1PX (021-236 9441).

The Coventry Community Cancer Fund

Eligibility: Firstly, Macmillan nurses; secondly, people and families of people with cancer or cancer-related diseases living within 15 to 20 miles of Coventry city centre.

Types of grants: Grants have been given towards beds, washing machines, specialised medical aids for individuals, as well as towards the cost of nursing care.

Annual grant total: Money is raised locally each year and totalled £18,000 in 1993.

Applications: Applications can only be made through Macmillan nurses. No other referrals and no direct applications will be accepted.

Correspondent: D R Sarginson, Sarginsons, 11 Warwick Row, Coventry CV1 1EQ (0203-553181).

The Coventry Freemen's Charity

Eligibility: Freemen and their dependants who are in need and live within seven miles of St Mary's Hall, Coventry.

Types of grants: £39 quarterly to individuals who are 67 or over, or a lump sum grant to other applicants.

West Midlands

Annual grant total: Between £150,000 and £200,000 in about 1,300 grants.

Applications: In writing to the correspondent.

Correspondent: D J Evans, Clerk, Abbey House, Manor Road, Coventry CV1 2FW (0203-257317).

The Margery Fry Benevolent Fund

Eligibility: People who have suffered a restriction on their liberty by order of any court having criminal jurisdiction and who require assistance with accommodation needs.

Types of grants: Welfare grants to individuals or organisations needing funding for accommodation needs.

Annual grant total: In 1992/93, the trust had assets of £28,000 generating an income of £2,500. Grants totalled £13,000. It gives about six grants a year (out of about eight applications).

Applications: In writing to the correspondent.

Correspondent: F H Bayley, 3 The Maltings Court, 2 Anderson Road, Smethwick, Warley, West Midlands B66 4AR (021-434 3200).

The Grantham Yorke Trust

Eligibility: People under 25 who live in the West Midlands, in particular the Birmingham area.

Types of grants: One-off or recurrent grants according to need.

Annual grant total: According to the Charity Commission, in 1990 the trust had an income of £194,000. No more recent information is available.

Applications: In writing to the correspondent.

Correspondent: D L Turfrey, Martineau Johnson, St Philips House, St Philips Place, Birmingham B3 2PP (021-200 3300).

The Florence Juckes Memorial Trust Fund

Eligibility: People in need living within a 50-mile radius of Birmingham city centre.

Types of grants: Grants range from £30 to £150, but are generally £100 or less. Recent grants have included £30 for shoes for a disabled child and £100 towards car insurance for a disabled man.

Annual grant total: £1,000 in 1991/92.

Applications: In writing to the correspondent. Applications should be submitted directly by the individual. They are considered in September and March.

Correspondent: Miss A E Bond, 42 Whitehouse Way, Solihull, West Midlands B91 1SE (021-779 5337).

The Lant Trust

Eligibility: People in need, especially the elderly, living in the ecclesiastical parishes of Berkswell (St John the Baptist), Balsall Common (St Peter) and Temple Balsall (St Mary). The trust also augments three clergy stipends, and helps maintain some playing fields.

Types of grants: Probably one-off and recurrent grants according to need.

Annual grant total: In 1991, the trust's income was £20,000. Grants totalled about £10,000, including £6,000 in 50 relief-in-need grants to individuals and £4,000 to organisations. The trust may regularly have a surplus of income over expenditure. We have been unable to obtain more up-to-date information.

Applications: In writing to the correspondent.

Correspondent: Mr Dumbleton, c/o Rotherham & Co, 8–9 The Quadrant, Coventry CV1 2EG (0203-227331).

The James Frederick & Ethel Anne Measures Charity

Eligibility: (a) Applicants must usually originate in the West Midlands; (b) applicants must show evidence of self-help in their application; (c) trustees have a preference for disadvantaged people; (d) trustees have a dislike for students who have a full local authority grant and want finance for a different course or study; (e) trustees favour grants towards the cost of equipment; (f) applications by individuals in cases of hardship will not usually be considered unless sponsored by a local authority, health professional or other welfare agency.

Types of grants: One-off or recurrent grants according to need. Grants are usually between £50 and £500.

Annual grant total: £36,000 in 1992/93, 170 grants.

Applications: In writing to the correspondent. No reply to unsuccessful applicants unless an sae is enclosed.

Correspondent: D J K Nichols, Messrs Tyndallwoods & Millichip, Solicitors, 51–52 Calthorpe Road, Edgbaston, Birmingham B15 1RH (021-624 4000).

The Thomas Pargeter of Foxcote Charity & the John Wand Bequest

Eligibility: Women who have never been married, who are over 55 and live in their own homes. Preference for those living in the West Midlands area, but other areas of the country would be considered.

Types of grants: Annuities of £240, paid in quarterly instalments of £60, reviewed annually.

Annual grant total: £13,400 in 1992.

Applications: On a form available from the correspondent to be submitted directly by the individual and including two referees. Applications are considered in March and September.

Correspondent: Mrs Heddwen Harris, Clerk, 19 De Montfort Road, Hinckley, Leicestershire LE10 1LQ (0455-636602).

The Temple Balsall Amalgamated Charities

Eligibility: People in need who live in the ecclesiastical parishes of Temple Balsall and Balsall Common.

Types of grants: Grants are given "when, for whatever reason, illness, accident, bereavement etc. a sudden need arises; or when reduced circumstances and rising prices turn necessities into luxuries". The trust gives about 20 recurrent grants to individuals, five special grants to individuals, and eight grants to local organisations.

Annual grant total: The trust had an income of £5,000 in 1990.

Applications: In writing to the correspondent at any time. A trustee will then visit the applicant.

Correspondent: DW Hill, Clerk, 74 Broad Oaks Road, Solihull, West Midlands B991 1HZ (021-456 2525).

The Eric W Vincent Trust Fund

Eligibility: People in need living within a radius of 20 miles of Halesowen.

Types of grants: One-off grants. Grants are NOT given for second degrees or towards salaries in organisations.

Annual grant total: In 1990/91, the trust had assets of £650,000 with an income of about £44,000, but only some of this is available for relief-in-need to individuals.

Applications: Trustees normally meet five times a year. Applications should be in writing either directly by the individual or through a social worker, citizen's advice bureau or other welfare agency.

Correspondent: Mrs J Stephen, Clerk, 4–5 Summer Hill, Halesowen, West Midlands B63 3BU.

● Bilston

The Bilston Relief-in-Need Charity

Eligibility: People in need living in the ecclesiastical parish of Bilston and the area of the former borough of Bilston.

Types of grants: Generally one-off grants where help cannot be obtained from any other source.

Annual grant total: About £1,500.

Applications: Applications, in writing to the correspondent, can be submitted by the individual, through a recognised referral agency (eg. social worker, citizen's advice bureau or doctor) or other third party.

Correspondent: Rev P J Chapman, St Leonard's Vicarage, Dover Street, Bilston, West Midlands WV14 6AW (0902-491560).

● Birmingham

The Banner's Trust

Eligibility: Men and widows in need living in the city of Birmingham.

Types of grants: Clothing grants of about £100.

Annual grant total: £2,000 to £3,000.

Applications: Applicants must be nominated by trustees, doctors or by the Council for Old People.

Correspondent: Mrs Martin, Lee Crowder, 24 Harborne Road, Edgbaston, Birmingham B15 3AD (021-456 4477).

Other information: The trust can also give apprenticing grants, but this is done through certain colleges, applicants should not apply direct.

The Frances Lynn Betteridge Memorial Trust Fund

Eligibility: Children and young people under 18 who are in need and live in, or close to, the city of Birmingham. Preference will be given to those within the city.

Types of grants: One-off grants have been given for outings, holidays and special equipment. Grants are not given for clothing and toys.

Annual grant total: In 1992/93, the trust gave grants averaging £25 per child and £50 per family. In total about £6,000 was given in 113 grants.

Applications: Applicants must be nominated by a social worker.

Correspondent: Miss Beverley Tulloch, Social Service Department, The Directorate, Louisa Ryland House, 44 Newhall Street, Birmingham B3 3PL (021-235 3923).

The Birmingham Children's Holiday Fund

Eligibility: Children and young people aged 5 to 19 who live in Birmingham.

Types of grants: Towards holidays/outings for children in need as a result of social, emotional or environmental deprivation, who are known to social workers of the Child Advisory Social Work Service in Birmingham. Grants are also given towards day trips, adventure camps, caravan holidays, school/educational holidays/trips. Grants range from £20 to £100.

Grants are not given to children not known to the Child Advisory Social Work Service.

Annual grant total: In 1993, the trust had an income of £3,400 and gave 100 grants totalling £3,200.

Applications: Referrals are made via a social worker from the Child Advisory Social Work Service.

Correspondent: David Lake, Secretary, Child Advisory Social Work Service (South), 74 Balden Road, Harborne, Birmingham B32 2EH (021-428 1166).

The Birmingham Royal Institution for the Blind

Eligibility: Registered blind people who live in Birmingham.

Types of grants: One-off grants up to £200. Grants are not given for items that should be covered by the DSS or Social Services Department or for structural alterations to property.

Annual grant total: £3,000 in 45 grants.

Applications: Preferably through a social worker, although individuals can apply directly on a form available from the correspondent. Grants of up to £100 are considered in the Vision Services Department and larger grants by a small committee.

Correspondent: Mrs J Hancox, Vision Services Department, 62 Woodville Road, Harborne, Birmingham B17 9AX (021-428 5080).

The Baron Davenport Emergency Grant

Eligibility: Needy widows, spinsters and children under 21 whose fathers are dead, who live in the city of Birmingham. In practice, applications from women who are unmarried but who have children are not accepted.

Types of grants: One-off grants of £40 to £100 depending on need. Mainly for clothing, household essentials and convalescence.

Annual grant total: £2,000.

Applications: In writing to the correspondent. Applications can be submitted directly by the individual or through a social worker, citizen's advice bureau or other welfare agency. If the need is covered by the Social Fund, the applicant should approach them first. Applications are considered throughout the year.

Correspondent: The Personal & Financial Counselling Service, BVSC, 138 Digbeth, Birmingham B5 6DR (021-643 4343).

Other information: For information on Baron Davenport's Charty Trust, see entry in the Midlands general section.

The George Fentham (Birmingham) Trust

Eligibility: People in need who have lived in the city of Birmingham for a long time.

Types of grants: One-off or recurrent relief-in-need grants to individuals.

Annual grant total: In 1990, the trust had assets of £375,000 and an income of £48,000. About 20 grants of between £150 and £400 were given to individuals in need. The trust also gives grants to organisations.

Applications: In writing to the correspondent. Applications should be made through a social worker, citizen's advice bureau or other welfare agency.

Correspondent: Mrs A E Holmes, Lee Crowder, 24 Harborne Road, Edgbaston, Birmingham B15 3AD (021-456 4477).

The Charity of Jane Kate Gilbert

Eligibility: People of at least 60 years of age and in need who have lived in Birmingham for at least two years.

Types of grants: Quarterly pensions of £10 (currently £40 a year to 32 people).

Annual grant total: About £1,300.

Applications: On a form available from the correspondent. Applications can be

West Midlands

submitted directly by the individual but should include a letter from a social worker, doctor, minister of religion or other third party.

Correspondent: Louisa Nisbett, Clerk, Central Executive Department, The Council House, Birmingham B1 1BB (021-235 9944).

The Handsworth Charities including the Charity of William Stevenson

Eligibility: People living in the ancient parish of Handsworth (now in Birmingham) which covers Kingstanding.

Types of grants: One-off grants of about £90 for travel expenses to and from hospital, outfits and tools to enter a trade, profession or calling, and general necessities for people in need. Regular pensions are given to elderly people.

Annual grant total: In 1993, about 20 grants were given totalling nearly £2,000. Christmas grants were also given to 9 pensioners. The trust regularly has a surplus of income over expenditure.

Applications: In writing to the correspondent.

Correspondent: G R De'Ath, Clerk, Shakespeares, Solicitors, 10 Bennetts Hill, Birmingham B2 5RS (021-632 4199).

The CB & AB Holinsworth Fund of Help

Eligibility: People in need who live in the city of Birmingham.

Types of grants: One-off grants to help recovery from sickness are given for convalescence or help in the home. Generally no grants for bills or debts. In 1993, grants ranged from £50 to £250.

Annual grant total: In 1993, the trust gave grants totalling about £9,000.

Applications: On a form available from the correspondent. Applications are considered throughout the year. Individuals should apply through an organisation, not directly.

Correspondent: Louisa Nisbett, Clerk, Central Executive Department, The Council House, Birmingham B1 1BB (021-235 9944).

The Charity of Joseph Hopkins

Eligibility: People who live in the city of Birmingham.

Types of grants: Clothing vouchers at Christmas. Applications from individuals cannot be considered and grants are only made via registered charities. Grants range between £100 and £500.

Annual grant total: In 1992/93, the trust had assets of £387,000 generating a net income of £67,000. Grants totalled £65,000.

Applications: On a form available from the correspondent to be submitted directly by the charity. Applications are considered twice yearly.

Correspondent: H B Carslake, Clerk, Martineau Johnson, St Philips House, St Philips Place, Birmingham B3 2PP (021-200 3300).

The Charity of Harriet Louisa Loxton

Eligibility: People in need through old age, infirmity or any other circumstance who live in Birmingham.

Types of grants: One-off grants according to need.

Annual grant total: Between October 1992, when the trust started, to December 1993, a total of 81 grants were given totalling £104,000.

Applications: Applications must be made through officers of the Birmingham Social Services Department.

Correspondent: The Director of Social Services, Strategic Planing Section, Level 5, Louisa Ryland House, 44 Newhall Street, Birmingham B3 3PL (021-235 2711).

Other information: The trust was established from proceeds of the sale of Icknield, a property donated to the city by Harriet Louisa Loxton for use as a home for elderly people.

The Robert Stevens Charity

Eligibility: Individuals and families in need where statutory help is not available and who live in the ecclesiastical parish of St Mary's, Moseley and "other districts of Birmingham".

Types of grants: One-off grants ranging from £30 to £100. Grants have been given towards a special car seat for a disabled child, clothing and other essentials, and school uniform for children.

Annual grant total: About £1,300 in 1993.

Applications: In writing to the correspondent, usually through referral by social services and other national or local organisations. Applications are considered in February, May, September and November.

Correspondent: Miss M M Brown, Secretary, 6 Salisbury Close, Moseley, Birmingham B13 8JX (021-442 4246).

● Bradley

The Greenway Benefaction Trust

Eligibility: People in need living in the Bradley area of the borough of Wolverhampton.

Types of grants: Towards the cost of holidays, convalescence, toys, entertainment etc..

Annual grant total: In 1992/93, the trust had an income of £1,100. No grants appear to have been given nor, as in previous years, does it seem to have spent all of its income.

Applications: Applications can be submitted by the individual or through a recognised referral agency (eg. social worker, citizen's advice bureau or doctor) and are considered as received.

Correspondent: The Director of Legal & Admin. Services, Wolverhampton Borough Council, Finance Department, Civic Centre, St Peter's Square, Wolverhampton WV1 1RL (0902-27811 ext. 5027).

● Bushbury

The Bushbury United Charities

Eligibility: People in need living in the ancient and rural parishes of Bushbury.

Types of grants: Annual grants.

Annual grant total: £11,500 in 395 grants in 1990.

Applications: In writing to the correspondent. Applications are considered once a year.

Correspondent: The Chairman of the Trustees, The Rectory, 382 Bushbury Lane, Wolverhampton WV10 8JP.

● Castle Bromwich

The Dame Mary Bridgeman Charity

Eligibility: People in need living in the ecclesiastical parishes of St Mary, St Margaret and St Clement, Castle Bromwich.

Types of grants: Grants range from £25 to £750.

Annual grant total: In 1990/91, the trust's income was £6,100. Expenditure totalled £5,300 in 21 grants (not all to individuals).

Applications: In writing to the correspondent, directly by the individual or through a social worker or other welfare agency, or through a third party such as church, school or parent. Applications are considered mainly in May and October.

Correspondent: P B Jackson, Secretary, 147 Chester Road, Castle Bromwich, Birmingham B36 0AE (021-747 2498).

● **Coventry**

The Children's Boot Fund

Eligibility: School-children in the city of Coventry, aged 4 to 16.

Types of grants: Grants for school footwear for children in need. No other type of help is given. Grants are made direct to footwear suppliers in the form of vouchers.

Annual grant total: In 1993, the trust had an income of £13,000 and an expenditure of £9,700. 469 grants totalled £9,100.

Applications: Referrals are made by local schools to the executive committee which meets four times a year in February, May, September and December.

Correspondent: P R H Hancock, Hon. Secretary, 19 Priorsfield Road, Kenilworth CV8 1DA (0926-54818).

The Coventry Charity for Special Relief

Eligibility: People in need living in the city of Coventry.

Types of grants: One-off grants up to £200 according to need. Grants have recently been given towards a cooker, children's shoes, a robotron reading system and payment of a gas bill. No grants for an individual's holiday, council tax payments or to buy tens machines.

Annual grant total: In 1992, the trust had assets of £52,000 producing an income of £4,400. 50 grants to individuals totalled £5,400.

Applications: On a form available from the correspondent. Applications can be submitted by the individual or through a recognised referral agency (eg. social worker, citizen's advice bureau or doctor) and are considered three times a year.

Correspondent: The City Secretary, The Council House, Earl Street, Coventry CV1 5RR (0203-833031).

The Coventry Convalescent Fund

Eligibility: People who have been patients in Coventry hospitals.

Types of grants: Payments are made only towards convalescence recommended by a doctor or social worker, and may occasionally include the cost of patients' travel to and from the convalescent home. Payments are made direct to convalescent homes rather than to the individual. In 1992/93, 14 patients were helped and 37 weeks of convalescence paid for.

Annual grant total: In 1990/91, the trust's income was £3,700 including donations of £2,000. Expenditure totalled about £4,000. No more recent information available.

Applications: Applications can only be made via a social worker on a form provided by the trust. They are considered at any time.

Correspondent: Mrs A D Pendle, Secretary, 124 Rochester Road, Coventry CV5 6AG (0203-675495).

The Coventry Nursing Trust

Eligibility: People in need living in the city of Coventry.

Types of grants: Grants for the relief of sickness are mainly given to help with night sitting costs, although day sitting is also provided for. Help with day-to-day expenses is not given.

Annual grant total: About £12,000.

Applications: In writing to the correspondent.

Correspondent: Mrs E A Martin, Clerk, 44 Madeira Croft, Chapelfields, Coventry CV5 8NY (0203-711082).

The Dunsmoor Day Nursery & Maternity Home (also known as the Dunsmoor Charity)

Eligibility: Expectant mothers, mothers with babies, and mothers of young children under the age of 16 and living in the city of Coventry.

Types of grants: One-off grants averaging about £50 for baby equipment, bedding etc..

Annual grant total: In 1993, grants totalled around £3,000.

Applications: In writing to the correspondent.

Correspondent: Miss E Mathews, Mander, Hadley & Co, Solicitors, 1 The Quadrant, Coventry CV1 2DW (0203-631212).

The General Charities of the City of Coventry

Eligibility: People in need living in the city of Coventry.

Types of grants: One-off and recurrent grants to individuals in need, gifts to pensioners and interest-free loans to freemen of the city of Coventry.

Annual grant total: In 1993, the trust had an income of about £200,000. Grants totalled £177,000, including £52,000 to pensioners over 70 and over £55,000 for a variety of relief-in-need purposes. A further £70,000 was given to organisations.

Applications: Must be made through statutory bodies.

Correspondent: The Clerk, Old Bablake, Hill Street, Coventry CV1 4AN (0203-222769).

Other information: The charities receive income from Sir Thomas White's Charity including the allocation for the Sir Thomas White's Loan Fund in Coventry.

The Lord Mayor's Common Good Fund

Eligibility: Mainly elderly people who live in Coventry.

Types of grants: Welfare grants, typically about £50, up to a usual maximum of £200.

Annual grant total: About £1,200.

Applications: In writing to the Lord Mayor. Applications are usually considered within two weeks.

Correspondent: The Lord Mayor's Secretariat, Lord Mayor's Office, Council House, Earl Street, Coventry CV1 5RR (0203-833100).

The Dr William MacDonald of Johannesburg Trust

Eligibility: People in need who live in Coventry.

Types of grants: One-off welfare grants, typically about £50, usual maximum £200.

Annual grant total: About £2,000.

Applications: In writing to the Lord Mayor. Applications are usually considered within two weeks.

Correspondent: The Lord Mayor's Secretariat, Lord Mayor's Office, Council House, Earl Street, Coventry CV1 5RR (0203-833100).

The Charity of John Moore

Eligibility: People in need, generally elderly, living in the city of Coventry.

Types of grants: Grants of up to £15 usually given in December and March.

Annual grant total: About £2,000.

West Midlands

Applications: The money is distributed by the five trustees to suitable people either directly or through local churches.

Correspondent: C Adams, Sarginsons, 11 Warwick Row, Coventry CV1 1EQ (0203-553181).

The Penderels Trust Fund

Eligibility: People who are disabled and living independently in the community in the city of Coventry.

Types of grants: This trust is exceptional in the size of the grant it gives to individuals. In 1992/93, £191,500 was given, mainly to 17 individuals (many appear to have been regular beneficiaries) and to support the continuation of a Community Services Volunteer Scheme supporting 15 people. Grants can be to individuals, couples and to carers.

Annual grant total: About £191,500 in 1992/93.

Applications: In writing to the correspondent.

Correspondent: The Manager, 474 Woodway Lane, Potters Green, Coventry CV2 2LW (0203-226575).

Samuel Smith Charity, Coventry

Eligibility: People in need who live in Coventry and the ancient parish of Bedworth.

Types of grants: One-off grants and pensions according to need.

Annual grant total: About £31,000.

Applications: Applications can be made in writing to the correspondent, but most beneficiaries are referred by the charity's almoner.

Correspondent: J C B Leech, Trustee, Kidsons Impey, Park House, Station Square, Coventry CV1 2NS (0203-256333).

Spencer's Charity

Eligibility: Elderly ladies in need living in the city of Coventry.

Types of grants: Pensions of £10 a month.

Annual grant total: About £20,000 to between 160 and 170 beneficiaries.

Applications: In writing to the correspondent.

Correspondent: G T W Foottit, c/o Browetts Solicitors, 23 Bayley Lane, Coventry CV1 5RJ (0203-553311).

The Tansley Charity Trust

Eligibility: Elderly or infirm women living in the city of Coventry.

Types of grants: One-off grants up to £200 according to need. Help has recently been given to buy a speech synthesizer, for telephone installation, payment of a television licence and gas bill, and with the cost of group holidays. No grants for the payment of council tax or to buy a tens machine.

Annual grant total: In 1993, the trust had assets of £88,000 producing an income of £7,000. Total expenditure was £10,400. Grants of up to £200 were given to 47 individuals and totalled £8,000.

Applications: On a form available from the correspondent. Applications can be submitted by the individual or through a recognised referral agency (eg. social worker, citizen's advice bureau or doctor) and are considered three times a year.

Correspondent: The City Secretary, The Council House, Earl Street, Coventry CV1 5RR (0203-833031).

The Harry Weston Memorial Fund

Eligibility: Old age pensioners living in the city of Coventry.

Types of grants: Television licences and rental and other items to relieve need.

Annual grant total: In 1992, the trust had an income of £1,500. Grants were given to 15 people totalling £750. The income for 1993 was expected to be £2,500.

Applications: In writing to the correspondent.

Correspondent: A W Parsons, 56 Kenilworth Road, Leamington Spa, Warwickshire CV32 6JW (0926-420604).

Darlaston

The Darlaston Relief-in-Sickness Fund

Eligibility: People in need living in Darlaston.

Types of grants: One-off or recurrent grants according to need.

Annual grant total: No information available.

Applications: In writing to the correspondent.

Correspondent: C J Forester, Messrs Haden, Stretton, Slater & Miller, 43 Church Street, Darlaston, Wednesbury, West Midlands WS10 8EA.

Other information: This entry has not been confirmed by the trust.

Dudley

The Baron Davenport Emergency Grant

Eligibility: Needy widows, spinsters and children under 21 whose fathers are dead, who live in Dudley.

Types of grants: One-off emergency grants.

Annual grant total: About £2,000.

Applications: Applications are usually made through a social worker or a citizen's advice bureau, but they can be made directly.

Correspondent: Mrs G C Cooper, Gen. Secretary, Dudley Council for Voluntary Service, 7 Albion Street, Brierly Hill, West Midlands DY5 3EE (0384-73381).

Other information: For information on Baron Davenport's Charity Trust, see entry in the Midlands general section.

The Dudley Charity

Eligibility: People in need living in the old county borough of Dudley (as constituted on 31st March, 1965).

Types of grants: Grants are given direct to the individual and via local clergy. In 1992/93, £6,300 was given direct to individuals in food and clothing vouchers; £1,600 to 10 local parishes, to be given to individuals in need by the respective vicars; and £2,000 was given in eight payments for specific items for named people or through organisations.

Annual grant total: In 1992/93, the trust had assets of £98,000 generating an income of £9,200. Grants totalled £9,900.

Applications: In writing to the correspondent or through local clergy.

Correspondent: D C Jones, Secretary, Swinford House, Albion Street, Brierley Hill, West Midlands DY5 3EL (0384-75611).

The Reginald Unwin Dudley Charity

Eligibility: Mainly elderly and chronically sick people in need living in the area administered by Dudley Metropolitan Council.

Types of grants: Grants for emergency needs ranging from £35 to £500.

Annual grant total: In 1992/93, the trust's income was £5,500 which was given in about 40 grants.

Applications: On an application form available by writing to the correspondent.

Correspondent: R J Little, 27 Priory Close, Dudley, West Midlands DY1 3ED.

West Midlands

Foleshill

The Foleshill Aid-in-Sickness Fund

Eligibility: People in need living in Foleshill.

Types of grants: One-off grants.

Annual grant total: About £2,000 in about 10 grants.

Applications: In writing to the correspondent.

Correspondent: Peter Cooper, 11 Unicorn Lane, Eastern Green, Coventry CV5 7LN (0203-474061).

Meriden

The Meriden United Charities

Eligibility: People in need who have lived in Meriden for at least the two years before their application.

Types of grants: One-off or recurrent grants according to need.

Annual grant total: In 1991, the trust's income was £1,100; five grants totalled £500.

Applications: In writing to the correspondent.

Correspondent: Alan Barker, Clerk, Francis Webb, Chartered Accountants, Melrose House, 53 Walsgrave Road, Coventry CV2 4HE (0203-221080).

Sandwell

The Fordath Foundation

Eligibility: People in need living in the borough of Sandwell.

Types of grants: About 50 one-off grants ranging from £25 to £200 to cover a wide range of need including holidays, funeral expenses, furniture, heating bills, essential clothing and equipment.

Annual grant total: £5,500 in 1993.

Applications: Applications should be made through Sandwell Social Services, the West Midlands Probation Service, the WRVS or similar welfare agency. Applications are considered throughout the year, funds permitting.

Correspondent: J Sutcliffe, Kebroyd, 22 Mount Pleasant, Derrington, Stafford ST18 9NB (0785-47035).

The Mayor's General Fund

Eligibility: People in need living in the area covered by Sandwell Metropolitan Borough Council.

Types of grants: Generally small grants (usually about £25, but up to £100) to help with one-off financial needs (eg. clothing, fuel bills etc.).

Annual grant total: About £1,000.

Applications: In writing to the correspondent through a social worker, citizen's advice bureau or other welfare agency. Applications are considered at any time. Letters must be addressed to the Mayor of Sandwell.

Correspondent: Michael Kean-Price, Mayor's Officer, Mayor's Parlour, Sandwell Council House, Oldbury, Sandwell, West Midlands B69 3DE (021-569 3050).

The George & Thomas Henry Salter Trust

Eligibility: People in need living in the borough of Sandwell.

Types of grants: Weekly cash payments totalled £200 and welfare assistance £1,500.

Annual grant total: The income of the George & Henry Salter Trust is divided equally for relief-in-need and education. In 1989, the income for relief-in-need purposes was £22,700. Grants totalled £4,100 leaving a surplus of £18,600. No more recent information available.

Applications: Initially by letter to the correspondent. The trustees interview all new applicants (unless their application is made through a social worker, who should write giving full details of the applicant's circumstances). The trustees meet monthly.

Correspondent: Mrs Styler, Clerk, Lombard House, Cronehills Linkway, West Bromwich B70 7PL (021-553 3286).

Solihull

The Baron Davenport Emergency Grant

Eligibility: Needy widows, spinsters and children under 21 whose fathers are dead, who live in the metropolitan borough of Solihull.

Types of grants: One-off emergency grants for widows, unmarried women and fatherless children who are in need.

Annual grant total: About £2,000.

Applications: Applications are made through referrals from the social services/housing departments, the probation service or other recognised welfare agencies, and not through direct personal application.

Correspondent: Andrew Moore, General Manager, Solihull Council for Voluntary Service, Alice House, 10 Homer Road, Solihull, West Midlands B91 3QQ (021-704 1619).

Other information: For information on Baron Davenport's Charity Trust, see entry in the Midlands general section.

Stourbridge

The Palmer & Seabright Charity

Eligibility: Elderly people in need living in the parish of Stourbridge.

Types of grants: The 1988 report of the trustees stated: "The activities of the charity during the year is to make grants not exceeding £4.80 [a week] to needy people (chiefly old age pensioners) on Supplementary Benefit or financially helping students towards the cost of books, instruments etc. whilst attending university or college."

Annual grant total: In 1988, the trust had an income of £15,000. Grants to individuals for relief-in-need and education totalled £7,300, leaving a further £5,600 unspent. It is thought the income for 1992 was nearly £19,000, it is not known how much was given in grants. See Other information below.

Applications: In writing to the correspondent.

Correspondent: Roger Kendrick, Wall, James & Davis, 19 Hagley Road, Stourbridge, West Midlands DY8 1QW (0384-370911).

Other information: The correspondent insists that the charity does not wish to be included in the Guide and so will not update the financial information. However, it is our policy to include all publicly registered charities of relevance.

Sutton Coldfield

The Sutton Coldfield Municipal Charities - General Charity

Eligibility: People in need living in the Four Oaks, New Hall and Vesey wards of Sutton Coldfield.

Types of grants: In 1992/93, as well as maintaining almshouses, the General Charity gave grants for children's clothing totalling £66,400 and "Other grants" totalling £1,291,000. It is not known what proportion of "Other grants" were given to individuals compared to organisations. The trust prefers to give one-off grants.

West Midlands

Annual grant total: In 1992/93, the income available for distribution was £628,000 (from assets of £6,500,000).

Applications: On a form available from the correspondent or in writing initially. Applications should be made directly by the individual and are considered from September to July.

Correspondent: The Clerk, Lingard House, Fox Hollies Road, Sutton Coldfield B76 8RJ (021-351 2262).

Tettenhall

The Tettenhall Relief-in-Need & Educational Charity

Eligibility: People in need living in the parish of Tettenhall as constituted on 22nd June 1888.

Types of grants: Usually £25 at Christmas to each individual.

Annual grant total: In 1990/91, the trust's income was £1,900; 48 grants to individuals totalled £1,200.

Applications: In writing to the correspondent. Applications should be made through a social worker, citizen's advice bureau or other welfare agency, doctors or senior citizen's organisations. They are considered in November and June, but in emergencies applications can be considered quickly.

Correspondent: L Haworth, 46 Knights Avenue, Tettenhall, Wolverhampton WV6 9QA (0902-752679).

Walsall

The Baron Davenport Emergency Grant

Eligibility: Needy widows, spinsters and children under 21 whose fathers are dead, who live in the borough of Walsall.

Types of grants: One-off emergency grants ranging from £10 to £120. Grants have been given towards payment of heating bills, minor urgent repairs to property (especially where safety is a factor), help towards the cost of bedding and winter clothes.

Annual grant total: £1,300 in 20 grants in 1992/93.

Applications: On a form available from the correspondent. Applications are considered in January, March, May, July, September and December.

Correspondent: K Buckler, Chief Officer, Walsall Guild for Voluntary Service, 50 Lower Hall Lane, Walsall WS1 1RJ (0922-38825).

Other information: For information on Baron Davenport's Charity Trust, see entry in the Midlands general section.

The Blanch Woolaston Walsall Charity

Eligibility: People in need living in the borough of Walsall.

Types of grants: One-off grants, firstly for people under 21 towards employment training, and then grants for general hardship, usually paid at Christmas.

Annual grant total: In 1992/93, grants totalled £1,350. Around £1,200 was given in £2 and £3 Christmas gifts to needy people nominated by the seven trustees. Students received grants of £50/£60.

Applications: In writing to the correspondent.

Correspondent: The Director of Legal & Admin. Services, Walsall Metropolitan Borough Council, Civic Centre, Darwall Street, Walsall WS1 1TP (0922-650000).

Wednesfield

The Wednesfield Parochial Charity

Eligibility: People in need living in the ecclesiastical parish of St Thomas, Wednesfield.

Types of grants: One-off or recurrent grants according to need.

Annual grant total: In 1992, the trust's income was £2,100. Grants included £600 to individuals. (A further £260 was distributed via local clergy, £535 was given at Christmas to social services and £320 was given to five organisations).

Applications: In writing to the correspondent.

Correspondent: The Rector, The Rectory, 9 Vicarage Road, Wednesfield, Wolverhampton WV11 1SB (0902-731462).

West Bromwich

The Charles Akrill Trust

Eligibility: People in need who live in the old county borough of West Bromwich.

Types of grants: Grants for the relief of sickness, aids for blind people and essential equipment for disabled people.

Annual grant total: In 1992, the trust had assets of £59,000 and an income of £7,000. Grants for 1993, totalled about £6,500.

Applications: In writing to the correspondent.

Correspondent: D G Smith, Secretary, 58 Catholic Lane, Sedgley, Dudley (0902-884500).

The Charity of Jane Patricia Eccles

Eligibility: Elderly women in need living within the old West Bromwich boundary.

Types of grants: Generally one-off grants to meet specific needs eg. mobile phone, shower, central heating for elderly or disabled people.

Annual grant total: £1,200.

Applications: Applications must be made through, and include a letter of support from a church minister or welfare agency.

Correspondent: Mrs J E Wakeman, 2 Waddington Avenue, Great Barr, Birmingham B43 5JG (021-357 4415).

The K A Macaulay Trust

Eligibility: People in need living in West Bromwich.

Types of grants: To enable people to buy a house for his or her occupation.

Annual grant total: In 1992/93, the trust had an income of £1,600. No grants were given.

Applications: In writing to the correspondent. Applications should be made directly by the individual and are considered at any time.

Correspondent: J M A Price, Secretary, c/o West Bromwich Building Society, 374 High Street, West Bromwich B70 8LR (021-525 7070).

Wolverhampton

The Baron Davenport Emergency Grant

Eligibility: Needy widows and children under 21 whose fathers are dead, who have lived in Wolverhampton for 10 years.

Types of grants: One-off grants for emergencies only where statutory help is not available. Grants are usually to a maximum of £150.

Annual grant total: About £2,000 in 1993.

Applications: Applications can only be made through voluntary and statutory organisations based in Wolverhampton, and are considered every six weeks.

Correspondent: The General Secretary, Wolverhampton Voluntary Sector Council, 2-3 Bell Street, Wolverhampton WV1 3PR (0902-773761/2).

Other information: For information on Baron Davenport's Charity Trust, see entry in the Midlands general section.

The Power Pleas Trust

Eligibility: Mainly young people with muscular dystrophy and similar diseases living in the borough of Wolverhampton.

Types of grants: To "relieve children and young people suffering from muscular dystrophy and other similar diseases and handicaps generally and in particular in the purchase and provision of outdoor electric wheelchairs and such other aids as trustees may from time to time decide".

Annual grant total: No information available.

Applications: In writing to the correspondent.

Correspondent: Mrs Valerie Rendell, 44 Torvale Road, Wightwick, Wolverhampton WV6 8NL (0902-761951).

● **Yardley**

The Yardley Great Trust

Eligibility: People living in the ancient parish of Yardley in the city of Birmingham. This includes the wards of Yardley, Acocks Green, Fox Hollies, Billesley, Hall Green and part of the wards of Hodge Hill, Shard End, Sheldon, Small Heath, Sparkhill, Moseley, Sparkbrook and Brandwood. (A map is produced by the trust outlining the beneficial area.)

Types of grants: "The trust will help most organisations and individuals (through an agency) within its benefit area, excepting that help which is something the local authority or a government department should provide." The trust also provides sheltered accommodation for the elderly.

Annual grant total: In 1992, the trust had assets of about £10 million, mainly in almshouses. Grants total up to £100,000 each year, about £30,000 was given in 80 grants to individuals in 1992.

Applications: On a form available from the correspondent. Applications should be submitted through a social worker, citizen's advice bureau or other welfare agency or through a third party such as a local priest, headteacher, councillor, MP etc.. They are considered each month.

Correspondent: L K Moreton, Clerk, Old Brookside, Yardley Fields Road, Stechford, Birmingham B33 8QL (021-784 7889).

7. South West

The Avon & Somerset Constabulary Benevolent Fund

Eligibility: Serving and retired police members of the Avon & Somerset Constabulary and their dependents.

Types of grants: One-off grants up to £2,000 for equipment and house repairs; interest-free loans up to £3,000 to cover debts or other urgent needs.

No grants for private medical treatment or legal representation.

Annual grant total: About £20,000 in 1993.

Applications: Applications must be submitted with a report and recommendation by a force welfare officer. They can be considered at any time.

Correspondent: P Roberts, Force Welfare Officer, Avon & Somerset Constabulary Headquarters, Valley Road, Portishead, Bristol BS20 8QJ (0272-454372).

The J H Beckly Handicapped/Sick Children's Fund

Eligibility: Children under 18 who live in the city of Plymouth or district of Caradon, Cornwall and who are sick or disabled.

Types of grants: Generally one-off grants.

Annual grant total: In 1993, the trust had assets of £102,000 and an income of £7,600. Grants ranging from £50 to £500 were given to 25 individuals.

Applications: In writing to the correspondent giving brief details of income and outgoings of the applicant's parent/guardian. Applications should be made through a welfare agency or other third party.

Correspondent: T J P Emerson, Foot & Bowden, 70-76 North Hill, Plymouth, Devon PL4 8HH (0752-663416).

The Devon & Cornwall Aid for Girls Trust

Eligibility: Girls who live in the counties of Devon and Cornwall. There is a preference for orphans (that is those who have lost either or both parents), but any other girl in need can apply.

Types of grants: One-off and recurrent grants according to need.

Annual grant total: £9,800.

Applications: In writing to the correspondent.

Correspondent: F G Uglow, Flat 36, 8 Grand Parade, The Hoe, Plymouth, Devon PL1 3DF (0752-674800).

The Mine Accident Fund for Cornwall & Devon

Eligibility: Miners (and their dependants) in Cornwall and Devon who are suffering from injuries received directly or indirectly in connection with their employment, but who are not entitled to compensation under the Workmen's Compensation Act 1906 or any amending act.

Types of grants: Mostly recurrent grants of £5 a week (£260 a year) and some one-off grants.

Annual grant total: In 1992, the trust had an income of £1,500. Total expenditure was £2,000. Grants of between £25 and £260 were given to 16 individuals and totalled £1,950.

Applications: In writing to the correspondent including financial circumstances and all state benefits and other charitable grants received. Applications can be submitted directly by the individual or through a social worker, citizen's advice bureau or other welfare agency. They are considered in May and October.

Correspondent: J C Beling, c/o Carnon Consolidated Ltd, South Crofty Mine, Dudnance Lane, Pool, Redruth, Cornwall TR15 3QH (0209-714821).

South West/Avon

The Plymouth & Cornwall Cancer Fund

Eligibility: People in need who live in the county of Cornwall and within a radius of 40 miles of Plymouth Civic Centre in Devon. Priority to people who are poor, sick, infirm or elderly, and those who have cancer (or related diseases), as well as in-patients and out-patients of any hospital controlled by the Plymouth & District Hospital Management Committee or any of its successors in title.

Types of grants: One-off and recurrent grants according to need.

Annual grant total: In 1991, the fund had an income of £14,500 of which £4,500 was given in hardship grants and the rest towards research.

Applications: In writing to the correspondent.

Correspondent: Mr Crocker, Whiteford Crocker Solicitors, 111 The Ridgeway, Plympton, Plymouth PL7 3AA (0752-335994).

Avon

The Bristol Municipal Charities

Eligibility: People in need who for the last five years have lived within a 10-mile radius of Bristol city centre.

Types of grants: Quarterly allowances and one-off grants for emergencies, clothing, household equipment, furniture, medical equipment and aids for disabled people. No grants for debts or telephones (another trust covers these). Only one grant per applicant per year and there is a limit of four yearly grants.

Annual grant total: In 1992/93, the trust had assets of £4,600,000 producing an income of £500,000. Total expenditure for the year was £530,000. The annual grant total amounted to £400,000 of which £252,000 was given to 2,250 individuals in relief-in-need grants ranging from £35 to £1,000.

Applications: Applications, on a form available from the correspondent, should be submitted through a recognised referral agency (social worker, citizen's advice bureau, doctor, clergy etc.) and are considered daily.

Correspondent: The Secretary General, Orchard Street, Bristol BS1 5EQ (0272-290084).

The Grateful Society

Eligibility: Women over 50 who have lived in Avon for at least 10 years.

Types of grants: Regular allowances and occasional gifts.

Annual grant total: In 1991, the trust had assets of £300,000 and an income of £40,000. Expenditure totalled £33,000 including £27,000 in 58 relief-in-need grants.

Applications: Applications, on a form available from the correspondent, can be submitted directly by the individual or through a recognised referral agency (eg. social worker, citizen's advice bureau or doctor) and are considered throughout the year.

Correspondent: Charles Wyld, Hon. Secretary, c/o Burges Salmon, Narrow Quay House, Prince Street, Bristol BS1 4AH (0272-276567).

The Peter Herve Benevolent Institution

Eligibility: People aged 60 and over who are in need, are of "the middle ranks of life" and who live in a 25-mile radius of the Exchange in Bristol. People of former independence or profession, tutors and governesses or people who once supported elderly relatives are given some preference.

Types of grants: One-off and recurrent grants according to need.

Annual grant total: About £6,000.

Applications: In writing to the correspondent.

Correspondent: Tim Baines, Coopers & Lybrand, 66 Queen Square, Bristol BS1 4JP (0272-292791).

Bath

The Bath Municipal Charities

Eligibility: People in need and those who are sick and in need who live in or very near Bath.

Types of grants: One-off grants only, generally up to £1,000. One of the charities makes grants for the benefit of mentally disabled children (under 18) in need of special educational treatment.

Annual grant total: In 1990, the charities had an income of £40,000 and expenditure of around £10,000.

Applications: On a form available from the Almoner, Mrs C Bayntun-Coward, 4 Chapel Court, Bath BA1 1SZ (0225-443117). Applications should be made either by the individual or through a social worker, citizen's advice bureau or other welfare agency.

Correspondent: Mr Elston, Clerk, Midland Bridge Road, Bath BA1 2HQ (0225-448494).

The Mayor of Bath's Relief Fund

Eligibility: People in need who live in Bath.

Types of grants: One-off grants for a wide range of needs.

Annual grant total: In 1992/93, the trust had assets of £63,000 and an income of £4,700. 16 grants were made totalling £2,530.

Applications: On a form available from the correspondent. Applications can be submitted directly by the individual or through a social worker, citizen's advice bureau or other welfare agency. They are considered throughout the year.

Correspondent: Colin M Goater, Corporate Services Division, City Treasurer's Department, Bath City Council, Guild Hall, High Street, Bath BA1 5AW (0225-461111 ext. 2341).

The Monmouth Street Society, Bath

Eligibility: The "deserving poor" who live in Bath.

Types of grants: One-off and recurrent grants up to £150 for food, solid fuel, kitchen appliances, furniture, television licence, outstanding debts such as electricity, gas, rent, water rates, telephone (where essential).

Annual grant total: In 1992, the trust's income was £6,200. 35 relief-in-need grants totalled £6,300 (£2,830 in one-off grants and £3,300 in pensions).

Applications: Preference for personal applications, but will accept any received through social workers and such like. All cases are investigated by a member of the society, and are considered throughout the year.

Correspondent: The Hon. Secretary, 4 Chapel Court, Bath BA1 1SQ.

The St John's Hospital, Bath

Eligibility: People in need living in Bath. There are no age restrictions.

Types of grants: One-off grants only with no fixed maximum but generally not more than £500. Help is given towards gas and electricity bills and domestic equipment, and other requests are considered.

Annual grant total: In 1993, 600 relief-in-need grants were given, totalling £120,000. The budget for 1994 is £120,000.

Applications: On a form available from Mrs C Bayntun-Coward, Almoner, 4 Chapel Court, Bath BA1 1SL (0225-443117). Applications can be made at any time through a social worker, citizen's advice bureau or other welfare agency. The almoner visits applicants at home and meets with two trustees twice-weekly to decide on awards.

Correspondent: Q T S Elston, Clerk, Midland Bridge Road, Bath BA1 2HQ (0225-448494).

● **Bristol**

The Anchor Society

Eligibility: Elderly people in need who live in Bristol.

Types of grants: One-off and recurrent grants according to need (usually up to £500).

Annual grant total: About £4,000 in one-off grants; about £14,000 is given in annuities.

Applications: On a form available from the correspondent.

Correspondent: J S Ledbury, Hon. Secretary, Anchor House, 13–14 Eaton Crescent, Clifton, Bristol BS8 2ES (0272-737421).

The Bristol Benevolent Institution

Eligibility: Elderly people living in their own homes with small fixed incomes and little or no capital. Applicants must be over 65 and have lived in Bristol for more than 30 years.

Types of grants: Recurrent grants mainly within the level disregarded by the DSS when calculating benefits. 600 annuitants receive between £260 and £520 a year.

Annual grant total: In 1992/93, grants totalling £250,000 were given to individuals.

Applications: Referrals to the correspondent or directly by the individual in writing.

Correspondent: The Secretary, 45 High Street, Nailsea, Bristol BS19 1AW (0275-810365).

The Bristol Caledonian Society Benevolent Fund

Eligibility: People in need who are connected with Scotland by birth, parentage or marriage, who live in Bristol and district.

Types of grants: Annual grants.

Annual grant total: In 1992/93, the trust had an income of £1,100. £920 was given to annuitants.

Applications: In writing to the correspondent.

Correspondent: Mrs J Phelps, Treasurer, 43 Cleeve Hill, Downend, Bristol BS16 6ET (0272-562215).

The Bristol Corn Trade Guild

Eligibility: Members of the guild and their dependants.

Types of grants: One-off or recurrent grants according to need, up to £500.

Annual grant total: £3,200 in 20 to 25 grants in 1992.

Applications: In writing to the correspondent.

Correspondent: A C Gulland, 2 Blenheim Court, 6 Beaufort Park, Woodlands, Almondsbury, Bristol BS12 4NE (0454-618008).

The Bristol (St John the Baptist & St Ambrose) Charity

Eligibility: People in need who live in the parishes of St John the Baptist and St Ambrose, in Bristol.

Types of grants: One-off and recurrent grants according to need.

Annual grant total: About £1,000 for individuals; the remainder of the income is spent on almshouses.

Applications: In writing to the correspondent.

Correspondent: D W Ratcliffe, c/o Messrs Osborne Clarke, 30 Queen Charlotte Street, Bristol BS99 7QQ (0272-230220).

The Dolphin Society

Eligibility: People in need and/or at risk through sickness, ill-health, disability or poverty and who live in Bristol. Preference is given to elderly people.

Types of grants: Help towards telephone installations, minicoms and lifeline necklaces.

Annual grant total: In 1992/93, grants to about 400 individuals totalled £35,000.

Applications: Usually through the social services. If directly from the individual the application must be supported by a doctor, clergy etc. (not necessary if elderly).

Correspondent: Maureen Nicholls, Administrator, 45 High Street, Nailsea, Bristol BS19 1AW (0275-810365).

The Federation of Master Builders (Bristol Branch) Benevolent Fund

Eligibility: Elderly and infirm members of the building trade who live or have worked in Bristol, and their dependants. New entrants training in the construction industry in the Bristol area are also eligible.

Types of grants: Pensions and one-off grants to the above.

Annual grant total: About £1,400.

Applications: In writing to the correspondent. Applications can be submitted directly by the individual and are considered quarterly.

Correspondent: J W A Chapman, Regional Director, 83 Alma Road, Clifton, Bristol BS8 2DP (0272-736891).

The Lord Mayor of Bristol's Christmas Appeal for Children

Eligibility: Children under 16 who are in need and who live in the city of Bristol.

Types of grants: One-off grants in the form of vouchers.

Annual grant total: According to the Charity Commission in 1992 the trust had an income of £55,500.

Applications: Through a social worker or service club.

Correspondent: B Simmonds, Hon. Treasurer, Priestlands, Hambrook, Bristol BS16 1RN (0272-566010).

The Redcliffe Parish Charity

Eligibility: People in need who live in the city of Bristol.

Types of grants: One-off grants only up to a maximum of £60. "The trustees generally limit grants to families or individuals in particular financial stress rather than continuing need." Grants are typically given for cooker repairs, items for a new baby, children's school trips.

Annual grant total: In 1992/93, the trust's assets generated an income of £5,800. Relief-in-need grants to individuals totalled £4,900.

Applications: In writing to the correspondent. Applications should be submitted on the individual's behalf by a social worker, citizen's advice bureau or appropriate third party, and will usually be considered once a month, but always 12 times a year. Ages of family members should be supplied in addition to financial circumstances and the reason for the request.

Avon/Cornwall

Thomas Beames' Charity

Eligibility: People of pensionable age who are in need and live in the ancient parish of St Augustine with St George in Bristol.

Types of grants: Regular allowances only, distributed monthly.

Annual grant total: In 1991, the trust had an income of £3,500.

Applications: In writing to the correspondent.

Correspondent: J Heal, Secretary, Messrs Heal Solicitors, 14 John Street, Bristol BS1 2HX (0272-260773).

Langford

Charles Graham Stone's Relief-in-Need Charity

Eligibility: People in need who live in Langford, Avon.

Types of grants: Grants for specific needs.

Annual grant total: In 1993, the trust had an income of £3,700. It is not known how much was given in grants to individuals in need.

Applications: In writing to the correspondent.

Correspondent: F R Darby, Treasurer, Brinsea Cottage, Congresbury, Bristol BS19 5JL (0934-852287).

Newton St Loe

The Henry Smith Charity

Eligibility: People in need who live in Newton St Loe, and who have done so for at least five years.

Types of grants: Annual grants of food vouchers and clothing tickets.

Annual grant total: In 1993, the trust had £1,350 income allocated by Henry Smith's (General Estate) Charity. All of this was given in grants.

Applications: In writing to the correspondent. Applications should be submitted directly by the individual by 25th September, for payment in November/December each year.

Correspondent: Mrs J Ringham, 51 Claysend Cottages, Newton St Loe, Bath BA2 9DE.

Stanton Prior

The Henry Smith Charity

Eligibility: People in need who have lived in Stanton Prior for more than three years.

Types of grants: Grants are given in token form to people in rented accommodation.

Annual grant total: About £600.

Applications: In writing to the correspondent.

Correspondent: R A Hardwick, Poplar Farm, Stanton Prior, Bath BA2 9HX (0761-470382).

Thornbury

The Thornbury Town Trust

Eligibility: People in need who live in the parish of Thornbury.

Types of grants: One-off grants, usually of £25. Grants are not given for educational purposes.

Annual grant total: In 1993, the trust had an income of £25,000. Expenditure totalled £9,200, with 45 grants to individuals totalling £1,100.

Applications: On a form available from the correspondent. Applications can be submitted directly by the individual or through a social worker, citizen's advice bureau or other welfare agency. They are considered in November.

Correspondent: J T Ovens, Clerk, 48 Gloucester Road, Thornbury, Bristol BS12 1JQ (0454-412829).

Cornwall

The Blanchminster Trust

Eligibility: People who live in the parishes of Bude, Stratton and Poughill (the former urban district of Bude-Stratton).

Types of grants: Generally one-off grants for the relief of need, hardship or distress.

Annual grant total: In 1992, the trust had assets of £665,000 and an income of about £216,000. Expenditure totalled £159,000 with 62 relief-in-need grants totalling £32,000. In 1991, 140 relief-in-need grants totalled £109,000.

Applications: On a form available from the correspondent. Applications are considered monthly and should be submitted directly by the individual.

Correspondent: Owen A May, Clerk, Blanchminster Building, 38 Lansdown Road, Bude, Cornwall EX23 8EE (0288-352851 [answerphone service]).

The Lizzie Brooke Charity

Eligibility: People in need who live in West Cornwall.

Types of grants: One-off grants up to £500.

Annual grant total: In 1993, the trust had an income of £9,000. 93 grants to individuals totalled £8,000.

Applications: On a form available from the correspondent. Applications should be submitted through a social worker, citizen's advice bureau or other welfare agency. They are considered at any time.

Correspondent: Mrs W A Stone, Hon. Secretary, Woodside, 8 Tredarvah Road, Penzance TR18 4LE (0736-64908).

The Cornwall Retired Clergy, their Widows & Dependants Fund

Eligibility: Retired clergy and the widows and unmarried children of deceased clergy who were licensed in the diocese of Truro.

Types of grants: One-off and recurrent grants according to need.

Annual grant total: In 1992, the trust had an income of £3,000. Total expenditure was £1,100. No grants were made to individuals.

Applications: In writing to the correspondent.

Correspondent: Rev P B Denny, Tralee, The Crescent, Truro TR1 3ES (0872-74492).

The Cornwall Seamen's Benevolent Trust

Eligibility: Distressed merchant seamen or fishermen who live in Cornwall, or their widows and dependants.

Types of grants: One-off grants of at least £50.

Annual grant total: In 1992, about 70 grants totalling £10,000 were made.

Applications: On a form available from the correspondent. Applications can be submitted by the individual, a social worker, citizen's advice bureau or the trust's representative.

Correspondent: C C Jago, 25 Budock Terrace, Falmouth, Cornwall TR11 3ND (0326-311782).

Cornwall/Devon

The Levant Mine Fund

Eligibility: Miners in Cornwall who were injured in the Levant Mine Disaster of 20th October 1919 and the relatives and dependants of miners killed or injured in the disaster. After making such provision the fund can be used for the relief of miners in need who are suffering from injuries received directly or indirectly in connection with their employment, and their dependants.

Types of grants: One-off and recurrent grants ranging from £25 to £260 a year according to need.

Annual grant total: In 1992, the trust had assets of £23,300 and an income of £3,200. 42 relief-in-need grants totalled £2,900.

Applications: In writing to the correspondent giving financial circumstances (including all state benefits and other charitable grants). Applications can be submitted directly by the individual or through a social worker, citizen's advice bureau or other welfare agency. They are considered in May and October.

Correspondent: J C Beling, c/o Carnon Consolidated Ltd, South Crofty Mine, Dudnance Lane, Pool, Redruth, Cornwall TR15 3QH (0209-714821).

● **Gunwalloe**

The Charity of Thomas Henwood

Eligibility: People in need who live in the parish of Gunwalloe.

Types of grants: One-off or recurrent grants according to need, including grants to provide nurses and to help people recovering from illness. All by periodic distribution.

Annual grant total: In 1993, the trust had an income of £5,600. Grants to individuals totalled £5,000.

Applications: In writing to the trustees.

Correspondent: The Vicar of Gwynwalloe, The Rectory, St Mawgan-in-Meneage, Helston, Cornwall TR12 6AD (0326-221293).

● **Helston**

The Helston Welfare Trust

Eligibility: People in need who live in area administered by Helston Town Council.

Types of grants: One-off or recurrent grants according to need. Grants may be given for all kinds of need including help with fuel bills, television licence fees, furniture, clothing, travel expenses for hospital visiting, telephone installation, food for special diets and equipment for disabled people.

Annual grant total: In 1992/93, the trust had an income of £860; no grants were given.

Applications: In writing to the correspondent. Applications can be submitted directly by the individual or through a third party. They are considered as received.

Correspondent: T B Gooding, Clerk, The Guildhall, Helston, Cornwall TR13 8ST.

● **Launceston**

The Launceston Relief-in-Sickness Fund

Eligibility: People who are sick, convalescing, disabled and infirm and who live in the former borough of Launceston.

Types of grants: One-off grants for medical fees, travel expenses to and from hospital, and other needs.

Annual grant total: Over £1,000.

Applications: In writing to the correspondent.

Correspondent: J F Moir, Peter Peter & Sons, Solicitors, Westgate, Launceston, Cornwall PL15 9AD (0566-772451).

● **Liskeard**

The United Charities of Liskeard

Eligibility: For the relief-in-need fund, people in need who live in the town of Liskeard (formerly the borough of Liskeard). For the relief-in-sickness fund, people in need who live in Liskeard, the parish of Dobwalls with Trewidland (formerly the parish of Liskeard) and the parishes of Menheniot and St Cleer.

Types of grants: One-off and recurrent grants according to need.

Annual grant total: About £1,800 in 1988.

Applications: In writing to the correspondent.

Correspondent: Miss B J Berryman, Clerk, 3 Westwood, Liskeard, Cornwall PL14 6DG (0579-342180).

Other information: This entry has not been confirmed by the trust.

Devon

Edward Blagdon's Charity

Eligibility: People in need who live in Tiverton and Washfield.

Types of grants: One-off grants only, ranging from £15 to £100.

Annual grant total: £800 in 12 grants.

Applications: Directly by the individual to the trustees. Applications are considered monthly.

Correspondent: Tom Penny, Gotham House, Phoenix Lane, Tiverton, Devon EX16 6LT (0884-242111).

The Mrs E L Blakeley Marillier Annuity Fund

Eligibility: Ladies over 55 who are in reduced circumstances and are not of the Roman Catholic faith or members of the Salvation Army. Preference is given to women from the counties of York and Devon and in particular the towns of Scarborough and Torbay.

Types of grants: Annuities ranging from £100 to £520.

Annual grant total: In 1990/91, the trust had an income of £19,000; annuities totalled £13,000.

Applications: In writing to the correspondent. The trustees are actively looking for new annuitants.

Correspondent: Mr James, Messrs Hooper & Wollen, Carlton House, Torquay, Devon TQ1 1BS.

Other information: This entry is repeated in the North Yorkshire section of the book.

The Brownsdon & Tremayne Estate Charity (also known as the Nicholas Watts Trust)

Eligibility: For the Browsdon Fund, men in need who live in Devon, with a preference for Tavistock; for the Tremayne Estate Charity, people in need generally who live in Tavistock. Applicants should normally be owner/occupiers.

Types of grants: One-off grants. In addition to general relief of need, the trustees prefer to help towards the maintenance of homes owned by beneficiaries (eg. providing new carpets) although the trust does not assist with mortgage repayments.

Annual grant total: In 1992/93, the Brownsdon Trust gave grants totalling

Devon

£12,000 and the Tremayne Trust about £3,600 in 45 grants of about £80.

Applications: On a form available from the correspondent. The trustees advertise for applications in July, to be considered in September. Applications can be submitted directly by the individual.

Correspondent: M E S Stewart, Osborne House, 10 Watts Road, Tavistock, Devon PL19 8LF (0822-612822).

The Devon & Exeter Benevolent Medical Society Fund

Eligibility: Medical practitioners who have worked in Devon and their dependants.

Types of grants: One-off and recurrent grants according to need.

Annual grant total: No information available.

Applications: On a form available from the correspondent. Applications can be submitted by the individual or through a recognised referral agency (eg. social worker, citizen's advice bureau or doctor) and are considered throughout the year. They must be supported by two referees, one of whom must be a medical practitioner.

Correspondent: The Senior Caseworker, Royal Medical Benevolent Fund, 24 King's Road, Wimbledon, London SW19 8QN (081-540 9194).

The Northcott Devon Foundation

Eligibility: People in need who live in Devon.

Types of grants: Primarily one-off grants up to £500, to those suffering hardship and distress relating to disability, illness, bereavement or exceptional disadvantage. Grants will not be made for relieving community charge, taxes, or other public funds, and repayment of debt is not normally considered.

Annual grant total: In 1992/93, the trust had a disposable income of £232,000; grants to 480 individuals totalled £142,000.

Applications: On a form available from the correspondent. All applications must be supported in writing by an authorized representative of a local statutory or voluntary agency, or by a reputable independent referee. They are considered monthly.

Correspondent: G C Halliday, Secretary, South Lodge, Belvedere, Burgmann's Hill, Lympstone, Exmouth, Devon EX8 5HP (0395-269204).

Other information: The trust also gives to organisations and young people living in Devon who are of limited means and are undertaking philanthropic activity which is not part of a formal education or training programme.

The Parish Lands Charity (Highweek)

Eligibility: People in need over the age of 65 who live in the parish of Highweek in Newton Abbot, and Newton Bushell.

Types of grants: One-off Christmas grants of £40.

Annual grant total: About £2,800.

Applications: In writing to the correspondent or by recommendation by a trustee.

Correspondent: B W Manley, 1 Castlewood Avenue, Highweek, Newton Abbot, Devon TQ12 1NX (0626-61674).

The Tavistock, Whitchurch & District Nursing Association

Eligibility: Sick or needy people living in Tavistock, Whitchurch and district.

Types of grants: Mainly one-off grants of £30 to £40 according to need (eg. help with heating and water bills, travel to medical appointments etc.). Grants can occasionally be recurrent.

Annual grant total: In 1992/93, the trust had an income of £1,600 and gave 60 grants totalling £1,500.

Applications: Can be submitted by the individual, through a social worker, citizen's advice bureau etc., doctor, district nurse, health visitor, church or town councillor. Applications are considered in May and November.

Correspondent: J Montgomery, 24 Chollacott Close, Tavistock, Devon PL19 9BW (0822-612837).

Barnstaple

The Barnstaple Municipal Charities

Eligibility: People in need living in Barnstaple.

Types of grants: One-off or recurrent grants according to need.

Annual grant total: £38,700.

Applications: In writing to the correspondent.

Correspondent: M Steele, 429 Carrington Terrace, Yeo Vale, Barnstaple, Devon EX32 7AF (0271-46354).

The Barnstaple & North Devon Dispensary Fund

Eligibility: Sick and poor people who live in the borough of Barnstaple and district (ie. within a seven mile radius of Barnstaple).

Types of grants: One-off or recurrent grants according to need.

Annual grant total: In 1993, the trust had an income of £10,000. It is not known how much was given in grants to individuals.

Applications: In writing to the correspondent.

Correspondent: Miss I G Hibbs, Clerk, 28 Beaufort Walk, Gorwell Barnstaple, North Devon EX32 7JB (0271-75821).

Bideford

The Bideford Bridge Trust

Eligibility: People in need who live in Bideford and neighbourhood.

Types of grants: One-off grants.

Annual grant total: No information available.

Applications: In writing to the correspondent.

Correspondent: P R Sims, 24 Bridgeland Street, Bideford, Devon EX39 2QB (0237-473122).

Bratton Fleming

The Bratton Fleming Relief-in-Need Charity

Eligibility: People in need living in the parish of Bratton Fleming. Applications from those living outside the parish will NOT be considered.

Types of grants: One-off or recurrent grants between £25 and £50.

Annual grant total: In 1990, the trust had an income of £1,500. 28 relief-in-need grants were given totalling £1,100.

Applications: In writing to the correspondent by the individual or a third party on their behalf to be considered in June and December.

Correspondent: The Rector, The Rectory, Bratton Fleming, Barnstaple, Devon EX31 4RT (0598-710807).

Brixton

The Brixton Feoffee Lands Charity

Eligibility: People in need who live in the parish of Brixton, near Plymouth.

Types of grants: One-off or recurrent grants according to need.

Annual grant total: Up to £14,000, half of which is for the benefit of the poor of the parish, the remainder to the parish church.

Applications: In writing to the correspondent. Applications can be submitted directly by the individual or through a social worker, citizen's advice bureau or other welfare agency or third party. They are considered throughout the year.

Correspondent: Mrs S Axell, 15 Cherry Tree Drive, Brixton, Plymouth PL8 2DD (0752-880262).

Broadclyst

The Broadclyst Relief-in-Need Charity

Eligibility: People in need who live in the parish of Broadclyst.

Types of grants: One-off grants ranging from £15 to £50.

Annual grant total: In 1992/93, the trust had an income of about £1,000. £700 was given in 35 grants to individuals in need.

Applications: On a form available from the correspondent. Applications should be submitted directly by the individual. They are considered in December.

Correspondent: The Vicar, Chairman, The Vicarage, Broadclyst, Exeter EX5 3EW (0392-61280).

Broadhempston

The Broadhempston Relief-in-Need Charity

Eligibility: People in need who live in the parish of Broadhempston.

Types of grants: One-off or recurrent grants of £5 to £30 for food, fuel, "expenses and gifts" for those in hospital or housebound, aids for children with disabilities and special needs, families who have financial hardship and elderly people needing assistance with paying fuel bills.

Annual grant total: £1,600 in 1992/93.

Applications: In writing to the correspondent directly by the individual to be considered in June and December.

Correspondent: Mrs R Brown, Meadows, Broadhempston, Totnes, Devon TQ9 6BW (0803-813130).

Budleigh Salterton

The Fryer Welfare Trust

Eligibility: People living in the local authority boundary of Budleigh Salterton.

Types of grants: One-off grants between £100 and £500, and loans.

Annual grant total: In 1990/91, the trust's assets combined with those of the Fryer Recreational Trust were £41,000, generating an income for both trusts of £3,300. One relief-in-need grant of £400 was given for furnishings for a flat. Grants are also given to organisations.

Applications: In writing to the correspondent at any time. Applications can be submitted directly by the individual or through a social worker, citizen's advice bureau or other welfare agency.

Correspondent: W K H Coxe, Council Chambers, Budleigh Salterton, Devon EX9 6RL (0395-442223).

The Budleigh Salterton Nursing Association

Eligibility: People who live in the parish of Budleigh Salterton and are sick, convalescent, disabled or infirm.

Types of grants: One-off grants are given for medical items, services and facilities. Recent grants have been given for a wheelchair, raised bed, and access ramp. Grants will not be given for rates or council/government taxes.

Annual grant total: In 1992/93, the trust had an income of £2,100. Eight relief-in-need grants of £50 to £500 were given totalling £1,200.

Applications: In writing to the correspondent at any time including details of the nature of the illness, doctor's name, an indication of why funds are unavailable and family details eg. number of children to help, whether the spouse is disabled, unemployed or separated. Applications can be submitted directly by the individual, through a social worker, citizen's advice bureau or other appropriate third party (eg. a doctor) and are considered all year round.

Correspondent: Mrs Mary Perriam, Hillcrest, Hayes Lane, Otterton, Budleigh Salterton, Devon EX9 7JS (0395-68410).

Cornwood

The Reverend Duke Yonge Charity

Eligibility: People in need who live in the parish of Cornwood.

Types of grants: Recent grants have included help towards treatment in a privately run hospice, domestic aids such as a special chair and special shower unit, convalescence and Christmas gifts.

Annual grant total: In 1993, the trust had assets of £73,000 and an income of about £13,000. Around 175 relief-in-need grants totalled about £7,000.

Applications: In writing to the correspondent. Local trustees are expected to make themselves aware of any need. Applications are considered throughout the year.

Correspondent: Miss E E Balkwill, Coulstons Keep, Lutton, Cornwood, Ivybridge, Devon PL21 9SJ (0752-837295).

Crediton

The Crediton Relief-in-Need Charity

Eligibility: People in need who live in Crediton town and Crediton Hamlets.

Types of grants: One-off grants according to need.

Annual grant total: About £5,000 in 1993.

Applications: In writing to the correspondent.

Correspondent: D Wagg, Community Office, Organ House, Church Lane, Crediton, Devon EX17 2AH (0363-777798).

Culmstock

Culmstock Fuel Allotment Charity

Eligibility: People in need who live in the ancient parish of Culmstock.

Types of grants: One-off or recurrent grants according to need.

Annual grant total: About £3,500 in 1992/93.

Applications: In writing to the correspondent.

Correspondent: Mrs B P Spratt, Clerk, Lynwood, Culmstock, Cullompton, Devon EX15 3JJ (0884-840913).

Devon

Dartmouth

Dartmouth Trust Lands

Eligibility: People in need who live in the ancient parish of St Petrox, Dartmouth.

Types of grants: Preferably one-off grants.

Annual grant total: In 1993, the trust had an income of £25,700. It is currently finding it difficult to distribute all this income to people in need.

Applications: In writing to the correspondent.

Correspondent: H D Bastone, Clerk, 4 Thurlestone Gardens, Mount Boone, Dartmouth, Devon TQ6 9HG (0803-834395).

Exeter

The Exeter Dispensary & Aid-in-Sickness Fund

Eligibility: Sick poor people who live in Exeter.

Types of grants: One-off grants for convalescence, help with fuel bills, and "amenities not available from public funds".

Annual grant total: About £26,000.

Applications: Applications should be made through a social worker or doctor.

Correspondent: D W Fanson, Hon. Secretary, 85 Beacon Lane, Whipton, Exeter EX4 8LL (0392-56381).

The Exeter Municipal Charities

Eligibility: People in need who live in the city of Exeter.

Types of grants: One-off grants averaging £25, mainly towards children's clothing.

Annual grant total: In 1991, the total expenditure of the trust was about £6,000.

Applications: On a form available from the correspondent. Applications can be submitted directly by the individual, or on their behalf through a social worker, citizen's advice bureau or other welfare agency. Details of financial circumstances and any special needs should be supplied together with three references from, for example, a doctor, social worker, health visitor etc..

Correspondent: M R King, Clerk, 22 Southernhay East, Exeter EX1 1QU (0392-213613).

The Exeter Relief-in-Need Charity

Eligibility: People in need who live in Exeter.

Types of grants: One-off grants ranging from £25 to £50, towards clothing, bedding, tools for apprentices etc..

Annual grant total: £4,250 in about 90 grants in 1993.

Applications: On a form available from the correspondent, either directly by the individual or through a social worker, health visitor etc.. Applications are considered quarterly.

Correspondent: M R King, Clerk, Exeter Municipal Charities, 22 Southernhay East, Exeter EX1 1QU (0392-213613).

The St Edmunds on the Bridge Parish Charity

Eligibility: People in need who live in the parish of St Edmunds on the Bridge, Exeter.

Types of grants: Small one-off and recurrent grants according to need.

Annual grant total: £750.

Applications: In writing to the correspondent at any time. Applications can be submitted directly by the individual or through a social worker, citizen's advice bureau or appropriate third party.

Correspondent: G R S Simey, 8 Cathedral Close, Exeter EX1 1EW (0392-74126).

Exminster

The Exminster Parish Lands

Eligibility: People in need living in the parish of Exminster.

Types of grants: One-off grants ranging from £50 to £150 and loans to families (including single parent families) according to need.

Annual grant total: £600 to 8 individuals in 1992.

Applications: In writing to the correspondent. Applications can be submitted throughout the year directly by the individual or by a social worker, citizen's advice bureau, other welfare agency or another third party (eg. doctor, priest). They should outline the applicant's background and need for a grant.

Correspondent: K A Beer, Highfield, Aboveway, Exminster, Nr Exeter EX6 8DT (0392-832674).

Exmouth

The Exmouth Welfare Trust

Eligibility: People living in the urban district of Exmouth who are convalescent, disabled or infirm.

Types of grants: One-off grants according to need.

Annual grant total: £1,000.

Applications: In writing to the correspondent.

Correspondent: G M Williams, Cae Mor, 1a Seafield Avenue, Exmouth, Devon EX8 3NJ.

Gittisham

The Beaumont Charity

Eligibility: People in need who live in the parish of Gittisham.

Types of grants: Quarterly pensions in March, June, September and December with a bonus at Christmas. One-off grants have been given for holidays and a mobile telephone for a disabled beneficiary. Grants and pensions range between £30 and £100.

Annual grant total: In 1991, the trust had assets of £10,300, and an income of £3,300. 73 relief-in-need grants totalled £2,300.

Applications: In writing to the correspondent at any time throughout the year. Applications can be submitted directly by the individual.

Correspondent: Mrs P S Land, Messrs Dunnings, Solicitors, 130 High Street, Honiton, Devon EX14 8JR.

Great Torrington

The Great Torrington Poors Charities

Eligibility: People in need who live in Great Torrington.

Types of grants: Probably one-off or recurrent grants according to need.

Annual grant total: In 1993, the trust had an income of £76,000; it is not known how much of this was given in grants to individuals.

Applications: In writing to the correspondent.

Correspondent: C J Styles, The Town Hall Office, High Street, Torrington, Devon EX38 8HN.

Holsworthy

The Poor's Land/Charity of Peter Speccott

Eligibility: People in need who live in Holsworthy, generally widows aged 60 or over and widowers of 65 or over, although younger people can be helped.

Types of grants: Generally payments of £15 twice-yearly.

Annual grant total: In 1992/93, the trust had an income of £1,800, of which £1,700 was disbursed to 56 recipients.

Applications: A list of beneficiaries is kept by the trustees and considered at the June and December trustees' meetings. When a beneficiary dies or moves out of the area new people are added to the list.

Correspondent: L M Yelland, Fairways, Kingswood Meadow, Holsworthy, Devon EX22 6HG (0409-253012).

Honiton

The Honiton United Charities

Eligibility: People in need aged 65 or over who live in the borough of Honiton.

Types of grants: Pensions of £7 a quarter for single people, and £10 a quarter for married couples.

Annual grant total: In 1990, the trust had an income of £6,500. 120 relief-in-need grants totalled £4,200. No more recent information available.

Applications: In writing to the correspondent including details of income and savings. Applications can be submitted directly by the individual and are usually considered in March and September.

Correspondent: R M P Howe, Steward, 130 High Street, Honiton, Devon EX14 8JR (0404-41221).

Kingsbridge

The Dodbrooke Parish Charity

Eligibility: People in need who live in the parish of Kingsbridge.

Types of grants: One-off grants and pensions to elderly people.

Annual grant total: About £8,000.

Applications: In writing to the correspondent, though usually through trustees.

Correspondent: D Tucker, 6 Alvington Terrace, Kingsbridge, Devon TQ7 1HD (0548-853845).

Litton Cheney

The Litton Cheney Relief-in-Need Trust

Eligibility: People in need who live in the parish of Litton Cheney.

Types of grants: The trust distributes annual grants at the beginning of December, but can also make one-off emergency grants at any time eg. where there is a serious illness in the family.

Annual grant total: In 1992, the trust had an income of £2,600 and expenditure of £2,400. Grants of between £100 and £150 and totalling £2,400 were given to 21 individuals.

Applications: Applications, on a form available from the correspondent, should be submitted directly by the individual, and are considered throughout the year.

Correspondent: B Prentice, Steddings, Chalk Pit Lane, Litton Cheney, Dorchester, Dorset DT2 9AN (0308-482535).

Morebath

The Charity of John Brooke

Eligibility: People in need who live in Morebath.

Types of grants: One-off or recurrent grants according to need.

Annual grant total: About £3,000.

Applications: In writing to the correspondent.

Correspondent: Rev P Ockford, The Vicarage, Bampton, Tiverton, Devon EX16 9NG.

Other information: This entry has not been confirmed by the trust.

Netherexe

The Christopher Hill Charity

Eligibility: People in need who live in the former parish of Netherexe.

Types of grants: Recurrent grants at Christmas ranging between £118 and £276. From a total adult population of 30 people, seven households are currently supported.

Annual grant total: £1,100 in eight grants in 1992. In addition, the trust pays up to a quarter of its yearly income to supplement the rector's income.

Applications: On a form available from the correspondent. Applications can be submitted directly by the individual.

Correspondent: Colin Bond, Trustee, Fortescue Crossing, Thorverton, Exeter EX5 5JN (0392-841512).

Other information: This entry has not been confirmed by the trust.

Newport

The Newport Charity

Eligibility: People in need who are 65 or over and live in the ecclesiastical parish of Newport.

Types of grants: Vouchers paid in December and June to spend in local shops and worth about £5 - £7 for single people and £7 - £10 for married couples.

Annual grant total: £1,600.

Applications: In writing to the correspondent.

Correspondent: D Pickard, Lawnswood, 17 Hillcrest Road, Barnstaple, Devon EX32 9EP (0271-43738).

Ottery St Mary

The Non-Ecclesiastical Charity of Thomas Axe

Eligibility: Sick and poor people living in Ottery St Mary.

Types of grants: One-off grants in "marriage portions", and aids for elderly and disabled people. Recurrent support cannot be given.

Annual grant total: In 1993, the trust had an income of £1,400. 90 relief-in-need grants totalled £1,250.

Applications: In writing to the correspondent directly by the individual, or through a social worker, citizen's advice bureau or other welfare agency. Applications are considered in March, June, September and December although urgent requests can be considered at any time. Requests for marriage portions should be submitted on an application form available from the correspondent.

Correspondent: G B Charter, Ravenhill, Longdogs Lane, Ottery St Mary, Devon EX11 1HX (0404-814798).

Other information: The trust also gives loans to those starting a business or increasing stock, and helps those entering a trade or profession.

The Ottery Feoffee Charity

Eligibility: People in need who live in Ottery St Mary.

Types of grants: One-off or recurrent grants according to need.

Devon

Annual grant total: The annual endowment income is £7,500. Up to half of this may be given to individuals, but most is used to run and maintain almshouses.

Applications: In writing to the correspondent.

Correspondent: R J O Lovell, 7 Broad Street, Ottery St Mary, Devon EX11 1BS (0404-812228).

Paignton

The Parish Lands or Second Poor's Charity

Eligibility: Poor people who live in Paignton.

Types of grants: Beneficiaries receive one or two payments a year.

Annual grant total: About £1,000.

Applications: Beneficiaries are recommended by the trustees.

Correspondent: E F Barbet, 37 Kings Road, Paignton, Devon TQ3 2AN (0803-550145).

Plymouth

Joseph Jory's Charity

Eligibility: Widows over 50 who are in need and have lived in the city of Plymouth for the last seven years.

Types of grants: Pensions paid quarterly. Amounts vary according to available income. In 1992 the amount was £315. Currently the vacancies are not filled, but available funds are used to increase the amount paid to existing beneficiaries.

Annual grant total: In 1992, the trust's income was £9,000. Relief-in-need grants totalled £7,000 in 22 pensions.

Applications: On a form available from the correspondent giving details of weekly income, to be submitted directly by the individual. Two testimonials should be enclosed with the application.

Correspondent: D J Gabbitass, Deptford Chambers, 62-64 North Hill, Plymouth PL4 4EP (0752-663295).

The Ladies Aid Society & the Eyre Charity

Eligibility: Widows and spinsters who were born, have lived or now live in Plymouth. Women who are divorced are not eligible for grants.

Types of grants: Annuities of £85 quarterly to each recipient.

Annual grant total: In 1992, the trusts had assets of £79,000, and an income of £11,000. Annuities totalled £11,000.

Applications: Applications are considered in March, June, September and December. They should be submitted through a social worker, citizen's advice bureau, clergy, doctor, solicitor or similar third party.

Correspondent: Mrs J M Stephens, The Rectory, Thurlestone, Kingsbridge, Devon (0548-560232).

The Charity of William Rowe

Eligibility: People in need who live in Plymouth.

Types of grants: One-off grants of £25 to £250 for clothing and education.

Annual grant total: In 1992/93, the trust had an income of £1,500. Two relief-in-need grants totalled £300.

Applications: In writing to the correspondent directly by the individual. Applications are usually considered in April and September.

Correspondent: Mrs J Gibbons, Clerk, Charity Trustee's Office, Greenbank House, Freedom Fields Hospital, Plymouth PL4 7JG (0752-663107).

Plympton

The Maudlyn Lands Charity & Others

Eligibility: People who live in the ancient parish of Plympton St Mary.

Types of grants: One-off or recurrent grants according to need.

Annual grant total: In 1993, the trust had assets of £100,000, and an income of £6,300. Grants totalled £6,250.

Applications: In writing to the correspondent.

Correspondent: S Edgcumbe, 241 Ridgeway, Plympton, Plymouth PL7 3HP (0752-336750).

Sandford

The Sandford Relief-in-Need Charity

Eligibility: People in need who live in Sandford.

Types of grants: One-off grants of £30 to £300 to repair broken/damaged household items, towards bereavement etc. or recurrent grants of £10 a month (currently to 31 households) according to need. The trust no longer gives winter grants towards fuel bills or television licences.

Annual grant total: In 1993, about £5,000 was given to individuals.

Applications: In writing to the correspondent.

Correspondent: Mrs D Edworthy, 7 Snows, Sandford, Crediton, Devon EX17 4NJ (0363-775511).

Sheepwash

The Bridge Land Charity

Eligibility: People in need who live in the parish of Sheepwash.

Types of grants: One-off or recurrent grants according to need.

Annual grant total: In 1992/93, the trust had an income of £1,500. The correspondent states: "[It is] many years since we made any type of grant. Money is mostly disbursed in annual outings for children in the village."

Applications: In writing to the correspondent.

Correspondent: B Thomas, Mermaid House, The Square, Sheepwash, Beaworthy, North Devon EX21 5NE (0409-23213).

Silverton

The Silverton Parochial Charity

Eligibility: People in need in the parish of Silverton.

Types of grants: One-off or recurrent grants according to need.

Annual grant total: In 1992, the trust had an income of £18,000. Expenditure totalled £6,000, leaving £12,000 unallocated in the year.

Applications: In writing to the correspondent. Applications are considered at any time.

Correspondent: C A Williams, Henbury, Old Butterleigh Road, Silverton, Devon EX5 4JE (0392-860408).

South Brent

The South Brent Parish Lands Charity

Eligibility: People in need who live in the parish of South Brent.

Types of grants: One-off or recurrent grants and Christmas gifts. Grants can be £10 to £500 and can be for a variety of needs including hospital transport/travel costs and special treatment to adults and/or children where the family is desperately in need of help.

Annual grant total: In 1993, the trust had an income of £34,000, £31,000 of which is divided equally between local organisations, educational grants and welfare grants.

Applications: On a form available from the correspondent and can be submitted by the individual or through a local health centre/social worker/educational welfare officer.

Correspondent: J I G Blackler, Luscombe Maye Chartered Surveyors, Fore Street, South Brent, Devon TQ10 9BQ (0364-73651).

● **Topsham**

The Charities of John Shere & Others

Eligibility: People in need who have lived in the parish of Topsham for at least three years.

Types of grants: Regular monthly allowances of £3 a calendar month plus a Christmas bonus of £30, a fuel bonus of £17 in February and a holiday bonus of £17 in June.

Annual grant total: In 1992/93, the charities had assets of £62,400 and an income of £16,600. Relief-in-need grants totalling £9,000 were given to 97 individuals.

Applications: On a form available from the correspondent. Applications can be submitted directly by the individual and are considered in March each year.

Correspondent: J S Powell, Secretary, 3 Premier Place, Exeter EX2 4LB.

● **Torbay**

The Leonora Carlow Trust Fund

Eligibility: Children up to 18 who have physical or mental disabilities and live in Torbay.

Types of grants: One-off grants for special equipment such as wheelchairs, bath hoists and car seats. No grants for telephones.

Annual grant total: In 1992/93, the trust had an income of £1,500. Relief-in-need grants, usually between £50 and £250, were given to 16 individuals and totalled £1,000.

Applications: In writing to the correspondent by the individual or through a social worker, citizen's advice bureau or other welfare agency. Applications are considered throughout the year, and should include details of help sought from any other source and the outcome.

Correspondent: The Town Clerk, Town Hall, Torquay TQ1 3DR (0803-218082).

● **Torquay**

The Annie Toll Bequest

Eligibility: Women in need who live in Torquay.

Types of grants: Recurrent grants of up to £20 a month and one-off payments according to need. The hire costs of a television for an elderly beneficiary have recently been met by the trust.

Annual grant total: In 1992, the trust had assets of £52,000, with an income of £3,100. 17 relief-in-need grants totalled £3,300.

Applications: In writing to the correspondent.

Correspondent: F G Hazell-Smith, South Cliff, Headland Road, Torquay TQ1 1RD.

Dorset

The Beaminster Charities

Eligibility: People in need who live in Beaminster, Netherbury and Stoke Abbott.

Types of grants: One-off and recurrent grants according to need. The trustees will, however, consider any application.

Annual grant total: In 1992, the trust had assets of £140,000 and an income of £12,000. £3,300 was given in relief-in-need grants to 41 individuals.

Applications: Applications can be submitted in writing to the correspondent by the individual or through a recognised referral agency (social worker, citizen's advice bureau or doctor etc.).

Correspondent: J Groves, 24 Church Street, Beaminster, Dorset DT8 3BA (0308-862313).

The Boveridge Charity

Eligibility: Poor single people, widows/widowers or spinsters/bachelors, who have lived in the ancient parish of Cramborne (which includes the present parishes of Cramborne-cum-Boveridge, Wimborne St Giles, Alderholt, Verwood, Ferndown, West Farley and Edmondsham) for at least two years. For people who live in Boveridge there is a preference for pensions, for which the minimum age is 65 for men and 60 for women.

Types of grants: Pensions and one-off grants. Grants have been given for holiday recuperation after sickness, travel to see a specialist in London for medical reasons, alterations to a cottage to provide facilities on the ground floor for an infirm pensioner, and provision of a special medical bed.

Annual grant total: In 1993, up to 12 grants totalling £1,000 were made, along with 12 pensions of £7 per week totalling about £4,000.

Applications: In writing to the correspondent.

Correspondent: P S James, James Harris, The Estate Office, 33 West Borough, Wimborne, Dorset BH21 1LT (0202-882336).

The Dorset Police Welfare Fund

Eligibility: Serving or retired members of the Dorset Police, special constabulary, police cadets, traffic wardens and civilian staff or their dependants who are in need.

Types of grants: One-off grants according to need.

Annual grant total: £5,500.

Applications: In writing to the correspondent.

Correspondent: J K Blueman, Welfare Officer, Police Headquarters, Winfrith, Dorchester, Dorset DT2 8DZ.

The Sir Henry Edwards Gift Charity

Eligibility: People in need who live in the former borough of Weymouth and Melcombe Regis as it was on 31st March, 1974.

Types of grants: One-off and recurrent grants according to need.

Annual grant total: About £5,000.

Applications: In writing to the correspondent.

Correspondent: C I Thompson, Messrs Batten & Co, 60 St Thomas Street, Weymouth, Dorset DT4 8HB (0305-774666).

The Alfred Lodder Charity

Eligibility: Women in need who are members of the Church of England and aged over 60 or unable to work and who live in Colehill, Holt, Kingston Lacy and Wimborne.

Dorset

Types of grants: Quarterly payments of £12 or £13 to about 4 people.

Annual grant total: The trust had an income of over £1,000 in 1993.

Applications: In writing to the correspondent.

Correspondent: Mrs M A Brace, 2 Cobbs Road, Colehill, Wimborne, Dorset BH21 2RL (0202-885932).

William Williams Charity

Eligibility: People in need who live in the ancient parishes of Blandford Forum, Shaftesbury and Sturminster Newton.

Types of grants: One-off and recurrent grants according to need.

Annual grant total: In 1988, the charity's income was over £100,000; it gave over £30,000 in grants (including grants to organisations). No more recent information is available.

Applications: In writing to the correspondent.

Correspondent: O B N Paine, Andrews Son & Huxtable, 31 High West Street, Dorchester, Dorset DT1 1UP (0305-251707).

Blandford Forum

The Blandford Forum Charities

Eligibility: People in need who live in the borough of Blandford Forum.

Types of grants: One-off grants for necessities, recuperative holidays and occupational training.

Annual grant total: Between 120 and 130 grants are given totalling about £13,000.

Applications: In writing to the correspondent.

Correspondent: J Brown, Clerk, 22 Lockeridge Close, Blandford Forum, Dorset DT11 7TT (0258-454018).

Bournemouth

The Bournemouth Blind Aid Society

Eligibility: Blind or partially sighted people who live in Bournemouth.

Types of grants: One-off grants according to need.

Annual grant total: The trust has an income of £5,000, but probably not all of this is given in grants to individuals.

Applications: In writing to the correspondent.

Correspondent: D Cook, 29 Gleneagles, Fairway Drive, Christchurch, Dorset BH23 1JZ.

The MacDougall Trust

Eligibility: People in need who live in Bournemouth and the surrounding area.

Types of grants: One-off grants for all kinds of need.

Annual grant total: About £5,000.

Applications: Usually through social services.

Correspondent: Mrs A Kirby, 36 Dorset Lake Avenue, Lilliput, Parkstone, Poole, Dorset BH14 8JD.

Bridport

The Bridport Charities

Eligibility: People in need aged 60 or over who live in the borough of Bridport and surrounding parishes and have done so for at least two years.

Types of grants: One-off or recurrent grants according to need.

Annual grant total: In 1992, the trust had an income of £19,000. Only two grants were given to individuals totalling £50.

Applications: On a form available from the correspondent. Applications should be submitted directly by the individual.

Correspondent: Mrs V J Smith, 5 Hillingdon, Bridport, Dorset DT6 3DH (0308-423283).

Charmouth

The Charmouth United Charities

Eligibility: People in need who live in the parish of Charmouth.

Types of grants: One-off or recurrent grants according to need. Grants have been given for hospital travel and funeral expenses. Annual coal or grocery vouchers are given to selected people.

Annual grant total: In 1993, the trust had an income of £2,500. Grants to individuals totalled £2,250.

Applications: In writing to the correspondent or other trustees. Applications can be submitted directly by the individual or through a third party such as a rector, doctor or trustees. They are considered throughout the year.

Correspondent: D H M Carter, Secretary, 2 Parkway, Lower Sea Lane, Charmouth, Bridport, Dorset DT6 6LP (0935-26044 work/0297-60910 pm).

Christchurch

Legate's Charity

Eligibility: People in need who live in Christchurch borough.

Types of grants: Allowances of £2.75 a week for single people and £4.00 a week for married couples. One-off grants may be awarded depending on circumstances.

Annual grant total: In 1993, the trust had an income of over £6,000 and gave nine one-off grants and 25 weekly allowances totalling over £5,000.

Applications: On a form available from the correspondent. New applications are considered quarterly; for people under 50, applications are reviewed annually; all others reviewed every three years.

Correspondent: The Clerk, The Town Clerk's Department, Civic Offices, Bridge Street, Christchurch, Dorset BH23 1AZ (0202-486321).

The Mayor's Goodwill Fund

Eligibility: People in need who live in the borough of Christchurch.

Types of grants: Food parcels at Christmas to elderly and/or needy people and potted plants to lonely or recently bereaved people. The fund can also make donations in exceptional cases of hardship at other times of the year.

Annual grant total: In 1993/94, the trust gave 148 parcels and 42 plants to a total value of £2,300.

Applications: In writing to the correspondent preferably through a social worker, citizen's advice bureau or other welfare agency. Applications are considered in November/December.

Correspondent: The Mayor's Secretary, Civic Offices, Bridge Street, Christchurch, Dorset BH23 1AZ (0202-486321 ext. 368).

Other information: Grants are also given to Christchurch-based groups and voluntary organisations to help with Christmas activities.

Corfe Castle

The Corfe Castle Charities

Eligibility: People in need who live in the parish of Corfe Castle, including the village of Kingston.

Types of grants: One-off grants or loans to relieve sickness, infirmity or distress including rental of emergency lifelines, help with recuperative hospital costs and payment of travel expenses for patients/ visiting relatives to hospital.

Dorset/Gloucestershire

Annual grant total: In 1993, about £10,000 was given in grants some of which may have been given to students on vocational education courses.

Applications: In writing to the correspondent. The trustees meet every two months to decide on applications, but emergency requests are dealt with as they arise.

Correspondent: Mrs Clarke, 58 East Street, Corfe Castle, Wareham, Dorset BH20 5EQ (0929-480093).

● Dorchester

The Dorchester Relief-in-Need Charity

Eligibility: People in need who live in the ecclesiastical parish of Dorchester.

Types of grants: One-off and recurrent grants according to need.

Annual grant total: £2,300 in 1991/92.

Applications: Applications should be submitted through a social worker, health visitor, citizen's advice bureau, clergy and similar third parties. There is no form and applications are considered throughout the year.

Correspondent: R C Burnett, 48 Herringston Road, Dorchester, Dorset DT1 2BT (0305-265496).

● Poole

The Poole Children's Fund

Eligibility: Needy, deprived and disabled children up to 18 who live in the borough of Poole.

Types of grants: To provide holidays, educational or recreational opportunities. Grants range from £10 to £80.

Annual grant total: £1,400 in education and relief-in-need grants to 60 children in 1991. Grants range between £10 and £55 and are one-off. Loans may be available in some cases.

Applications: On a form available from the correspondent completed by a third party. Applications are considered throughout the year. Applications should include details of family structure including ages, reason of application; any other sources of funding which have been tried; what agencies (if any) are involved in helping the family, and any Statutory Orders (eg. care orders) pertaining to the child or their family members.

Correspondent: Jane Underhill, Secretary, 5 Park Road, Poole, Dorset BH5 2SH.

Other information: This entry has not been confirmed by the trust.

● Shaftesbury

The John Foyles Charity

Eligibility: People in need who live in the parish of Holy Trinity, Shaftesbury.

Types of grants: One-off grants.

Annual grant total: In 1991, the trust had assets of £16,000, and an income of £3,100. Five relief-in-need grants totalled £500. In recent years the trust seems to have withheld the bulk of its annual income rather than giving it in grants.

Applications: In writing to the correspondent at any time. Applications can be submitted directly by the individual or through an appropriate third party.

Correspondent: A B G Traill, 35 Bell Street, Shaftesbury, Dorset SP7 8AF (0747-852343).

● Sturminster Newton

The Sturminster Newton United Charities

Eligibility: People in need who live in the parish of Sturminster Newton.

Types of grants: Recurrent grants of £12 at Christmas.

Annual grant total: In 1993, the trust had an income of £1,200, all of which was given in 100 relief-in-need grants.

Applications: In writing to the correspondent by the individual or an appropriate third party. Applicants who the trustees know to be "self-supporting" are not awarded grants.

Correspondent: E Rose, 54 Green Close, Sturminster Newton, Dorset DT10 1BL (0258-472304).

● Tarrant Gunville

The Edwin Lucas Trust

Eligibility: "Residents of Tarrant Gunville of long-standing respectability." (In practice widows/widowers).

Types of grants: To relieve special needs eg. transport to hospital/nursing home by applicant or visiting relatives, solid fuel during cold weather and television licences. Christmas bonuses are also given to widows/widowers.

Annual grant total: The trust has an annual income of about £900. The average grant total in the last four years has been £500.

Applications: In writing to the correspondent by or on behalf of the individual. Applications are considered at any time.

Correspondent: James Farquharson, Chairman, Marlborough Farmhouse, Eastbury Estates, Tarrant Gunville, Dorset (0258-830312).

● Wimborne Minster

The Higden Hall Habgood & Brown Charity

Eligibility: People in need living in the ancient parish of Wimborne Minster.

Types of grants: One off grants.

Annual grant total: £500.

Applications: In writing to the correspondent.

Correspondent: Mrs M A Brace, 2 Cobbs Road, Colehill, Wimborne, Dorset BH21 2RL (0202-885932).

Other information: This entry has not been confirmed by the trust.

Gloucestershire

The Barnwood House Trust

Eligibility: Physically and mentally disabled people with special needs who live in the county of Gloucestershire and have a strong Gloucestershire connection.

Types of grants: Adaptions, equipment and other necessities related to special needs arising from the person's disability.

Annual grant total: The trust has a grants budget of £1 million, but over half of this is given to organisations. In 1993, the trust gave grants to 1,200 individuals.

Applications: By referral only. The key professional who knows the applicant's circumstances and need should complete the trust's application form.

Correspondent: Mrs C M Ellson, The Manor House, 162 Barnwood Road, Gloucester GL4 7JX (0452-611292).

Ann Cam's Charity

Eligibility: People who as a result of age, ill health or some other infirmity can no longer support themselves and who live within a 20-mile radius of Dymock.

Types of grants: Pensions of about £100 a year paid half yearly.

Annual grant total: About £1,600.

● Gloucestershire

Applications: On a form available from the correspondent. Should be submitted before June each year.

Correspondent: W H Masefield, Secretary, R & C B Masefield, Worcester Road, Ledbury, Hereford & Worcester HR8 1PN (0531-632377).

Sylvanus Lyson's Charity

Eligibility: Clergymen of the Church of England and their widows and dependents who are in need and have served in the diocese of Gloucester.

Types of grants: One-off and recurrent grants according to need.

Annual grant total: £60,000 in 65 grants, although not all to individuals.

Applications: In writing to the correspondent.

Correspondent: N A M Smith, c/o Messrs Wellingtons, 4 College Green, Gloucester GL1 2LU (0452-301903).

Other information: The trust also supports religious and other charitable work of the Church of England in the diocese of Gloucester.

The Charity of Lord Redesdale

Eligibility: Members of the Church of England or people in regular attendance at divine service, living in the ancient parishes of Batsford, Bourton-on-the-Hill, Blockley, Great Wolford, Moreton-in-Marsh, Little Wolford and Snowshill. Applicants should be aged 60 or over, or aged 40 or over if disabled in war.

Types of grants: Grants have been given towards help in bereavement, illness and loss of possessions in fire.

Annual grant total: £1,500 in 1990.

Applications: In writing to the correspondent.

Correspondent: M Hughes-Hallett, Secretary, Batsford Estate Office, Moreton-in-Marsh, Gloucestershire GL56 9QF (0608-650722).

Other information: This entry is repeated in the Warwickshire section of the book.

● Bisley

The Bisley Charities for the Poor

Eligibility: People in need who live in the ancient parish of Bisley.

Types of grants: One-off or recurrent grants according to need.

Annual grant total: In 1991/92, the trust had an income of £6,000. It is not known how much was given in grants to individuals in need.

Applications: In writing to the correspondent.

Correspondent: Mrs M R Hartwell, Secretary, Prospect Cottage, Bisley, Stroud, Gloucestershire GL6 7AB (0452-770600).

● Cheltenham

The Cheltenham Aid-in-Sickness & Nurses Welfare Fund

Eligibility: 1. Domiciliary nurses, past or present, who are in need and have worked or lived in the Cheltenham area. 2. People in need who are sick, convalescent, disabled or infirm who live in Cheltenham and neighbourhood.

Types of grants: One-off grants range from £30 to £100. They are given towards clothing, essential items of furniture, beds and bedding, washing machines, cookers, floor covering, appliances for disabled people, telephone installation etc..

Annual grant total: In 1992/93, the trust had an income of £10,600. Grants in category (1) totalled £3,600 in 60 grants; in category (2) totalled £2,400.

Applications: On a from available from the correspondent. Applications should be submitted through a social worker, citizen's advice bureau, health visitor, community nurse or other welfare agency. They are considered throughout the year.

Correspondent: Mrs A A Turner, Secretary, Cheltenham Family Welfare Association, 21 Rodney Street, Cheltenham GL50 1HX (0242-522180).

Other information: The Association also administers The Gooding Fund from which grants are given to individuals in need. The income of the fund is about £700 a year.

● Cirencester

The Smith's Cirencester Poor Charity

Eligibility: People in need who live within five miles of Cirencester.

Types of grants: One-off grants of around £50 towards items for people with disabilities and recurrent grants of about £10 a week paid quarterly.

Annual grant total: About 15 people receive recurrent grants and 2 or 3 receive one-off grants totalling up to £8,000.

Applications: By nomination from a trustee or in writing to the correspondent, generally through a welfare organisation.

Correspondent: Mrs J E Powell, 7 Dollar Street, Cirencester GL7 2AS (0285-651212).

● Gloucester

The Fluck Convalescent Fund

Eligibility: Women and children (boys under 16) who live in the city of Gloucester or its immediate neighbourhood, who are poor, sick or convalescent after illness or surgical operation.

Types of grants: One-off grants between £20 and £200 for recuperative holidays, clothing, bedding, fuel, food and medical or other aids. Grants will not be made for the repayment of a debt already incurred.

Annual grant total: About £20,000.

Applications: Applications in writing to the correspondent must be submitted by a responsible sponsor such as social services, health officer, doctor etc..

Correspondent: The Clerk, c/o Whitemans, Solicitors, 33-37 Brunswick Road, Gloucester GL1 1JQ (0452-411601).

The Gloucester District Nursing Charities

Eligibility: People in need who are sick or disabled and live in the city of Gloucester and the immediately adjoining parishes.

Types of grants: One-off and recurrent grants according to need.

Annual grant total: £17,000 in 1993.

Applications: In writing to the correspondent.

Correspondent: E G Davis, Clerk, 15a Heathville Road, Gloucester GL1 3DS (0452-525728).

The United Charity of Palling Burgess

Eligibility: People in need who live in the city of Gloucester.

Types of grants: One-off and recurrent grants according to need.

Annual grant total: 25 grants totalling about £1,100.

Applications: In writing to the correspondent. Applications should be submitted through a social worker, minister of religion or similar third party.

Correspondent: D S Bayliss, Clerk, 23 Hill Hay Road, Maston, Gloucester GL4 9LS (0452-21800).

● Tewkesbury

The Gyles Geest Charity

Eligibility: People in need who live in the borough of Tewkesbury.

Types of grants: Annual distribution in December of £17 vouchers to be used in local shops for groceries etc.. Recipients are usually retired or old age pensioners.

Annual grant total: In 1992/93, the trust gave 400 grants totalling £6,800.

Applications: On a form available from the correspondent. Applications should be submitted directly by the individual to be considered in November.

Correspondent: E A Hughes, Clerk, 23 Elmvil Road, Newtown, Tewkesbury, Gloucestershire GL20 8DD (0684-294493).

Somerset

The Somerset County Bowling Association Benevolent Fund

Eligibility: Somerset bowlers who are or have been members of subscribing clubs affiliated to the county association and their widows who are in need.

Types of grants: One-off grants ranging from £75 to £250.

Annual grant total: In 1992/93, the trust had an income of £1,200; nine grants totalled £1,175.

Applications: Club committees wishing to make a recommendation should obtain a form from the correspondent. Applications are considered throughout the year.

Correspondent: B A Jones, 2 Norton Hall, Norton Down, Stratton-on-the-Fosse, Bath BA3 4RW (0761-412853).

The Somerset Local Medical Benevolent Fund

Eligibility: Medical practitioners practising or having practised in Somerset, and their dependants in need.

Types of grants: One-off or recurrent grants according to need.

Annual grant total: In 1992/93, the trust had an income of £10,300. Grants to individuals totalled £3,150. Grants were also given to medical charities.

Applications: In writing to the correspondent. Applications can be submitted directly by the individual, or through a social worker, citizen's advice bureau or other welfare agency or a general medical practitioner.

Correspondent: Dr R S Tiner, Secretary, 10 Pine Close, Taunton TA1 2SD (0823-282055).

● Axbridge

The William Spearing Charity & Others

Eligibility: People in need who live in the town of Axbridge.

Types of grants: Annual Christmas gifts of £25 to elderly people.

Annual grant total: £1,260 in 44 grants in 1992.

Applications: In writing to the correspondent by the beginning of November.

Correspondent: F Jarmany, Axbridge Parochial Charity, Maricourt, St Mary's Street, Axbridge, Somerset BS26 2BN.

● Bridgwater

The Manchip Trust

Eligibility: People in need over retirement age who live in Bridgwater.

Types of grants: Annuities paid quarterly.

Annual grant total: In 1991, the trust had an income of £2,000. Eight annuitants received between £236 and £286.

Applications: Through the local office of Somerset Social Services. Applications should be submitted on a form available from the correspondent. Applicants should have savings of less than £500.

Correspondent: Miss E M Willett, c/o the Universal Beneficent Society, 6 Avonmore Road, London W14 8RL (071-602 6274).

The Tamlin Charity

Eligibility: Elderly people over retirement age who are in need and live in Bridgwater.

Types of grants: Quarterly instalments.

Annual grant total: £1,600 in 1993 to 40 beneficiaries.

Applications: On a form available from a trustee or from the correspondent.

Correspondent: Richard Young, Clerk, 5 Channel Court, Burnham-on-Sea, Somerset TA8 1NE.

● **Gloucestershire/Somerset** ●

● Cannington

The Cannington Combined Charity

Eligibility: People in need who live in the parish of Cannington.

Types of grants: Grants to meet regular or one-off bills where applicants cannot receive additional assistance from any other source. Recent grants have been for recreational equipment for disabled people, decorating, gardening and fuel bills for elderly and disabled people.

Annual grant total: In 1992, the trust had an income of £2,200. 15 relief-in-need grants totalled £1,520.

Applications: On a form available from the correspondent. Applications can be submitted directly by the individual, through a social worker, family member, doctor or similar third party. Trustees meet quarterly in January, April, August and November.

Correspondent: Miss C A Roberts, 6 Mount Road, Nether Stowey, Bridgwater, Somerset (0278-732789).

Other information: This trust has been formed by the Henry Rogers Charity absorbing four smaller Cannington charities.

● Compton Martin

William Webb's & Others' Charities

Eligibility: People in need aged over 60 who live in the ancient parish of Compton Martin in Somerset.

Types of grants: One-off grants of a minimum of £15.

Annual grant total: No information available.

Applications: In writing to the correspondent. Applications are considered in December and can be submitted directly by the individual.

Correspondent: M Sinden, Clerk to the Parish Council, Huntsdown, Yew Tree Lane, Compton Martin, Bristol BS18 6JS.

● Edington

The Jat Luttrell Memorial Charity

Eligibility: People in need who live in Edington.

Types of grants: Probably one-off and recurrent grants according to need.

Annual grant total: About £6,000.

Somerset

Applications: In writing to the correspondent.

Correspondent: Mrs A Auld, West Close, Church Road, Edington, Bridgewater, Somerset TA7 9JT (0278-722418).

Ilchester

The Ilchester Relief-in-Need & Educational Charity

Eligibility: People in need who live in the parish of Ilchester. Preference is given to men over 50.

Types of grants: One-off grants usually of about £50.

Annual grant total: In 1993, the trust had an income of £18,000. Grants to individuals in need totalled £1,900.

Applications: On a form available from the correspondent. Applications can be submitted directly by the individual or through a social worker, citizen's advice bureau, other welfare agency or third party.

Correspondent: Mrs J M Hill, Clerk, Greystones, Podimore, Yeovil, Somerset BA22 8JH (0935-840640).

Porlock

The Henry Rogers Charity (Porlock Branch)

Eligibility: People in need who live in the rectorial manor of Porlock.

Types of grants: Monthly and one-off grants.

Annual grant total: In 1993, the trust's income was £1,480. 125 grants to individuals totalled £1,460.

Applications: On a form available from the correspondent. Applications are considered throughout the year, and should be submitted directly by the individual.

Correspondent: L S R Perkins, Higherbourne, Porlock, Minehead, Somerset TA24 8PU (0643-862332).

Rimpton

The Rimpton Relief-in-Need Charities

Eligibility: People in need who live in the parish of Rimpton.

Types of grants: One-off or recurrent grants according to need.

Annual grant total: The trust had an income of £3,200 in 1992.

Applications: In writing to the correspondent.

Correspondent: G L Burrows, Treasurer, Old Hall House, Rimpton, Yeovil, Somerset BA22 8AD (0935-851300).

Shapwick

The Henry Smith Charity

Eligibility: People in need who live in Shapwick.

Types of grants: One-off and recurrent grants according to need.

Annual grant total: £500 to £600.

Applications: In writing to the correspondent.

Correspondent: M Motum, Home Farm House, Station Road, Shapwick, Bridgwater, Somerset TA7 9NJ.

Street

The George Cox Charity

Eligibility: People in need who live in the parish of Street.

No applications from people living outside the parish can be considered.

Types of grants: Generally one-off grants of £30 to £75 paid through the social services. Help is given towards holidays; repair of domestic appliances such as washing machines and cookers; equipment for the frail elderly such as visual aids and helping hand; second hand furniture and carpets; hospital visiting travel costs; heaters and fires for the elderly, and debt payments.

Annual grant total: In 1993, the trust had an income of £2,000. 40 grants to individuals totalled £1,400.

Applications: Applications in writing can be submitted through a recognised referral agency (eg. social worker, citizen's advice bureau or doctor) or other third party, and are considered throughout the year.

Correspondent: P A Preston, Clerk, 10 Seymour Road, Street, Somerset BA16 0SP (0458-43501).

Taunton

The Taunton Aid in Sickness Fund

Eligibility: Sick poor people who live in the old borough of Taunton and civil parish of Trull, with priority to those living within a four-mile radius of St Mary's Church, Taunton. The area of benefit was increased in 1993.

Types of grants: One-off grants, ranging from £8 to £500 according to need.

Annual grant total: In 1992/93, the trust had an income of £13,000, after expenditure on a laundry service and maintaining property. 52 grants were given to individuals totalling £7,000.

Applications: On a form available from the correspondent either submitted directly by the individual or through a third party. Applications are considered throughout the year.

Correspondent: N N Banks, Secretary, Apsley House, Billet Street, Taunton, Somerset (0823-259101).

Trull

The Trull Parish Lands Charity

Eligibility: People in need who live in the parish of Trull.

Types of grants: One-off or recurrent grants according to need.

Annual grant total: In 1993, the trust had an income of £4,400 to be distributed to individuals in need.

Applications: In writing to the correspondent.

Correspondent: W P Morris, Clerk, Dodson Harding, 11 Hammet Street, Taunton TA1 1RJ (0823-331293).

Yeovil

The Marsh Trust

Eligibility: Children in need who live in the ecclesiastical parishes of Holy Trinity and St Michael and All Angels, and the former ecclesiastical parish of St John the Baptist, all in Yeovil.

Types of grants: One-off grants only.

Annual grant total: £825.

Applications: In writing to the correspondent.

Correspondent: T D George, Porter Bartlett Mayo (Ref. TDG), Solicitors, The Close, Church Path, Yeovil BA20 1HH (0935-24581).

Wiltshire

The Julius Silman Charitable Trust

Eligibility: Disadvantaged people in need who live in the Wiltshire area.

Types of grants: One-off grants ranging from £50 to £500.

Annual grant total: About £40,000, of which about £10,000 can be given to individuals. In 1992, 20 grants were given to individuals totalling £3,000.

Applications: In writing to the correspondent. Applications should be submitted directly by the individual. They are considered 3/4 times a year.

Correspondent: J Silman, Courtlands, Corsham, Wiltshire SN13 9QT (0249-730216).

● **Aldbourne**

The Poors' Gorse Charity

Eligibility: Elderly people in need who live in the parish of Aldbourne.

Types of grants: One-off grants for fuel.

Annual grant total: 120 grants totalling over £1,000.

Applications: In writing to the correspondent.

Correspondent: Miss J Wootton, 4 Castle Street, Aldbourne, Marlborough, Wiltshire SN8 2DA.

● **Ashton Keynes**

The Ashton Keynes Charity

Eligibility: Elderly people in need who live in Ashton Keynes.

Types of grants: Grants to pensioners.

Annual grant total: About £2,000.

Applications: In writing to the correspondent.

Correspondent: R Smith, Clerk, Amberley, 4 Gosditch Road, Ashton Keynes, Swindon SN6 6NZ (0285-861461).

● **Bishopstone**

The Bishopstone United Charities

Eligibility: Elderly people and widows who live in the parish of Bishopstone near Swindon.

Types of grants: Yearly grants of coal to about 14 people (or the equivalent in money to elderly people in electrically heated council accommodation), and annual allowances of £40.

Annual grant total: About 18 grants totalling £1,500.

Applications: To the correspondent; trustees meet twice-yearly to consider applications and review existing benefits.

Correspondent: A G Parrett, Seymour House, Bishopstone, Swindon.

Other information: This information has not been confirmed by the trust.

● **Chippenham**

The Chippenham Borough Lands Charities

Eligibility: People in need who live in the civil parish of Chippenham.

Types of grants: One-off and recurrent grants upwards of £100. Recent grants have included help with respite care, car conversions and wheelchairs.

Annual grant total: The charity's endowment is about £3 million which generated an income of £250,000 in 1991/92. £275,000 was disbursed in grants (including grants to organisations).

Grants are not given in any circumstances where the trustees consider the award to be a substitute for statutory provision.

Applications: On a form available from the correspondent. Applications are considered every six weeks and can be submitted directly by the individual or though a social worker, citizen's advice bureau or other welfare agency.

Correspondent: B D Coombs, Clerk, 16 Market Place, Chippenham, Wiltshire SN15 3HW (0249-658180).

● **Cricklade**

The Cricklade United Charities

Eligibility: People in need who live in the parish of St Sampson's, Cricklade.

Types of grants: One-off or recurrent grants according to need.

Annual grant total: About £1,000.

Applications: Considered once a year after a public advertisement for Christmas grants.

Correspondent: G W Freeth, 46 High Street, Cricklade, Swindon, Wiltshire SN6 6BX (0793-750501).

Other information: The charity hopes to widen its scope.

● **East Knoyle**

The East Knoyle Charities

Eligibility: People in need who live in the parish of East Knoyle and in exceptional circumstances people who live immediately outside the parish.

Types of grants: One-off grants only, usually for heating bills, but any need is considered, including grants to school-leavers for tools, working clothes and books.

Annual grant total: 35 grants totalling £1,200.

Applications: At any time to the correspondent or any other trustee.

Correspondent: G G S Chambers, Turnpike Cottage, Shaftesbury Road, East Knoyle, Salisbury, Wiltshire SP3 6AT (0747-830476).

● **Marlborough**

The Herbert Leaf Charity

Eligibility: People in need who live in the parish of Marlborough.

Types of grants: One-off grants only.

Annual grant total: In 1992/93, the trust had an income of £3,400. Grants to individuals totalled £1,200.

Applications: In writing to the correspondent. Applications are usually considered in July each year and can be submitted directly by the individual.

Correspondent: A W Skittrall, Marlborough Town Council, Council Offices, 5 High Street, Marlborough, Wiltshire SN8 1LP (0672-512487).

● **Salisbury**

The William Botley Charity

Eligibility: Women in need who live in the city of Salisbury.

Types of grants: One-off grants to meet all kinds of emergency and other needs that cannot be met from public funds. Recent grants have been given for essential items such as good quality reconditioned cookers, washing machines, refrigerators, school clothing and shoes, holidays and wheelchairs.

Annual grant total: Around 180 grants totalling £7,500 in 1993.

Applications: Applications are considered on the first Friday of every

Wiltshire

month. Application forms, available from the correspondent, are required 15 days before. Preferably, applications should be sponsored by a recognised professional who is aware of statutory entitlements and capable of giving advice/supervision on budgeting etc..

Correspondent: H P L Saunders, Clerk, Trinity Hospital, Trinity Street, Salisbury SP1 2BE (0722-25640).

The Salisbury City Almshouse & Welfare Charities

Eligibility: People in need who live in Salisbury and district.

Types of grants: Generally one-off grants to meet all kinds of emergency or other needs that cannot be met from public funds. Recent grants have been given for essential items such as good quality reconditioned cookers, washing machines, refrigerators, school clothing and shoes, holidays and wheelchairs.

Annual grant total: Over 150 grants totalling about £11,500 in 1993.

Applications: Applications are considered on the first Friday of each month. Application forms, available from the correspondent, are required 15 days before. Preferably, applications should be sponsored by a recognised professional who is aware of statutory entitlements and is capable of giving advice/ supervision in budgeting etc..

Correspondent: H P L Saunders, Clerk, Trinity Hospital, Trinity Street, Salisbury SP1 2BE (0722-325640).

Trowbridge

The Cecil Norman Wellesley Blair Charitable Trust

Eligibility: People in need who live in the civil parish of Trowbridge.

Types of grants: One-off grants only, mainly in the form of Christmas vouchers.

Annual grant total: £3,000 to £3,500.

Applications: In writing to the correspondent, occasionally on referral through social services, citizen's advice bureau etc..

Correspondent: M Ridley, Castle House, Castle Street, Trowbridge, Wiltshire BA14 8AX.

Dr C S Kingston Fund

Eligibility: People in need who live in urban district of Trowbridge.

Types of grants: One-off grants only.

Annual grant total: 17 grants totalling £2,000 were given in 1993.

Applications: In writing to the correspondent including details of the need, the applicant's resources and other benefits available. Applications can be submitted directly by the individual or through a social worker, citizen's advice bureau or other welfare agency. They are considered at any time.

Correspondent: Matthew Ridley, Castle House, Castle Street, Trowbridge, Wiltshire BA14 8AX (0225-755621).

Warminster

The Warminster Relief-in-Need Charity

Eligibility: People in need who live in Warminster.

Types of grants: About 25 individuals receive Christmas grants of £7 and/or one-off grants of up to £50.

Annual grant total: In 1992, the trust's income was about £1,900, including £1,100 from Henry Smith's (General Estate) Charity.

Applications: In writing to the correspondent.

Correspondent: Miss M E Wynne, 12 Beckford Close, Warminster, Wiltshire BA12 9LW (0985-212546).

Westbury

The Henry Smith Charity

Eligibility: People in need who live in Westbury.

Types of grants: One-off or recurrent grants according to need.

Annual grant total: Probably about £1,000.

Applications: In writing to the correspondent.

Correspondent: Messrs Pinniger Finch & Co, Solicitors, Church Street, Westbury, Wiltshire BA13 3BX. (0373-823791).

Other information: The correspondent did not wish to have an entry in the Guide and stated that the trust is not open for people to make applications for grants.

8. South East

The Berkshire Nurses & Relief-in-Sickness Fund

Eligibility: 1. People in need through sickness or disability who live in the county of Berkshire and those areas of Oxfordshire formerly in Berkshire.

2. Nurses and midwives employed as district nurses in the county of Berkshire and those areas of Oxfordshire formerly in Berkshire and people employed before August 1980 as administrative and clerical staff by Berkshire County Nursing Association.

Types of grants: One-off grants only towards household accounts (excluding those below), holidays, some medical aids, special diets, clothing, wheelchairs, electronic aids for disabled people, hospital travel costs, prescription season tickets etc..

No grants for rent or mortgage payments, community charge, water rates, funeral bills, on-going payments such as nursing home fees or any items thought to be the responsibility of statutory authorities.

Annual grant total: In 1992/93, the trust had an income of £49,000. £3,400 was given in grants to retired nurses; £24,000 to 223 individuals; and £6,000 to organisations.

Applications: On a form available from the correspondent. Applications should be made through a social worker, citizen's advice bureau or other welfare agency and supported by a member of the statutory authorities. They are considered as received.

Correspondent: Mrs R Pottinger, Hon. Secretary, 26 Montrose Walk, Fords Farm, Calcot, Berkshire RG3 5YH (0734-424556).

The German Society of Benevolence

Eligibility: People who are or were citizens of the German Federal Republic, the German Democratic Republic or Austria, and dependants of the above. Applicants must live in Greater London, Essex, Hertfordshire, Kent or Surrey.

Types of grants: Pensions and small one-off grants for heating, clothing and other needs, but not for relief of rates and taxes.

The society can make no commitment to renew payments.

Annual grant total: £3,000.

Applications: Applications are considered from individuals in need or from agencies acting on their behalf.

Correspondent: Mrs L Little, c/o The German Welfare Council, 59 Birkenhead Street, London WC1H 3BB (071-278 6955).

Other information: This society should not be confused with the German Welfare Council, which is an advisory body only. This entry is repeated in the London section of the book.

The B V MacAndrew Trust

Eligibility: People in need who live in East and West Sussex.

Types of grants: One-off grants.

Annual grant total: In 1991/92, the trust had an income of £5,000.

Applications: In writing to the correspondent at any time. Applications should be made through a social worker, citizen's advice bureau or other welfare agency.

Correspondent: Eric S Diplock, Hon. Solicitor, Lanes End House, 15 Prince Albert Street, Brighton BN1 1HY (0273-23231).

Other information: This entry has not been confirmed by the trust, but the address is correct according to the Charity Commission.

The Sussex Police Charitable Fund

Eligibility: Retired police officers of the Sussex Police Authority and their widows or dependants who live in Sussex. Preference for members of the fund, but the management committee can help police pensioners who are not members but who otherwise qualify for help.

Types of grants: One-off grants for any type of need such as aids, adaptations, holidays and hospital travel expenses. Discretionary loans may be given to serving officers subscribing to the fund who are facing financial difficulties. Loans are repayable from salary at source per pay period.

No grants towards debt repayment.

Annual grant total: In 1991, the fund had assets of £224,000 and an income of £46,000. 80 grants to individuals totalled £36,000.

Applications: In writing to the correspondent.

Correspondent: Mrs C A MacFie, Force Welfare Officer, Sussex Police Headquarters, Malling House, Lewes, East Sussex BN7 2DZ (0273-475432).

The Maurice Winston Charitable Trust

Eligibility: People in need, particularly single elderly people living in their own homes, the deaf or hard of hearing, and physically disabled people not in the care of any local authority. Applicants must live in East or West Sussex.

Types of grants: Grants for domestic help, aids, appliances, convalescence and other necessities and comforts.

Annual grant total: £2,800 in 1991.

Applications: On a form available from the correspondent.

Correspondent: Margaret Christie, 95 Western Road, Hove BN3 1FA (0273-734977).

Bedfordshire

● Bedfordshire

The Wootton Charities

Eligibility: People in need, particularly elderly people or single parent families, who live in Wootton and Stewartby.

Types of grants: One-off and recurrent grants of £10 to £20 distributed at Christmas and in the summer according to need.

Annual grant total: In 1993, around 50 people received grants totalling about £1,500, a few of which may have been given for educational purposes.

Applications: In writing to the correspondent by the individual or submitted by a charities committee member. Applications are usually considered in July and November.

Correspondent: Mrs J Sherwood, Clerk, 157 Bedford Road, Wootton, Bedford MK43 9BA (0234-840249 - before 3pm weekdays; 0234-852797 - after 3.30pm).

● Bedford

The Municipal Charities & the Bedford & District Aid in Sickness Charity

Eligibility: People in need who live in the borough of Bedford.

Types of grants: Pensions; annual grants towards fuel bills and other necessities; occasional one-off grants.

Annual grant total: About £9,000 in 70 pensions; £1,000 in annual grants.

Applications: In writing to the correspondent.

Correspondent: The Clerk, c/o The Chief Executive, Bedford Borough Council, Town Hall, Bedford MK40 1SJ (0234-267422).

● Dunstable

The Dunstable Poor's Lands Charity

Eligibility: People in need who live in the old borough of Dunstable.

Types of grants: Grants are made annually on Maundy Thursday mostly to elderly people on Income Support or other benefit.

Annual grant total: In 1993, the trust had an income of £5,000. Grants to 362 individuals in need totalled £4,300

Applications: Directly by the individual to the trustees on Maundy Thursday following distribution.

Correspondent: Mrs B Royce, Clerk, Grove House, High Street North, Dunstable, Bedfordshire LU6 (0582-607895).

The Dunstable Welfare Trust

Eligibility: People in need who live in Dunstable.

Types of grants: One-off grants ranging from £50 to £100.

Annual grant total: About £500.

Applications: In writing to the correspondent through a social worker, citizen's advice bureau or other welfare agency or clergy. Applications are considered every month.

Correspondent: The Rector, 77 High Street South, Dunstable, Bedfordshire LU6 3SF (0582-696725).

● Husborne Crawley

The Husborne Crawley Charities of the Poor

Eligibility: People in need who live in the ancient parish of Husborne Crawley.

Types of grants: Grants of £100 are given to all pensioners for fuel and a Christmas gift, in death grants to relatives and to other people in need.

Annual grant total: £5,700 in 1993.

Applications: In writing to the correspondent directly by the individual. They are considered in May and December.

Correspondent: C T Lousada, Chairman, Estate Office, Crawley Park, Husborne Crawley, Bedford MK43 0NN (0908-282860).

● Kempston

The Kempston Charities

Eligibility: People in need who live in Kempston (including Kempston rural).

Types of grants: Grants are only given for a specific purpose eg. a particular piece of equipment.

Grants are not given for general purposes or running costs.

Annual grant total: In 1992, the trust had an income of £11,000. About £800 was given in 15 grants to individuals.

Applications: In writing to the correspondent. Applications should be made directly by the individual. They are considered in February, June and November.

Correspondent: Mrs N Darwood, 113 High Street, Kempston, Bedford MK42 7BP (0234-855167).

Other information: Grants are also given to local schools and institutions.

● Luton

The Emily Ada Sibthorpe Trust

Eligibility: Women over 60 and men over 65 who are in need and live in Luton.

Types of grants: One-off grants for small items, telephone bills, repairs, alterations and comforts.

Annual grant total: In 1990/91, the trust's income was £3,400. 25 relief-in-need grants to individuals totalled £3,800.

Applications: In writing to the correspondent through the social services department.

Correspondent: Director of Business Services, Bedfordshire County Council, County Hall, Bedford MK42 9AP (0234-363222).

● Ravensden

The Ravensden Town & Poor Estate

Eligibility: People in need who live in the parish of Ravensden.

Types of grants: Grants of £30 to £35 are given to widows, widowers and others in need at Christmas and on their birthday. One-off grants are also given for special need.

Annual grant total: The trust had an income of £4,400 in 1992. 32 grants to individuals totalled £1,800.

Applications: In writing to the correspondent. Applications can be submitted directly by the individual. They are considered in November, although urgent cases can be responded to at any time.

Correspondent: P C Wallinger, Clerk, 16 Crofton Close, Bedford MK41 8AJ (0234-267169).

● Shefford

The Charity of Robert Lucas for the Poor & for Public Purposes

Eligibility: People in need who live in the ancient township of Shefford.

Types of grants: Probably one-off or recurrent grants according to need.

Annual grant total: In 1992, the trust had an income of £37,000. Expenditure totalled £28,000; it is not known how much of this was given in grants to individuals.

Applications: In writing to the correspondent. Applications should be submitted directly by the individual and are considered throughout the year.

Correspondent: Mrs L M Davis, Clerk, 9 Queen Elizabeth Close, Shefford, Bedfordshire SG17 5LE (0462-814992).

Berkshire

The Berkshire Clergy Charity

Eligibility: Clergy in need who work or have worked in the Archdeaconry of Berkshire, and their dependants.

Types of grants: Grants according to need.

Annual grant total: £6,300 in 1993.

Applications: In writing to the correspondent or to the appropriate rural dean.

Correspondent: D G Wheeler, 30 Moor Copse Close, Earley, Reading RG6 2NA (0734-261489).

The Finchamstead & Barkham Relief-in-Sickness Fund

Eligibility: People in need who are sick, convalescing, mentally/physically disabled or infirm and who live in the civil parishes of Finchamstead and Barkham.

Types of grants: Usually one-off grants towards the cost of medical, nursing and domestic sevices, and for appliances. Help is also given for those caring for or visiting sick or disabled people. "The terms of the trust do not permit the offer of continuing support but the committee is always glad to consider a repeat application where need recurs or continues."

Annual grant total: 6 to 10 grants totalling £2,500.

Applications: Application can be made directly by the individual through any member of the committee who will be personally responsible for assessing eligibility. Applications can be submitted at any time.

Correspondent: Dr J K Dewhurst, Fourwinds, The Ridges, Finchamstead, Wokingham, Berkshire RG11 3SY (0734-732783);
or Miss A Billing (0734-733736);
Mrs M Rimmer (0734-782477);
Rev K Humphreys (0734-730030).

The Polehampton Charities

Eligibility: People in need who live in Twyford and Ruscombe.

Types of grants: One-off grants for necessities and convalescence. Grants range from £50 to £200.

Annual grant total: In 1992, the charities had assets of over £500,000 and an income of £21,000. Over 60 relief-in-need grants to individuals totalled £5,000.

Applications: In writing to the correspondent, including details of income and expenditure. Applications can be submitted directly by the individual or through a social worker or other welfare agency.

Correspondent: Peter M Hutt, Clerk, Addington House, 73 London Street, Reading, Berkshire RG1 4QB (0734-581441).

The Reading Municipal Church Charities

Eligibility: See below.

Types of grants: A number of different charities operate from the same address; two are for relief-in-need purposes:

1. Archbishop Laud's Marriage Portions Charity – grants to girls who attend church, who were born or live in the district of Reading or the parish of Wokingham and are about to get married.

2. Edward Simeon's Clothing Charity – grants for clothing to children who live in the borough of Reading. Applicants must be referred by the vicar.

Annual grant total: No information available.

Applications: In writing to the correspondent.

Correspondent: The Clerk, 1 Friar Street, Reading RG1 1DA (0734-587111).

● **Binfield**

The Fritillary Trust

Eligibility: People in need who live in Binfield.

Types of grants: One-off grants only.

Annual grant total: In 1993, the trust's income was £7,000 and grants totalled £4,300.

Applications: In writing to the correspondent.

Correspondent: The Trustees, Hambros Trust Company Limited, 41 Tower Hill, London EC3N 4HA (071-480 5000).

● **Burnham**

The Cornelius O'Sullivan Fund

Eligibility: People in need who are sick, convalescent, disabled or infirm and live in or near the parish of Burnham.

Types of grants: One-off grants of about £500 for pilgrimages or donations towards specialist medical equipment.

Annual grant total: In 1993, the trust had assets of £10,000 producing an income of £1,900. Grants of about £500 were given to 4 individuals and totalled £3,400.

Applications: Applications can be submitted by the individual, through a recognised referral agency (eg. social worker, citizen's advice bureau or doctor) or other third party, and are considered in January and September.

Correspondent: Mrs J Carter, Head Teacher, Our Lady of Peace RC Middle School, Derwent Drive, Slough, Berkshire SL1 6HW (0628-666715).

● **Datchet**

The Datchet United Charities

Eligibility: People in need who live in the ancient parish of Datchet, with a preference for the elderly.

Types of grants: One-off and recurrent grants according to need.

Annual grant total: In 1992/93, around 150 grants were given totalling over £500.

Applications: Through welfare agencies on behalf of the individual. All referrals are vetted by social workers.

Correspondent: J H Reader, Clerk, 38 London Road, Datchet, Berkshire SL3 9JN (0753-542376).

● **Earley**

The Earley Charity

Eligibility: People in need who live in the ancient liberty of Earley and the immediate neighbourhood.

Types of grants: One-off grants for relief of poverty, sickness, disablement, housing needs, elderly and infirm people, and carers.

Berkshire/Buckinghamshire

Annual grant total: In 1993, 200 grants totalling £42,750 were made. In addition a separate annual distribution of £12,000 was made to 150 people to help with fuel bills. Grants are usually limited to a maximum of £500 but in special cases can be increased.

Applications: On a form available from the correspondent. Applications are considered every 6 weeks.

Correspondent: L G Norton, Clerk, The Liberty of Earley House, Strand Way, Earley, Reading RG6 4EA (0734-755663).

● Eton

The Eton Poor's Estate

Eligibility: People over 60 who are in need in the ancient parish of Eton.

Types of grants: Weekly grants of £1.50 and grants of £200 for a particular need.

Annual grant total: In 1992, the trust had an income of £34,000, of which £14,000 was given in grants to individuals.

Applications: In writing to the correspondent. Applications are considered in May and December.

Correspondent: J Gidney, 15 High Street, Eton, Windsor, Berkshire SL4 6AX (0753-869991).

Other information: The trust also supports a day centre for the elderly.

● Reading

The Reading Dispensary Trust

Eligibility: People in need who are suffering from physical or mental disability or infirmity and who live in Reading and the surrounding area.

Types of grants: One-off grants for recuperative holidays, services and special items.

Annual grant total: £55,000, although not all this was given in grants to individuals.

Applications: On a form available from the correspondent.

Correspondent: D H Comerford, Clerk, 16 Wokingham Road, Reading RG6 1JQ (0734-265698).

St Laurence Charities for the Poor

Eligibility: People in need who live in the parish of St Laurence in Reading.

Types of grants: One-off or recurrent grants according to need.

Annual grant total: In 1990, the trust had an income of £30,000. Most of the income is given to charities rather than individuals.

Applications: In writing to the correspondent. Applications should be submitted directly by the individual for consideration in November.

Correspondent: John M James, Treasurer, c/o Vale & West, Victoria House, 26 Queen Victoria Street, Reading RG1 1TG (0734-573238).

● Shinfield

The Godson's Charity

Eligibility: People in need who wish to emigrate and who currently live in the London borough of Greenwich; Tenbury Wells in Hereford and Worcester and Shinfield in Berkshire. The majority of applications are received from Greenwich.

Types of grants: One-off grants up to £1,000 for those in need and wishing to emigrate (especially where the applicant has a new job to go to).

Annual grant total: Two grants totalling £1,500 were given in 1992. (The total expenditure of the trust was £3,500.) The trust has assets of £80,000, generating an income of £6,500.

Applications: Directly by the individual on a form available from the correspondent. Details of the proposed destination, occupation, and financial circumstances must be given. Applications are considered as they are received.

Correspondent: Anne Gregory, c/o Teredo Petroleum plc, 13–14 Hanover Street, London W1R 9G (071-495 5916).

Other information: This entry is repeated in the Midlands and London sections of the book.

● Slough

The Slough Good Causes Fund

Eligibility: People in need (usually those in receipt of social security benefit) who live in Slough and district. Applications will not be considered from outside this area.

Types of grants: Usually one-off grants of about £50 for emergency needs eg. for heating, lighting and telephone bills getting out of control, school uniforms, children's clothes and buggies.

Annual grant total: About 90 grants totalling £3,800.

Applications: On a form available from the correspondent, submitted through a social worker or other welfare agency. Applications are considered at any time.

Correspondent: A Hailer, General Secretary, The Day Centre, William Street, Slough, Berkshire SL1 1XX.

● Sunninghill

The Sunninghill Fuel Allotment

Eligibility: People in need who live in the parish of Sunninghill.

Types of grants: One-off grants only.

Annual grant total: Over £40,000.

Applications: In writing to the correspondent.

Correspondent: T R Clark, 8 Woodend Drive, Ascot, Berkshire SL5 9BG.

● Wokingham

The Wokingham United Charities

Eligibility: People in need who live in the parishes of Wokingham Town and Wokingham Without.

Types of grants: One-off grants between £25 and £150.

Annual grant total: In 1991/92, the trust's income was £2,800. 21 relief-in-need grants totalled £3,600.

Applications: In writing to the correspondent. Applications are considered each month and can be submitted directly by the individual, or through a social worker, head teacher or similar third party.

Correspondent: P Robinson, Clerk, 66 Upper Broadmoor Road, Crowthorne, Berkshire RG11 7DF (0344-762637).

Buckinghamshire

The Stoke Mandeville & Other Parishes Charity

Eligibility: People in need who live in the parishes of Stoke Mandeville, Great and Little Hampden and Great Missenden.

Types of grants: Annual Christmas grant to all pensioners and one-off grants to disabled people for specific needs.

Buckinghamshire

Annual grant total: In 1990, the trust had an income of £108,000. Of this, 10 elevenths is for the people living in the parish of Stoke Mandeville and one eleventh for people living in the other parishes listed above. Not all the income is used for grants to individuals.

Applications: In writing to the correspondent.

Correspondent: G Crombie, Secretary, Blackwells, Great Hampden, Great Missenden, Bucks HP16 9RJ (0494-488240).

● Aylesbury

The Charity of Elizabeth Eman

Eligibility: Women in need in the following order of priority:

1) widows born in the former borough of Aylesbury as constituted immediately before 1st April 1974;
2) widows living in the present district of Aylesbury Vale;
3) women living in the present district of Aylesbury Vale.

Types of grants: Allowances of £5 a week paid four times a year. Grants are for life.

Annual grant total: About £39,000. The trust currently supports 150 pensioners.

Applications: On a form available from the correspondent after a public advertisement. Applications can be submitted directly by the individual or through a social worker or other welfare agency, or by a member of the individual's immediate family. Original birth, marriage and death certificates should be included. Applications are usually considered in January.

Correspondent: R P Keighley, Clerk, Messrs Horwood & James, 7 Temple Square, Aylesbury (0296-87361).

William Harding's Charity

Eligibility: People in need who live in Aylesbury, but see below. Applications from outside Aylesbury cannot be considered.

Types of grants: Probably relief-in-need payments to elderly people only.

Annual grant total: In 1991, the trust's income was £3.6 million. Expenses totalled about £410,000, with a further £296,000 given out, no explanation is given as to the large surplus. Of the expenditure, general grants totalled £46,000 and alms £38,000. Other grants were for broadly educational purposes.

Applications: In writing to the correspondent.

Correspondent: Mr Leggett, Messrs Parrott & Coales, Solicitors, 14 Bourbon Street, Aylesbury HP20 2RS (0296-82244).

● Calverton

The Charity of the Unknown Donor

Eligibility: People over 65 and in need who live in the ecclesiastical parish of All Saints, Calverton.

Types of grants: One-off and recurrent grants according to need.

Annual grant total: In 1993, the trust had assets of £50,000 generating an income of £3,200. Total expenditure was £4,200. 29 grants were given to individuals totalling £3,200.

Applications: On a form available from the correspondent. Applications are considered in June and December.

Correspondent: Miss K Phillips, 79 High Street, Stony Stratford, Milton Keynes MK11 1AU (0908-563232).

● Great Marlow

The Myers Marlow Benevolent Fund

Eligibility: People in need who live in Great Marlow.

Types of grants: Usually one-off grants.

Annual grant total: About £10,000 given in relief-in-need and education grants to individuals.

Applications: On a form available from the correspondent or health visitors.

Correspondent: The Secretary, Little Stone House, High Street, Marlow, Buckinghamshire SL7 1AN (0628-482266).

● High Wycombe

The High Wycombe Central Aid Society

Eligibility: People in need who live in the borough of High Wycombe.

Types of grants: One-off grants towards fuel debts, clothes, holidays, spectacles, telephone installation, decorating materials etc.. The trust also has a second hand furniture warehouse and clothes and soft furnishings store.

Annual grant total: In 1991/92, the trust had an income of £22,000 of which £2,000 was given out in about 40 relief-in-need grants of between £25 and £100.

Applications: In writing to the correspondent. Applications can be submitted directly by the individual or through a social worker, citizen's advice bureau or other welfare agency. They are considered on the first Monday of each month. Clients are visited in their homes by the trust caseworker who makes recommendations to the committee.

Correspondent: Mrs M Mitchell, Secretary, 1–3 Cornmarket, High Wycombe, Buckinghamshire HP11 2BW (0494-535890).

● Hulcote

The Salford Town Lands

Eligibility: People in need who live in the parish of Hulcote and Salford.

Types of grants: One-off or recurrent grants according to need.

Annual grant total: In 1992, the trust had an income of £5,600. £3,600 was given in 51 grants to individuals.

Applications: In writing to the correspondent. Applications can be submitted directly by the individual or through any other parishioner. They are considered each month.

Correspondent: G M Knudsen, Treasurer, Aspley Hall Farm, Hulcote, Milton Keynes MK17 8BP (0908-583265).

● Iver

The Iver Heath Sick Poor Fund

Eligibility: People who are sick, convalescing, physically or mentally disabled or infirm and who live in the Iver Heath ward of the parish of Iver and part of the parish of Wexham.

Types of grants: Grants for clothing, medical needs, home help, fuel, lighting and other necessities.

Annual grant total: About 26 grants totalling £1,800.

Applications: In writing to the correspondent.

Correspondent: The Rector, The Rectory, Pinewood Close, Iver Heath, Buckinghamshire SL0 0QL (0753-654470).

Other information: This entry has not been confirmed by the trust.

The Iver & Richings Park Sick Poor Fund

Eligibility: Sick people in need living in Iver Village and Richings Park.

Buckinghamshire/Cambridgeshire

Types of grants: Recurrent grants of £25 to £100 to elderly sick people. One-off grants are given for crises, the provision of domicillary chiropody for those virtually housebound and occasional help with heating costs.

Annual grant total: In 1992, the trust had assets of £24,000 and an income of £1,400, all of which was given in 46 grants.

Applications: In writing to the correspondent by a social worker, citizen's advice bureau or other appropriate third party on behalf of the individual. Applications are considered in April and October but emergencies can be considered immediately.

Correspondent: Mrs J Gaastra, Clerk, 36 Syke Cluan, Iver, Buckinghamshire SL0 9EH (0753-653508).

The Iver United Charities

Eligibility: People in need who live in the parishes of Iver and Iver Heath.

Types of grants: Heating grants generally only for those aged 65 or over, although in special circumstances help is given with fuel bills to those who are younger such as a recent award to a young person with AIDS. About £400 is set aside for one-off grants for other needs.

Annual grant total: In 1992, the trust had assets of £26,000 and an income of £3,000. About 180 grants totalled £2,300.

Applications: For heating grants: on a form available from the correspondent directly by the individual to be considered in November. For other grants: in writing to the correspondent by a social worker, health visitor, vicar, district nurse or other appropriate third party on behalf of the individual.

Correspondent: Mrs J Gaastra, Clerk, 36 Syke Cluan, Iver, Buckinghamshire SL0 9EH (0753-653508).

● **Pitstone**

The Pitstone Town Lands Charity Estate

Eligibility: Elderly people in need who live in Pitstone.

Types of grants: One-off grants for fuel, bus fares, outings, travel to or from hospital, spectacles, chiropody and other necessities.

Annual grant total: About £6,000.

Applications: In writing to the correspondent.

Correspondent: Mrs C Martell, 22 Chequers Lane, Pitstone, Leighton Buzzard, Beds LU7 9AG (0296-668389).

● **Wolverton**

The Catherine Featherstone Charity

Eligibility: People in need who live in the ancient parish of Wolverton.

Types of grants: One-off or recurrent grants according to need ranging from £100 to £150.

Annual grant total: In 1993, the trust had an income of £5,500. 20 grants to individuals totalled £4,600.

Applications: In writing to the correspondent. Applications are considered in April and December.

Correspondent: Miss K Phillips, Secretary, 79 High Street, Stony Stratford, Milton Keynes, Bucks MK11 1AU (0908-563232).

● **Wooburn**

The Wooburn, Bourne End & District Relief-in-Sickness Charity

Eligibility: People who live in Wooburn and neighbouring areas who are sick, convalescing, physically or mentally disabled or infirm.

Types of grants: One-off grants for telephone installation, help with nursing costs, convalescence, holidays, home help and other necessities.

Annual grant total: Over £3,000.

Applications: In writing to the correspondent.

Correspondent: Mrs D A Heyes, 11 Telfton Close, Bourne End, Bucks (0628-523498).

Cambridgeshire

The Farthing Trust

Eligibility: People in need, with a priority given to those either personally known to the trustees or recommended by those personally known to the trustees.

Types of grants: One-off and recurrent grants according to need.

Annual grant total: In 1992, £30,000 was divided between individuals in need and other charitable purposes.

Applications: In writing to the correspondent. Applicants will only be notified of a refusal if an sae is enclosed.

Correspondent: C H Martin, 48 Ten Mile Bank, Littleport, Ely, Cambridgeshire CB6 1EF.

Other information: The trusts states that it receives 20 letters a week and is able to help one in a 100. There would seem little point in applying unless a personal contact with a trustee is established.

The Swaffham Prior Parochial Charities

Eligibility: People in need in the parishes of Swaffham Prior and Reach.

Types of grants: One-off grants ranging from £10 to £100.

Annual grant total: In 1992, the trust had an income of £6,000, of which £2,400 was given in 198 grants to individuals.

Applications: In writing to the correspondent, including details of need and sources of existing aid. Applications can be submitted directly by the individual or through a third party such as a social worker, citizen's advice bureau, relations and friends.

Correspondent: M J Fox, Clerk, Rivendell, 30 High Street, Swaffham Prior, Cambridge CB5 0LD (0638-742003).

Other information: Grants are also given to local organisations for equipment etc..

The Upwell Isle Charity

Eligibility: People in need who live in the parish of Upwell (on the Isle of Ely) and the parish of Christchurch.

Types of grants: One-off grants only ranging from £9 to £30.

Annual grant total: In 1993, the trust had an income of £3,100. 120 relief-in-need grants totalled £2,200.

Applications: In writing to the correspondent. Applications should be submitted directly by the individual and are considered in December.

Correspondent: Mrs W J Judd, Clerk, 27 Hallbridge Road, Upwell, Wisbech, Cambridgeshire PE14 9DP (0945-773668).

● **Buckden**

The Buckden Relief-in-Need Charity

Eligibility: People in need who live in the parish of Buckden.

Types of grants: One-off grants between £25 and £200.

Annual grant total: About £700 to £1,000.

Applications: In writing to the correspondent.

Cambridgeshire

Correspondent: Martin Dean, 19 Glebe Lane, Buckden, Huntingdon, Cambridgeshire PE18 9TG (0480-810333).

Burwell

The Burwell Poors Fen Charity

Eligibility: Retired people over 65 who are in need and live in the ancient parish of Burwell.

Types of grants: One gift a year to one retired person per household provided they are on the electoral roll. One or two grants are also given to people with severe disabilities. In 1993, the grant per person was £6, although this can vary according to the income available to the charity.

Annual grant total: In 1992/93, the trust's income was £2,800. It gave 497 grants totalling about £3,000.

Applications: In writing to the correspondent directly by the individual. Applications are considered from March to October.

Correspondent: Ray Elwood, Rickards, 33 Pound Close, Burwell, Cambridge CB5 0EP (0683-743516).

Cambridge

The Foundation of Edward Storey

Eligibility: Unsupported women in need who are at least 40 years of age and who qualify for assistance under either or both of the undermentioned categories:

(a) Clergymen's Widows Branch, in the following order of priority:

1. Widows of clergymen of the Church of England;
2. Dependants of clergymen of the Church of England;
3. Women deacons and deaconesses of the Church of England;
4. Missionaries of the Church of England;
5. Other women closely involved with the work of the Church of England (including divorced, separated and deserted wives of clergymen of the Church of England).

(b) Parish Almspeople's Branch: eligible people living within the city of Cambridge boundary.

Types of grants: Grants and pensions (which are annually reviewed) to qualified applicants.

Annual grant total: £149,000 in 1992/93. Grants under category (a) totalled about £70,000 and under (b) about £25,000; pensions under (a) totalled about £30,000 (about 90 pensions) and under (b) £24,150 (about 60 pensions).

Applications: By application form and sponsorship by, for example, Diocesan Widows' Officers, Diocesan Visitors, clergy, social workers etc.. Applications are considered bi-monthly by trustees.

Correspondent: The Clerk to the Trustees, Storey's House, Mount Pleasant, Cambridge CB3 0BZ (0223-64405).

Other information: This entry is repeated in the Occupational section of the book.

Chatteris

The Chatteris Feoffee Charity

Eligibility: People in need who have lived in Chatteris for at least 10 years.

Types of grants: £15 grants given annually in January/February.

Annual grant total: About £2,000, of which about £700 is given to individuals.

Applications: In writing to the correspondent.

Correspondent: The Clerks, Messrs Brian, Hawden & Co, Solicitors, 1 Wood Street, Chatteris, Cambridgeshire (0354-692212).

Downham

The Downham Feoffee Charity

Eligibility: People in need who live in the ancient parish of Downham.

Types of grants: One-off and recurrent grants according to need.

Annual grant total: About £5,000.

Applications: In writing to the correspondent.

Correspondent: W D Crawley, Clerk, 14 Vineyards Way, Ely, Cambridgeshire CB7 4QQ.

Fenstanton

The Fenstanton Town Trust

Eligibility: People in need who live in Fenstanton.

Types of grants: One-off grants for specific items.

Annual grant total: £1,100; of this £400 was given as a relief-in-need grant.

Applications: In writing to the correspondent. Applications can be submitted directly by the individual or by an appropriate third party, to be considered in February (although decisions can be made throughout the year if necessary).

Correspondent: Mrs A Sinclair-Russell, Burwen House, Wentworth, Ely, Cambridgeshire CB6 3QE (0353-778452).

Haddenham

The Haddenham Charities

Eligibility: People in need who live in the parish of Haddenham.

Types of grants: Mainly hampers and cash grants at Christmas, also one-off grants.

Annual grant total: In 1988, the trust spent £810 on Christmas hampers, £90 on Christmas grants, and £180 on cash grants to people in need.

Applications: In writing to the correspondent.

Correspondent: The Clerk, 2 Station Road, Haddenham, Ely, Cambridgeshire CB6 3XD.

Other information: This entry has not been confirmed by the trust.

Ickleton

The Ickleton United Charities (Relief-in-Need Branch)

Eligibility: People in need who live in the parish of Ickleton, Cambridgeshire.

Types of grants: One-off grants for fuel costs and necessities, and gift vouchers at Christmas.

Annual grant total: 50 grants totalling about £1,500.

Applications: In writing to the correspondent.

Correspondent: R J Herbert, Treasurer, Hovells, 10 Frogge Street, Ickleton, Saffron Walden, Essex CB10 1SH.

Landbeach

Rev Robert Masters for Widows Trust

Eligibility: Women in need who live in the parish of Landbeach, with a preference for widows. (The trust is hoping to amend the objects to include men.)

Types of grants: One-off and recurrent grants according to need.

Cambridgeshire

Annual grant total: In 1992/93, the trust had an income of £900. No grants were given.

Applications: In writing to the correspondent.

Correspondent: G Hayward, Secretary, North Farm, Landbeach, Cambridge CB4 4ED.

Leverington

The Leverington Relief-in-Sickness Fund

Eligibility: People who live in the parish of Leverington and who are sick, convalescing, disabled or infirm.

Types of grants: One-off grants for medical purposes.

Annual grant total: No information available.

Applications: In writing to the correspondent.

Correspondent: Mrs J Ostler, Clerk, Birdbeck House, Station Road, Wisebech St Mary, Wisbech, Cambridgeshire PE13 4RY (0945-410076).

The Town Lands Charity

Eligibility: People in need who live in the parish of Leverington.

Types of grants: One-off grants only.

Annual grant total: About £4,000.

Applications: In writing to the correspondent.

Correspondent: Mrs J Ostler, Clerk, Birdbeck House, Station Road, Wisebech St Mary, Wisbech, Cambridgeshire PE13 4RY (0945-410076).

Little Wilbraham

The Johnson Bede & Lane Charitable Trust

Eligibility: People in need who live in the civil parish of Little Wilbraham.

Types of grants: One-off grants only between £15 and £100. Recent awards have included small Christmas grants and help with heating costs for elderly people, help with a family where the wage-earner is off work for a considerable time owing to an accident, and help with educational expenses such as books and tools.

Annual grant total: In 1991/92, the trust's income was £2,800. About 50 relief-in-need grants totalled £2,000.

Applications: In writing to the correspondent directly by the individual or by a third party such as a social worker, citizen's advice bureau or neighbour. Applications can be considered at any time, but particularly in May and November.

Correspondent: Mrs Mary Frend, 31 Rectory Farm Road, Little Wilbraham, Cambridge CB1 5LB (0223-811731).

Pampisford

The Pampisford Relief-in-Need Charity

Eligibility: People in need who live in the parish of Pampisford.

Types of grants: One-off grants including a taxi service for hospital attendance, bus passes for retired and disabled people and Christmas gifts for elderly and disabled people.

Annual grant total: In 1992, the income of the trust was £5,300. Expenditure totalled £8,100 including £3,000 in grants to individuals including Christmas gifts, taxi fares and village amenities.

Applications: In writing to the correspondent. Applications can be submitted directly by the individual, through a social worker, citizen's advice bureau or other welfare agency, or through a third party, usually a relative or friend. Applications are considered as the need arises.

Correspondent: D F Lee, Clerk, Garden House, Mill Farm, Pampisford, Cambridgeshire CB2 4EQ (0223-837497).

Peterborough

The Florence Saunders Relief-in-Sickness Charity

Eligibility: People who live in the area of the former city of Peterborough and who are sick, convalescent, infirm or disabled.

Types of grants: One-off and recurrent grants between £100 and £300. No grants for repayment of debts.

Annual grant total: In 1990/91, the trust had assets of £60,000, generating an income of £6,400. Seven grants to individuals totalled £1,400 leaving a surplus of £2,000.

Applications: In writing to the correspondent throughout the year.

Correspondent: K J Waterfield, Hon. Secretary, Stephenson House, 15 Church Walk, Peterborough PE1 2TP (0733-343275).

Ramsey

The Ramsey Welfare Charities

Eligibility: People in need who live in Ramsey.

Types of grants: One-off or recurrent grants according to need.

Annual grant total: In 1992, the trust had an income of £4,500, it is not known how much of this was given to individuals.

Applications: In writing to the correspondent.

Correspondent: Mrs G A Stratton, Clerk, 76 Hollow Lane, Ramsey, Huntingdon, Cambs PE17 1DQ (0487-813786).

Soham

The Soham Relief-in-Need Charity

Eligibility: People in need of all ages who live in the parish of Soham.

Types of grants: One-off grants have been given to individuals recommended by the citizen's advice bureau and Cambridgeshire Social Services to pay pressing debts and buy clothing.

Annual grant total: In 1992, the charity had an income of £10,400. Expenditure totalled £8,500 including £172 in three grants to individuals.

Applications: In writing to the correspondent directly by the individual or through a social worker or other welfare agency. Applicants should include a financial statement giving details of assets and liabilities, and reasons in support of the application. They are considered in February and November.

Correspondent: J R Ennion, 3 Churchgate Street, Soham, Ely, Cambridgeshire CB7 5DS (0353-720317).

Stetchworth

The Stetchworth Relief-in-Need Charity

Eligibility: People in need who live in the parish of Stetchworth and have done so for at least two years.

Types of grants: One-off grants ranging from £10 to £50 according to need. For example, grants have been given towards electricity bills, fuel, groceries (through an account at the local community shop) and transport to hospital.

Cambridgeshire/East Sussex

Annual grant total: In 1993, the trust had an income of £1,900. £2,100 was given in 37 relief-in-need grants.

Applications: On a form available form the correspondent or the Elmsmere Centre, Stetchworth. "We welcome information from anyone who knows someone in need." Applications are considered at any time.

Correspondent: Mrs F R L Swann, 8 Vicarage Lane, Woodditton, Newmarket, Suffolk CB8 9SG (0638-730859).

● Sutton

The Sutton Poors' Land Charity

Eligibility: People in need who live in the parish of Sutton.

Types of grants: Generally Christmas vouchers of £10 to £50 and occasional one-off grants to people in need or for further education.

Annual grant total: About 100 grants totalling up to £4,500; a small proportion is given for educational purposes.

Applications: In writing to the correspondent, considered at any time.

Correspondent: Ann Sinclar-Russell, Burwell House, Wentworth, Ely, Cambridgeshire CB6 3QE (0353-778452).

● Swaffham Bulbeck

The Swaffham Bulbeck Relief-in-Need Charity

Eligibility: People in need who live in the parish of Swaffham Bulbeck.

Types of grants: One-off grants in kind or in cash, usually not more than £15 each.

Annual grant total: About £1,200.

Applications: In writing to the correspondent or through the trustees.

Correspondent: Mrs C Ling, 43 High Street, Swaffham Bulbeck, Cambridge CB5 0HP.

● Swavesey

Thomas Galon's Charity

Eligibility: People in need who live in the parish of Swavesey.

Types of grants: One-off grants for hospital travel expenses, fuel costs and other needs.

Annual grant total: £4,500 in 1991.

Applications: In writing to the correspondent.

Correspondent: Mrs Patricia Howard, Greenside Close, Swavesey, Cambridgeshire.

● Walsoken

The Walsoken United Charities

Eligibility: People in need who are 60 or over and have lived in Walsoken for at least two years.

Types of grants: One-off grants in the form of cash (limited to £10 per household), gifts in kind and loans.

Annual grant total: £3,100 in 1991.

Applications: In writing to the correspondent.

Correspondent: D Mews, Clerk, Fraser Southwell, 28–29 Old Market, Wisbech, Cambridgeshire PE13 1ND (0945-582664).

● Whittlesey

The Whittlesey Charity

Eligibility: People in need who live in the ancient parishes of Whittlesey Urban and Whittlesey Rural.

Types of grants: Annual cash grants. In 1993 about 100 grants were given of £20 a person, plus a number of one-off grants.

Annual grant total: The net income of the charity for each year is distributed the following year. It is divided between relief-in-need, education and public purposes. In 1993, the income (for distribution in 1994) was £9,000 for each of the above three branches. Most of this is allocated at the May trustees' meeting.

Applications: In writing to the correspondent. Applications are considered in February, May, August and November, but urgent applications can be dealt with at fairly short notice.

Correspondent: R H Hinton, 14 London Street, Whittlesey, Peterborough PE7 1BP (0733-203384).

● Whittlesford

The Charities of Nicholas Swallow & Others

Eligibility: People in need who live in the parish of Whittlesford.

Types of grants: One-off cash grants at Christmas; help towards hospital travel costs and school trips.

Annual grant total: The trustees preferred not to update the financial information (grants previously totalled £1,600).

Applications: Directly by the individual in writing to the correspondent.

Correspondent: T W Grigg, 12 Scotts Gardens, Whittlesford, Cambridgeshire CB2 4NR (0223-834500).

East Sussex

The Catharine House Trust

Eligibility: Elderly or sick people of limited means in need of medical or surgical treatment and convalescent or other accommodation. Priority is given to people living in the Hastings and St Leonards area of East Sussex.

Types of grants: Grants towards the cost of treatment, convalescence, accomodation and travel.

Annual grant total: £25,000.

Applications: In writing to the correspondent.

Correspondent: Mrs Hawke, Secretary, 70 Hoads Wood Road, Hastings, East Sussex TN34 2BA (0424-426543).

The Doctor Merry Memorial Fund

Eligibility: People who are ill and live in the Eastbourne Area Health Authority.

Types of grants: One-off grants for nursing home care, help with Lifeline rentals and medical equipment.

Annual grant total: In 1992/93, the trust's assets were £105,000, generating an income of £7,300. 35 relief-in-need grants to individuals totalled about £6,400.

Applications: On a form available from the applicant's doctor. Applications are considered throughout the year.

Correspondent: Mrs B E Winch, 6 The Lawns, St Mary's Close, Willingdon, East Sussex BN22 0ND (0323-503724).

● Battle

The Battle Charities

Eligibility: People in need who live in Battle.

Types of grants: Payments for fuel, and Christmas parcels.

Annual grant total: About £1,000.

Applications: In writing to the correspondent.

East Sussex/Essex

Brighton

The Brighton District Nursing Association Trust

Eligibility: People in need through sickness who live in Brighton, and nurses in need (whether retired or still working) who live or work in Brighton.

Types of grants: One-off grants for items in respect of medical treatment and for convalescence; some limited allowances for retired or sick nurses.

Annual grant total: About £55,000, but not all of this is given to individuals.

Applications: In writing to the correspondent, preferably supported by a doctor or health visitor.

Correspondent: The Secretary, c/o Fitzhugh Gates, 3 Pavilion Parade, Brighton BN2 1RY.

Eastbourne

The Mayor's Discretionary Fund & The Mayor's Fund, Eastbourne

Eligibility: Adults and children in need who live in the borough of Eastbourne.

Types of grants: One-off grants for urgent needs, usually of £25 to £500.

Annual grant total: About 25 grants totalling £3,000.

Applications: Considered on receipt, usually but not necessarily through social workers or health visitors.

Correspondent: The Mayor's Personal Assistant, The Town Hall, Grove Road, Eastbourne, East Sussex BN21 4UG (0323-410000 ext. 5020).

Hastings

The Isabel Blackman Foundation

Eligibility: People in need, particularly elderly, blind or disabled people, who live in Hastings and district.

Types of grants: One-off and recurrent grants according to need.

Annual grant total: 50 grants totalling about £75,000.

Applications: In writing to the correspondent.

Correspondent: A K Vint, Secretary, 13 Laton Road, Hastings, East Sussex TN34 2ES (0424-431756).

Other information: This entry has not been confirmed by the trust.

The Hastings & St Leonard's District Nursing Association & Aid-in-Sickness Trust

Eligibility: People in need who are sick and live in the borough of Hastings.

Types of grants: One-off grants in the form of payments to suppliers for essential furniture and household items (as deemed by the trustees and including cookers, washing machines, beds, carpets, baby items and bedding), and travel costs to/from hospital.

Annual grant total: In 1992/93, the trust had an income of £4,500. Grants of between £5 and £250 were given to 67 individuals and totalled £4,500.

Applications: Applications, on a form available from the correspondent, should be submitted through a recognised referral agency (eg. social worker, citizen's advice bureau or doctor) and are considered throughout the year.

Correspondent: Mrs J A Fletcher, Clerk, Hastings Area Community Trust, 48–49 Cambridge Gardens, Hastings, East Sussex TN34 1EN (0424-718880).

Hove

The Margaret & Alfred Denny Christmas Charity

Eligibility: People in need who are over 70 and live in the borough of Hove.

Types of grants: One-off grants or food parcels up to a value of £10 given to about 300 people at Christmas.

Annual grant total: About £3,000.

Applications: In writing to the correspondent. Beneficiaries are normally referred by voluntary agencies such as Rotary or the Community Care Council. Applications are considered on the first Monday of November.

Correspondent: The Clerk, Hove Borough Council, Town Hall, Norton Road, Hove BN3 4AH (0273-775400).

Newick

The Newick Distress Fund

Eligibility: People in need who live in the village of Newick.

Types of grants: One-off or recurrent grants according to need.

Annual grant total: £700 in 1990.

Applications: In writing to the correspondent or one of the trustees.

Correspondent: G I Clinton, Dolphin Cottage, 3 High Hurst Close, Newick, East Sussex BN8 4NJ (0273-207171).

St Leonards

The Sarah Brisco Charity

Eligibility: People in need who live in the parish of St Peter and St Paul, St Leonards-on-Sea.

Types of grants: One-off cash grants and gifts in kind.

Annual grant total: The trust has assets of £36,000 and an income of £6,000. In 1992, 45 relief-in-need grants to individuals totalled £1,440.

Applications: In writing to the correspondent. Applications should be submitted directly by the individual and are considered at any time.

Correspondent: D A Ray, 6 Clarence Road, St Leonards-on-Sea, East Sussex TN37 6SD (0424-439556).

Warbleton

The Henry Smith Charity

Eligibility: People in need who live in the parish of Warbleton.

Types of grants: One-off and recurrent grants according to need.

Annual grant total: Probably about £1,000.

Applications: In writing to the correspondent.

Correspondent: D E Phillips, 3 Clock Tower Court, Park Avenue, Bexhill-on-Sea TH39 3HP.

Essex

The Sarah Chamberlayne Charity

Eligibility: Widows/unmarried women who are at least 50 years old; elderly men; physically/visually disabled people of either sex, and children who have lost both parents or children who are mentally/physically disabled or infirm. Applicants must live in Southam and Long Itchington in Warwickshire or Hatfield Broad Oak and Ugely in Essex.

Types of grants: Quarterly annuities of £14 or £15 to 30 individuals.

Annual grant total: About £1,800.

Applications: In writing to the correspondent.

Correspondent: J M P Hathaway, Clerk, Messrs Heath & Blenkinsop, Solicitors, 13 Old Square, Warwick CV34 4RA (0926-492407).

Other information: This entry is repeated in the Warwickshire section of the book.

The Kay Jenkins Trust

Eligibility: People in need, especially elderly people, who live in Great and Little Leighs.

Types of grants: One-off grants in kind, and help with heating and transport costs.

Annual grant total: About £1,000.

Applications: In writing to the correspondent.

Correspondent: The Rector, Great Leighs Rectory, Boreham Road, Great Leighs, Chelmsford CM3 1PP (0245-361218).

Braintree

The Braintree United Charities

Eligibility: People in need who live in the parish of Braintree.

Types of grants: One-off and recurrent grants according to need.

Annual grant total: About £1,000.

Applications: On a form available from the correspondent.

Correspondent: R Hume, c/o Cunnington, Solicitors, Great Square, Braintree, Essex CM7 7UD (0376-326868).

Broomfield

Broomfield United Charities

Eligibility: People in need who live in the ancient parish of Broomfield.

Types of grants: One-off grants according to need.

Annual grant total: In 1990/91, the trust had an income of £15,000. It is not known how much was given in grants to individuals in need.

Applications: In writing to the correspondent.

Correspondent: A C Hardy, Secretary, 28 Jubilee Avenue, Broomfield, Chelmsford, Essex CM1 5HE (0245-440243).

Colchester

The Colchester Lying-In Charity

Eligibility: Poor or expectant mothers who live in Colchester.

Types of grants: One-off grants, up to £40, to provide comforts and benefits before, during and after childbirth.

Annual grant total: About £1,000, but few eligible applications have been received recently.

Applications: In writing to the correspondent.

Correspondent: The Town Clerk's Department, Colchester Borough Council, Town Hall, High Street, Colchester CO1 1PJ (0206-712210).

The Colchester Society for the Blind

Eligibility: Blind people living in Colchester.

Types of grants: One-off or recurrent grants according to need. Occasional holiday grants are given, as are annual grants to help with heating in the winter.

Annual grant total: No information available.

Applications: In writing to the correspondent.

Correspondent: Mrs G F Hallett, Secretary, 15 Roddam Close, Colchester, Essex CO3 3UN (0206-574933).

Dovercourt

The Henry Smith Charity

Eligibility: People in need who live in Dovercourt.

Types of grants: One-off or recurrent grants according to need.

Annual grant total: Probably about £1,000.

Applications: In writing to the correspondent.

Correspondent: J O Jackson, 4 Dove Crescent, Dovercourt, Harwich CO12 4QX.

East Bergholt

The East Bergholt United Charities

Eligibility: People in need who live in East Bergholt.

Types of grants: One-off grants. If no cases of hardship are brought to the attention of the trustees, they usually give £15 each at Christmas to about 20 old age pensioners who are known to have small incomes. These are not given to the same person two years running, though additional help can be given if needed.

Annual grant total: In 1992, the trust had an income of £1,100 available for grants.

Applications: In writing to the correspondent, although most cases are brought to the attention of the trustees.

Correspondent: Mrs M D Whittle, Clerk, Talavera, Gaston Street, East Bergholt, Nr. Colchester, Essex CO7 6SB (0206-298316).

East Tilbury

East Tilbury Relief-in-Need Charity

Eligibility: People in need who live in the parish of East Tilbury.

Types of grants: One-off and recurrent grants according to need.

Annual grant total: In 1991, the trust had an income of £7,000. It is not known how much was given in grants to individuals in need.

Applications: In writing to the correspondent.

Correspondent: R F Fowler, Treasurer, 44–46 Orsett Road, Grays, Essex RM17 5ED (0375-373828).

Halstead

Helena Sant's Residuary Trust Fund

Eligibility: People in need who live in the parish of Halstead, St Andrew with Holy Trinity who have at any time been a member of the Church of England.

Types of grants: One-off or recurrent grants according to need. Grants can be given in money or gifts in kind.

Annual grant total: In 1993, the trust had an income of £6,800. Half the income is available for relief of those in need and half for furthering the work of the Church of England in the parish.

Applications: In writing to the correspondent.

Correspondent: M R R Willis, Trustee, Greenway, Church Street, Gestingthorpe, Halstead, Essex CO9 3AX (0787-461893).

Essex/Hampshire

Harley

The Harlow Community Chest

Eligibility: Individuals and families in desperate financial need, particularly where a small financial contribution will help to arrest the spiral of debt. Applicants must live in Harlow.

Types of grants: One-off grants up to £150 for the payment of outstanding bills such as fuel and telephone bills for people in special need; clothing (eg. for unemployed young people going for a job interview); household items (eg. repair of cooker) and help towards funeral expenses, removal costs, lodging deposits and nursery fees. Only one grant to an individual/family can be made in any one year.

No grants for housing rents or rates.

Annual grant total: About 200 grants totalling £15,000.

Applications: Applications, on a form available from the correspondent, should be submitted through a recognised referral agency (eg. social worker, citizen's advice bureau or doctor) or other third party, and are considered on the first Wednesday of each month. Emergency payments of £25 can be made between meetings.

Correspondent: Dr George Torkildsen, Rosemont, 31 Hare Street, Harlow, Essex CM19 4AY (0279-422489 or 0279-439681 work).

Saffron Waldon

The Saffron Waldon United Charities

Eligibility: People in need who live in Saffron Walden.

Types of grants: All types of help can be considered.

Annual grant total: In 1990, the trust had an income of £33,500. It is not known how much was given in grants to individuals. Grants are also given to organisations.

Applications: In writing to the correspondent.

Correspondent: G R Lard, Secretary, 4 Park Lane, Saffron Walden, Essex CB10 1DA (0799-526514).

Other information: This is the latest information available at the Charity Commission, but the entry has not been confirmed by the trust.

Thaxted

The Thaxted Relief-in-Need Charities

Eligibility: People in need who live in the parish of Thaxted.

Types of grants: Probably one-off and recurrent grants according to need.

Annual grant total: In 1986, the trust gave £700 in vouchers for poor people and £160 in funeral grants. There was a further £2,000 unallocated during the year. No more recent information available.

Applications: In writing to the correspondent.

Correspondent: H Saych, 10 St Clements, Thaxted, Essex (0371-830367).

Hampshire

The Farnborough (Hampshire) Welfare Trust

Eligibility: People in need who live in the Cove and Farnborough area.

Types of grants: One-off and recurrent grants mainly to the elderly at Christmas. Grants are generally between £20 and £50.

Annual grant total: In 1992, the trust's income was £2,500. 80 to 100 relief-in-need grants totalled £2,000.

Applications: In writing to the correspondent either directly by the individual or by a third party. Applications are considered in early December.

Correspondent: M R Evans, Bowmarsh, 45 Church Avenue, Farnborough, Hampshire.

The Hampshire Constabulary Welfare Fund

Eligibility: Members (including cadets), pensioners and civilian employees of the Hampshire Constabulary and their dependants, and any serving or retired member of any police force in the UK having some connection with Hampshire.

Types of grants: One-off or recurrent grants or loans according to need.

Annual grant total: In 1991, the fund had an income of £114,000.

Applications: Through local police welfare officers.

Correspondent: Mike King, Secretary, West End Police Station, West End, Southampton (0703-463517).

The C V Hollis Trust

Eligibility: Spinsters over 40 who are in need and live in Hampshire or the Isle of Wight. Preference for the daughters of professional men.

Types of grants: One-off grants ranging from £50 to £100 for special purposes (such as a second hand gas cooker) and £4 weekly pensions.

Annual grant total: In 1990/91, the trust had an income of £5,000. 13 relief-in-need grants totalled £1,100 and six pensions totalled £1,300.

Applications: In writing to the correspondent, including full details of income/expenditure and the specific need. Applications are considered as required.

Correspondent: Mrs L Hayden, 3 Winchester Close, Newport, Isle of Wight PO30 1DR (0983-521368).

The Penton Trust

Eligibility: People in need who are 65 or over and live in a 12-mile radius of Basingstoke Town Hall.

Types of grants: Regular allowances to enable people to live in comfortable rented accommodation or, for those living in their own home, to be able to afford domestic help. The trust states that it "should consider favourably and if possible give priority to, claims of people who have an unmarried daughter living with, and keeping house for, them so that such a daughter might be released from her responsibility and be free to enjoy her own life".

Annual grant total: 60 grants totalling about £12,000.

Applications: In writing to the correspondent.

Correspondent: R D Edwards, Clifton House, Monk Sherbourne, Basingstoke, Hampshire.

Other information: This entry has not been confirmed by the trust.

The Poor Ladies' Holiday & Relief Fund

Eligibility: Women in need aged 40 to 90 living in Hampshire. There may be a preference for residents of Southampton.

Types of grants: Regular Christmas and summer grants. Emergency gifts in times of illness or distress. Grants range from £100 to £190. Grants are NOT given to students.

Hampshire

Annual grant total: In 1993, the trust had an income of £2,300. 13 relief-in-need grants totalled £3,900.

Applications: On a form available from the correspondent. Applicants should be recommended by a social worker, citizen's advice bureau, doctor etc.. They are considered in May and November.

Correspondent: Mrs J Hammond, Dwiley Mill, Botley, Southampton, Hampshire SO3 2BP (0489-860217).

The Scale Charity

Eligibility: Blind people over 30 who were born and have lived in Hampshire for at least five years.

Types of grants: Mainly pensions.

Annual grant total: In 1990/91, the trust had an income of £4,000. Annuities totalled £800.

Applications: On a form available from the correspondent.

Correspondent: The City Manager's Office, Floor 3, Civic Offices, Portsmouth PO1 2AL (0705-834059).

The Southampton Charitable Trust

Eligibility: People who are sick and poor and who live in the area administered by Southampton Borough Council.

Types of grants: One-off grants only ranging from £50 to £250. Grants can be given bedding, comforts, food, fuel and medical or other aids. Help has also been given towards the cost of holidays or obtaining domestic help.

Annual grant total: £7,500 in 1992, but most of this is given to organisations. Two grants were given to individuals totalling £350.

Applications: In writing to the correspondent. Applications can be submitted directly by the individual or through a social worker, citizen's advice bureau or other welfare agency or third party. The trustees meet in April and October, but applications can be dealt with outside these meetings.

Correspondent: K R Ball, Clerk, Charter Court, Third Avenue, Southampton SO9 1QS (0703-702345).

The Three Parishes Fund

Eligibility: People in need who live in the parishes of Headley, Whitehill, Grayshott and Lindford.

Types of grants: One-off grants.

Annual grant total: No information available.

Applications: In writing or by application form available from the correspondent. Applications are considered at any time and can be submitted directly by the individual, or by a social worker, doctor, clergy or similar third party.

Correspondent: G Wilson, Fremont, 23 Taylor's Lane, Lindford, Bordon, Hampshire GU35 0SW (0420-472899).

The Winchester Children's Holiday Trust

Eligibility: Children in need who live in the area administered by Winchester City Council and surrounding districts.

Types of grants: Grants to help with the cost of holidays, outings and other educational visits.

Annual grant total: About £12,000. Help is given to 200 to 300 children.

Applications: In writing to the correspondent.

Correspondent: David Smith, Lower Boredean Farm, Langrish, Petersfield, Hampshire GU32 1ER.

The Winchester Rural District Welfare Trust

Eligibility: People in need who live in Winchester Rural District. This includes the parishes of Beauworth, Bighton, Bishops Sutton, Bramdean, Cheriton, Chilcomb, Compton, Crawley, Headbourne Worthy and Abbotts Barton, Hursley, Itchen Stoke and Ovington, Itchen Valley, Kilmeston, Kings Worthy, Littleton, Micheldever, New Alresford, Northington, Old Alresford, Olivers Battery, Owslebury, Sparsholt, Tichborne, Twyford, and Wonston. It does NOT include the city of Winchester.

Need as far as the trust is concerned may arise where assistance required is not available from public funds, or not available in time from public funds.

Types of grants: One-off grants for example towards bedding, clothing, special food, fuel and heating appliances, telephone, nursing requirements, house repairs, transport and convalescent care.

Immediate assistance may be obtained in any particular parish from the local trustee. The names and addresses of these trustees are widely circulated. If in doubt contact local clergy or the correspondent.

Annual grant total: In 1992/93, the trust's income was £2,100 including £700 allocated by Henry Smith's (General Estate) Charity. Relief-in-need grants to individuals totalled £2,100.

Applications: In writing to the correspondent. Applications should be submitted through a social worker, citizen's advice bureau or other welfare agency or through a local parish trustee. They are considered at any time.

Correspondent: Mrs M C Browne, Clerk, 69 Tower Street, Winchester, Hampshire SO23 8TA (0962-865730).

Other information: This trust was formed by merging the endowments of 26 charities in 25 parishes in the Winchester Rural District. The trust has an information sheet outlining the area of benefit and support available.

● Alverstoke

The Alverstoke Trust

Eligibility: People in need who live in Alverstoke.

Types of grants: One-off and recurrent grants according to need.

Annual grant total: About £700 in about eight grants.

Applications: In writing to the correspondent.

Correspondent: G W Hill, Clerk, Hauraki, 7 Alvara Road, Alverstoke, Gosport, Hampshire PO12 2HY (0705-581847).

Other information: The above information appeared in the previous edition of this Guide. The trustees chose not to update it.

● Fareham

The Fareham Welfare Trust

Eligibility: People in need who live in the ecclesiastical parishes of St Paul, St John and Holy Trinity, all in Fareham.

Types of grants: One-off and recurrent grants according to need. Help has been given towards clothing, furniture, food, cookers and washing machines.

Grants are not given where a statutory award is an entitlement/available.

Annual grant total: In 1993, the trust had an income of about £7,900. Total expenditure was about £6,000. Grants up to a maximum of £100 were given to 70 individuals and totalled £5,800.

Applications: Applications should be submitted through a recognised referral agency (eg. social worker, citizen's advice bureau or doctor) or trustee. They are considered throughout the year. Details of the individuals income and circumstances must be included.

Hampshire

Correspondent: Mrs Anne Butcher, Clerk, 44 Old Turnpike, Fareham, Hampshire PO16 7HA (0329-235186).

Harting

The Henry Smith Charity

Eligibility: People in need who live in Harting.

Types of grants: One-off or recurrent grants according to need.

Annual grant total: About £1,000.

Applications: In writing to the correspondent.

Correspondent: K D Hughes, 33 South Acre, South Harting, Petersfield, Hampshire GU31 5LL.

Hawley

The Hawley Almshouse & Relief-in-Need Charity

Eligibility: People in need who have lived in the parish of Hawley for at least one year. Beneficiaries are generally women aged 60 or over and men aged 65 or over.

Types of grants: Generally one-off grants for needs that cannot be met from any other source. Help is given towards very high heating bills during extremely cold weather and the installation of equipment such as chair-lifts.

Annual grant total: About £5,000.

Applications: Considered in February, May, August, and November, but grants of up to £100 can be made at any time in emergencies. Applications can be submitted directly by the individual or by an appropriate third party such as a social worker or close family member.

Correspondent: Mrs C Spence, Secretary, Trustees' Office, Ratcliffe House, Hawley Garden Cottages, Hawley Road, Black-water, Camberley, Surrey GU17 9DD (0276-33515).

Other information: The trust also provides warden-operated individual accommodation for elderly people in the parish.

Isle of Wight

The Mary Pittis Charity for Widows

Eligibility: Widows who are aged 60 and over, who live on the Isle of Wight and express Christian beliefs.

Types of grants: One-off grants ranging from £100 to £200, towards heating bills, contribution to a new cooker and rental for the WightCare emergency telephone system etc..

Annual grant total: In 1993, the trust had an income of £7,000. Grants to 21 individuals totalled £2,800.

Applications: On a form available from the correspondent. Applications can be made directly, through a welfare agency or a minister of religion. They are considered at any time.

Correspondent: Messrs Roach Pittis, Trustees' Solicitors, 64 Lugley Street, Newport, Isle of Wight PO30 5EU (0983-524431).

Portsmouth

The Brogden Appeal Trust

Eligibility: Elderly or infirm people living in the city of Portsmouth as constituted on 31st March, 1974.

Types of grants: The provision and maintenance of personal contact call systems.

Annual grant total: £3,000 was spent on the above in 1987/88. No more recent information available.

Applications: In writing to the correspondent.

Correspondent: The City Manager's Office, Floor 3, Civic Offices, Portsmouth PO1 2AL (0705-834059).

The Montague Neville Durnford & Saint Leo Cawthan Memorial Trust

Eligibility: People over 60 who are in need and who live in the city of Portsmouth. Preference to ex-naval men and their widows.

Types of grants: Annual grants of between £40 and £50 paid in March. One-off grants may be given in exceptional circumstances.

Annual grant total: In 1993, annual grants totalling £3,000 were made to 60 individuals. No one-off grants were given.

Applications: In writing to the correspondent. Applications are considered in October.

Correspondent: The Manager's Office, Floor 3, Civic Offices, Portsmouth PO1 2AL (0705-834059).

The Isaac & Annie Fogelman Relief Trust

Eligibility: People of the Jewish faith aged 40 and over who live in Portsmouth.

Types of grants: One-off and recurrent grants according to need.

Annual grant total: In 1993, grants totalled £3,400 to 12 individuals.

Applications: In writing to the correspondent.

Correspondent: L J Guyer, Warner Goodman & Streat, 66 West Street, Fareham, Hampshire PO16 0JR.

The Lord Mayor of Portsmouth's Charity

Eligibility: The objects of the charity change annually with the change of Lord Mayor.

Types of grants: Details of grants to individuals, if any, are advertised in the local press.

Annual grant total: About £12,000.

Applications: In writing to the correspondent directly by the individual.

Correspondent: The Lord Mayor's Secretary, Civic Offices, Guildhall, Guildhall Square, Portsmouth PO1 2AJ (0705-822251).

The John Wallace Peck Trust

Eligibility: People in need who live in Portsmouth.

Types of grants: One-off and recurrent grants according to need.

Annual grant total: £1,600 in 1990/91.

Applications: In writing to the correspondent. Applications are considered in May/June.

Correspondent: The City Manager's Office, Floor 3, Civic Offices, Portsmouth PO1 2AL (0705-834059).

Ryde

The Ryde Sick Poor Fund

Eligibility: Sick people in need who live in the former borough of Ryde.

Types of grants: One-off grants only. The trust is unable to give recurrent grants.

Annual grant total: 30 to 40 grants totalling about £1,800.

Applications: In writing to the correspondent.

Correspondent: A Searle, Clerk, Myrtle Cottage, 45 St Michaels Road, St Helens, Isle of Wight (0983-873791).

Southampton

The Southampton Relief-in-Need Charity

Eligibility: People in need who live in the ecclesiastical parish of Southampton (in practice, the city centre).

Types of grants: One-off grants only.

Annual grant total: 80 to 90 grants totalling about £8,000.

Applications: In writing to the correspondent.

Correspondent: H F B Clark, Beaufort, Lainston Close, Weeke, Winchester SO22 5LJ (0962-854883).

Winchester

The Winchester Welfare Charities

Eligibility: People in need or distress, or who are sick, convalescing, disabled or infirm, who live in Winchester and its immediate surroundings and are over 60.

Types of grants: The trust gives annuities paid quarterly, winter fuel payments in December and emergency grants throughout the year. These one-off grants (typically £25 to £50) have been towards repairs to an electric wheelchair, special shoes for disabled people and repairs to a washing machine etc.. Help can also be given for furniture, bedding, clothing, food, fuel and nursing requirements.

Annual grant total: In 1993, the trust had an income of £2,400 and gave £1,600 in 53 grants to individuals.

Applications: When an annuitant vacancy arises applications should be submitted through one of the six trustees. Recipients of Christmas vouchers are nominated by the trustees and the social services department. Applications for emergency payments should be made through a social worker, citizen's advice bureau or similar third party.

Correspondent: D Shaw, Hon. Clerk, Winchester City Offices, Colebrook Street, Winchester, Hampshire SO23 9LJ (0962-848221).

Other information: A leaflet is available from the correspondent.

Wotton

The Henry Smith Charity

Eligibility: People in need who live in the ancient parish of Wotton.

Types of grants: One-off or recurrent grants ranging from £100 to £300.

Annual grant total: In 1993, the trust received £8,500 income, allocated by Henry Smith's (General Estate) Charity. Grants to 36 individuals totalled £4,380.

Applications: In writing to the correspondent.

Correspondent: Mrs I Devoil, Berrylands, Hook Lane, Fareham, Hampshire PO14 4LP (0489-583773).

Hertfordshire

The Bowley Charity for Deprived Children

Eligibility: Deprived children who live in south west Hertfordshire (in practice the immediate area around Three Rivers District Council plus Watford District Council).

Types of grants: Grants for clothing and safety equipment eg. fire guard.

Annual grant total: £5,500 in about 100 grants.

Applications: On a form available from the correspondent.

Correspondent: The Secretary, c/o Parsonage Close, Abbots Langley, Hertfordshire WD5 0BQ (0923-265238).

The Dacorum Community Trust

Eligibility: People in need who live in the district of Dacorum (the area around Hemel Hempstead).

Types of grants: Generally one-of grants and loans, especially to disabled people. Grants range from £100 to £1,000.

Annual grant total: £7,000 in 41 grants in 1992/93.

Applications: On a form available from the correspondent. Applications can be submitted by the individual or through a recognised referral agency (eg. social worker, citizen's advice bureau or doctor) and are considered in March, June, September and December.

Correspondent: G Wyton, Clerk, 3 St Mary's Road, Hemel Hempstead, Hertfordshire HP2 5HL (0442-231396).

The Hertfordshire Charity for Deprived Children

Eligibility: Deprived children up to the age of 17 living in Hertfordshire (excluding the Watford area).

Types of grants: One-off grants generally for holidays (not overseas), clothing (eg. school or cub uniforms or general clothing), and equipment (eg. a baby buggy, cot, washing machine or cooker where this would improve the quality of life for the child). Grants range between £30 and £250.

Annual grant total: In 1992/93, the trust's income was £10,000. 223 grants to individuals totalled £13,000.

Applications: On a form available from the correspondent. Applications should be made through a health visitor, social worker, probation officer or similar third party. Trustees meet in June and November, but applications can be considered between meetings and approved on by two trustees.

Correspondent: Richard Errington, Clerk, Fourfields, Rosedale Way, Cheshunt, Hertfordshire EN7 6JG.

The Hertfordshire Convalescent Trust

Eligibility: People who are sick and who live in Hertfordshire.

Types of grants: One-off grants for "the elderly, the young, the chronic sick, the carers and the cared for." Grants are for fees for short care only (not for equipment or transport costs). Grants for convalescence at convalescent homes, short stay at nursing homes, two week's holiday for carers and cared for, and for families in need. Awards are up to £400. The trust organises two holidays a year serving a different area of the county each time.

Annual grant total: In 1992, the trust had assets of £396,000, generating an income of £44,000. 160 relief-in-need grants totalled £34,000.

Applications: Applications are considered throughout the year and can be made by the individual or through a social worker, citizen's advice bureau or other appropriate third party. An application form is available form the correspondent.

Correspondent: Mrs Janet Bird, Administrator, 140 North Road, Hertford SG14 2BZ (0992-505886).

The Hertfordshire County Nursing Trust

Eligibility: Nurses working in the community, either practicing or retired, who live in Hertfordshire.

Types of grants: One-off and recurrent grants according to need.

Annual grant total: In 1991, the trust had an income of £40,000, but only part is available for individuals.

Hertfordshire/Kent

Applications: In writing to the correspondent.

Correspondent: Alasdair Shand, Timber Hall, Cold Christmas, Ware, Hertfordshire SG12 7SN (0920-466086).

The Hertfordshire Society for the Blind

Eligibility: Registered blind and partially sighted people living in Hertfordshire.

Types of grants: One-off grants up to £60, where funding is not available from statutory sources. Grants are given towards domestic equipment, telephone installation, magnifiers, holiday/respite care, moving expenses and heating etc..

Annual grant total: In 1992/93, the trust had assets of £320,000 and an income of £95,000. Expenditure totalled £114,000 including £9,700 in grants to individuals.

Applications: In writing to the correspondent. Applications can be submitted directly by the individual or through a social worker, citizen's advice bureau or other third party. They are considered daily.

Correspondent: Mervyn D Terrett, Secretary, HCC Trinity Centre, Fanhams Hall Road, Ware, Hertfordshire SG12 7PS (0992-588145).

● Buntingford

The Buntingford Relief-in-Need Charity

Eligibility: People in need who live in the parish of Buntingford.

Types of grants: One-off or recurrent grants according to need.

Annual grant total: In 1990, the trust had an income of £6,800. £5,600 was given in grants to individuals in need.

Applications: In writing to the correspondent.

Correspondent: Mrs J W Bailey, Clerk, Longmead, Buntingford, Hertfordshire SG9 9EF (0763-271208).

● Watford

The Watford Mayor's Fund

Eligibility: Retired people in need who live in the borough of Watford.

Types of grants: £10 vouchers are given just before Christmas, redeemable in local food stores or against gas/electricity bills.

Annual grant total: In 1992/93, the trust had an income of £3,550. Grants totalled £5,900 to 591 individuals.

Applications: In writing to the correspondent including confirmation that the nominee exists solely on state benefits. Applicants must be nominated by a third party such as doctors, social services, community associations etc..

Correspondent: The Mayor of Watford (FAO Sue Sleeman), International & Civic Officer, Watford Borough Council, Town Hall, Watford WD1 3EX (0923-226400 ext. 2830).

● Wormley

The Wormley Parochial Charity

Eligibility: People in need who live in the parish of Wormley as it was on 31st March, 1935.

Types of grants: Generally Christmas grants in kind; occasionally cash grants from £10 to £75.

Annual grant total: In 1992, the trust had an income of £3,900 and £1,950 was given in 91 grants to individuals.

Applications: In writing to the correspondent by any third party. Applications are considered in November.

Correspondent: J D Liggatt, The Old Manor House, High Road, Wormley, Hertfordshire EN10 6DU (0992-463747).

Kent

The Appleton Trust (Canterbury)

Eligibility: People in need connected with the Church of England in the diocese of Canterbury.

Types of grants: One-off grants ranging between £50 and £3,000.

Annual grant total: In 1992/93, grants totalling £27,000 were given to 30 to 40 individuals and local Christian organisations.

Applications: In writing to the correspondent. Applications should be submitted directly by the individual to be considered in January, March, June, September and December.

Correspondent: Miss R A Collins, Clerk, Diocesan House, Lady Wootton's Green, Canterbury CT1 1NQ (0227-459401).

The Canterbury United Municipal Charities

Eligibility: People in need who live within the boundaries of what was the county borough of Canterbury.

Types of grants: Pensions of £52 a year to about 20 pensioners; fuel and clothing tickets given in December each year, and other one-off grants according to need.

Annual grant total: About £1,500.

Applications: In writing to the correspondent.

Correspondent: G B Cotton, Clerk, 2 Castle Street, Canterbury CT1 2QH (0227-456731).

The Christmas Gift Fund for the Old City of Canterbury

Eligibility: Elderly people in need who live in the former county borough of Canterbury (as it was in March 1974).

Types of grants: Christmas parcels.

Annual grant total: £10,000 distributed in about 800 parcels.

Applications: In writing to the correspondent.

Correspondent: W E Elvy, 60 St Stephen's Hill, Canterbury CT2 7AR.

The Kent County Football Association Benevolent Fund

Eligibility: Injured, ill or incapacitated players who are in need and involved in football in the area of Kent as at 1908.

Types of grants: One-off grants according to need.

Annual grant total: In 1992, the trust had an income of £3,800, of which £3,000 was given in grants to individuals.

Applications: On a form available from the correspondent.

Correspondent: K T Masters, Secretary, 69 Maidstone Road, Chatham, Kent ME4 6DT (0634-843824).

The Dorothy Parrott Memorial Trust Fund

Eligibility: People in need who live in the area administered by Sevenoaks town council and adjoining parishes.

Types of grants: One-off and recurrent grants ranging from £50 to £100 according to need. Grants have been given towards outstanding water, gas and electricity bills, school and baby clothes, shoes, telephone installation, transport for special treatment, special equipment eg. a bed and a medical lamp,

Kent

and replacement of lost keys. Grants also given for council tax payments or rent arrears.

Annual grant total: In 1993, the trust had assets of £27,000 and income of £2,100. 39 relief-in-need grants totalled £2,000.

Applications: Either direct to the correspondent or through a social worker, citizen's advice bureau or similar third party, including a general history of the family. Applications are considered in January, April, July and October. Urgent cases can be dealt with in 48 hours.

Correspondent: C F Coston, Barnwell, 11 Kingwood Road, Dunzon Green, Sevenoaks, Kent TN13 2XE (0732-462248).

The Sir Thomas Smythe's Charity

Eligibility: People in financial need who live in the following parishes in Kent:

Bidborough: St Lawrence.
Darenth: St Margaret.
Dunton Green: St John.
Hildenborough: St John the Evangelist.
Langton Green: All Saints.
Otford: St Bartholomew.
Rusthall: St Paul.
Shorne: St Peter and Paul.
Southborough: St Peter, St Thomas, St Matthew.
Speldhurst: St Mary the Virgin and St John the Evangelist, Groombridge.
Sutton-at-Home: St John the Baptist.
Swanley: St Paul, St Mary.
Tonbridge: St Peter and St Paul with St Saviour, St Stephen.
Tunbridge Wells: Holy Trinity, Christ Church, St John, St James, St Peter, King Charles the Martyr, St Barnabas, St Luke.
Wilmington: St Michael and All Angels.

Types of grants: One-off and recurrent grants according to need. One-off grants typically £50 to £250. Regular allowances are usually £300 a year.

Annual grant total: About £90,000, of which £70,000 is in the form of regular allowances. Around 400 grants are given, 300 of which are recurrent. However, please note that the charity has been badly affected by the recession and no applications can be considered at present.

Applications: Applications must be made through the local trustee of the particular parish concerned, whose name can be obtained from the correspondent below. They are considered quarterly, but emergency grants can be made between meetings.

Correspondent: The Charities Clerk, The Skinners' Company, Skinners' Hall, 8 Dowgate Hill, London EC4R 2SP (071-236 5629).

● Borden

The Barrows Eleemosynary Charity

Eligibility: People in need who live in the ancient ecclesiastical parish of Borden. Preference for people of 60 years or over.

Types of grants: One-off grants and twice-yearly allowances to pensioners. Occasional grants are made to disabled and other people in the parish. Grants typically range from £50 to £200.

Annual grant total: In 1992, the trust had assets of £302,000, generating an income of £12,000. Relief-in-need grants to 55 individuals totalled £6,900. The trust also gives grants to organisations.

Applications: On a form available from the correspondent. Applications should be submitted directly by the individual to be considered in April and October.

Correspondent: J V Clarke, Clerk, c/o George Webb & Co, 43 Park Road, Sittingbourne, Kent ME10 1DX (0795-470556/7).

● Canterbury

Streynsham's Charity

Eligibility: People who live in the ancient parish of St Dunstan's, Canterbury.

Types of grants: One-off grants.

Annual grant total: Over £10,000.

Applications: In writing to the correspondent.

Correspondent: Mrs J L McCulloch, Clerk, Langley, 13 South Canterbury Road, Canterbury CT1 3LH.

● Dover

The R V Coleman Trust

Eligibility: People who live in Dover and the immediate neighbourhood and who are sick, convalescing, mentally or physically disabled or infirm.

Types of grants: Over 100 one-off and recurrent grants according to need. Grants have been given for periods in nursing homes, for specific needs such as wheelchairs, for telephone facilities in extreme cases and for convalescent holiday breaks.

Annual grant total: £35,000 in 1991.

Applications: Usually made via doctors or social workers. Direct applications are not encouraged. When they do occur, applicants are given a certificate which must be filled in by their doctor. Applications considered continuously.

Correspondent: P W Sherred, 110 Maison Dieu Road, Dover, Kent CT16 1RT (0304-206850).

● Folkstone

The Folkestone Municipal Charities

Eligibility: People in need, particularly the elderly, who live in the area of the former borough of Folkestone.

Types of grants: One-off grants of £25 to £500 for most types of need (eg. telephone installation, help after a burglary, loss of a purse/wallet, shoes for needy children, gas/electricity bills, household repairs).

Annual grant total: In 1990/91, the trust had assets of £975,000, and an income of £194,000. 26 relief-in-need grants totalled £5,000. We have not been able to update this information.

Applications: In writing to the correspondent, including age, length of residence in beneficial area, financial circumstances and receipt of benefits. Applications should preferably be through a social worker, citizen's advice bureau or other welfare agency, and can be submitted at any time.

Correspondent: The Secretary, c/o Age Concern, Victoria Grove, Folkestone, Kent.

● Fordwich

The Fordwich United Charities

Eligibility: People in need who live in Fordwich.

Types of grants: One-off grants for heating of £40 each.

Annual grant total: 14 grants totalling about £550.

Applications: In writing to the correspondent.

Correspondent: C B Wacher, Furley Page Fielding & Barton Solicitors, 39 St Margaret's Street, Canterbury CT1 2TX (0227-763939).

● Herne Bay

The Herne Bay Parochial Charities

Eligibility: People in need who live in Herne Bay.

Types of grants: Both one-off and regular grants during the year and at Christmas.

237

Kent

Annual grant total: Over £1,500 in monthly payments to 17 beneficiaries and 40 Christmas gifts.

Applications: In writing, or by telephone in an emergency, to the correspondent.

Correspondent: J Craig King, 158 High Street, Herne Bay, Kent CT6 5NP (0227-373874).

● Hothfield

The Thanet Charity

Eligibility: People in need who live in the parish of Hothfield.

Types of grants: One-off or recurrent grants according to need.

Annual grant total: £4,600 in 1990/91.

Applications: In writing to the correspondent. Applications can be submitted directly by the individual or through a social worker, citizen's advice bureau or other third party. They are considered throughout the year.

Correspondent: Mrs V Foad, Robertsdane, Hastingleigh, Nr Ashford, Kent TN25 5HE (0233-750281).

● Leigh

The Leigh United Charities

Eligibility: People in need, generally on Income Support, who live in Leigh and the Hollenden portion of Leigh in Hildenborough.

Types of grants: Christmas gifts and grants for food and fuel of £15 to £50.

Annual grant total: In 1993, the trust had assets of £150,000, and an income of £25,000. 150 relief-in-need grants to individuals totalled £20,000.

Applications: Applications are considered in November or as required, and are submitted personally to the trustees.

Correspondent: W S Crocker, Eastern Bungalow, High Street, Leigh, Tonbridge, Kent TN11 8RP (0732-832580).

● Maidstone

The Edmett, Swain & Hanson Charity

Eligibility: People in need, preferably over 60, who live in the former borough of Maidstone (as it was before April 1974).

Types of grants: Christmas gifts and about 30 pensions of £45.50 a quarter.

Annual grant total: Over £2,000.

Applications: On a form available from the correspondent.

Correspondent: R P Rogers, 72 King Street, Maidstone, Kent ME14 1BL (0622-690077).

The Hollands-Warren Charitable Trust

Eligibility: People in need of temporary medical and nursing services in their own homes and/or domestic help, who live in the borough of Maidstone.

Types of grants: Grants towards the cost of such services and/or domestic help.

Annual grant total: In 1992/93, the trust had an income of £51,000. Most of this is already committed to local causes. No grants to individuals were made, but the trust had a surplus of £7,000.

Applications: In writing to the correspondent. Applications should be submitted directly by the individual.

Correspondent: G A W Bracher, Trustee, Somerfield House, 59 London Road, Maidstone, Kent ME16 8JH (0622-690691).

Other information: The trust states: "The trustees do not have funds to monitor individual applications. Accordingly funds are allocated in bulk and individual applications are only considered via personal recommendation by a trustee".

The Maidstone Relief-in-Need Charities

Eligibility: People in need who live in the former borough of Maidstone.

Types of grants: Annual distribution of about 300 winter vouchers of £9.00 each and weekly grants of between £4 and £10. Also, special one-off grants up to £100.

Annual grant total: In 1992/93, £1,600 was given in Christmas vouchers, £480 in cash grants and £245 in special grants.

Applications: Winter voucher recipients are nominated by trustees. Applications for weekly or special grants should be made through a social worker, health visitor, doctor or similar third party on a form available from the correspondent.

Correspondent: The Clerk, Maidstone Borough Council, 5–11 London Road, Maidstone, Kent ME16 8HR (0622-602000).

● Rochester

The William Mantle Trust

Eligibility: People in need who are over 60 and were either born in that part of Rochester which lies to the south and east of the River Medway, or have at any time lived in that part of the city for a continuous period of not less than 15 years.

Types of grants: Pensions.

Annual grant total: In 1992/93, the trust had an income of £6,500. It is not known how much was given in grants to individuals in need.

Applications: In writing to the correspondent.

Correspondent: Mrs B A Emery, Clerk, Administrative Offices, Watt's Almshouses, Maidstone Road, Rochester, Kent ME1 1SE (0634-842194).

● Sevenoaks

The Kate Drummond Trust

Eligibility: People in need who live in Sevenoaks and the neighbourhood.

Types of grants: Probably one-off or recurrent grants according to need.

Annual grant total: In 1992/93, the trust had an income of £5,000. It is not known how much was given for the relief-in-need of individuals.

Applications: In writing to the correspondent.

Correspondent: The Vicar, St Nicholas Rectory, Rectory Lane, Sevenoaks, Kent TN13 1JA (0732-740340).

● Tunbridge Wells

Miss Ethel Mary Fletcher's Charitable Bequest

Eligibility: Elderly people in need who live in the Tunbridge Wells area.

Types of grants: Weekly allowances only. The charity states that funds are "fully committed, permanently" and presumably will therefore not respond to any applications.

Annual grant total: About £2,000.

Applications: See Types of grants above.

Correspondent: P Badwell-Purefoy, c/o Thomson, Snell & Passmore, 3 Lonsdale Gardens, Tunbridge Wells, Kent TN1 1NX (0892-510000).

● Wilmington

The Wilmington Parochial Charity

Eligibility: People in need who live in the parish of Wilmington.

Types of grants: Grants are given twice a year ie. a grocery voucher and small cash grant at Christmas and a heating grant at Easter.

Annual grant total: In 1993, the trust had assets of £120,000 and an income of £9,000, one fifth of which is for education. £7,000 was given in grants of £25 to £100 to 185 individuals in need.

Applications: On a form available from the correspondent for consideration in February and November.

Correspondent: S J Stringer, 13 Meadow Walk, Wilmington, Dartford, Kent DA2 7BP (0322-226335).

Norfolk

The Callibut's Estate & the Hillingdon Charities

Eligibility: People in need who live in Hillingdon and East Walton.

Types of grants: Probably one-off and recurrent grants according to need.

Annual grant total: Over £1,000, divided equally between the parishes of Hillingdon and East Walton.

Applications: In writing to the correspondent.

Correspondent: D J Borley, Clerk to the Parish Council, Denmar, Fakenham Road, Hillingdon, Kings Lynn, Norfolk.

Other information: This entry has not been confirmed by the trust.

The King's Lynn & West Norfolk Borough Charity

Eligibility: People in need who live in the borough of King's Lynn and West Norfolk.

Types of grants: One-off grants only.

Annual grant total: In 1992, the trust had assets of £135,000 generating an income of £8,000. It is not known how much was given in grants to individuals.

Applications: On a form available from the correspondent. Applications should be submitted through a social worker, doctor or similar third party. They are considered in January, April, July and October.

Correspondent: Veronica Stiles, 54 Park Road, Hunstanton, Norfolk PE36 5DL (0485-533352).

The Lord Mayor's New Horizons Fund

Eligibility: Physically and mentally disabled people who live in Norfolk.

Types of grants: One-off grants up to £200. Grants have been given for driving lessons, car adaptation, training courses, holidays at centres catering specifiically for disabled people, household equipment and computer equipment.

Annual grant total: About £2,300 in 25 grants.

Applications: On a form available from the correspondent. Individuals may apply directly but a sponsor is needed such as a doctor, teacher, clergy etc.. Applications are considered quarterly.

Correspondent: David Crowe, 56 London Road, Wymondham, Norfolk NR18 9BP (0953-604885).

The Earl of Northampton's Charity

Eligibility: Elderly people in need who live in Castle Rising and Shotsam in Norfolk and Greenwich, London.

Types of grants: Pensions up to £10 a week.

Annual grant total: £18,000 in pensions.

Applications: In writing to the correspondent.

Correspondent: The Clerk to the Mercers' Company, Mercers Hall, Ironmonger Lane, London EC2V 8HE (071-726 4991).

Other information: This entry is repeated in the London section of the book.

The Shelroy Trust

Eligibility: People in need who live in Norfolk.

Types of grants: One-off grants to elderly or disabled people for equipment that is not available through the NHS. Grants range from £50 to £500.

Annual grant total: In 1991/92, the trust had assets of £310,000 and an income of £16,000. Relief-in-need grants to individuals totalled £4,500 (36 grants).

Applications: In writing to the correspondent. Applications can be made directly by the individual or through a social worker, citizen's advice bureau or other third party. They are considered at any time.

Correspondent: A Callf, 25 The Street, Brundall, Norwich NR13 5AA (0603-712565).

Other information: The trust also encourages youth projects with Christian or medical emphasis overseas.

The West Winch Town Yard Charity

Eligibility: People in need who live in West Winch and Setchey.

Types of grants: Generally one-off and recurrent grants in the form of coal to the value of £29 at Christmas.

Annual grant total: In 1993, the trust's income was £2,600. 26 grants totalling £760 were given.

Applications: In writing to the correspondent to be considered in September/October. Applications should be submitted directly by the individual and should indicate whether the applicant is retired or unemployed.

Correspondent: F H Fuller, 42 Hall Lane, West Winch, King's Lynn PE33 0PP (0553-840302).

● **Barton Bendish**

The Barton Bendish Poor's Charity

Eligibility: Widows and people in need who live in Barton Bendish.

Types of grants: Grants of £40 towards funeral expenses or travel to hospitals. Christmas payments for fuel costs.

Annual grant total: In 1991, the trust's income was £1,100. Relief-in-need grants to 21 individuals totalled £840.

Applications: The five trustees are well known and can be approached personally. Applications can also be submitted in writing to the correspondent at any time throughout the year.

Correspondent: Mrs Freda Rumball, Clerk, Barton Bendish Parish Council, 45 Church Road, Barton Bendish, King's Lynn, Norfolk PE33 9DP (0366-347324).

● **Beeston**

The Beeston Fuel Charity

Eligibility: Pensioners in need who live in the parish of Beeston and have done so for at least five years.

Types of grants: Fuel grants, generally one-off, from a minimum of £22 for widows over 60 and pensioners over 65. People burning coal receive coal while people burning oil receive a cheque equal to the coal prices.

Norfolk

Annual grant total: In 1993, the trust had assets an income of £1,100. Relief-in-need grants to individuals totalled over £1,000.

Applications: In writing to the correspondent by a third party on the applicant's behalf. Applications are considered in December.

Correspondent: Brian Potter, Beeston Village, General Store, King's Lynn PE32 2NG.

● Buxton

The Charity of Sir John Picto & Others

Eligibility: People in need who live in the parish of Buxton with Lammas with Little Hautbois.

Types of grants: One-off and recurrent grants according to need.

Annual grant total: In 1992/93, the trust had an income of £6,400. It is not known how much was given in grants to individuals in need.

Applications: In writing to the correspondent.

Correspondent: D W Smithson, Clerk, Avandix, Crown Road, Buxton, Norwich NR10 5EN (0603-279203).

● Diss

The Diss Parochial Charities Poors Branch

Eligibility: People in need who live in Diss.

Types of grants: Bereavement grants of £100 accounted for £2,000 in 1993. Other grants have been given towards vehicle adaptation and a motorised wheelchair.

Annual grant total: Expenditure totalled £7,500 in 1993, but not all of this was for individuals in need.

Applications: In writing to the correspondent. Referrals are often made by the town health centre, but also by the DSS, schools, churches and other bodies.

Correspondent: H R Judd, Clerk, 7 Whytehead Gardens, Diss, Norfolk IP22 3HB (0379-644080).

● East Dereham

The East Dereham Relief-in-Need Charity

Eligibility: People in need who live in East Dereham.

Types of grants: About 20 one-off grants ranging from £50 to £75 towards clothing, heating and hospital travel, and 300 to 400 vouchers given at Christmas.

Annual grant total: In 1992, the trust had £1,320 income, allocated by Henry Smith's (General Estate) Charity.

Applications: In writing to the correspondent.

Correspondent: Mr Parker, Case & Dewing, Estate Agents, Quebec Street, Dereham, Norfolk NR19 2DJ (0362-692004).

● East Ruston

East Ruston Poor's Allotment

Eligibility: People in need who live in the parish of East Ruston.

Types of grants: Fuel or a cheque equivalent to pensioners at Christmas and other grants according to need.

Annual grant total: In 1992/93, the trust had an income of £10,200. Grants to 52 households totalled £2,500.

Applications: Should be made directly by the individual to any trustee.

Correspondent: Tony Billett, The New Vicarage, Camping Field Lane, Stalham, Norwich NR12 9DT.

● Feltwell

The Edmund Atmere Charity

Eligibility: People, generally over 70, who have lived in Feltwell for at least 10 years.

Types of grants: Annual one-off grants of around £6 a year to elderly people and one-off payments for emergency needs.

Annual grant total: In 1991, the trust had assests of £6,200 and an income of £2,200. 146 relief-in-need grants totalled £1,300.

Applications: In writing to the correspondent.

Correspondent: E A Lambert, Hill Farm, Feltwell, Thetford, Norfolk (0842-828156).

● Foulden

The Foulden Parochial Charities

Eligibility: People in need who live in Foulden.

Types of grants: Probably one-off and recurrent grants according to need.

Annual grant total: £1,400.

Applications: In writing to the correspondent.

Correspondent: Mrs S J Tolman, Secretary, 27 Vicarage Road, Foulden, Thetford, Norfolk IP26 5AB.

Other information: According to the Charity Commission the address is correct, but the entry has not been confirmed by the trust.

● Garboldisham

The Garboldisham Parish Charities

Eligibility: People in need who live in the parish of Garboldisham. Generally, this is covered by the Relief-in-Need Fund, although widows and those over 65 who have lived in the parish for over two years may qualify for allowances from the Fuel Allotment Charity.

Types of grants: One-off and recurrent grants according to need.

Annual grant total: About £3,000, but not all of this is given in relief-in-need grants.

Applications: Applications can be submitted directly by the individual including specific details of what the grant is required for. Applications are usually considered in July and December.

Correspondent: P Girling, Treasurer, Smallworth, Garboldisham, Diss, Norfolk IP22 2RQ (0953-81646).

● Gayton

The Gayton Fuel Allotments

Eligibility: Widows and widowers who have lived in Gayton for at least five years.

Types of grants: Annual grants of £14 to help with the cost of fuel.

Annual grant total: In 1993, the trust had an income of £1,100, all of which was given in about 80 grants to individuals.

Applications: In writing to the correspondent directly by the individual for consideration in October.

Correspondent: N F Bradshaw, Clerk, 14 Birch Road, Gayton, Kings Lynn, Norfolk PE32 1UN (0553-636321).

● Gaywood

The Gaywood Poors' Allotment

Eligibility: People in need who live in the ecclesiastical parish of Gaywood.

Norfolk

Types of grants: Annual grants of £5 given in December to help with the cost of fuel. Emergency grants up to £100 are given for short term needs.

Annual grant total: About 500 grants totalling £2,500.

Applications: In writing to the correspondent. Applications for emergency grants are generally made through a social worker.

Correspondent: L W A Barratt, Clerk, Pleasant Holme, 3 The Green, South Wootton, King's Lynn PE30 3LD (0553-671456).

Great Hockham

The Great Hockham Fuel & Furze Trust

Eligibility: People in need who live in the parish of Great Hockham.

Types of grants: Grants to help with the cost of fuel (eg. cheque payable to local electricity board).

Annual grant total: In 1993, the trust had an income of £1,400. Grants of £40 were given to 29 individuals and totalled £1,160.

Applications: Directly by the individual in writing to the correspondent or through a third party on their behalf (eg. relative or neighbour). Applications are considered in October/November.

Correspondent: P N P Gray, Scotgate Cottage, Watton Road, Great Hockham, Thetford, Norfolk IP24 1PD (0953-498375).

Halvergate

The Halvergate Town Lands Charity

Eligibility: People in need who live in the parish of Halvergate and Tunstall.

Types of grants: One-off and recurrent grants according to need.

Annual grant total: In 1992/93, the trust had an income of £4,600. Total expenditure was £5,100. Grants of between £40 and £55 were given to 43 individuals and totalled £2,250.

Applications: In writing to the correspondent.

Correspondent: B F Phillips, Cartref, Marsh Road, Halvergate, Norwich NR13 3QB (0493-700306).

Harling

The West Harling Road Allotment Gardens Trust

Eligibility: Women in need who live in the parish of Harling.

Types of grants: One-off and recurrent grants according to need. Recently grants have been given for travel costs for hospital visiting, fuel costs where the husband is chronically sick, and help immediately following a bereavement.

Annual grant total: In 1990/91, the income of the trust was £650. The trust gave seven relief-in-need grants to individuals totalling £450.

Applications: In writing to the correspondent at any time.

Correspondent: David R Gee, Clerk, Hanworth House, Market Street, East Harling, Norwich NR16 2AD (0953-717652).

Hilgay

The Hilgay Feoffee Charity

Eligibility: People in need who live in the parish of Hilgay.

Types of grants: One-off and recurrent grants according to need (including coal). Grants range from £25 to £75.

Annual grant total: In 1991, the charity had an income of £4,100. £1,400 was given in relief-in-need grants to individuals.

Applications: In writing to the correspondent, directly by the individual or by a third party aware of the circumstances.

Correspondent: J E Clarke, 21 London Road, Downham Market, Norfolk PE38 9AP (0366-387387).

Other information: The charity also gives grants to the two schools in the parish.

Horstead

The Horstead Poor's Land Charity

Eligibility: People in need who live in Horstead with Stanninghall.

Types of grants: One-off and recurrent grants according to need.

Annual grant total: In 1992/93, grants totalling £8,830 were made, not all of which was given in grants to individuals.

Applications: Applications, in writing to the correspondent, can be submitted directly by the individual, through a recognised referral agency (eg. social worker, citizen's advice bureau or doctor) or other third party, and are considered throughout the year.

Correspondent: W B Lloyd, 7 Church Close, Horstead, Norwich NR12 7ET (0603-737632).

King's Lynn

The King's Lynn Charities for the Poor

Eligibility: People in need who live in King's Lynn.

Types of grants: One-off grants according to need.

Annual grant total: The trust has an income of about £600.

Applications: In writing to the correspondent.

Correspondent: M J Pellizzaro, Clerk, Mapus, Smith & Lemmon, 48 King Street, King's Lynn, Norfolk PE30 1HE (0553-774761).

Kirby Cane

The Kirby Cane Charities

Eligibility: Widows and widowers who live in Kirby Cane.

Types of grants: One-off grants at Christmas, presently of £30.

Annual grant total: In 1993, the trust had an income of £1,100 and gave 15 grants of £30 totalling £450.

Applications: In writing to the correspondent directly by the individual. Applications are considered in December.

Correspondent: Mrs B J Pye, Clerk, The Kennels, Yarmouth Road, Raveningham, Norfolk NR14 6NN (0508-548422).

Little Dunham

The Little Dunham Relief-in-Need Charities

Eligibility: People in need who live in Little Dunham who are on state pensions, low income or unemployed.

Types of grants: Usually one-off cheques made out to fuel companies, but other needs are also considered.

Annual grant total: In 1992, the trust had an income of £2,000. Grants of about £50 were given to 26 people totalling £1,300.

Applications: The trustees usually depend on their local knowledge, but also consider direct approaches from village

Norfolk

residents. Applications are considered in October or November each year.

Correspondent: Mrs H Heslin, Clerk, The Barn, Barrow Holes Lane, Little Dunham, Kings Lynn, Norfolk PE32 2DP (0760-724495).

Lyng Heath

The Lyng Heath Charity

Eligibility: People in need living in the village of Lyng Heath.

Types of grants: One-off and recurrent grants between £25 and £40 to help with heating costs.

Annual grant total: In 1992/93, the trust's income was £1,400. 16 relief-in-need grants totalled £460.

Applications: In writing to the correspondent at any time. Applications can be submitted directly by the individual or through a social worker, citizen's advice bureau or other welfare agency. Applicants should include their date of birth, how long they have lived in the village and any other relevant information. Applications are considered in November/December.

Correspondent: R S Burton, Hon. Secretary, 19 Richard Haggard Close, Shipdham, Thetford, Norfolk IP25 7LL (0362-820558).

Marham

The Marham Poors Allotment Trust

Eligibility: People in need, particularly pensioners, widows and the long-term sick who live in Marham.

Types of grants: Two vouchers of £15 and £20 are given to be spent at the village shop, butcher, milkman or coal merchant. The trust has also recently given grants towards some young people's medical needs.

Annual grant total: About 76 grants totalling £2,300.

Applications: By adding the name to a list in the local post office and shops or by approaching a trustee. The closing date for "dole coal" is 31st October.

Correspondent: Dave Watson, 32 Hillside, Marham, Kings Lynn, Norfolk PE33 9JJ (0760-337777).

Other information: The income for the trust comes from land donated to the town. Anglia Water have 145 acres of it which they rented on a 99-year lease; they only have five years remaining. Anglia Water are currently paying £131 a year for this and were renting out shooting rights for £240 a year; this has now been stopped.

Northwold

The Northwold Combined Charity for the Needy & the Charity of Edmund Atmere

Eligibility: People in need who live in Northwold.

Types of grants: Probably one-off and recurrent grants according to need.

Annual grant total: About £4,500 in 1993.

Applications: In writing to the correspondent.

Correspondent: Mrs J Norris, 25 West End, Northwold, Norfolk IP26 5LE (0366-728296).

Norwich

The Norwich Consolidated Charities

Eligibility: People in need who live within the city boundary of Norwich.

Types of grants: One-off grants for welfare according to need. Loans are also available for tradesmen starting in business.

Annual grant total: About £37,000 in 170 grants to individuals. Around 90% of applications are granted.

Applications: On a form available from the correspondent. Applications are considered by the trustees at five committee meetings each year.

Correspondent: N A Ogilvie, Administrator, 10 Golden Dog Lane, Magdalen Street, Norwich NR3 1BP (0603-621023).

The Norwich Town Close Estate Charity

Eligibility: Freemen of Norwich and their families who are in need.

Types of grants: One-off and recurrent grants according to need.

Annual grant total: £15,000 in about 100 grants.

Applications: On a form available from the correspondent.

Correspondent: N A Ogilvie, Administrator, 10 Golden Dog Lane, Magdalen Street, Norwich NR3 1BP (0603-621023).

Other information: This trust also gives about £85,000 for education to individuals and £300,000 to charities dealing with education. See *The Educational Grants Directory*.

Old Buckenham

The Old Buckenham United Eleemosynary Charity

Eligibility: People in need who live in Old Buckenham, Norfolk. Preference for pensioners (over 65) but others are considered.

Types of grants: Normally recurrent grants in coal or cash in lieu for those without coal fires. Grants are currently 5cwt or £28 and distributed yearly in early December. Cases considered to be of exceptional need can be given more.

Annual grant total: £1,600, usually to about 60 to 70 families.

Applications: For new applicants, in writing to the correspondent following posted notices around the parish each autumn. Applications are usually considered early November.

Correspondent: D C Hardy, 4 Sutherland Chase, Blythewood, Ascot, Berkshire SL5 8TF (0344-25382).

Pentney

The Pentney Charities

Eligibility: People in need who live in the parish of Pentney.

Types of grants: One-off grants to individuals and organisations for the general benefit of the inhabitants of Pentney.

Annual grant total: In 1992/93, the trust had an income of £6,400. 51 relief-in-need grants to individuals totalled £1,200 and £800 to organisations.

Applications: In writing to the correspondent. Applications are considered in May and November.

Correspondent: Mrs Susan Smalley, Falgate Farm, Narborough Road, Pentney, King's Lynn, Norfolk PE32 1JD (0760-337534).

Saham Toney

The Saham Toney Fuel Allotment & Perkins Charity

Eligibility: People in need who have lived in Saham Toney for at least two years.

Types of grants: Grants between £50 and £80 to help with the cost of fuel.

Norfolk

Annual grant total: In 1992, the trust's income was £6,700. 59 relief-in-need grants to individuals totalled £4,200.

Applications: On a form available from the correspondent giving details of dependants and income. Applications are considered in June.

Correspondent: Mrs J S Glenn, 12 The Terrace, Richmond Road, Saham Toney, Thetford, Norfolk IP25 7ER (0953-881317).

● Saxlingham

The Saxlingham District Charity

Eligibility: People in need who are sick, disabled or infirm and who live in Saxlingham.

Types of grants: One-off and recurrent grants according to need.

Annual grant total: About £2,300.

Applications: In writing to the correspondent.

Correspondent: Dr J Fox, Ivy Farm, Foxhole, Saxlingham Thorpe, Norfolk NR15 1VG (0508-492929).

The Saxlingham United Charities

Eligibility: People in need aged 70 or over who have lived in the village of Saxlingham for five or more years.

Types of grants: Recurrent grants for coal and electricity.

Annual grant total: In 1992/93, the trust's income was £2,400. 22 grants totalling £1,600 were given, although not all were for relief-in-need.

Applications: In writing to the correspondent. Applications can be submitted directly by the individual and are usually considered in September/October.

Correspondent: Mrs E Hollingworth, 17 Kensington Close, Saxlingham, Nethergate, Norwich NR15 1TR (0508-499503).

● Shipdham

The Shipdham Parochial & Fuel Allotment

Eligibility: People in need who have lived in Shipdham for two years.

Types of grants: One-off and recurrent grants according to need.

Annual grant total: £6,000 in about 140 grants.

Applications: On an application form available from the correspondent.

Correspondent: Rev F W Irwin, Shipdham Rectory, Thetford, Norfolk IP25 7LX (0362-820234).

● South Creake

The South Creake Charities

Eligibility: People in need who live in South Creake.

Types of grants: Mostly annual grants of £28 towards fuel.

Annual grant total: £2,500 given in grants to 76 households for relief-in-need and education.

Applications: In writing to the correspondent.

Correspondent: Miss E Sands, 2 Bluestone Crescent, South Creake, Fakenham, Norfolk NR21 9LZ (0328-823227).

● Stow Bardolph

The Stow Bardolph Town Lands & Poors Charity

Eligibility: People in need who live in the parish of Stow Bardolph, with preference for elderly people. Households where one person is working are excluded.

Types of grants: Fuel vouchers.

Annual grant total: In 1992/93, the trust's income was £2,200. 60 relief-in-need grants totalled £2,500.

Applications: In writing to the correspondent. Applications can be submitted directly by the individual and are usually considered in December.

Correspondent: Mrs P Golds, Reeve Cottage, Wards Chase, Stowbridge, King's Lynn PE34 3NN (0366-387387).

● Swanton Morley

Thomas Barrett's Charity

Eligibility: Elderly people in need who live in Swanton Morley.

Types of grants: One-off and recurrent grants according to need.

Annual grant total: £750 in 40 grants.

Applications: In writing to the correspondent directly by the individual. Applications are considered in November or December.

Correspondent: H G Cator, Old Bank of England Court, Queen Street, Norwich NR2 4TA (0603-767606).

● Thetford

The Henry Smith Charity

Eligibility: People in need who live in Thetford.

Types of grants: Grants of about £10 at Christmas only for coal, fuel, heating etc..

Annual grant total: In 1992, the trust received £1,100 income, allocated by Henry Smith's (General Estate) Charity.

Applications: An advertisement is placed in the Thetford & Brandon Times in October inviting applications.

Correspondent: A V Hughes, Municipal Offices, Kings House, Thetford, Norfolk IP24 2AP.

● Thurne

The Thurne Poor Allotment

Eligibility: People in need who live in Thurne.

Types of grants: Grants to help with the cost of fuel.

Annual grant total: Over £1,000.

Applications: In writing to the correspondent.

Correspondent: D W George, Abbey Farm, Thurne, Great Yarmouth, Norfolk NR29 3BY.

● Tilney All Saints

The Tilney All Saints Parish Lands Charity

Eligibility: People in need who live in the ancient parish of Tilney All Saints.

Types of grants: Two-thirds of the trust's income is distributed in Christmas grants to widows and widowers. The remaining income is given to any charitable purpose that benefits the people of the parish.

Annual grant total: £1,100 in 1991.

Applications: In writing to the correspondent.

Correspondent: Mrs E Constable, Elm House, Station Road, Clenchwarton, King's Lynn, Norfolk PE34 4DH (0553-764003).

● Walpole

The Walpole St Peter Poor's Estate

Eligibility: People in need aged 16 and over who live in Walpole St Peter and Walpole Highway.

Norfolk

Types of grants: One-off and recurrent grants ranging from £50 to £100. For example grants are given towards heating costs and travel expenses.

Annual grant total: 4 grants totalling £2,900 in 1993.

Applications: In writing to the correspondent. Applications should be submitted directly by the individual and are considered in November.

Correspondent: Mrs P M Winkley, Cricket Willow, Church Road, Walpole St Peter, Wisbech PE14 7NU (0945-780242).

● Watton

The Watton Relief-in-Need Charity

Eligibility: People in need who live in Watton.

Types of grants: One-off grants only.

Annual grant total: £2,500.

Applications: In writing to the correspondent.

Correspondent: C H Cadman, 19 Priory Road, Watton, Norfolk IP25 6PQ (0953-882015).

● Welney

The Bishop's Land Charity

Eligibility: People in need, particularly those over 65 who live in Welney.

Types of grants: £15 per person each year.

Annual grant total: £1,155 in 77 grants in 1993.

Applications: By attending, in person, the William Marshall School usually on the 2nd Saturday of December.

Correspondent: Mrs D L Houghton, Ash Farm, Tipsend, Welney, Wisbech, Cambridgeshire PE14 9SF.

William Marshall's Charity

Eligibility: Widows in need who live in the parish of Welney.

Types of grants: Grants of £240 each year.

Annual grant total: £6,600 in 28 grants in 1993. One third of the income goes to individuals, a third to the parish church and a third to organisations.

Applications: In writing to the correspondent. The list of recipients is reviewed quarterly.

Correspondent: R J Brooks, Town Hall, Littleport, Ely CB6 1LU (0353-860281).

● Wereham

The Wereham Relief-in-Need Charity

Eligibility: Men over 65 and women over 60 in need who live in Wereham and have done so for at least one year. Applications are restricted to one per household.

Types of grants: Electricity stamps worth about £20. Grants can be recurrent.

Annual grant total: In 1992, the trust had an income of £1,000. £930 was given to 48 individuals.

Applications: In writing to the correspondent for consideration in November.

Correspondent: Mrs E A M Baddock, Clerk, Chile House, St Margarets Hill, King's Lynn PE33 9AN (0366-500233).

● West Walton

The West Walton Poors' Charity

Eligibility: People in need who live in West Walton.

Types of grants: Mainly Christmas grants to pensioners.

Annual grant total: £3,500 in 1991.

Applications: In writing to the correspondent.

Correspondent: W R Knowles, Messrs Dawbarns Solicitors, 1 York Row, Wisbech, Cambridgeshire PE13 1EA (0945-61456).

● Witton

The Witton Charity

Eligibility: Widows in need who live in Witton.

Types of grants: One-off and recurrent grants according to need.

Annual grant total: £2,000.

Applications: In writing to the correspondent.

Correspondent: Mrs L F Tompkins, Shootersway, Heath Road, Ridlington, North Walsham, Norfolk NR28 9NZ (0692-650500).

● Wiveton

The Ralph Greenaway Charity

Eligibility: People in need who are over 60 and have lived in the parish of Wiveton for at least three years. Preference is given to widows.

Types of grants: Small weekly pensions and fuel grants to any other elderly person in need. Help is occasionally given for educational purposes.

Annual grant total: In 1992/93, the trust had an income of £1,700. Pensions of £1.25 a week were given to 8 individuals.

Applications: Applications, on a form available from the correspondent, should be submitted directly by the individual and are considered in June and November. The names of two referees should be included.

Correspondent: P Veitch, 1 Meadow View, The Street, Wiveton, Holt, Norfolk NR25 7TJ (0263-741016).

● Woodton

The Woodton United Charities

Eligibility: People in need who live in the parish of Woodton.

Types of grants: One-off and recurrent grants according to need. Grants were given to help with a funeral (£50), hospital visits (£20), sick or disabled people in homes (£35) etc.. Regular grants are made during the winter months.

Annual grant total: In 1992, the trust had an income of £1,600. Grants were given to 14 individuals and totalled £800.

Applications: In writing to the correspondent for consideration each month.

Correspondent: J V Cowan, Long Barn, Hempnall Road, Woodton, Bungay, Suffolk NR35 2LR (0508-44624).

● Wretton

The Jane Forby Charity

Eligibility: People in need who live in the parish of Wretton.

Types of grants: One-off and recurrent grants according to need. Grants range from £40 to £70.

Annual grant total: In 1992/93, the charity had an income of £1,800. Relief-in-need grants to individuals totalled £1,200.

Applications: In writing to the correspondent, directly by the individual or by a third party aware of the circumstances. Applications are considered in November.

Correspondent: J E Clarke, 21 London Road, Downham Market, Norfolk PE38 9AP (0366-387387).

Oxfordshire

The Appleton Trust (Abingdon)

Eligibility: People in need who live in Appleton or Eaton.

Types of grants: One-off and recurrent grants for fuel, bereavement payments (£100) and for special hardships.

Annual grant total: About £1,300.

Applications: "Being a small community, the trustees are familiar with the circumstances of most villagers. If a family is in need, we become aware of it via the grapevine, and in an emergency the chairman and treasurer are empowered to give financial aid immediately."

Correspondent: The Rector, Appleton Rectory, Abingdon, Oxfordshire OX13 5JS (0865-862458).

Ducklington & Hardwick with Yelford Charity

Eligibility: People in need who live in the parishes of Ducklington, Hardwick and Yelford.

Types of grants: One-off grants towards heating for elderly people, assistance with playgroup fees, funeral expenses, conversion of rooms for elderly and disabled people, provision of telephone, spectacles, school holiday assistance and assistance with rent arrears.

Annual grant total: In 1993, the trust had an income of £4,700. 16 grants to individuals totalled £2,800.

Applications: In writing to the correspondent. Applications can be submitted directly by the individual or by a third party. They are considered at any time.

Correspondent: Mrs A P Shaw, Clerk, 127 Abingdon Road, Standlake, Witney, Oxfordshire OX8 7QN (0865-300615).

The Faringdon United Charities

Eligibility: People in need who live in the parishes of Faringdon, Littleworth, Great and Little Coxwell, all in Oxfordshire.

Types of grants: One-off and recurrent grants. Help is given towards pre-school playgroup fees, equipment for those with disabilities, Christmas grants to homes for the elderly or those with learning difficulties and grants to local clergy for visiting the sick. Grants cannot be given for nursing/retirement home fees, as the trust cannot commit itself to long-term support.

Annual grant total: In 1992/93, the trust had assets of £58,800 producing an income of £12,000. 70 grants of between £100 and £200 were given to individuals and organisations and totalled £9,600.

Applications: In writing to the correspondent or by telephone to the trustees throughout the year. Applications can be submitted either by the individual or by a third party on their behalf.

Correspondent: W R Jestico, Clerk, Critchleys, 10 Marlborough Street, Faringdon, Oxfordshire SN7 7JP (0367-240226).

The Lockinge & Ardington Relief-in-Need Charity

Eligibility: People in need who live in the parish of Lockinge and part of the parish of Ardington included in the hamlet of Ginge.

Types of grants: One-off and recurrent grants between £30 and £60.

Annual grant total: In 1990/91, 19 grants were given to individuals totalling £800. We have been unable to obtain more up-to-date information.

Applications: In writing to the correspondent by the individual. Applications are considered in May and November, although urgent cases can be considered at any time.

Correspondent: G K Belcher, Secretary, Lockinge Estate Office, Ardington, Wantage, Oxfordshire OX12 8PP.

Other information: This entry has not been confirmed by the trust.

The Oxford & District Good Neighbours' Fund

Eligibility: People in need who live in Oxford and surrounding areas.

Types of grants: Usually up to £50.

Annual grant total: Over £4,000.

Applications: On a form available from the correspondent. Applications can be dealt with quickly if necessary.

Correspondent: F G Ingram, 36 Saunders Road, Cowley, Oxford OX4 2EF (0865-716365).

Tetsworth Cozens Bequest

Eligibility: Widows or spinsters in need who live in the parishes of Tetsworth, Great Hasley, Lewknor, Poscombe and Stoke Talmage.

Types of grants: Regular allowances of 75 pence a week paid monthly plus a Christmas gift (from any unallocated income) of about £50.

Annual grant total: In 1993, the trust had an income of £3,250. Total expenditure was £3,000.

Applications: Either directly by the individual or through a third party, on a form available from the correspondent. Applications are considered at any time and should be supported by two referees.

Correspondent: H W Thynne, 10 Silver Street, Tetsworth, Oxen OX9 7AR (0844-281320).

● Banbury

The Banbury Charities – Bridge Estate

Eligibility: People in need who live in the former borough of Banbury as it was in 1974.

Types of grants: "Any charitable purposes for the general benefit of the inhabitants of Banbury." In 1992, the trust gave £47,000 to groups/organisations, mainly to help establish local groups and charities. £16,000 was given to individuals.

Annual grant total: In addition to the above, the trustees are also in charge of two smaller trusts that have an income of over £40,000, but which give grants totalling less than £40,000 in education grants to individuals and organisations.

Applications: In writing to the correspondent.

Correspondent: The Clerk, 36 West Bar, Banbury, Oxfordshire OX16 9RU (0295-251234).

● Bletchingdon

The Bletchingdon Charity

Eligibility: People in need who live in the parish of Bletchingdon, in particular the elderly and infirm.

Types of grants: Grants to elderly and infirm people at Christmas and Easter towards fuel bills and other needs. Help is given for travel, chiropody and television licences. Otherwise one-off grants for social welfare, education and relief-in-sickness according to need.

Annual grant total: 273 grants totalling £4,240 were made in 1993.

Applications: Generally as the trustees see a need, but applications can be made in writing to the correspondent by the

Oxfordshire

individual or by a social worker, doctor, or welfare agency.

Correspondent: H B Marsden, Chairman, Quincotts, Islip Road, Bletchingdon, Kidlington, Oxfordshire OX5 3DP (0869-350235).

Other information: The charity also seeks to support any educational, medical and social needs that will benefit the village community as a whole.

Burford

The Burford Relief-in-Need Charity

Eligibility: People in need who live within five miles of the Tolsey, Burford.

Types of grants: One-off grants according to need. The trust may give grants to relieve sudden distress, travel expenses for hospital visiting, towards fuel bills, television licences, furniture, bedding, clothing, essential household items, services such as decorating, repairs, meals on wheels etc. and recuperative holidays. Grants range from £5 to £500. Receipts are required for grants towards the cost of equipment.

Annual grant total: In 1992, the trust had an income of £2,500. Grants to 46 individuals totalled £916.

Applications: In writing to the correspondent directly by the individual, including full name, address, age, and the number of years the applicant has lived in Burford or their connection with Burford.

Correspondent: Miss M J Parker, Secretary, 3 Petheri Piece, Burford, Oxon OX18 4NH (0993-823031).

Cassington

The Cassington Parochial Charities

Eligibility: People in need who live in Cassington with priority given to almshouse tenants.

Types of grants: Probably one-off grants.

Annual grant total: No information available.

Applications: In writing to the correspondent, usually by a social worker.

Correspondent: Miss S J Partridge, Clerk, 53 Eynsham Road, Cassington, Witney, Oxon OX8 1DJ (0865-881275).

Eynsham

The Eynsham Consolidated Charity

Eligibility: People in need who live in the ancient parish of Eynsham (which covers Eynsham and part of Freeland).

Types of grants: One-off grants mainly for pensioners to help with heating costs. Grants are also given towards playgroup fees, equipment for those with disabilities and financial help following bereavement. The trust does not give recurrent grants or loans.

Annual grant total: In 1992, the trust had an income of £2,600. 31 relief-in-need grants totalled £1,680.

Applications: In writing to the correspondent. Applications can be made by the individual or by a third party. They are considered in February, May, September and November.

Correspondent: R N Mitchell, 20 High Street, Eynsham, Witney, Oxfordshire OX8 1HB.

Oxford

The City of Oxford Charities

Eligibility: People in need who have lived in the city of Oxford for at least five years.

Types of grants: One-off grants for all kinds of need.

Annual grant total: The charities have an annual income of over £30,000 but not all of this is given in grants to individuals.

Applications: Considered quarterly. There can be a quick response for emergency applications for amounts of less than £100.

Correspondent: D J V Wright, Clerk, 20 St Michael's Street, Oxford OX1 2EA (0865-792300).

Sibford Gower

The Town Estate Charity

Eligibility: People in need who live in the civil parish of Sibford Gower and Birdrop.

Types of grants: One-off and recurrent grants towards things like telephone provision. The trust also provides free home chiropody treatment.

Annual grant total: In 1993, the trust had an income of about £18,000. About £1,200 was given in grants to individuals. Grants are also given to organisations and schools in the area.

Applications: In writing to the correspondent.

Correspondent: P H Baadsgaard, Quince Cottage, Bonn's Lane, Sibford Gower, Banbury, Oxfordshire OX15 5RT.

Souldern

The Souldern United Charities

Eligibility: People in need who live in the parish of Souldern.

Types of grants: Annual recurrent grants of £15 for coal or groceries.

Annual grant total: About £600 in about 40 grants.

Applications: In writing to the correspondent.

Correspondent: J Talbot, The Barn, Souldern, Bicester, Oxfordshire OX6 9JP (0869-345450).

Steventon

The Steventon Allotments & Relief-in-Need Charity

Eligibility: People in need who live in Steventon.

Types of grants: One-off grants only.

Annual grant total: The trust's income is £85,000 a year, but most of this is not given to individuals.

Applications: In writing to the correspondent. The trust advertises regularly in the local parish magazine.

Correspondent: Carole Rogers, Clerk, Maple Rose Cottage, Milton Hill, Abingdon, Oxfordshire OX13 6AG (0865-791122).

Thame

The Thame Welfare Trust

Eligibility: People in need of all ages who live in Thame.

Types of grants: Mainly one-off but some recurrent grants according to need.

Annual grant total: The charity's income is over £2,000 a year. This is given to individuals for relief-in-need and education.

Applications: Mainly through social workers, probation officers, teachers, or a similar third party.

Correspondent: P V Playford, 22 Cedar Crescent, Thame, Oxfordshire (0844-212393).

Oxfordshire/Suffolk

● **Wallingford**

The Wallingford Municipal & Relief-in-Need Charities

Eligibility: People in need who live in the former borough of Wallingford.

Types of grants: One-off grants for necessities.

Annual grant total: About £3,500.

Applications: On a form available from the correspondent.

Correspondent: B W Picken, Clerk, 9 St Martin's Street, Wallingford, Oxfordshire OX10 0AL (0491-35373).

Suffolk

The Stowmarket Relief Trust

Eligibility: People in need who live in the town of Stowmarket. Also subject to the availability of income, people who live in the civil parishes of Stowupland, Creeting St Peter, Badley, Combs, Great Finborough, Onehouse, Haughley and Old Newton with Dagworth.

Applicants must have approached all sources of statutory benefit. People on Income Support will normally qualify. People in full-time paid employment will not normally qualify for assistance, but there are possible exceptions. People with substantial capital funds are also ineligible.

Types of grants: Normally one-off, but recurrent grants have been given in exceptional circumstances. Grants are available for virtually any purpose for which a need can be established. Examples of recent grants given include for or towards family and recuperative holidays; expenses to visit people in hospital; electricity or gas accounts; sewerage and water charges; council tax; rent arrears; buying or repairing electrical appliances; beds, bedding, clothing, footwear; adapting homes for disabled people; telephone installation charges and rental; wheelchairs for disabled people; decorating or repairing houses/fixtures and medical aids.

Annual grant total: In 1992/93, the trust had an income of £53,000. £42,000 was given in grants directly to or for the benefit of people in need.

Applications: On a form available from the correspondent. Unless there are exceptional circumstances, applications are only accepted from formal organisations or individuals on behalf of the prospective beneficiary, who have knowledge of his/her needs and family and financial circumstances eg. social worker, probation officer, citizen's advice bureau, doctor, welfare organisations etc.. Applications are usually dealt with within 10 to 14 days of receipt.

Correspondent: R J James, Clerk, 5 Oak Road, Stowupland, Stowmarket, Suffolk IP14 4DP (0449-615657).

The Suffolk Association for the Care & Resettlement of Offenders

Eligibility: People in need who are or have suffered a legal restriction on their liberty, and their families, who live in Suffolk.

Types of grants: One-off grants towards rehabilitation and education. Grants usually range from £10 to £70. Sums of money are not usually paid direct, but itemised bills will be met directly by SACRO.

Applicants are usually already being supported by, or are known to, SACRO, and should have exhausted all possible sources of statutory funds. Grants are not given towards payment of debts, fines or legal costs.

Annual grant total: Up to £2,000 if funds allow.

Applications: In writing to the correspondent. All applications must be supported by a probation officer or other professional person.

Correspondent: T H Grantham, Chief Executive, 32 Silent Street, Ipswich, Suffolk IP1 1TF (0473-213140).

● **Brockley**

The Brockley Town & Poor Estate

Eligibility: People in need who live in Brockley, including elderly people of limited means; the widowed; families where the father is out of work, ill or otherwise unable to provide, and the poorest people in the village.

Types of grants: Recurrent grants of £60, usually as rebates on electricity bills.

Annual grant total: In 1992, the trust gave 21 grants of £60 totalling over £1,200.

Applications: In writing to the correspondent. Applications are considered in December.

Correspondent: Mrs E M Coe, Suttons Farm, Brockley, Bury St Edmunds, Suffolk IP29 4AG (0284-830256).

● **Bungay**

The Bungay Town Trust

Eligibility: People in need who live in Bungay.

Types of grants: One-off and recurrent grants according to need.

Annual grant total: About £1,000.

Applications: In writing to the correspondent.

Correspondent: D Sprake, Clerk, Sprake & Kingsley, 16 Broad Street, Bungay, Suffolk NR35 1EN (0986-892721).

● **Bury St Edmunds**

The Old School Fund

Eligibility: Widows in need who live in Bury St Edmunds.

Types of grants: Probably one-off and recurrent grants according to need.

Annual grant total: About £4,000 in 1985, the most recent year for which information is available, but not all of this was given to widows in need.

Applications: In writing to the correspondent.

Correspondent: C P V Creagh, 80 Guildhall Street, Bury St Edmonds, Suffolk IP33 1QB.

Other information: This entry has not been confirmed by the trust.

● **Carlton Colville**

The Carlton Colville Fuel & Allotment Charity

Eligibility: People in need, normally over 70, who receive the basic state pension and live in the ancient parish of Carlton Colville.

Types of grants: Recurrent grants (£43 in 1993) normally for fuel and heating costs and exceptionally for transport and outings.

Annual grant total: In 1992, the trust had an income of £12,000. Total expenditure was £9,000. 182 individual grants of £40 totalled £7,280.

Applications: On a form available from the correspondent. Applications can be submitted by the individual throughout the year, although they are usually considered in April.

Correspondent: M Soloman, 59 The Street, Carlton Colville, Lowestoft, Suffolk NR33 8JP (0502-586102).

247

Suffolk

Cavendish

The George Savage Charity

Eligibility: People in need who live in Cavendish, or who are connected with the village and wish to return.

Types of grants: One-off and recurrent grants according to need.

Annual grant total: About £2,000.

Applications: In writing to the correspondent.

Correspondent: B T Ambrose, Chairman, Nether Hall, Cavendish, Sudbury, Suffolk CO10 8BX.

Chediston

The Chediston United Charities, Town & Poors' Branch

Eligibility: People in need who live in the civil parish of Chediston.

Types of grants: One-off and recurrent grants ranging from £5 to £100. Grants are given for alarm systems for elderly people, Christmas gifts, and to each child of school age or younger.

Annual grant total: In 1990/91, the trust had assets of £15,000 and an income of £2,500. 60 relief-in-need grants to individuals totalled £2,000.

Applications: In writing to the correspondent. They are considered throughout the year, although mainly in November. The trust has no formal application procedure as requests are usually made personally to the trustees.

Correspondent: Michael Stanton, Clerk, Hedgerows, Chediston, Halesworth, Suffolk IP19 0AZ (0986-875514).

Corton

The Corton Poors' Land Trust

Eligibility: People in need who live in the ancient parish of Corton.

Types of grants: Grants include Christmas gifts for elderly people, grants for chiropody treatment, taxi fares to hospital, and a recent payment for Piper Lifeline system installation and rent.

Annual grant total: Recently the trust has only given out about 20% of its income in grants (around £4,000 in 1992/93). The accumulated income is to be used to build almshouse bungalows for local people.

Applications: In writing to the correspondent. Applications can be submitted at any time directly by the individual or by an appropriate third party.

Correspondent: B N H Blake, 28 Corton Long Lane, Lowestoft, Suffolk NR32 5HA (0502-730665).

Dennington

The Dennington Consolidated Charities

Eligibility: People in need who live in the parish of Dennington.

Types of grants: One-off and recurrent grants according to need including travel expenses for hospital visiting of relatives; installation of telephone for emergency help calls for the elderly and infirm; Christmas grant to needy pensioners. Grants range from £25 to £100.

The trust does not make loans.

Annual grant total: In 1992, the trust had an income of £12,000. Expenditure totalled £10,000 including £2,300 in 60 grants to individuals.

Applications: In writing to the correspondent. Applications are considered throughout the year.

Correspondent: P H de Whalley, Clerk, Bell House, Dennington, Woodbridge, Suffolk IP13 8BZ (0728-75679).

Dunwich

Dunwich Pension Charity

Eligibility: People in need who live in the parish of Dunwich.

Types of grants: One-off grants towards fuel costs, help in cases of sickness etc..

Annual grant total: In 1992, the trust had an income of £12,700. Grants to individuals totalled £2,600, leaving £8,000 unallocated for the year.

Applications: In writing to the correspondent, including details of capital, income, the special need and statutory help available. Applications can be made directly by the individual or through a third party.

Correspondent: Major P F Rodwell, Clerk, Abbots Hill, Holton Road, Halesworth, Suffolk IP19 8HG (0986-873161).

Framlingham

The Florence Pryke Charity

Eligibility: People in need who live in Framlingham.

Types of grants: One-off grants for hospital visits, to relieve sudden distress, sickness or infirmity, or for fuel and other needs. Grants are usually for £20 to £25.

Annual grant total: In 1992/93, the trust's income was £1,275. 22 relief-in-need grants to individuals totalled £535.

Applications: In writing to the correspondent either directly by the individual or through a social worker, district nurse, doctor, or welfare agency. Applications are considered monthly, but emergencies can be acted on straight away.

Correspondent: S H Baines, Park Cottage, 8 College Road, Framlingham, Woodbridge, Suffolk IP13 9EP (0728-723452).

Gisleham

The Gisleham Relief-in-Need Charity

Eligibility: People in need who live in the parish of Gisleham.

Types of grants: One-off or recurrent grants according to need, usually of £50.

Annual grant total: In 1993, the trust had an income of £5,900. 38 grants to individuals totalled £1,900, leaving £4,000 unallocated for the year.

Applications: In writing to the correspondent.

Correspondent: N A Finch, Secretary, Shandwick, Gisleham, Lowestoft, Suffolk NR33 8DT (0502-569414).

Gislingham

The Gislingham United Charity

Eligibility: People in need who live in Gislingham.

Types of grants: One-off or recurrent grants according to need.

Annual grant total: In 1993, the trust had an income of £2,200. About 50 grants to individuals totalled £1,800.

Applications: In writing to the correspondent. Applications should be submitted directly by the individual and are considered as they occur.

Correspondent: R Moyes, 6 Broadfields Road, High Street, Gislingham, Eye, Suffolk IP23 8HX (0379-783778).

Halesworth

The Halesworth United Charities

Eligibility: People in need who live in the ancient parish of Halesworth.

Types of grants: One-off grants, generally to local organisations but some help also given directly to individuals for items such as furniture, bedding, clothing, heating appliances and recuperative holidays.

Annual grant total: £2,800 in 1992, of which about £500 was to individuals.

Applications: Directly by the individual in writing to the correspondent, including the reason a grant is required or the cost of service provision, full financial details ie. income/expenditure and, if applicable, those of the applicant's parents.

Correspondent: J R Strange, Messrs Rodwell & Co, 52 The Thoroughfare, Halesworth, Suffolk IP19 8AR (0986-872513).

Ipswich

The John Dorkin Charity

Eligibility: People in need who live in the ancient parish of St Clement, Ipswich (broadly speaking the south eastern sector of Ipswich bounded by Back Hamlet/Foxhall Road and the River Orwell). Preference for the widows and children of seamen.

Types of grants: One-off grants.

Annual grant total: In 1993, the charity's accumulated income amounted to £30,000. Grants to individuals totalled £10,000.

Applications: In writing to the correspondent at any time, giving details of financial circumstances.

Correspondent: N J Bonham-Carter, 32 Lloyds Avenue, Ipswich, Suffolk IP1 3HD (0473-213311).

Lakenheath

The Charities of George Goward & John Evans

Eligibility: People in need who live in the parish of Lakenheath in Suffolk.

Types of grants: One-off grants for medical and domestic equipment, heating and telephone bills, transport, clothing, television licences, removal fees and computer equipment for special needs pupils.

Annual grant total: About £1,800 in 9 grants in 1992.

Applications: In writing by a social worker, citizen's advice bureau, similar welfare agency or doctor, and should be submitted for the meetings in March, June and September.

Correspondent: Mrs E M Crane, 3 Roughlands, Lakenheath, Brandon, Suffolk IP27 9HA (0842-860445).

The Lakenheath Consolidated Charities

Eligibility: People in need who live in Lakenheath.

Types of grants: Usually one-off grants. Most grants are given to elderly people.

Annual grant total: About £7,000.

Applications: In writing to the correspondent.

Correspondent: P Crane, Clerk, 28 Roughlands, Lakenheath, Suffolk IP27 9HA (0842-860157).

Lowestoft

The Lowestoft Charity Board, Relief-in-Need Charity & Eleesmosynary Charity of John Wilde

Eligibility: People in need who live in the old borough of Lowestoft.

Types of grants: One-off grants only for items of clothing, furniture, course fees for an unemployed person, deposit for rented flat etc.. No recurrent grants.

Annual grant total: In 1992/93, the trust had an income of about £6,500. Total expenditure was £4,600, although it is not known how much of this was in relief-in-need grants to individuals as the trust also supports organisations.

Applications: On a form available from the correspondent. Applications can be submitted by the individual, or by a social worker, welfare agency or similar third party. They are considered as they are received.

Correspondent: John M Loftus, Clerk, Lowestoft Charity Board, 148 London North Road, Lowestoft, Suffolk NR32 1HF (0502-565146).

Melton

The Melton Trust

Eligibility: People in need who live in the ecclesiastical parish of Melton.

Types of grants: One-off and recurrent grants according to need, including Christmas gifts and bereavement tokens. Applicants must have obtained all possible statutory help.

Annual grant total: In 1993, £7,000 was given in grants to 353 people.

Applications: In writing to the correspondent. Applications can be submitted directly by the individual or through a third party. They are considered as they arrive.

Correspondent: A A Calder, Clerk, Holmwood, Melton Hill, Woodbridge, Suffolk IP12 1AX (0394-383644).

Mildenhall

The Mildenhall Parish Charities

Eligibility: People in need who live in the parish of Mildenhall.

Types of grants: One-off grants.

Annual grant total: About £5,000.

Applications: In writing to the correspondent either directly by the individual or a recognised third party.

Correspondent: T Coombs, Clerk, The Pavilion, Recreation Way, Mildenhall, Bury St Edmunds IP28 7HG (0638-713493 [24 hour telephone]).

Pakenham

The Pakenham Charities

Eligibility: People in need who live in Pakenham.

Types of grants: One-off and recurrent grants according to need.

Annual grant total: Under £5,000.

Applications: In writing to the correspondent.

Correspondent: K Heeps, Church Hill, Pakenham, Bury St Edmunds, Suffolk.

Other information: This entry has not been confirmed by the trust.

Reydon

The Reydon Poors' Allotment Charity

Eligibility: People in need who live in the parish of Reydon.

Types of grants: One-off and recurrent grants according to need. Grants have been given for travel expenses to hospital for treatment or visiting, school meals, college fees/travel, stairlift, powered

Suffolk/Surrey

wheelchair, Christmas hampers, fuel, cooking stove and new roof.

Annual grant total: £7,500 in 56 grants in 1992/93.

Applications: In writing to the correspondent. Applications can be submitted directly by the individual or through a third party. They are considered at any time.

Correspondent: Stanley Copperwheat, Mistley Thorn, Halesworth Road, Reydon, Southwold, Suffolk IP18 6NR (0502-723181).

● Risby

The Lancelot Danby & Others Charity

Eligibility: People in need who live in the parish of Risby.

Types of grants: One-off and recurrent grants according to need, primarily for the purchase of winter fuel.

Annual grant total: In 1992/93, the trust had an income of £5,000. Grants of between £40 and £100 were given to about 40 individuals.

Applications: In writing to the correspondent. Applications can be submitted by the individual, through a recognised referral agency (eg. social worker, citizen's advice bureau or doctor) or other third party and are considered in October.

Correspondent: Mrs P Wallis, 3 Woodland Close, Risby, Bury St Edmunds (0284-810649).

Other information: Occasionally grants are given to higher education students from Risely and in cases of emergency.

● Rushbrooke

Lord Jermyn's Charity

Eligibility: People in need who are over 60 and live in Rushbrooke.

Types of grants: One-off or recurrent grants according to need.

Annual grant total: In 1990/91, the trust had an income of £5,000. It is not known how much was given in grants to individuals in need.

Applications: In writing to the correspondent.

Correspondent: W C Belinger, Secretary, 1 Poplar Meadow, Rushbrooke, Bury St Edmunds, Suffolk IP30 0EW (0284-386276).

● Stanton

The Stanton Poors' Estate Charity

Eligibility: People in need who live in the parish of Stanton and who are in receipt of statutory benefits.

Types of grants: Vouchers redeemable at local shops for Christmas. Grants up to about £30 are also given for special needs at other times.

Annual grant total: £2,400 in 108 grants in 1992/93.

Applications: In writing or by telephone or personal call to the secretary. The charity advertises in a local newsletter which is distributed to every house in the parish in October each year. Applications are then considered in November.

Correspondent: A S Peacock, Secretary, 22 Drovers Rise, Shepherds Grove Park, Stanton, Bury St Edmunds, Suffolk IP31 2BW (0359-51016).

● Stutton

The Charity of Joseph Catt

Eligibility: People in need who live in the parish of Stutton.

Types of grants: One-off grants to help with fuel, hospital travel expenses, convalescent holidays, household goods, clothing, and telephone helplines.

Annual grant total: In 1992, the trust had an income of £9,000 and a total expenditure of £7,500. Grants totalling £7,000 were given to 94 individuals.

Applications: Applications can be submitted by the individual, through a recognised referral agency (eg. social worker, citizen's advice bureau or doctor) and are considered at any time.

Correspondent: K R Bales, Chairman, 34 Cattsfield, Stutton, Ipswich, Suffolk IP9 2SP (0473-328179).

● Sudbury

The Sudbury Municipal Charities

Eligibility: People in need who live within the old borough boundaries of Sudbury.

Types of grants: Ascension Day gifts for pensioners; Christmas Day gifts for men aged 65 or over, and special consideration to one-off cases of hardship. Grants range from £100 to £300.

Annual grant total: In 1993, the trust's income was £8,800; it gave £1,030 in Ascension Day gifts (171 beneficiaries) and £540 in Christmas Day gifts (18 beneficiaries). A further £2,900 was given in grants to organisations.

Applications: In writing to the correspondent for an application form. Applications can be submitted by the individual and are considered in February, April, July, October and December.

Correspondent: A C Walters, Clerk, Longstop Cottage, The Street, Lawshall, Bury St Edmunds IP29 4QA (0284-828219).

● Walberswick

The Walberswick Common Lands

Eligibility: People in need who live in Walberswick.

Types of grants: One-off and recurrent grants according to need.

Annual grant total: £2,500 in over 100 grants given to individuals for relief-in-need and education in 1987, the most recent year for which information is available.

Applications: In writing to the correspondent.

Correspondent: R G Bunscombe, Belle Vue, The Terrace, Walberswick, Southwold, Suffolk IP18 6TZ (0502-722359).

Surrey

The Association for Helping Poor Ladies

Eligibility: Elderly ladies in need who live in the former urban district of Walton and Weybridge, and who are over 60.

Types of grants: Usually one-off grants ranging from £25 to £300.

Annual grant total: £6,100 in 46 grants in 1993.

Applications: In writing to the correspondent. Applications should be submitted directly by the individual or through a social worker, citizen's advice bureau or other welfare agency. They are considered at any time.

Correspondent: Mrs Jan Wickens, Clerk, Elm Grove, Hersham Road, Walton-on-Thames, Surrey KT12 1LH (0932-252656).

John Beane's Guildford & Dorking Eleemosynary Charity

Eligibility: People in need living in areas covered by Guildford Borough Council, Waverley Borough Council and Mole Valley District Council.

Types of grants: One-off or recurrent grants according to need for children's clothing, domestic appliances, fuel, furniture etc..

Annual grant total: In 1992/93, the trust had an income of £15,000, and £17,000 was given in grants to individuals.

Applications: On a form available from the correspondent, preferably accompanied by a letter from a social worker, health visitor, citizen's advice bureau or similar third party.

Correspondent: C E Fullagar, 55–56 Quarry Street, Guildford, Surrey GU1 3UE (0483-62901).

The Dempster Trust

Eligibility: People in need who live in Farnham and surrounding villages.

Types of grants: One-off grants only. Help is not given towards rent, rates or household bills.

Annual grant total: In 1993, the trust had an income of £14,000. It is not known how much was given in grants to individuals in need.

Applications: In writing to the correspondent, either directly or through doctors, social workers, hospitals etc..

Correspondent: Mrs J P Baker, Clerk, Stream Cottage, 73 Bridgefield, Farnham, Surrey GU9 8AW (0252-726430).

The Frimley Fuel Allotments

Eligibility: People in need who live in the area of Frimley – OldCamberley – Mytchett. This consists of the wards of Old-Dean, Town, St Michaels, St Pauls, Watchetts, Frimley, Frimley-Green, Mytchett, Heatherside and Parkside.

Types of grants: One-off grants generally given directly to people in need and not to organisations providing a service. Help has been given towards fuel bills, to enable elderly people to live in their own homes, and to provide discretionary funds for headteachers for the direct benefit of pupils from poor families.

Annual grant total: In 1992/93, grants ranged from £40 to £1,000 and totalled about £55,000.

Applications: On a form available from the citizen's advice bureau or from the social service centres, submitted through a social worker or other welfare agency or neighbour. Applications should be returned to the respective social service centre by 20th November, though urgent applications can be considered at any time if supported by the councillor for the ward, the respective social service centre, or by a doctor or health visitor.

Correspondent: P E Collins, 157 Frimley Road, Camberley, Surrey GU15 2PZ (0276-22866).

Other information: The trusts income is derived from the Pine Ridge Golf Centre, an 18-hole golf course and driving range developed on 164 acres of land leased from the charity trustees.

The trust also provides a useful "Notes for applicants" on the back of the application form and a leaflet about the charity.

The Nugent Charitable Trust

Eligibility: Sick, disabled or elderly people in need who live in Godalming and south west Surrey.

Types of grants: One-off and recurrent grants according to need.

Annual grant total: The trust's income is about £7,000.

Applications: In writing to the correspondent.

Correspondent: Lord Nugent of Guildford, Blacknest Cottage, Dunsfold, Near Godalming, Surrey GU8 4PE.

The Reigate & Banstead Care Committee for Chest & Vascular Diseases

Eligibility: People in need who have chest and vascular diseases and live in the borough of Reigate and Banstead.

Types of grants: One-off grants of £25 to £30 to help with heating and telephone bills, clothing, bedding, etc.. Regular assistance is given to two or three people.

Annual grant total: In 1993, the trust gave grants totalling about £1,000.

Applications: On a form available from Surrey County Council Social Services.

Correspondent: Margaret Quine, Borough Secretary's Department, Reigate & Banstead Borough Council, Town Hall, Castlefield Road, Reigate, Surrey RH2 0SH (0737-242477).

The Henry Smith Charity

Eligibility: People in need who live in Ash and Normandy.

Types of grants: One-off or recurrent grants according to need.

Annual grant total: In 1992, the trust received £2,100 income, allocated by Henry Smith's (General Estate) Charity.

Applications: In writing to the correspondent through a social worker, citizen's advice bureau or other welfare agency.

Correspondent: J G Ades, 87 Oxenden Road, Tongham, Surrey GU10 1AR (0252-23909).

The Henry Smith Charity

Eligibility: People in need who live in Camberley, Deepcut, Frimley, Frimley Green and Mytchett.

Types of grants: Usually one-off grants to meet identified need.

Annual grant total: In 1992/93, the trust gave £930 in six grants.

Applications: In writing to the correspondent either directly or through a third party. They are considered throughout the year.

Correspondent: P R Trott, Clerk, Surrey Heath Borough Council, Surrey Heath House, Knoll Road, Camberley, Surrey GU15 3HD (0276-686252).

The Henry Smith Charity

Eligibility: Widows or people over 60 who are in need, of good character and have lived in the parishes of Long Ditton and Tolworth for the past five years.

Types of grants: Grants of £25 (in 1994) to be spent on coal or coke, clothing or footwear at named retailers.

Annual grant total: In 1993, the trust had an income of £3,000, allocated by Henry Smith's (General Estate) Charity.

Applications: In writing to the appropriate correspondent.

Correspondent: *For Tolworth:* D G Reynolds, 30 Douglas Road, Surbiton, Surrey KT6 7SA (081-399 1548); *For Long Ditton:* R L Howard, 19 Orchard Avenue, Thames Ditton, Surrey KT7 0BB (081-398 3247).

The Henry Smith Charity

Eligibility: People in need who live in Send and Ripley.

Types of grants: One-off or recurrent grants according to need.

Annual grant total: In 1992, the trust received £2,800 income, allocated by Henry Smith's (General Estate) Charity.

Applications: In writing to the correspondent.

Surrey

Correspondent: H L Powell-Cullingford, Hay Place, Kiln Lane, Ripley, Surrey GU23 6EX (0483-225303).

The Henry Smith Charity (I Wood Estate)

Eligibility: People in need who live in Chertsey, Addlestone, New Haw and Lyne.

Types of grants: Fuel vouchers to elderly people which can be used as part payment of fuel bills.

Annual grant total: In 1993, the trust had an income of £14,750, allocated by Henry Smith's (General Estate) Charity.

Applications: In writing to the correspondent.

Correspondent: B Fleckney, c/o Civic Offices, Runnymede Borough Council, Station Road, Addlestone, Surrey KT15 2XL.

The Surrey Voluntary Association for the Blind

Eligibility: Blind and partially-sighted people who live in the administrative county of Surrey.

Types of grants: One-off grants for most kinds of need, including holidays. The association awards standard holiday grants of £20. General grants have no set maximum, but are usually under £200. Grants are given for equipment and a sudden domestic need such as a high fuel bill or an urgent household repair. Interest-free loans are occasionally given.

Annual grant total: In 1992/93, the association had assets of £695,000, generating an income of £91,000. Total expenditure for the year was £67,000. General grants to individuals totalled £6,500 (108 grants); holiday grants totalled £8,500 (325 grants).

Applications: On a form available from the correspondent. Applications can be submitted at any time by the individual or through a social worker, welfare agency, club or any recognised organisation for blind or partially-sighted people.

Correspondent: D C Jones, General Secretary, Rentwood, School Lane, Fetcham, Leatherhead, Surrey KT22 9JX (0372-377701).

The Witley Charitable Trust

Eligibility: People in need who live in the parishes of Witley and Milford which may include Grayswood.

Types of grants: One-off or recurrent grants according to need. Telephone, electricity and gas debts (up to about £150) can be paid usually via social services. Medical appliances not available through the Health Service can be purchased eg. £250 was paid for mobile oxygen. At Christmas eight, £20 grants/hampers were given. Grants are also given for educational purposes and to organisations.

No grants to pay taxes or to contribute to public funds.

Annual grant total: In 1993, the trust had an income of over £4,000, £2,400 of which was received from Henry Smith's (General Estate) Charity. Nine individuals received grants totalling nearly £1,200.

Applications: On a form available from the correspondent or other trustees, to be submitted through nurses, doctors, social workers, citizen's advice bureau etc. but not directly by the individual. Applications are considered in February and September.

Correspondent: K C Murfitt, Tyrella, Manor Lea Road, Milford, Godalming, Surrey GU8 5EF (0483-417152).

The Wonersh Charities

Eligibility: People in need who live in the parish of Wonersh, Shamley Green and Blackheath. (There is a preference for elderly people.)

Types of grants: Four grants of £55 to £90 a year to 34 recipients. Christmas grants and vouchers are also given.

Annual grant total: In 1993, the trust had an income of £3,000 most of which was received from Henry Smith's (General Estate) Charity. Grants totalled £2,200.

Applications: In writing to the correspondent preferably through a third party eg. citizen's advice bureau, trustee, local clergy or other similar organisation.

Correspondent: Miss C M Glover, 17 Josephs Road, Guildford, Surrey GU1 1DN (0483-64533).

● Abinger

The Henry Smith Charity

Eligibility: People in need who live in the parish of Abinger.

Types of grants: One-off or recurrent grants according to need.

Annual grant total: In 1992, the trust received £12,800 income, allocated by Henry Smith's (General Estate) Charity.

Applications: In writing to the correspondent either directly by the individual or through a third party. Applications are considered at any time.

Correspondent: Mrs V Hepplewhite, Badger's Mount, Hoe Lane, Abinger Hammer, Dorking, Surrey RH5 6RS.

● Albury

The Henry Smith Charity

Eligibility: People in need who live in Albury.

Types of grants: One-off or recurrent grants according to need.

Annual grant total: In 1993, the trust received £3,600 income, allocated by Henry Smith's (Warbleton Estate) Charity.

Applications: In writing to the correspondent.

Correspondent: Mrs B A D Prentis, Greensward Cottage, Albury, Guildford, Surrey GU5 9DJ.

● Alford

The Henry Smith Charity

Eligibility: People in need who live in Alfold and have done so for at least five years.

Types of grants: Grocery vouchers worth £30 for exchange in the village store.

Annual grant total: In 1992, the trust received £1,150 income, allocated by Henry Smith's (General Estate) Charity.

Applications: The correspondent states: "no applications required".

Correspondent: F G G Field, Martyns, Linersh Wood, Bramley, Guildford, Surrey GU5 0EE (0483-892237).

● Banstead

The Henry Smith Charity

Eligibility: People in need who live in the parish of Banstead.

Types of grants: One-off grants according to need.

Annual grant total: In 1992, the trust received £4,800 income, allocated by Henry Smith's (General Estate) Charity.

Applications: In writing to the correspondent. Applications should be submitted through a social worker, citizen's advice bureau or other welfare agency. They are considered in February and November.

Correspondent: Mrs E White, 5 Sutton Lane, Banstead, Surrey SM7 3QW (0737-352926).

Surrey

Betchworth

Betchworth United Charities

Eligibility: People in need who live in the old parish of Betchworth including Brockham.

Types of grants: Twice yearly distribution to pensioners according to need, plus consideration for special need.

Annual grant total: In 1992, the trust received £16,000 income, allocated by Henry Smith's (General Estate) Charity.

Applications: In writing to the correspondent.

Correspondent: Mrs V F Houghton, Brick Field, 20 Kiln Lane, Betchworth, Surrey RH3 7LX (0737-843342).

Bisley

The Henry Smith Charity

Eligibility: People in need who live in Bisley and have done so for at least three years.

Types of grants: One-off or recurrent grants according to need.

Annual grant total: In 1992, the trust had an income of £1,800, allocated from Henry Smith's (General Estates) Charity.

Applications: In writing to the correspondent.

Correspondent: Mrs P K Hockley, Appledore, 2 Queens Close, Bisley, Surrey GU24 9AL (0483-487798).

Bletchingley

The Henry Smith Charity

Eligibility: People in need who live in Bletchingley.

Types of grants: One-off or recurrent grants according to need.

Annual grant total: In 1993, the trust received £12,800 income, allocated by Henry Smith's (General Estate) Charity.

Applications: In writing to the correspondent.

Correspondent: Mrs C A Bolshaw, Cleves, Castle Street, Bletchingley, Surrey RH1 4QA (0883-743000).

Bramley

The Henry Smith Charity

Eligibility: People in need who live in the vicinity of Bramley.

Types of grants: One-off or recurrent grants according to need.

Annual grant total: In 1993, the trust received £2,100 income, allocated by Henry Smith's (General Estate) Charity.

Applications: In writing to the correspondent.

Correspondent: D Morley, 6 Brambles Park, Bramley, Surrey GU5 0BA (0483-894138).

Byfleet

The Byfleet Pensions Fund

Eligibility: Elderly people in need who have lived in the parish of Byfleet (as it was on 1st November 1918) for at least two years before applying.

Types of grants: Monthly pensions for as long as the beneficiary lives in the parish. Vacancies for pensions are infrequent.

Annual grant total: About £1,400 in 1993 (three pensions of £39 per month).

Applications: By letter or telephone to the correspondent. Applicants will be visited and assessed.

Correspondent: Mrs M A Jones, Clerk, c/o Stoop Court, Leisure Lane, West Byfleet, Surrey KT14 6HF (0932-340943).

Capel

Henry Smith's Charity

Eligibility: People in need who live in Capel.

Types of grants: One-off or recurrent grants according to need.

Annual grant total: In 1992, the trust received £1,400 income, allocated by Henry Smith's (General Estate) Charity.

Applications: In writing to the correspondent.

Correspondent: A E Posner, Fermain, Beare Green, Dorking, Surrey RH5 4QE (0306-711386).

Carshalton

The Carshalton Aid-in-Sickness Fund

Eligibility: People in need who live in the former urban district of Carshalton.

Types of grants: One-off or recurrent grants according to need.

Annual grant total: About £2,000 in 1993.

Applications: In writing to the correspondent.

Correspondent: Mrs Hilda Harding, Clerk, 1 St Mary's Court, 56 Bute Road, Wallington, Surrey SM6 8BU (081-647 7154).

Charlwood

Henry Smith's Charity

Eligibility: Disabled people or those over 65 and in need who live in the old parish of Charlwood.

Types of grants: One-off or recurrent grants. Help is given in the form of an annual gift of £30 to disabled people and those over 65, and, for example, towards the cost of television licences and "community alarms".

Annual grant total: In 1993, the trust received £8,000 income, allocated by Henry Smith's (General Estate) Charity. £2,350 was given to 65 individuals.

Applications: Applications can be submitted by the individual, through a recognised referral agency (eg. social worker, citizen's advice bureau or doctor) or other third party, and are generally considered in November. Details of any disability or special need should be given.

Correspondent: Mrs J M Shelley, 4 Norwood Hill Road, Charlwood, Horley, Surrey RH6 0ED (0293-862646).

Chertsey

The Chertsey Combined Charity

Eligibility: People in need who live in the electoral divisions of the former urban district of Chertsey.

Types of grants: One-off and recurrent grants according to need.

Annual grant total: In 1987/88, the trust's income was £41,000; it gave £10,000 in fuel vouchers, £8,000 in Christmas grants and two other grants of £1,000 each to individuals. The surplus of unallocated income for the year was £15,000. According to the Charity Comission in 1993, the trust had an income of £56,000.

Applications: On a form available from the correspondent.

Correspondent: M R O Sullivan, Secretary, PO Box 89, Weybridge, Surrey KT13 8HW.

Other information: This entry has not been confirmed by the trust.

Surrey

Chessington

The Chessington Charities

Eligibility: People in need who live in the parish of St Mary the Virgin, Chessington.

Types of grants: Usually one-off grants plus Christmas gifts to elderly people who are on basic income and Income Support.

Annual grant total: In 1992, the trust received £3,200 income, allocated by Henry Smith's (General Estate) Charity.

Applications: In writing to the correspondent.

Correspondent: Mrs A Hollis, 26 Bolton Road, Chessington, Surrey KT9 2JB (081-397 4733).

Chiddingfold

The Henry Smith Charity

Eligibility: People in need who live in Chiddingfold.

Types of grants: Christmas vouchers distributed in November/December, which can be used only in local shops.

Annual grant total: In 1993, the trust received £3,000 income, allocated by Henry Smith's (General Estate) Charity.

Applications: The vouchers are distributed immediately after the charity receives the grant from the main Henry Smith Charity in London. No money is available the rest of the year.

Correspondent: P J Heavens, Lindfield, Ridgley Road, Chiddingfold, Surrey GU8 4QW.

Chobham

The Chobham Poor Allotment Charity

Eligibility: People in need who live in the ancient parish of Chobham which includes the civil parishes of Chobham and West End.

Types of grants: One-off grants between £20 and £100 for gas and electricity bills, holidays and grocery vouchers.

Annual grant total: About 350 grants totalling £19,000 in 1992/93.

Applications: On a form available from the correspondent. Applications should be submitted directly by the individual in October for annual grants. Special cases can be considered at any time.

Correspondent: R V Steer, 37 Cedar Close, Bagshot, Surrey GU19 5AB (0276-473689).

The Henry Smith Charity

Eligibility: People in need who live in the ancient parish of Chobham.

Types of grants: Annual distribution to 300 to 350 people.

Annual grant total: About £4,000.

Applications: In writing to the correspondent.

Correspondent: R V Steer, 37 Cedar Close, Bagshot, Surrey GU19 5AB (0276-473689).

Cobham

The Henry Smith Charity

Eligibility: People in need who live in the ancient parish of Cobham.

Types of grants: One-off or recurrent grants according to need.

Annual grant total: In 1993, the trust had an income of £7,000, allocated by Henry Smith's (General Estate) Charity.

Applications: In writing to the correspondent.

Correspondent: D C Taylor, Appleton, 4 Cedar Avenue, Cobham, Surrey KT11 2AB.

Crowhurst

The Henry Smith Charity

Eligibility: People in need who live in Crowhurst (Surrey).

Types of grants: One-off or recurrent grants according to need.

Annual grant total: In 1993, the trust received £3,200 income, allocated by Henry Smith's (Worth Estate) Charity.

Applications: In writing to the correspondent.

Correspondent: Mrs P Cook, Church Farm Cottage, Crowhurst, Lingfield, Surrey RH7 6LR (0342-834121).

Dorking

The Henry Smith Charity

Eligibility: People in need who live in Dorking.

Types of grants: One-off or recurrent grants according to need. Grants are also given to local homes for elderly people.

Annual grant total: About 4 to 6 individuals receive around £1,000.

Applications: In writing to the correspondent, usually referred through social services or a citizen's advice bureau.

Correspondent: D Matanle, Homefield, 5 Fortyfoot Road, Leatherhead, Surrey KT22 8RP (0372-370073).

Dunsfold

The Henry Smith Charity

Eligibility: People in need who live in Dunsfold and who have done so for the past five years.

Types of grants: Grocery vouchers for £35 exchangeable in the village store.

Annual grant total: In 1992, the trust received £2,100 income, allocated by Henry Smith's (General Estate) Charity.

Applications: In writing to the correspondent. They are considered in December.

Correspondent: F G G Field, Martyns, Linersh Wood, Bramley, Guildford, Surrey GU5 0EE (0483-892237).

East & West Horsley

Lady Noel Byron's Nursing Association

Eligibility: People in need who live in the parishes of East and West Horsley.

Types of grants: One-off or recurrent grants according to need for medically related purposes only. This has included grants towards buying wheelchairs, first aid equipment, a special matress, convalescence and counselling.

Annual grant total: In 1992/93, the trust had an income of £5,000. Nine grants to individuals totalled £3,500.

Applications: In writing to the correspondent. Applications can be made directly by the individual or through a social worker, other welfare agency or third party. They are considered in November.

Correspondent: J R Miles, Chairman, Postboys, Cranmore Lane, West Horsley, Leatherhead, Surrey KT24 6BX (0483-284141).

Henry Smith's Charity

Eligibility: People in need who live in East Horsley.

Types of grants: One-off or recurrent grants according to need.

Annual grant total: In 1993, the trust received £700 income, allocated by Henry Smith's (General Estate) Charity.

Applications: In writing to the correspondent.

Correspondent: Mrs A Jackson, Sable Lodge, Pine Walk, East Horsley, Surrey KT24 5AG (0486-54844).

East Molesey

The Henry Smith Charity

Eligibility: People in need who live in East Molesey St Mary.

Types of grants: One-off or recurrent grants according to need.

Annual grant total: Probably about £1,000.

Applications: In writing to the correspondent.

Correspondent: Rev Don Adams, The Vicarage, St Mary's Road, East Molesey, Surrey KT8 0ST (081-979 1441).

The Henry Smith Charity

Eligibility: People aged over 60 who are in need and live in East Molesey St Paul.

Types of grants: One-off grants of £20 to single people and £30 to married couples paid around Christmas.

Annual grant total: In 1993, the trust had an income of about £600 to £700, allocated by Henry Smith's (General Estate) Charity. All of this was distributed to 33 households.

Applications: In writing to the correspondent.

Correspondent: Mrs J Porter, 4 Hurst Lane, East Molesey, Surrey KT8 9EB (081-979 3849).

Effingham

The Henry Smith Charity

Eligibility: People in need who live in Effingham.

Types of grants: One-off or recurrent grants according to need. Grants are generally of £50 to £100; many grants are given at Christmas.

Annual grant total: About £2,000 divided between 20 to 30 people.

Applications: In writing to the correspondent.

Correspondent: C E W Crouch, 85 Woodlands Road, Little Bookham, Leatherhead, Surrey KT23 4HL (0372-452232).

Egham

The Egham United Charity

Eligibility: People in need who live in the ancient parish of Egham.

Types of grants: One-off grants to alleviate immediate need.

Annual grant total: About £1,000.

Applications: On a form available from the correspondent.

Correspondent: G A J Cameron, Clerk, 20 Willow Walk, Englefield Green, Surrey TW20 0DQ.

Epsom

The Epsom Parochial Charities

Eligibility: People in need who live in the ancient parish of Epsom.

Types of grants: One-off or recurrent grants according to need.

Annual grant total: £11,000 in 1993, but not all of this was given to individuals.

Applications: On a form available from the correspondent. Applications can be submitted directly by the individual and are usually considered in February, May, August and November.

Correspondent: Mrs M West, Clerk, 38 Woodcote Hurst, Epsom, Surrey KT18 7DT.

Esher

The Henry Smith & Lynch Charity

Eligibility: People in need who live in the ancient parish of Esher.

Types of grants: Annual grants of £45 towards fuel bills for elderly or sick people or families with young children who are living on low pensions or Income Support. Emergency grants of £45 to £75 towards for example nursery school fees, a second hand bike (to enable the applicant to get to work) and a double buggy.

Annual grant total: In 1993, the trust had an income of £3,600, allocated by Henry Smith's (General Estate) Charity. 37 grants totalled £1,730. The trust has £5,000 available for distribution in 1993/94.

Applications: In writing to the correspondent. Applications can be submitted directly by the individual or through a third party. Annual grants are considered in November/December, emergency grants at any time.

Correspondent: Mrs G B Barnett, Clerk, 24 Pelhams Walk, Esher, Surrey KT10 8QD.

Ewell

The Ewell Parochial Trusts

Eligibility: People in need who live in the ancient ecclesiastical parish of Ewell and the liberty of Kingswood.

Types of grants: One-off or recurrent grants according to need.

Annual grant total: In 1992, the trust had an income of £61,000, it is not known how much of this was given in grants to individuals.

Applications: In writing to the correspondent.

Correspondent: Geoffrey Berry, 2 Portway Crescent, Ewell, Epsom, Surrey KT17 1SX (081-393 5979).

Gatton

The Henry Smith Charity

Eligibility: People in need who live in the parish of Gatton.

Types of grants: One-off or recurrent grants according to need.

Annual grant total: In 1993, the trust received £3,200 income, allocated by Henry Smith's (Worth Estate) Charity.

Applications: In writing to the correspondent.

Correspondent: Rev R J M Grosvenor, The Rectory, Gatton Bottom, Merstham, Surrey RH1 3BH (0737-643755).

Godstone

The Henry Smith Charity

Eligibility: People in need who live in the parish of Godstone (Blindley Heath, South Godstone and Godstone Village).

Types of grants: Food vouchers and electricity stamps given in December and February according to need. One-off grants are given mainly for urgent medical attention. Grants are also given to local organisations.

Annual grant total: In 1993, the trust received £8,000 income, allocated by Henry Smith's (General Estate) Charity. Total expenditure was £6,200, of which £4,700 was given to 135 households (29 families and 106 single people).

Surrey

Applications: In writing to the correspondent or through local trustees, doctors, social workers, the British Legion or local grocers.

Correspondent: Mrs P Rodgers, 61 Hickmans Close, Godstone, Surrey RH9 8EB (0883-743182).

Guildford

The Guildford Relief-in-Need Charities

Eligibility: People in need who live in Guildford.

Types of grants: Weekly and one-off grants for clothing, furniture, holidays and other necessities.

Annual grant total: £47,000.

Applications: On a form available from the correspondent preferably accompanied by a letter from a social worker, health visitor or similar third party.

Correspondent: C E Fullagar, 56 Quarry Street, Guildford, Surrey GU1 3UE (0483-62901).

The Guildford Relief-in-Sickness Charity

Eligibility: People living in Guildford who are sick or convalescing and who are in recognised need.

Types of grants: One-off grants for convalescent holidays, coal, clothing, nursing home fees and medical appliances.

Annual grant total: £3,400.

Applications: On a form available from the correspondent preferably accompanied by a letter from a social worker, health visitor or similar third party.

Correspondent: C E Fullagar, 56 Quarry Street, Guildford, Surrey GU1 3UE (0483-62901).

The Mayor of Guildford's Christmas Distress Fund

Eligibility: People in need who live in the borough of Guildford.

Types of grants: Probably one-off or recurrent grants according to need.

Annual grant total: £11,000.

Applications: In writing to the correspondent.

Correspondent: The Mayor's Secretary, The Mayor's Parlour, Millmead House, Guildford, Surrey GU2 5BB.

Hambledon

The Henry Smith Charity

Eligibility: People in need who live in Hambledon.

Types of grants: An annual grant is made to Hambledon Parish Coucil who distribute it at Christmas to about 35 people.

Annual grant total: In 1992, the trust received £525 income, allocated by Henry Smith's (General Estate) Charity.

Applications: In writing to the correspondent.

Correspondent: P A Vacher, The Country Counter, Salt Lane, Hyde Stile, Godalming, Surrey GU8 4DF (0483-416746).

Hascombe

The Henry Smith Charity

Eligibility: People, generally pensioners, in need who live in Hascombe.

Types of grants: Generally grants given at Christmas.

Annual grant total: In 1993, the trust received £1,800 income, allocated by Henry Smith's (General Estate) Charity, of which £700 is held in reserve. £1,000 was given in 22 grants to individuals.

Applications: In writing to the correspondent.

Correspondent: F W Moss, Clerk of Hascombe Parish Council, Pembroke, The Drive, Godalming, Surrey GU7 1PF (0483-421415).

Headley

The Henry Smith Charity

Eligibility: People in need who live in Headley.

Types of grants: Annual and one-off grants according to need.

Annual grant total: In 1992, the trust received £6,400 income, allocated by Henry Smith's (General Estate) Charity.

Applications: In writing to the correspondent or trustees.

Correspondent: The Secretary, Sunnyside, Tot Hill, Headley, Epsom, Surrey KT18 6PY (0372-377556).

Horley

The Henry Smith Charity

Eligibility: Single people and married couples aged 75 and over and who have lived in the parish of Horley and Salfords for a minimum of 25 years.

Types of grants: Grants are given as vouchers for Waitrose Ltd.

Annual grant total: In 1992, the trust received £8,000 income, allocated by Henry Smith's (General Estate) Charity.

Applications: In writing to the correspondent.

Correspondent: Miss A Middlecote, 26 Victoria Close, Horley, Surrey RH6 7AP (0293-782425).

Other information: Grants are also given to first year students for books.

Horne

The Henry Smith Charity

Eligibility: People in need who live in the ancient parish of Horne.

Types of grants: One-off or recurrent grants according to need.

Annual grant total: In 1992, the trust received £8,000 income, allocated by Henry Smith's (General Estate) Charity.

Applications: In writing to the trustees.

Correspondent: Mrs D Ledwidge, Secretary, Hilarion, Wilmots Lane, Horne, Horley, Surrey RH6 9JR (0342-842823).

Horsell

The Henry Smith Charity

Eligibility: People in need who live in the parish of Horsell.

Types of grants: The trust distributes electricity savings stamps (to a value of £17) to help towards the quarterly bills.

Annual grant total: In 1992, the trust received £700 income, allocated by Henry Smith's (General Estate) Charity. £680 was given in 40 grants.

Applications: In writing to the correspondent. Applications should be submitted through a social worker, citizen's advice bureau or other welfare agency or third party eg. vicar. They are considered in December.

Correspondent: M S Couper, 17 Pine Close, Horsell, Woking, Surrey GU21 4SJ (0483-770920).

Surrey

Leatherhead

The Leatherhead United Charities

Eligibility: People in need who live in the area of the former Leatherhead urban district council.

Types of grants: One-off grants. Help towards heating bills for the elderly, unexpected expenditure (eg. damage caused by fire/flooding) and children's clothing.

Annual grant total: In 1992, the trust had assets of £500,000 generating an income of £64,000. Total expenditure was £62,000. Grants ranging from £50 to £1,000 were given to 50 individuals and totalled £5,300. In 1992, the trust was allocated about £22,000 by Henry Smith's (General Estate) Charity.

Applications: On a form available from the correspondent and submitted through a recognised referral agency (eg. social worker, citizen's advice bureau or doctor) giving details of income and the names of two referees. Applications are considered monthly.

Correspondent: D Mantale, Homefield, 5 Fortyfoot Road, Leatherhead, Surrey KT22 8RP (0372-370073).

Leigh

The Henry Smith Charity

Eligibility: People in need who live in Leigh.

Types of grants: The trust has a list of all people over 65; each receives support at Christmas in the form of food vouchers, or help with gas and electricity. Gifts may also be given at Easter in the years when the trust receives more income.

Annual grant total: In 1993, the trust received £6,400 income, allocated by Henry Smith's (General Estate) Charity.

Applications: In writing or by telephone to the correspondent, or through a third party.

Correspondent: Mrs J Sturt, Fortune Farmhouse, Mynthurst, Leigh, Reigate, Surrey RH2 8RJ (0293-862225).

Merstham

The Henry Smith Charity

Eligibility: People in need who live in the parish of Merstham.

Types of grants: One-off or recurrent grants according to need, ranging from £30 to £40.

Annual grant total: In 1993, the trust received £4,800 income, allocated by Henry Smith's (General Estate) Charity. 67 grants totalled £3,200, but not all was given to individuals.

Applications: On a form available from the correspondent. Applications are considered in December/January.

Correspondent: C C Morris, The Cottage, Quality Street, Merstham, Surrey RH1 3BB (0737-642012).

Newdigate

The Henry Smith Charity

Eligibility: People in need who live in the parish of Newdigate.

Types of grants: One-off or recurrent grants according to need.

Annual grant total: In 1992, the trust received £8,000 income, allocated by Henry Smith's (General Estate) Charity.

Applications: In writing to the correspondent.

Correspondent: Miss B Norman, 4 Oaks, Village Street, Newdigate, Dorking, Surrey RH5 5DH.

Nutfield

The Henry Smith Charity

Eligibility: People in need who live in Nutfield.

Types of grants: One-off grants ranging from £25 to £40.

Annual grant total: In 1993, the trust received £6,400 income, allocated by Henry Smith's (General Estate) Charity. 89 grants totalled about £6,000, but not all were to individuals.

Applications: In writing to the correspondent. Applications are considered in December and can be submitted by anyone who knows of someone in need.

Correspondent: Miss N E Kempsell, 1 Church Hill, Nutfield, Redhill, Surrey RH1 4JA (0737-822227).

Ockley

The Henry Smith Charity

Eligibility: People in need who live in Ockley.

Types of grants: Annual gift of cash or coal worth £80. Special grants for special needs ranging from £100 to £200.

Annual grant total: In 1993, the trust received £9,600 income, allocated by Henry Smith's (General Estate) Charity. 50 grants to individuals totalled £2,700. Other grants are given to organisations.

Applications: In writing to the correspondent. Applications can be submitted directly by the individual or through a third party. They are considered at any time.

Correspondent: R Coates, Orchard Cottage, Friday Street, Ockley, Dorking, Surrey RH5 5TE.

Oxted

The Henry Smith Charity

Eligibility: People in need who live in Oxted.

Types of grants: One-off or recurrent grants according to need.

Annual grant total: In 1992, the trust received £6,400 income, allocated by Henry Smith's (General Estate) Charity.

Applications: In writing to the correspondent.

Correspondent: S Cowlard, 2 Oakleigh Court, Church Lane, Oxted, Surrey RH8 9PT (0883-717752).

Peper Harow

The Henry Smith Charity

Eligibility: People in need who live in Peper Harow.

Types of grants: Grants of about £40 paid at Christmas and Easter.

Annual grant total: About 10 people receive grants totalling £800 to £1,000.

Applications: In writing to the correspondent or by word of mouth through the trustees, local shopkeepers, doctor, social services etc..

Correspondent: F Parsons, Somerset Farm, Shackleford Road, Elstead, Godalming, Surrey GU8 6LB (0252-702404).

Pirbright

The Pirbright Relief-in-Need Charity

Eligibility: People in need who live in the parish of Pirbright.

Types of grants: One-off or recurrent grants for a variety of needs, including buying or renting medical equipment to use at home.

Annual grant total: About £1,000 in 1992/93.

Surrey

Applications: In writing to the correspondent directly by the individual, social worker, citizen's advice bureau, other welfare agency or third party.

Correspondent: P B Lawson, Stanemore, Rowe Lane, Pirbright, Surrey GU24 0LX (0483-472842).

● Puttenham

The Henry Smith Charity

Eligibility: People in need who live in Puttenham or, exceptionally, immediately outside the parish.

Types of grants: One-off or recurrent grants according to need.

Annual grant total: In 1992, the trust received £700 income, allocated by Henry Smith's (General Estate) Charity.

Applications: To the correspondent or any other trustee.

Correspondent: P B Smith, Farm Cottage, The Heath, Puttenham, Guildford, Surrey GU3 1AJ (0483-810352).

● Pyrford

The Pyrford Charities

Eligibility: People in need who live in the ancient parish of Pyrford.

Types of grants: Vouchers given for food, fuel or clothing.

Annual grant total: £2,700 in 29 grants in 1992/93.

Applications: In writing to the correspondent either directly or through a third party. Applications are considered in October/November.

Correspondent: Mrs D M Mossini, Charleroi, 1 Floyds Lane, Pyrford, Woking, Surrey GU22 8TF (0932-344041).

● Shalford

The Henry Smith Charity

Eligibility: People in need who live in Shalford.

Types of grants: One-off or recurrent grants according to need, ranging from £25 to £50.

Annual grant total: About £2,000 in 49 grants in 1992/93.

Applications: In writing to the correspondent, with recommendation by a doctor, citizen's advice bureau or other third party. Applications are considered in March.

Correspondent: J D Surrey, 39 Summersbury Drive, Shalford, Guildford, Surrey GU4 8JG (0483-574473).

● Shere

The Shere Charity for Relief-in-Need

Eligibility: People in need who live in the parish of Shere (this includes Gomshall, Peaslake and Holmbury St Mary).

Types of grants: One-off or recurrent grants according to need, where assistance cannot be obtained elsewhere.

Annual grant total: In 1992, the trust received £16,000 income from by Henry Smith's (General Estate) Charity.

Applications: In writing to the correspondent.

Correspondent: R C Callingham, Clerk, 3 Pilgrims Way, Shere, Guildford, Surrey GU5 9HR (0486-412450).

● Shottermill

The Henry Smith Charity

Eligibility: People in need who live in the parish of Shottermill.

Types of grants: One-off or recurrent grants according to need. A distribution is usually made at Christmas, but emergencies can be considered at other times.

Annual grant total: In 1993, the trust received £700 income, allocated by Henry Smith's (General Estate) Charity.

Applications: In writing to the correspondent.

Correspondent: T A Gittins, 61 Shepherds Way, Liphook, Hants GU30 7HH.

● Staines

The Staines Parochial Charities

Eligibility: People in need who live in the urban district of Staines.

Types of grants: One-off and recurrent grants according to need.

Annual grant total: About £5,000.

Applications: In writing to the correspondent.

Correspondent: The Director of Finance, Spelthorne Borough Council, Council Offices, Knowle Green, Staines, Middlesex TW18 1XB (0784-446221).

● Stoke D'Abernon

The Henry Smith Charity

Eligibility: People in need who live in Stoke D'Abernon.

Types of grants: One-off or recurrent grants according to need.

Annual grant total: In 1992, the trust had an income of £1,800, allocated by Henry Smith's (General Estate) Charity.

Applications: In writing to the correspondent.

Correspondent: Mrs H C Lee, Beggars Roost, Blundel Lane, Stoke D'Abernon, Cobham, Surrey KT11 2SF (0932-863107).

● Sunbury

The Sunbury Fuel Allotment Trust

Eligibility: People on a limited income, particularly pensioners. Applicants must live in the parish of St Mary's Church, Sunbury-on-Thames and must either have been born there or have lived in the parish for a large number of years.

Types of grants: Allowances of £40 to £45, or 5 bags of household coal or 4 bags of smokeless fuel whichever is preferred, delivered two weeks before Christmas.

Annual grant total: In 1990/91, the trust's income was £3,100. 32 relief-in-need grants totalled about £1,200.

Applications: On a form available from the correspondent. Applications can be submitted directly by the individual or by a social worker, citizen's advice bureau or other welfare agency. They are considered in November.

Correspondent: Mrs J Fiddes, 31a Warren Road, Ashford Common, Ashford, Middlesex TW15 1TU (0932-787559).

● Tandridge

The Henry Smith Charity

Eligibility: People in need who live in the parish of Tandridge.

Types of grants: One-off grants of about £100.

Annual grant total: In 1992, the trust received £6,400 income, allocated by Henry Smith's (General Estate) Charity. Grants to 20 individuals totalled £2,000.

Applications: In writing to the correspondent. Applications should be submitted directly by the individual. They are considered in November.

Thorpe

The Henry Smith Charity

Eligibility: People in need who live in the ancient parish of Thorpe.

Types of grants: In 1992/93, 12 grants of solid fuel to the value of £42 were given. Other one-off and recurrent grants are occasionally given according to need.

Annual grant total: In 1992/93, the trust had an income of £3,600, allocated by Henry Smith's (General Estate) Charity. 58 grants to individuals totalled £2,400.

Applications: In writing to the correspondent by the end of October. Applications are considered in November.

Correspondent: B J Price, Clerk, 29 Grange Road, Egham, Surrey TW20 9QP.

Thursley

The Thursley Charities

Eligibility: People in need who live in the parish of Thursley and that part of the parish of Haslemere formerly in the parish of Thursley.

Types of grants: According to need.

Annual grant total: In 1993, the trust received £2,450 income, allocated by Henry Smith's (General Estate) Charity.

Applications: In writing to the correspondent.

Correspondent: B E Camp, Hollies, Thursley, Godalming, Surrey GU8 6QN (0252-703408).

Walton-on-the-Hill

The Henry Smith Charity

Eligibility: People in need who live in Walton-on-the-Hill.

Types of grants: One-off or recurrent grants according to need.

Annual grant total: In 1992/93, the trust received £3,200 income, allocated by Henry Smith's (General Estate) Charity.

Applications: In writing to the correspondent.

Correspondent: Mrs J I Woodhouse, 9 Evesham Road, Reigate, Surrey RH2 9DF (0737-244083).

Correspondent: Mrs C Scott, Goulds Farm, Hare Lane, Lingfield, Surrey RH7 6JA.

West Clandon

The Henry Smith Charity

Eligibility: People in need who live in West Clandon, and have done so for at least five years.

Types of grants: Gifts are in the form of vouchers for a local supermarket and are distributed annually in late November or early December.

Annual grant total: In 1992, the trust received £1,750 income, allocated by Henry Smith's (General Estate) Charity.

Applications: In writing to the correspondent.

Correspondent: Mrs V B Golden, 68 Meadowlands, West Clandon, Guildford, Surrey GU4 7TB (0483-222843).

West Horsley

The Henry Smith Charity

Eligibility: People in need who live in West Horsley.

Types of grants: One-off or recurrent grants according to need.

Annual grant total: £600 to £700.

Applications: In writing to the correspondent.

Correspondent: Mrs Mollie Lewendon, Clerk to the Parish Coucil, Lansdowne, Silkmore Lane, West Horsley, Surrey KT24 6JB.

West Molesey

The Henry Smith Charity

Eligibility: People in need who live in West Molesey.

Types of grants: One-off grants, usually under £50 paid at Christmas.

Annual grant total: In 1992, the trust received £2,000 income, allocated from Henry Smith's (General Estate) Charity.

Applications: In writing to the correspondent.

Correspondent: Rev W A J Yeend, The Vicarage, 518 Walton Road, West Molesey, Surrey KT8 0QF (081-979 2805).

Weybridge

The Weybridge Parochial Charities

Eligibility: People in need who live in the ancient parish of Weybridge.

Types of grants: The proceeds of the charities, cash from one and vouchers from the other, are jointly distributed at Christmas. The gifts are generally divided between the number of appplicants, with preference to those considered to be particularly needy. A small amount of benefit is retained for distribution during the year in the event of a particularly needy recipient coming to the attention of the trustees.

Annual grant total: In 1990/91, the trust had an income of £4,600. 234 relief-in-need grants totalled £4,000. In 1992, the trust received income of £3,600, from Henry Smith's (General Estate) Charity.

Applications: On a form available from the correspondent or from the Weybridge Library at the beginning of October. The closing date is the first week of November.

Correspondent: D W Jenkins, Clerk, The Civic Centre, High Street, Esher, Surrey KT10 9SD (0372-474474).

Woking

The Henry Smith Charity

Eligibility: People in need who live in the ancient parish of Woking.

Types of grants: One-off grants only according to need.

Annual grant total: In 1992, the trust received £3,500 income, allocated by Henry Smith's (General Estate) Charity.

Applications: In writing to the correspondent or through the vicar.

Correspondent: M Shawcross, White Wickets, Onslow Crescent, Woking, Surrey GU22 7AY (0483-714474).

Worplesden

Worplesden Parish Charities (including the Henry Smith Charity)

Eligibility: People in need who live in the parish of Worplesden.

Types of grants: Vouchers of £35 to buy coal, clothing or groceries at Christmas.

Annual grant total: In 1993, the trust distributed £1,715.

Applications: Apply when the distribution is advertised within the parish (normally in October/November each year).

Correspondent: J D Culverwell, 1 Worplesdon St Mary, Perry Hill, Worplesdon, Guildford GU3 3RE (0483-232575).

West Sussex

The Ashington, Wiston & Warminghurst Sick Poor Fund

Eligibility: People who are sick or poor and who live in the administrative county of West Sussex. Preference for those living in the parishes of Ashington, Wiston and Warminghurst (all as constituted on 1st April 1993).

Types of grants: One-off grants, normally given for food, medicines, extra bedding, fuel, domestic help etc..

Annual grant total: In 1993, the trust had an income of £5,000. Out of a total expenditure of £11,000, two grants were given to individuals totalling £175.

Applications: On a form available from the correspondent. Applications can be submitted directly by the individual or through a social worker, citizen's advice bureau or other welfare agency. They are considered in May and November.

Correspondent: Mrs J Turner, Senior Administrative Assistant, Chichester Health Authority, Royal West Sussex Hospital, Broyle Road, Chichester PO19 4AS (0243-781411 ext 207).

The West Sussex County Nursing Benevolent Fund

Eligibility: Firstly, retired community nursing staff in need who have worked in West Sussex. Secondly, people who are sick, convalescent, disabled or infirm and live in West Sussex.

Types of grants: One-off and recurrent grants according to need, ranging from £18 to £900. Grants are given to provide or pay for items or services which will alleviate the suffering or assist the recovery of beneficiaries in cases where assistance is not readily available from any other source.

Annual grant total: £12,000 in 36 grants in 1993.

Applications: On a form available from the correspondent. Applications can be submitted directly by the individual or through a third party. They are considered in May and November.

Correspondent: Mrs J Turner, Senior Administration Assistant, Chichester Health Authority, Royal West Sussex Hospital, Broyle Road, Chichester PO19 4AS (0243-781411 ext. 207).

Other information: The fund also sponsors places on care of dying courses for community nursing staff in West Sussex.

● Chichester

The Chichester Welfare Trust

Eligibility: People who are in need, sick, disabled or infirm and live in the city of Chichester.

Types of grants: Cash grants or provision of items such as furniture, bedding, clothing, food, fuel, loan of services or facilities. Care is taken not to duplicate benefits provided by social services. A limited amount of cash is held for immediate use in cases of emergency.

Annual grant total: No information available.

Applications: On a form available from the correspondent.

Correspondent: Cliff Spawton, Manor Barn, Appledram Lane South, Fishbourne, Chichester PO20 7PE (0243-789301).

● East Grinstead

The East Grinstead Relief in Sickness Charity

Eligibility: People in need who are sick, convalescent, disabled or infirm and live in East Grinstead.

Types of grants: Usually one-off grants ranging from about £20 to £100. Grants have been given towards the provision of lifeline phones, hospital travel, medical equipment, glasses, prescriptions and expenses for parents of ill children.

Grants are not given towards housing, council tax or anything the statutory services should provide.

Annual grant total: In 1992/93, the trust had an income of £1,610 (usually about £750). 41 families received grants totalling £1,925.

Applications: On a form available from the correspondent. Applications are usually made through a district nurse or health visitor. They are considered at any time.

Correspondent: Mrs M A Hooker, Treasurer, 61 Fulmar Drive, East Grinstead, West Sussex RH19 3NN (0342-321292).

● Horsham

The Innes Memorial Fund

Eligibility: Poor and sick people in need who live in Horsham.

Types of grants: One-off and recurrent grants according to need.

Annual grant total: The trust's income is about £12,000.

Applications: In writing to the correspondent.

Correspondent: Mrs P Eastland, Clerk, 12 Coolhurst Lane, Horsham, West Sussex RH13 6DH (0403-63289).

Other information: This entry has not been confirmed by the trust.

● Loxwood

The Cordelia Molineux Smallpiece Bequest

Eligibility: People in need who live in the parish of Loxwood.

Types of grants: Probably one-off or recurrent grants according to need.

Annual grant total: In 1993, the trust had an income of £6,000. It is not known how much was given in grants to individuals in need.

Applications: In writing to the correspondent.

Correspondent: Mrs B I Walker, Secretary, Martlets, Pond Copse Lane, Loxwood, Billingshurst, West Sussex RH14 0SF (0403-752777).

● Midhurst

The Pest House Charity

Eligibility: People in need who live in the parish of Midhurst.

Types of grants: One-off or recurrent grants according to need.

Annual grant total: In 1993, the trust had an income of £8,250. Grants to individuals in need totalled £5,300.

Applications: In writing to the correspondent.

Correspondent: D R Rudwick, Clerk, 6 Heathfield Gardens, Midhurst, West Sussex GU29 9HG (0730-814659).

9. London

The Benevolent Society for the Relief of the Aged and Infirm Poor

Eligibility: People over 60 years of age who are needy and infirm and live in the London area only.

Types of grants: Commonly grants are given for the replacement or acquisition of essential personal or household items eg. clothing, shoes, cookers, heaters etc.; assistance with the cost of optical and orthopaedic items that are not available free on the NHS, and gas/electricity bills that can no longer be managed. Grants typically range from £50 to £500.

Annual grant total: In 1993, the trust had assets of about £95,000 and an income of £8,000. 50 individual relief-in-need grants totalling £7,000 were made.

Applications: In writing to the correspondent including a full statement of income, expenditure, assets, liabilities, the need and estimates of cost together with details of other applications pending. Applications can be submitted by the individual, their spouse, a family member or friend, or through a recognised referral agency (social worker, citizen's advice bureau or doctor etc.) and are considered in March, June, September and December.

Correspondent: T J Berner, Hon. Secretary, 107 Elborough Street, Southfields, London SW18 5DS (081-870-9303).

Other information: Applications should be accompanied by details of income, expenditure, assets and liabilities, together with an estimate of the cost of the item(s) required/the purpose for which the grant is to be used.

The Benevolent Society of St Patrick

Eligibility: Poor Irish people irrespective of creed or politics who live in the London postal area.

Types of grants: Grants for clothing, essential household items, fuel bills, convalescence, visit to families at time of bereavement, and general assistance for hardship caused by illness or unemployment. Help has been given towards summer outings for children and elderly people. The normal maximum grant is £100.

Annual grant total: About £8,000.

Applications: Only through welfare organisations, charitable institutions or local authorities.

Correspondent: The Grants Administrator, Family Welfare Association, 501-505 Kingsland Road, Dalston, London E8 4AU (071-254 6251).

The Cripplegate Foundation

Eligibility: People in need who live or work in the ancient parish of St Giles, Cripplegate, together with the former parish of St Luke's, Old Street (the present-day City of London and the southern part of the borough of Islington respectively).

Types of grants: Grants for all kinds of need up to a usual maximum of £500.

Annual grant total: The trust gives about £900,000 in grants, including about £130,000 to individuals.

Applications: The foundation employs a staff of three and welcomes a preliminary approach by telephone or in writing to establish if an application is likely to be considered.

Correspondent: The Clerk to the Governors, 87 Worship Street, London EC2A 2BE (071-247 2106).

The Isaac Davies Trust

Eligibility: People of the Jewish faith who live in London.

Types of grants: One-off and recurrent grants according to need.

Annual grant total: No information is available.

Applications: In writing to the correspondent.

Correspondent: Miss E Cashdan, Secretary, Woburn House, Upper Woburn Place, London WC1H 0EZ (071-387 4300).

The Emanuel Hospital Charity

Eligibility: Poor, sober and honest people over 56 who are members of the Church of England and for at least two years have lived in the following areas: (i) the city of Westminster (with priority for that area north of the Thames river but south of Oxford Street and Bayswater Road); (ii) the royal borough of Kensington & Chelsea (with priority for that area north of the Thames river and east of Chelsea Creek); (iii) the borough of Hillingdon (with priority for that area known as the parish of Hayes).

Types of grants: The charity gives "Lady Dacre" pensions of £258 a year to elderly people who, in addition to the qualifications above, have a maximum income of £75 a week for single applicants and £115 a week for married couples. One-off grants are also made.

Annual grant total: £19,000 out of an income of £70,000.

Applications: On a form available from the correspondent which should be returned along with supporting documentation. Help and advice may be sought from local welfare agencies (eg. Age Concern) and churches.

Correspondent: Kevin Lee, Clerk, PO Box 270, Guildhall, London EC2P 2EJ (071-332 1405).

Other information: The charity has a surplus of income over expenditure of about £51,000 a year which it reinvests. It can now give more pensions and publicizes its activities and details of pension vacancies in local papers, through welfare agencies and churches within the beneficial areas.

• London

Friends of the Sick (also known as Chevrat Bikkur Cholim)

Eligibility: Jewish people in need who live in London and who are incapacitated through accident, ill health, old age, childbirth etc..

Types of grants: Grants for care and comfort. Probably one-off or recurrent grants according to need.

Annual grant total: In 1992, the trust had an income of £84,000. Most of the income is used to provide Jewish nurses and home helps. Only a small part is available for individual grants.

Applications: In writing to the correspondent.

Correspondent: Mrs E Weitzman, General Secretary, 463a Finchley Road, London NW3 6HN (071-435 0836).

The German Society of Benevolence

Eligibility: People who are or were citizens of the German Federal Republic, the German Democratic Republic or Austria, and dependants of the above. Applicants must live in Greater London, Essex, Hertfordshire, Kent or Surrey.

Types of grants: Pensions and small one-off grants for heating, clothing and other needs, but not for relief of rates and taxes. The society can make no commitment to renew payments.

Annual grant total: £3,000.

Applications: Applications are considered from individuals in need or from agencies acting on their behalf.

Correspondent: Mrs L Little, c/o The German Welfare Council, 59 Birkenhead Street, London WC1H 3BB (071-278 6955).

Other information: This society should not be confused with the German Welfare Council, which is an advisory body only. This entry is repeated in the South East general section of the book.

Help a London Child

Eligibility: Children and young people under 18 who live in Greater London.

Types of grants: HALC may only distribute money to registered charities. However individuals may apply but must nominate a charity willing to accept the money on their behalf should they be successful.

Grants awarded in respect of children have ranged from help with the cost of specialised equipment for severely disabled children to a holiday for a family of four children who had suffered serious deprivation. No help for holidays outside the UK.

Annual grant total: £700,000 in 1991/92, but almost all goes to organisations.

Applications: On a form available from 1st January from the administrator upon receipt of a 9" x 4" sae. Would-be beneficiaries should send in their applications by the beginning of May. HALC's Allocations Meeting takes place at the beginning of July. Applicants are informed in early August whether or not they have been successful.

Correspondent: Aletheia Gentle, Administrator, c/o Capital Radio plc, Euston Tower, London NW1 3DR (071-608 6203).

Other information: Help a London Child (HALC) was started in 1975 by Capital Radio as a fundraising appeal to help disadvantaged and underprivileged children in London.

The Hornsey Parochial Charities

Eligibility: People in need who live in the ancient parish of Hornsey in Haringey and Hackney which comprises N8 and parts of N2, N4, N6, N10 and N16.

Types of grants: One-off grants for all kinds of need provided funding is not available from statutory or other sources. Weekly allowances for elderly people are also available.

Annual grant total: In 1990, the trust's income was £96,000 (including the educational portion of the trust). Grants totalled £64,000. No more recent information available.

Applications: Individuals can phone or write for an application form which, on being returned, can usually be dealt with within a month. However, the trust is already overburdened with applications.

Correspondent: John Bailey, Clerk, 47 The Chine, London N10 3PX (081-883 9031).

The London Bereavement Relief Society

Eligibility: Widows and widowers in need who live within London postal districts.

Types of grants: Small cash grants to help with the initial problems of bereavement.

Annual grant total: In 1993, 27 grants were made to 18 clients with dependent children. Grants totalled £3,100.

Applications: In writing from a social worker or any other responsible person. Applications must be submitted within four months of bereavement. A meeting will then be arranged with Mrs Idle, the society's visitor.

Correspondent: W N Barr, Secretary, 175 Tower Bridge Road, London SE1 2AH (071-407 7585).

The London Electricity Benevolent Society

Eligibility: Members and retired members of the society or widows/widowers of deceased members, and current employees of London Electricity irrespective of where they live.

Types of grants: One-off grants and short-term loans according to need. In 1993, Christmas gifts of £20 totalled £3,400 and ordinary grants totalled £6,000 including grants towards a washing machine, electric blanket, spectacles, help with the purchase of a wheelchair and expenses at the time of bereavement.

Annual grant total: In 1993, the trust's income was £21,000 and gave grants totalling £9,000.

Applications: On a form available from the correspondent and can be submitted by the individual. Applications are considered all year round.

Correspondent: The Secretary, 81-87 High Holborn, London WC1V 6NU (071-242 9050).

The Metropolitan Society for the Blind

Eligibility: Registered blind and partially sighted people who live in the 12 central London boroughs or the City of London.

Types of grants: The society's primary function is as a full-time home-visiting agency on which it spends almost half its income; it also offers a small-scale escort service conducted by volunteer car drivers, normally in the London area. Some general welfare grants are made (£15,000 in 1992). The society can also help with a wide variety of aids and equipment, including radio sets; it awards a number of pensions (£13,000 in 1992), but no further pensions will be awarded.

Annual grant total: £28,000 in 1992.

Applications: On a form available from the correspondent. Applications should be made through welfare, voluntary, church or similar organisations. The secretary can be contacted between 9.30 am and 4 pm on weekdays.

Correspondent: The Secretary, 4th Floor, Duke House, 6-12 Tabard Street, London SE1 4JT (071 403 6184/6571).

The Metropolitan Visiting & Relief Association

Eligibility: People in need who live in the boroughs of Camden, Greenwich, Hackney, Hammersmith & Fulham, Islington, Kensington & Chelsea, Lambeth, Lewisham, Southwark, Tower Hamlets, Wandsworth, Westminster and the City of London.

Types of grants: One-off grants for almost every kind of need, but not fines, rent arrears, council tax, water rates and funeral expenses. The most common requests are for help with fuel bills, children's clothing and holidays, but more unusual needs can also be met. Grants usually range from £100 to £200.

Annual grant total: £6,000.

Applications: Through a social worker on a form available from the correspondent. These forms must be signed by the Church of England vicar of the applicant's parish (although the applicant need not be a churchgoer).

Correspondent: The Grants Administrator, Family Welfare Association, 501-505 Kingsland Road, London E8 4AU (071-254 6251).

Other information: The Family Welfare Association administers a wide variety of funds that can potentially meet most cases of individual need nationally. See the entry in the National and general charities section of the book.

The Mary Minet Trust

Eligibility: People in need who are sick, convalescent, disabled or elderly and infirm and live in the boroughs of Southwark and Lambeth.

Types of grants: Grants in the range of £50 to £150 for such items as telephones, orthopaedic aids, furniture, nursing costs and convalescent holidays. The trust cannot help with debts of any kind. Assistance from members of the applicant's family or anyone with a legal or moral obligation to the applicant shall be taken into account by the trustees when considering a grant.

Annual grant total: £11,500 in 76 grants in 1992/93, out of an income of £13,000.

Applications: Via social services, citizen's advice bureaux, hospitals or doctors. The trustees meet quarterly in March, June, September and December, but emergency grants can be dealt with quickly. Before considering an application, the trustees require:

- Name, age and address of the applicant;
- State of health
- Financial situation;
- Particulars of members of the family who might be expected to support or help the applicant and their reasons for not doing so;
- Any other relevant information eg. medical or professional.

Correspondent: Dr A Clark-Jones, Hon. Secretary, 54-56 Knatchbull Road, London SE5 9QY (071-274 2266).

Queen Adelaide's Fund

Eligibility: People who are receiving or within the previous five years have received treatment or training in respect of mental distress and who either live in Greater London or the former county of Middlesex, or who received such treatment or training there.

Types of grants: One-off grants of less than £100 towards needs including clothing, furnishing, telephone installation and holidays. No grants can be made to repay debts or arrears of any kind and every source of statutory funding (ie. DSS/social services) must have been applied to and have proved not to have helped.

Annual grant total: In 1993, over £12,000 was given to about 250 applicants.

Applications: On a form available from the correspondent. Applications must be made through, or supported by, a social worker or other professional worker who has worked with the applicant in respect of their mental disorder. Trustees meet at the end of March, June, September and December.

Correspondent: Barry Watts, c/o MIND, Granta House, 15-19 Broadway, Stratford, London E15 4BQ (071-637 0741).

The St George Dragon Trust

Eligibility: People in need who live in the boroughs of Hammersmith & Fulham, Kensington & Chelsea and Wandsworth.

Types of grants: One-off grants of £50 to £200 are given to people who are moving from Special Needs Housing Association into independent accommodation. Applicants should not be eligible for community care grants and have minimum resources to buy furniture for their home.

Annual grant total: In 1992, the trust had an income of £7,700. 21 grants to individuals totalled £4,000.

Applications: In writing to the correspondent through the Special Needs Housing Association staff. Applications are considered in March, June, September and December.

Correspondent: D Savill, Clerk, The Basement, 706 Fulham Road, London SW6 5SB (071-731 6570).

The Sheriffs' & Recorders' Fund

Eligibility: People on discharge from prison who are in need, and temporary relief to their families in distress during their imprisonment. Applicants must live in the Metropolitan Police area or Greater London area.

Types of grants: Usually one-off grants.

Annual grant total: £56,000 in 1992.

Applications: Must be on a form available from the correspondent or through probation offices/social worker.

Correspondent: David Elias, Administrator, c/o Central Criminal Court, Old Bailey, London EC4M 7EH (071-248 3277).

The Society for the Relief of Distress

Eligibility: People in need who live in the boroughs of Camden, Greenwich, Hackney, Hammersmith & Fulham, Islington, Kensington & Chelsea, Lambeth, Lewisham, Southwark, Tower Hamlets, Wandsworth, Westminster and the City of London.

Types of grants: One-off grants, usually of £25 to £100, for "any cases of sufficient hardship or distress, whether mental or physical." Grants may be given towards essential household items and clothing but seldom for convalescent holidays, funeral expenses or debts.

Annual grant total: £8,000.

Applications: Through social workers, citizen's advice bureaux, registered charities and church organisations only. Applications submitted by individuals will not be considered.

Correspondent: Mrs D Hughes, Hon. Secretary, 5 Dunsany Road, London W14 OJP.

The South London Relief-in-Sickness Fund

Eligibility: People in need through sickness, disability or infirmity who live in the boroughs of Lambeth and Wandsworth.

Types of grants: One-off grants normally up to £100.

Annual grant total: £7,000 in 1992.

Applications: Only through a social worker, doctor, clergy or welfare agency. The trustees meet twice a year but grants can also be dealt with at the chairman's discretion.

Correspondent: Andrew Cottell, Clerk, London Borough of Wandsworth, Wandsworth Town Hall, High Street, London SW18 (081-871 6010).

Sarah Rachael Titford's Charity

Eligibility: A spinster/widow aged over 60 whose income, except state benefits, does not exceed £1,750 a year, who believes "in the Lord Jesus Christ" and "desires to obey Him in general conduct" and who lives in London especially Westminster and the borough of Southwark.

Types of grants: One-off or recurrent grants according to need.

Annual grant total: £7,250 in 1992/93.

Applications: In writing to the correspondent.

Correspondent: Rev B W Amey, Secretary, 2 Sussex Road, Harrow, Middlesex HA1 4LX (081-427 3411).

Vacher's Endowment

Eligibility: People in need who are over 50 and who live or have lived in Greater London, and their dependants. Preference has to be given to those who have been engaged in some trade or profession on their own account in Greater London, and to people who either live or have lived in the area of the united parishes of St Margarets and St John Westminster. Preference also to members of or regular worshipers at a Protestant Christian church.

Types of grants: Quarterly pensions of £50 or £75 and one-off grants up to £500.

Annual grant total: £12,600 in 1992.

Applications: Application forms and further information may be obtained from the correspondent in writing.

Correspondent: Sir Reginald Pullen, Warden's House, 42 Rochester Row, London SW1P 1BU (071-828 3131).

Barking & Dagenham

The Avenue Trust Fund

Eligibility: People of retirement age who live in the Rush Green area of Dagenham and Romford.

Types of grants: One-off grants ranging from £100 to £200. Provision is also made for recently widowed people in the area.

Annual grant total: In 1993, the trust had assets of £32,000 producing an income of £4,000. Grants totalled £1,500.

Applications: Applications can be submitted by the individual or through a recognised referral agency (eg. social worker, citizen's advice bureau or doctor) and are considered monthly. Reasons for requesting financial assistance and supporting evidence of circumstances and residence are required.

Correspondent: M F Booth, Hon. Secretary, Barking & Dagenham Old People's Welfare Association, White House, 884 Green Lane, Dagenham RM8 1BX (081-592 4500 ext. 2891).

The Barking & Dagenham Mayor's Fund

Eligibility: People in need who live in Barking and Dagenham.

Types of grants: Grants, usually between £10 and £50, for a variety of needs. Some are given through local welfare agencies and social services departments. Examples include Christmas gifts for pensioners, travel expenses in cases of hardship, holiday expenses for children in need, household goods, and the payment of debts incurred by people on probation.

Annual grant total: £1,800 in 1992/93, of which £1,000 was given to individuals.

Applications: In writing to the correspondent.

Correspondent: Miss J Allen, Mayor's Secretary, London Borough of Barking & Dagenham, Civic Centre, Dagenham RM10 7BN (081-592 4500).

The Barking General Charities

Eligibility: People in need who live in the Barking area.

Types of grants: Small one-off grants can be made for most types of need.

Annual grant total: £1,000 to £2,000.

Applications: In writing to the correspondent, either through social services or a similar welfare agency or directly by the individual. Trustees meet infrequently.

Correspondent: A K Glenny, Clerk, Messrs Hatten Asplin Channer & Glenny, Radial House, 3-5 Ripple Road, Barking, Essex IG11 7NG (081-591 4131).

The William Ford & Dagenham United Charities

Eligibility: People in need who live in the ancient parish of Dagenham.

Types of grants: Gift vouchers between £20 and £40 at Christmas.

Annual grant total: £1,100 in 55 grants in 1992/93.

Applications: In writing to the correspondent through the social worker, citizen's advice bureau or other welfare agency. Details of any disability should be included if appropriate.

Correspondent: W C Smith, Chief Executive, Civic Centre, Dagenham RM10 7BN (081-592 4500).

Barnet

The Finchley Charities

Eligibility: Elderly people who live in the former borough of Finchley (as it was before 1st April 1965), now in the borough of Barnet.

Types of grants: One-off grants only, but beneficiaries can submit subsequent applications. The trust also provides over 170 flatlets for elderly people in the area.

Annual grant total: In 1992, the trust's income was £266,000; £20,000 was given in grants, but not all to individuals.

Applications: In writing to the correspondent.

Correspondent: F H Jex, Clerk, 3 Caddington Road, London NW2 1RP (081-452 7598).

The William Jackson Trust

Eligibility: Poor widows who live in East Barnet and have done so for at least 20 years.

Types of grants: An annual grant is given rather than a fixed pension. In 1990, the grant was £150, but this may vary according to the number of applicants.

Annual grant total: £1,750.

Applications: In writing to the correspondent.

Correspondent: The Rector, The Rectory, Church Hill Road, East Barnet, Hertfordshire EN4 8XD (081-368 3840).

The Douglas Martin Trust

Eligibility: People in need who live in the Barnet area.

Barnet/Bexley

Types of grants: The trust gives a large number of one-off grants to individuals (average £50) for a wide variety of purposes, especially for or towards the cost of essential household equipment and furniture, or to relieve hardship where debts have been incurred through accidents, illness, etc..

Annual grant total: In 1990, the trust's income was £41,000; grants totalled £26,000, most of which was given to individuals for relief in need or education grants.

Applications: ONLY through Barnet Social Services. The correspondent should NOT be contacted directly.

Correspondent: J A Lorenz, Administrator, 18 Central Circus, London NW4 3AS (081-202 6333).

Other information: The correspondent states: "all funds are being more than fully extended through applications from local council social services".

The Mayor of Barnet's Benevolent Fund

Eligibility: People in need who live in the London borough of Barnet.

Types of grants: One-off grants usually ranging from £50 to £150. Grants are given towards household items, furniture, clothing, household debts and maintenance for students.

Annual grant total: In 1992/93, the fund had an income of £6,000 and gave £2,500 in 12 grants.

Applications: In writing to the correspondent. Applications can be submitted directly by the individual or by a third party. They are considered at any time.

Correspondent: The Grants Unit, Chief Executive's Directorate, Town Hall, The Burroughs, Hendon, London NW4 4BG (081-202 8282 ext. 2092).

The Eleanor Palmer's Charity

Eligibility: People in need who live in the former urban districts of Barnet and East Barnet.

Types of grants: One-off or recurrent grants according to need. (The trust concentrates on joint housing projects and running its own almshouses.)

Annual grant total: About £7,000.

Applications: In writing to the correspondent.

Correspondent: Richard Piert, Clerk, 106b Wood Street, Barnet, Hertfordshire EN5 4BY (081-441 3222).

The Valentine Poole Charity

Eligibility: People in need who live in the former urban districts of Barnet and East Barnet.

Types of grants: In 1992/93, £9,000 was given in pensions of up to £10 a week paid monthly. £17,000 was given in one-off grants, of which about £1,400 was given to elderly people towards holidays, telephone and replacing/repairing broken equipment. (About £1,600 was given to individuals for educational purposes and £14,000 was given to organisations.)

Annual grant total: £26,000 in 1992/93, of which £10,000 was given to individuals in need.

Applications: In writing to the correspondent.

Correspondent: Mrs M G Lee, The Forum Room, Ewen Hall, Wood Street, Barnet, Herts EN5 4BW (081-441 6893).

The Henry Smith Charity

Eligibility: People in need who live in Chipping Barnet.

Types of grants: Vouchers to elderly people and families in need, mostly at Christmas. Amounts range from £15 to £25.

Annual grant total: £1,000 in 63 grants in 1992/93.

Applications: In writing to the correspondent. Applications should be submitted through a social worker, citizen's advice bureau or other welfare agency. They are considered in November.

Correspondent: L J Adams, Treasurer, 2 Oaklands Lane, Arkley, Barnet EN5 3JN (081-440 9942).

The West Hendon & Colindale Relief-in-Sickness Charity

Eligibility: People in need who live in West Hendon and Colindale wards.

Types of grants: Grants of £25 to £50 where there is no appropriate payment from statutory sources. The trust can help with nursing care for non-carcinogenic terminal illnesses, assistance to people needing holidays to alleviate extreme stress, material goods in an emergency, transport, items of specialized nursing equipment which cannot be provided by any other means.

Annual grant total: £400 in 1988 from an income of £600. No more recent information available.

Applications: By phone or in writing to the correspondent including full details.

Correspondent: Miss Diana Hopwood, Secretary, 4 Flower Lane, Mill Hill, London NW7 2JB (081-959 1563).

Bexley

The Bexley Mayor's Fund

Eligibility: People in need who live in the borough of Bexley.

Types of grants: Grants for a variety of needs (eg. towards an electric wheelchair for a severely disabled man and to buy new clothes for an elderly person whose home had been damaged in a fire). There can be an immediate response in emergency cases.

Annual grant total: In 1992/93, grants totalled about £6,000 part of which went to a local carers association. The amount given to individuals is not known.

Applications: In writing to the correspondent. In practice, many applications are referred by the council's social services department who also vet all applications from individuals.

Correspondent: The Mayor, London Borough of Bexley, Civic Offices, Broadway, Bexleyheath, Kent DA6 7LB (081-303 7777).

The Samuel Edward Cook Charity for the Poor

Eligibility: People in need who live in Bexleyheath.

Types of grants: About 25 one-off grants a year to individuals and families.

Annual grant total: £1,500 in 1993.

Applications: Direct or through a welfare agency. Allocation of the funds is at the discretion of the Minister of Trinity Baptist Church.

Correspondent: Rev D G Barter, 75 Standard Road, Bexleyheath, Kent (081-303 5858).

The John Payne's Charity

Eligibility: Elderly people who live in the ancient parish of East Wickham.

Types of grants: Grants for fuel bills and essential needs such as gas fire installation. Five pensions of £2 a week are paid plus summer and Christmas bonuses; one or two vacancies may exist.

Annual grant total: £900 in 1993.

Applications: Directly in writing to the correspondent or through Age Concern or a similar agency.

Correspondent: The Headmistress, Clerk, Foster's Primary School, Upper Wickham Lane, Welling, Kent (081-854 1092).

Brent

The Kingsbury Charity

Eligibility: People in need who live in the ancient parish of Kingsbury.

Types of grants: Most of the charity's expenditure is on almshouses. Recent grants to individuals have included £100 towards the cost of a trip to Lourdes and £100 to help a family with a six year old child suffering from leukaemia.

Annual grant total: £3,000 in 1990/91, including grants to organisations.

Applications: Applications are normally made through social services, doctor, teacher, church etc. and are considered every six weeks.

Correspondent: J B Jordan, Hon. Secretary, 55 Grove Crescent, Kingsbury, London NW9 0LS (081-205 2101).

The Wembley Samaritan Fund

Eligibility: Poor sick people in the former urban district of Wembley.

Types of grants: Most of the grant total is spent on providing holidays for disabled people. Grants are also made for items such as heaters and bedding for sick or elderly people.

Annual grant total: About £3,000 out of a total income of £4,000 in 1993. Most grants were for £200 to £300 towards Lifeline necklaces or holidays.

Applications: By telephone or in writing to the correspondent. A visit by two trustees to the applicant will be arranged.

Correspondent: Miss J Hancock, 31 Lily Gardens, Alperton, Wembley, Middlesex HA0 1DL (081-998 3488).

Bromley

The Bromley Relief-in-Need Charity

Eligibility: People in need who live in the ancient parish of Bromley (this does not cover all the present borough).

Types of grants: One-off grants of £50 to £100 including help with debt and fuel bills. In recent years the charity has been receiving too few applications to dispose of its income and a surplus of several thousand pounds has accumulated.

Annual grant total: The trust's income is about £1,000 a year, but see above.

Applications: Only through social services or similar welfare agency, citizen's advice bureau, doctor, headteacher etc..

Correspondent: M Cox, Clerk, 15 Rayford Avenue, Lee, London SE12 0NF (081-857 3346).

Camden

The Ancient Parish of St Andrew Holborn - Charities Administered from the Guild Church of St Andrew

The Guild Church of St Andrew Holborn is the administrative base for the three charities described below. The limited beneficial area and objects of these charities were making it increasingly difficult for beneficiaries to be found and all the money to be spent. The trustees have therefore simplified and extended the charities' schemes.

Applications: Applications on a form available from the correspondent can be submitted by the individual, through a recognised referral agency (eg. social worker, citizen's advice bureau or doctor) or other third party, and are considered regularly.

Correspondent: Ian Gray, Clerk, 5 St Andrew Street, London EC4A 3AB (071-583 7394).

(i) Isaac Duckett - St Andrew Holborn Branch

Eligibility: People over 60 who have lived or worked in the Holborn area of the London borough of Camden (north west portion of the city of London) for at least the past 3 years.

Types of grants: Pensions and one-off grants are given.

Annual grant total: In 1992/93, the trust had an income of £32,000 and a total expenditure of £19,000. Grants ranging between £50 and £350 were given to 68 individuals and totalled £17,000.

(ii) The St Andrew Holborn City Foundation

Eligibility: People in need who have lived or worked in the Holborn area of the London borough of Camden (north west portion of the city of London) for at least the past 3 years.

Types of grants: One-off grants.

Annual grant total: In 1992, the trust had an income of £12,000 and a total expenditure of £8,400. Grants ranging between £85 and £700 were given to 23 individuals and totalled £7,300.

(iii) The Hoxton Estate Charity

Eligibility: People who have lived or worked for at least the past three years in the liberties of Saffron Hill, Hatton Garden or Ely Rents in the ancient parish of St Andrew, Holborn, now in the borough of Camden.

Types of grants: After administrative costs the trust allocates its money in the following proportions: 75% in pensions to elderly people in need; 25% on relief-in-need.

Annual grants total: In 1992, the trust had an income of £30,000. Grants of between £150 and £450 were given to 80 individuals and totalled £23,000.

The Bloomsbury Dispensary

Eligibility: Sick or ill people who live in Bloomsbury.

Types of grants: One-off grants for the relief of sickness and illness (this does not include pregnancy). No grants for debt repayments.

Annual grant total: In 1992, grants totalled £4,500.

Applications: In writing to the correspondent.

Correspondent: Mrs J Rustage, Secretary, 17a Macklin Street, Drury Lane, London WC2B 5NR (071-405 1878).

The Dibdin Bread Charity

Eligibility: Elderly people in need who live in the former metropolitan borough of Holborn.

Types of grants: Pensions of £15 per month.

Annual grant total: £1,000 to 6 beneficiaries from an income of around £2,600.

Applications: To the correspondent.

Correspondent: Mrs J Rustage, Secretary, 17a Macklin Street, Drury Lane, London WC2B 5NR (071-405 1878).

Camden/City of London

The Hampstead Wells & Campden Trust

Eligibility: People in need who live in the former metropolitan borough of Hampstead.

Types of grants: Pensions and one-off grants including help with clothing, furniture, fuel and heating, holidays, removals and travel expenses, television and telephones, and occasionally for education and help with debts.

Annual grant total: £90,000 (ie. £52,000 in 165 pensions and 400 one-off grants totalling £38,000).

Applications: Applications should normally be sponsored by a statutory or voluntary organisation, or by a person familiar with the circumstances of the case eg. social worker, doctor, clergyman. To apply for a weekly pension, the sponsoring person or body should outline the case and complete an application form. Office hours: 10am to 1pm Mon, Wed, Fri and 10am to 4pm Tues, Thurs.

Correspondent: Mrs Sheila A Taylor, Clerk, 62 Rosslyn Hill, London NW3 1ND (071-435 1570).

The Mayor of Camden's Charity Trust Fund

Eligibility: People in need who live in the borough of Camden or immediate neighbourhood.

Types of grants: One-off or recurrent grants according to need.

Annual grant total: Since 1st June 1993, £15,500 has been given in grants, mostly to individuals.

Applications: On a form available from the correspondent, either directly or through social workers.

Correspondent: The Mayor's Officer, Mayor's Parlour, Town Hall, Euston Road, London NW1 2RU (071-278 4444 ext. 5130).

The St Pancras Welfare Trust

Eligibility: People in need who live in the old metropolitan borough of St Pancras (NW1, NW5, N19 and parts of WC1 and NW3).

Types of grants: One-off grants, usually between £50 and £200, for a wide range of needs.

Annual grant total: £60,000 in 1993, including grants to organisations.

Applications: Through social workers, hospitals, voluntary organisations etc.. Applications are considered quarterly, but emergency grants for sums up to £150 can be considered more quickly.

Correspondent: Pam Warren, Clerk, 38a Belsize Grove, London NW3 4TR (071-483 4493).

Stafford's Charity

Eligibility: People in need who live in the Holborn and Clerkenwell areas of central London, roughly between Southampton Row (WC1), Farringdon Road (EC1), Guildford Street (WC1) and High Holborn and Holborn Viaduct.

Types of grants: Pensions to people who have lived in the above area for three years. Quarterly pensions of £300 a year were paid to about 150 pensioners. The pensions are paid unequally with higher sums paid during the winter months. Usually only people in receipt of supplementary benefit or rate/rent rebate will be considered; the health of the applicant is taken into consideration. It is likely that the pension level will remain unchanged or reduce during the next year or so.

Grants are usually paid to assist with debts, furniture or clothing and with occasional holidays.

Annual grant total: In 1992/93, the trust's income was about £75,000; grants totalled about £50,000 ie. £45,000 in pensions and £5,000 in one-off grants.

Applications: On a form available from the correspondent. A meeting is arranged after the form has been completed during which information on the form is checked and an attempt is made to assess the applicant's needs.

Correspondent: A Tahourdin, Secretary, Simmonds Church Smiles & Co, 13 Bedford Row, London WC1R 4BU (071-242 9971).

Other information: Owing to financial pressures the number of pensions is being limited to 150 with a waiting list operating. Grant payments are not being restricted but are carefully screened. It is hoped that the disposable income of the charity will increase in 1994/95 and relieve this tight financial policy.

The Matthew Wistrich Trust

Eligibility: Children and young people up to the age of 25 who are physically disabled or have learning difficulties, and their families who live in Camden.

Types of grants: Grants for clothing, travel, holidays and equipment.

Annual grant total: £3,200 in 1991, from an income of £5,000.

Applications: By referral from social workers.

Correspondent: The Grants Administrator, Family Welfare Association, 501-505 Kingsland Road, Dalston, London E8 4AU (071-254 6251).

City of London

The Aldgate Freedom Foundation

Eligibility: People over 60 and in need in the freedom part of the parish of St Botolph, Aldgate.

Types of grants: Recurrent grants of £32.50 per quarter plus a £30 Christmas gift. Help is also given to hospitals within the city and St Botolph's church.

Annual grant total: In 1992, the trust had assets of £562,000 producing an income of £34,000. Total expenditure was £31,000. Grants of £160 were given to 56 individuals and totalled £9,000.

Applications: On a form available from the correspondent, either directly by the individual or through a third party. Details of income/capital/expenditure and length of residence in the parish must be included. Applications are considered at any time.

Correspondent: H L Gledhill, St Botolph's Church, Aldgate, London EC3N 1AB (071-283 1670/1950).

The City Chapter & Percy Trentham Charity

Eligibility: People at least 60 years old who live or have lived or worked in the City of London including Glasshouse Yard.

Types of grants: Cash grants up to £400. About 26 regular grants to people over 80 who are in poor health.

Annual grant total: £4,000.

Applications: Only through a social worker, welfare officer or clergyman. Applications for regular grants are processed twice a year; all other applications are dealt with as they are received.

Correspondent: Mrs F Meek, Hon. Secretary, 56b Venner Road, London SE26 5EL.

Other information: This entry has not been confirmed by the trust. The similar but smaller Hammond Pension Charity is administered with the above. Its beneficial area is the ancient parish of St Andrew Holborn.

The Ada Lewis Winter Distress Fund

Eligibility: Poor and distressed people who live or work, or have lived or worked, in the City of London area, and their dependants.

Types of grants: Annual grants of £100.

Annual grant total: £3,000.

Applications: Usually through the welfare officers of the Corporation of London.

Correspondent: Alan Page, Town Clerk's Office, Corporation of London, PO Box 270, Guildhall, London EC2P 2EJ (071-606 3030).

The Mitchell City of London Charity

Eligibility: People in need who live or work, or have lived/worked, in the City of London, and their widows or children.

Types of grants: Pensions and one-off grants.

Annual grant total: £19,500 in 1992/93 (ie. £7,900 in grants and £11,570 in pensions). £32,000 was transferred to the Educational Foundation.

Applications: In writing to the correspondent.

Correspondent: J Keyte, Clerk, The Lodge, 23 Old Lodge Lane, Purley, Surrey CR8 4DJ.

Croydon

The Annie Jane Knowles & Edward George Bates Pension Fund for the Blind

Eligibility: Blind people who live in the borough of Croydon.

Types of grants: Pensions.

Annual grant total: About £1,000 (16 pensions are currently being awarded).

Applications: To the correspondent via Croydon Voluntary Association for the Blind.

Correspondent: Bruce Middlemiss, Borough Secretary, Taberner House, Park Lane, Croydon CR9 3JS (081-686 4433 ext. 5693).

The St John the Baptist Charitable Fund

Eligibility: People in need through poverty or sickness who live in the parish of St John the Baptist, Purley.

Types of grants: One-off grants, usually ranging from £50 to £250.

Annual grant total: £2,200 in eight grants in 1992/93, but some of these were to organisations.

Applications: Direct to the correspondent or through the parish priest of St John the Baptist church. Applications are considered in November.

Correspondent: P Bunce, 4 Highclere Close, Kenley, Surrey CR8 5JU (081-660 7301).

Ealing

The Acton (Middlesex) Charities

Eligibility: People in need who live in the former ancient parish of Acton (to 1899) and borough of Acton. The area of benefit covered is:
Postal district W3 – except the area west of the District railway from Chiswick Park to Acton Town stations.
Postal district W4 – from the west side of Woodstock Road to the west ie. most of Bedford Park, Thorney Hedge Road, Silver Crescent and Chiswick Road.
Postal district NW10 – from Victoria Road west to Park Royal Road and north to the Wesley Estate.

Types of grants: Mostly to individuals and to a few organisations with services and facilities for those in distress or need.

Annual grant total: This charity has been reorganised and amalgamated with others. No financial information is currently available.

Applications: Referral from clergy, doctors, health visitors or other professional people.

Correspondent: The Rector, St Mary's Church, Acton, London W3.

The Ealing Aid-in-Sickness Trust

Eligibility: People in need who live in the borough of Ealing.

Types of grants: One-off or recurrent grants according to need.

Annual grant total: £2,660.

Applications: On a form available from the correspondent.

Correspondent: Mr Barber, Clerk, 25 Golden Manor, Hanwell, London W7 3EE (081-579 2921).

The Ealing Philanthropic Institution

Eligibility: Elderly, sick and needy people who live in Ealing W5 and W13 postal districts.

Types of grants: Christmas gifts and one-off grants.

Annual grant total: The trust's income was £5,000 in 1992/93; grants totalled £4,900, about half of which was given for outings. Christmas gifts totalled £925 and £350 was given in one-off grants. £1,200 was given to organisations.

Applications: In writing to the correspondent either directly by the individual or through a third party.

Correspondent: P F Jacobsen, Secretary, 137 Coldershaw Road, West Ealing, London W13 9DU (081-567 7482).

The Eleemosynary Charity of William Hobbayne

Eligibility: People in need who live in the Hanwell (London W7) area.

Types of grants: One-off or recurrent grants according to need.

Annual grant total: In 1990, the trust's income was £57,000. Grants totalled £22,000, but this included grants to organisations.

Applications: Local sponsoring bodies apply on an application form which has to be completed by the sponsor and sent in the first instance to the correspondent.

Correspondent: Mr Barber, Clerk, 25 Golden Manor, Hanwell, London W7 3EE (081-579 2921).

The Hanwell Philanthropic Institution

Eligibility: People in need who live in the London W7 postal area.

Types of grants: The institution tends to concentrate on socially based activities such as visits, outings, Christmas parties and Christmas boxes, but can help if cases of individual need arise.

Annual grant total: About £6,000 in 1993.

Applications: In writing to the correspondent.

Correspondent: David Lane, Hon. Secretary, 18 Thornwell Court, Bishop's Road, Hanwell, London W7 2PR (081-567 7753).

The Mayor's Christmas Fund

Eligibility: People in need who are 70 or over, live in the borough of Ealing and are in receipt of Income Support.

Ealing/Enfield/Greenwich

Types of grants: Christmas gifts of £10 in 1993 (£20 for applicants over 90 years old). Owing to a shortage of funds these will probably be reduced. Occasional one-off emergency grants can also be made. Grants are only given to people in private or rented accommodation. Those who live in residential homes or hospitals are not eligible.

Annual grant total: No information available.

Applications: Applications are processed at Christmas for individual gifts. For emergency grants applications can be considered when they are received.

Correspondent: Mrs A V Snow, Mayoral Officer, Mayor's Parlour, Town Hall, New Broadway, Ealing, London W5 2BY (081-579 2424 ext. 42234/6).

Enfield

The Edmonton Aid-in-Sickness & Nursing Fund

Eligibility: People in need who live in Edmonton.

Types of grants: One-off grants for fuel and heating costs, clothing, furniture and convalescence. No recurrent grants.

Annual grant total: £4,000 in 68 grants in 1992.

Applications: Through social services, citizen's advice bureaux, nurses, health visitors, hospitals and doctors. Applications are received at any time and are dealt with immediately and without formality. Grants over £50 are considered at a trustees' meeting.

Correspondent: David Firth, Hon. Secretary, 178 Wellington Road, Enfield, Middlesex EN1 2RT (081 360 3659).

The Old Enfield Charitable Trust

Eligibility: People in need, hardship or distress who live in the ancient parish of Enfield.

Types of grants: Grants are distributed either directly to individuals or through a welfare agency or suitable third party. The first priority of the charity is relief of need with grants being given for a wide range of necessities.

Annual grant total: £100,000 in 1993/94, out of an income of £325,000.

Applications: On a form available on written request from the correspondent. Applications can be made either directly or through social services, probation service, hospitals, clinics and clergy. Applicants writing directly are subsequently visited and assessed.

Correspondent: Mrs N D Forkgen, Clerk, 10a Church Street, Enfield, Middlesex EN2 6BE (081-367 8941).

Other information: The Enfield Parochial Charity and The Hundred Acres Charity were merged to form this charity on 1st April 1994.

Greenwich

The Charity of Sir Martin Bowes

Eligibility: People in need who live in the borough of Greenwich.

Types of grants: Both one-off grants and regular allowances are given.

Annual grant total: In 1992/93, the trust's income was £7,500 with grants totalling £7,000.

Applications: Through the Director of Social Services, London Borough of Greenwich.

Correspondent: The Clerk, Worshipful Company of Goldsmiths, Goldsmiths' Hall, Foster Lane, Cheapside, London EC2V 6BN (071-606 8971).

Godson's Charity

Eligibility: People in need who wish to emigrate and who currently live in the London borough of Greenwich; Tenbury Wells in Hereford and Worcester and Shinfield in Berkshire. The majority of applications are received from Greenwich.

Types of grants: One-off grants up to £1,000 for those in need and wishing to emigrate (especially where the applicant has a new job to go to).

Annual grant total: Two grants totalling £1,500 were given in 1992. (The total expenditure of the trust was £3,500.) The trust has assets of £80,000, generating an income of £6,500.

Applications: Directly by the individual on a form available from the correspondent. Details of the proposed destination, occupation, and financial circumstances must be given. Applications are considered as they are received.

Correspondent: Anne Gregory, c/o Teredo Petroleum plc, 13–14 Hanover Street, London W1R 9HG (071-495 5916).

Other information: This entry is repeated in the Midlands and South East sections of the book.

The Greenwich Charities for the Blind & Disabled

Eligibility: Blind, partially-sighted and disabled people who live or are regularly employed in the borough of Greenwich, and blind and partially-sighted people who live within the London area. Preference will be given to applicants living alone.

Types of grants: Generally grants of up to £250, but not normally towards rent arrears, rates, food, clothing/footwear, heating or lighting, except under exceptional circumstances.

Annual grant total: £10,000.

Applications: On a form available from the correspondent. Applications can be made directly by the individual or through a social worker. Details of income/expenditure and charitable assistance received within the past year must be included. No application will be considered where an alternative statutory source of funding is available.

Correspondent: Steve Potter, Budget Monitoring Officer, c/o Greenwich Social Services, 4th Floor, Nelson House, 50 Wellington Street, Woolwich SE18 6PY (081-854 8888 ext. 3065).

The Earl of Northampton's Charity

Eligibility: Elderly people in need who live in Castle Rising and Shotsam in Norfolk and Greenwich, London.

Types of grants: Pensions up to £10 a week.

Annual grant total: £18,000 in pensions.

Applications: In writing to the correspondent.

Correspondent: The Clerk to the Mercers' Company, Mercers Hall, Ironmonger Lane, London EC2V 8HE (071-726 4991).

Other information: This entry is repeated in the Norfolk section of the book.

The Woolwich & Plumstead Relief-in-Sickness Fund

Eligibility: Sick people in need who live in the borough of Greenwich, with an emphasis on the Woolwich and Plumstead areas.

Types of grants: Grants up to about £200 to help with a wide range of need. Application should arise out of sickness, but this can be interpreted widely. The trust has recently been giving particular

Greenwich/Hackney/Hammersmith & Fulham

attention to younger families and single mothers where sickness or disability have imposed financial hardship, or where a partner is in prison. It cannot help with debts, rates or rent.

Annual grant total: £4,800.

Applications: In writing to the correspondent either direct or through health visitors, district nurses, social services or welfare agencies. Although most applications are received around Christmas, they can be dealt with as and when received.

Correspondent: Miss J A Waugh, Secretary, 64 Kidbrooke Park Close, Blackheath, London SE3 0EG (081-856 6012).

Hackney

Mr John Baker's Trust

Eligibility: Poor widows and unmarried women over 50 who have lived for at least five years in the parish of Christchurch, Spitalfields in the borough of Hackney.

Types of grants: Pensions.

Annual grant total: In 1993, the trust had an income of £3,600. Pensions totalling about £2,300 were paid to 13 individuals.

Applications: In writing to the correspondent.

Correspondent: The Clerk to the Brewers' Company, Brewers' Hall, Aldermanbury Square, London EC2V 7HR (071-606 1301).

The Hackney Parochial Charities

Eligibility: People in need who live in the former metropolitan borough of Hackney (as it was before 1970).

Types of grants: Grants are given to sick, disabled and elderly people for bedding, clothing, heating appliances, furniture, and towards the cost of aid and treatment (but not when this should be the responsibility of the statutory authorities eg. provision of wheelchairs for amputees). The cost of fares to visit long-stay patients can also be met in the case of close relatives. Grants have also been given for holidays for widows with small children and single parent families;and for gifts at Christmas for children in need.

Grants are one-off, generally of £100 to £250, although individuals can apply annually. No grants for statutory charges (rent, rates, gas, electricity, telephone charges).

Annual grant total: In 1993, the trust gave about £75,000 in grants, £30,000 to organisations and about £45,000 to over 150 individuals.

Applications: In writing to the correspondent. The trustees meet in March, June, September and November and as grants cannot be made between meetings it is advisable to make early contact with the correspondent.

Correspondent: A D M Sorrell, Clerk, 81-83 High Road, London N22 6BE (081-888 0155).

The United Charities of Saint Leonard's, Shoreditch

Eligibility: People in need who live in Hackney including Shoreditch and Stoke Newington and have done so for at least three years.

Types of grants: 49 charities have been united into four funds. The two largest, The General Charity and Lloyd Thomas House, are concerned mainly with almshouses, although it is believed that grants for the relief of hardship in the parish generally can also be made from them.

Annual grant total: £2,800 in 1988, the most recent year for which information is available.

Applications: In writing to the correspondent.

Correspondent: J Houlstrom, Clerk, 113 Geffrye Street, Hackney, London E2 8JA (071-729 0924).

Other information: This information is the most up to date available at the Charity Commission, but no response was received from the correspondent.

Hammersmith & Fulham

Dr Edward's & Bishop King's Fulham Charity

Eligibility: People in need who live in the former metropolitan borough of Fulham and have done so for at least two years prior to applying for a pension.

Types of grants: One-off grants and pensions according to need.

Annual grant total: In 1993, grants to individuals totalled £122,000, consisting of £35,000 in pensions, £85,000 in one-off grants and £2,000 in pensioners' Christmas parcels/vouchers.

Applications: On a form available from the correspondent submitted either directly or through social welfare agencies. One-off grants are paid via voluntary organisations, the local authority or direct to companies for wheelchairs, holidays and essential household equipment.

Correspondent: Maria Blackmore, Director, Percy Barton House, 33–35 Dawes Road, London SW6 7DT (071-386 9387).

The Fulham Philanthropic Society

Eligibility: People in need who live in Fulham.

Types of grants: Small one-off grants usually up to £20 for most types of need, but bills will not be paid under any circumstances.

Annual grant total: £650.

Applications: Either direct or through social services.

Correspondent: Mrs Channan, 99 Kenyon Street, Fulham, London SW6 6LA (071 385 3286).

The Hammersmith Relief-in-Sickness Fund

Eligibility: People in need who are physically/mentally ill or disabled and live in the former borough of Hammersmith.

Types of grants: One-off grants are made for the relief of sickness (including disablement, infirmity and convalescence), where the applicant is also in financial need. Grants can be considered for clothing, furnishings, bedding, household appliances, reasonable fuel arrears, fares for hospital visits, removals and for recuperative holidays or fares to stay with relatives.

No grants for telephone, fuel or council tax bills, decorating materials, educational fees or arrears and debts which cannot be substantiated.

Annual grant total: In 1992/93, the trust had assets of £69,000 generating an income of £6,800. Total expenditure was £5,800. Grants of up to £40 were given to 97 individuals and totalled £4,000.

Applications: On a form available from the correspondent to be submitted through a recognised referral agency (eg. social worker, citizen's advice bureau, housing association or doctor). They are considered each month.

Applications should be supported by a letter from a doctor, medical centre or hospital confirming the applicant's illness or disability and the extent of their need. Details of other charities or official sources approached for assistance should be included.

Correspondent: Mrs J O'Loughlin, Secretary, 196a Blythe Road, West Kensington, London W14 0HH (071-602 1221).

The Mayor of Hammersmith & Fulham's Appeal Fund

Eligibility: People in need who live in the borough of Hammersmith & Fulham.

Types of grants: Christmas gift vouchers for elderly people and single-parent families, and grants to pay for holidays for single parents or people with disabilities. Grants range from £25 to £50.

Annual grant total: £4,000 to £5,000.

Applications: In writing to the correspondent.

Correspondent: The Mayor, Mayor's Office, Room 201, Town Hall, King Street, London W6 9JU (081-748 3020 ext. 2013).

Haringey

The Mayor's Benevolent Fund

Eligibility: People in need who live in the borough of Haringey.

Types of grants: This is an emergency fund to help elderly, sick and distressed people and children in need. It makes one-off grants only up to £100 usually for specific items such as kettles or clothing. Some money is given at Christmas to in-patients in the borough's hospitals.

Annual grant total: £4,200 in 1990/91, including £3,600 in emergency payments and £600 in Christmas gifts and lunches.

Applications: In writing to the correspondent.

Correspondent: The Mayor's Office, Civic Centre, High Road, Wood Green, London N22 4LE (081-975 9700 ext. 2962).

The Tottenham Aid-in-Sickness Fund

Eligibility: People in need who live in the former borough of Tottenham.

Types of grants: One-off grants only for the relief of sickness.

Annual grant total: In 1992/93, the trust's income was £9,000; grants totalled £7,500.

Applications: On a form available from the correspondent. Applicants are usually referred through social services, Age Concern or citizen's advice bureaux.

Correspondent: Carolyn Banks, Principal Committee Secretary, Corporate Services, Civic Centre, Wood Green, London N22 4LE (081-975 9700 ext. 2919).

The Tottenham District Charity

Eligibility: People in need, especially the elderly, who live in the urban district of Tottenham as constituted on 28th February 1896 which is largely the postal districts of N15 and N17.

Types of grants: One-off grants to poor, elderly, sick or disabled people to reduce need, hardship or distress. Grants are to help with clothes, carpets, essential household items etc.. Pensions of £10 a month paid quarterly to elderly people. Christmas and Easter gifts are also given.

No grants for education or debts.

Annual grant total: In 1993, the trust's income was £77,000. Expenditure was £78,000, of which grants totalled £21,000 and pensions and bonuses totalled £46,000.

Applications: On a form available from the correspondent, which should be submitted through a third party such as social services or advice bureau.

Correspondent: Carolyn Banks, Principal Committee Secretary, Corporate Services, Civic Centre, Wood Green, London N22 4LE (081-975 9700 ext. 2919).

The Wood Green (Urban District) Charity

Eligibility: People in need who lived in the urban district of Wood Green (as constituted in 1896, roughly the present N22 postal area) for at least seven years.

Types of grants: Pensions and small one-off grants.'

Annual grant total: In 1991, the trust's income was £13,000. Grants totalled £9,000 including £8,000 in pensions and £1,000 in small grants.

Applications: In writing to the correspondent. Applications are considered in January, April, July and October.

Correspondent: Carolyn Banks, Clerk, Corporate Services, Civic Centre, Wood Green, London N22 4LE (081-862 2919).

Harrow

The Mayor of Harrow's Charity Fund

Eligibility: People in need who live in the borough of Harrow.

Types of grants: Small one-off grants.

Annual grant total: No information available.

Applications: Individuals and families are usually referred through social services, although applications can be made directly to the correspondent.

Correspondent: The Mayor's Secretary, Civic Centre, Harrow HA1 2UH (081-863 5611).

Hillingdon

The Harefield Parochial Charities

Eligibility: People in need who live in the ancient parish of Harefield.

Types of grants: One-off grants only of between £10 and £60. Grants are not given to students in further and higher education.

Annual grant total: Over £2,000.

Applications: In writing to the correspondent.

Correspondent: Mrs D South, Treasurer, 2 Meadow View, Springwell Lane, Harefield, Middlesex UB9 6PQ (0895-822387).

The Uxbridge United Welfare Trusts

Eligibility: People in need who live in the old urban district of Uxbridge.

Types of grants: One-off grants either in cash or for furniture, equipment, clothing and help with fuel bills. No grants for rent or rates.

Annual grant total: £40,000 in 1988, but not all of this was given to individuals. No more recent information available.

Applications: On a form available from the correspondent. Applications can be submitted directly by the individual or through a third party. They are considered each month.

Correspondent: The Chairman, Trustee Room, Woodbridge House, New Windsor Street, Uxbridge UB8 2TY (0895-232976).

Hounslow

The Brentford & Chiswick Merged Charities

Eligibility: People in need who live in Brentford and Chiswick.

Types of grants: One-off grants for items such as telephone installation and bedding. Small pensions to two pensioners and Christmas gifts of £10 to widows have been made. The trust states: "more and more help is being given towards heating bills, but this has to be restricted due to the lack of funds". This was before VAT was introduced on fuel bills.

Annual grant total: About £14,000, most of which is given in educational grants.

Applications: In writing to the correspondent.

Correspondent: Mrs Thelma Lewis, Clerk, 285 Staines Road, Hounslow TW4 5AL (081-570 9789).

Other information: The trustees also administer the Brentford and Chiswick Relief in Need and Sick Poor Persons Funds. These funds have small budgets of about £300 to £400 each a year. One-off grants are requested quite often through agencies such as citizen's advice bureaux, social services, hospital welfare departments or money advice bureaux. These charities are not allowed to make grants towards relief of rates, council taxes or public funds.

The Brentford Relief-in-Need Charity

Eligibility: People in need who live in the former ecclesiastical parish of St Faith, Brentford and the united parish of Brentford, St Lawrence with St Paul & St George.

Types of grants: One-off grants only for items such as removal expenses, medical equipment, holidays and decorating materals.

Annual grant total: In 1992, the trust had assets of £13,000 producing an income of £1,100. Grants ranging from £20 to £250 were given to 6 individuals and totalled £670.

Applications: Preference is given to applications made through a recognised referral agency (social worker, citizen's advice bureau, doctor etc.) and are considered upon receipt.

Correspondent: The Rector of the Parish of Brentford, 3 The Butts, Brentford, Middlesex TW8 8BJ (081-568 6502).

The Hanworth Poors Land Trust & Coal Fund

Eligibility: People in need who live in the ancient parish of Hanworth.

Types of grants: Each year grants are made to about 10 families and a few individuals.

Annual grant total: The trust had an income of £1,500 in 1992.

Applications: Only through referral by social services, health visitors, probation officers, citizen's advice bureaux and Welcare.

Correspondent: E J Pittman, 6 Shakespeare Way, Hanworth, Middlesex TW13 7PE.

Other information: This entry has not been confirmed by the trust.

The Isleworth United Charities

Eligibility: People in need who live in the ancient parish Isleworth.

Types of grants: One-off grants only, from £25 upwards, depending on need.

Annual grant total: In 1993, the trust had an income of about £1,500 to £2,000. About 6 grants were given. The trust regularly has a surplus of income over expenditure.

Applications: In writing to the correspondent.

Correspondent: Mrs Worboys, Clerk, Clerk's Office, Tolson Lodge, North Street, Old Isleworth TW7 6BY (081-569 9200).

Islington

Richard Cloudesley's Charity

Eligibility: People in need who live in the ancient parish of St Mary Islington (roughly the modern borough, excluding the area south of the Pentonville and City Roads).

Types of grants: One-off grants, typically of £50, to help with cases of sickness or disability only.

Annual grant total: £250,000 including about £52,000 to individuals in 1991.

Applications: Applications should be made through the social services, doctor, citizen's advice bureau or similar agency. Applications on behalf of individuals are administered by Miss Kerala Thomson, Honorary Almoner, c/o 166 Upper Street, London N1 1XU (081-883 5809).

Correspondent: K Wallace, Clerk, c/o Richards Butler, Beaufort House, 15 St Botolph Street, London EC3A 7EE (071-247 6555).

The Finsbury Relief-in-Sickness Charity

Eligibility: Sick, convalescent and disabled people who live in Finsbury.

Types of grants: One-off grants according to need. Help has been given towards the cost of clothing, gas and electric bills, bedding, cookers, washing machines and floor coverings. Grants will not be given towards holidays, telephone bills, rent, council tax, television licences or education.

Annual grant total: In 1993, grants of between £50 and £100 were given to 34 individuals and totalled about £2,000.

Applications: Applications, on a form available from the correspondent, should be submitted through social services, hospitals, citizen's advice bureaux or similar agencies, and are considered quarterly from January onwards.

Correspondent: Doreen Scott, c/o IVAC, 322 Upper Street, London N1 2XQ (071-226 4862).

Lady Gould's Charity

Eligibility: People in need who live in Highgate (ie. the N6 postal district and part of the N2, N8, N10 and N19 districts).

Types of grants: Normally one-off generally under £500. Exceptionally recurrent grants will be considered.

Annual grant total: In 1993, about £30,000.

Applications: On a form available from the correspondent.

Correspondent: J Talbot, Secretary, Bower Cotton & Bower, 36 Whitefriars Street, London EC4Y 8BH (071-350 3040).

The Islington Relief-in-Need Charities

Eligibility: People in need who live in Islington.

Types of grants: One-off grants ranging from £25 to £75 towards clothing, fuel, bedding, cookers and essential household items etc.. No grants towards telephone, rent, council tax bills or television licences.

Annual grant total: In 1993, the trust gave grants to 104 people totalling over £6,000.

Applications: In writing through social services, hospitals, citizen's advice bureaux and similar agencies for

Islington/Kensington & Chelsea

consideration in January, April, July and October.

Correspondent: Doreen Scott, c/o IVAC, 322 Upper Street, London N1 2XQ (071-226 4862).

The Islington Relief-in-Sickness Charity

Eligibility: Sick, convalescent and disabled people who live in Islington.

Types of grants: One-off grants of between £25 and £100 towards clothing, gas and electric bills, bedding, furniture, cookers, washing machines and floor covering. No grants for holidays, telephone bills, rent, council tax or television licences.

Annual grant total: About 17 individuals received grants totalling £1,000.

Applications: In writing through social services, hospitals, citizen's advice bureaux and similar agencies for consideration in January, April, July and October.

Correspondent: Doreen Scott, c/o IVAC, 322 Upper Street, London N1 2XQ (071-226 4862).

Dame Alice Owen's Eleemosynary Charities

Eligibility: Poor widows who are over 50 and live in the parishes of St Mary, Islington and St James, Clerkenwell and have done so for at least two years.

Types of grants: Pensions of £20 a month to about 5 people.

Annual grant total: All the income is distributed totalling about £1,200.

Applications: The local vicar and social services are told when vacancies arise, but direct applications can be made.

Correspondent: The Clerk, The Worshipful Company of Brewers, Brewers' Hall, Aldermanbury Square, London EC2V 7HR (071-606 1301).

The Saint Luke's Parochial Trust

Eligibility: People in need, particularly the elderly, who live in the ancient parish of St Luke's, Old Street in the former metropolitan borough of Finsbury.

Types of grants: Pensions for the elderly, with allowances of £3 a week for a single person and £4 a week for a married couple. Rates are at present being reviewed. Note that applicants for pensions must have lived in the parish for 5 years before application, or for 15 years out of the previous 30. Elderly people who once lived within the beneficial area but were forced to move away because of the war, slum clearance or similar cause will also be considered. The trust also provides grants, mainly for the elderly, for television licences, Christmas gifts and individual help where necessary.

Annual grant total: In 1993, the trust's income was £992,000. Grants totalled £153,000 including £118,000 on pensions and related benefits and £35,000 on other benefits including grants and holidays.

Applications: To the correspondent at any time.

Correspondent: K C S Wood, Chief Executive, 90 Central Street, London EC1V 8AQ (071-250 4144).

Other information: The main expenditure of the trust is on the running of a leisure centre for elderly people living within its area of benefit.

The St Sepulchre (Finsbury) United Charities

Eligibility: Elderly people in need who live in the parish of St Sepulchre, Islington (EC1 and N1).

Types of grants: Pensions.

Annual grant total: In 1991, the trust's income was £20,000; pensions totalled £17,000 and one-off grants £30. In 1992, the trust received £1,100 of its income from Henry Smith's (General Estate) Charity.

Applications: In writing to the correspondent.

Correspondent: P S Rust, Secretary, 61 West Smithfield, London EC1A 9EA (071-606 5711).

Kensington & Chelsea

The Campden Charities

Eligibility: People in need who live in the royal borough of Kensington and Chelsea, north of the Fulham Road.

Types of grants: *1. Grants given direct to individuals in need:* Pensions to people in need who are over 70 and who have lived in the parish for at least seven years. The current pension is £280 a year. Christmas and birthday presents, television licences, holidays and other sundries are distributed. The authorised number of pensions is 650. In 1991/92, pensions and gifts totalled £243,000.

2. Grants given to individuals in need through agencies which have applied on their behalf: These grants vary a great deal in size and purpose from quite small sums for children's clothing and pocket money to large sums for equipment and the settling of debts. A total of £105,000 was awarded to 683 people.

Annual grant total: In 1992, the trust's income was £1.4 million. Grants totalled £1.8 million including £105,000 in relief-in-need payments to individuals.

Applications: Preliminary telephone enquiries are welcomed. Specific application forms are available for social work organisations seeking pensions or charitable relief for individuals in the parish. Applications are considered by the case committee, the education committee or the board of trustees as appropriate. Each of these meets monthly (except during August).

Correspondent: The Clerk, 27a Pembridge Villas, London W11 3EP (071-243 0551).

Other information: The charities also make grants to organisations (totalling £807,000 in 1992/93). See *A Guide to the Major Trusts*.

The Chelsea Non-Ecclesiastical Charities

Eligibility: Poor people, particularly elderly women, who live in Chelsea.

Types of grants: One-off grants, usually about £30.

Annual grant total: £850 out of an income of £1,100 in 1987. No more recent information available.

Applications: In writing to the correspondent.

Correspondent: Miss B M Towle, 17 Meriden Court, Chelsea Manor Street, London SW3 3TT (071-352 5032).

Other information: The trust states: "We have many more requests for help than we can possibly accept". Ineligible applications will not therefore be considered.

The Nicholas Freeman Memorial Trust

Eligibility: Elderly, disabled and disadvantaged people in need who live in Kensington and Chelsea.

Types of grants: Grants for services, equipment and other needs such as personal alarm units.

Annual gran total: In 1993, the trust had an income of £67,000. £12,000 was given in grants to individuals in need. Grants are limited by an on-going commitment to fund alarms already installed.

Kensington & Chelsea/Kingston-upon-Thames/Lambeth

Applications: In writing to the correspondent.

Correspondent: The Administrator, 19-27 Young Street, London W8 5EH (071-937 8045).

The Kensington District Nursing Trust

Eligibility: Sick people in need who have lived for at least two years in the former borough of Kensington.

Types of grants: Grants for equipment, essential items etc.. During the winter heating allowances are given. Some grants are also given to local organisations. The trust cannot fund rent, rates (except water rates) or hire-purchase debts or fines.

Annual grant total: In 1993, the trust gave grants to 180 individuals totalling £23,500.

Applications: On a form available from the correspondent. Applications must be submitted through social services, district nurses, health visitors or doctors. The case committee sits monthly (except August).

Correspondent: Mrs J Forbes, Clerk, 27a Pembridge Villas, London W11 3EP (071-229 3538).

Kingston-upon-Thames

The Kingston-upon-Thames Association for the Blind

Eligibility: Blind and partially sighted people who live in Kingston-upon-Thames.

Types of grants: Grants given include help towards holidays and house repairs.

Annual grant total: £5,500.

Applications: In writing to the correspondent.

Correspondent: Jonathan Cooper, 52 Barnfield Avenue, Kingston-upon-Thames KT2 5RE (081-546 4899).

The Kingston-upon-Thames Central Aid Society

Eligibility: People in need who live in the borough of Kingston-upon-Thames.

Types of grants: In 1991/92, 600 grants were made for the relief of need, especially in cases of sickness or emergencies (eg. repair/replacement of household furniture, help with bedding, clothing, dentures or spectacles, fares, removals, heating bills, rent or rate arrears, and television licences). Help can also be provided towards much-needed convalescent holidays. Christmas gifts, toys and food parcels are also distributed.

Annual grant total: £23,000 in 1990/91.

Applications: In writing directly by the individual or through a welfare agency, social services and similar agencies.

Correspondent: Mrs M Chapman, Director Secretary, Parman House, 36a Fife Road, Kingston-upon-Thames KT1 1SY (081-546 6187).

Other information: The society has extensive links with the area's voluntary sector (it is represented on old people's welfare committees, SSAFA and Kingston Care Committee for Chest Heart and Stroke Association) and can offer advice or arrange visits from its Fife Road offices. Office hours are Mon, Wed, Fri 10.00 am to 4.00 pm and Tues, Thurs 10.30 am to 12.30 pm.

William Nicholl's Charity

Eligibility: People in need who live in the former borough of Kingston-upon-Thames as constituted until 1964.

Types of grants: Fuel vouchers and pensions. However, the trustees have decided not to issue any further pensions until 1995 when applications from the reserve list will be considered.

Annual grant total: £2,600 in 1994, including 200 fuel vouchers of £10 and four weekly pensions of £3.

Applications: Applications for fuel vouchers in writing to the correspondent which will then be forwarded to the trustees, local organisations or ward councillors. Vouchers are issued via local organisations and ward councillors from about January to March each year.

Correspondent: A R Bessant, Clerk, The Guildhall, Kingston-upon-Thames, Surrey KT1 1EU (081-547 5021).

Lambeth

The Brixton Dispensary

Eligibility: People in need through mental or physical illness who live in the 11 ecclesiastical parishes in and around the centre of Brixton.

Types of grants: One-off grants, usually between £50 and £100, towards cookers, heating and convalescent holidays. Christmas gifts of £25, mainly for sick and elderly people. Generally no grants for debts.

Annual grant total: In 1993, the trust had an income of £2,275 and total expenditure of £1,900. Grants ranging from £50 to £100 were given to 15 individuals and totalled £1,640.

Applications: Applications should be submitted through a recognised referral agency (social worker, citizen's advice bureau, doctor etc.) and are considered by the trustees three times a year. The chairman can deal with emergency applications at any time.

Correspondent: Mrs M F Stedman, Clerk, 1 Kett Gardens, London SW2 1SS (071-652 0457).

Other information: Applicants should detail their name and address, type of sickness and income.

The Clapham Relief-in-Need Charity

Eligibility: People in need who live in the former parish of Clapham, or exceptionally, immediately outside this area (generally the postal districts of SW4 and parts of SW8 and SW12). Preference will be given to former tradesmen or those employed in trading businesses and their wives, widows, husbands and widowers, and dependent children.

Types of grants: Grants up to £150 are made towards the cost of fuel, heating appliances, bedding, clothing, special dietary foods, surgical appliances and convalescent holidays. No help will be given where sufficient benefit is obtainable from public sources.

Annual grant total: In 1992/93, the trust had an income of about £11,000 and gave £4,700 in grants.

Applications: On a form available from the correspondent. Applications should be sent through a recognised referral agency (social worker, citizen's advice bureau or doctor). They are considered in February, May, July and October.

Correspondent: R F Harding, Clerk, 19 Highfield Park, Marlow, Bucks SL7 2DE (0628-486293).

The Lambeth Endowed Charities

Eligibility: People in need who live in the borough of Lambeth (although in very exceptional cases the trustees may grant relief to people otherwise eligible who live immediately outside the beneficial area).

Types of grants: Grants for individuals fall into several categories: grants to individuals or families in urgent need; quarterly grants between to people with extraordinary needs, mostly disabled people; monthly payments to chronically sick and disabled patients, and quarterly pensions for pensioners.

In addition the Electric Wheelchair Loan Scheme enables disabled people to receive wheelchairs.

No grants where debts or bills have already been incurred; where funds are available from a statutory or other source; where applicants (individuals or organisations) live or operate outside the area of benefit; to students aged 25 and above.

Annual grant total: In 1992, 509 grants ranging from £30 to £770 were given to individuals in need and totalled £56,500.

Hayle's Charity also gave 10 grants to individuals in need, including specialised equipment for disabled people, totalling about £4,000.

Applications: On a form available from the correspondent. Applications are normally considered in February, June, September and November and should reach the correspondent at least one month beforehand for consideration at the next meeting. Applications must be supported by a recognized welfare agency or citizen's advice bureau, or by a doctor, social worker or minister of religion. For further help or advice contact the correspondent or Jenny Field, Fieldworker.

Correspondent: Rev D I S Jones, Clerk, 127 Kennington Road, London SE11 6SF (071-735 1925).

The Lambeth Mayor's Fund

Eligibility: People in need who live in the borough of Lambeth.

Types of grants: Grants, usually £20 to £30, where help is not available from the relevant statutory bodies. They are decided by the Mayor.

Annual grant total: £5,000 to £6,000.

Applications: Applicants are usually referred by social workers, citizen's advice bureaux etc., but individuals may also write directly.

Correspondent: The Mayor, Lambeth Town Hall, Brixton Hill, London SW2 1RW (071-926 1000).

The Thrale Almshouse & Relief-in-Need Charity

Eligibility: People in need who live within the ancient parish of Streatham.

Types of grants: One-off grants up to £250 according to need (not educational or replacing or abating statutory benefits).

Annual grant total: £4,000.

Applications: In writing to the correspondent.

Correspondent: The Clerk, c/o The Family Welfare Association, 501-505 Kingsland Road, London E8 4AU.

Lewisham

The Deptford Pension Society

Eligibility: Elderly people who have lived in the old London borough of Deptford for at least 7 years.

Types of grants: Pensions of £7 per month to 45 individuals.

Annual grant total: About £3,800 in 1993.

Applications: In writing to the correspondent.

Correspondent: Mrs Alison Claremont-Davies, Hon. Secretary, c/o All Saints' Church, 105 New Cross Road, London SE14 5DJ (071-639 2889).

The '56 Aid Club

Eligibility: People in need who live in the parish of Sydenham in Lewisham.

Types of grants: One-off grants according to need.

Annual grant total: £1,900 in 1989/90, out of an income of £3,200.

Applications: Directly by the individual in writing to the correspondent. It is an advantage if the applicant is known by a member of the club.

Correspondent: J McCarthy, Secretary, 15 Watlington Grove, Sydenham, London SE26 5RR.

The William Hatcliffe Non-Educational Charity

Eligibility: People in need, particularly elderly and disabled people, who have lived in the ancient parish of Lee in Lewisham for at least five years.

Types of grants: Regular allowances (currently £146 a year).

Annual grant total: No information available.

Applications: In writing to the correspondent.

Correspondent: D J Swales, 39 Brownhill Road, Catford, London SE6 2HB (081-697 8528).

Merton

The Mitcham United Charities

Eligibility: People in need who live in the Mitcham area, and have done so for two years.

Types of grants: Christmas gifts and one-off grants ranging from £50 to £100 for specific items such as household items and heating bills.

Annual grant total: About £2,000.

Applications: On a form available from the correspondent. Applications can be submitted directly by the individual or through a social worker, citizen's advice bureau or other welfare agency. They are considered bi-monthly.

Correspondent: Mrs B Bull, Age Concern (Merton), 277 London Road, Mitcham, Surrey CR4 3NT (081-648 5792).

The Lady Tyrrell Giles Gift

Eligibility: Women of the upper, middle and professional classes, with a preference for applicants who have or have had connections with the borough of Wimbledon.

Types of grants: One-off grants only ranging from £100 to about £1,000.

Annual grant total: In 1992/93, the trust had assets of £65,000 and an income of £5,000. 12 relief-in-need grants to individuals totalled £10,000.

Applications: On a form available from the correspondent. Applications can be submitted directly by the individual or through a social worker, citizen's advice bureau or other welfare agency. They are considered throughout the year.

Correspondent: The Charities Clerk, The Skinners' Company, 8 Dowgate Hill, London EC4R 2SP (071-236 5629).

The Wimbledon Guild of Social Welfare

Eligibility: People in need who live in Wimbledon and part of SW20 (the old borough of Wimbledon).

Types of grants: One-off grants of up to £200 for the relief of most sorts of need, such as household equipment, furniture, minor household repairs, clothing, bedding and occasionally towards holiday costs.

Annual grant total: £8,500 in 1992/93.

Applications: On a form available from the correspondent. Applications should be submitted through a social worker,

● Merton/Newham/Redbridge/Richmond-upon-Thames

citizen's advice bureau or other welfare agency. They are considered each month.

Correspondent: The Head of Social Work Dept., The Guild House, 30-32 Worple Road, Wimbledon, London SW19 4EF (081-946 0735).

Newham

The Mary Curtis Maternity Charity

Eligibility: Poor women who live in the borough of Newham.

Types of grants: Welfare grants before and after confinement.

Annual grant total: About £3,000.

Applications: In writing to the correspondent.

Correspondent: Geoffrey Hooper, Chairman, South West Ham Child Welfare Society, c/o Mansfield House University Settlement, 310 Barking Road, London E13 8HL (071-476 1505).

Redbridge

The Ilford Charities

Eligibility: Elderly people who live in the borough of Redbridge, Ilford.

Types of grants: Christmas grants to the elderly. In 1993, 213 elderly people received a £20 grant on 2nd December.

Annual grant total: £4,300 in 1993.

Applications: Details are advertised locally in day centres etc.. Application forms are available from the Town Hall during the first three weeks in October. The form asks for brief details of age, how long the applicant has lived in Ilford or other districts administered by Redbridge, income, expenses etc..

Correspondent: Lois Geary, Clerk, Information Centre, Town Hall, High Road, Ilford, Essex IG1 1DD (081-478 3020 ext. 2126).

Other information: The charity is also responsible for publicising and finding elderly beneficiaries for the annual visit of members of the Worshipful Company of Poulters who distribute a £10 note to each of the 80 people at a ceremony attended by the Mayor in the Town Hall in June of each year. Applications forms are available during the first three weeks in April.

Richmond-upon-Thames

The Barnes Relief-in-Need Charity and The Bailey & Bates Trust

Eligibility: People in need who live in East Sheen, London SW14.

Types of grants: Small grants to pensioners up to a maximum of £200.

Annual grant total: About £3,800.

Applications: In writing to the correspondent.

Correspondent: T M Sutton-Mattocks, Clerk, Bank Chambers, 1 Rocks Lane, Ranelagh Gardens, Barnes, London SW13 0DE (081-876 8811/2/3).

The Barnes Workhouse Fund

Eligibility: People in need who live in the ancient parish of Barnes (in practice SW13).

Types of grants: One-off grants only.

Annual grant total: £60,000 in 1989/90, out of an income of £106,000, but only £220 was given in grants to individuals. We have been unable to obtain more up-to-date information.

Applications: Applications can be submitted by the individual or preferably, through a recognised referral agency (eg. social worker, citizen's advice bureau or doctor) or other third party.

Correspondent: T M Sutton-Mattocks, Clerk, Bank Chambers, 1 Rocks Lane, Ranelagh Gardens, Barnes, London SW13 0DE (081-876 8811/2/3).

The Hampton Fuel Allotment Charitable Trust

Eligibility: Primarily people in need who are sick, convalescent, disabled or infirm and live in the ancient town of Hampton, ie. the present area of Hampton and of Hampton Hill; also the former borough of Twickenham and the remainder of the present borough of Richmond-upon-Thames.

Types of grants: See below.

Annual grant total: About £2,000,000 in 1991. This includes £107,000 to individuals in need of which £69,000 was for heating grants, £7,000 for emergency alarm systems and the remaining £31,000 for various items and facilities.

Applications: On a form available from the correspondent.

Correspondent: A W B Goode, Clerk, 15 Hurst Mount, High Street, Hampton, Middlesex TW12 2SA (081-941 7866).

The Hampton Wick United Charity

Eligibility: People in need who live in Hampton Wick and most of South Teddington, especially the parishes of St John the Baptist, Hampton Wick and St Mark, South Teddington.

Types of grants: One-off grants (with the possibility of future re-application).

Annual grant total: Around £20,000 in 1992/93, of which about two-thirds was given in grants to individuals.

Applications: In writing to the correspondent. The trustees normally meet three times a year to consider applications.

Correspondent: R R H Ellison, Clerk, Stane Cottage, Westlands, Birdham, Nr Chichester, West Sussex PO20 7HJ (0243-512476).

The Petersham United Charities

Eligibility: People in need who live in the parish of Petersham.

Types of grants: Pensions and grants of £100 to £250, including Christmas and birthday gifts and heating allowances. No grants where statutory funding is available.

Annual grant total: About £3,000 including education grants.

Applications: In writing to the correspondent by the individual. Applications are considered in January, April, July and October.

Correspondent: R M Robinson, Clerk, Dixon Ward & Co, 16 The Green, Richmond, Surrey TW9 1QD (081-940 4051).

The Richmond Aid-in-Sickness Fund

Eligibility: People in need who live in the borough of Richmond.

Types of grants: One-off and recurrent grants for bedding, fuel bills, rent/funeral expenses, recuperative holidays Christmas parcels and gifts and small cash grants.

Annual grant total: In 1992, the trust had an income of £3,200. Grants ranging from £75 to £150 were given to 9 individuals. Christmas parcels were also given to 77 households. The total value distributed to individuals was £2,200.

Applications: In writing to the correspondent for monthly consideration.

Correspondent: R M Robinson, Clerk, Dixon Ward & Co, 16 The Green, Richmond, Surrey TW9 1QD (081-940 4051).

The Richmond Charities Almshouses

Eligibility: People in need who live in the former borough of Richmond.

Types of grants: Small, one-off grants for relief of need, hardship and distress, welfare of widows, and provision of pensions.

Annual grant total: £1,800 in 1989. No more recent information available.

Applications: Either direct or through social services, citizen's advice bureaux, doctors etc..

Correspondent: H R Stinson, Clerk, 9 The Green, Richmond, Surrey TW9 1PU (081-948 4188).

The Richmond Parish Lands Charity

Eligibility: People in need who live in Richmond, Kew and North Sheen (NOT the whole borough of Richmond).

Types of grants: 1. *Small grants* for people in financial need, up to a maximum of £250 (with few exceptions).

2. *Grants for people with physical disability.* Each case is considered on its merits; there is no stated maximum.

3. *Warm campaign:* heating vouchers for elderly people on low incomes.

Annual grant total: 1. About £20,000. 2. Variable. 3. About £42,000.

Applications: Must be through nominated welfare organisations, mainly citizen's advice bureaux and social services. NO DIRECT APPLICATIONS ARE CONSIDERED.

Correspondent: The Clerk, The Vestry House, 21 Paradise Road, Richmond, Surrey TW9 1SA.

Other information: It is hoped to extend the benefit area for SMALL GRANTS ONLY to East Sheen and Ham/Petersham during 1994.

The Richmond Philanthropic Society

Eligibility: People in need who live in the former parish of Richmond upon Thames.

Types of grants: Small one-off grants to a maximum of £50.

Annual grant total: According to the Charity Commission, in 1991 the trust had an income of £8,400.

Applications: Only through social services or a welfare agency.

Correspondent: Edward J Harrison, 6 Gloucester House, Courtlands, Sheen Road, Richmond, Surrey TW10 5BB (081-940 6314).

Other information: This is the most up to date information at the Charity Commission. The entry has not been confirmed by the trust.

Ann Elizabeth Savage's General Charities

Eligibility: Widows who live in the ancient parish of Kingston-upon-Thames.

Types of grants: Annuities of about £100 given to 12 people and occasional one-off grants. Grants are also given to organisations.

Annual grant total: About £1,500 to individuals in 1993.

Applications: In writing to the correspondent or through All Saints and St John the Evangelist churches.

Correspondent: The Vicar of Kingston, 15 Woodbines Avenue, Kingston-upon-Thames, Surrey KT1 2AZ (081-546 2644).

The Henry Smith Charity

Eligibility: People in need who live in the old borough of Richmond.

Types of grants: Usually one-off grants.

Annual grant total: In 1993, the trust received £2,800 income, allocated from Henry Smith's (General Estate) Charity.

Applications: In writing to the correspondent, from referring bodies such as social services, health authority, citizen's advice bureau etc..

Correspondent: Miss Joan E Newell, 9 The Green, Richmond, Surrey TW9 1PU (081-948 4188).

Southwark

The Camberwell Consolidated Charities

Eligibility: Elderly people in need who live in Camberwell, Peckham and Dulwich.

Types of grants: About 430 pensions of £30 a year paid in instalments of £5 every two months.

Annual grant total: £13,000 in 1988, the most recent year for which information is available.

Applications: Vacancies are advertised by social services area offices, Age Concern etc.. Application forms are also available at the town hall. Trustees usually meet in May and November to consider new pensions.

Correspondent: Evelyn Jarrett, Clerk, Town Hall, Peckham Road, London SE5 8UB (071-525 5000).

The Camberwell Provident Dispensary Fund

Eligibility: People in need who live within a two-mile radius of the church of St Giles, Camberwell.

Types of grants: About 20 one-off grants to sick poor people towards holiday expenses, food, clothing, fuel and medical expenses. No grants for the relief of rates or taxes.

Annual grant total: Around £600 in 1993.

Applications: On a form available from the correspondent. Must be endorsed by a social worker, doctor etc..

Correspondent: Rev Andrew Davey, St Luke's Vicarage, 123 Farnborough Way, London SE15 6HL (071-703 5587).

The Christ Church United Charities

Eligibility: Elderly people in need who live in the former metropolitan borough of Southwark (ie. the northern part of the present borough of Southwark).

Types of grants: Pensions for elderly people (£45,000), Christmas parties (£8,500) and gifts (£2,700). Summer holidays for pensioners accounted for £60,000.

Annual grant total: About £115,000 in 1992/93.

Applications: In writing to the correspondent.

Correspondent: W F Plowright, Clerk, Charities Section, Municipal Offices, 151-153 Walworth Road, London SE17 1RY (071-525 2128/2129).

The Joseph Collier Holiday Fund

Eligibility: People aged 60 or over who live in the former metropolitan borough of Southwark (ie. the northern part of the present borough of Southwark).

● Southwark/Sutton

Homeowners, whether bought by themselves or on their behalf, are excluded.

Types of grants: Yearly one-off grants towards the cost of recuperative holidays in the UK or travel expenses to visit a relative.

Annual grant total: £1,400 in 1989, out of an income of £7,000. We have been unable to obtain more up-to-date figures.

Applications: Applicants should collect a form, in person, from the office on Monday or Thursday mornings. Applications are considered monthly. Forms are not issued to any other party.

Correspondent: Mrs J D Crossman, Charities Section, Municipal Offices, 151–153 Walworth Road, London SE17 IRY (071-525 2128/2129).

The Mayor of Southwark's Common Good Trust

Eligibility: People in need who live in the borough of Southwark.

Types of grants: Grants to individuals with disabilities for specific items such as electric wheelchairs. Also, smaller emergency grants eg. to elderly people facing sudden large heating bills or single-parent families needing children's clothing.

Annual grant total: About £17,500.

Applications: In writing to the correspondent. Applications should preferably come from or be supported by a welfare agency or social worker. They should include full details of family/financial/health background and details of other sources of funds, including whether a previous application has been made to this trust. Applications can be made at any time and are normally dealt with within one month.

Correspondent: The Secretary, The Town Hall, 31 Peckham Road, London SE5 8UB (071-525 7347).

The Peckham & Kent Road Pension Society

Eligibility: People who have lived in Peckham, SE15 for at least five years, are receiving Income Support and are over 60 (women) or 65 (men).

Types of grants: Monthly pensions of £7. The correspondent states that the trust's resources are already stretched by its pension commitments.

Annual grant total: £6,500 in 1993.

Applications: In writing to the correspondent. Applications should be made through social services, doctor etc..

A recommendation from an existing grantee is helpful.

Correspondent: L R Clayton, 2 Clayhill Cottages, Lamberhurst, Kent TN3 8AY (0892-890247).

The Rotherhithe Consolidated Charities

Eligibility: People in need who live in the ancient parish of St Mary's, Rotherhithe.

Types of grants: The trust pays an annual pension of £91 to about 450 pensioners, and gives other one-off grants.

Annual grant total: £111,000 in 1992.

Applications: On a form available from the correspondent. Applications can be submitted directly by the individual or by a third party. They are considered at any time.

Correspondent: B D Claxton, Hardcastle Burton, 19 Amwell Street, Hoddesdon, Herts EN11 8TS (0992-444466).

Other information: In 1988, the charity sold one of its properties for £1,250,000 so the trust's income has more than doubled since 1987. The trustees are proposing a new scheme to provide holidays for its pensioners (probably costing about £60,000 a year). They have also written to the Charity Commission to change the trust's constitution to increase the scope of grants.

St Olave's United Charity, incorporating the St Thomas & St John Charities

Eligibility: People in need who live in Bermondsey and Rotherhithe (ie. SE1 and SE16).

Types of grants: 650 elderly people are currently receiving pensions, and a further grant is made before Christmas. One-off grants can be made for a wide variety of need, including clothes, musical instruments and holidays.

Annual grant total: In 1993, the trust had an income of about £270,000. Around £20,000 was given in grants to individuals in need and £40,000 to organisations.

Applications: Pension applications are dealt with four times a year. There is a waiting list. Applications should be in writing outlining the need.

Correspondent: Mrs S Broughton, Secretary, 6-8 Druid Street, Tooley Street, London SE1 2EU (071-407 2530).

Rebecca Flower Squire's Bequest & Others

Eligibility: People in need who live in the ancient parish of St Mary Newington.

Types of grants: One-off grants to a maximum of £150.

Annual grant total: In 1992, the trust received £1,150 income, allocated from Henry Smith's (General Estate) Charity.

Applications: In writing to the correspondent. The trustees meet in the spring and autumn.

Correspondent: The Rector, 57 Kennington Park Road, London SE11 4JQ (071-735 1894).

The Emily West Temple Trust

Eligibility: Poor people under 25 who live in the following (in order of priority): the parish of Christchurch, Southwark; the former borough of Southwark.

Types of grants: One-off grants only.

Annual grant total: £2,500.

Applications: In writing to the correspondent.

Correspondent: Canon P B Challen, Christchurch Industrial Centre, 27 Blackfriars Road, London SE1 8NY (071-928 4707).

Sutton

The Beddington & Wallington Relief Fund For the Sick & Infirm

Eligibility: People in need who live in Beddington and Wallington.

Types of grants: Grants up to £30 for services or towards the cost of essential items or equipment (no cash grants are given and receipts are needed as proof of purchase). Christmas parcels are distributed.

Annual grant total: £900 in 1988. The trust has not updated this information.

Applications: In writing and only on referral from social services or welfare agencies such as Age Concern and WRVS.

Correspondent: Miss M Mansfield, 51 Fairlawnes, Maldon Road, Wallington, Surrey SM6 8BG (081-647 9551).

Tower Hamlets

The Henderson Charity

Eligibility: Pensioners who live in the hamlets of Ratcliff and Shadwell, and the parish of St George's-in-the-East, Stepney. Applicants must be long-standing residents of the beneficial area, and there is a maximum income requirement.

Types of grants: Pensions of £15 a month for single people and £20 a month for married couples.

Annual grant total: About £10,000 in 1991.

Applications: Vacancies are advertised locally and through social services and appropriate welfare agencies. Application forms when an election is due can be obtained from social services or the correspondent.

Correspondent: Charles Westover, Taylor Joynson Garrett, Solicitors, Carmelite, 50 Victoria Embankment, Blackfriars, London EC4Y 0DX (071-353 1234).

The Trevor Huddleston Fund for Children

Eligibility: Children in need who live on the Isle of Dogs. Where necessary help can be given to their parents and families.

Types of grants: About 100 grants a year between £10 and £150 to cover basic needs.

Annual grant total: About £5,000 in 1993.

Applications: Mostly through schools, social services and churches, but individuals may also apply directly.

Correspondent: Rev Nicholas Holtam, Christ Church Vicarage, Manchester Road, London E14 3BN (071-987 1915).

The Stepney Relief-in-Need Charity

Eligibility: People in need who live within the boundaries of the following area in Stepney: Jubilee Street on the west, Mile End Road on the north, Grand Union Canal on the east and Commercial Road on the south.

Types of grants: Christmas parcels, heating allowances and a monthly payment to pensioners. Under the scheme governing the charity, there can be no additions to the present list of pensioners. Other one-off grants are also given.

Annual grant total: £3,000 in 1992/93. Grants were also made to Stepney Neighbourhood Social Services (£4,200) to disburse to individuals who apply to them for help.

Applications: In writing to the correspondent. The trustees usually meet four times a year.

Correspondent: Mrs J Partleton, Clerk, Rectory Cottage, 5 White Horse Lane, Stepney, London E1 3NE (071-720 3598).

Miss Vaughan's Spitalfields Charity

Eligibility: People in need who live in the ecclesiastical parishes of Christchurch with All Saints Spitalfields, St Matthew Bethnal Green and St Leonard Hoxton.

Types of grants: Originally the clothing and support of poor mechanics and weavers in Spitalfields, unable from illness or any calamity to work. Now grants are given to individuals and families who are convalescing, unemployed or disabled, large families on a low income etc..

Annual grant total: About £1,000.

Applications: To a member of the clergy from the above mentioned parishes.

Correspondent: Philip Whitehead, 45 Quilter Street, London E2 7BF.

Waltham Forest

The Waltham Forest Handicapped Trust

Eligibility: Disabled people who live in the borough of Waltham Forest.

Types of grants: The trust makes grants for a variety of needs and can also give advice about sources of statutory funding.

Annual grant total: £1,100 in 1990/91.

Applications: In writing to the correspondent via social services or other welfare agencies.

Correspondent: Mrs L Bell, London Borough of Waltham Forest, Adult Disabilities, 2b Hatch Lane, Chingford, London E4 6NG (081-524 5271).

The Walthamstow Almshouse & General Charities

Eligibility: People in need living in the former borough of Walthamstow.

Types of grants: One-off grants only, following confirmation that funds for the required purpose are not available from social services or any other source.

Annual grant total: The trust had an income of £585,000. Most of this is used for almshouse purposes. Only 1% (£5,000) in the 15 month period up to 31st March 1993 was given to individuals. A further £21,000 was given to other charitable and caring institutions.

Applications: In writing to the correspondent, only through the social services departments of the borough of Waltham Forest.

Correspondent: The Clerk, Monoux Hall, Church End, Walthamstow, London E17 9RL (081-520 0295).

Wandsworth

The Battersea United Charities

Eligibility: People in need who live in the former borough of Battersea.

Types of grants: Small grants for those in urgent need, particularly elderly poor people.

Annual grant total: About £5,000, but most of this is for education grants.

Applications: In writing to the correspondent.

Correspondent: T W Ottway, Clerk, Battersea District Library, Lavender Hill, London SW11 1JB (081-871 7466).

The Harold Carter Bequest

Eligibility: People in need who live in north Battersea.

Types of grants: Grants up to £250 a year.

Annual grant total: £2,500 in 1990/91, the most recent year for which informtion is available.

Applications: Through referral from social services, charities and schools. A preliminary phone call to discuss the application is welcomed.

Correspondent: D Jesson-Dibley, St Mary's Parochial Church Council, 72 Albany Mansions, Albert Bridge Road, London SW11 4PQ (071-228 7506).

The Peace Memorial Fund

Eligibility: Children under 16 who live in the borough of Wandsworth.

Wandsworth/Westminster

Types of grants: Grants towards holidays (mainly in the UK).

Annual grant total: Grants to individuals for relief-in-need and education totalled £6,000 in 1993 (about 100 grants).

Applications: Through organisations only eg. Wandsworth Borough Council, scouts and cubs groups, schools and local churches.

Correspondent: Gareth Jones, Town Hall, Room 153, Wandsworth High Street, London SW18 2PU (081-871 7520).

The Putney Creche

Eligibility: Mothers with children up to the age of seven who live in the Putney and Wandsworth areas.

Types of grants: One-off grants to mothers who might have experienced matrimonial problems and are now experiencing financial difficulties in bringing up infant children. Grants up to £35 where there is one child in the family and up to £60 where there are two or more. If help is still needed after six months, a further payment of up to half the above values can be made.

Annual grant total: About 125 grants were given totalling around £6,000 in 1993.

Applications: For economic reasons distributions are only made through recognised welfare organisations in the area. Application forms can be obtained from the correspondent.

Correspondent: Mrs A Smalley, Messrs Russell-Cooke Potter & Chapman, 2 Putney Hill, London SW15 6AB (081-789 9111).

The Putney Relief Committee

Eligibility: Elderly people and families who are in need and who live in Putney.

Types of grants: Monthly payments, fuel allowances and Christmas gifts. Grants for special cases are also available.

Annual grant total: £2,500 in 1988. No more recent information available.

Applications: By personal recommendation from clergy, social workers, health visitors, doctors etc.. Note that the address below is for mailing purposes only.

Correspondent: The Secretary, c/o Eileen Lecky Health Centre, 2 Clarendon Drive, London SW15 1AA.

Other information: This entry has not been confirmed by the trust.

The Wandsworth Children's Fund

Eligibility: Children under 16 who live in the borough of Wandsworth and the parts of the old borough which included Streatham and parts of Clapham.

Types of grants: One-off grants towards the cost of baby equipment, clothing and convalescent holidays. No grants for general furnishings, debts or adult holidays.

Annual grant total: In 1990/91, the trust's income was £3,200; grants totalled £1,500.

Applications: Only through social workers, health visitors, education welfare officers, school teachers and youth club leaders. Application forms are available from the correspondent, and applications are considered in March, June and September.

Correspondent: Mrs B Giles, Clerk, 42 Rosemead Avenue, Mitcham, Surrey CR4 1EY (081-764 1690).

The Wandsworth Combined Charity

Eligibility: Elderly people in need who live in the ancient parish of Wandsworth, ie. the present wards of Fairfield, Earlsfield, Southfield, West Hill, Springfield, part of Thamesfield and part of East Putney.

Types of grants: Pensions only.

Annual grant total: In 1989, the trust's income was £9,600; grants totalled £7,000. In 1992, the trust received £2,200 income, allocated by Henry Smith's (General Estate) Charity. No further information available.

Applications: Via social services, Age Concern, local clergy or by direct enquiry to the correspondent. Vacancies are advertised locally.

Correspondent: A V Rashbrook, Clerk, H E Rashbrook & Son, 91 East Hill, Wandsworth, London SW18 2QD (081-874 2211).

Other information: The Wandsworth Consolidated Charities, the Charity of Francis Millington and a small educational charity were amalgamated in January 1992 to form the Wandsworth Combined Charity.

Westminster

The Bengough Charity

Eligibility: Elderly women in need, with preference for those who live in the parish of St Matthew, Westminster.

Types of grants: Pensions paid quarterly and one-off grants towards eg. heating, lighting and mobility aids. Grants are also available to organisations towards the provision of accommodation especially for women who are communicants of the Church of England and regular attenders at St Matthews.

Annual grant total: In 1992, the trust had assets of £470,000 and an income of £32,000. Grants and accommodation were given to five individuals totalling £23,000.

Applications: On a form available from the correspondent.

Correspondent: Sir Reginald Pullen, Warden's House, 42 Rochester Row, London SW1P 1BU (071-828 3131).

The Charity of A J G Cross

Eligibility: People who are sick and in need and live in south Westminster.

Types of grants: One-off grants (average about £70, maximum £100) for heating, fuel, clothing, convalescence, holidays, travel, home repairs, aids and appliances. Also occasional grants towards more expensive items (eg. electric wheelchairs).

Annual grant total: 40 grants totalling £2,500 were made in 1993.

Applications: The charity does not deal directly with individuals. Applications, on a form available from the correspondent, should be submitted via a social worker, physiotherapist, occupational therapist, hospital or welfare organisation together with a covering letter. Grants for up to £100 are dealt with immediately; larger amounts are considered twice yearly at the trustees' meetings. All grants are distributed through social services, hospitals etc., not given directly to individuals.

Correspondent: Mrs E Garwood, 68 Arncliffe Drive, Heelands, Milton Keynes MK13 7LH (0908-319460).

Isaac Duckett's Charity (St Clement Danes Branch)

Eligibility: People who are or have been employed in the city of Westminster, with preference for the parish of St Clement Danes. Preference for people who are qualified as, who are or have been

Westminster

domestic servants, housekeepers or resident caretakers.

Types of grants: One-off grants and pensions. In 1992/93, pensions of £5 per week were given and grants of up to £200.

Annual grant total: The trust is currently revising its grant making policies and in future will be dispersing funds through other charitable organisations. For this reason it has requested an annual grant total not be given in case it misleads potential applicants.

Applications: On a form available from the correspondent.

Correspondent: The Clerk, St Mary-le-Strand, 171 Strand, London WC2R 2LS (071-836 3205).

The Hyde Park Place Estate Charity (Civil Trustees)

Eligibility: People in need who live in the borough of Westminster.

Types of grants: One-off grants to individuals and families for all kinds of need. No recurrent grants are given, but beneficiaries can reapply if there is further need.

Annual grant total: £202,000 in 1992/93, including grants to organisations.

Applications: In writing to the correspondent. Applications on behalf of individuals need the recommendation of a trustworthy person/organisation. Applications are often processed within a few days but may be held over to the next half-yearly meeting if large-scale funding is involved.

Correspondent: Miss E Crichton, Clerk, St George's Vestry, 2a Mill Street, London W1R 9LB (071-629 0874).

The Paddington Welfare Charities

Eligibility: People who are sick or in need who live in the former metropolitan borough of Paddington (roughly the north-west corner of the city of Westminster, bounded by Edgware Road and Bayswater Road).

Types of grants: Generally one-off grants for specific requests such as services or facilities; furniture and household equipment; clothing; arrears with telephone, gas and electricity bills and holiday breaks to alleviate the person's situation. In 1992, about £23,000 was given to individuals and organisations.

A monthly pension scheme is also in operation paying a total of £10,000 a year to up to 75 local residents nominated by Age Concern. Food and fuel coupons (worth about £3) are also given to local vicars and social work agencies for them to distribute. The total value of the coupons totals about £2,000 a year. There is no maximum or minimum grant. Pensions are at least £12 a month.

All clergy in the parish can participate in the distribution of Christmas gifts. Most receive about £100 to distribute in amounts of £5 or £10 per recipient. Part of the cost of this scheme are met by the William Whitley Christmas Gifts Charity. The total value of these gifts was over £1,500 in 1992. The clergy are also given £50 each to distribute during the rest of the year; this costs £1,000.

Over £1,500 is given to the social services to distribute in emergency grants or loans.

Annual grant total: At least £39,000 was given in 1992, some of which was given to organisations to provide services to beneficiaries and some to organisations to distribute on the charities' behalf.

Applications: In writing through social services and welfare agencies only. Applications are normally dealt with within two to three weeks.

Correspondent: Sarah Carter, Assistant Clerk, City of Westminster, PO Box 240, Westminster City Hall, Victoria Street, London SW1E 6QP (071-798 2735).

Other information: The calls on the welfare fund during the last few years of recession have greatly intensified. The trust has set monthly cash limits and a system of prioritising the more pressing applications.

The St Clement Danes Parochial Charities

Eligibility: The parish of St Clement Danes in Westminster, but if there are no suitable applicants, the city of Westminster.

Types of grants: One-off grants to a maximum of £200 and quarterly pensions. In 1993, the charity gave 29 pensions of £5 a week.

Annual grant total: About £7,500 in 1993.

Applications: On a form available from the correspondent.

Correspondent: The Clerk, St Mary-le-Strand Office, 171 Strand, London WC2R 2LF (071-836 3205).

The St Mary-le-Strand Charity

Eligibility: People in need who have lived in the city of Westminster for more than a year, with priority for the parish of St Mary-le-Strand.

Types of grants: One-off grants of about £100 to individuals in need and regular allowances to elderly people in need.

Annual grant total: The charity's income was £84,000 in 1992; relief-in-need grants and grants to welfare organisations totalled about £48,000 and pensions £3,200. It is thought that about £5,000 was given to individuals in need.

Applications: Applications must come from social workers or welfare agencies where a case worker is already working with the potential beneficiary.

Correspondent: Mrs Anne Butters, Clerk, 171 Strand, London WC2R 2LS (071-836 3205).

The St Marylebone Health Society

Eligibility: Families with children of school age and under who live in the former borough of St Marylebone in the city of Westminster ie. east of Edgware Road and north of Oxford Street in NW1 or W1.

Types of grants: Holidays for parents and their children are arranged and paid for. Grants are usually sufficient to pay for one week at a holiday centre, including fares and food allowance if self-catering. (In 1992, most families went to the Haven Caister Holiday Centre, Great Yarmouth during the school summer holidays.) The applicant should have lived in the beneficial area for two years. Overseas holidays and families without children cannot be funded.

Other grants (length of residence qualification not necessary) totalling £5,700 in 1992 were made for beds, bedding, household equipment, children's equipment, clothing etc.. Grants average about £100; the maximum is about £300. Christmas grants, ranging from £10 for a single parent and small child to around £40 for a large family, are made in the form of grocery vouchers.

Grants are not given to adults not caring for children, to assist elderly people or to students.

Annual grant total: £19,000 in 1992 to 172 families (ie. 231 adults and 447 children).

Applications: Via social workers, educational welfare officers and health visitors, using the application form available from the correspondent. Holiday applications by March if possible. Other applications at any time.

Correspondent: Mrs M North, Hon. Secretary, 9 Hunting Gate Close, Enfield, Middlesex EN2 7EF (081-367 6704).

Westminster

The United Charities of St Paul's, Covent Garden

Eligibility: People in need who live in the city of Westminster.

Types of grants: One-off grants ranging from £50 to £180. Monthly payments to about 12 people. Grants can be paid directly or through hospitals, health authorities, family service units or an early intervention service.

Annual grant total: About £4,000.

Applications: In writing to the correspondent.

Correspondent: C G Snart, Clerk, William Sturges, Alliance House, 12 Caxton Street, London SW1H OQY (071-222 1391).

United Westminster Almhouses

Eligibility: Elderly people in need who live in the city of Westminster.

Types of grants: Pensions and one-off grants.

Annual grant total: In 1992, the trust's income was £320,000 and expenditure £296,000. Most of this went on maintaining almshouses and Extra Care Unit. £14,000 was given in out-pensions and grants and £2,000 was given in benefits to its almspeople.

Applications: On a form available from the correspondent.

Correspondent: Sir Reginald Pullen, Warden's House, 42 Rochester Row, London SW1P 1BU (071-828 3131).

The Waterloo Parish Charity for the Poor

Eligibility: People in need who live in the parish of Waterloo, St John & St Andrew.

Types of grants: Small grants for living expenses and domestic items, although the charities' combined income is already overstretched.

Annual grant total: About £1,000.

Applications: Usually through social workers.

Correspondent: Irene Page, St John's Vicarage, 1 Secker Street, London SE1 8UF (071-633 9819).

The Westminster Amalgamated Charity

Eligibility: People in need who live or work in the borough of Westminster.

Types of grants: Grants are given for heating, holidays and holiday fares, clothing, household equipment and furnishing, and other forms of real need.

Annual grant total: In 1992, the trust's income was £258,000. Grants totalled £190,000 including £39,000 in grants to individuals.

Applications: In writing to the correspondent through a welfare agency, doctor, social services or similar third party.

Correspondent: P Bircher, Clerk, 4-5 Gough Square, London EC4A 3DE (071-353 9991).

National and general charities

This section includes all the entries which could not be tied to a particular occupation, disability or locality. It starts with an index which divides the various charities into general groups classified according to their beneficiaries (eg. children, elderly etc.) with a separate category for trusts that specifically give grants for convalescence/holidays.

Applicants should note that many of the trusts are under the "General" heading. This is because they can give to a wide range of people, so if applicants are unable to find help from other sources in the Guide then they should be able to approach one or more of these. However, most of these charities still have restrictions on who they can help; applicants should not simply send off indiscriminate applications to any charity under the General heading, rather they should first consider carefully whether they are eligible. Also, these trusts are still the best known and so they tend to receive most applications.

After the index come the entries which are arranged alphabetically.

Index of National and general charities

Children/Young People
Athlone Trust
Buttle Trust
Care Trust
Family Welfare Association
Lubricators Charitable Trust
Norwood Child Care
E C Roberts Charitable Trust

Convalescence/Holidays
Frederick Andrew Convalescence Trust
Family Holiday Association
Ogilvie Charities
Pearson's Holiday Fund
Lloyd Thomas Charity for Women & Girls
Victoria Convalescent Trust Fund

Elderly
Percy Bilton Charity Limited
Care Trust
Counsel & Care for the Elderly
Deakin Institution
Charles Dixon Pension Fund
Family Welfare Association
Friends of Elderly & Gentlefolk's Help
Home Warmth for the Aged
Lubricators Charitable Trust
Middlesex King Edward VII Memorial Fund
John Murdoch Trust
National Benevolent Institution
Northern Ladies Annuity Society
Royal United Kingdom Beneficent Association
St Andrew's Society for Ladies in Need
Society for Assistance of Ladies in Reduced Circumstances
Unity Fund for the Elderly
Universal Beneficent Society
Wireless for Bedridden
see also Widows/Widowers/Single People and Women

Ethnic & Foreign Communities in Britain
Anglo-Arab Aid Ltd
Association of Vietnamese Residents in the UK
Catholic Council for Polish Welfare
Ibero-American Benevolent Society
King Edward VII British/German Foundation
Muslim Welfare Board
Netherlands Benevolent Society
Polish Naval Association Welfare Fund
Rhodesians Worldwide Assistance Fund
Royal Belgian Benevolent Society
Scandinavian Benevolent Society
Society of Friends of Foreigners in Distress
Swiss Benevolent Society
Zakat Committee

General
Thomas Betton's Charity for Pensions & Relief-in-Need
C B Charitable Trust
Carnegie Hero Trust Fund
Late Baron F A D'Erlanger's Charitable Trust
Mark Davies Injured Riders Fund
Alfred de Rothschild Charity
Dibs Charitable Trust
Drake Charity Trust
Francis Drake Fellowship
Family Welfare Association
Farthing Trust
David Finnie & Alan Emery Charitable Trust
R L Glasspool Charitable Trust
Grut Charitable Trust
Guild of Aid for Gentlepeople
Homelife DGAA
Imperial Society of Knights Bachelor Sunfund
Johnston Family Fund
William Johnston Trust Fund
Heinz & Anna Kroch Foundation
Hoper-Dixon Trust
James Scott Law Charitable Fund

283

● **National and general charities**

League of Helping Hand
Professional Classes Aid Council
Royal Air Forces Escaping Society Charitable Fund
Royal Scottish Corporation
Royal United Kingdom Beneficent Association (RUKBA)
Sainsbury Family Charitable Trusts
St Martin-in-the-Field's Vicar's Relief Fund
Salvation Army
Henry Smith Charity
Mrs Smith & Mount Trust
Society of St Vincent de Paul
Straits Settlement & Malay States Benevolent Society
Sir John Sumners's Trust
Triangle Trust 1949 Fund
S C Witting Trust
Women's Royal Voluntary Service (WRVS) Trust
Worshipful Company of Cordwainer

Holidays (see Convalescence/Holidays)

Masons (see Orders, Masonic, Buffaloes)

Orders (Masonic, Buffaloes)
Grand Charity (of Freemasons under United Grand Lodge of England)
New Masonic Samaritan Fund
Royal Antediluvian Order of Buffaloes Grand Lodge of England War Memorial Annuities
Royal Masonic Benevolent Institution

Prisoners/Former Prisoners
Aldo Trust
Matthew Trust
National Association for Care & Resettlement of Offenders (NACRO)
Royal London Aid Society
Paul Stephenson Memorial Trust

Religion

Christian Science
Morval Foundation

Jewish
Annie Arbib Trust
George Julian Egerton Fund
Nathan & Adolphe Haendler Charity
Holmleigh Trust
Jewish Aged Needy Pension Society
Jewish Care
Jewish Refugees Charitable Trust
Helen Lucas Fund
Norwood Child Care

Protestant
Charity of Anne Farrar Brideoake
Deakin Institution
Charles Dixon Pension Fund
Mylne Trust
Arthur Townrow Fund

Victims of Crime
Matthew Trust

Widows/Widowers/Single People
Broadlands Home Trust
Crossley Fund
Deakin Institution
John Murdoch Trust
Ogilvie Charities
Perry Fund
Widow's Friend Society
see also Women

Women
Annie Arbib Trust
Broadlands Home Trust
Deakin Institution
Sir Thomas Devitt's Endowment Fund
Helen Lucas Fund
Morris Beneficent Fund
Northern Ladies Annuity Society
Perry Fund
Royal Society for the Relief of Indigent Gentlewomen of Scotland
St Andrew's Society for Ladies in Need
Society for Assistance of Ladies in Reduced Circumstances
Lloyd Thomas Charity for Women & Girls
Arthur Townrow Fund
see also Widows/Widowers/Single People

The Aldo Trust

Eligibility: People in need who are being held in detention pending their trial or after their conviction. The applicant must still be serving the sentence.

Types of grants: One-off grants, generally up to a maximum of £10.

Annual grant total: In 1989, £6,000 was given. The benefactor has since died and the amount of future income is unsure.

Applications: Applications must be made through prison service personnel (eg. probation, chaplaincy, education), and should include the name and number of the prisoner, age, length of sentence and expected date of release. Applicants can apply once each year. No applications direct from prisoners will be considered.

Correspondent: Annie Smith, Welfare/Insurance Administrator, c/o NACRO, 169 Clapham Road, London SW9 0PU (071-582 6500).

Other information: The trust appears to be admirably flexible and wide-ranging in its grants. It has given grants for recreational purposes, including for musical instruments, radios and record players, clothing, games, hobbies, arts and budgerigars.

The Frederick Andrew Convalescent Trust

Eligibility: Broadly, professional women who are working or retired.

Types of grants: One-off grants for convalescence only. Grants range from £150 to £500.

Annual grant total: The trust's income is £50,000 to £60,000. £40,000 of this is given to individuals.

Applications: On a form available from the correspondent. Applications are considered throughout the year and can be submitted by the individual or through a recognised referral agency (social worker, citizen's advice bureau or doctor etc.). Applications must be countersigned by a doctor.

Correspondent: C T Prichard, Andrew & Co, St Swithin's Square, Lincoln LN2 1HB (0522-512123).

Other information: This entry is repeated in the Sickness and disability charities section of the book.

Anglo-Arab Aid Ltd

Eligibility: Arab families who are in need, whether born in Arab countries or not.

Types of grants: One-off and recurrent grants according to need.

National and general charities

Annual grant total: In 1992, the trust had an income of £36,000, of which £13,000 was given in grants to individuals.

Applications: In writing to the correspondent.

Correspondent: Mrs N Al-Kutoubi, General Secretary, 3 Frognal Close, Hampstead, London NW3 6YD (071-794 8557).

The Annie Arbib Trust

Eligibility: Jewish women in need.

Types of grants: One-off and recurrent grants according to need. About 25 grants are given at present.

Annual grant total: £15,000 in 1989, the most recent year for which we have information.

Applications: By letter or recommendation.

Correspondent: Miss H E Hyman, Secretary, 5 Verity House, Hamilton Terrace, London NW8 9YB (071-624 5335).

The Association of Vietnamese Residents in the UK

Eligibility: Vietnamese people living in the UK who are in need.

Types of grants: One-off grants ranging from £50 to £500.

Annual grant total: In 1991, expenditure totalled £1,500, of which £400 was given to individuals for relief-in-need. (The major part of the income is used to produce a newsletter, Huong Venguon.)

Applications: In writing to the correspondent. Applications should be submitted directly by the individual and can be in Vietnamese.

Correspondent: Dr P N Luu, 15 Melrose Avenue, Mitcham, Surrey CR4 2EH.

The Athlone Foundation

Eligibility: Needy ADOPTED children in the UK under the age of 18, on the application of their parents.

Types of grants: One-off grants according to need.

Annual grant total: £12,000 in 1993, although most of this was given in education grants.

Applications: In writing to the correspondent. Applications are considered in May and November.

Correspondent: J J Tobin, 14 New Street, London EC2M 4TR (071-972 9720).

Thomas Betton's Charity for Pensions & Relief-in-Need

Eligibility: Poor people.

Types of grants: One-off grants only. No grants for holidays or clothing.

Annual grant total: About £10,000 is given in up to 100 grants.

Applications: On a form available from the correspondent through a social worker. Applications are considered throughout the year.

Correspondent: The Secretary, Ironmongers Hall, Barbican, London EC2Y 8AA (071-606 2725).

The Percy Bilton Charity Limited

Eligibility: 1. Elderly people.

2. Disabled/handicapped people: both children and adults whether in a family unit or living alone.

3. People suffering from a medical illness where treatment is required either by hospital or in cases of genuine illness being dealt with by a doctor. Guidance notes are available upon receipt of an sae.

Types of grants: Grants are usually between £20 and £1,000. Christmas hampers are also given. The trust states: "Whilst the following list gives the more general requests for assistance, it is by no means complete. Therefore more unusual requests will be considered provided they do not fall outside current criteria given below:

Laundry equipment, transport, aids and adaptations, certain visiting expenses, the purchase of heating equipment, bedding, general items of clothing, telephone installations (not rental), refrigerators, furniture and furnishings, holidays (only if an applicant has not taken a holiday within the last two years)."

The trust will not consider any of the following:

- General cases of hardship falling outside the stated criteria above.
- Requests for foreign holidays or visits.
- Educational grants.
- Debts of any kind, including gas, electricity and rent arrears.
- TV and car licences.
- Nursing fees.
- Funeral expenses.
- Applications found to be requesting re-imbursements of any nature.
- Requests for school uniforms.
- Continuing donations over a specified period.

Annual grant total: About £140,000 in 800 grants together with about 3,500 Christmas hampers.

Applications: "Applications are received only from social workers in social services departments and hospitals.

Applications must include the following information before they can be processed:

- Full name and address of applicant, including names and ages of children.
- Status, whether married/divorced/single parent etc..
- Income of applicant.
- Brief history to present day.
- Requirement and an estimation of the cost.
- If any other charities or organisations have been approached please state.
- Please quote amounts received from statutory sources (ie. DSS) or other charitable funding within the past six months.
- Please state clearly the name of the authority to which the cheque should be made payable in the event of a grant being issued."

Correspondent: Mrs J A Beasley, Bilton House, Uxbridge Road, London W5 2TL (081-579 2829).

Other information: This entry is repeated in the Sickness and disability charities section of the book.

The Charity of Ann Farrar Brideoake

Eligibility: Communicant members of the Church of England in the dioceses of York, Liverpool and Manchester.

Types of grants: Generally recurrent bursaries, usually between £100 and £300. Beneficiaries may be assisted as long as they remain in need, but each case is reviewed annually. There are about 150 regular beneficiaries and about 12 new beneficiaries are added each year.

Annual grant total: Over £60,000.

Applications: On a form available from the correspondent. The form must be countersigned by a local vicar.

Correspondent: A B Anderson, 8 Blake Street, York YO1 1XJ (0904-625678).

• **National and general charities**

The Broadlands Home Trust

Eligibility: Needy widows or single women over 40; poor girls entering a trade or occupation (but not graduates).

Types of grants: Regular allowances of £4 a week for widows and spinsters in poor circumstances but not in residential care; small grants for books and clothes for girls for further training. One-off grants range from £50 to £100.

Annual grant total: In 1990/91, the trust had an income of £8,500. Pension payments totalled £5,500 and 12 relief-in-need grants totalled £1,000.

Applications: In writing to the correspondent, including date of birth, full details of income and expenditure, specific needs and a reference. Applications are considered twice a year in May and November.

Correspondent: Mrs L Hayden, 3 Winchester Close, Newport, Isle of Wight (0983-521368).

The Buttle Trust

Eligibility: See below.

Types of grants: The trust policy is to assist children and young people (under the age of 21) brought up in the Christian religion whose circumstances come within the following criteria:

1. (a) Adopted children facing special problems, especially those problems arising subsequent to adoption having taken place;

(b) Children who have been de facto adopted or privately fostered by a relative or family friend, the guardian(s) being unable to provide adequately for their needs;

(c) Young people who, through no fault of their own, have had to leave the family home, who are living solo, and whose circumstances can be vouched for independently.

2. Other children and young people who are both deprived of normal family life, and suffering from some compelling or exceptional misfortune.

3. Students under the age of 25 (see *The Educational Grants Directory*).

4. 10% of the trust's distributable income is set aside for grants to organisations (see *A Guide to the Major Trusts*).

The trust gives priority to helping individual children and young people at a time of acute social crisis. Most grants are therefore for 'maintenance' purposes. In exceptional circumstances, school fee awards are made to provide for an acute boarding need or to ensure stability for a child already at a fee-paying institution.

Annual grant total: £1,460,000 in 1992/93.

Applications: Applications should be made initially by letter from a social worker, health visitor, school, clergy or the like (or direct from the parent or guardian), detailing the name(s) and address(es) of the parent(s) or guardian(s), the name(s) and date(s) of birth of the child(ren), and the qualifying misfortune. No application form is sent out until an initial letter has been received and considered in principle. Applications are considered monthly and should be addressed as follows:

For applicants in England: The Director, The Buttle Trust, Audley House, 13 Palace Street, London SW1E 5HS.

For applicants in Wales: The Regional Secretary, Whitecross House, Whitecross Street, Monmouth, Gwent NP5 3BY.

For applicants in Scotland: The Regional Secretary, Baltic Chambers, 50 Wellington Street, Glasgow G2 6SB.

For applicants in Northern Ireland: The Regional Secretary, 28 Victoria Road, Holywood, Belfast BT18 9BG.

Correspondent: The Director, Audley House, 13 Palace Street, London SW1E 5HS (071-828 7311).

Other information: The trust was founded by the Rev W F Buttle in 1953. It is a Christian foundation and where possible every beneficiary should be brought up within the context of Christian family life. It publishes useful Notes for the guidance of social agencies or others applying for a Buttle Trust grant.

The C B Charitable Trust

Eligibility: Europeans who live or have lived in Kenya and their dependants in need.

Types of grants: Generally recurrent grants to elderly people; occasional one-off grants. Grants range from £100 to £400.

Annual grant total: In 1992, the trust had assets of £67,000 and an income of £6,300. Grants totalled £5,200.

Applications: In writing to the correspondent. Applications should include precise details of time spent in Kenya and should be submitted directly by the individual. They are considered throughout the year.

Correspondent: James A C Smith, The Copse, Post Grove, Upper Enham, Andover SP11 6JB (0264-357487).

The Care Trust

Eligibility: People in need, with a special emphasis on children and elderly people.

Types of grants: Grants according to need, typically £100 and up to a maximum of £1,000.

Annual grant total: £3,000.

Applications: In writing to the correspondent through a social worker, citizen's advice bureau or other welfare agency.

Correspondent: P L Gallaher, 3 Mulcaster Street, St Helier, Jersey JE2 3NJ.

The Carnegie Hero Fund Trust

Eligibility: Heroes and their families (that is people who have suffered financial loss or have been injured - or the families of people who have been killed - in performing acts of heroism in saving human life in peaceful pursuits in the British Isles and territorial waters). About five to six new cases are recognised each year.

Types of grants: One-off and recurrent grants according to need.

Annual grant total: About 200 families are on the trust's books; not all receive grants every year. In 1993, the trust gave about £100,000 in grants.

Applications: Direct applications are rare; recommendations are usually submitted by the police or by other organisations and the trustees also nominate suitable applicants through the press.

Correspondent: Mr Runciman, Secretary, Abbey Park House, Dunfermline, Fife KY12 7PB (0383-723638).

Other information: The trust was established in 1908 by Andrew Carnegie, who made a great fortune from steel. His Birthplace Museum in Dunfermline displays the Roll of Honour of the Hero Fund Trust, now containing the names of over 6,000 heroes and heroines.

The Catholic Council for Polish Welfare

Eligibility: People of Polish origin who are in need and who do not come within the scope of other funds.

Types of grants: One-off and recurrent grants according to need.

Annual grant total: About £1,500.

Applications: In writing to the correspondent, preferably through a social worker, citizen's advice bureau or other welfare agency.

Correspondent: O M Stepan, Hon. Secretary, 14 Collingham Gardens, London SW5 0HT (081-992 3328).

Counsel & Care for the Elderly

Eligibility: People over retirement age.

Types of grants: Lump sum grants typically for fuel bills, telephone installation, emergency alarms, and other needs which are not met by the Social Fund. The capital limit is £1,500.

Annual grant total: £45,000 in 1993, plus monies administered on behalf of other trusts.

Applications: In writing to the correspondent.

Correspondent: The Administration Department, Twyman House, 16 Bonny Street, London NW1 9PG (071-485 1566).

Other information: This charity provides an advice service (including 21 fact sheets) for elderly people on matters including help at home, accommodation and finance (including ensuring elderly people are receiving their full DSS entitlements).

The Crossley Fund

Eligibility: Poor widows and spinsters of at least 50 years of age.

Types of grants: Help with RENT ONLY; grants up to £2.50 a week.

Annual grant total: £2,000.

Applications: Usually made with the assistance of welfare organisations or third parties such as vicars. A form is sent to likely applicants on request. Applications are considered at any time.

Correspondent: Mrs Sheila Norris, 4 The Grove, Wannock Lane, Lower Willingdon, East Sussex BN20 9SP (0323-484049).

Other information: The correspondent states "We receive lots of inappropriate applications; we can only help older people with rent ".

The Late Baron F A D'Erlanger's Charitable Trust

Eligibility: People in need.

Types of grants: One-off and recurrent grants (either monthly or quarterly) according to need.

Annual grant total: About £150,000.

Applications: In writing to the correspondent.

Correspondent: F J Mulhearn, 37 Great James Street, London WC1N 3HB (071-242 4304).

The Mark Davies Injured Riders Fund

Eligibility: People injured in horse-related accidents (excluding professional jockeys and those injured in the horse racing industry).

Types of grants: One-off and recurrent grants according to need, ranging from £150 to £8,000. Grants have been given towards mortgage and hire purchase payments, wheelchairs, therapy beds, stable and home help, travel, second hand cars, chair lifts, house adaptations etc.. Interest free loans have also been given.

Annual grant total: In 1993, the trust had an income of £47,000. 24 grants to individuals totalled £29,000.

Applications: In writing to the correspondent or to Mrs Jane Davies, Little Woolpit, Ewhurst, Cranleigh, Surrey GU6 7NP (0483-277344/268623). Applications can be submitted directly by the individual or by a third party. They are considered at any time.

Correspondent: M Franklin, Fund Accountant, BEC Stoneleigh, Kenilworth, Warwickshire CV8 2LR (0203-696697).

The Alfred de Rothschild Charity

Eligibility: People unable to pay in full for medical treatment of a special nature.

Types of grants: Generally one-off grants; typically £300, usual maximum £500.

Annual grant total: About £9,000 given in around 20 grants.

Applications: In writing to the correspondent.

Correspondent: The Administrator, 57 Elm Park Mansions, Park Walk, London SW10 0AP.

Other information: This entry is repeated in the Sickness and disability charities section of the book. This entry has not been confirmed by the trust, but the address is correct according to the latest information on file at the Charity Commission.

The Deakin Institution

Eligibility: Ladies who live in the UK, have never been married, are in reduced circumstances and who are members of the Church of England or of a church having full membership of the Council of Churches for Britain and Ireland. Grants are not usually given to ladies under 55 years of age.

Types of grants: Annuities, usually £260 a year, paid half yearly. No one-off grants.

Annual grant total: About £45,000 in 172 grants in 1992/93. The income of the trust was £54,000.

Applications: On a form available from the correspondent submitted directly by the individual. Applications are considered in October.

Correspondent: Michael L Chadwick, The Annexe, The Manor House, 260 Ecclesall Road South, Sheffield S11 9UZ (0742-621251).

Sir Thomas Devitt's Endowment Fund

Eligibility: Women of the upper, middle and professional classes in financial need.

Types of grants: Pensions ranging from £288 to £1,600 a year. No one-off grants.

Annual grant total: In 1992/93, the trust had assets of £35,000 with an income of £2,700. Virtually the whole of the income was given in nine pensions.

Applications: On a form available from the correspondent. Applications can be submitted directly by the individual or through a social worker, citizen's advice bureau or other welfare agency. It is unlikely that any new applications will be successful for the foreseeable future.

Correspondent: The Clerk to the Skinners' Company, Skinners' Hall, 8 Dowgate Hill, London EC4R 2SP (071-236 5629).

The Dibs Charitable Trust

Eligibility: People in need.

Types of grants: One-off grants for the relief of immediate distress only, ranging from £25 to £250. No pensions or annuities. Grants are not given for furniture/fixtures and fittings, travel abroad, education or holidays.

Annual grant total: £31,000 in 200 grants in 1990.

Applications: In writing through a local social services department or similar recognised body. They are considered throughout the year.

Correspondent: C H Davis/A M W Davis, c/o 10a Angel House, 20-32

● **National and general charities**

Pentonville Road, London NW1 9XD (071-833 2594).

The Charles Dixon Pension Fund

Eligibility: Merchants who are married men, widowers or bachelors of good character, who are members of the Church of England and who are not less than 60 years of age. Applicants must live in Bristol, Liverpool or London.

Types of grants: Pensions of up to £1,500 a year.

Annual grant total: £7,500 in 1993 in eight pensions.

Applications: On an application form when a vacancy is advertised in the press. Applications can be submitted directly by the individual or through a social worker, citizen's advice bureau, other welfare agency or a third party such as a clergyman.

Correspondent: The Treasurer, The Society of Merchant Venturers, Merchants' Hall, The Promenade, Clifton, Bristol BS8 3NH (0272-738058).

The Drake Charity Trust

Eligibility: Male level green bowlers in need who are members of a bowling club.

Types of grants: One-off and recurrent grants, generally worth £100 to £200, according to need.

Annual grant total: In 1993, the trust gave 15 grants totalling £2,200.

Applications: In writing to the correspondent, requesting an application form. Full details of income and expenditure are needed. Applications should be submitted through the bowling club.

Correspondent: Dennis F Cousins, 102 Malford Grove, South Woodford, London E18 2DQ (081-989 3810).

Other information: The trust works closely with the Francis Drake Fellowship. See entry below.

The Francis Drake Fellowship

Eligibility: Widows and dependants of members of the fellowship. Grants are given to needy dependants of deceased bowling members.

Types of grants: One-off and recurrent grants according to need. There is a sliding scale of grants depending on surplus income. If after general household/living expenses (excluding food, clothing etc.) the applicant has a surplus of under £50 per week, grants are £300; if the surplus income is between £50 and £70, grants are £250.

Annual grant total: In 1992, the trust gave 86 grants totalling £26,000, £3,800 of which was to dependent children.

Applications: In writing to the correspondent, requesting an application form. Applications should be submitted through the bowling club's Francis Drake Fellowship delegate.

Correspondent: Ron Norris, Treasurer, 8 Lowlands, Hatfield, Herts AL9 5DY.

Other information: The trust works closely with the Drake Charity Trust. See entry above.

The George Julian Egerton Fund

Eligibility: Jewish ladies and gentlemen of good family who are in reduced circumstances and in their middle or old age.

Types of grants: One-off or recurrent grants according to need.

Annual grant total: £6,500.

Applications: In writing to the correspondent. Applications can be submitted directly by the individual.

Correspondent: The Secretary, 221 Golders Green Road, London NW11 9DQ (081-458 3282).

The Family Holiday Association

Eligibility: Families who are referred by social workers, health visitors or other caring agencies as desperate for a weeks' holiday break. Applicants must not have had a holiday within the past four years, unless there are exceptional circumstances.

Types of grants: Grants are paid to the agency for a holiday of the family's choice (usually holiday camp, caravan or a stay with relatives). The total cost of the holiday is paid (holiday camp costs, food and travel expenses).

Annual grant total: In 1993, the trust gave £345,000 to about 900 families.

Applications: As early as possible (preferably Nov/Dec). Social workers should apply by letter requesting an application form and enclose a STAMPED ADDRESSED ENVELOPE. Applications must be referred by a welfare agency; those made directly by the individual are not accepted. Grants are calculated on the basis of the kind of holiday the family would choose, so precise costings are helpful. This is a fundraising charity. Funds are often exhausted by the end of February, so it is important to apply early.

Correspondent: The Administrator, Hertford Lodge, East End Road, London N3 3QE (081-349 4044).

The Family Welfare Association

Eligibility: People in need.

Types of grants: "Almost every kind of need can be met, as a wide variety of trust funds are administered by the FWA. Fuel bills, clothing, particularly children's clothing, household needs and holidays are most commonly requested, but we can also help with more unusual needs such as electronic aids.

"We cannot help with rent arrears, council tax, funeral expenses, fines, or expenses already covered by statutory funds.

"The FWA also administers pensions to elderly people and the amalgamation of a number of old pension funds has enabled us to make half-yearly grants to approximately 150 pensioners."

Annual grant total: About £700,000 given in about 3,500 grants.

Applications: "Application must be made by a social worker on behalf of a client as part of an overall treatment plan. The Grants Administrator is first contacted by letter and given a brief outline on the need. If funds are available and an application can be accepted, the application form is sent to the social worker. When this has been returned and processed it is then considered by the Grants Committee at their weekly meeting. Emergency applications will be accepted by telephone.

"Grants Committee members are experienced workers from various branches of social work, who can also advise on additional statutory benefits to which the client may be entitled. Payment in all cases is made either to the referring agency or intermediary and not direct to the beneficiaries."

Correspondent: Grants Administrator, 501-505 Kingsland Road, Dalston, London E8 4AU (071-254 6251).

The Farthing Trust

Eligibility: People in need. Those either personally known to the trustees or recommended by those personally known to the trustees have priority.

Types of grants: One-off and recurrent grants according to need.

National and general charities

Annual grant total: £30,000 in 1992 was divided between individuals in need and other charitable purposes.

Applications: In writing to the correspondent. Applicants will only be notified of a refusal if an sae is enclosed.

Correspondent: C H Martin, 48 Ten Mile Bank, Littleport, Ely, Cambridgeshire CB6 1EF.

Other information: The trusts states that it receives 20 letters a week and is able to help one in a 100. There would seem little point in applying unless you can establish a personal contact with a trustee.

The David Finnie & Alan Emery Charitable Trust

Eligibility: People in need.

Types of grants: One-off grants according to need.

Annual grant total: In 1991, the trust's income was £60,000; it gave £37,000 in grants. In 1993, 10 to 12 grants of between £200 and £1,000 were given to individuals. The trust also gives grants to organisations.

Applications: In writing to the correspondent.

Correspondent: The Trustees, Stoy Hayward, 8 Baker Street, London W1M 1DA (071-486 5888).

The Friends of the Elderly & Gentlefolk's Help

Eligibility: People in need who are over retirement age, preferably on Income Support or a retirement pension, with no more than £3,000 in savings.

Types of grants: One-off and recurrent grants according to need. Grants are given for clothing and most essential household furnishings and appliances. There is a special fund for winter warmth.

No grants for funerals, telephone bills or council tax. Loans are not given.

Annual grant total: £240,000 (plus other trust funds).

Applications: On a form available from the correspondent.

Correspondent: Mrs Rosemary Faux, Welfare Director, 42 Ebury Street, London SW1 0LZ (071-730 8263).

Other information: The main activity of the charity is the management of 13 residential homes, several of them with nursing wings.

The R L Glasspool Charity Trust

Eligibility: People in need.

Types of grants: Small one-off grants only, primarily for household equipment, clothing and holidays.

Annual grant total: £113,000 in 1992/93.

Applications: In writing to the correspondent, through the social services, probation service, citizen's advice bureau or hospital social work department.

Correspondent: Mrs F Moore, Secretary, 298 Hoe Street, Walthamstow, London E17 9QD (081-520 4354).

The Grand Charity (of Freemasons under the United Grand Lodge of England)

Eligibility: Personal petitioners must be indigent freemasons under the United Grand Lodge of England, or their dependants (ie. widows, dependent children under 21, and spinster daughters or spinster sisters who are incapacitated or over 60).

Types of grants: Lump sums, which may be disbursed over not less than twelve months, are made available. The average grant to personal petitioners in 1993 was £1,127. Annuities are not granted.

Annual grant total: £1,594,000 to 1,414 individuals in 1993.

Applications: In writing to the correspondent.

Correspondent: The Secretary, 60 Great Queen Street, London WC2B 5AZ (071-831 9811).

Other information: 1. Personal applicants whose masonic link is not under the United Grand Lodge of England should apply to the appropriate Grand Lodge. If applicants do not have appropriate addresses, the Secretary above will be able to help.

2. Much practical help and financial support in personal distress and for local charity is given independently of the Grand Charity by individual lodges and Provincial Grand Lodges. Addresses are available from the Secretary above.

3. The Grand Charity gives substantial support to operating charities, including national (but not local) non-masonic charities, as well as to individuals.

4. There is also the Masonic Trust for Girls and Boys to help children of any age (including adopted children and step-children) of freemasons under the United Grand Lodge of England. See entry in *The Educational Grants Directory*.

5. See also the separate entries for the Royal Masonic Benevolent Institution and the New Masonic Samaritan Fund in this Guide.

The Grut Charitable Trust

Eligibility: "Individuals suffering from the effects of illness or poverty." Children in need and elderly people are given particular consideration.

Types of grants: Grants generally up to £100.

Annual grant total: About £25,000 given in about 1,500 grants.

Applications: In writing to the correspondent. Applications should be supported by a recognised body, local authority or social welfare organisation.

Correspondent: The Secretary, Poole & Co, Solicitors, Dolphin House, 21 Hendford, Yeovil, Somerset BA20 1TP (0935-24381).

The Guild of Aid for Gentlepeople

Eligibility: People of gentle birth or good education who have no call on a trade or professional benevolent fund. "The Guild can help all age groups - many who have support are younger disabled people with dependent children."

Types of grants: One-off grants and weekly allowances according to need. Grants are given to people living in their own home or in residential/nursing homes.

The guild does not make loans or clear debts.

Annual grant total: In 1992, the guild had assets of £1.2 million and a total expenditure of £208,000 including £152,000 in relief-in-need grants to individuals.

Applications: On a form available from the correspondent. Applications can be submitted directly by the individual or by a third party such as a social worker or other welfare agency.

Correspondent: The Secretary, 10 St Christopher's Place, London W1M 6HY (071-935 0641).

Other information: The guild is operated alongside the Professional Classes Aid Council. See separate entry.

National and general charities

The Nathan & Adolphe Haendler Charity

Eligibility: Poor Jews who have come to take refuge in the UK or Eire.

Types of grants: One-off and recurrent grants or loans according to need.

Annual grant total: £12,000.

Applications: In writing to the correspondent. Urgent applications can be dealt with at any time.

Correspondent: The Central British Fund for World Jewish Relief, Drayton House, 30 Gordon Street, London WC1H 0AN (071-387 3925).

The Holmleigh Trust

Eligibility: Jewish people in need.

Types of grants: Distribution of goods only. No monetary grants are given, nor any help with education.

Annual grant total: Goods worth £200,000 were distributed in the four year period up to 1988. No more recent information available.

Applications: Applications are only accepted when direct recommendation is received from rabbis involved in the communal social benefit scheme.

Correspondent: A Barnett, 154 Holmleigh Road, London N16 5PY (081-800 5489).

Home Warmth for the Aged

Eligibility: Elderly people, men over 65 and women over 60, at risk from the cold in winter.

Types of grants: Provision of heating appliances, bedding, clothing and solid fuel, and to pay fuel debts where the supply has been disconnected and in certain cases recommended by a doctor or social worker. One-off grants only. No grants to pensioners who have younger members of the family living with them.

Annual grant total: £12,000 in 1992/93.

Applications: Through social workers, doctors, nurses etc. only, to whom grants are returned for disbursement. If there is an armed forces connection, applications should be made through SSAFA (see separate entry). Applications made directly by individuals are not considered.

Correspondent: The General Secretary, Sea Haze, Gorsethorn Way, Fairlight, East Sussex TN35 4BQ (0424-813515).

Homelife DGAA (formerly The Distressed Gentlefolk's Aid Association)

Eligibility: British or Irish people who are "distressed gentlefolk". This is broadly interpreted as people of professional or similar background or connection.

Types of grants: Grants according to need (although "grants are made in accordance with scales which are not published"). Grants may be one-off gifts or regular allowances (within the limits of the DSS disregard). They may be given for telephone rental, television rental and licence, and for help with nursing or residential care home fees.

Grants are not normally given for the settlement of debts, education, private medical expenses or funeral expenses.

Annual grant total: About £700,000 given in around 1,000 grants.

Applications: On a form available from the correspondent. Applications can be submitted directly by the individual or through a social worker, citizen's advice bureau or similar welfare agency. Applications should be made in the first instance to specific or professional funds where appropriate.

Correspondent: Mrs M E Yeats, Director of Casework, Vicarage Gate House, Vicarage Gate, London W8 4AQ (071-229 9341).

Other information: The association also runs its own residential and nursing homes. For information contact Miss H M Funston, Admissions Officer.

The Hoper-Dixon Trust

Eligibility: "This small trust was established by a man about to become a member of the English Province of the Order of Preachers, commonly known as the Dominicans, and is intended to assist the poor in the parishes of the three churches in Newcastle, Leicester and London maintained and run by that order of Roman Catholic priests. Objects of the charity are referred to the trustees by the pastoral clergy of the three churches involved."

Types of grants: One-off and recurrent grants according to need.

Annual grant total: In 1992/93, the trust had an income of £16,000. 12 grants totalled £7,000.

Applications: Only considered if made through the parish priest. Applications addressed to the correspondent below will NOT be processed.

Correspondent: The Trustees Solicitor, Messrs Farrer & Co, 66 Lincoln's Inn Fields, London WC2A 3JX (071-242 2022).

The Ibero-American Benevolent Society

Eligibility: Subjects or citizens of all Spanish or Portuguese speaking countries, whilst in the UK, and the wives or widows and children of the above.

Types of grants: Usually one-off grants of £50 to £500 for a wide range of needs (eg. washing machines, cookers, telephone installation/bills in certain circumstances). No education grants.

Annual grant total: 19 grants totalling £5,000 in 1993.

Applications: In writing to the correspondent. Applications can be made directly by the individual or through a social worker, citizen's advice bureau, the Spanish Consulate or a minister of the church.

Correspondent: J A Lopez-Ruiz, Secretary, c/o Banco Bilbao Vizcaya, 100 Cannon Street, London EC4N 6EH (071-623 3060).

The Imperial Society of Knights Bachelor Sunfund

Eligibility: Individuals or families who by reason of disaster or unforeseen misfortune are subject to particular hardship for which they have no financial resources or any help from other recognised sources or charities.

Types of grants: One-off grants up to £500.

Annual grant total: Probably about £15,000.

Applications: In writing to the correspondent. All applications should be made through a charity or recognised welfare agency, not direct from the individual unless endorsed by a responsible body.

Correspondent: Robert M Esden, Clerk, 21 Old Buildings, Lincoln's Inn, London WC2A 3UJ (071-405 1860).

The Jewish Aged Needy Pension Society

Eligibility: Members of the Jewish community aged 60 or over, who have known better circumstances.

Types of grants: About 60 to 70 pensions of up to £5 per week for all kinds of need.

Annual grant total: £18,000 in 1993.

Applications: In writing to the correspondent.

Correspondent: Mrs S A Taylor, Secretary, 34 Dalkeith Grove, Stanmore, Middlesex HA7 4SG (081-958 5390).

Jewish Care

Eligibility: Elderly, mentally ill, visually impaired and physically disabled people and their families who live in London and the south-east of England and are of the Jewish faith.

Types of grants: Jewish Care (which includes the former Jewish Welfare Board, Jewish Blind Society and the Jewish Home and Hospital at Tottenham) is the largest Jewish social work agency, providing a range of services, both domiciliary and residential. Financial assistance is not a normal part of the board's work, though some such expenditures are inevitably associated with its social work service. (See also the George Julian Egerton Fund at the same address.)

Annual grant total: "Small".

Applications: In writing to the correspondent either direct by the individual or through a social worker.

Correspondent: The Director of Social Services, 221 Golders Green Road, London NW11 9DW (081-458 3282).

Other information: This entry is repeated in the Sickness and disability charities section of the book.

The Jewish Refugees Charitable Trust

Eligibility: Refugees from Nazi oppression and their children who are settled in the UK.

Types of grants: One-off and recurrent grants according to need. Most kinds of need can be considered.

Annual grant total: No information available. Most of the income is used to fund a day centre.

Applications: In writing to the correspondent.

Correspondent: Mrs Rossen, Administrator, 1 Hampstead Gate, 1a Frognall, London NW3 6AL (071-431 6161).

The Johnston Family Fund

Eligibility: Members of the upper and middle classes who through no fault of their own have fallen into impoverished circumstances, and widows and daughters of such people. No male under 50 and no female under 40 will benefit.

Types of grants: One-off and recurrent grants according to need. Grants usually range from £500 to £1,000. No grants for education.

Annual grant total: In 1992, the trust had assets of £212,000 and an income of £17,000. Total expenditure was £11,000 in seven relief-in-need grants to individuals.

Applications: By letter only to the correspondent. Applications are considered throughout the year.

Correspondent: J N L Packer, Secretary, Nigel Packer & Co, 1st Floor, Royal Liver Building, Pier Head Liverpool L3 1HU.

The William Johnston Trust Fund

Eligibility: People in need.

Types of grants: One-off and recurrent grants according to need. Grants range from £100 to £2,000. Grants are not given for education.

Annual grant total: In 1992, the trust had assets of £283,000 with an income of £23,000. Total expenditure was £24,000 including £23,500 in 22 relief-in-need grants to individuals.

Applications: By letter only to the correspondent. Applications are considered throughout the year.

Correspondent: J N L Packer, Secretary, Nigel Packer & Co, 1st Floor, Royal Liver Building, Pier Head Liverpool L3 1HU.

The King Edward VII British-German Foundation (United Kingdom)

Eligibility: Needy people of German nationality in the UK, or minors with at least one parent of German birth.

Types of grants: Mainly one-off grants between £50 and £100.

Annual grant total: In 1990/91, the trust had assets of £42,000 and income of £26,000. Expenditure totalled £17,000 including £1,100 in 12 relief-in-need grants to individuals. (Most grants are in the form of educational scholarships.) The correspondent has confirmed that the entry is correct but was unwilling to update the financial information.

Applications: In writing, including full details, to the correspondent. Applications can be submitted directly by the individual or through a social worker, citizen's advice bureau or other welfare agency.

Correspondent: The Secretary, 23 Falcondale Road, Westbury-on-Trym, Bristol BS9 3JS (0272-623613).

The Heinz & Anna Kroch Foundation

Eligibility: Individuals suffering severe financial hardship.

Types of grants: This foundation gives money to new and existing projects in the field of medical research. Part of its income is also used to give support to individual cases of severe hardship in the form of one-off grants, which can be to help clear debts to enable the client get back on their feet. No grants are given to students, for holidays, or drug-related problems.

Annual grant total: In 1992/93, the foundation had assets of £1.4 million with an income of £125,000. Total expenditure was £95,000, of which £68,000 was given in grants of between £100 to £500.

Applications: Must be made through the social services or similar welfare agencies. Applications must include full details of circumstances including income and expenditure and are considered throughout the year.

Correspondent: Mrs H Astle, Administrator, PO Box 17, Worsley, Manchester M28 2SB (061-793 4201).

The James Scott Law Charitable Fund

Eligibility: People in need.

Types of grants: Grants towards the cost of specific medical aids.

Annual grant total: £4,000, but some of this is given in educational grants.

Applications: In writing to the correspondent.

Correspondent: R H Wilson, Secretary, Merchants' Hall, 22 Hanover Street, Edinburgh EH2 2EP (031-225 7202).

The League of the Helping Hand

Eligibility: People of "gentle birth" and "good character" who are in financial need caused through physical or mental illness.

Types of grants: Regular grants of up to £10 a week, plus one-off grants ranging from £100 to £250, typically for heating, bedding, television licences, telephone connection, hospital travel, replacement equipment and furnishings. A small number of beneficiaries are granted £10 a week for a shortfall in nursing home fees (currently 25 beneficiaries). Holiday grants are limited to convalescence or to enable carers to have a break.

Grants are not at present given for computers, electric wheelchairs or

National and general charities

holidays except for the two categories stated above.

Annual grant total: In 1992/93, the trust had assets of £941,000 and an income of about £95,000. Expenditure totalled under £22,000, of which only £520 was given in grants of £25 to £250 to individuals in need. In the previous edition of this Guide we stated that about £68,000 was given to 90 regular pensioners together with a limited number of one-off grants.

Applications: Applications should be submitted through a third party on a form available from the correspondent. A doctor's letter stating applicant's ill-health must accompany the application as must details of family and financial situation. Details are required as to how much is needed and what for, who else has been approached and how much has been realised. They are considered every six weeks.

Correspondent: Mrs I Goodland, 226 Petersham Road, Petersham, Richmond, Surrey TW10 7AL (081-940 7303).

The Lubricators Charitable Trust

Eligibility: Children and elderly people in need.

Types of grants: One-off and recurrent grants according to need. Grants range from £50 to £10,000 and are only given where there is no public assistance available.

Annual grant total: In 1993, grants to individuals totalled £10,000 and members nominated their own charities to receive grants at Christmas totalling £10,000.

Applications: In writing to the correspondent.

Correspondent: P D Smithson, c/o Messrs Amhurst Brown, Colombotti, 2 Duke Street, St James's, London SW1Y 6BJ (071-930 2366).

The Helen Lucas Fund

Eligibility: "Distressed gentlewomen" in need, with a preference for women of the Jewish faith.

Types of grants: One-off grants according to need, usually under £500.

Annual grant total: About £15,000.

Applications: In writing to the correspondent, but preferably through a social worker, Jewish Care or other welfare agency.

Correspondent: Mrs Anita Kafton, Hon. Secretary, 16 Sunny Hill, London NW4 4LL (081-203 3567).

The Matthew Trust

Eligibility: Patients and former patients at special hospitals; mentally ill people in prisons and those discharged; victims of aggression; one-parent families and those who are socially disadvantaged with mental health problems; people who are mentally ill generally. There is a preference for those who have been treated under a Mental Health Act Order.

Types of grants: (a) For patients from special hospitals: financial assistance with rehabilitation, legal and taxation advice, medical/psychiatric specialist counselling, clothing for work purposes, private fees for educational and professional courses, equipment for accommodation.

(b) For patients in special hospitals and regional secure units and prisoners with mental health conditions: assistance with fees for educational courses; where appropriate, legal assistance for mental health review tribunals and independent psychiatric reports; financial assistance to families of patients and prisoners and counselling.

(c) For victims of violent crimes: payment for private counselling sessions, installation of telephones, installation of security equipment to the home, cash grants.

(d) Individuals who are socially disadvantaged with mental health problems: grants to assist financial difficulties given mainly to keep the family in tact, plus counselling, liaison with local authorities and government departments.

Grants range from £50 to £1,000.

Annual grant total: In 1992/93, the trust had an income of £94,000, of which 12% to 15% (about £12,000) is given in grants. About 140 grants of £20 to £700 were distributed.

Applications: On a form available from the correspondent submitted through a social worker, citizen's advice bureau or other probation service, mental health teams; also from other voluntary organisations and statutory bodies including a declaration that all other sources have been exhausted first.

Correspondent: Peter Thompson, Director, PO Box 604, London SW6 3AG (071-736 5976) (FAX 071-731 6961).

Other information: This entry is repeated in the Sickness and disability charities section of the book.

The Middlesex King Edward VII Memorial Fund

Eligibility: Children aged between six and 16 and who live in the former county of Middlesex (as constituted in 1912), north west London and the home counties.

Types of grants: Grants for holidays or convalescence at the seaside or in the country (holidays must be in the UK). Grants range from £50 to £100 per individual.

Annual grant total: £5,500 in 1992.

Applications: In writing to the correspondent through a social worker, welfare agency or other third party such as a head teacher. Information should include details of the circumstances of the child, why the holiday is of particular benefit, financial circumstances of parent(s)/guardian(s), dates, cost and location of proposed holiday. Applications are considered at any time but always around April and June.

Correspondent: A J G Moore, Hon. Secretary, 2nd Floor, Room 215, Glen House, 200 Tottenham Court Road, London W1P 9LA (071-580 5191).

The Morris Beneficent Fund

Eligibility: Distressed gentlewomen recommended by members of the fund.

Types of grants: Grants according to need. At the end of 1990, 24 women were receiving annuities.

Annual grant total: About £30,000.

Applications: On an application form supplied by a member. No unsolicited applications will be considered.

Correspondent: The Secretary, Flat 6, Pine Trees Court, Hassocks, West Sussex BN6 8NW.

Other information: There is at present a waiting list and no new applications can be considered.

The Morval Foundation

Eligibility: Elderly Christian Scientists who are members of the Mother Church.

Types of grants: One-off and recurrent grants according to need.

Annual grant total: £26,000 in 1993/94.

Applications: On a form available from the correspondent.

Correspondent: The Secretary, 20 Summerfield, West Farm Avenue, Ashtead, Surrey KT21 2LF.

The John Murdoch Trust

Eligibility: Needy bachelors and widowers who, either as amateurs or professionals, have pursued science in any of its branches, and who are at least 55 years old.

Types of grants: Yearly allowances of about £1,000 to £2,000.

Annual grant total: No information available.

Applications: Considered as they are received.

Correspondent: The Secretary, c/o The Royal Bank of Scotland plc, Private Trust & Taxation Office, 2 Festival Square, Edinburgh EH3 9SU (031-523 2648).

Other information: This entry is repeated in the Occupational charities section of the book.

The Muslim Welfare Board

Eligibility: Sick, poor and elderly Muslims.

Types of grants: Probably one-off and recurrent grants according to need, and for the rehabilitation of Muslims sentenced to imprisonment.

Annual grant total: About £10,000 in 1993, of which £500 to £1,000 was given to individuals.

Applications: In writing to the correspondent.

Correspondent: G Shabbir, Secretary, 248 Brockley Road, London SE4 2SF (081-691 2942).

The Mylne Trust

Eligibility: Protestants who are or who have been involved in evangelistic work. This includes missionaries both past and present, married ordinands with dependent children (who are given priority) and other Christian workers at the trustees' discretion.

Types of grants: Annual and one-off grants.

Annual grant total: In 1992/93, the trust had assets of £799,000 with an income of £64,000. Grants to individuals totalled £67,000.

Applications: On a form available from the correspondent to be submitted directly by the individual including a passport size photograph of the applicant certified as a true likeness. Applications are considered each month.

Correspondent: The Secretary, Messrs Bells, Potter & Kempson, 11 South Street, Farnham, Surrey GU9 7QX (0252-733733).

Other information: This entry is repeated in the Occupational charities section of the book.

The National Association for the Care & Resettlement of Offenders (NACRO)

Eligibility: Probation clients and their families.

Types of grants: One-off grants only, usually of around £25 to match a grant from the Probation Be-friending Fund. NACRO is not permitted to match funding given by other charities.

Annual grant total: About £50,000, much of which is spent on providing advice and information.

Applications: Only through the probation service, social service departments, citizen's advice bureau and registered charities.

Correspondent: A Smith, Welfare Administrator, 169 Clapham Road, London SW9 0PU (071-582 6500).

The National Benevolent Institution

Eligibility: Elderly retired gentlefolk (generally over 60 or over 50 if disabled). "Qualification under the terms of the NBI charter is interpreted quite liberally. Birth, education and way of life, particularly service to others, are taken into consideration."

Types of grants: The main activity of the institution is the provision of annuities to elderly gentlefolk. Once in receipt of an annuity (up to £10 a week), modest grants towards household expenses, convalescence etc. may be made. Help towards nursing home and rest home fees (up to £1,040 a year) is also available.

Grants are not given to pay debts.

Annual grant total: In 1992, the institution had assets of £5.3 million and an income of £362,000. Total expenditure was £365,000 including £226,000 in relief-in-need grants to individuals. There are over 500 regular annuitants receiving up to £10 per week.

Applications: On a form available from the correspondent. The committee meets monthly.

Correspondent: The Secretary, 27d Leinster Square, London W2 4NQ (071-723 0021).

The Netherlands Benevolent Society

Eligibility: People in need living in the UK who are at least one half Dutch, or are married to a Dutch born person.

Types of grants: One-off and recurrent grants for general financial need. Regular allowances are usually about £40 a month for couples or families, and £32 a month for single people. One-off grants range from £25 to £200.

Annual grant total: In 1992, the society had assets of £226,000 and an income of £28,000. Total expenditure was £23,000 including £13,000 in relief-in-need grants to individuals.

Applications: In writing to the correspondent.

Correspondent: The Administrator, 7 Austin Friars, London EC2N 2EJ (081-546 4732).

The New Masonic Samaritan Fund

Eligibility: Freemasons, their families and dependants who are in both financial and medical need.

Types of grants: The fund's policy is to provide support at whichever hospital is most appropriate. Help is only given if the applicant cannot obtain treatment on the NHS without undue delay or hardship.

Annual grant total: £1.5 million to £2 million a year.

Applications: On a form available from the correspondent. The trustees meet each month (usually the first Thursday) to decide on applications received in the previous 30 days.

Correspondent: The Secretary, 26 Great Queen Street, London WC2B 5BB (071-404 1550).

The Northern Ladies Annuity Society

Eligibility: Ladies in need who live in the counties of northern England. Applicants must be over the age of 65 and must have an annual income of no more than £6,000. (This includes any interest gained on capital and any income from part-time employment.)

Types of grants: Annual grants paid quarterly only to annuitants of the society. Awards range from £260 to £520 a year. Cold weather and Christmas grants may also be given depending on the income and numbers being supported. The trust does not give one-off grants.

● **National and general charities**

Annual grant total: In 1993, the trust's income was over £100,000; grants were given to between 100 and 120 individuals and totalled around £35,000.

Applications: On a form available from the correspondent. Applications can be submitted directly by the individual and are considered in January, from March to July and September to November.

Correspondent: Mrs Joan Davies, Secretary, 178 Portland Road, Jesmond, Newcastle-upon-Tyne NE2 1DJ (091-232 1518).

Norwood Child Care

Eligibility: Jewish children and their families. This is a national trust but has a preference for London and the south east.

Types of grants: According to need, but no regular allowances. Grants towards the celebration of Jewish religious festivals, social need and holidays.

Annual grant total: In 1993, about 1,000 grants were given totalling £118,000.

Applications: Grants are recommended by Norwood Child Care staff who are working with the family.

Correspondent: The Executive Director, Jewish Care, Norwood House, Harmony Way, off Victoria Road, Hendon, London NW4 2DR (081-203 3030).

Other information: Grants are made in conjunction with a comprehensive welfare service. Norwood Child Care provides a range of social services for Jewish children and families, including social work, day facilities, residential and foster care.

The Ogilvie Charities

Eligibility: There are various categories of Eligibility:

(i) People in straitened circumstances, particularly (although not exclusively): (a) those living in Ipswich and Leiston, Suffolk; (b) former governesses or female teachers; (c) widows with dependent children.

(ii) Disadvantaged children living in London who are in need of a holiday in the country.

(iii) Adults in need of a recuperative holiday (especially those tired out by nursing or long hours of work, continued worry, or suffering from nervous breakdown), for whom a period of rest would be beneficial and who would be helped thereby to renew their own health and strength. There may be a preference for those whose exhaustion is due to their intensive care of others.

Types of grants: Generally one-off grants for holidays mainly for carers needing a break away from the people they are caring for; those in extreme need of essential items (such as cots, beds and bedding), particularly people who have been recently widowed, with dependent children. Requests must be for needs for which there is no statutory provision.

No grants towards education or training, holidays abroad or where statutory bodies have a clear responsibility.

Annual grant total: In 1992, the trust had assets of £385,000, generating an income of £39,000. Grants ranging from £50 to £250 were given to 159 individuals and totalled £25,000.

Applications: Through a social worker, community nurse or other welfare agency. No forms are issued, but details of need, recommended solution, dates (if applicable), if second hand items are available, which other charities have been approached and applicant's weekly income and expenditure must be given. A preliminary telephone call may be useful. Office hours are 9 am to 1 pm, 2 pm to 4 pm, Mondays to Fridays.

Correspondent: The General Manager, The Gate House, 9 Burkett Road, Woodbridge, Suffolk IP12 4JJ (0394-388746).

Pearson's Holiday Fund

Eligibility: School children aged 4 to 16 years inclusive.

Types of grants: Grants for children's holidays only. Grants are £25 a week while on holiday, or lump sums for groups. The fund only supports holidays in the UK.

Annual grant total: In 1992, the trust had an income of £64,000. Grants up to £500 were given to 4,100 individuals and totalled £53,000.

Applications: The fund does not deal with the family or child directly, rather through social workers, doctors, health visitors, teachers etc.. Applications should include details of where the holiday will be taken and will be considered between October and March.

Correspondent: Robert Heasman, General Secretary, Box 123, Bishop's Waltham, Hampshire SO3 1ZE (0489-893260).

The Perry Fund

Eligibility: Single elderly ladies from professional families, whether widows or unmarried.

Types of grants: One-off and recurrent grants according to need. No grants for education.

Annual grant total: About £9,000 in 1993.

Applications: In writing to the correspondent, enclosing an sae.

Correspondent: J L Riches, St Leonards House, St Leonards Close, Bridgnorth, Shropshire.

Other information: The entry above is more or less a copy of the one which appeared in the first edition of the Guide. The correspondent states: "All that the previous entry in the Directory has achieved is to produce a stream of totally unsuitable applications from students requesting assistance with various courses. ... The applications number one or two a week throughout the year and not one single application has come within the terms of the trust which although clearly set out in the Directory are equally clearly not read by prospective applicants!" As a consequence the correspondent asked that the trust be deleted from that edition. However, we aim to include all publicly registered charities of relevance and having included the trust the correspondent reported that he had received fewer inappropriate applications. We would continue to urge all our readers to be discerning in which trusts they apply to for funds.

The Polish Naval Association Welfare Fund

Eligibility: Polish citizens or ex-citizens and their dependants who are in need.

Types of grants: One-off or recurrent grants according to need.

Annual grant total: In 1992, the trust had an income of £34,000, it is not known how much of this was given in grants to individuals.

Applications: In writing to the correspondent.

Correspondent: Lt Cdr K Zubkowski, Trustee, 14 Collingham Gardens, London SW5 0HS (071-370 2659).

The Professional Classes Aid Council

Eligibility: People of professional background who have no specific fund to turn to when in distress. Grants are also given for the welfare of children of the above.

Types of grants: Weekly allowances and one-off gifts according to need.

Annual grant total: In 1992, the trust had assets of £859,000 and an income of

£277,000. Total expenditure was £252,000. Relief-in-need grants of £50 to £500 a year (up to £10 per week) were given to 600 individuals. About £70,000 was given for educational purposes.

Applications: On a form available from the correspondent. Applications can be submitted by the individual or by other third parties for consideration throughout the year except August.

Correspondent: The Secretary, 10 St Christopher's Place, London W1M 6HY (071-935 0641).

Other information: The Professional Classes Aid Council is operated alongside the Guild of Aid for Gentlepeople. See separate entry.

The Rhodesians Worldwide Assistance Fund

Eligibility: People formerly resident in Rhodesia (now called Zimbabwe), and their dependants who are in need.

Types of grants: Grants are awarded mainly to elderly people on Income Support who require assistance for a specific need which the DSS are not able to provide. Grants are also given on compassionate grounds, where individuals are in financial difficulties through no fault of their own and to disabled people.

No education grants.

Annual grant total: In 1991, the trust had an income of £22,000, it is not known how much of this was given in grants to individuals.

Applications: In writing addressed to the Trustees, RWAF. Applications are considered quarterly.

Correspondent: P Hagelthorn, Fund Administrator, Box 260, West Lavington, Devizes, Wiltshire SN10 4QZ (0380-818381).

The E C Roberts Charitable Trust

Eligibility: Poor children and orphans, especially those with disabilities.

Types of grants: One-off or recurrent grants according to need.

Annual grant total: £24,000 in 1991/92.

Applications: The trust states that its income is fully committed until 1996. "No applications please."

Correspondent: Miss H A G Tyler, Trustees' Solicitor, Messrs Brutton & Co, Cambridge House, 132 High Street, Portsmouth PO1 2HR (0705-812711).

The Royal Air Forces Escaping Society Charitable Fund

Eligibility: People in need who live in Europe and who have been recognised "helpers". Also dependants of a helper who lost their life through assisting members of the RAF, dominion air forces or allied forces serving within the framework of the RAF to evade and escape during World War 2.

Types of grants: One-off or annual grants according to need, ranging from £50 to £250.

Annual grant total: In 1992, the trust had an income of £46,000. £9,000 was given in 76 grants to individuals.

Applications: In writing to the correspondent. Applications should be made directly by the individual, through the Air Attache at the British Embassy or through the fund's country representatives or colleague European organisations.

Correspondent: Wing Cmdr I R Cooper, Treasurer, Ministry of Defence, Room 6/10 Metropole Building, Northumberland Avenue, London WC2N 5BL (071-218 9351).

The Royal Antediluvian Order of Buffaloes, Grand Lodge of England War Memorial Annuities

Eligibility: Members of the order and their dependants.

Types of grants: Annuities, though the Grand Lodge may have other charitable funds available for one-off grants.

Annual grant total: Considerably more than £50,000.

Applications: Applications should be made through the member's lodge. All assistance originates at the local lodge level; if its resources are inadequate, the lodge may then seek assistance at provincial or ultimately national level. For dependants of deceased members, it is necessary to give the lodge to which he belonged. If its name and number is known, the correspondent below will probably be able to identify a current local telephone number or address. If only the place is known, this may still be possible, but not in all cases, particularly when the lodge concerned does not belong to this Grand Lodge group.

Correspondent: W A Hartmann, Grand Secretary, Grove House, Harrogate, North Yorkshire HG1 4LA (0423-502438).

Other information: The Grand Lodge of England is the largest of 15 separate and independent Buffalo groups in the country. They appear to exist for mutual sociability and support and for the support of their local communities. There are over 3,500 local lodges, all of which may be concerned to help members, dependants and perhaps others in time of need or distress. This fund was established as a tribute to members of the order who died during the 1st World War.

The Royal Belgian Benevolent Society

Eligibility: Poor Belgians who live in Britain, and their close dependants.

Types of grants: One-off grants and regular allowances.

Annual grant total: About £3,000, most of which is given to students.

Applications: In writing to the correspondent.

Correspondent: The Secretary, 60 Knightsbridge, London SW1X 7LF (071-235 2121).

The Royal London Aid Society

Eligibility: Offenders, both before and after discharge from prison, their families and young people "at risk" (that is young people under a supervision order or who have come to the attention of the police). The society is national but preference is given to London and the South East.

Types of grants: One-off grants for example for education, tools and specialist clothing. There is a preference for items that will help with employment. Grants have also been given for education, clothing, furniture, training courses etc. to people discharged from prison and their families.

Annual grant total: In 1991, the society had assets of £392,000 with an income of £47,000. Expenditure totalled £43,000 including £13,000 in 122 relief-in-need grants to individuals.

Applications: On a form available from the correspondent. All applications must be supported by some authority and grants are made through that authority (not directly to the beneficiary). Applications are considered in March, June, September and December.

Correspondent: G McCarthy, 84 Upney Lane, Barking, Essex IG11 9LR (081-594 4240/2168).

National and general charities

The Royal Masonic Benevolent Institution

Eligibility: Freemasons (usually over 60 years of age, unless unemployed due to incapacity) of the English Constitution (England, Wales and certain areas overseas) and their dependants.

Types of grants: Regular assistance to beneficiaries living in their own homes. Annuities are paid quarterly and can be for life, up to the maximum disregard figure (currently £520 per year) for social benefit purposes. Annuitants living in their own house may also be eligible for low-interest loans to renovate their house.

Annual grant total: In 1992, the trust had assets of £42.5 million and an income of £16.7 million. Grants ranging from £52 to £640 were given to 2,500 individuals and totalled £1.1 million.

Applications: On a form available from the correspondent, usually submitted through the lodge of the relevant freemason. Applications are considered every month except August.

Correspondent: The Chief Executive, 20 Great Queen Street, London WC2B 5BG (071-405 8341).

Other information: The institution has a team of Welfare Visitors covering the whole of England and Wales and also runs 15 homes (three more opening soon) catering for 1,000 older freemasons.

The Royal Scottish Corporation

Eligibility: Generally, Scots living within 35 miles of Charing Cross, London. Specifically: "An applicant for relief must have been born in Scotland or be a child of parents one of whom was born in Scotland. A widow whose husband was born in Scotland may be eligible for relief. Relief may be granted only to applicants resident or found within a radius of thirty-five miles of Charing Cross."

Types of grants: One-off and recurrent grants according to need.

Annual grant total: In 1993, the trust had an income of £550,000 and gave 600 to 700 grants totalling £350,000.

Applications: By letter to the correspondent.

Correspondent: Wing Commander Alan Robertson, 37 King Street, Covent Garden, London WC2E 8JS (071-240 3718).

Other information: The corporation also administers the Kinloch Bequest for Scottish ex-servicemen and their dependants (see entry in the Services and ex-services charities section of the book), and a fund for serving Scottish soldiers, especially those from the Aldershot Garrison (see entry for St Andrew's Scottish Soldiers Club Fund).

The Royal Society for the Relief of Indigent Gentlewomen of Scotland

Eligibility: Needy, widowed or unmarried gentlewomen, over 50, of Scottish birth or education who have a professional/business background and who have savings of less than £8,000. Applicants need not live in Scotland.

Types of grants: See entry in the Scotland general section of the book.

The Royal United Kingdom Beneficent Association (RUKBA)

Eligibility: Elderly and infirm people in need who come from a professional background and live in the British Isles, particularly those "who have served their generation in a professional capacity, in devoted service to others or in one of many humanitarian causes. They need to be over pensionable age, or be over 40 and unable to work through infirmity. In addition, their assessed income needs to be below the limits set by RUKBA's committee. These levels are revised regularly and are currently £5,295 for a single person and £9,002 for a married couple."

Types of grants: Annuities, which are granted for life (unless there is an unexpected and considerable improvement in their circumstances) and are up to a maximum of £1,152 a year, are the main form of help.

The association does not give one-off grants.

Annual grant total: £4,296,000 to about 4,950 regular beneficiaries in 1993. Over 600 new annuities were awarded in 1993.

Applications: In the first instance the applicant should write to the correspondent describing their occupational background and giving a brief description of their circumstances. Arrangements will then be made for the applicant to be visited by one of the association's 700 honorary secretaries. Applications are considered bi-monthly.

Applications can also be made from people in residential/nursing homes who are unable to meet the balance of "reasonable" fees. In such cases, the income limit is not necessarily applied but capital resources have to be reduced to £3,000 before a case can be considered.

Correspondent: The Applicants Officer, 6 Avonmore Road, London W14 8RL (071-602 6274; fax 071-371 1807).

Other information: RUKBA has four residential and nursing homes with 181 beds at present and has 77 flats and bungalows for disabled elderly people. This entry is repeated in the Occupational charities section of the book.

The Sainsbury Family Charitable Trusts

Eligibility: People in need. Small grants can be made to individuals in need (eg. for fuel debts), provided that applications are via an appropriate welfare agency and that every other possible source of help has been approached.

Types of grants: One-off grants, not usually exceeding £250.

Annual grant total: Grants to individuals totalled £175,000 in 1992.

Applications: In writing to the correspondent at any time through a social worker or other welfare agency. Applicants should state what other sources of funding have been approached, both statutory and non-statutory. There are no application forms.

Correspondent: H L de Quetteville, 9 Red Lion Court, London EC4A 3EB (071-410 0330).

Other information: There are a number of Sainsbury Family Charitable Trusts administered from the same office and for which a single application is sufficient. They include The Linbury Trust; The Headley Trust; The Monument Trust; The Gatsby Charitable Foundation and The Elizabeth Clark Charitable Trust.

St Andrew's Society for Ladies in Need

Eligibility: Single, elderly ladies (over 60) from a well-educated and/or professional background who are in reduced circumstances.

Types of grants: Regular weekly grants from £5 to £10 a week; special grants towards heating costs, moving expenses or medication etc.; holiday grants to help with convalescent holidays.

Annual grant total: About £42,000.

Applications: On a form available from the correspondent, submitted directly by the individual or by a third party with the power of attorney. They are considered in February, April, June and October.

Correspondent: Mrs M Pope, General Secretary, 20 Denmark Gardens, Holbrook, Ipswich, Suffolk IP9 2BG (0473-327408).

National and general charities

The St Martin-in-the-Fields' Vicar's Relief Fund

Eligibility: People in need, especially those who live in London and other inner city areas.

Types of grants: One-off grants for all kinds of need, especially immediate crises. Grants have been given for furnishing, domestic appliances, arrears, clothing, telephone, prams etc..

Grants are not given knowingly where the money is to be held for any length of time (eg. waiting for other funding) by the agency; the money is not given until it is to be used. The average grant is £50.

Grants are not given for travel abroad for almost any reason; large expensive items such as wheelchairs, computers or cars; arrears in excess of £600 to £800, or educational pursuits (ie. funding of students, undergraduate or postgraduate).

Annual grant total: About £90,000 given in about 1,900 grants.

Applications: In writing to the correspondent. Applications must be made through a social worker. Further information is available from the correspondent. An sae should be sent if a reply is required. Applications are considered throughout the year.

Correspondent: The Administrator, St Martin-in-the-Fields, 6 St Martin's Place, London WC2N 4JH (071-930 1781 recorded message only).

The Salvation Army

Eligibility: People in need.

Types of grants: All grants are in the form of specific practical assistance such as needs in the home (to make the home more habitable) to those being helped by the Army. Local branches can give a little financial assistance but more usually help with items. The head office can generally give up to £250 and not usually over £350. No grants for educational purposes or to return people to their homeland.

Annual grant total: About £700,000.

Applications: Those seeking help should approach any local branch. These can usually be found in the telephone book. Applications to head office must be supported by a report from a welfare organisation such as a citizen's advice bureau or social worker etc..

Correspondent: The Chief Secretary, 105-109 Judd Street, Kings Cross, London WC1H 9TS (071-383 4230).

Other information: The Salvation Army is probably the biggest single welfare organisation in Britain. Its most characteristic feature is the provision of direct practical help. Financial assistance is usually only a small and incidental part of its work. The Army is most unlikely to make grants to people in need other than those with whom it is already in contact.

The Scandinavian Benevolent Society

Eligibility: Norwegians and Danes who live in the UK.

Types of grants: There are currently about 20 pensioners each receiving £5 or £10 a week. The trust also makes one-off payments of £50 to £200 towards telephone installation, clothing, heating costs and television licences etc.. No grants for educational purposes or to top up fees for nursing/residential homes.

Annual grant total: In 1993, the trust had assets of about £190,000 with an income of around £20,000. Total expenditure was about £23,000 including £18,500 in relief-in-need grants to individuals.

Applications: Must be made through Norwegian or Danish churches/embassies, social services department, citizen's advice bureau, doctor, vicar or other such person or welfare agency. The trustees meet every three months, but payments can be made more promptly in certain cases.

Correspondent: Mrs V K Goodhart, Secretary, 68 Burhill Road, Hersham, Walton-on-Thames, Surrey KT12 4JF (0932-244916).

Other information: The society helps particularly the elderly in need of financial support and families in need. However all applications for help will be considered. The society can also help with re-patriation.

The Henry Smith Charity

Eligibility: This charity distributes about £500,000 a year (1992) for the relief of need, divided unequally among about 175 independent parochial Smith Charities, mostly in southern England.

Types of grants: These local Smith charities either operate independently or have been merged into combined charities, a part of whose income derives from Smith funds. The income received from the Smiths funds appears to vary greatly, from a few pounds to several thousand pounds. Where these local charities have a distributable income of over £500 to individuals in need they have a separate entry in the relevant section of this book.

All applications must be made at the local level.

The Mrs Smith & Mount Trust

Eligibility: People in need.

Types of grants: One off grants to support:

(1) "The successful continuity of family life by offering appropriate funding to the central carer. The concept of the family is wider than the single household and may include other dependants for whom the carer takes responsibility.

(2) Those who have been in care who are entering independent life in the community.

(3) Individuals who have needed short term residential care upon their return to the community.

"NOTE: The trustees will consider applications for lone parents or couples, who have more than one child or other dependent kin who have a disability or long term illness, who are in receipt of Invalidity Benefit or have been on long term benefit."

British Home Stores/Mothercare Vouchers are given towards clothing, unless there is no store nearby or if the applicant has special needs. Grants towards holidays will only be for convalescent holidays or for the families of those involved caring for a sick or invalid person.

Grants are given for a wide variety of needs except gas, electricity, rent, money borrowed or lent, house repairs, rates, telephone bills, debts of any kind or funeral expenses. Applications relating to any of these will not even receive a reply.

Annual grant total: £104,000 in 1993.

Applications: On a form available from the correspondent which should be submitted by a qualified social worker or similar. A "Guide to Applicants" is available from the trust and its use is recommended before an application is made. Grants will be made out to the sponsoring organisation who will be responsible for the use of the funds.

Correspondent: The Administrator, c/o Pothecary & Barratt, Box MST, White Horse Court, 25c North Street, Bishop's Stortford, Hertfordshire CM23 2LD (0279-506421).

Other information: The Mrs Smith Trust and the Mount Trust have amalgamated. The Mrs Smith Trust gives grants to individuals, the Mount Trust to organisations for projects.

National and general charities

The Society for the Assistance of Ladies in Reduced Circumstances

Eligibility: Elderly (above retirement age) and infirm ladies living on their own, who are on a low income and who are domiciled in the British Isles.

Types of grants: Monthly allowances (to a maximum of £10 a week, but dependent on applicant's age) to assist ladies who are living in their own homes. Those who have moved to rest homes or nursing homes because of failing health can also be helped.

Annual grant total: About £160,000 was given in around 500 grants in 1993.

Applications: In writing to the correspondent.

Correspondent: The Secretary, Lancaster House, 25 Hornyold Road, Malvern, Hereford & Worcester WR14 1QQ (0684-574645).

The Society of Friends of Foreigners in Distress

Eligibility: Foreigners from countries which are not part of the British Commonwealth, the former British Empire nor from the USA. Applicants must be living in or around Greater London.

Types of grants: One-off grants of up to £50 and weekly allowances for elderly people. No grants to top-up fees for nursing/residential homes or to students.

Annual grant total: In 1993, the trust had assets of over £100,000 with an income of around £20,000. About £8,500 was given in about 40 relief-in-need grants to individuals.

Applications: Should be submitted by a social worker, citizen's advice bureau or equivalent welfare agency.

Correspondent: Mrs V K Goodhart, Secretary, 68 Burhill Road, Hersham, Walton-on-Thames, Surrey KT12 4JF (0932-244916).

The Society of St Vincent de Paul

Eligibility: Anyone in need following a visit by a member of the society. Although this is a Catholic charity it is completely non-denominational in its operation.

Types of grants: Small donations of goods or money to alleviate temporary need, dependent on local assessment and availability of funds. Friendship to anyone in need is a fundamental principle of the society. Direct financial relief is incidental to this. "We are the largest UK distributor of EC surplus beef and butter to those already receiving benefit. We also give cold weather payments for excessive fuel costs; travel vouchers to sick relatives; help with holidays for families in need; subsidies for children to go to our one-week summer camps; and help for homeless and unemployed people."

No recurrent grants or grants for education.

Annual grant total: In 1993, the society's income was about £2 million about half of which was distributed in relief-in-need grants to individuals.

Applications: Applications can be made through the central office at the address below or usually through any local priest. All applicants will be visited by a volunteer from the society before any award is made.

Correspondent: The Secretary, Damascus House, The Ridgeway, London NW7 1EL (081-906 1339).

Other information: There are about 2,000 parish groups in England and Wales, with around 20,000 members. Most of the income is raised locally by members and distributed locally by them.

The Paul Stephenson Memorial Trust

Eligibility: Discharged prisoners who are in need.

Types of grants: Probably one-off or recurrent grants according to need.

Annual grant total: In 1991, the trust had an income of £4,000. It is not known how much was given in grants to individuals in need.

Applications: In writing to the correspondent.

Correspondent: The Hon. Secretary, c/o Mason Collins Solicitors, 8-10 Cricket Green, Mitcham, Surrey CR4 4LA (081-648 4044).

Other information: This correspondent is correct, but the other information, obtained from the Charity Commission, has not been confirmed by the trust.

The Straits Settlement & Malay States Benevolent Society

Eligibility: Retired persons who have lived in the Far East for a minimum of two years, and their dependants.

Types of grants: Both one-off and recurrent grants according to need. The society tends to support Europeans and dependants of Europeans, although this is not exclusively so.

Annual grant total: £20,000 in 1989, the most recent year for which information is available.

Applications: Applications should be sponsored by a subscriber.

Correspondent: J H Wilson, Ernst & Young, 400 Capability Green, Luton LU1 3LU.

Other information: The society's funds are fully committed and the society does not wish to incur further administration costs in replying to applications which cannot at present be considered.

Sir John Sumner's Trust

Eligibility: People in need.

Types of grants: "Voluntary quarterly grants."

Annual grant total: £10,000.

Applications: Personal applications must be completed on forms available from the trust and generally supported by an appropriate welfare agency.

Correspondent: A C Robson, Secretary, 8th Floor, Union Chambers, 63 Temple Row, Birmingham B2 5LT.

The Swiss Benevolent Society

Eligibility: Swiss nationals who live in the consular district of the Swiss Embassy in London (mainly the Greater London area and the south of England).

Types of grants: One-off and recurrent grants according to need. The trust also gives pensions and holiday grants for children of Swiss nationality to go to Switzerland for their holidays.

No student grants.

Annual grant total: £28,000 in 1992.

Applications: By personal or third party (eg. Swiss Embassy, Swiss church etc.) application to the correspondent. Applications are considered monthly and require proof of Swiss nationality.

Correspondent: Mrs D Hardaway, 31 Conway Street, London W1P 5HL (071-387 2173).

The Lloyd Thomas Charity for Women & Girls

Eligibility: Poor women and girls in desperate need of a holiday.

Types of grants: Grants up to about £100 towards the cost of a holiday. Only in exceptional circumstances can a person be considered for a grant if they have had a holiday within the last three years.

Annual grant total: In 1990/91, the trust had an income of £4,000. Expenditure totalled £2,635 including £1,700 in 15 grants as above.

Applications: Through a social worker or other welfare agency including income, health, personal situation and year of last holiday. Applications are considered year round though generally from November to May.

Correspondent: Fiona Hills, c/o FHA, Hertford Lodge, East End Road, London N3 3QE (081-349 4044).

The Arthur Townrow Fund

Eligibility: Spinsters in England over 40 years of age who are in need, of good character and are members of the Church of England or of a Protestant dissenting church that acknowledges the doctrine of the Holy Trinity.

Types of grants: About 360 regular allowances of £5 a week. One half of the pensions granted must be paid to women living in Chesterfield, Bolsover and North East Derbyshire. The remaining grants may be paid anywhere in England but only to those over the age of 40. Allowances will not be made to those with an income greater than £3,865 a year.

Annual grant total: £70,000.

Applications: In writing to the correspondent, requesting an application form.

Correspondent: P I King, Secretary, 24 Gluman Gate, Chesterfield, Derbyshire S40 1UA (0246-208081).

Other information: This entry is repeated in the Derbyshire section of the book.

The Triangle Trust 1949 Fund

Eligibility: People in severe financial need.

Types of grants: One-off grants ranging from £100 to £500 for the alleviation of poverty.

Grants are not given for private medicine or education, holidays, overseas educational trips, nursing home fees or loans.

Annual grant total: In 1992/93, the trust had assets of £5 million and an income of £363,000. Expenditure totalled £374,000 including £79,000 in 500 grants to individuals, £20,000 for a special project, £76,000 in 254 recurrent grants, £36,000 for education, and £123,000 to 25 registered charities.

Since these figures were published, the trustees have made some changes to their policy and guidelines. Applications are no longer considered for educational and recurrent grants and the funds available for registered charities are confined to special projects initiated by the trustees. It is not possible for responses to be made to unsolicited appeals from registered charities.

Applications: Applications should be submitted through a social worker, citizen's advice bureau or other welfare agency. They are considered in March, June, September and November.

Correspondent: The Secretary, Glaxo House, Berkeley Avenue, Greenford, Middlesex UB6 0NN (081-966 8285/071-493 4060).

The Unity Fund for the Elderly

Eligibility: Elderly people (over 65) in need.

Types of grants: One-off grants for example towards small building repairs or improvements, telephone installation, door entry systems and appliances.

Annual grant total: In 1993, the trust had an income of £14,500. 61 grants to individuals totalled £9,000.

Applications: In writing to the correspondent. Applications should be submitted through a social worker, citizen's advice bureau or other welfare agency. They are considered at any time.

Correspondent: D H T Rowcliffe, Secretary, Meadowland Cottage, Coxgrove Hill, Pucklechurch, Bristol BS17 3NL (0272-372477).

The Universal Beneficent Society

Eligibility: Elderly people over retirement age and living at home. Priority is given to those over 75. Beneficiaries are usually housebound, living alone and have savings of less than £500.

Types of grants: On going quarterly annuities of £166 to £260 a year given for life while beneficiaries live in their own homes.

Annual grant total: In 1992, the total expenditure was £142,000 including £121,000 in 600 relief-in-need grants to individuals.

Applications: On a form available from the correspondent. All applications must come through social workers, statutory or voluntary. Applications are considered in February, April, June, August and December.

Correspondent: Miss E M Willett, Almoner, 6 Avonmore Road, London W14 8RL (071-602 6274).

The Victoria Convalescent Trust Fund

Eligibility: People in need.

Types of grants: Grants towards the cost of convalescent or recuperative holidays. Grants are paid direct to registered convalescence or nursing homes.

Annual grant total: About £50,000 in 250 to 300 grants.

Applications: Only accepted from those responsible for the medical treatment, **not** the individual.

Correspondent: A C Winter, Chairman, 62 Wilson Street, London EC2A 2BU.

Other information: This entry is repeated in the Sickness and disability charities section of the book.

The Widow's Friend Society

Eligibility: Protestant Christian widows aged 60 or over who are in need.

Types of grants: Pensions.

Annual grant total: In 1992, the trust had an income of £22,500. Grants to individuals totalled £31,500.

Applications: Trust funds are fully committed. No new grant applications can currently be considered.

Correspondent: T J Dennett, Chief Executive, The Aged Pilgrims Friend Society, 175 Tower Bridge Road, London SE1 2AL (071-407 5466).

Wireless for the Bedridden

Eligibility: Housebound invalids and housebound elderly people who are unable to afford a television or radio set for themselves.

Types of grants: Radio and television (black and white or colour) sets are available, as may be help with the initial television licence fee.

Annual grant total: In 1993, 200 radios and 700 television sets were given.

Applications: On the official application form available from the correspondent and supported by a sponsor from an appropriate welfare agency. Applications are considered weekly.

Correspondent: The Secretary, 159a High Street, Hornchurch, Essex RM11 3YB (0708-621101).

Other information: This entry is repeated in the Sickness and disability charities section of the book.

National and general charities

S C Witting Trust

Eligibility: People in need.

Types of grants: One-off grants (typically ranging from £30 to £50) for most kinds of needs to individuals and families on state benefits or low income. Grants are given to help with the cost of necessities such as clothing, basic furniture and other household items.

No grants for payment of debts.

Annual grant total: £45,000 was given in 315 grants in 1991.

Applications: Applications by letter to the correspondent must come from social workers or citizens' advice bureaux; the trust cannot respond to applications from individuals. Letters (no telephone calls) should include the following information:

1. Names and ages of individuals, and of members of a family unit.

2. Financial circumstances of individuals or families (income, benefits etc.).

3. What the money is wanted for, the approximate amount needed, and to whom a cheque should be made payable. (Cheques will be sent to the social worker's department, not to individual recipients.)

4. Whether an approach has been made to any other charity or local authority, and whether any money has already been raised.

5. Whether the applicant has received help from the Witting Trust before; if so, when?

6. The urgency of the need. If the request is for assistance with a holiday, the date and place that this is planned.

Correspondent: Jenny Ingram, Administrator, c/o Friends House, Euston Road, London NW1 2BJ.

The Women's Royal Voluntary Service (WRVS) Trust

Eligibility: People in need.

Types of grants: The WRVS does not give financial grants. However, it runs more than 450 clothing stores to which applications can be made for this kind of practical help.

Applications: Through the local WRVS office. See below.

Correspondent: The Secretary, 234-244 Stockwell Road, London SW9 9SP (071-416 0146 ext. 2057).

Other information: The WRVS provides, in conjunction with local authorities, a wide range of welfare facilities. These include meals on wheels, books on wheels, old people's clubs, luncheon clubs, hospital tea bars and shops, trolley services, social and rural transport schemes, welfare for offenders, children's and family holidays and residential care homes for the elderly.

Local WRVS Offices

North West Division

597 Stretford Road, Old Trafford, Manchester M16 9BX (061-872 7492). *Director:* Mrs E Holmes.

North East Division

1st Floor, Enterprise House, Valley Street, Darlington, Co Durham DL1 1GY (0325-465848). *Director:* Mrs M Duff.

Central Division

36 Regent Street, Nottingham NG1 5DA (0602-475917). Director: Mrs E Flowerdew.

South East Division

11 St Chad's Street, London WC1H 8BG (071-837 1132). *Director:* Mrs C Mayers.

South West Division

Exwick Cottage, The Village, Clyst St Mary, Exeter EX5 1BR (0392-877597). *Director:* Mrs C Cribb.

Scottish Division

19 Grosvenor Crescent, Edinburgh EH12 5EL (031-337 2261). *Director:* Mrs E Ross.

Welsh Headquarters

26 Cathedral Road, Cardiff CF1 9LJ (0222-228386). *Director:* Mrs M S Gibbons.

The Worshipful Company of Cordwainers

Eligibility: The company administers a number of small trusts the eligibility of which varies. Specific trusts exist for people who are "poor and distressed", people who are blind, people who are deaf and dumb, widows of clergymen, spinsters in the Church of England, ex-servicemen and widows of those who served in the merchant or armed forces.

Types of grants: Pensions and one-off grants depending on the trust and the circumstances.

Annual grant total: In 1991, the trust's had a combined income of £17,000. It is not known how much of this was given in grants to individuals.

Applications: In writing to the correspondent.

Correspondent: The Clerk to the Worshipful Company of Cordwainers, Eldon Chambers, 30 Fleet Street, London EC4Y 1AA (071-353 4309).

Other information: The trusts administered include the Charity of John Came, the Charity of Elizabeth Love and the James Milner Trust.

The Zakat Committee

Eligibility: Muslim people in need who live in the UK (temporarily resident or otherwise).

Types of grants: Grants of £100 to £500 to individuals.

Annual grant total: The trust gives over 1,000 grants to individuals each year probably totalling about £500,000. Grants are also given to Muslim organisations.

Applications: On a form are available from the correspondent. Applications are considered monthly. Applicants may only apply once in any six month period.

Correspondent: H Shuweik, Secretary, Regents Park Mosque, 146 Park Road, London NW8 7RG (071-724 3363).

Other information: Muslims in need can also approach their own local mosque for support, most of which collect donations to redistribute to poorer members of their community.

Charities for the relief of the poor

Editors' note: This Charity Commission leaflet CC4 entitled Charities for the Relief of the Poor *gives excellent advice to charity trustees and administrators on a range of difficult areas. It has been reproduced with the permission of the Controller of Her Majesty's Stationery Office.*

Introduction

This leaflet gives guidance to trustees of charities whose purposes include the relief of the poor. In particular the leaflet gives advice on:

- General duties of trustees
- The modern meaning of "poor"
- Assisting people who receive State benefits
- The Social Fund
- What trustees can do to make their charity more effective
- Small charities
- Applying for a Scheme
- Ways in which trustees can help poor people
- Making grants to other charities

General duties of trustees

1. The trustees of all charities should regularly review their use of the charity's funds, so as to ensure that the money is spent most effectively in carrying out the purposes of the charity. This review is particularly important for trustees of charities for the relief of the poor, because of continuing change in economic and social circumstances and in the nature of public provision for people affected by it, and the especial vulnerability of the poor at such times. Trustees should ask themselves whether they are in fact relieving poverty, and whether they are spending the charity's funds in the way most helpful to the charity's beneficiaries.

2. Rather than try to spread the charity's resources thinly among as many people as possible, trustees should consider whether it might not be more effective in relieving poverty to target their funds so as to give larger benefits to a smaller number of people who are most in need.

3. At the same time trustees must remember that the benefits given to individuals should be what is actually required to relieve their need. To give people benefits which more than relieve their need would not be fulfilling the purposes of the charity and would be an improper use of charity funds.

4. A charity's funds may be spent only for the purposes set out in the charity's governing document (ie. the trust deed, constitution, Scheme of the Commissioners, conveyance, will or other document describing the charity's purposes and, usually, how it is to be administered). Some governing documents may still lay down the precise means by which the beneficiaries' poverty can be relieved (eg. the provision of clothing or grants of particular sums at particular times of the year). However, there are many more ways nowadays than there used to be in which charity trustees can help relieve poverty.

5. If trustees consider that the means laid down in the governing document are unduly restrictive, they should consider modifying the governing document either by using section 74 of the Charities Act 1993 (if it is applicable to their charity) or applying to the Commission for a Scheme. These procedures are discussed in paragraphs 25 to 29 of this leaflet.

6. If the trustees consider that either:

- There is a lack of needy people in the charity's area of benefit; or
- The income is too small to be of practical use;

they should consider the advice given in paragraphs 23 and 24 and paragraphs 25 to 29 respectively, of this leaflet.

Modern meaning of "poor"

7. A person does not necessarily have to be destitute to qualify as "poor". Anyone who is in a condition of need, hardship or distress might be eligible for help, and it is up to trustees to make their own judgement as to whether a particular person qualifies for assistance. **Generally speaking, anyone who cannot afford the normal things in life which most people take for granted would probably qualify for help.** A person who normally has an acceptable standard of living, but is suffering temporary hardship perhaps because of an accident, a death in the family, or other setback, could also qualify for help.

8. People may qualify for assistance from the charity whether or not they are eligible for State benefits. Each person's actual needs and financial circumstances must be assessed individually. Some people who already receive their full entitlement of State benefits may need additional help. Equally, some people who are not entitled to State benefits may sometimes need help because of particular circumstances.

Assisting people who receive State benefits

9. When trustees of a charity for the relief of the poor are thinking about assisting people who are already receiving State benefits, they should take care not to use the charity's funds in a way which would replace assistance which these people are already receiving from the State.

10. To use the charity's funds in this way would not make the people any better off: it would simply mean that they were getting from a charity what they had previously been receiving from the State. In effect the charity would be relieving the State, not the beneficiary.

11. The charity's funds must be applied in a way which would actually benefit the recipients in addition to any assistance they receive from the State.

12. When assessing a person's income and financial circumstances, trustees

Charities for the relief of the poor

should count as part of that income any State benefits they know the person is **entitled** to receive. Where such benefits have not been claimed, the trustees should encourage the applicant to do so. Trustees **should not** make payments to a person who is entitled by law to receive the money from the State under the system of statutory benefits.

13. However, trustees may use charity funds to relieve temporary need where there is a delay in receiving statutory benefits. If people are still in need even after receiving all State benefits to which they are entitled, then charitable funds may be used to relieve that continuing need.

14. In order to make the most effective use of the charity's funds, trustees should take the trouble to learn about the system of State benefits, how a person's State benefits may be affected by receiving a grant from a charity and the gaps in the State benefits system which can be filled by payments from charities.

15. Leaflets are available from local offices of the Benefits Agency about the State benefits available to the elderly, disabled, sick, unemployed, those on low incomes, and single-parent families.

16. Trustees should keep in regular contact with local Benefits Agency offices and with the Social Services Department of their local authority. In this way trustees can learn about the help available to poor people from public funds. By consulting about specific cases trustees can find out how to help a person from charitable funds without affecting any State benefits which that person may be receiving.

The Social Fund

17. The Benefits Agency also administers the Social Fund which is intended to help people meet exceptional expenses from their regular income. Many of these payments are made in the form of interest-free loans instead of grants. Nobody has a right in law to a loan or grant from the Social Fund - it is up to the officers administering it to decide whether an applicant's circumstances are such that a loan or grant can be made.

18. For the reasons explained in paragraphs 9 to 16 of this leaflet, charitable funds should not be used as a substitute for benefits to which a person has a statutory right. Nevertheless, in determining whether a loan or a grant may be made, Social Fund officials are in some circumstances also obliged by law to consider whether an applicant could be helped from another source, such as a charity.

19. **The risk that applicants might be shunted from social security office to charity and vice versa must at all costs be avoided.**

20. When an applicant has been referred by a Benefits Agency official to a charity, trustees must assume that the Social Fund cannot help in that particular case, and that the official was acting in the knowledge of the help the charity was likely to give and not on the basis of mere speculation. Should trustees feel that a particular office or officer is using the availability of charitable funds to avoid Social Fund expenditure, their concern should be raised with the official concerned and subsequently if necessary at a higher level. The office should be informed clearly of what the trustees' policy is in the selection of applicants for benefit from the charity's funds.

21. Should individuals still be referred to a charity contrary to agreed policy, the trustees may wish to consider joining with the individuals concerned to secure whatever help they may be entitled to.

22. There are circumstances where trustees can make payments to a person even if that person has been promised a Social Fund loan. These are:

- Where the person is in **urgent need** and cannot wait for the Social Fund money to be made available (although crisis loans are normally paid on the day of claim);
- Where they believe that a Social Fund loan will not succeed in relieving the person's need, because the person cannot afford to pay back the loan in the time required. In this case the trustees could give the person a grant instead of a loan or they could give a loan on more favourable terms than the Social Fund loan- this is an exception to the general principle stated above that charitable funds should not replace State funds;
- Where the Social Fund loan promised will be too little to relieve the person's need, and the trustees are in a position fully to relieve that need.

What trustees can do to make their charity more effective

23. Trustees of some charities for the relief of the poor may find it difficult to spend all the charity's income in the way the governing document demands. This may be because the level of poverty in the charity's area of benefit has significantly decreased in recent times, and there are fewer needy people. In these circumstances, trustees should take positive steps to search for potential beneficiaries, for example by:

- Asking the local Benefits Agency office and Social Services Department to let them know of any people living within the charity's area of benefit whose needs cannot fully be met by State payments;
- Advertising in local newspapers;
- Contacting trustees of other charities and voluntary organisations, particularly those involved in welfare.

24. If trustees:

- Continue to have difficulty in finding beneficiaries after having taken these steps; or
- Are restricted by the governing document of the charity to helping in ways which are outmoded or inappropriate to present needs; or
- Consider that the charity's income is too small to be of practical use;

then there are a number of courses of action which they could take to enable them to apply the charity's funds in a more effective way. These are explained in the following paragraphs.

Small charities

25. Under section 74 of the Charities Act 1993, charities (other than exempt charities and charitable companies) with an annual income of £5,000 or less, which do not own land subject to a restriction that it must be used for the purpose of the charity, may resolve:

- To modify the trusts so as to bring them up to date but keeping them as similar to the original trusts as is practical; or
- To transfer the charity's property to one or more other charities with similar purposes.

26. Under section 75 of that Act, charities (other than exempt charities and charitable companies) with an annual income of £1,000 or less and having no land, may also resolve to spend their charity's capital as well as its income, thus eventually ending the charity when all the funds have been spent.

27. There are special rules about the procedures for these resolutions which are set out in our leaflet **Small Charities (CC44).**

Applying for a Scheme

28. Trustees of other charities for the relief of the poor should consider applying to the Commission for a Scheme. If the Commission agrees that changes are needed to the charity's governing

Charities for the relief of the poor

document, a Scheme will be made which will do one or more of the following:

- Extend the charity's area of benefit so that the trustees have more potential beneficiaries to choose from;
- Amend the purposes of the charity to enable the trustees to apply the income in a variety of ways primarily for the benefit of poor people;
- Amalgamate the charity with one or more other charities for the relief of poverty.

29. For further information, please read our leaflet **Making a Scheme (CC36)**

Ways in which trustees can help poor people

30. There are a number of ways in which trustees may be able to give assistance of real value to people in need. If the charity's purposes are couched in general terms then any or all of these options may be open to the trustees, but some governing documents are specific about the ways in which the founder intended the poor to be helped. If trustees are in any doubt as to whether they have the power to assist in a particular way, they should contact the Commission for advice. Some examples of how poor people may be assisted are listed below, and others will no doubt occur to trustees.

31. **Grants of money** in the form of:

- Weekly allowances for a limited period to meet a particular need;
- Special payments to relieve sudden distress;
- Payments of travelling expenses for visiting people, for example in hospital or a convalescent home, or a children's home, or in prison or other similar place, particularly where more frequent visits are desirable than payments from public funds will allow; and payments to meet consequential expenses - child-minding, accommodation, refreshments, etc.;
- Payments to other charities accommodating those in need in the area of the charity such as almshouses, or homes or hostels for the residence or care of old, infirm or homeless people;
- Payments to assist in meeting electricity, gas and water bills;
- Payment of television licence fees.

32. **The provision of items** (either outright or, if expensive and appropriate, on loan) such as:

- Furniture, bedding, clothing, food, fuel, heating appliances;
- Washing machines for widows with large families or radio or television sets for the lonely, the bedridden or the housebound.

33. **Payment for services** such as house decorating, insulation and repairs, laundering, meals on wheels, outings and entertainments, child-minding.

34. **The provision of facilities** such as:

- The supply of tools or books or payment of fees for instruction or examinations or of travelling expenses so as to help the recipients to earn their living;
- Provision of equipment and funds for recreational pursuits or training intended to bring the quality of life of the beneficiaries to a reasonable standard.

35. Further examples follow of the sort of additional help that can be given **when those in need are also sick, convalescent, disabled, handicapped or infirm,** whether mentally or physically.

36. **Grants of money** in the form of:

- Special payments to relieve sickness or infirmity;
- Payment of travelling expenses on entering or leaving hospitals, convalescent homes or similar institutions, or for out-patient consultations;
- Payment towards the cost of adaptations to the homes of disabled people;
- Payment of telephone installation charges and rentals.

37. **The provision of items** (either outright or, if expensive and appropriate, on loan) such as:

- Food for special diets, medical or other aids, nursing comforts;
- Wheelchairs for the disabled, handicapped or infirm.

38. **The provision of services** such as bathing, exchange of library books, foot care, gardening, hair washing, shaving, help in the home, nursing aid, physiotherapy in the home, reading, shopping, sitting-in, tape-recording for the housebound, travelling companions.

39. **The provision of facilities** such as:

- Arrangements for a period of rest or change of air; or
- Securing the benefits of any convalescent home or other institution or organisation; or
- Providing temporary relief for those having the care of the sick or handicapped person;
- Help for relatives and friends to visit or care for patients;
- Transport.

Making grants to other charities

40. As well as giving grants to individual people in need, or to organisations on behalf of those individual people, trustees can also make grants to other charities and organisations which offer help to the poor. In this case, however, trustees must ensure that any donation will be passed on, in cash or in kind, to persons who qualify as proper recipients according to the purposes of the donor charity.

41. On this basis, grants to almshouse charities, and other charities which cater exclusively for the poor, are permissible provided that the receiving charities operate in the same area of benefit as the donor charity.

42. Grants cannot be made by a charity for the relief of the poor to another charity if that charity's purposes and activities are other than the relief of poverty. Local charities which could not, therefore, be supported by a charity for the relief of the poor include village halls, recreation grounds and church restoration funds. Although poor people may use these facilities, the facilities are not primarily provided for the benefit of poor people. Other people who are not poor also use them and would therefore benefit from any money used to support them.

43. However, some local charities may cater only or mainly for poor people even though their purposes may not be strictly confined to the relief of poverty. For example, in a particularly deprived area most people attending a youth club or an old age pensioners' club may be poor, although membership of the club is not limited to the poor. If the trustees wish to give a general grant to another charity in such circumstances, they should find out whether in practice the charity's beneficiaries are poor persons. If they are, then a grant may be permissible. Even if a few people who are not poor will benefit, this will not prevent a grant if their benefit is merely incidental and unavoidable, and the bulk of the benefit is to poor people. Again, trustees should contact the Commission for advice if they are in any doubt.

44. A grant could also be made to another charity having a variety of purposes, one of which was relief of the poor. In such a case a grant could be made in support of that charity's work in relieving need but the grant would have to be made subject to the specific condition that it be applied by that charity in relieving need.

© *Crown copyright August 1993*

Index

This index is of the grant-making trusts included in this Guide. It does not include the army regimental associations or the sickness and disability advice organisations except where they also have specific funds for the relief of need; details of these are given in the relevant sections of the book.

Abbott: Abbott Memorial Trust	138
Aberdeen: Aberdeen Disabled People's Trust	106
Aberdeen: Aberdeen Widows' & Spinsters' Benevolent Fund	106
Abergwili: Abergwili Relief-in-Need Charity & Others	121
ABTA: ABTA Benevolent Fund	20
Accrington: Accrington Relief-in-Need Charity	159
Action: Action for Blind People	75
Acton: Acton (Middlesex) Relief-in-Need Charity	268
Actors:	
Actors' Benevolent Fund	20
Actors' Charitable Trust	20
Adams: Kate Adams Trust	185
Adamson: Adamson Trust	96
Addlethorpe: Addlethorpe Parochial Charity	175
Aged:	
Aged Christian Friend Society of Scotland	96
Aged & Infirm Ministers' Fund	21
Ainslie: Ainslie, Sir Samuel Chisholm & Fraser Hogg Bequests (see Charities Administered by Midlothian District Council)	113
Airborne: Airborne Forces Security Fund	60
Aircrew: Aircrew Association Charitable Fund	60
Airth: Airth Benefaction Trust	96
Akrill: Charles Akrill Trust	202
Alcester: Alcester Wednesday Night Over 70's Fund	190
Aldborough: Aldborough, Boroughbridge & District Relief-in-Sickness Fund	132
Aldgate: Aldgate Freedom Foundation	267
Aldo: Aldo Trust	284
Alexander: Alexander Mortification Fund	111
Alfreton: Alfreton Welfare Trust	168
Allan: James Allan of Mid-Beltie (Widows' Fund)	106
Allen: Mary Ellen Allen Charity	169
Alnwick: Alnwick & District Relief-in-Sickness Fund	135
Alverstoke: Alverstoke Trust	233
Alzheimer's: Alzheimer's Disease Society	75
Amalgamated: Amalgamated Engineering & Electrical Union – Electrical, Electronic, Telecommunication & Plumbing Section	21
Ambleside: Ambleside Welfare Charity	152
Ambulance: Ambulance Services Benevolent Fund	21
Anchor: Anchor Society	205
Ancient: Ancient Parish of St Andrew Holborn	266
Anderson: Anderson Bequest	111
Andrew: Frederick Andrew Convalescent Trust	76, 284
Anglo-Arab: Anglo-Arab Aid	284
Angus: Charities Administered by Angus District Council	117
Annandale & Eskdale: Charities Administered by Edinburgh Voluntary Organisations' Council	110
Appleton:	
Appleton Trust (Abingdon)	245
Appleton Trust (Canterbury)	236
Arbib: Annie Arbib Trust	285
Architects: Architects Benevolent Society	21
Arden: Arthur Arden Charities & Others	187
Argyll:	
Argyll & Bute District Charities	114
Argyll Naval Fund	109
Arlish: Arlish & Chambers Charity	134
Armchair: Armchair	171
Army:	
Army Benevolent Fund	60
Army Catering Corps Association Benevolent Fund	60
Arnison: Arnison Fund	139
Arnold: Edmund Arnold's Charity	178
Arthritis: Arthritis Care	76
Artists: Artists' General Benevolent Institution	21
Ashby-de-la-Zouch: Ashby-de-la-Zouch Relief-in-Sickness Fund	172
Ashington: Ashington, Wiston & Warminghurst Sick Poor Fund	260
Ashton:	
Mrs Frances Ashton's Charity	21
John Ashton & Ellis Smethurst Charities	144
Ashton Keynes Charity	219
Associated: Associated Society of Locomotive Engineers & Firemen (ASLEF) Orphans' Fund	21
Association:	
Association for Helping Poor Ladies	250
Association of Her Majesty's Inspectors of Taxes Benevolent Fund	21
Association of Jewish Ex-servicemen & Women	61
Association of Optical Practitioners Charitable Fund	22
Association for the Relief of Incurables in Glasgow & the West of Scotland	96
Association of Royal Navy Officers	61
Association for Spina Bifida & Hydrocephalus (ASBAH)	76
Association of Teachers & Lecturers Benevolent Fund	22
Association of University Teachers Benevolent Fund	22
Association of Vietnamese Residents in the UK	285
Aston-cum-Aughton: Aston-cum-Aughton Charity Estate	137
Ataxia: Ataxia	76
Atherton: Atherton Trust	186
Athlone: Athlone Trust	285
Atmere: Edmund Atmere Charity	240
ATS: ATS & WRAC Benevolent Funds	61
Auchray: Auchray Fund (see Charities Administered by Moray District Council)	108
Authors: Authors' Contingency Fund	22
Auxiliary: Auxiliary Fund of the Ministers' Retirement Fund of the Methodist Church	22
Avenel: Avenel Trust	110
Avenue: Avenue Trust Fund	264
Avery: Jane Avery Charity	174
Avon: Avon & Somerset Constabulary Benevolent Fund	203
Backhouse: Agnes Backhouse & Dorothy Barrow Annuity Trusts	152
Badley: Badley Memorial Trust	195
Bailey: Ernest Bailey Charity	169
Baine: Baine's Charity	157
Baker: Mr John Baker's Trust	270
Bakers: Bakers' Benevolent Society	22
Balderton: Balderton Parochial Charity	184
Baltic: Baltic Exchange Charitable Society	22
Banbury: Banbury Charities - Bridge Estate	245
Banff: Banff & Buchan District Charities	108
Bankers: Bankers Benevolent Fund	22
Banking: Banking Insurance & Finance Union Benevolent Fund	22
Banner: Banner's Trust	197
Barbers: Barbers' Amalgamated Charity	23
Barclay: Thomas Barclay Bequest (see Charities Administered by Edinburgh Voluntary Organisations' Council)	110
Barford: Barford Relief-in-Need Charity	192
Barking:	
Barking & Dagenham Mayor's Fund	264
Barking General Charities	264

Index

Barnes:
- Ellen Barnes Charitable Trust — 186
- Barnes Relief-in-Need Charity — 276
- Barnes Samaritan Charity — 152
- Barnes Workhouse Fund — 276

Barnsley:
- Barnsley Prisoner of War Fund — 137
- Barnsley Tradesmen's Benevolent Institution — 137

Barnstaple:
- Barnstaple Municipal Charities — 208
- Barnstaple & North Devon Dispensary Fund — 208

Barnwood: Barnwood House Trust — 215
Barrett: Thomas Barrett's Charity — 243
Barristers: Barristers' Benevolent Fund — 23
Barron: Thomas Metcalfe Barron Charity — 129
Barrow: Barrow-Thornbarrow Charity — 151
Barrows: Barrows Eleemosynary Charity — 237

Barton:
- Barton Bendish Poor's Charity — 239
- Barton-upon-Humber Relief-in-Sickness Fund — 130

Bates: John Heggs Bates' Charity for Convalescents — 172
Bath: Bath Municipal Charities — 204
Batley: Batley Town Mission — 141
Battersea: Battersea United Charities — 279
Battle: Battle Charities — 229
Batty: Samuel Watson Batty Trust — 143
Bayne: James Bayne Charitable Trust — 153
Beacon: Beacon Centre for the Blind — 195
Beames: Thomas Beames' Charity — 206
Beaminster: Beaminster Charities — 213
Beane: John Beane's Guildford & Dorking Eleemosynary Charity — 251
Beardsley: Beardsley's Relief-in-Need Charity — 190

Beaumont:
- Beaumont Charity — 210
- Beaumont & Jessop Relief-in-Need Charity — 144
- Charity of Letitia Beaumont — 150

Becker: Mrs Becker's Charity for Clergy — 23
Beckly: J H Beckly Handicapped/Sick Children's Fund — 203
Beddington: Beddington & Wallington Relief Fund for the Sick & Infirm — 278
Beeston: Beeston Fuel Charity — 239
Beeton: Beeton, Barrick & Beck Relief-in-Need Charity — 130
Beighton: Beighton Relief-in-Need Charity — 137

Belfast:
- Belfast Association for the Blind — 94
- Belfast Central Mission — 94
- Belfast Sick Poor Fund — 96

Bell: Sir Hugh & Lady Bell Memorial Fund — 128
Ben: Ben - Motor & Allied Trades Benevolent Fund — 23

Benevolent:
- Benevolent Fund of HM Inspectors of Schools — 23
- Benevolent Fund of the Institution of Mechanical Engineers — 23
- Benevolent Fund for Nurses in Scotland — 96
- Benevolent Society of the Licensed Trade of Scotland — 97
- Benevolent Society for the Relief of the Aged & Infirm Poor — 261
- Benevolent Society of St Patrick — 261

Bengough: Bengough Charity — 280
Bentinck: Bentinck Benevolent Fund — 24
Bequest: Bequest of Miss Marjorie Williams — 124

Beresford: Beresford Trust — 24

Berkshire:
- Berkshire Clergy Charity — 223
- Berkshire Nurses & Relief-in-Sickness Fund — 221

Berwick: Berwick-upon-Tweed Guild of Freemen — 135
Berwickshire: Charities Administered by Berwickshire District Council — 103
Betchworth: Betchworth United Charities — 253
Betteridge: Frances Lynn Betteridge Memorial Trust Fund — 197
Betton: Thomas Betton's Charity for Pensions & Relief-in-Need — 285
Beveridge: Miss Beveridge Trust (see Charities Administered by Edinburgh Voluntary Organisation's Council) — 110
Bexley: Bexley Mayor's Fund — 265
Bideford: Bideford Bridge Trust — 208
Biggart: Biggart Trust — 97

Bilston: Bilston Relief-in-Need Charity — 197

Bilton:
- Bilton Poors' Land & Other Charities — 193
- Percy Bilton Charity Limited — 76, 285

Bingham: Bingham United Charities — 184
Bingley: Bingley Diamond Jubilee Relief-in-Sickness Charity — 141
Birkenhead: Birkenhead Relief-in-Sickness Fund — 162

Birmingham:
- Birmingham Children's Holiday Fund — 197
- Birmingham Jewish Welfare Board — 195
- Birmingham & Midland Cinematograph Trade Benevolent Fund — 195
- Birmingham Royal Institution for the Blind — 197
- Birmingham & Three Counties Trust for Nurses — 165

Bishop: Bishop's Land Charity — 244
Bishopstone: Bishopstone United Charities — 219
Bisley: Bisley Charities for the Poor — 216
Black: Black's Bequest (see Charities Administered by Berwickshire District Council) — 103
Blackman: Isabel Blackman Foundation — 230

Blackpool:
- Blackpool, Fylde & Wyre Society for the Blind — 157
- Blackpool Ladies' Sick Poor Association — 158

Blackstock: Blackstock Trust — 103
Blackwood: Blackwood Trust — 97
Blagdon: Edward Blagdon Charity — 207

Blair:
- Cecil Norman Wellesley Blair Charitable Trust — 220
- J T Blair's Charity — 153

Blakeley: Mrs E L Blakeley - Marillier Annuity Fund — 132
Blakesley: Blakesley Parochial Charities — 178
Blanchminster: Blanchminster Trust — 206
Blandford: Blandford Forum Charities — 214
Bletchingdon: Bletchingdon Charity — 245
Bloomsbury: Bloomsbury Dispensary — 266
Blunt: Mary Anne & Ruth Blunt's Charity — 180
Blyth: Blyth Benevolent Trust — 97
Body: Body Postive — 77

Bolton:
- Bolton & District Nursing Association — 154
- Bolton Poor Protection Society — 154

Bond: James Bond Charity — 159
Book: Book Trade Benevolent Society — 24
Bookbinders: Bookbinders' Charitable Society — 24

Bookmakers: Bookmakers Employees Benevolent Fund — 24
Boot: Boot Trade Benevolent Society — 24
Booth: Booth Charities — 156
Botley: William Botley Charity — 219
Bournemouth: Bournemouth Blind Aid Society — 214
Boveridge: Boveridge Charity — 213
Bowes: Charity of Sir Martin Bowes — 269
Bowley: Bowley Charity for Deprived Children — 235
Bowness: Bowness Trust — 152
Bowsher: John Bowsher's Charity for Bachelors — 121
Brackley: Brackley United Feoffee Charity — 178

Bradford:
- City of Bradford Fund for the Disabled — 141
- Bradford & District Wool Association Benevolent Fund — 141
- Bradford Gentlewomen's Pension Fund — 141
- Bradford Jewish Benevolent Society — 141
- Bradford Spinsters' Endowment Fund — 143

Braintree: Braintree United Charities — 231
Bramhope: Bramhope Trust — 144
Bramley: Bramley Poors' Allotment & Other Charities — 142
Brampton: Brampton Bierlow Welfare Trust — 136
Bratton: Bratton Fleming Relief-in-Need Charity — 208
Braunston: Braunston Town Lands Charity — 179
Brechin: Brechin Victoria Nursing Association — 117

Brecknock:
- Brecknock Association for the Welfare of the Blind — 124
- Brecknock Welfare Trust — 124

Brentford:
- Brentford & Chiswick Merged Charities — 272
- Brentford Relief-in-Need Charity — 272

Brideoake: Charity of Anne Farrar Brideoake — 285
Bridge: Bridge Land Charity — 212
Bridgeman: Dame Mary Bridgeman Charity — 198
Bridlington: Bridlington Charity Trustees — 130
Bridport: Bridport Charities — 214
Bright: Beatrice Eveline Bright Trust — 182
Brighton: Brighton District Nursing Association Trust — 230
Brington: Brington Chauntry Estate — 179
Brisco: Sarah Brisco Charity — 230

Bristol:
- Bristol Benevolent Institution — 205
- Bristol Caledonian Society Benevolent Fund — 205
- Bristol Corn Trade Guild — 205
- Bristol Municipal Charities — 204
- Bristol (St John the Baptist & St Ambrose) Charity — 205

British:
- British Airline Pilots' Association Benevolent Fund (BALPA) — 24
- British Antique Dealers' Association Benevolent Fund — 25
- British College of Optometrists Benevolent Fund — 25
- British Commonwealth Ex-Services League — 61

Index

British Dental Association Benevolent Fund	25
British Diabetic Association	77
British Epilepsy Association	77
British Hairdressers' Benevolent & Provident Institution	25
British Jewellery, Giftware & Leathergoods Benevolent Society	25
British Kidney Patient Association	77
British Limbless Ex-Servicemen's Association	61
British Motoring Sport Relief Fund	25
British Office Systems & Stationery Federation Benevolent Fund	25
British Polio Fellowship	77
British Rail Staff Assistance Fund	26
British Telecom Benevolent Fund	26
Brittle: Brittle Bone Society	77
Brixton:	
Brixton Dispensary	274
Brixton Feoffee Lands Charity	209
Broadclyst: Broadclyst Relief-in-Need Charity	209
Broadhempston: Broadhempston Relief-in-Need Charity	209
Broadlands: Broadlands Home Trust	286
Brockley: Brockley Town & Poor Estate	247
Brogden: Brogden Appeal Trust	234
Bromley: Bromley Relief-in-Need Charity	266
Bromwich: Thomas Bromwich Charity	195
Brook: Charles Brook Convalescent Fund	144
Brooke:	
Charity of John Brooke	211
Lizzie Brooke Charity	206
Brooke Poor's Land	173
Broomfield: Broomfield United Charities	231
Brotherton: Brotherton Charity Fund	147
Brough: Joseph Brough Benevolent Association	126
Broughty: Broughty Ferry Benevolent Fund	117
Browne: Winifrede Browne's Charity	177
Brownlow: Lawrence Brownlow Charity	153
Brownsdon: Brownsdon & Tremayne Estate Charity	207
Bruce: Bruce Charitable Trust	105
Brunt: Brunt's Charity	184
Buccleuch: Buccleuch Place Trust (see Charities Administered by Edinburgh Voluntary Organisation's Council)	110
Buchanan: Buchanan Society	97
Buckden: Buckden Parochial Charity	226
Buckland: Lord Buckland Trust	123
Budleigh: Budleigh Salterton Nursing Association	209
Builders: Builders' Benevolent Institution	26
Bungay: Bungay Town Trust	247
Buntingford: Buntingford Relief in Need Charity	236
Burford: Burford Relief-in-Need Charity	246
Burma: Burma Star Association	62
Burton:	
Reg Burton Fund	173
Burton & South Derbyshire Charity for the Sufferers of Multiple Sclerosis	167, 189
Burton-on-Trent Sick Poor Fund	189
Burwell: Burwell Poors Fen Charity	227
Bury: Bury Relief-in-Sickness Fund	154
Bushbury: Bushbury United Charities	198
Butchers': Butchers' & Drovers' Charitable Institution	26
Butterfield: Butterfield Trust	141
Buttle: Buttle Trust	286
Byfield: Byfield Poors' Allotment	179
Byfleet: Byfleet Pensions Fund	253
Byron: Lord Byron's Nursing Association	254
Caersws: Caersws Community Care Fund	124
Callibut: Callibut's Estate & the Hillingdon Charities	239
Calverley: Calverley Charity	140
Calverton: Calverton Jane Pepper & Poor Lands Charity	184
Cam: Ann Cam's Charity	215
Camberwell:	
Camberwell Consolidated Charities	277
Camberwell Provident Dispensary Fund	277
Cameron: Cameron Fund	26
Camp: John & Anne Camp's Charity	180
Campden: Campden Charities	273
Cancer:	
Cancer Help Society (Wales)	119
Cancer & Leukaemia in Childhood Trust (CLIC)	78
Cancer Relief Macmillan Fund	78
Cannington: Cannington Combined Charity	217
Canterbury: Canterbury United Municipal Charities	236
Cantley: Cantley Poors' Land	137
Capital: Capital Charitable Trust	110
Cardiff:	
Cardiff Caledonian Society	124
Cardiff Charity of Special Relief	125
Care:	
Care & Action Trust for Children with Handicaps	119
Care Trust	286
Carlisle: Carlisle Sick Poor Fund	152
Carlow: Leonora Carlow Trust Fund	213
Carlton: Carlton Colville Fuel & Poors' Allotment Charity	247
Carnegie: Carnegie Hero Fund Trust	286
Carperby: Carperby Poor's Land Charity	133
Carr: Carr Trust	189
Carshalton: Carshalton Aid-in-Sickness Fund	253
Carter:	
Carter's Charity for the Poor of Wilford	186
Harold Carter Bequest	279
Cassington: Cassington Parochial Charities	246
Cathedral: Cathedral Nursing Society Charitable Trust	139
Catherine: Catherine House Trust	229
Catholic: Catholic Council for Polish Welfare	286
Catt: Charity of Joseph Catt	250
Cavell: Edith Cavell & Nation's Fund for Nurses	26
CB: CB Charitable Trust	286
Century: Century Benevolent Fund	26
Ceramic: Ceramic Industry Welfare Society	27
Certified: Certified Accountants' Benevolent Association	27
Chalker: Henry & Ada Chalker Trust	146
Challenger: Challenger Children's Fund	97
Chalmers: George, James & Alexander Chalmers Trust	107
Chamberlain:	
John Chamberlain Permanent Benevolent Fund for Aged & Infirm Members of the Brush Trade	27
Charity of Leonard Chamberlain	131, 134
Chamberlayne: Sarah Chamberlayne Charity	190, 230
Champney: Margaret Champney Rest & Holiday Fund	78
Chapel: Chapel Allerton & Potternewton Relief-in-Need Charity	144
Chapman: John William Chapman Charitable Trust	137
Charities: Charities Fund	140
Charity: Charity of the Unknown Donor	225
Charlton: Charlton Bequest & Dispensary Trust	139
Charmouth: Charmouth United Charities	214
Chartered:	
Chartered Accountants' Benevolent Association	27
Chartered Institute of Journalists Orphan Fund	27
Chartered Institute of Loss Adjusters Benevolent Fund	27
Chartered Institute of Management Accountants' Benevolent Fund	27
Chartered Institute of Patent Agents' Incorporated Benevolent Association	27
Chartered Institution of Building Services Engineers Benevolent Fund	27
Chartered Society of Physiotherapy Members' Benevolent Fund	28
Chartered Society of Queen Square	78
Chatteris: Chatteris Feoffee Charity	227
Chediston: Chediston United Charities, Town & Poors' Branch	248
Chelsea: Chelsea Non-Ecclesiastical Charities	273
Cheltenham: Cheltenham Aid-in-Sickness & Nurses Welfare Fund	216
Chemical: Chemical Engineers' Benevolent Fund	28
Chertsey: Chertsey Combined Charity	253
Chessington: Chessington Charities	254
Chester:	
Chester Parochial Relief-in-Need Charity	149
Chester Sick Poor Fund	149
Cheyne: Gordon Cheyne Trust Fund	107
Chichester: Chichester Welfare Trust	260
Children:	
Children's Boot Fund	199
Children's Charity Circle	142
Children's Community Holidays	94
Children's Leukaemia Appeal	78
Chippenham: Chippenham Borough Lands Charities	219
Chobham: Chobham Poor Allotment Charity	254
Christ:	
Christ Church Fund for Children	162
Christ Church United Charities	277
Christie: Robert Christie Bequest Fund	110
Christmas: Christmas Gift Fund for the Old City of Canterbury	236
Chronicle: Chronicle Cinderella Fund	157
Church:	
Church of England Pensions Board	28
Church of Ireland Retirement Trust	94
Church Schoolmasters & Schoolmistresses' Benevolent Institution (CSSBI)	28
Church of Scotland Ministers' Orphan Fund	97
Cinema: Cinema & Television Benevolent Fund	28
City:	
City Chapter & Percy Trentham Charity	267
City of Oxford Charities	246

Index

Civil:
   Civil & Public Services Association Benevolent Fund — 28
   Civil Service Benevolent Fund — 29
Clackmannan: Clackmannan District Charitable Trust — 104
Clapham: Clapham Relief-in-Need Charity — 274
Clarke: Elizabeth Clarke & Wigston Relief-in-Need Funds — 174
Clayton: Clayton, Taylor & Foster Charity — 147
Cloudesley: Richard Cloudesley's Charity — 272
Clover: Emily Clover Trust — 162
Coal:
   Coal Industry Benevolent Trust — 29
   Coal Trade Benevolent Association — 29
Cockermouth: Cockermouth Relief-in-Need Charity — 152
Cockpen: Cockpen, Lasswade & Falconer Bequest (see Charities Administered by Midlothian District Council) — 113
Coddington: Coddington United Charities — 184
Cohen: Myrtle Cohen Trust Fund — 29
Colchester:
   Colchester Lying-In Charity — 231
   Colchester Society for the Blind — 231
Cole: Charities of Susanna Cole & Others — 165
Coleman: R V Coleman Trust — 237
Coles: Coles & Rice Charity — 180
Collier: Joseph Collier Holiday Fund — 277
Colvill: Colvill Trust — 117
Commandos: Commandos' Benevolent Fund — 62
Commercial:
   Commercial Travellers of Scotland Benevolent Fund for Widows & Orphans — 97
   Commercial Travellers' Benevolent Institution — 29
Community: Community Shop — 145
Concert: Concert Artistes' Association — 29
Confectioners: Confectioners' Benevolent Fund — 29
Congleton: Congleton Municipal Charities — 149
Conroy: Conroy Trust — 160
Convalescent: Convalescent & Holiday Fund — 160
Cook: Samuel Edward Cook Charity for the Poor — 265
Cooper: Cooper & Lancaster Annuities — 136
Corah:
   Leslie Corah Memorial Trust — 172
   J Reginald Corah Foundation Fund — 172
Corfe: Corfe Castle Charities — 214
Corkhill: John Lloyd Corkhill Charity — 160
Corn: Corn Exchange Benevolent Society — 30
Cornwall:
   Cornwall Retired Clergy, Widows of Clergy & their Dependants Fund — 206
   Cornwall Seamen's Benevolent Trust — 206
Corporation: Corporation of the Sons of the Clergy — 30
Corstorphine: Corstorphine & Cramond Bequests — 112
Corton: Corton Poors' Land Trust — 248
Corwen: Corwen College Pension Charity — 119
Cottam: Cottam Charities — 158
Cotton:
   Cotton Districts Convalescent Fund — 133, 142, 147, 167
   Cotton Industry Benevolent Fund — 30

Counsel: Counsel & Care for the Elderly — 287
Coventry:
   Coventry Charity for Special Relief — 199
   Coventry Community Cancer Fund — 195
   Coventry Convalescent Fund — 199
   Coventry Freeman's Charity — 195
   Coventry Nursing Trust — 199
Cox: George Cox Charity — 218
Craigcrook: Craigcrook Mortification — 97
Crediton: Crediton Relief-in-Need Charity — 209
Crerar: Alastair Crerar Trust for Single Poor — 98
Cresswell: Eliza Ann Cresswell Memorial — 168
Crewe: Lord Crewe's Charity — 126
Cricketers: Cricketers Association Charity — 30
Cricklade: Cricklade United Charities — 219
Cripplegate: Cripplegate Foundation — 261
Crisis: Crisis Fund of Voluntary Service Aberdeen — 107
Crosby: Crosby Ravensworth Relief-in-Need Charities — 152
Cross: Arthur John Graham Cross Charity — 280
Crossley: Crossley Fund — 287
Crosthwaite: Lady Crosthwaite Bequest Fund — 128
Crusaid: Crusaid — 78
Culmstock: Culmstock Fuel Allotment Charity — 209
Cumbria:
   Cumbria Constabulary Benevolent Fund — 151
   Cumbria Miners' Welfare Trust Fund — 151
Curie: Marie Curie Memorial Foundation — 98
Curtis: Mary Curtis Matenity Charity — 276
Customs: Customs & Excise Orphans' & Widows' Fund — 30
Cystic: Cystic Fibrosis Trust — 78

D'Erlanger: Late Baron F A D'Erlanger's Charitable Trust — 287
Dacorum: Dacorum Community Trust — 235
Danby: Lancelot Danby Charities & Others — 250
Dance: Dance Teachers' Benevolent Fund — 30
Dargie: Mrs Marie Dargie Trust — 117
Darleston: Darleston Relief-in-Sickness Fund — 200
Dartmouth: Dartmouth Trust Lands — 210
Datchet: Datchet United Charities — 223
Davenport:
   Baron Davenport Charity Trust — 165
   Baron Davenport Emergency Grant (Birmingham) — 197
   Baron Davenport Emergency Grant (Dudley) — 200
   Baron Davenport Emergency Grant (East Staffs) — 188
   Baron Davenport Emergency Grant (Malvern) — 170
   Baron Davenport Emergency Grant (North Warwickshire) — 190
   Baron Davenport Emergency Grant (Nuneaton & Bedworth) — 191
   Baron Davenport Emergency Grant (Redditch) — 170
   Baron Davenport Emergency Grant (Rugby) — 193
   Baron Davenport Emergency Grant (Solihull) — 201
   Baron Davenport Emergency Grant (Stafford) — 188

   Baron Davenport Emergency Grant (Staffordshire, Warwickshire & Worcestershire) — 165
   Baron Davenport Emergency Grant (Stratford) — 194
   Baron Davenport Emergency Grant (Tamworth) — 190
   Baron Davenport Emergency Grant (Walsall) — 202
   Baron Davenport Emergency Grant (Warwick) — 194
   Baron Davenport Emergency Grant (Warwickshire) — 165
   Baron Davenport Emergency Grant (Wolverhampton) — 202
Daventry: Daventry Consolidated Charities — 179
Davidson: Davidson Charity Trust — 139
Davies:
   Charity of Arthur Vernon Davies for the Poor — 155
   Isaac Davies Trust — 261
   Mark Davies Injured Riders Fund — 287
de Rothschild: Alfred de Rothschild Charity — 79, 287
de Sousa: Margaret de Sousa Deiro Fund — 79
Deakin: Deakin Institution — 287
Dempster: Dempster Trust — 251
Dennington: Dennington Consolidated Charities — 248
Denny: Margaret & Alfred Denny Christmas Charity — 230
Deptford: Deptford Pension Society — 275
Derbyshire: Lucy Derbyshire Annuity Fund — 182
Devitt: Sir Thomas Devitt's Endowment Fund — 287
Devon:
   Devon & Cornwall Aid for Girls Trust — 203
   Devon & Exeter Benevolent Medical Society Fund — 208
Dewsbury: Dewsbury & District Sick Poor Fund — 142
Dibdin: Dibdin Bread Charity — 266
Dibs: Dibs Charitable Trust — 287
Dickinson: Mary Dickinson Charity — 182
Digby: Simon Lord Digby Relief-in-Need Charity — 192
Dinas: Dinas Powis Relief-in-Sickness Fund — 125
Diocesan: Diocesan Institutions of Chester, Manchester, Liverpool & Blackburn — 147
Disablement: Disablement Income Group Scotland — 98
Diss: Diss Parochial Charities Poors Branch — 240
Dixon: Charles Dixon Pension Fund — 288
Dodbrooke: Dodbrooke Parish Charity — 211
Dolphin: Dolphin Society — 205
Domestic: Domestic Servants Benevolent Institution — 30
Donald: Donald Trust — 107
Dorchester: Dorchester Relief-in-Need Charity — 215
Doris: Howard Doris Trust — 109
Dorkin: John Dorkin Charity — 249
Dorrington: Dorrington Welfare Charity — 175
Dorset: Dorset Police Welfare Fund — 213
Downham: Downham Feoffee Charity — 227
Drake:
   Drake Charity Trust — 288
   Francis Drake Fellowship — 288
Drapers: Drapers' Consolidated Charity — 31
Driving: Driving Instructors Accident & Disability Fund — 31

307

Index

Dronfield:
Dronfield Nightingales — 167
Dronfield Relief-in-Need Charity — 168
Drummond: Kate Drummond Trust — 238
Duckett:
Issac Duckett's Charity (St Clement Danes Branch) — 280
Issac Duckett - St Andrew Branch (see Ancient Parish of St Andrew Holborn) — 266
Ducklington: Ducklington & Hardwick with Yelford Charity — 245
Dudley:
Dudley Annitsford Aged People's Treat Fund — 136
Dudley Charity — 200
Reginald Unwin Dudley Charity — 200
Dugdale: Henry Percy Dugdale Charity — 144
Dunblane: Dunblane Coal Fund — 104
Dunchurch: Dunchurch & Thurlaston Community Trust — 191
Dundee:
City of Dundee District Charities — 117
Dundee Indigent Sick Society — 117
Dunfermline: Charities Administered by Dunfermline District Council — 105
Dunsmoor: Dunsmoor Day Nursery & Maternity Home (also known as the Dunsmoor Charity) — 199
Dunstable:
Dunstable Poor's Lands Charity — 222
Dunstable Welfare Trust — 222
Dunwich: Dunwich Pension Charity — 248
Durnford: Montague Neville Durnford & Saint Leo Cawthan Memorial Trust — 234

Ealing:
Ealing Aid-in-Sickness Trust — 268
Ealing Philanthropic Institution — 268
Earley: Earley Charity — 223
East:
East Bergholt United Charities — 231
East Dereham Relief-in-Need Charity — 240
East Grinstead Relief in Sickness Charity — 260
East Knoyle Charities — 219
East Retford Relief-in-Need Charity — 186
East Ruston Poor's Allotment — 240
East Tilbury Relief in Need Charity — 231
Eaton: Eaton Fund for Artists, Nurses & Gentlewomen — 31
Eccles: Charity of Jane Patricia Eccles — 202
Echo: Echo Goodfellow Fund — 160
Edinburgh:
Edinburgh Children's Holiday Fund — 112
Edinburgh Coal Fund (see Charities Administered by Edinburgh Voluntary Organisations' Council) — 110
Edinburgh Cripple Aid Society — 110
Edinburgh Discharged Prisoners Aid Society (see Charities Administered by Edinburgh Voluntary Organisations' Council) — 111
Edinburgh Medical Missionary Society Hawthornbrae Trust — 112
Edinburgh Merchants Company Endowment Trust — 110
Edinburgh Royal Infirmary Samaritan Society — 112
Edinburgh Society for Relief of Indigent Old Men — 112
Edmett: Edmett, Swain & Hanson Charity — 238
Edmonds: William Edmonds Fund — 163
Edmonton: Edmonton Aid-in-Sickness & Nursing Fund — 269

Edridge: Edridge Benevolent Fund — 31
Educational: Educational Institute of Scotland Benevolent Fund — 98
Edward: Edward's Bequest — 187
Edwards:
Dr Edwards' & Bishop King's Fulham Charity — 270
Sir Henry Edwards Gift Charity — 213
Egerton: George Julian Egerton Fund — 288
Egham: Egham United Charity — 255
Electrical: Electrical & Electronic Industries Benevolent Association — 31
Electronic: Electronic Aids for the Blind — 79
Eleemosynary: Eleemosynary Charity of William Hobbayne — 268
Elkington: Maud Elkington Charitable Trust — 166
Elliot: Samuel Elliot Bequest (see Charities Administered by Annandale & Eskdale Council) — 104
Eman: Charity of Elizabeth Eman — 225
Emanuel: Emanuel Hospital Charity — 261
Emmandjay: Emmandjay Charitable Trust — 140
Endowment: Endowment Fund — 185
Engineering: Engineering Employers' Federation Benevolent Fund — 31
Engineers: Engineers' & Managers' Association (EMA) Benevolent Fund — 32
English: English National Opera Benevolent Fund — 32
Entertainment: Entertainment Artistes' Benevolent Fund — 32
Enville: Enville Poor's Charity — 189
Epsom: Epsom Parochial Charities — 255
Equity: Equity Trust Fund — 32
Estate: Estate Charity of Lady Leveson's — 166
Eton: Eton Poor's Estate — 224
Evans:
Freeman Evans St Davids Day Denbigh Charity — 121
Freeman Evans St David's Day Ffestiniog Charity — 122
Les Evans Holiday Fund for Sick & Handicapped Children — 79
Ewell: Ewell Parochial Trust — 255
Ex-Services: Ex-Services Mental Welfare Society — 62
Exeter:
Exeter Dispensary, Aid-in-Sickness — 210
Exeter Municipal Charities — 210
Exeter Relief-in-Need Charity — 210
Exminster: Exminster Parish Lands — 210
Exmouth: Exmouth Welfare Trust — 210
Eynsham: Eynsham Consolidated Charity — 246

Faculty: Faculty of Advocates 1985 Charitable Trust — 98
Family:
Family Fund — 79
Family Holiday Association — 288
Family Welfare Association — 288
Fareham: Fareham Welfare Trust — 233
Faringdon: Faringdon United Charities — 245
Farlow: Farlow James & Williams Charity — 187
Farmers: Farmers' Benevolent Institution — 174
Farnborough: Farnborough Welfare Trust — 232
Farrar: Mary Farrar's Benevolent Trust Fund — 143
Farthing: Farthing Trust — 226, 288
Fearnside: Susannah Fearnside's Charity — 132
Featherstone: Catherine Featherstone Charity — 226

Federation: Federation of Master Builders (Bristol Branch) Benevolent Fund — 205
Fenstanton: Fenstanton Town Trust — 227
Fentham: George Fentham (Birmingham) Trust — 197
Feoffees: Feoffees of the Common Lands of Rotherham — 137
Ferryhill: Ferryhill Station, Mainsforth & Bishop Middleham Aid-in-Sickness Charity — 129
Field: Olive & Norman Field Charity — 132
Fife: Fife, Kinross & Clackmannan Charitable Society — 115
Fifty:
Fifty Fund — 185
'56 Aid Club — 275
Finchamstead: Finchamstead & Barkham Relief-in-Sickness Fund — 223
Finchley: Finchley Charities — 264
Finnie: David Finnie & Alan Emery Charitable Trust — 289
Finsbury: Finsbury Relief-in-Sickness Charity — 272
Fire: Fire Services National Benevolent Fund — 32
Fisher:
Fisher Institution — 138
Jane Fisher Trust — 151
Fishmongers: Fishmongers' & Poulterers' Institution — 32
Fleetwood: Fleetwood Fishing Industry Benevolent Fund — 159
Fleming:
Fleming Bequest — 106
Jane Turner Fleming Charity — 135
Fletcher: Miss Ethel Mary Fletcher's Charitable Bequest — 238
Fluck: Fluck Convalescent Fund — 216
Flynn: Paul Flynn Memorial Fund — 80
Fogelman: Isaac & Annie Fogelman Relief Trust — 234
Foleshill: Foleshill Aid-in-Sickness Fund — 201
Folkestone: Folkestone Municipal Charity — 237
Football: Football Association Benevolent Fund — 32
Forbes:
Forbes Fund — 107
Dr Forbes (Inverness) Trust — 109
Forby: Jane Forby Charity — 244
Forces: Forces Help Society & Lord Roberts Workshops — 62
Ford:
Joseph Ford's Trust — 133
William Ford & Dagenham United Charities — 264
Fordath: Fordath Foundation — 201
Fordwich: Fordwich United Charities — 237
Forester: Lady Forester Trust — 148, 166
Forres: Forres Poor Fund & Others (see Charities Administered by Moray District Council) — 108
Foster: Alfred Foster Settlement — 33
Foulden: Foulden Parochial Charities — 240
Foundation: Foundation of Edward Storey — 33, 227
Fountain: Fountain Nursing Trust — 137
Foxton: Foxton Dispensary — 157
Foyles: John Foyles Charity — 215
Frampton: Frampton United Charities — 176
Franklin: Sir George Franklin's Pension Charity — 138
Fraser: Miss Jane Campbell Fraser's Trust — 113
Freeman: Nicholas Freeman Memorial Trust — 273

308

Index

Friends:
  Friends of the Clergy Corporation 33
  Friends of the Elderly &
    Gentlefolk's Help 289
  Friends of the Sick 262
Frimley: Frimley Fuel Allotments 251
Friskney: Friskney United Charities 176
Fritillary: Fritillary Trust 223
Fry: Margery Fry Benevolent Fund 196
Fryer: Fryer Welfare Trust 209
Fuel: Fuel Fund of Voluntary Service
  Aberdeen 107
Fulham: Fulham Philanthropic Society 270
Furness: Furness Seamen's Pension Fund 128
Furnishing: Furnishing Trades
  Benevolent Association 33

Gainsborough: Gainsborough
  Dispensary Charity 176
Galon: Thomas Galon's Charity 229
Garboldisham: Garboldisham Parish
  Charities 240
Gardeners: Gardeners' Royal Benevolent
  Society 33
Gardner:
  Dr Gardner's Trust for Nurses 187
  Grace Gardner Trust 134
  Gardner's Trust for the Blind 80
Gargrave: Gargrave Poor's Land Charity 133
Garlthorpe: Garlthorpe Charity 130
Garrett: Dr Garrett Memorial Trust 154
Garston: Garston & Grassendale Fund
  for the Sick & Convalescent 163
Garthgwynion: Garthgwynion Charities 123
Gayton:
  Gayton Fuel Allotments 240
  Gayton Relief-in-Need Charity 179
Gaywood: Gaywood Poors' Allotment 240
Geest: Gyles Geest Charity 217
General:
  General Charities of the City of
    Coventry 199
Gent: Charity of Priscilla Gent & Others 192
German: German Society of
  Benevolence 221, 262
Gibson:
  Gibson, Simpson & Brockbank
    Annuities Trust 159
  Gibson's Charity 117
Gilbert: Charity of Jane Kate Gilbert 197
Gilbertson: Gilbertson Trust 114
Gill: Francis Butcher Gill's Charity 182
Girling: Girling (Cwmbran) Trust 122
Girls: Girls' Welfare Fund 160
Gisleham: Gisleham Relief-in-Need
  Charity 248
Gislingham: Gislingham United Charity 248
Glasgow:
  Glasgow Angus & Mearns
    Benevolent Society (see Charities
    Administered by City of Glasgow
    Society of Social Services) 115
  Glasgow Benevolent Society (see
    Charities Administered by City of
    Glasgow Society of Social Services) 115
  Glasgow Bute Benevolent Society 114
  City of Glasgow Native Benevolent
    Association 115
  Charities Administered by Glasgow
    District Council 115
  Charities Administered by City of
    Glasgow Society of Social Services 115
  Glasgow Dumbartonshire Benevolent
    Association (see Charities
    Administered by City of Glasgow
    Society of Social Services) 115

  Glasgow Dumfriesshire Society (see
    Charities Administered by City of
    Glasgow Society of Social Services) 115
  Glasgow Jewish Welfare Board 115
  Glasgow Kilmarnock Society (see
    Charities Administered by City of
    Glasgow Society of Social Services) 115
  Glasgow Seaman's Friend Society 115
  Glasgow Society of Sons of Ministers
    of the Church of Scotland 98
  Glasgow & West of Scotland Society
    for the Blind 98
Glasspool: R L Glasspool Charity Trust 289
Gloucester: Gloucester District Nursing
  Charities 216
Godson: Godson's Charity 171, 224, 269
Golborne: Golborne Charities 154
Goldie: Grace Wyndham Goldie (BBC)
  Trust Fund 34
Goldminers: Goldminers OAP Outing &
  Christmas Fund 168
Goldsborough: Goldsborough Poor's
  Charity 132
Goldsmiths: Goldsmiths' Silversmiths' &
  Jewellers' Benevolent Society 34
Goodall: Goodall Trust 143
Goodman: Valentine Goodman Estate
  Charity 178
Goodwin:
  Stuart Goodwin Charity 185
  Sir Stuart & Lady Florence Goodwin
    Charity 186
Goores: John Goore's Charity 164
Goosnargh: Goosnargh & Whittingham
  United Charity 157
Gordon: Gordon District Charities 108
Gould: Lady Gould's Charity 272
Gourock: Gourock Coal & Benevolent
  Fund 116
Governesses: Governesses' Benevolent
  Society of Scotland 98
Gow:
  Ian Gow Memorial Fund 94
  Neil Gow Charitable Trust 116
Goward: Charities of George Goward &
  John Evans 249
Gowland: Ralph Gowland Trust 129
Gowthorpe: Charles Wright Gowthorpe
  Fund & Clergy Augmentation Fund 182
Grampian: Charities Administered by
  Grampian Regional Council 106
Grand:
  Grand Charity (of Freemasons under the
    United Grand Lodge of England) 289
  Grand Lodge of Antient, Free &
    Accepted Masons of Scotland 99
  Grand Order of Water Rats Charities
    Fund 34
  Grand Prix Mechanics Charitable Trust 34
Grandborough: Grandborough & Sutton
  Charities 192
Grant: Grant, Bagshaw, Rogers &
  Tidswell Fund 147
Grantham:
  Grantham Aid-in-Sickness Fund 176
  Grantham Yorke Trust 196
Grateful: Grateful Society 204
Gratrix: Gratrix Charity 153
Great:
  Great Hockham Fuel Allotment 241
  Great Torrington Poors Charities 210
Greenaway:
  Ralph Greenaway Charity 244
  Greenway Benefaction 198

Greenwich:
  Greenwich Charities for the Blind &
    Disabled 269
  Greenwich Hospital 62
Gregson: Gregson Memorial Annuities 148
Gresford: Gresford Colliery Disaster
  Relief Fund 119
Griffiths: Sir Percival Griffiths' Tea
  Planters Trust 34
Grimsby: Grimsby Fishermen's
  Dependants' Fund 130
Grut: Grut Charitable Trust 289
Guide: Guide Dogs for the Blind
  Association 80
Guild:
  Guild of Aid for Gentlepeople 289
  Guild of Air Pilots' & Navigators'
    Benevolent Fund 34
  Guild of Guide Lecturers Benevolent
    Fund 34
Guildford:
  Guildford Relief-in-Need Charities 256
  Guildford Relief-in-Sickness Charity 256
Gurney: Gurney Fund for Police
  Orphans 35
Gwent: Gwent Charitable Fund 121
Gwynedd: Gwynedd Children's Heart
  Association 122

Hackney: Hackney Parochial Charities 270
Haddenham: Haddenham Charities 227
Hadrian: Hadrian Trust 126
Haemophilia: Haemophilia Society 80
Haendler: Nathan & Adolphe Haendler
  Charity 290
Haig:
  Earl Haig Fund (Scotland) 99
  John & Margaret Haig Bequest (see
    Charities Administered by
    Midlothian District Council) 113
Hairdressers: Hairdressers' Children's
  Welfare Fund 35
Halesworth: Halesworth United
  Charities 249
Halifax:
  Halifax Society for the Blind 143
  Halifax Tradesmen's Benevolent
    Institution 143
Hall: George & Clara Ann Hall Charity 136
Halvergate: Halvergate Town Lands
  Charity 241
Hamilton: Janet Hamilton Fund 115
Hammersmith: Hammersmith Relief-
  in-Sickness Fund 270
Hampshire:
  Hampshire Constabulary Welfare
    Fund 232
  Hampshire & Isle of Wight Military
    Aid Fund (1903) 63
Hampstead: Hampstead Wells &
  Campden Trust 269
Hampton:
  Hampton Fuel Allotment Charitable
    Trust 276
  Hampton Wick United Charity 276
Hamsterley: Hamsterley Poors' Land &
  Stock Charity 129
Handicapped: Handicapped Children's
  Aid Committee 80
Handsworth: Handsworth Charities 198
Hankinson: Charity of Mary Hankinson 158
Hanwell: Hanwell Philanthropic
  Institution 268
Hanworth: Hanworth Poors Land Trust
  & Coal Fund 272
Harding: William Harding's Charity 225

309

Index

Hardwick: Ben Hardwick Memorial Fund — 80
Harefield: Harefield Parochial Charities — 271
Harlow: Harlow Community Chest — 232
Harper: Harper Annuities — 185
Harpole: Harpole Parochial Charities — 179
Harris:
  Harris Charity — 157
  James Edward Harris Trust — 119
Harrison:
  Harrison & Potter Trust — 145
  Margaret Harrison Trust — 168
Harrogate: Harrogate Good Samaritan Fund — 132
Hastings:
  Hastings Benevolent Fund — 35
  Hastings & St Leonard's District Nursing Association & Aid-in-Sickness Trust — 230
Hatcliffe: William Hatcliffe Non-Educational Charity — 275
Hatton: Hatton Consolidated Charities — 191
Hawley: Hawley Almshouse & Relief-in-Need Charity — 234
Hay: Douglas Hay Trust — 99
Hayward: R S Hayward Trust — 103
Head: Francis Head Bequest — 35
Hearing: Hearing Dogs for the Deaf — 80
Heath: Heath Memorial Trust Fund — 188
Heckmondwike: Heckmondwike & District Fund for the Needy Sick — 143
Help: Help A London Child — 262
Helston: Helston Welfare Trust — 207
Henderson: Henderson Charity — 279
Henwood: Charity of Thomas Henwood — 207
Hereford:
  Hereford Municipal Charities — 170
  Hereford Open House Charity Dart League — 170
Herne: Herne Bay Parochial Charities — 237
Herrick: Miss Herrick's Annunity Fund & the Herrick Fund for Widows & Single Women Afflicted with Incurable Diseases — 172
Hertfordshire:
  Hertfordshire Charity for Deprived Children — 235
  Hertfordshire Convalescent Trust — 235
  Hertfordshire County Nursing Trust — 235
  Hertfordshire Society for the Blind — 236
Herve: Peter Herve Benevolent Institution — 204
Hesselwood: Hesselwood Children's Trust (Hull Seamen's & General Orphanage) — 129, 174
Heywood:
  Heywood Charities — 154
  Heywood Relief-in-Need Trust Fund — 154
Higden: Higden Hall Habgood & Brown Charity — 215
Higgins: Terrence Higgins Trust — 81
High: High Wycombe Central Aid Society — 225
Hilgay: Hilgay Feoffee Charity — 241
Hill:
  Christopher Hill Charity — 211
  Mary Hill Trust — 171
  Rowland Hill Benevolent Fund — 35
Hilton: Hilton & Dawson Charity — 129, 133
Hodson: Frank Hodson Foundation Ltd — 185
Holford: John Holford's Charity — 148
Holidays: Holidays for Fatherless Children — 128
Holinsworth: C B & A B Holinsworth Fund of Help — 198
Hollands-Warren: Hollands Warren Charitable Trust — 238
Hollis: C V Hollis Trust — 232
Hollon: Mary Hollon Annuity & Relief-in-Need Fund — 136
Holmleigh: Holmleigh Trust — 290
Holt: Charity of Ann Holt — 143
Holywood: Holywood Trust — 104
Home: Home Warmth for the Aged — 290
Homelife: Homelife DGAA — 290
Honiton: Honiton United Charities — 211
Honourable: Honourable Company of Master Mariners — 35
Hoper-Dixon: Hoper-Dixon Trust — 290
Hopkins: Charity of Joseph Hopkins — 198
Hornsby: Hornsby Professional Cricketers Fund — 35
Hornsey: Hornsey Parochial Charities — 262
Horstead: Horstead Poors Land Charity — 241
Horticultural: Horticultural Trades Association Benevolent Fund — 35
Hospital: Hospital of God — 126
Hotel: Hotel & Catering Benevolent Association — 36
Hounsfield: Hounsfield Pension — 136
Household:
  Household Cavalry Central Charitable Fund — 63
  Household Division Queen's Silver Jubilee Trust — 63
Hoxton: Hoxton Estate Charity (see Ancient Parish of St Andrew Holborn) — 266
Hoylake: Hoylake & West Kirby Aid-in-Sickness Fund — 163
Huddersfield: Huddersfield Orphan Home Endowment — 144
Huddleston: Trevor Huddleston Fund for Children — 279
Hull:
  Hull Aid-in-Sickness Fund — 131
  Hull Fisherman's Trust Fund — 131
Hunstone: Hunstone's Charity — 175
Hunter:
  George Hunter Trust (see Charities Administered by Annandale & Eskdale District Council) — 104
  John Routledge Hunter Memorial Fund — 135, 140
Huntington: Huntington's Disease Association — 81
Hurst: Arthur Hurst Will Trust — 36
Husborne: Husborne Crawley Charities of the Poor — 222
Hutchinson: Rev Matthew Hutchinson's Charity — 133
Huyton: Huyton with Roby Distress Fund — 163
Hyde: Hyde Park Place Estate Charity — 281

Ibero: Ibero-American Benevolent Society — 290
Ickleton: Ickleton United Charities (Relief-in-Need Branch) — 227
Ilchester: Ilchester Relief-in-Need & Educational Charity — 218
Ilford: Ilford United Charities — 276
Imperial: Imperial Society of Knights Bachelor Sunfund — 290
Incorporated:
  Incorporated Association of Organists Benevolent Fund — 36
  Incorporated Association of Preparatory Schools Benevolent Fund — 36
  Incorporated Brewers' Benevolent Society — 36
  Incorporated Society of Musicians Benevolent Fund — 36
  Incorporated Society of Valuers & Auctioneers Benevolent Fund — 36
Independent: Independent Living (1993) Fund — 81
Indigent: Indigent Old Women's Society — 112
Injured: Injured Jockeys Fund — 36
Innes: Innes Memorial Fund — 260
Institute:
  Institute of Chartered Secretaries & Administrators Benevolent Fund — 37
  Institute of Clayworkers Benevolent Fund — 37
  Institute of Company Accountants Benevolent Fund — 37
  Institute of Financial Accountants Benevolent Fund — 37
  Institute of Football Management & Administration Charity Trust — 37
  Institute of Health Services Management Benevolent Fund — 37
  Institute of Legal Executive Benevolent Funds — 37
  Institute of Marine Engineers Guild of Benevolence — 38
  Institute of Petroleum 1986 Benevolent Fund — 38
  Institute of Physics Benevolent Fund — 38
  Institute of Public Relations Benevolent Fund — 38
  Institute of Quarrying Benevolent Fund — 38
Institution:
  Institution of Civil Engineers Benevolent Fund — 38
  Institution of Electrical Engineers Incorporated Benevolent Fund — 38
  Institution of Mining & Metallurgy Benevolent Fund — 39
  Institution of Plant Engineers Benevolent Fund — 39
  Institution of Professionals, Managers & Specialists Benevolent Fund — 39
  Institution of Structural Engineers Benevolent Fund — 39
Insurance:
  Insurance Benevolent Fund — 39
  Insurance Orphans' Fund — 39
International: International Dance Teachers' Association Benevolent Fund — 39
Invalids: Invalids at Home — 81
Inverness:
  Charities Administered by Inverness District Council — 109
  Inverness Benevolent Fund & Seasonal Comforts Scheme (see charities Administered by Inverness District Council) — 109
  Inverness District Benevolent Fund & Seasonal Comforts Scheme (see Charities Administered by Inverness District Council) — 109
Irving: Irving Trust to Relieve Distress — 158
Isleworth: Isleworth United Charities — 272
Islington: Islington Relief-in-Need Charities — 272
Islington: Islington Relief-in-Sickness Charity — 272
Iver:
  Iver Heath Sick Poor Fund — 225
  Iver & Richings Park Sick Poor Fund — 225
  Iver United Charities — 226

Jackson: William Jackson Trust — 264
Jamieson:
  Jamieson Charity — 116
  Dr Robert Jamieson Bequest Fund — 114
  George Jamieson Fund — 106

Index

Jenkins: Kay Jenkins Trust — 231
Jenkinson: David Jenkinson Memorial Fund — 82
Jennifer: Jennifer Trust for Spinal Muscular Atrophy — 82
Jermyn: Lord Jermyn's Charity — 250
Jewels: Jewels for Children — 82
Jewish:
Jewish Aged Needy Pension Society — 290
Jewish AIDS Trust — 82
Jewish Care — 82, 291
Jewish Refugees Charitable Trust — 291
Johnson:
Johnson Bede & Lane Charitable Trust — 228
Christopher Johnson & the Green Charity — 184
Johnston:
Johnston Family Fund — 291
William Johnston Trust Fund — 291
Johnstone: Johnstone Wright Fund — 112
Joicey: Rose Joicey Fund — 126
Joint: Joint Industrial Council & the Match Manufacturing Industry Charitable Fund — 40
Jopp: Henry John Jopp Fund — 107
Jory: Joseph Jory's Charity — 212
Juckes: Florence Juckes Memorial Trust Fund — 196

Kay: Louisa Alice Kay Fund — 154
Keith:
Keith Coal Funds & the Keith Poor Funds (see Charities Administered by Moray District Council) — 108
Keith Nursing Funds (see Charities Administered by Moray District Council) — 108
Kempston: Kempston Charities — 222
Kenilworth:
Kenilworth Carnival Comforts Fund — 192
Kenilworth United Charities — 192
Kensington: Kensington District Nursing Trust — 274
Kent: Kent County Football Association Benevolent Fund — 236
Kesteven: Kesteven Children in Need — 176
Kettering: Kettering Charities for the Poor — 179
King:
King Edward VII British-German Foundation — 291
King Edward VII Sister Purvis Convalescent Fund — 128
King George's Pension Fund for Actors & Actresses — 40
King James VI Hospital Fund — 118
King's:
King's Lynn Charities for the Poor — 241
King's Lynn & West Norfolk Borough Charity — 239
Kingsbury: Kingsbury Charity — 266
Kingston: Dr C S Kingston Fund — 220
Kingston-upon-Thames:
Kingston-upon-Thames Association for the Blind — 274
Kingston-upon-Thames Central Aid Society — 274
Kington: Kington United Charities — 170
Kinlock: Kinlock Bequest — 63
Kirby: Kirby Cane Charities of Bonfellow & Potts — 241
Kirkby: Kirkby Lonsdale Relief-in-Need Charity — 152
Kirkcaldy: Kirkcaldy Charitable Trust — 105

Kirke: Kirke's Charity — 145
Kitchings: Kitchings General Charity — 175
Knaresborough: Knaresborough Relief-in-Need Charity — 133
Knight: Knight's House Charity — 150
Knowles: Annie Jane Knowles & Edward George Bates Pension Fund for the Blind — 268
Kroch: Heinz & Anna Kroch Foundation — 291
Krull: Bonno Krull Fund — 40
Kyle: Kyle & Carrick District Charities — 116

Ladies:
Ladies' Aid Fund — 160
Ladies Aid Society & the Eyre Charity — 212
Lakenheath: Lakenheath Consolidated Charities — 249
Laleston: Laleston Relief-in-Sickness Charity — 123
Lamb: John William Lamb Charity — 183
Lambert: Charity of John Lambert — 174
Lambeth:
Lambeth Endowed Charities — 274
Lambeth Mayor's Fund — 275
Lancashire: Lancashire County Nursing Trust — 158
Lancaster: Lancaster Charity — 159
Langley: Charities of Peter Langley & Others — 188
Lant: Lant Trust — 196
Lathom: Peter Lathom's Charity — 158
Launceston: Launceston Relief-in-Sickness Fund — 207
Lavender: Lavender's Charity — 169
Law:
James Scott Law Charitable Trust — 291
Law Society of Scotland Benevolent Fund — 99
Leaf: Herbert Leaf Charity — 219
League: League of the Helping Hand — 291
Leamington: Leamington Fund — 193
Leather: Leather & Hides Trades' Benevolent Institution — 40
Leatherhead: Leatherhead United Charities — 257
Leeds:
Leeds Benevolent Society for Single Ladies — 145
Leeds District Aid-in-Sickness Fund — 145
Leeds Family Holiday Fund — 145
Leeds Jewish Welfare Board — 140
Leeds Poors' Estate — 146
Leeds Tradesmen's Trust — 146
Lees: Sarah Lees Relief Trust — 155
Legate: Legate's Charity — 214
Leicester:
Leicester Aid-in-Sickness Fund — 173
Leicester Charity Organisation — 172
Leicester Freemen's Estate — 172
Leicester Indigent Old Age Society — 173
Leicestershire: Leicestershire County Nursing Association — 172
Leigh: Leigh United Charities — 238
Leith:
Leith Aged Mariners' Fund — 111
Leith Benevolent Association — 111
Leukaemia: Leukaemia Care Society — 82
Levant: Levant Mine Fund — 207
Leverington: Leverington Relief-in-Sickness Fund — 228
Lewis: Ada Lewis Winter Distress Fund — 268
Library: Library Association Benevolent Fund — 40
Lighthouse: Lighthouse Club Benevolent Fund — 40

Lincoln:
Lincoln General Dispensary Fund — 175
Lincoln Municipal Relief-in-Need Charities — 176
Lincolnshire: Lincolnshire Police Charitable Fund — 175
Lindow: Lindow Workhouse Charity — 151
Lindsay: Misses Elizabeth & Agnes Lindsay Fund — 118
Lineham: Henry & Elizabeth Lineham Charity — 180
Linnecar: Linnecar Trust — 121
Lipton: Frances Lipton Memorial Fund (see Charities Administered by City of Glasgow Society of Social Services) — 115
Litchborough: Litchborough Parochial Charities — 180
Little:
Little Dunham Relief-in-Need Charities — 241
Andrew & Mary Elizabeth Little Charitable Trust — 99
Litton: Litton Cheney Relief-in-Need Trust — 211
Liverpool:
Liverpool Caledonian Association — 160
Liverpool Children's Welfare Trust — 161
Liverpool Corn Trade Guild — 163
Liverpool Cotton Association Ltd Benevolent Fund — 163
Liverpool Customs & Excise Benevolent Society — 161
Liverpool Governesses' Benevolent Institution — 40
Liverpool Ladies Institution — 161
Liverpool Merchants' Guild — 161
Liverpool Provision Trade Guild — 161
Liverpool Queen Victoria District Nursing Association (LCSS) — 161
Liverpool Queen Victoria District Nursing Association (PSS) — 161
Liverpool Wholesale Fruit & Vegetable Trust — 163
Liversage: Liversage Trust — 169
Llandenny: Llandenny Charities — 122
Llandough: Llandough LATCH — 124
Llanidloes:
Llanidloes & DistrictCommunity Nurses' Comforts Fund Committee — 124
Llanidloes Relief-in-Need Charity — 124
Lloyd: W M & B W Lloyd Trust — 158
Lloyds: Lloyd's Benevolent Fund — 40
Lloyds: Lloyds Patriotic Fund — 63
Local: Local Aid for Children & Community Special Needs — 125
Lockerbie: Lockerbie Trust (see Charities Administered by Annandale & Eskdale District Council) — 104
Lockinge: Lockinge & Ardington Relief-in-Need Charity — 245
Lodder: Alfred Lodder Charity — 213
London:
London Bereavement Relief Society — 262
City of London Linen Trades Association — 28
London Electricity Benevolent Society — 262
London Shipowners' & Shipbrokers' Benevolent Society — 41
Londonderry: Londonderry Methodist City Mission — 94
Long:
Long Buckby United Charities — 180
Long Lawford Pension & Relief-in-Need Charity — 193
Long Sutton Consolidated Charity — 177

Index

Lord:
- Lord Mayor of Bristol's Christmas Appeal for Children — 205
- Lord Mayor of Portsmouth's Charity — 234
- Lord Mayor's Common Good Fund — 199
- Lord Mayor's Family Holiday Fund — 154
- Lord Mayor's New Horizons Fund — 239

Loughborough: Loughborough Welfare Trusts — 173
Lowestoft: Lowestoft Charity Board, Relief-in-Need Charity & Eleesmosynary Charity of John Wilde — 249
Lowton: Lowton Charities — 159
Loxton: Charity of Harriet Louisa Loxton — 198
Lubricators: Lubricators Charitable Trust — 292

Lucas:
- Edwin Lucas Trust — 215
- Helen Lucas Trust — 292
- Charity of Robert Lucas for the Poor — 222

Lund: Lucy Lund Holiday Grants — 140
Lupton: Lupton & Poor's Land Charity — 184
Luttrell: Jat Luttrell Memorial Trust — 217
Lyall: Lyall Bequest — 99
Lymn: Lymn Relief-in-Sickness Fund — 149
Lyng: Lyng Heath Charity — 242
Lyson: Sylvanus Lyson's Charity — 216
Lytham: Lytham St Annes's Relief-in-Sickness Charity — 159

MacAndrew: B V MacAndrew Trust — 221
Macaulay: K A Macaulay Trust — 202
Macclesfield: Macclesfield Relief-in-Sickness Fund — 149
Macdonald: Henry Macdonald Fund — 105

MacDonald:
- Macdonald Bequest — 106
- Dr William MacDonald of Johannesburg Trust — 199

MacDougall: MacDougall Trust — 214
Macfarlane: Macfarlane Trust — 83
McGibbon: John McGibbon Fund — 112
MacKensie: William MacKensie Trust — 118
McKune: James McKune Mortification — 105
McLaren: McLaren Fund for Indigent Ladies — 99
McLean: Annie Ramsay McLean's Trust for the Elderly — 99
McRobert: McRobert Mortification - Gamrie & Forglen — 108
MacWatt: MacWatt Bequest (see Charities administered by Berwickshire District Council) — 103
Maerdy: Maerdy Children's Welfare Fund — 123
Magic: Magic Circle Benevolent Fund — 41
Maidstone: Maidstone Relief-in-Need Charities — 238
Malam: Edward Malam Convalescent Fund — 188

Manchester:
- Dean of Manchester Crossland Fund — 155
- Manchester District Nursing Institution Fund — 153
- Manchester Jewish Soup Kitchen — 153
- Manchester Jews Benevolent Society — 153
- Manchester Relief-in-Need Children's Relief-in-Need Charities — 155

Manchip: Manchip Trust — 217
Mantle: William Mantle Trust — 238
Manufacturing: Manufacturing Confectioners' Commercial Travellers' Association Benevolent Fund — 41
Marham: Marham Poors Allotment — 242

Marine: Marine Society — 41

Market:
- Market Harborough Town Estate & Bates Charity — 173
- Market Research Benevolent Association — 41

Marsh: Marsh Trust — 218
Marshall: William Marshall's Charity — 244
Martin: Douglas Martin Trust — 264
Masters: Rev Robert Masters for Widows Trust — 227
Massey: Dr Issac Massey's Charity — 166
Master: Master Tailors' Benevolent Association — 41
Matthew: Matthew Trust — 83, 292
Maudlyn: Maudlyn Lands Charity — 212

Mayor:
- Mayor of Barnet's Benevolent Fund — 265
- Mayor of Bath's Relief Fund — 204
- Mayor of Bebington's Benevolent Fund — 162
- Mayor of Blackpool's Welfare Services Fund — 158
- Mayor of Camden's Charity Trust Fund — 267
- Charity known as the Mayors Fund — 171
- Mayor of Great Grimsby's Fund — 131
- Mayor of Guildford's Christmas Distress Fund — 256
- Mayor of Hammersmith & Fulham's Appeal Fund — 271
- Mayor of Harrow's Charity Fund — 271
- Mayor of Southwark's Common Good Trust — 278
- Mayor of Tameside's Distress Fund — 157
- Mayor's Benevolent Fund (Haringey) — 271
- Mayor's Christmas Fund — 268
- Mayor's Discretionary Fund & Mayor's Fund, Eastbourne — 230
- Mayor's Fund for Necessitous Children — 139
- Mayor's General Fund — 201
- Mayor's Goodwill Fund — 214

Mayors: Mayors Fund Society of Stratford-upon-Avon — 194
Measures: James Frederick & Ethel Anne Measures Charity — 196
Medical: Medical Aid Trust — 83
Mellor: Mellor Fund — 153
Melton: Melton Trust — 249
Mendicants: Mendicants, Merthyr Tydfil Charity — 123

Merchant:
- Merchant Taylors' Charity — 134
- Merchant Taylors' Company — 41

Merevale: Merevale Sickness Fund — 191
Meriden: Meriden United Charities — 201
Merry: Doctor Merry Memorial Fund — 229

Merseyside:
- Charities Administered by Merseyside Jewish Welfare Council — 164
- Merseyside Police Orphans' Fund — 162

Merton: Zachary Merton & George Woofindin Convalescent Trust — 138, 176

Metcalfe:
- Metcalfe Shannon Trust — 63
- Metcalfe Smith Trust — 146

Methodist:
- Methodist Child Care Society — 94
- Methodist Local Preachers' Mutual Aid Association — 41

Metropolitan:
- Metropolitan Police Civil Staff Welfare Fund — 41
- Metropolitan Police Combined Benevolent Fund — 42
- Metropolitan Society for the Blind — 262
- Metropolitan Visiting & Relief Association — 263

Micklegate: Micklegate Strays Charity — 134
Mid-Glamorgan: Mid-Glamorgan County Blind Welfare Association — 123
Middlesex: Middlesex King Edward VII Memorial Fund — 292

Middleton:
- Charity of Miss Eliza Clubley Middleton — 131
- Middleton Cheney United Charities — 180
- Middleton Relief-in-Need Charity — 155

Midgley: William & Sarah Midgley Charity — 146
Midlothian: Charities Administered by Midlothian District Council — 113
Mildenhall: Mildenhall Parish Charities — 249
Mine: Mine Accident Fund for Cornwall & Devon — 203
Minet: Mary Minet Trust — 263
Mitcham: Mitcham United Charities — 275
Mitchell: Mitchell City of London Charity — 268
Mobility: Mobility Trust — 83
Molyneaux: Ann Molyneaux Charity — 164
Molineux: Cordelia Molineux Smallpiece Bequest — 260

Monk:
- Joseph & Lucy Monk's Trust — 150
- Joseph Monk Christmas Gift Trust — 150

Monmouth:
- Monmouth Charity — 122
- Monmouth Street Society, Bath — 204

Montgomery: Montgomery Welfare Fund — 124
Moonzie: Moonzie Parish Trust — 105
Moore: Charity of John Moore — 199
Moray: Charities Administered by Moray District Council — 108
Morden: Morden College — 42
Morgan: Junius S Morgan Benevolent Fund — 42
Morley: Morley Guild of Help — 146
Morpeth: Morpeth Dispensary — 136
Morris: Morris Beneficent Fund — 292
Morval: Morval Foundation — 292
Moser: Moser Benevolent Trust Fund — 142
Motability: Motability — 83
Motor: Motor Neurone Disease Association — 84
Mottram: Mottram St Andrew United Charities — 149
Moulton: Moulton Poors' Land Charity — 177
Mountgarret: Viscount Mountgarret Permanent Trust — 142
Mountsorrel: Mountsorrel Relief-in-Need Charity — 174
Multiple: Multiple Sclerosis Society of Great Britain — 84

Municipal:
- Municipal Charities & Bedford & District Aid in Sickness Charity — 222
- Municipal Charities of Chesterfield — 168
- Municipal Charities of Stratford-upon-Avon, Relief-in-Need Charity — 194

Murdoch: John Murdoch Trust — 42, 293
Murray: Matilda Murray Trust — 107

Musicians:
- Musicians Benevolent Fund — 42
- Musicians' Social & Benevolent Council — 42

Muslim: Muslim Welfare Board — 293
Myers: Myers Marlow Benevolent Trust — 225
Mylne: Mylne Trust — 43, 293
Napton: Napton Charities — 193
Nash: Nash Charity — 63

Index

National:
- National Advertising Benevolent Society ... 43
- National Amalgamated Stevedores & Dockers Benevolent Fund ... 131
- National Association for the Care & Resettlement of Offenders (NACRO) ... 293
- National Association of Cooperative Officials' Benevolent Fund ... 43
- National Association of Master Bakers ... 43
- National Association of Schoolmasters Union of Women Teachers Benevolent Fund ... 43
- National Benevolent Institution ... 293
- National Benevolent Society of Watch & Clock Makers ... 43
- National British & Irish Millers' Benevolent Society ... 43
- National Caravan Council Benevolent Fund ... 44
- National Dairymen's Benevolent Institution ... 44
- National Deaf Children's Society ... 84
- National Deaf-Blind League ... 84
- National Eczema Society ... 84
- National Federation of Fish Friers Benevolent Fund ... 44
- National Federation of Retail Newsagents Convalescence Fund ... 44
- National Federation of Sub-Postmasters Benevolent Fund ... 44
- National Foundation for Incurably Sick Children ... 84
- National Grocers' Benevolent Fund ... 45
- National Health Service Pensioners' Trust ... 45
- National Union of Journalists Provident Fund ... 45

Navy: Navy Special Fund ... 64
Neath: Neath Nursing Association ... 125
Nelson: Nelson District Nursing Association Fund ... 159
Netherlands: Netherlands Benevolent Society ... 293

New:
- New Appeals Organisation for the City & County of Nottingham ... 183
- New Masonic Samaritan Fund ... 293
- New Town Dispensary Trust (see Charities administered by Edinburgh Voluntary Organisations' Council) ... 111

Newark: Newark Municipal (General) Charities ... 185
Newcastle: Newcastle-under-Lyme United Charities ... 189
Newick: Newick Distress Fund ... 230
Newport: Newport Charity ... 211
Newspaper: Newspaper Press Fund ... 45
Newsvendors: Newsvendors' Benevolent Institution ... 45
Newtownabbey: Newtownabbey Methodist Mission ... 95
Nicholl: William Nicholl's Charity ... 274
Nightingale: Florence Nightingale Aid-in-Sickness Trust ... 84
Nimmo: William Brown Nimmo Charitable Trust ... 111
Nineteen: 1930 Fund for District Nurses ... 45
Nithsdale: Nithsdale District Charities ... 105
Non-Ecclesiastical: Non-Ecclesiastical Charity of Thomas Axe ... 211

Norris:
- Norris Charity ... 123
- Evelyn Norris Trust ... 45

North:
- Charities Administered by North East Fife District Council ... 105
- North Eastern Prison After Care Society ... 127
- North Staffordshire Convalescent & Incurable Fund ... 188
- North Staffordshire Miners Convalescent & Relief Fund ... 188
- North Wales Fund for Needy Psychiatric Patients ... 119
- North Wales Police Benevolent Fund ... 119
- North Wales Society for the Blind ... 120
- North West Police Benevolent Fund ... 148

North-East: North-East Area Mineworkers' Convalescent Fund ... 127

Northampton:
- Northampton Municipal Church Charities ... 178
- Earl of Northampton's Charity ... 239, 269

Northamptonshire: Northamptonshire Medical Charity ... 178
Northcott: Northcott Devon Foundation ... 208

Northern:
- Northern Counties' Charity for the Incapacitated ... 127, 148
- Northern Counties Orphans' Benevolent Society ... 127, 151
- Northern Ireland Children's Holiday Schemes ... 95
- Northern Ladies Annuity Society ... 293
- Northern Police Orphans' Trust ... 45

Northwold: Northwold Combined Charity for the Needy & the Charity of Edmund Atmere ... 242

Norwich:
- Norwich Consolidated Charities ... 242
- Norwich Town Close Estate Charity ... 242

Norwood: Norwood Child Care ... 294
Not: Not Forgotten Association ... 64

Nottingham:
- Nottingham Annuity Charity ... 183
- Nottingham Children's Welfare Fund ... 183
- Nottingham Gordon Memorial Trust for Boys & Girls ... 185

Nottinghamshire:
- Nottinghamshire Constabulary Benevolent Fund ... 183
- Nottinghamshire Miners' Welfare Trust Fund ... 183

Nugent: Nugent Charitable Trust ... 251
NUMAST: NUMAST Welfare Fund ... 46
Nuneaton: Nuneaton Poors' Piece Charity ... 193

Nurses:
- Nurses Fund for Nurses ... 46
- Nurses Memorial to King Edward VII Edinburgh Committee ... 99

O'Leary: Tim O'Leary Special Fund ... 46
O'Sullivan: Cornelius O'Sullivan Fund ... 223
Oban: Oban & District Trust for the Disabled ... 114
Officers: Officers' Association & the Officers' Families Fund ... 64
Officers: Officers' Association (Scottish Branch) ... 100
Ogilvie: Ogilvie Charities ... 294
Oilseed: Oilseed, Oil & Feedingstuffs Trades Benevolent Association ... 46

Old:
- Old Buckenham United Eleemosynary Charity ... 242
- Old Enfield Charitable Trust ... 269
- Old Parish Charities ... 181
- Old Park Ward Old Age Pensioners' Fund ... 169
- Old School Fund ... 247

Oldbury: Oldbury Nurses' Pension Trust Fund ... 166

Oldham:
- Oldham Distress Fund ... 155
- Oldham United Charities ... 155

Oliver: Ada Oliver Will Trust ... 84
Oswestry: Oswestry Dispensary Fund ... 187
Ottery: Ottery Feoffee Charity ... 211
Ottringham: Ottringham Charities ... 132
Ouchterlony: Ouchterlony Old Men's Indigent Sick Society ... 118
Overseas: Overseas Service Pensioners' Benevolent Society ... 46
Owen: Dame Alice Owen's Eleemosynary Charities ... 273
Oxford: Oxford & District Good Neighbours' Fund ... 245

Paddington: Paddington Welfare Charities ... 281
Page: Page's Fund ... 181
Paisley: Paisley's Former Town Council Charitable Funds ... 116
Pakenham: Pakenham Charities ... 249

Palmer:
- Eleanor Palmer's Charity ... 265
- Palmer & Seabright Charity ... 201

Pampisford: Pampisford Relief-in-Need Charity ... 228
Pargeter: Thomas Pargeter of Foxcote Charity & the John Ward Bequest ... 196

Parish:
- Parish Lands Charity (Highweek) ... 208
- Parish Lands or Second Poor's Charity ... 212
- Parish Piece Charity ... 173

Parkinson: Parkinson's Disease Society ... 85

Parrott:
- Dorothy Parrott Memorial Trust Fund ... 236
- James Parrott Charity ... 148

Patrick: Joseph Patrick Memorial Trust ... 85
Pattishall: Pattishall Parochial Charities ... 181

Pattullo:
- Gertrude Muriel Pattullo Trust for the Elderly ... 117
- Gertrude Muriel Pattullo Trusts for Handicapped Boys & Girls ... 116

Pawnbrokers Pawnbrokers' Charitable Institution ... 46
Payling: George Henry Francis Payling's Charity ... 185
Payne: John Payne's Charity ... 265
Peace: Peace Memorial Fund ... 279
Pearson: Pearson's Holiday Fund ... 294
Peck: John Wallace Peck Trust Fund ... 234
Peckham: Peckham & Kent Road Pension Society ... 278
Penderels: Penderels Trust Fund ... 200
Pendlebury: Sir Ralph Pendlebury's Charity for Orphans & the Elderly ... 156
Pension: Pension Fund of the Incorporated Society of Authors, Playwrights & Composers ... 46
Pentney: Pentney Charities ... 242
Penton: Penton Trust ... 232
Pepper: John Pepper Charity ... 189
Performing: Performing Right Society Members' Fund ... 46

Perry:
- Perry Fund ... 294
- Perry Trust Gift Fund ... 183

Persehouse: Persehouse Pensions Fund ... 166
Perth: Perth Indigent Old Men's Society ... 118
Pest: Pest House Charity ... 260

313

Index

Peter: Peter Benevolent Fund	118	
Peterhead: Peterhead Coal Fund	109	
Petersham: Petersham United Charities	276	
Petrie: Mrs Margaret Petrie's Mortification	118	
PGA: PGA European Tour Benevolent Fund	47	
Pharmaceutical: Pharmaceutical Society's Benevolent Fund	47	
Pickles: H T Pickles Benevolent Fund	47	
Picto: Charity of Sir John Picto & Others	240	
Pirbright: Pirbright Relief-in-Need Charity	257	
Pitstone: Pitstone Town Lands Charity Estate	226	
Pittis: Mary Pittis Charity for Widows	234	
Plymouth: Plymouth & Cornwall Cancer Fund	204	
Polehampton: Polehampton Charities	223	

Police:
- Police Aided Clothing Scheme of Edinburgh — 113
- Police Dependants' Trust — 47

Police-Aided: Police-Aided Children's Relief-in-Need Fund — 150

Polish:
- Polish Air Force Association Benevolent Fund — 64
- Polish Naval Association Welfare Fund — 294
- Polish Soldiers Assistance Fund — 64

Ponton: Ponton House Association (see Charities Administered by Edinburgh Voluntary Organisations' Council) — 111

Poole: Poole Childrens Fund — 215
Poole: Valentine Poole Charity — 265
Poor: Poor Ladies' Holiday Relief Fund — 232

Poors:
- Poor's Charity of Margaret Evans — 125
- Poors' Estate Charity & Others — 131
- Poors' Gorse Charity — 219
- Poor's Land/Charity of Peter Speccott — 211
- Poor's Plot Charity — 194

Positively: Positively Partners & Positively Children — 85
Pottery: Pottery & Glass Trade Benevolent Institution — 47
Power: Power Pleas Trust — 203

Presbyterian:
- Presbyterian Orphan Society — 95
- Presbyterian Old Age Fund, Women's Fund & Indigent Ladies Fund — 95

Preston: Preston Relief-in-Need Charity — 159
Price: Lucy Price Relief-in-Need Charity — 192
Priestman: Sir John Priestman Charity Trust — 127

Printers:
- Printers' Charitable Corporation — 47
- Printers' Community Fund — 140

Pritt: Pritt & Corlett Funds — 164

Professional:
- Professional Classes Aid Council — 47, 294
- Professional Footballers Association Accident Fund — 48
- Professional Footballers Association Benevolent Fund — 48

Protestant: Protestant Orphan Society for the Counties of Antrim & Down (Inc) — 95
Provision: Provision Trade Benevolent Institution — 48
Pryke: Florence Pryke Charity — 248

Putney:
- Putney Creche — 280
- Putney Relief Committee — 280

Pyncombe: Pyncombe Charity — 48
Pyrford: Pyrford Charities — 258

Queen:
- Queen Adelaide Naval Fund — 64
- Queen Adelaide's Fund — 263
- Queen Alexandra Sanatorium Fund & Allied Funds — 85
- Queen's Nursing Institute — 48

Quiller: Quiller Bequest (see Charities Administered by Edinburgh Voluntary Organisations' Council) — 111

Railway: Railway Benevolent Institution — 48
Ramsbottom: Ramsbottom Aid-in-Sickness Fund — 155, 160
Ramsey: Ramsey Welfare Charities — 228
Rank: Joseph Rank Benevolent Fund — 131
Ravensden: Ravensden Town & Poor Estate — 222
Rawlet: Rawlet Trust — 190
Raygill: Raygill Trust — 133

Reading:
- Reading Dispensary — 224
- Reading Municipal Church Charities — 223

Rector: Rector & Four & Twenty of Bedale — 133
Redcliffe: Redcliffe Parish Charity — 205
Redesdale: Charity of Lord Redesdale — 191, 216
Referees: Referees Association Members Benevolent Fund — 49
Reid: John Reid Mortification Fund — 113
Reigate: Reigate & Banstead Care Committee for Chest & Vascular Diseases — 251
Rendlesham: Rendlesham Benevolent Fund — 49
Research: Research Education & Aid for Children with Terminal Illness — 85
Retired: Retired Ministers' House Fund — 95
Reydon: Reydon Poors' Allotment Charity — 249
Rhodes: Betty Rhodes Fund — 85
Rhodesians: Rhodesians Worldwide Assistance Fund — 295
Rhonnda: Rhondda Blind Welfare Society — 123
Rhymney: Rhymney Trust — 123

Richards:
- Admiral of the Fleet Sir Frederick Richards Memorial Fund — 65
- Rev Dr George Richards Charity — 49

Richmond:
- Richmond Aid-in-Sickness Fund — 276
- Richmond Charities Almshouses — 277
- Richmond Parish Lands Charity — 277
- Richmond Philanthropic Society — 277

Rimpton: Rimpton Relief-in-Need Charities — 218
RMT: RMT (National Union of Rail, Maritime & Transport Workers) Orphan Fund — 49
Road: Road Haulage Association Benevolent Fund — 49
Roade: Roade Feoffees & Chivalls Charity — 181

Roberts:
- E C Roberts Charitable Trust — 295
- Evan & Catherine Roberts Charity — 120
- Samuel Roberts Trust — 138

Robertson: Mair Robertson Benevolent Fund — 118

Robinson:
- Robinson Memorial Gift — 139
- Thomas Robinson Charity — 163

Rochdale:
- Rochdale Fund for Relief-in-Sickness — 156
- Rochdale United & Ladies Charities — 156

Rogers: Henry Rogers Charity (Porlock Branch) — 218
Ross: Ross & Cromarty District Charities — 109
Rosslyn: Rosslyn Park Injury Trust Fund — 85
Rotherham: Rotherham Borough Co-Ordinating Committee for the Blind & Partially Sighted — 138
Rotherhithe: Rotherhithe Consolidated Charities — 278
Rowe: Charity of William Rowe — 212
Rowland: Emma Rowland Fund — 154
Roxburghshire: Roxburghshire Landward Benevolent Trust — 103

Royal:
- Royal Agricultural Benevolent Institution — 49
- Royal Air Force Benevolent Fund — 65
- Royal Air Forces Association — 65
- Royal Air Forces Escaping Society Charitable Fund — 295
- Royal Alfred Seafarers' Society — 49
- Royal Antediluvian Order of Buffaloes — 295
- Royal Armoured Corps War Memorial Benevolent Fund — 65
- Royal Army Medical Corps Charitable Funds — 66
- Royal Army Service Corps & Royal Corps of Transport Benevolent Fund — 66
- Royal Artillery Charitable Fund — 66
- Royal Ballet Benevolent Fund — 50
- Royal Belgian Benevolent Society — 295
- Royal Blind Pension Society of the UK — 85
- Royal British Legion — 66
- Royal British Legion, Scotland — 100
- Royal British Legion Women's Section — 66
- Royal College of Midwives Benevolent Fund — 50
- Royal College of Midwives' Scottish Board — 100
- Royal Electrical & Mechanical Engineers Corps Benevolent Fund — 67
- Royal Incorporation of Architects in Scotland — 100
- Royal Institution of Chartered Surveyors Benevolent Fund — 50
- Royal Institution of Naval Architects Benevolent Fund — 50
- Royal Leicestershire, Rutland & Wycliffe Society for the Blind — 166
- Royal Literary Fund — 50
- Royal Liverpool Seamen's Orphan Institution — 50
- Royal London Aid Society — 295
- Royal Masonic Benevolent Institution — 296
- Royal Medical Benevolent Fund — 50
- Royal Medical Foundation of Epsom College — 50
- Royal Metal Trades Benevolent Society — 51
- Royal National Institute for the Blind — 86
- Royal National Mission to Deep Sea Fishermen — 51
- Royal Naval Benevolent Society — 67
- Royal Naval Benevolent Trust — 67
- Royal Naval Reserve (V) Benevolent Fund — 67
- Royal Navy & Royal Marine Branch & Special Duties Officers' Benevolent Fund — 68
- Royal Opera House Benevolent Fund — 51
- Royal Patriotic Fund Corporation — 68
- Royal Pioneer Corps Benevolent Fund — 68
- Royal Scottish Agricultural Benevolent Institution — 100
- Royal Scottish Corporation — 296
- Royal Seamen's Pension Fund — 51

Index

Royal Signals Association Benevolent Fund — 68
Royal Society for Home Relief to Incurables, Edinburgh (General Fund) — 100
Royal Society for the Relief of Indigent Gentlewomen of Scotland — 100
Royal Society of Chemistry Benevolent Fund — 51
Royal Society of Musicians — 51
Royal Theatrical Fund — 52
Royal United Kingdom Beneficent Association (RUKBA) — 52, 296
Royton: Royton Sick & Needy Fund — 156
Ruabon: Ruabon & District Relief in Need Charity — 120
RUC: RUC Benevolent Fund — 95
Rugby:
  Rugby Football Union Charitable Fund — 52
  Rugby Relief-in-Need Charity — 193
  Rugby Welfare Charities — 193
Runcorn: Runcorn General War Relief Fund — 150
Rural: Rural, Agricultural & Allied Workers' Benevolent Fund — 52
Rycroft: Rycroft Children's Fund — 127, 148, 167
Ryde: Ryde Sick Poor Fund — 234

Saffron: Saffron Waldon United Charities — 232
Saham: Saham Toney Fuel Allotment & Perkins Charity — 242
Sailors:
  Sailors' Families Society — 52
  Sailors' Orphan Society of Scotland — 101
Sainsbury: Sainsbury Family Charitable Trusts — 296
St Andrew:
  St Andrew Holborn City Foundation (see Ancient Parish of St Andrew Holborn) — 266
  St Andrew's Scottish Soldiers Club Fund — 68
  St Andrew's Society for Ladies in Need — 296
St Andrews: St Andrews Welfare Trust — 106
St Chad: St Chad's Consolidated Charities — 188
St Clement: St Clement Danes Parochial Charities — 281
St Cyrus: St Cyrus Benevolent Fund — 118
St Dunstan: Saint Dunstan's — 68
St Edmund: St Edmunds on the Bridge Parish Charity — 210
St George: St George Dragon Trust — 263
St Giles: Saint Giles Charity Estate — 181
St John:
  St John the Baptist Charitable Fund — 268
  St John's Hospital, Bath — 204
  St John & Red Cross Joint Committee — 69
St Laurence: St Laurence Charities for the Poor — 224
St Leonard: St Leonard's Hospital Charity — 143
St Luke: St Luke's Parochial Trust — 273
St Margaret: St Margaret's Select Vestry — 173
St Martin: St Martin-in-the-Fields' Vicar's Relief Fund — 297
St Mary-le-Strand: St Mary-le-Strand Charity — 281
St Marylebone: St Marylebone Health Society — 281
St Michael: Charity of St Michael-le-Belfry — 134
St Olave: St Olave's United Charity — 278
St Pancras: St Pancras Welfare Trust — 267
St Sepulchre: St Sepulchre (Finsbury) United Charities — 273

Salisbury: Salisbury City Almshouse & Welfare Charities — 220
Salford:
  City of Salford Relief-in-Distress Fund — 156
  Salford Town Lands — 225
Salt: Sir Titus Salt's Charity — 141
Salter: George & Thomas Henry Salter Trust — 201
Salvation: Salvation Army — 297
Sandal: Sandal Magna Relief-in-Need Charity — 146
Sanders: William Sanders Charity — 121
Sanderson: Sanderson's Womens' Pension Fund — 147
Sandford: Sandford Relief-in-Need Charity — 212
Sant: Helena Sant's Residuary Trust Fund — 231
Sargent: Malcolm Sargent Cancer Fund for Children — 86
Saunders: Florence Saunders Relief-in-Sickness Charity — 228
Savage:
  Ann Elizabeth Savage's General Charities — 277
  George Savage Charity — 248
Sawley: Sawley Charities — 169
Saxlingham:
  Saxlingham District Charity — 243
  Saxlingham United Charities — 243
Scaldwell:
  Scaldwell Charity — 181
  Scaldwell Relief-in-Need Charity — 181
Scale: Scale Charity — 233
Scandinavian: Scandinavian Benevolent Society — 297
Scarborough: Scarborough Municipal Charities — 134
Schoolmistresses: Schoolmistresses & Governesses Benevolent Institution — 53
Scientific: Scientific Relief Fund — 53
Scottish:
  Scottish Chartered Accountants' Benevolent Association — 101
  Scottish Cinematograph Trade Benevolent Fund — 101
  Scottish Grocers' Federation Benevolent Fund — 101
  Scottish Hide & Leather Trades Provident & Benevolent Society — 101
  Scottish Law Agents Society Benevolent Fund — 101
  Scottish Mining Disasters Relief Fund — 101
  Scottish Musicians' Benevolent Fund — 101
  Scottish National Institution for the War-Blinded — 101
  Scottish Secondary Teachers' Association — 101
  Scottish Trust for the Physically Disabled — 102
  Scottish Women's Land Army Welfare & Benevolent Fund — 102
Seamen: Seamen's Hospital Society — 53
Second: Second Post Office Relief Fund — 53
Sedgefield: Sedgefield & District Relief-in-Need Charity, Thomas Cooper's Charity, Howle Hope Estate — 129
Sefton: Sefton Association for the Deaf — 164
Semple: Semple Fund for Cancer Relief & Research — 114
Sense: Sense, the National Deaf-Blind & Rubella Association — 86
Sewing: Sewing Machine Trade Benevolent Fund — 53
Shanks: Shanks Bequest — 104

Shaw-Stewart: Lady Alice Shaw-Stewart Memorial Fund — 116
Shawcross: Charity of Harold Shawcross — 156
Sheffield: Sheffield West Riding Charitable Society — 136
Shelroy: Shelroy Trust — 239
Shepherd: Shepherd Fund — 107
Shere:
  Shere Charity for Relief-in-Need — 258
  Charities of John Shere & Others — 213
Sherriffs: Sherriffs' & Recorders' Fund — 263
Shewringe: Shewringe's Hospital & Robert Goulding's Charities — 171
Shipdham: Shipdham Parochial & Fuel Allotment — 243
Shipman: Thomas Stanley Shipman Charitable Trust — 173
Shipwrecked: Shipwrecked Mariners' Society — 53
Show: Show Business Benevolent Fund (Scotland) — 102
Shrewsbury:
  Shrewsbury & District Welfare Society — 187
  Shrewsbury Municipal Charities — 187
Shropshire: Shropshire Welfare Trust — 187
Sibbald: Dr J R Sibbald's Trust — 102
Sibthorpe: Emily Ada Sibthorpe Trust — 222
Siebel: Mary Elizabeth Siebel Charity — 183
Silman: Julius Silman Charitable Trust — 218
Silverstone: Silverstone Poors' Allotments — 181
Silverton: Silverton Parochial Charity — 212
Silverwood: Silverwood Trust — 54
Sim: James Sim of Cornhill Trust — 107
Simmons: Sydney Simmons Pension Fund — 54
Simpson:
  Simpson Trust — 108
  Mrs Simpson's Charity — 106
Skelland: William Barlow Skelland Charity for the Poor — 149
Skelton: Skelton Swindells Trust — 158
Slough: Slough Good Causes Fund — 224
Smart: Reverend W Smart's Charity — 179
Smedley: Richard Smedley's Charity — 167
Smith:
  Smith's Cirencester Poor Charity — 216
  Henry Smith Charity — 297
  Henry Smith Charity Alfrsiton Estate — 54
  Henry Smith Charity (local):
    Abinger — 252
    Albury — 252
    Alford — 252
    Ash & Normandy — 251
    Banstead — 252
    Bedworth — 192
    Bisley — 253
    Bletchingley — 253
    Bramley — 253
    Capel — 253
    Charlwood — 253
    Chertsey — 252
    Chiddingfold — 254
    Chipping Barnet — 265
    Chobham — 254
    Cobham — 254
    Crowhurst — 254
    Dorking — 254
    Dovercourt — 231
    Dunsfold — 254
    East Horsley — 254
    East Moseley (St Mary) — 255
    East Moseley (St Paul) — 255
    Effingham — 255
    Esher — 255

315

Index

Frimley	251
Gatton	255
Godstone	255
Hambledon	256
Harting	234
Hascombe	256
Headley	256
Horley	256
Horne	256
Horsell	256
Leigh	257
Long Ditton	251
Merstham	257
Newdigate	257
Newton St Loe	206
Nutfield	257
Ockley	257
Oxted	257
Peper Harow	257
Pershore	170
Puttenham	258
Richmond	277
Send & Ripley	251
Shalford	258
Shapwick	218
Shottermill	258
Stanton Prior	206
Stoke D'Abernon	258
Tandridge	258
Thetford	243
Thorpe	259
Walton on the Hill	259
Warbleton	230
Westbury	220
West Clandon	259
West Horsley	259
West Moseley	259
Woking	259
Worcester	171
Wotton	235
Mrs Smith & Mount Trust	297
Samuel Smith Charity, Coventry	200
Frederick William Smith's Charity	122
Smorthwaite: Smorthwaite Charity	134
Smythe: Sir Thomas Smythe's Charity	237
Social: Social Workers' Benevolent Trust	54
Society:	
Society at Aberdeen for the Benefit of Children of Deceased Clergymen of the Church of Scotland & Professors of the Universities of Scotland	102
Society for the Assistance of Ladies in Reduced Circumstances	298
Society for Benefit of Sons & Daughters of the Clergy of the Church of Scotland	102
Society of Chiropodists Benevolent Fund	54
Society of Friends & Foreigners in Distress	298
Society of Licensed Victuallers	54
Society of Motor Manufacturers & Traders Charitable Trust Fund	54
Society for Mucopolysaccharide Diseases	86
Society of Radiographers Benevolent Fund	54
Society for the Orphans of Ministers & Missionaries of the Presbyterian Church in Northern Ireland	95
Society for the Relief of Distress	263
Society for the Relief of Necessitous Protestant Ministers	55
Society for the Relief of Poor Clergymen	55
Society for Relief of Widows & Orphans of Medical Men	55
Society for the Relief of Widows & Orphans of Shipwrecked Mariners	128
Society of St Vincent de Paul	298
Society of Schoolmasters	55
Society for Welfare & Teaching of the Blind	102
Soham: Soham Relief-in-Need Charity	228
Soldiers: Soldiers', Sailors' & Airmen's Families Association (SSAFA)	69
Solicitors: Solicitors' Benevolent Association	55
Sollitt: Herbert William Sollitt Memorial Trust	176
Solomon: Jack Solomon's Charity Fund	55
Somerset: Somerset County Bowling Association Benevolent Fund	217
Somerset: Somerset Local Medical Benevolent Fund	217
Souldern: Souldern United Charities	246
South:	
South Brent Parish Lands	212
South Creake Charities	243
South London Relief-in-Sickness Fund	263
South Moss Foundation	162
South Shields Indigent Sick Society	139
South Wales Association for Spina Bifida & Hydrocephalus	120
South Wales Constabulary Benevolent Fund	120
South Warwickshire Welfare Trust	191
Southampton:	
Southampton Charitable Trust	233
Southampton Relief-in-Need Charity	235
Southport: Southport & Birkdale Provident Society	164
Southwell: Southwell Charities for the Poor & Sick Poor	186
Spalding: Spalding Relief-in-Need Charity	177
Spastics: Spastics Society	86
Spearing: William Spearing's Charities & Others	217
Speck: Speck Walker Annuity Fund	129, 134
Spencer: Spencer's Charity	200
Spilsby: Spilsby Feoffees Charities	177
Spittal: Spittal Bequest	103
Spondon: Spondon Relief-in-Need Charity	169
Sponne: Sponne & Bickerstaffe Charity	181
Squire: Rebecca Flower Squire's Bequest & Others	278
Stable: Stable Lads Welfare Trust	55
Stafford: Stafford's Charity	267
Staines:	
Staines Parochial Charities	258
Staines Trust	55
Stair: Earl of Stair Bequest (see Charities Administered by Midlothian District Council)	113
Stanley: Stanley St Peter Relief-in-Sickness Fund	147
Stanton: Stanton Poors' Estate Charity	250
Stead: Stead Benefaction Trust	103
Steel: Sir James Steel's Trust	113
Stephenson: Paul Stephenson Memorial Trust	298
Stepney: Stepney Relief-in-Need Charity	279
Stetchworth: Stetchworth Relief-in-Need Charity	228
Stevens: Robert Stevens Charity	198
Steventon: Steventon Allotments & Relief-in-Need Charity	246
Stickford: Stickford Relief-in-Need Charity	177
Stock:	
Stock Exchange Benevolent Fund	55
Stock Exchange Clerks Fund	56
Stockburn: Stockburn Memorial Trust	180
Stockport: Stockport Sick Poor Nursing Association	156
Stoddart: Stoddart Samaritan Fund	138
Stoke:	
Stoke Mandeville & Other Parishes	224
Stoke-on-Trent Children's Holiday Trust Fund	189
Stone: Charles Graham Stone's Relief-in-Need Charity	206
Stow: Stow Bardolph Town Lands Charity	243
Stowmarket: Stowmarket Relief Trust	247
Straits: Straits Settlement & Malay States Benevolent Society	298
Strathblane: Strathblane & Strathendrick District Welfare Trust	114
Streynsham: Streynsham's Charity	237
Stringer: Elizabeth Stringer Trust	164
Stroke: Stroke Association	86
Sturminster: Sturminster Newton United Charities	215
Sudbury: Sudbury Municipal Charities	250
Suffolk: Suffolk Association for the Care & Resettlement of Offenders	247
Sumner: Sir John Sumner's Trust	298
Sunbury: Sunbury Fuel Allotment Trust	258
Sunderland: Samuel Sunderland Relief-in-Need Charity	141
Sunninghill: Sunninghill Fuel Allotment	224
Sunshine: Sunshine Society	96
Surfleet: Surfleet United Charities	177
Surrey: Surrey Voluntary Association for the Blind	252
Sussex: Sussex Police Charitable Fund	221
Sutherland: Sutherland Bequest	108
Sutton:	
Sutton Coldfield Municipal Charities	201
Sutton Poors' Land Charity	229
Sutton St James United Charities	177
Swaffham:	
Swaffham Bulbeck Relief-in-Need Charity	229
Swaffham Prior Parochial Charities	226
Swallow: Charities of Nicholas Swallow & Others	229
Swansea: Swansea & District Friends of the Blind	125
Swiss:	
Swiss Benevolent Society	298
Swiss Relief Society	153
Tailors: Tailors' Benevolent Institute	56
Tamlin: Tamlin Charity	217
Tamworth: Tamworth Municipal Charities	190
Tancred: Tancred's Charities	56
Tansley: Tansley Charity Trust	200
Taunton: Taunton Aid in Sickness Fund	218
Tavistock: Tavistock, Whitchurch & District Nursing Association	208
Taylor:	
H A Taylor Fund	174
Charity of Lily Taylor	184
Miss M O Taylor's Trust	103
Teachers: Teachers' Benevolent Fund	56
Teesside: Teesside Emergency Relief Fund	128
Temple: Temple Balsall Amalgamated Charities	196
Tenby: Tenby Relief-in-Need & Pensions Charity	121
Tenovus: Tenovus Cancer Appeal	87

Index

Tetsworth: Tetsworth Cozens Bequest 245
Tettenhall: Tettenhall Relief-in-Need & Educational Charity 202
Textile: Textile Benevolent Fund 56
Thame: Thame Welfare Trust 246
Thanet: Thanet Charity 238
Thaxted: Thaxted Relief-in-Need Charities 232
Theatrical: Theatrical Ladies Guild of Charity 56
Third: Third Inglis Property Trust 103
Thomas: Lloyd Thomas Charity for Women & Girls 298
Thomson:
  Hanna & Margaret Thomson Trust 118
  Jessie Ann Thomson's Trust 108
  Joseph Thomson Mortification (see Charities Administered by Edinburgh Voluntary Organisations' Council) 111
Thornbury: Thornbury Town Trust 206
Thornton: Thornton Fund 56
Thorpe: Thorpe Trust 186
Thrale: Thrale Almshouse & Relief-in-Need Charity 275
Three: Three Parishes Fund 233
Thurne: Thurne Poor Allotment 243
Thursley: Thursley Charities 259
Thyne: William Thyne Trust (see Charities Administered by Edinburgh Voluntary Organisations' Council) 111
Tilney: Tilney All Saints Parish Lands Charity 243
Timber: Timber Trades Benevolent Society 57
Tippett: Michael Tippett Musical Foundation 57
Titford: Sarah Rachael Titford's Charity 264
Tobacco: Tobacco Trade Benevolent Association 57
Tod: Tod Bequest (see Charities Administered by Midlothian District Council) 113
Todd:
  Edith Emily Todd Trust 190
  Charity of Edith Todd 187
Todmorden:
  Todmorden Needy Sick Fund 146
  Todmorden War Memorial Fund 146
Toll: Annie Toll Bequest 213
Tottenham:
  Tottenham Aid-in-Sickness Fund 271
  Tottenham District Charity 271
Town:
  Town Estate Charity 246
  Town Lands Charity 228
  Town Moor Money Charity & Robert Bell Harrison's Legacy 139
  Town Welfare Committee 179
Townend: Ethel Maud Townend Charity 130
Townrow: Arthur Townrow Pensions Fund 168, 299
Towries: Robert Towries Charity 130
Trained: Trained Nurses Annuity Fund 57
Transport: Transport Benevolent Fund 57
Triangle: Triangle Trust 1949 Fund 299
Trinity: Trinity House Charities 57
Tripp: Charity of John Tripp 130
Trull: Trull Parish Lands Charity 218
Trustees: Trustees for the Freemen of the Borough & County of the Town of Haverfordwest 121
Tutbury: Tutbury General Charities 190
Tyne: Tyne Mariners' Benevolent Institution/Society of Widows & Orphans 139
Tyrrell: Lady Tyrrell Giles Gift 275

UK: UK Atomic Energy Authority Benevolent Fund 57
Underwood: Thomas Underwood's Charity 184
UNISON: UNISON Welfare Fund 58
United:
  United Charities of Liskeard 207
  United Charities of Saint Leonard's, Shoreditch 270
  United Charities of St Paul's, Covent Garden 282
  United Charity of All Saints 170
  United Charity of Palling Burgess 216
  United Charity of Saint Martin 171
  United Law Clerks Society 58
  United Westinster Almshouses 282
Unity: Unity Fund for the Elderly 299
Universal: Universal Beneficent Society 226
Upwell: Upwell Isle Charities 226
Ure: Ure Elder Fund for Widows 116
Uxbridge: Uxbridge United Charities 271

Vacher: Vacher's Endowment 264
Vaughan: Miss Vaughan's Spitalfields Charity 279
Vawer: William Vawer's Charity 121
Veterinary: Veterinary Benevolent Fund 58
Victoria: Victoria Convalescent Trust Fund 87, 299
Victory: Victory (Ex-Services) Benevolent Trust 69
Vincent: Eric W Vincent Trust Fund 196

Walberswick: Walberswick Common Lands 250
Wallingford: Wallingford Municipal & Relief-in-Need Charities 247
Wallsend: Wallsend Charitable Trust 140
Walpole: Walpole St Peter Poor's Estate 243
Walsh: John Walsh Fund 138
Walsoken: Walsoken United Charity 229
Waltham: Waltham Forest Handicapped Trust 279
Walthamstow: Walthamstow Almshouse & General Charities 279
Wandsworth:
  Wandsworth Children's Fund 280
  Wandsworth Combined Charities 280
Wansbeck: Wansbeck Appeal Trust Fund 136
Wappenham: Wappenham Poors' Land Charity 182
Warbrick: Richard Warbrick Charities 162
Warminster: Warminster Relief-in-Need Charity 220
Warrington:
  Warrington Children's Summer Camp 150
  Warrington Sick & Disabled Trust 150
Warsop: Warsop United Charities 186
Warwick:
  Warwick Municipal Charities - King Henry VIII Charity 194
  Warwick Provident Dispensary 194
Warwickshire:
  Warwickshire Constabulary Benevolent Fund 191
  Warwickshire Miners Convalescent & Benevolent Fund 191
Waterloo: Waterloo Parish Charity for the Poor 282
Watford: Watford Mayor's Fund 236
Watson: Watson Bequest (see Charities Administered by Berwickshire District Council) 103
Watton: Watton Relief-in-Need Charity 244

Webb:
  Webb Relief-in-Sickness Fund 149
  William Webb's & Others' Charities 217
Wednesfield: Wednesfield Parochial Charity 202
Welsh: Welsh Rugby Union Charitable Trust 120
Welton: Welton Town Lands Trust 182
Wembley: Wembley Samaritan Fund 266
Wereham: Wereham Relief-in-Need Charity 244
West:
  Emily West Temple Trust 278
  West Gate Benevolent Trust 186
  West Glamorgan County Blind Welfare Association 125
  West Harling Road Allotment Gardens Trust 241
  West Hendon & Colindale Relief-in-Sickness Charity 265
  West Kirby Charities 162
  West Riding Distress Fund 128
  West Sussex County Nursing Benevolent Fund 260
  West Walton Poors' Charity 244
  West Winch Town Yard Charity 239
Westgarth: Clara Westgarth Trust 150
Westminster: Westminster Amalgamated Charity 282
Weston: Harry Weston Memorial Fund 200
Weybridge: Weybridge Parochial Charities 259
Wheatcroft: Julie Wheatcroft Trust 109
White:
  Captain & Mrs White's Loan Fund 113
  Sir Thomas White's Charity 167
  Thomas White's Loan Fund (Northampton) 178
Whittlesey: Whittlesey Charity 229
Whitton: Whitton Trust 175
Whittuck: Whittuck Charity 142
Whitwam: Herbert Whitwam Trust 142
Widow: Widow's Friend Society 299
Widows:
  Widows' Fund of the Three Denominations 58
  Widows', Orphans' & Dependants' Society of the Church in Wales 120
Wigan: Wigan Town Relief-in-Need Charity 157
Williams:
  Elizabeth Williams' Charity 120
  Charities of Thomas Williams & Charles Price 122
  William Williams Charity 214
Willis: Henry & James Willis Trust 171
Wilmington:
  Wilmington Parochial Charity 238
  Wilmington Trust 131
Wilmslow: Wilmslow Aid Trust 151
Wilson: John Wilson Bequest 113
Wimbledon: Wimbledon Guild of Social Welfare 275
Winchester:
  Winchester Children's Holiday Trust 233
  Winchester Rural District Welfare Trust 233
  Winchester Welfare Charities 235
Wine:
  Wine & Spirits Trades' Benevolent Society 58
  Wine Trade Foundation 58
Winston: Maurice Winston Charitable Trust 221
Winterscale: Robert Winterscale Charity 134
Wireless: Wireless for the Bedridden 87, 299

317

Index

Wistrich: Matthew Wistrich Trust 267
Wither: Wither's Pension 138
Witley: Witley Charitable Trust 252
Witting: S C Witting Trust 300
Witton: Witton Charity 244
Wokingham: Wokingham United Charities 224
Wolverley: Wolverley & Cookley Anne A Mitchell Charity 171
Women: Women's Royal Voluntary Service (WRVS) Trust 300
Wonersh: Wonersh Charities 252
Wooburn: Wooburn, Bourne End & District Relief-in-Sickness Charity 226
Wood:
   Edward Wood Bequest 173
   James Wood Bequest and the James Wood & Christina Shaw Bequest 113
   John Theodore Wood Charity 122
   Wood Green (Urban District) Charity 271
Woodford: Woodford Charity Estate 182
Woodthorpe: Woodthorpe Relief-in-Need Charity 168
Woodton: Woodton United Charities 244
Woolaston: Blanch Woolaston Walsall Charity 202
Woolwich: Woolwich & Plumstead Relief-in-Sickness Fund 269
Wootton: Wootton Charities 222
Worcester: Worcester Consolidated Municipal Charity 171
Worcestershire: Worcestershire Cancer Aid Committee 169
Wormley: Wormley Parochial Charity 236
Worplesden: Worplesden Parish Charities 259
Worshipful:
   Worshipful Company of Cordwainers 300
   Worshipful Company of Farriers Charitable Trust 59
   Worshipful Company of Insurers Charitable Trust Funds 59
   Worshipful Company of Launderers Trust Funds 59
   Worshipful Company of Plaisterers 59
   Worshipful Company of Tallow Chandlers 59
Wrenbury: Wrenbury Consolidated Charities 149
Wrexham: Wrexham & District Relief-in-Need Charity 120
Wright: Jane Wright's Charity 135
WRNS: WRNS Benevolent Fund 69
Wybunbury: Wybunbury United Charites 151
Wylde: Anthony & Gwendoline Wylde Memorial Charity 167
Wymeswold: Wymeswold Parochial Charities 174

Yardley: Yardley Great Trust 203
Yelvertoft: Yelvertoft & District Relief in Sickness Fund 178
Yonge: Reverend Duke Yonge Charity 209
York:
   York Children's Trust 135
   York City Charities 135
   York Dispensary Sick Poor Fund & the Purey Cust Fund 135
   York Fund for Women & Girls 135
Yorkshire: Yorkshire County Bowling Association Benevolent Fund 128
Yorston: Mrs E W Yorston Bequest (see Charities Administered by Midlothian District Council) 113

Zakat: Zakat Committee 300